◆ ◆ ◆ ◆ ◆

Financial Reporting and Cost Control for Health Care Entities

◆ ◆ ◆ ◆ ◆

Financial Reporting and Cost Control for Health Care Entities

Thomas R. Prince

AUPHA Press / Health Administration Press
Ann Arbor, Michigan   1992

96   95   94   93   92   5   4   3   2   1

Library of Congress Cataloging-in-Publication Data

Prince, Thomas R.
    Financial reporting and cost control for health care entities / Thomas R. Prince.
        p.   cm.
    Includes bibliographical references and index.
    ISBN 0-910701-50-4 (hard : alk. paper)
    1. Health facilities—Finance.   2. Health facilities—Cost control.   I. Title
    [DNLM: 1. Costs and Cost Analysis—methods.   2. Financial Management
—methods.   3. Health Facilities—economics.   WX 157 P957f]
RA971.3.P73   1992   362.1'068'1—dc20
DNLM/DLC for Library of Congress   92-1452 CIP

The paper used in this publication meets the minimum requirements of American National Standard for Information Sciences—Permanence of Paper for Printed Library Materials, ANSI Z39.48-1984. ∞™

Health Administration Press
A division of the Foundation
    of the American College of
    Healthcare Executives
1021 East Huron Street
Ann Arbor, Michigan 48104-9990
(313) 764-1380

Association of University Programs
    in Health Administration
1911 North Fort Myer Drive, Suite 503
Arlington, VA 22209
(703) 524-5500

To Eleanor

Contents

Part I   Health Care Industry and External Financial Reports

List of Exhibits, Tables, and Figures

Exhibits

Tables

Figures

Foreword

Being associated with this important new contribution to the field of health care financial education is of particular personal pleasure. As a full-time health care industry practitioner of accounting and finance and a dedicated alumnus of Northwestern University's J. L. Kellogg School of management (hopefully a credit to rather than a debit of its accounting and finance departments), it is only appropriate to give something back to today's generation of health care industry finance people, albeit through this short foreword.

In this volume, Tom Prince captures the wide range of issues that health care entities and their finance staffs, as well as students of the field, need to understand. Entities that deliver health care services are truly distinctive in the business social value spectrum. In 1980, the AICPA acknowledged that hospitals are, in fact, business entities in terms of their conceptual framework. More than 20 percent of the nation's nongovernment hospitals today are for-profit business entities, as are most physician practices and a majority of long-term care and home care–related entities. To be successful in organizing, capitalizing, managing, and controlling health care entities requires the same financial and accounting acumen and the same reporting devices for managers and executive leadership that is required for success in any other complex business organization.

The U.S. health care system is viewed as being in a state of crisis—certainly because of less than adequate access to service by an important proportion of Americans, but even more so because of perceived high cost. Although changes in the delivery system may affect overall costs for the better, the greater opportunity, in my opinion, is in the potential for every deliverer of service to focus on efficiency and achieve a greater output per cost unit than they do at present. This text enables many new participants to have a hand in that process.

Tom Prince brings to his mission of education a significant background of consulting experience with hospitals and other health care entities. The matrices in this book, which help organize the diverse operations into understandable units, are indicative of his working experiences with the financial statements and management of many health delivery entities. The chapters dealing with cost control take the student along a well-documented path of managerial common sense and logic. Designed to meet the latest external reporting standards and the managerial needs of the health care industry of the 1990s, this book will help make the novice in health care financial reporting a knowledgeable communicator of financial information to management, the board director, and auditors alike.

Lloyd B. Morgan
Partner
Arthur Andersen
Chicago, Illinois

Preface

Financial reporting, cost control, and managerial analysis of health care entities are performed in a challenging and changing environment. Interactive political, social, and economic forces provide the structure for the health care industry, while legal developments and new competition affect the financial viability of selective services. A change in administrative rules by a governmental agency or an accreditation body may create new economic opportunities in this competitive environment as to where, how, when, and what health care services are provided. Federal, state, county, and local officials may adjust the structure because of shifts in public opinion regarding access, availability, quality, rights of coverage, cost, and financing. Other factors contributing to these structural adjustments are changes in technology, changes in medical practice, revised licensure guidelines, new legal arrangements, revised organizational forms, and new health care delivery systems.

An annual picture of the industry gives the illusion of a permanent structure in which to study health care financial management because of the maze of governmental statutes, legal opinions, administrative rules, and regulatory guidelines that address specific issues in the delivery of services. But a comparison of these annual pictures for a few years may show drastic shifts by payor in the specifics of health care financial management. Various third party payors emphasize different features in their respective annual negotiations, and there is a lead-lag relationship among the payors. Some major corporations became their own payor in the late 1980s and began to directly negotiate contracts with health care providers. These corporate efforts changed the dominant position among payors that the Medicare program had held for several years.

In projecting the health care facility's budget for the next year, institutional knowledge is of equal importance to technical information on the exact payment arrangements per type of episode of care by payor for the current year. The competitive health care environment has stimulated innovative approaches by third party payors to selective providers, and some of these efforts have produced major shifts in the annual mix and distribution of services in a given facility. Financial incentives are such that a given payor's behavior last year may not be indicative of potential outcomes for the coming year; thus, a periodic monitoring of services by payor for a given type of episode of care has become a requirement for economic survival.

The final draft of this manuscript was revised to reflect the efforts by the American Institute of Certified Public Accountants to update the 1972 *Hospital Audit Guide* and to cope with the measurement of future services in continuing-care retirement communities. AICPA's 1990 *Audit and Accounting Guide: Audits of Providers of Health Care Services* is examined with an emphasis on health maintenance organizations, home health agencies, ambulatory care centers, and parent-subsidiary relationships. AICPA's 1990 "Statement of Position 90-8: Financial Accounting and Reporting by Continuing-Care Retirement Communities" provides guidance on financial reporting procedures for refundable fees, nonrefundable fees, and the liability for future services. Governmental Accounting Standards Board issued in 1991 Statement No. 14, "The Financial Reporting Entity," which addresses joint ventures, criteria for recognizing a separate organization, the blending method of financial reporting, and consolidated statements.

The dynamics of the changing health care field were experienced in the author's attempts to cope with the differences between the exposure draft and the final copy of AICPA's *Audit and Accounting Guide.* For example, the suggested format of aggregated balance sheets was changed and some of the flexibility in reporting arrangements for ambulatory care and home health was eliminated in the final guide. Thus, although an anonymous reviewer found several discrepancies between this manuscript and the final guide, the particular issues cited were compatible with the proposed guide.

The study of health care financial reporting and cost control is more inclusive than the scope of AICPA's *Audit and Accounting Guide.* A given type of health care entity may not be subject to this audit guide, but the entity may be covered by one of four other audit guides depending on its legal structure and ownership. A university teaching hospital, for example, may be subject to a governmental audit guide, a for-profit audit guide, nonprofit audit guide, or the university's audit guide, depending upon the legal structure of the entity.

The assigned problems in this volume highlight some of the financial reporting differences among similar health care entities following diverse audit guides. An appreciation of these different sets of rules is important for properly interpreting these dissimilar financial statements and in comparing health care operations among various institutions. The overall objectives of these application problems are to test students' understanding of conceptual materials and to emphasize the unique procedures followed in the health care field.

The selection of materials covered in this volume is based upon more than two decades of professional experience in working with different types of health care facilities under various organizational and legal arrangements. As course materials were tested in class, additional exhibits were incorporated into the text because many of the J. L. Kellogg Graduate School of Management students had never seen the code structure applied by medical records personnel or the contents of the billing forms used by various health care providers. The technical notes used as the basis for this integrated volume are from two separate health care finance and accounting courses taught by the author at Northwestern University.

Expanded materials on the code structure for diseases, procedures, patients, and locations have been prepared so that DRGs for inpatients and CPT-4 codes for outpatients and clinic visits can be appreciated by individuals without experience in the health care industry. The introductory materials on the DRG GROUPER were modified after the Department of Health and Human Services made major revisions in the prospective payment system during 1988 and 1989. Some of the more onerous classifications have been changed so as to mitigate the damages to selective health care facilities because the initial DRG structure had insufficient medical input in its design. There are still major classification problems with priorities assigned to complications and comorbidities. The shortcomings in the DRG GROUPER have produced economic, financial, operational, and ethical problems in hospitals, and these issues are addressed in this volume.

The first of the three parts in this volume examines external financial reporting of health care entities. The materials are designed for readers without an introductory course in financial accounting. Balance sheets, statements of revenue and expenses, statements of changes in fund balance, and statements of cash flows are examined primarily from the perspective of not-for-profit entities. Nursing homes are used to illustrate financial reporting of investor-owned facilities. Some comparisons are made in the text between the financial accounting practices of health care entities versus business enterprise for the purpose of emphasizing institutional knowledge. Performance measures, liquidity, financial status, and leverage are the focus of the last chapter in the first part on financial statement analysis.

The second and third parts of this volume address management planning and control in health care entities. Essential components of management control are the capture of expenditure, revenue, and activity data by regular cost account and the aggregation of these data by temporary reporting cost centers under the responsibility-accounting construct. These statistical data include specific work-load units and relative-value measures that are used in performance evaluation by regular cost account. Inpatients are assessed by an acuity index, which is used in patient care management and nurse scheduling. These relative-value units and acuity measures permit refined variance analysis for cost centers and cost-volume analysis for revenue centers.

Intermediate analysis begins with the mapping of regular cost data and common cost centers into departmental management control system modules in which a different type of monitoring and assessment is performed. Fixed costs and minimum-volume monitoring are accomplished for patient care and quality assurance purposes. Comparisons of actual with budget for the mix and distribution of health care services are essential for high-quality care. Some integrated problems address the accumulation process, responsibility-accounting reporting arrangements, cost assignments, cost allocations, and traceability of transaction data. Problems have also been included on cost accounting practices for health care entities in the areas of patient acuity, nurse scheduling, work-load measurements, variance analysis, and cost-volume analysis.

Management of patient services, addressed in the third and final part of the book, consists of classifying and reporting episodes of care, case-mix management, and revenue center analysis. Standard reports are examined that compare treatment protocols by payor for an attending physician within a case-mix group. The last chapter presents an overall framework of health care analysis that integrates information on patient admissions, registration, financial data, order entry, test results, medical records, and charting. Assigned problems focus on management planning and control issues at the lower level of treatment protocol by payor. Problems are included that serve to integrate segments of the course with applications that are based on the actual cost, revenue, and utilization experiences of health care entities.

Financial statements, operational reports, and utilization measures for not-for-profit community hospitals from the database provided by The Merritt System® permit profile comparisons of selected financial data and capital structure ratios. Application of these ratios to aggregate data by panels of community hospitals show financial differences among groups of hospitals. The overall decline in financial profitability by the average community hospital between 1985 and 1988 is also reflected in these hospital data. The Merritt System's database is also used in this volume for illustrating financial measures of solvency for a sample of community hospitals and the distribution of individual hospital data within these overall averages.

This volume contains sufficient institutional materials that it can be used at the undergraduate or graduate levels without requiring previous courses in health care. The materials are presented at the introductory level in accounting. Individuals with a prior course in elementary accounting have some advantage in the preparation of cash flow statements and consolidated financial reports for the general case. After the mechanics are covered, the advantage of prior course experience in accounting disappears as the focus shifts to considering alternative cash flow and financial statement formats dependent upon the organizational and legal structure of the health care entity. Additional problems on restricted fund transactions and transfers have been included because of the dominant role that nonoperating revenues are currently having on the survival of hospitals and clinics.

Many graduate students take the health care accounting and finance course as an elective because they are considering working in the health care industry or being employed by a financial institution or consulting firm that provides services to health care entities. Some institutional materials for these students are included in the first three chapters and in Chapter 15. Health care majors will find that the orientation of the institutional materials is different than that in their health care policy courses.

The author is grateful to Van Kampen Merritt Investment Advisory Corporation, a Xerox Financial Services Company, for the use of the database management system provided by The Merritt System®. This unique data source permitted financial comparisons and illustrations that would otherwise not have been possible. Each telephone call to The Merritt System was promptly handled by the professional staff. Special thanks go to Ms. Lori Finney and Mr. Andy Oliver of Van Kampen Merritt for their significant support.

The author is indebted to many health care professionals in the Chicago area who provided guidance on changes in financial reporting practice. The four individuals telephoned most frequently are David Burik, president of the Tiber Group; Kenneth R. Herlin, partner at Ernst & Young; Terence M. Mieling, vice president and national director of health care at John Nuveen; and Lloyd B. Morgan, partner at Arthur Andersen & Co.

Particular appreciation is expressed to Terence M. Mieling, Lloyd B. Morgan, John M. Prince, and William G. Stotzer (Arthur Andersen & Co.) for their detailed review of the final manuscript. Two anonymous reviewers of the manuscript also made helpful suggestions. The responsibility for any errors or oversights must lie with the author. The author participated in proposed changes to the draft copy of the 1990 AICPA, *Audit and Accounting Guide,* but the use of the terms *revenue* and *income* as plural concepts was missed.

Colleagues and students at the J. L. Kellogg Graduate School of Management have assisted in many ways in the development of this volume. Their counsel and guidance is appreciated. Ms. Bonnie Lee, Joan P. Palmer, and Elaine R. Zimmerman provided outstanding secretarial and administrative assistance on this volume. The author is appreciative to Christina Bych, Sandra J. Crump, Tracy Flynn, and Edward Kobrinski for their help in preparing this volume.

Part I

Health Care Industry and External Financial Reports

1

Entities Providing Health Care Services to Individuals

Introduction

Americans consumed about 12 percent of gross national product (GNP) in 1990 for health care, and there are many indications that this demand for health care services will continue. National health care expenditures were 5.3 percent of GNP in 1960 and increased to 10.2 percent by 1982. With this expansion in health care expenditures, many new types of legal entities have been created to provide services to individuals. The dominant role of hospitals decreased from 47 percent of national health care expenditures in 1982 to less than 45 percent by 1986. Physician services and freestanding clinics experienced increasing growth during the late 1980s and were the beneficiaries of these shifts in national health care expenditures. Although the form and arrangement of some new constructs may vary by geographical area, health care expenditures are a significant part of the national economy, and excellent financial management of these entities has both public and societal benefits.

Health care entities encompass many diverse types of organizations engaged in the delivery of services, products, and goods for the public and private sectors. These health care entities run the gamut

- from the public health department of a governmental body to the physician office of a sole practitioner;
- from the federal psychiatric hospital to a physical therapy clinic in a continuing-care retirement community;
- from the university-based medical center to a rural health clinic;
- from the skilled nursing facility to a home health agency;

3

- from the proprietary ambulatory surgical center to a hospice owned by a religious group;
- from the environmental monitoring department of a governmental body to the city hospital council; and
- from the pharmaceutical corporation to the small housekeeping firm.

There are several diverse health care entities within the range of each set of comparisons.

National health care expenditures are partitioned between public health and personal health, and there are diverse health care entities within each partition that comply with various external financial reporting requirements. The focus of this chapter is on the financial statements of entities in the personal health category. This subset of health care entities does include the pharmaceutical companies, health care supply companies, surgical and medical equipment companies, insurance and financial services companies, contractors for health care services, housekeeping and maintenance service companies, and health care support companies. On the other hand, the health care officer at a commercial bank, for example, may direct a department that works exclusively in providing services to health care facilities. Although the department in the bank is totally committed to the health care industry, the organizational unit is probably not a separate corporation with external financial reporting requirements.

Entities Providing Health Care Services

The American Institute of Certified Public Accountants (AICPA) uses the primary focus of the organization as a way of distinguishing organizations in personal health care from other firms that may be associated with health care delivery or provide support services. Those entities whose principal operations consist of providing health care services to individuals (for example, a physician's office, a hospital, a nursing home, or a clinic) are recognized by the AICPA as providers of health care services and are within the scope of a specific audit and financial reporting guide.[1]

Individuals are often not aware of the various entities that are providing health care services to them. When an individual goes to the hospital for emergency treatment, the hospital entity is the physical location where this treatment occurs, and the patient receives a bill from the hospital entity for the emergency room (ER) visit. But most of the medical and health care services provided to the ER patient in the emergency area are delivered by nonhospital entities. There is usually a physician-group entity that is responsible for the emergency medical services, for which the patient is separately billed. If special outpatient or ancillary services are provided to the ER patient, such as an x-ray in the radiology department, then another physician-group entity is participating in the delivery of health care services. An ER patient may receive bills from three or four distinct entities for a single emergency room visit.

Many of these entities providing health care services were established because of governmental policy statements, reimbursement considerations, regulatory restrictions, license issues, and approval requirements. Clinics as nonhospital entities to service hospital patients were established to avoid reimbursement limits placed on hospital expenditures under the Economic Stabilization Program during the 1970s. A regulatory agency in 1980, for example, might delay or deny the approval of purchase of new hospital equipment for a leading medical center; in response, a group of physicians at the medical center may establish a separate entity that is not under the control of the regulatory agency. This new entity can purchase the equipment and can provide the services to patients at the medical center. A hospital approaching a limit on payment for inpatients under the old cost-based reimbursement system for Medicare patients might encourage the creation of new entities to provide selected services to patients. These new entities would directly bill patients for these services without having any impact on the hospital's Medicare cost report.

The multiple entities participating in providing health care services to an individual for a single hospital visit were, to a large extent, created because of existing governmental rules and regulations or in response to proposed guides or political comments. Some of these new entities may have an unusual organizational design, identified with other economic, legal, financial, and taxation issues rather than with the initial factors responsible for their establishment. The dynamics of this regulatory process, and the response in the form of new health care entities, have progressed to the point that governmental agencies are now preparing new sets of rules and approval mechanisms for these new non–hospital-based entities. The Medicare approval activities for rural health clinics, comprehensive outpatient rehabilitation facilities, hospices, and ambulatory surgical centers occurred between 1981 and 1983 and began to have an impact in 1984.[2]

Some providers of health care services to individuals may give the impression of being one type of entity when they are not. The reasons for this discrepancy may relate to legal, regulatory, and reporting requirements of the past that are no longer valid. In other cases, the variance represents the personal preferences of the founders of the health care entity. As an example, not all medical centers qualify as hospitals by the American Hospital Association (AHA) definition. The most distinguished example of this variance is the Mayo Clinic in Rochester, Minnesota. The Mayo Clinic is often described as "one of the world's leading medical centers." A visitor to Rochester soon discovers that the Mayo Clinic competes with the IBM plant for the greatest number of employees within that geographical area. The Mayo Clinic is not a hospital, but an important member of the Medical Group Management Association, located in Denver, Colorado.

A university-based medical center might be another example of an entity that differs from its implied status. A medical center may be owned by a state university and treated as if it were a department within the state government. The only certified financial statements prepared for this medical center may be based on governmental accounting reports for the state university. Another medical center may be owned by a private university and treated as if it were a department within the university, without full control over all its assets. The financial statements for these two types of medical centers may not resemble the balance sheet of a freestanding hospital or medical center; many of the assets employed may be reported by fund accounts within the university without being fully separated for the medical center.[3]

Characteristics of Selected Health Care Entities

Financial statements of health care entities are not uniform for all types of facilities providing services to individuals. Different AICPA financial reporting and audit guides govern these statements based on selected characteristics of a health care entity. There are three principal dimensions for partitioning these characteristics: (1) ownership, (2) control, and (3) type of facility. The intersection of these three dimensions can be further separated by the entity's status with respect to accreditation and Medicare approval condition. Accreditation and Medicare status may significantly influence certain reporting arrangements.

Exhibit 1.1 illustrates the three dimensions of ownership, control, and type of facility. The objective is not to be complete, but just to emphasize the different dimensions. The noncommunity hospital type of facility ($k = 2$), for example, is partitioned into 12 specifications in the AHA's *Guide to the Health Care Field*. Ownership, control, and type of facility must, at least, be concurrently considered if health care entities are to be partitioned into meaningful categories for financial reporting guides.[4]

Exhibit 1.1   Three-Dimensional Classification of Health Care Entities by Ownership, Control, and Type of Facility

$X_{i,j,k}$ = Health care entity

where i = ownership   (1–4)
j = control   (1–7)
k = type of facility   (1–16)

Ownership (i)	*Type of Facility* (k)
i = 1: federal government	k = 1: community hospital
i = 2: state and local government	k = 2: noncommunity hospital
i = 3: nongovernment	k = 3: outpatient clinic
not-for-profit	k = 4: ambulatory surgical unit
i = 4: investor-owned	k = 5: physical therapy facility
	k = 6: speech therapy facility
Control (j)	k = 7: occupational therapy facility
	k = 8: skilled nursing facility
j = 1: independent, freestanding	k = 9: intermediate care facility
corporation	k = 10: residential facility
j = 2: freestanding corporation	k = 11: home health agency
that is a subsidiary of	k = 12: rural health clinic
another health care entity	k = 13: hospice
(by ownership or control)	k = 14: health maintenance
j = 3: freestanding corporation	organization
that is jointly owned or	k = 15: comprehensive outpatient
controlled by other health	rehabilitation facility
care entities	k = 16: continuing care
j = 4: hospital-based facility	retirement community
that is not a legal entity	
j = 5: nonhospital-based facility	
that is not a legal entity	
j = 6: department, division, or	
unit of governmental body	
j = 7: freestanding corporation	
that is a subsidiary of a	
non–health care entity	

Ownership

The legal status of entities providing health care services to individuals consists of four distinct categories of ownership, depicted in Exhibit 1.1: (1) federal government, (2) state and local government, (3) non-government not-for-profit, and (4) investor-owned entities. The format and content of external financial statements are different for entities in different ownership categories.

Financial statements for a health care entity that is owned by the federal government and that does not use enterprise fund accounting (ownership $i = 1$) contain five types of information:

1. Appropriations
2. Expenditures
3. Fund balances
4. Cash collections, if applicable
5. Services provided.

This health care entity receives federal funds in response to the budgetary and appropriation process. The entity has mandated financial reports on its expenditures and the services it provides in carrying out the entity's mission. These federal government entities have been the leaders in productivity measures, human resource accounting, and statistical efforts to capture the services rendered. The traditional accounting usage of the concept "revenue recognition" is not, however, an integral part of the financial statements for federal health care entities. In place of "net patient service revenue," the financial statements for federal health care entities emphasize the statistical measures of services rendered, such as days of care, visits, tests, procedures, operations, activities, and treatments provided.

Health care entities owned by the state and local government (ownership $i = 2$) are similar only in the legal status of their origin. Some of these state and local government entities depend entirely on government funds for their economic existence, and their financial statements are very similar to those of related federal health care entities. Other state and local government entities charge patients for services and generate sufficient amounts of revenues so that they only seek approval (not funds) from the governmental body for expenditures. Other health care entities owned by the state and local government are primarily self-sufficient, but depend on government funds for supporting services to those patients without insurance coverage or without the ability to pay. Hospitals at a state penitentiary, at a state correctional facility, and at a state mental health institute are examples of the first group of entities, whose financial statements are very similar to those of related federal health care entities. State and local government community hospitals may be in either of the other two groups—fully self-sufficient or primarily self-sufficient. The statement of revenues and expenses for governmental health care entities in the last two groups are similar to those of related nongovernment not-for-profit entities; the balance sheets may be different, depending on the governmental entity, because of following guidelines from the Governmental Accounting Standards Board (GASB) instead of the Financial Accounting Standards Board (FASB) for nongovernment not-for-profit entities.

Nongovernment not-for-profit health care entities (ownership $i = 3$) that provide health care services to individuals are typically organized to comply with Section 501(c)(3) of the Internal Revenue Code and are exempt from federal income taxes on related income pursuant to Section 501(a). Many not-for-profit health care entities have been restructured in recent years and may have other related not-for-profit corporations that perform activities for them. Some of these restructuring activities have included entities organized under Section 501(c)(2) of the Internal Revenue Code for purposes of holding title to property, collecting income therefrom, and turning over the net income to an exempt organization. Health care entities have been restructured under other arrangements, but, for purposes of this discussion, the focus is on not-for-profit corporations under Section 501(c)(3) and the FASB required external financial statements.

An investor-owned health care entity (ownership $i = 4$) may exist as a regular corporation, a Subchapter S corporation, a partnership, a corporation with a single shareholder, or as a sole proprietorship. It is unusual to have a sole proprietorship whose principal operations consist of providing health care services to individuals and where the firm is not established as a corporation because of license and other considerations. Proprietary (investor-owned) health care entities must comply with the AICPA's generally accepted accounting principles and with the applicable FASB opinions related to financial statements, including all aspects of AICPA's *Audit and Accounting Guide: Audits of Providers of Health Care Services*. The AICPA has exempted nongovernment not-for-profit health care entities from certain rules and reporting procedures.[5]

Some organizational units providing health care services to individuals do not meet any of the four categories of ownership because the units are divisions or departments of other legal entities. Some private university–based hospitals and some state university–based hospitals are examples of this exception. Statements of revenues and expenses are frequently prepared for these divisions or departments in response to requirements of regulatory agencies; however, it is often not possible to prepare a meaningful balance sheet for those segments of larger entities. Hospital-based clinics and therapy units that may be remote from the parent hospital are additional examples of this exception; the balance sheets of the hospital are meaningful, but the statements do not show the separate assets of the clinics and the therapy units. These remote facilities are departments or divisions of the parent, and the assets employed in these facilities are merged with the overall assets of the hospital.

The four categories of ownership are useful in partitioning health care entities before examining their external financial statements. These categories of ownership represent the first of three dimensions in this discussion of characteristics of entities providing health care services to individuals.

Control

The health care industry has become very complex, and many non-government not-for-profit health care entities organized as $501(c)(3)$ corporations are not independent companies (control $j = 1$) as they first appear. The freestanding corporation may be a subsidiary of another health care entity (control $j = 2$) or the freestanding entity may be jointly owned or controlled by two or more health care entities (control $j = 3$). This second dimension in Exhibit 1.1 looks beyond the ownership status and focuses upon control. Who manages and directs the activities of that health care entity?

The concept of control varies with the ownership status, and hence control is presented as the second dimension in this framework. A federal government health care entity may be managed and directed on a day-to-day basis by a proprietary (for-profit) corporation, but there is some governmental agency, bureau, or department that has overall monitoring responsibility for this arrangement (control $j = 6$). Some federal prison hospitals have been managed this way for over a decade. This same type of relationship may exist between a state and local government health care entity and a proprietary corporation, but the dynamics of the monitoring role by the governmental office are significantly different. The response by the proprietary corporation is immediate, not after a formal inquiry has been conducted. Some state

and local government community hospitals are managed by proprietary corporations, but the options under control in Exhibit 1.1 do not
include further partitions that separate a government facility managed
by a proprietary organization from a facility managed by government
employees.

In some states, public welfare recipients must belong to a health
maintenance organization (HMO). Various health care entities in these
states have created their own HMOs for marketing reasons. The legal
ownership of the HMO does not relate to the health care entity. The
technical requirements for federal approval of the HMO may result
in the appearance of an independent organization when, in fact, the
HMO is an extension of the health care entity that created it. Many
HMOs are freestanding corporations that are subsidiaries of non–
health care entities (control j = 7), such as insurance companies.

The restructuring of health care organizations in the late 1970s
and early 1980s has created some unusual answers to this second
dimension of control. Many of these newly created nongovernment
not-for-profit health care entities are controlled by another nongovernment not-for-profit health care entity. In other cases, the nongovernment not-for-profit health care entity is controlled by two or more
nongovernment not-for-profit health care entities (control j = 3). Some
hospitals are controlled by a church, and the health care facility is not
a legal entity (j = 4). A nursing home is sometimes a "department" of
a hospital and is not a separate legal entity (j = 5).

This second dimension of control is directly related to the
AICPA's generally accepted accounting principles for financial statements in the areas of (1) consolidated statements and (2) related-
party disclosures. The absence of stock ownership in these 501(c)(3)
corporations has required the AICPA committees to address the issue
of "effective control" in place of legal ownership. While the AICPA
study group is reconsidering consolidated statements, the financial
statements of health care entities are beginning to include major notes
on activities of health care entities in which the reporting organization has some degree of control.[6] The related-party disclosures in
financial statements have also escalated due to technological developments, advancements in medical practice, and new government rules
for approving non–hospital-based facilities. Related-party disclosures
alert financial statement readers that certain transactions are not arm's
length and conducted in a normal free-market manner. These disclosures are similar to potential conflict-of-interest activities, where
physicians and administrative personnel in one health care entity are

responsible for directing economic gain to another health care entity in which they have a proprietary interest. The combined impact of these developments is such that the external financial statements for a given hospital may devote more space in notes to control and related-party disclosures than given in aggregate to the statements of revenues and expenses and the balance sheets.

Type of facility

The third dimension in the framework of Exhibit 1.1 focuses on the classification of the facility. AHA uses ten requirements to differentiate a hospital from a nursing home, a clinic, or other types of health care institutions.[7] The minimum requirements for identification as a hospital include the following:

- Six inpatient beds are continuously available for care of patients who are unrelated and who stay, on the average, more than 24 hours per admission.
- Patients are admitted to a hospital by physicians, and continuous nursing care is under the supervision of registered nurses.
- Pharmacy services are maintained in the hospital and supervised by a registered pharmacist.
- Medical records are maintained for each patient that are available for reference.

There are other medical, health, facility, and legal requirements for a hospital as defined by AHA.

AHA's definition of a hospital is the foundation of any classification system for separating facilities that are hospitals from all other facilities. Furthermore, many health care facilities that appear to be independent units are, in fact, hospital-based units and are included in AHA's annual survey data. For example, the 1,248 nursing-home–type units located in 6,720 hospitals in 1989 are not classified as "nursing homes" but are part of the hospitals' activities.[8]

The 1972 refinements in AHA's definitions included separating community hospitals from all other hospitals; this terminology has become the standard for the industry. All federal hospitals are excluded by this definition from being community hospitals. The 1972 definition of community hospitals (type of facility $k = 1$) also excludes all nonfederal hospitals for psychiatric, tuberculosis and other respiratory diseases, and long-term general and other special facilities (type of facility $k = 2$). The short-term hospital units at institutions were also excluded by this definition, and these excluded units are at colleges, universities, prisons, and state institutions. The excluded unit at an institution meets the technical requirements of being a hospital, but the facility is not open to the general public and might be identified as an infirmary, student health services, or a medical department.

Community hospitals, in comparison with noncommunity hospitals, are the dominant force in the field. AHA's *Hospital Statistics*, for example, reports the following data on facilities for 1989:[9]

Community hospitals	5,455
Noncommunity hospitals	1,265
Total hospitals	6,720

In the context of this three-dimensional framework in Exhibit 1.1, it is useful to report the hospital as a type of facility (third dimension) partitioned by ownership (first dimension). Table 1.1 presents the 1989 AHA data for hospitals by ownership. The 1,265 noncommunity hospitals (per Exhibit 1.1) include 42 hospital units at institutions. From a detailed study of AHA's data, it was determined that 17 units were at colleges and universities, 8 units were at state hospitals, several were at state penitentiaries, and the remainder were at state correctional centers.

Hospital-based clinics, therapy units, and ambulatory care centers are part of AHA's definition of hospitals, and these hospital-based outpatient facilities dominate the industry. Medicare had certified 709 freestanding ambulatory surgical centers ($k = 4$) by the end of 1986, while at the same time AHA's annual survey showed 5,243 hospital-based ambulatory surgical centers, including 4,961 community hospital–based ambulatory surgical centers.[10]

There are over 25,000 nursing homes in the United States, not including the 1,248 nursing-home–type units that are hospital based.[11] Health Care Financing Administration (HCFA) reported that 9,125 skilled nursing facilities (SNF) in 1987 ($k = 8$) were certified by Medicare or Medicaid for providing daily inpatient care by a health care professional under the direction of a physician. HCFA also reported that 5,600 intermediate care facilities (ICF) in 1987 ($k = 9$) were certified by Medicaid for providing daily health-related services to individuals whose mental and physical condition does not necessitate hospital or SNF care but who do require care above room and board.[12] An SNF is an inpatient facility where services are needed on a daily basis, are ordered by a physician, and require the skilled services of technical and professional personnel. An ICF is for patients who do

Table 1.1 Distribution of Community and Noncommunity Hospitals by Ownership for 1989

Community Hospitals	
Nongovernment not-for-profit community hospitals	3,220
State and local government community hospitals	1,466
Investor-owned (for-profit) community hospitals	769
Total	*5,455*
Noncommunity Hospitals	
Federal psychiatric hospitals	17
Federal general and other special hospitals	323
Nonfederal psychiatric nongovernment not-for-profit hospitals	127
Nonfederal psychiatric state and local government hospitals	258
Nonfederal psychiatric investor-owned hospitals	356
Nonfederal TB nongovernment not-for-profit hospital	1
Nonfederal TB state and local government hospitals	3
Nonfederal long-term nongovernment not-for-profit hospitals	63
Nonfederal long-term state and local government hospitals	55
Nonfederal long-term investor-owned hospitals	20
Nonfederal nongovernment not-for-profit hospital units of institutions	13
Nonfederal state and local government hospital units of institutions	29
Total	*1,265*

Source: AHA, *American Hospital Association Hospital Statistics, 1990–91 Edition* (1990), 16 and 20.

not require an SNF but have mental and physical requirements that are above the level of room and board and can only be provided through institutional facilities. A third type of nursing home, which is not certified by Medicare or Medicaid, provides custodial or personal care services (1) prescribed by a physician, (2) supervised by a registered nurse, and (3) provided by a qualified person ($k = 10$).

There are over 8,000 residential facilities that are not nursing homes according to the technical registration and certification requirements but that may provide custodial or personal care. Over 96 percent of the 8,000 residential facilities are proprietary.[13] HCFA reported in 1987 that 3,550 institutions for mentally retarded were approved for Medicaid participation.[14]

There are other aspects of Medicare approval that may influence the financial reports of health care entities. Given facilities in HCFA's provider-of-service file may interface with various types of health care delivery services. A comprehensive outpatient rehabilitation facility ($k = 15$) approved by Medicare may be located in a life-care retirement community or a continuing-care retirement community ($k = 16$). An outpatient physical therapy facility approved by Medicare may be in a residential care facility. In some states all Medicaid recipients are almost forced to join HMOs ($k = 14$); outpatient facilities run by these HMOs and approved by Medicaid are included in the HCFA file. In the case of physical therapy ($k = 5$), speech pathology ($k = 6$), occupational therapy ($k = 7$), hospices ($k = 13$), and ambulatory surgical centers, these freestanding units represent a smaller volume of facilities and services than the comparable hospital-based units. As previously cited, the 25,000 nursing homes are the major exception to this situation.

An HMO is a health care entity that combines the delivery of services and financing functions. This type of entity was encouraged by P. L. 93–222, the HMO Act of 1973 (December 1972), and many legislative efforts to stimulate the growth of this combined method of health care delivery. Some prepaid health care plans are very similar to HMOs without using that label for regulatory reasons. The external financial statements may be the same for the HMO or the prepaid health care plan.

It is more difficult to bring closure on the third dimension than on the first two dimensions for ownership and control. The requirements for being a hospital are specified by AHA, and the different types of hospitals are also defined by AHA. Furthermore, the Joint Commission on Accreditation of Healthcare Organizations (JCAHO) periodically evaluates programs and services of hospitals, and AHA's annual survey accumulates status data on licensure, membership, accreditations, and approvals. But, there is no single organization performing a similar function for nonhospital entities. There are independent organizations that evaluate programs and facilities in mental health and in ambulatory care.

Where Medicare has established approval or certification requirements for a nonhospital facility, then this information can be used in specifying these other types of facilities. These Medicare-approved freestanding entities are as follows:

- Skilled nursing facility ($k = 8$)
- Home health agency ($k = 11$)
- Outpatient physical therapy unit ($k = 5$)
- Outpatient speech pathology unit ($k = 6$)

- Portable x-ray unit
- End-stage renal disease facility
- Rural health clinic ($k = 12$)
- Comprehensive outpatient rehabilitation facility ($k = 15$)
- Ambulatory surgical center ($k = 4$)
- Hospice ($k = 13$)

Those nonhospital facilities for which Medicare does not have approval mechanisms are very difficult to classify. The state laws and regulations governing the granting of operating licenses for the same type of facility may vary significantly across states. This may result in erroneous classifications of nonhospital facilities in national studies that are based on state-administered labels.

Classification Framework

The application of the three-dimensional framework of Exhibit 1.1 is to the object or the entity being observed and how that entity is reported in financial statements. The actual legal status of the entity may be different from what appears to be the case; when that is the situation, the unit is probably not a legal entity and is designated by a control code (j) of 4 or 5. Examine the observations and specifications in Table 1.2 with careful attention to the structure in Exhibit 1.1. The last two observations emphasize the limitations of this framework, where the added dimension of a Medicare-approved facility is not shown. The objective in these examples is to relate what is being observed to the accounting entity for the financial statements where information on the health care organization is reported.

Entities and Financial Statements

Financial statements of most health care entities are compatible with the three-dimensional framework of ownership, control, and type of facility presented in Exhibit 1.1. These reports for not-for-profit and governmental health care entities consist of a balance sheet, a statement of revenue and expenses of general funds, a statement of changes in fund balances, and a statement of cash flows of general funds. Investor-owned health care entities follow similar reports of other investor-owned entities, such as a balance sheet, income statement, statement of

Table 1.2   Applications of the Three-Dimensional Framework of Exhibit 1.1

Observation	Specification
A rural health clinic that is not a separate legal structure but is a hospital-based facility for a state and local government community hospital	$X_{2,4,12}$
The consolidated financial statements for the state and local government community hospital that includes a rural health clinic	$X_{2,6,1}$
A psychiatric hospital owned by the federal government (see Exhibit 1.1)	$X_{1,6,2}$
A hospital unit at a state penitentiary (see Exhibit 1.1)	$X_{2,6,2}$
A skilled nursing facility that is not a separate corporation and is owned by a nongovernment not-for-profit community hospital	$X_{3,4,8}$
A skilled nursing facility that is a separate corporation and is proprietary	$X_{4,1,8}$
An ambulatory surgical unit that is a separate 501(c)(3) corporation jointly owned by two nongovernment not-for-profit community hospitals	$X_{3,3,4}$
A community hospital that is a separate 501(c)(3) corporation that is a subsidiary of another health care entity	$X_{3,2,1}$
A community hospital that is a separate 501(c)(3) corporation and is independent	$X_{3,1,1}$
A community hospital that is a separate 501(c)(3) corporation that is a subsidiary of private university	$X_{3,7,1}$
A hospice that is a separate 501(c)(3) corporation with a Medicare-approved program and is jointly owned by two nongovernment not-for-profit community hospitals	$X_{3,3,13}$
A hospice that is a separate 501(c)(3) corporation and is jointly owned by two nongovernment not-for-profit community hospitals	$X_{3,3,13}$

retained earnings, and cash flow statements. Certified financial statements for most entities are based on generally accepted accounting principles (GAAP) reported by the American Institute of Certified Public Accountants (AICPA), Financial Accounting Standards Board (FASB), and Governmental Accounting Standards Board (GASB).

The Financial Accounting Foundation (FAF) is the parent entity for both FASB and GASB and provides funding and administrative support for the two subsidiaries. The overlap between FASB and GASB had to be formally addressed by the parent entity, with early jurisdiction disputes favoring FASB. But FAF's board of trustees altered its position in November 1989 and gave GASB authority over financial reporting by all governmental entities.[15] FAF's board seeks comparability in financial reporting in both the public and private sectors. GASB has many issues to address under this new arrangement, and until GASB statements are released, state and local government health care entities are subject to both FASB and GASB as to format and disclosures on financial statements.

Certified financial statements of some health care entities are not based on GAAP but follow an other comprehensive basis of accounting (OCBOA). Some nonprofit clinics and ambulatory care units elect to use a cash method of accounting where revenue is not recognized until received and expenses are reported when paid. The financial statements of these entities based on OCBOA do not contain accounts receivables or accounts payables, and the AICPA now requires the titles of such financial reports to be different so a reader is immediately aware that GAAP is not being followed.[16] The AICPA suggests that the balance sheet and income statement under OCBOA for investor-owned health care entities might be titled "statement of assets and liabilities arising from cash transactions" and "statement of revenue collected and expenses paid." The statement of revenue and expenses for not-for-profit health care entities might also be "statement of revenue collected and expenses paid." Federal governmental agencies accept OCBOA statements from clinics as fully satisfying governmental program reporting requirements, including the use of grants and awards.

Entities and Funds

The organizational unit for which a set of financial statements is prepared is called an *accounting entity*. If the organizational unit is a corporation, there are legal requirements for submitting annual financial statements to the secretary of state for the geographical area where the corporation is incorporated. In this situation, the accounting entity is a legal entity and the boundaries of the organizational unit are defined by the corporation.

Many not-for-profit legal entities often contain two or more accounting entities providing health care services to individuals. This arrangement is illustrated by various parent-and-subsidiary relationships in the control dimension of the classification framework in Exhibit 1.1. In addition to the separation by parent and subsidiary, many not-for-profit health care entities must create separate accounting entities to satisfy the fiduciary responsibilities of donors and benefactors. Restricted gifts may impose terms and conditions on a health care entity that can only be accommodated by the creation of multiple accounting entities. In a recent study, 69 percent of 1,297 not-for-profit community hospitals had restricted funds.[17] The more differentiating factor is the number of restricted funds (and separate accounting entities) contained in a given nonprofit health care entity.

The AICPA uses the term *fund* to designate "a self-contained accounting entity set up to account for a specific activity or project."[18] Assets, liabilities, and fund balances are reported on a balance sheet for each accounting entity. When there are mutual funds, a combined statement is often prepared on which each fund is disclosed in a separate column or a separate section of the financial report. A sample hospital in Exhibit 1a of AICPA's *Audit and Accounting Guide* illustrates four funds (and accounting entities) under a common heading of "balance sheets."[19]

The control dimension of the classification framework in Exhibit 1.1 includes health care facilities that are not legal entities. Certified financial statements based on GAAP and OCBOA are prepared for non–legal entities. Some church-operated community hospitals are not separate legal entities; to some extent AHA's control code 21 in the *Guide to the Health Care Field* designates a church-operated hospital that is not a legal entity versus control code 23. For example, 81 of 339 community hospitals belonging to the Catholic Health Association in a 1990 study have the control code 23 designation.[20] Mergers and special financing arrangements for office buildings and nursing homes have created complex accounting entities for some not-for-profit community hospitals, but the basic financial statements continue to be by fund.

There are usually multiple accounting entities (funds) within a complex medical center, with each entity having its own set of financial statements. The most common separation of a health care facility's activities are between general funds and restricted funds.

General funds

General funds represent all resources not restricted to identified purposes by donors and grantors, including all assets whose use is limited, agency funds, and property and equipment related to the general operations of the hospital. The general funds account for all resources and obligations not recorded in donor-restricted funds. The assets and liabilities of general funds are classified as current or noncurrent in conformity with GAAP.[21]

AICPA's definition of general funds in the 1990 *Audit and Accounting Guide* is different from professional practice in the early 1980s.[22] Many nonprofit health care entities in the early 1980s had general unrestricted funds and board-designated funds. These two segments of general funds were used in special disclosures to donors as to what operations looked like in the absence of gifts, contributions, investment income, grants, awards, and other nonoperating activities. These segmented reports of the health care entity's general fund could be misleading, and the AICPA moved to change this practice by a phased approach. During the mid 1980s segmented reports were permitted, provided a complete general fund report was also given to the donor. Under the new *Audit and Accounting Guide*, board-designated assets are part of the general fund without any segmentation of the unrestricted fund balance.

Donor-restricted funds

If a hospital has a donor-restricted fund, there are at least two accounting entities: (1) general funds and (2) a donor-restricted fund. There are often three or four accounting entities for donor-restricted funds, depending on the legal documents accompanying the gifts, donations, and bequests. The following are typical donor-restricted funds:

- Specific-purpose funds
- Property and equipment funds (plant replacement and expansion funds; building construction funds; capital debt retirement funds)
- Endowment funds ("regular" endowment funds; term endowment funds)
- Research funds
- Student loan funds

Restricted contributions and gifts impose legal and fiduciary responsibilities on the health care entity's trustees to carry out the written specifications of donors. The special accounting required to support these legal and fiduciary responsibilities may be handled by a series of restricted funds, or the series can be pooled into a single restricted fund provided the detailed accounting system can support all required financial disclosures. If all of these donor gifts are aggregated into one restricted fund, that restricted fund is a single accounting entity. In the case of that restricted fund, the organizational boundaries of the accounting entity have been administratively determined rather than legally specified. An annual financial statement will be prepared for this single accounting entity. The trustee must be able to provide special reports to the donors of the restricted gifts included within this single accounting entity.

Consolidated statements

The business practice concept of consolidated statements is applied to health care institutions in some instances. During reorganization, many hospitals have created special corporations that own office buildings, laundries, data processing companies, health maintenance organizations, clinics, and management consulting firms. The business concept of consolidated statements is applied in combining these subsidiaries into the parent corporation. Consolidated financial statements are prepared for the parent corporation in this context.

The concept of consolidated statements does not apply to the combining of general funds and donor-restricted funds as a single entity. Such combining has no legal meaning or understanding—the accounting entities are not related. Donor-restricted funds, by their very nature, cannot be freely used to meet general obligations incurred by the general funds; therefore, it is inappropriate to present such a combination on a hospital financial statement that might be relied on by outsiders. It is common practice in disclosing financial statements to incorporate the self-balancing funds (general funds, donor-restricted funds, and endowment funds) as distinct balance sheets within combined statements. This reporting arrangement maintains the integrity of each separate entity while providing a combined overview of all funds.

Summary

Physician offices and hospitals have been augmented by many other types of entities providing health care services to individuals. Actions by governmental agencies, pending legislative proposals, and responses and reactions to economic, political, and social forces have created many new types of health care entities. Reimbursement considerations, regulatory restrictions, license issues, and approval requirements are factors that contribute to the legal form of the health care entity. Some health care entities appear to be different from their actual status because of these forces and factors.

Health care entities can be classified by ownership as federal government, state and local government, nongovernment not-for-profit, and for-profit or proprietary organizations. Some health care entities that appear to be freestanding are really a subsidiary or a joint venture of one or more other health care entities. There are two closely related issues of ownership and control that must be specified before the organizational nature of a health care entity is known. The third dimension in this framework is the type of health care entity, such as hospital, nursing home, freestanding clinic, HMO, home health agency, residential facility, physical therapy facility, comprehensive outpatient rehabilitation facility, and hospice. State laws may vary as to the label assigned to the same type of health care entity depending on its geographical location. The recent efforts by administrators of Medicare to certify various types of health care facilities has eliminated some of the identification issues through the guidelines and mandated approval documents.

Financial statements for nonprofit health care entities must be prepared for each legal entity and annually submitted to the appropriate secretary of state. That legal reporting relationship for registration purposes is different from the primary external disclosure arrangement for most nonprofit health care entities. A given nonprofit health care entity may contain multiple legal entities. Some nonprofit health care entities may be affiliated with a church or a university and do not themselves represent any legal entity.

The four basic financial statements (balance sheet, statement of revenue and expenses of general funds, statement of changes in fund balances, and statement of cash flows of general funds) are prepared for the nonprofit accounting entity. The typical certified financial statements are based on GAAP from the AICPA, FASB, and GASB. Some health care entities have certified financial statements with different titles because they are based on a cash method of accounting with the OCBOA designation within the auditor's certificate.

Most not-for-profit community hospitals have multiple accounting entities or funds for which financial statements must be prepared. The fiduciary responsibilities of restricted donations and gifts require a separation of general funds from restricted funds. The health care entity's trustees have fiduciary responsibilities imposed upon them by such restricted donations, which can be administratively handled in different ways. However, there must be a capability of providing special financial statements for each restricted fund as required. The 1990 *Audit and Accounting Guide* has eliminated segmented special reports for board-designated resources; such activities are part of general funds and are classified as "assets whose use is limited."[23] These are major changes from accounting practice in the mid-1980s.

Notes

1. Health Care Committee and the Health Care Audit Guide Task Force of the American Institute of Certified Public Accountants (AICPA), *Audit and Accounting Guide: Audits of Providers of Health Care Services* (New York: AICPA, 1990), ix.
2. V. Watkins and W. Kirby, "Health Care Facilities Participating in Medicare and Medicaid Programs, 1987," *Health Care Financing Review* 9 (Winter 1987): 101–5.
3. Governmental Accounting Standards Board (GASB) issued an exposure draft that provides guidance on accounting and reporting models used by public colleges and universities per *Journal of Accountancy* 172 (July 1991): 19. GASB also issued in 1991, "Statement No. 14 of the Governmental Accounting Standards Board—The Financial Reporting Entity," which is effective for financial statements for periods beginning after 15 December 1992. GASB Statement No. 14 (paragraph 47) provides a reporting arrangement for using both governmental and proprietary methods of accounting that might be followed in college and university operations.
4. The preface to AICPA *Audit and Accounting Guide* (p. ix) lists a broad spectrum of health care entities to which the guide applies. GASB issued in 1990, "Statement No. 11 of the Governmental Accounting Standards Board; Measurement and Basis of Accounting—Governmental Fund Operating Statements," which is effective for financial statements for periods beginning after 15 June 1994. Codification instructions (GASB Statement No. 11 paragraph 254) for the new measurement focus are not specified because current practices may not exist when this is implemented in 1994.
5. For example, FASB Statement No. 95, "Statement of Cash Flows," issued in November 1987, contained paragraph 69 excluding not-for-profit organizations. The 1990 *Audit and Accounting Guide* (paragraph 3.25) includes the statement of cash flows per FASB Statement No. 95, even though the initial exposure draft of the audit guide contained a different statement.
6. AICPA "Statement on Position 81-2, Reporting Practices Concerning Hospital-Related Organizations, August 1, 1981" (pp. 4–6) provided guidance for not-for-profit hospitals on consolidated statements and related-party disclosures. FASB Statement No. 57, "Related Party Disclosures, March 1982," encompassed all health care entities, but the statement did not contain any special guidance on related-party issues of not-for-profit

entities. AICPA *Audit and Accounting Guide* paragraph 13.8 removed any uncertainty about the applicability of FASB Statement No. 57, "Related Party Disclosures," in disclosing transactions between directors, management, medical staff, and other related parties.

7. American Hospital Association (AHA), *American Hospital Association Guide to the Health Care Field, 1990 Edition* (Chicago: AHA, 1990), A4–A5.

8. AHA, *American Hospital Association Hospital Statistics, 1990–91 Edition* (Chicago: AHA, 1990), 16.

9. AHA, *Hospital Statistics, 1990–91 Edition*, 12.

10. AHA, *Hospital Statistics, 1987 Edition.* (Chicago: AHA, 1988), 207.

11. *National Data Book and Guide to Sources, Statistical Abstract of the United States, 1988*, 108th Edition (Washington, DC: U.S. Government Printing Office, December 1987), 97, and *Hospital Statistics, 1990–91*, 14.

12. Watkins and Kirby, "Health Care Facilities," 101–5.

13. *National Data Book and Guide to Sources, Statistical Abstract of the United States, 1987*, 107th Edition (Washington, DC: U.S. Government Printing Office, December 1986), 99.

14. Watkins and Kirby, "Health Care Facilities," 101–5.

15. "FAF Alters Position on FASB-GASB Jurisdiction," *Journal of Accountancy* 169 (January 1990): 13.

16. AICPA "Statement on Auditing Standards No. 62—Special Reports" (New York: AICPA, 1989).

17. T. R. Prince, "Assessing Financial Outcomes of Not-For-Profit Community Hospitals," *Hospital & Health Services Administration* 36 (Fall 1991): 331–49.

18. AICPA, *Audit and Accounting Guide*, 259.

19. AICPA, *Audit and Accounting Guide*, 147–49.

20. The assistance of Dr. Edwin Fonner, Jr., director of research and information at the Catholic Health Association is appreciated, particularly with respect to providing some privileged information that serves as the basis for these comments on CHA member hospitals. The 339 hospitals are part of almost 600 CHA member entities the author had access to through the database of The Merritt System®.

21. AICPA, *Audit and Accounting Guide*, 18–19.

22. AICPA, *Audit and Accounting Guide*, 18–19.

23. AICPA *Audit and Accounting Guide* is used as a reference for change in practice for all health care entities. Some entities were covered by AICPA "Statement of Position 78-10, Accounting Principles and Reporting Practices for Certain Nonprofit Organizations, December 31, 1978," Subsequent AICPA statements of position changed the disclosures of other entities during the 1980s.

Additional Readings

Arrington, B., and C. C. Haddock. "Who Really Profits from Not-for-Profits?" *Health Services Research* 25 (June 1990): 291–304.

Fottler, M. D., J. D. Blair, C. J. Whitehead, M. D. Laus, and G. T. Savage. "Assessing Key Stakeholders: Who Matters to Hospitals and Why?" *Hospital & Health Services Administration* 34 (Winter 1989) 525–46.

Kralewski, J., G. Gifford, and J. Porter. "Profit vs. Public Welfare Goals in Investor-Owned and Not-for-Profit Hospitals," *Hospital & Health Services Administration* 33 (Fall 1988): 311–29.

Pauly, M. V. "Nonprofit Firms in Medical Markets," *American Economic Review* 77 (May 1987): 257–62.

Discussion Questions

1.1. Explain why the typical emergency room visit results in health care services being provided by multiple entities.

1.2. Using the three-dimensional classification of ownership, control, and type of facility defined in Exhibit 1.1, determine the specification ($X_{i,j,k}$ for the following observations:

- Student health clinic at a private university (clinic is not a corporation but appears in AHA's *Guide* as "hospital unit at institution")

- Continuing-care retirement community that is a separate 501(c)(3) corporation and is jointly controlled by two community hospitals

- Comprehensive outpatient rehabilitation facility that is a separate 501(c)(3) corporation and is a subsidiary of another health care entity

- Residential facility that is not a separate corporation but is a unit of the state government

- Community hospital that is a separate corporation, is independent, and is proprietary

- Speech therapy unit that is a freestanding, separate 501(c)(3) corporation and is a subsidiary of a nongovernment not-for-profit community hospital

- General hospital owned by the federal government primarily for military personnel and their dependents

1.3. Explain the difference in the external financial statements for a nursing-home–type unit and a nursing home. Assume the nursing home is a 501(c)(3) corporation and is owned by a non–health care entity.

1.4. In the health care industry, professionals in one health care entity may direct patients to another entity in which these same professionals have a proprietary interest. Explain the reasons for numerous related-party activities in health care.

1.5. Assume there is a not-for-profit community hospital and a nearby proprietary clinic that is owned by physicians who practice at the hospital, and these same physicians make major annual contributions to the hospital. Is this a related-party situation, or is the clinic a subsidiary of the hospital? In your answer address the issue of legal ownership versus effective control.

1.6. Many health care entities are not what they appear to be. Briefly summarize the major forces and factors that have created many unique health care entities.

1.7. Explain the difficulty in conducting a national study of a given type of freestanding clinic that is not subject to the approval mechanisms of Medicare or Medicaid.

1.8. How can a clinic have certified financial statements without disclosing the amount of outstanding obligations to creditors?

1.9. How does the title of a certified financial statement differ for GAAP versus OCBOA?

1.10. Explain the difference between an accounting entity and a legal entity as related to published annual financial statements.

1.11. Explain the difference between board-designated resources in a hospital and a specific-purpose donor-restricted fund.

1.12. Explain the appropriate use of consolidated statements in a health care entity. What is the proper interpretation of combining donor-restricted and general funds for a community hospital?

2

Balance Sheets and Fund Accounting

Introduction

Titles of certified financial statements signal the type of accounting principles that support the reports. Generally accepted accounting principles (GAAP) are associated with certified reports having the title "balance sheets." Health care entities following the cash method of accounting have titles like "statement of assets and liabilities arising from cash transactions." The auditor's certificate specifies that other comprehensive basis of accounting (OCBOA) is being followed.

Fund accounting is associated with nonprofit health care entities. The organizational unit comprising the boundaries of the accounting entity for a fund may be a legal entity or a non–legal entity or a portion of a legal or non–legal entity. Most not-for-profit hospitals have restricted donations that require the health care entity to have at least two funds or accounting entities: general funds and donor-restricted funds.

Limiting the focus of this chapter to balance sheets and fund accounting does not eliminate variation in financial reporting practices under GAAP. Some nonprofit health care entities are not accounting entities for which certified financial statements are prepared; the health care entity may be part of another corporation, such as a government, a medical school, a university, or a subsidiary of a corporation. There are different accounting and audit guides for a hospital that is a department at a private university versus one at a state university. Neither of these audit guides at university-based facilities are the same as *Audit and Accounting Guide: Audits of Providers of Health Care Services*. Some nonprofit health care entities are subject to the AICPA's *Audit of Voluntary Health and Welfare Organizations*; others must follow the AICPA's *Audits of Certain Nonprofit Organizations*.

Balance sheets for health care entities following the *Audit and Accounting Guide: Audits of Providers of Health Care Services* are the primary focus of this chapter. Some variations in reporting practices under other AICPA audit guides are illustrated to show noncomparability of GAAP balance sheets for similar health care entities operating under different organizational arrangements.

Fund Accounting

The AICPA defines a *fund* as "a self-contained accounting entity set up to account for a specific activity or project." This organizational unit (accounting entity) has assets, claims against those assets, and a net balance. The assets, by definition, must equal the liabilities, or claims against those assets, plus the net fund balance. This equality of assets versus liabilities and net fund balance for the accounting entity or fund is the meaning of being "self-contained."

The typical not-for-profit community hospital has three funds: (1) general funds, (2) specific-purpose funds, and (3) plant replacement and expansion funds. Some hospitals have a fourth fund, an endowment fund. There may be so many diverse restrictions placed on donations and gifts that the specific-purpose funds are separated into two or more funds.

Each of these funds is self-balancing, where the assets equal the liabilities plus the net fund balance. The asset accounts in the restricted funds are frequently fully invested, so there is no cash available for immediate payment or disbursements. The working capital in general funds is used for any required restricted fund disbursements and then transfers are recorded against the restricted fund. On the maturity of short-term investments, the actual cash transfer occurs between the restricted funds and the general funds.

The maturity date of short-term investments often does not coincide with the end of the fiscal period. Therefore, the certified balance sheets for multiple funds in a health care entity may contain a series of "due to" and "due from" amounts in the various funds that in aggregate are equal.

Financial Transactions

Within each self-balancing fund there is a standard relationship between net assets versus liabilities plus the net fund balance. This basic relationship is also called the *fundamental accounting equation.* For non-profit health care entities the accounting equation is as follows:

Assets = Liabilities + Fund balance

Investor-owned facilities have three accounts in place of net fund balance:

Assets = Liabilities + Capital stock
+ Paid-in surplus + Retained earnings

There are no general funds versus restricted funds in the accounting for investor-owned facilities.

To illustrate the mechanics of this fundamental accounting equation, assume that three foundations made unrestricted donations toward the establishment of a health care clinic in a metropolitan area, including gifts of a building, health care equipment, medical supplies, office equipment, and administrative supplies.[1] A commercial bank gave the new health care clinic a two-year loan, using as collateral the donated building. These transactions, captured in Exhibit 2.1, are separately explained.

Exhibit 2.1   Metropolitan Health Care Clinic: Transactions 1–7

Transactions	Assets	=	Liabilities	+ Net Fund Balance
(1)	+$120,000	=		+$120,000
(2)	+ 350,000	=		+ 350,000
(3)	(10,000)	=		(10,000)
(4)	+ 45,000	=	+$ 45,000	
(5)	+ 20,000	=	+ 20,000	
(6)	(45,000)	=	(45,000)	
(7)	+ 100,000	=	+ 100,000	
Balance	$580,000	=	$120,000	+$460,000

Transaction (1). Cash of $120,000 was received by the Metropolitan Health Care Clinic from two foundations, with the understanding that $10,000 of this amount would be paid for the legal fees and organizational cost of establishing the not-for-profit health care entity. A separate check was issued by the foundation for the $10,000 with a written statement of its purpose. The transaction is an increase in an asset account (cash) and an increase in the fund balance account for $120,000.

Transaction (2). A building was purchased for $350,000 by a foundation and immediately donated to the nonprofit health clinic. The clinic shows an increase of $350,000 in assets (building by $325,000 and land by $25,000) and an increase of $350,000 in net fund balance account for this economic event.

Transaction (3). The legal fees of establishing the clinic were paid. There is a decrease of $10,000 in assets (cash) and a decrease of $10,000 in net fund balance account from this transaction.

Transaction (4). Medical equipment and medical supplies costing $45,000 in total were purchased. This transaction for $45,000 increases assets (medical equipment by $30,000 and medical supplies by $15,000) and increases liabilities (individual vendors are recorded in a subsidiary file) with the same aggregate amounts for the two sides of the equation.

Transaction (5). Office equipment and administrative supplies costing $20,000 were purchased. This transaction increases assets (office equipment by $15,000 and office supplies by $5,000) and increases liabilities (individual vendor is recorded in a subsidiary file) for $20,000.

Transaction (6). The various vendors in transaction (4) are paid in full. The economic event is a reduction of $45,000 in assets (cash) and a reduction of $45,000 in liabilities (individual vendors are recorded as being paid in a subsidiary file).

Transaction (7). A commercial bank loans $100,000 to the clinic for 24 months that can be used as working capital. This transaction increases an asset (cash) by $100,000 and increases a liability (long-term note payable) by $100,000.

After these seven transactions were recorded, a balance sheet on 1 June 19X1 presents the details of the $580,000 in total assets for general funds as shown in Exhibit 2.2. Since operations have not begun, there can be no amortization or depreciation charges for the property and equipment in the new clinic.

The balance sheet (or statement of financial condition) presents the assets, liabilities, and fund balances for a given accounting entity. The total assets (the physical properties that the accounting entity owns or has an invested interest in) must equal the total liabilities (what is owed to others) plus the net fund balance (equity).[2] Metropolitan Health Care Clinic has $185,000 in current assets plus $395,000 in property and equipment for total assets of $580,000. The $20,000 in current liabilities plus $100,000 in long-term debt equals $120,000

Exhibit 2.2   Metropolitan Health Care Clinic: Balance Sheet of
General Funds, 1 June 19X1

Assets

Current assets:		
Cash and cash equivalents	$165,000	
Medical supplies	15,000	
Office supplies	5,000	
Total current assets		$185,000
Property and equipment:		
Land	$ 25,000	
Building	325,000	
Medical equipment	30,000	
Office equipment	15,000	
Property and equipment, net		395,000
Total assets		$580,000
Liabilities and Fund Balance		
Current liabilities:		
Accounts payable	$ 20,000	
Total current liabilities		$ 20,000
Long-term debt:		
Notes payable	100,000	
Total long-term debt		100,000
Fund balance		460,000
Total liabilities and fund balance		$580,000

in liabilities, plus $460,000 in net fund balance for a total of $580,000.
Exhibit 2.2 shows that the general funds are in balance at $580,000.

Accounting Entity Reports

Wilmette Community Hospital is a nongovernment not-for-profit hospital. There are three accounting entities at this hospital for which balance sheets must be prepared: (1) general fund, (2) specific-purpose
donor-restricted funds, and (3) plant replacement and expansion
donor-restricted funds.[3] Exhibit 2.3 presents the balance sheets for
these three funds for the years ended 31 December 19X2 and 31 December 19X1. Each balance sheet in Exhibit 2.3 represents a separate

report for a fund or an accounting entity in a given year in which the total assets equal the total liabilities plus the fund balance as follows:

- General funds

Year	Total Assets	=	Total Liabilities	+	Total Fund Balance
19X2	$102,843,000	=	$41,569,473	+	$61,273,527
19X1	$ 82,020,000	=	$28,764,036	+	$53,255,964

- Specific-purpose donor-restricted funds

Year	Total Assets	=	Total Liabilities	+	Total Fund Balance
19X2	$ 2,998,109	=	0	+	$2,998,109
19X1	$ 2,620,591	=	0	+	$2,620,591

- Plant replacement and expansion donor-restricted funds

Year	Total Assets	=	Total Liabilities	+	Total Fund Balance
19X2	$ 4,916,748	=	0	+	$4,916,748
19X1	$ 3,588,263	=	0	+	$3,588,263

Assets from the two donor-restricted funds are transferred to the general funds in accordance with the stipulations by the donors. Assume that the donors specified that certain types of health care expenses are to be financed by transfers from specific-purpose funds, but a problem arises because of timing. The actual amount of these expenses may not be known until the books are closed for the period. Estimates are made and funds may be advanced to finance these expenses; the differences are reported on the balance sheets as due to and due from various funds. In Exhibit 2.3, the general funds owe $494,042 to the plant replacement and expansion funds and $205,233 to the specific-purpose fund for a total of $699,275 as of 31 December 19X2.

The format and contents of the equity section are different when the health care entity is an investor-owned or proprietary facility. Fund balance is replaced by stockholders' equity section containing capital stock, paid-in surplus, and retained earnings.

Major Classifications for General Funds

Properties or assets in the general funds are divided into categories based on specific characteristics. *Current assets* for a hospital represent

Exhibit 2.3 Wilmette Community Hospital: Balance Sheets,
31 December 19X2 and 19X1

Assets	19X2	19X1
General Funds		
Current assets:		
Cash and cash equivalents	$ 450,794	$ 744,406
Assets whose use is limited and are required for current liabilities (notes omitted)	1,416,240	1,370,880
Patient accounts receivable, net of estimated uncollectibles of $403,808 in 19X2 and $397,162 in 19X1	11,500,603	9,731,390
Estimated third party payor settlements—Medicare	390,000	470,000
Inventory of supplies at lower of cost (first in, first out) or market	1,195,339	1,025,281
Other current assets	478,427	380,874
Total current assets	*15,431,403*	*13,722,831*
Assets whose use is limited (notes omitted):		
By board for capital improvements	11,950,687	7,452,490
By agreements with third party payors for funded depreciation	7,791,722	5,681,609
Under malpractice funding arrangement—held by trustee	1,996,495	1,296,495
Under indenture agreement—held by trustee	5,100,000	4,300,000
Total assets whose use is limited	*26,838,904*	*18,730,594*
Less assets whose use is limited and that are required for current liabilities	1,416,240	1,370,880
Noncurrent assets whose use is limited	*25,422,664*	*17,359,714*
Land	2,112,274	2,112,274
Land improvements	284,317	284,317
Buildings and improvements	44,839,982	45,641,540
Equipment	21,756,791	20,181,080
	68,993,364	*68,219,211*

Continued

Exhibit 2.3   Continued

Assets	19X2	19X1
Less accumulated depreciation and amortization	22,603,972	19,881,699
	46,389,392	*48,337,512*
Construction in progress	14,222,842	1,681,838
Property and equipment, net	*60,612,234*	*50,019,350*
Other assets:		
Deferred financing costs	1,376,699	918,105
Total assets	*$102,843,000*	*$82,020,000*

Liabilities and Fund Balances	19X2	19X1
General Funds		
Current liabilities:		
Current installments of long-term debt	$ 1,416,240	$ 1,370,880
Accounts payable	2,547,243	2,387,653
Accrued expenses	4,631,354	3,500,283
Retainage and construction accounts payable	890,500	71,500
Estimated third party payor settlement—Medicaid	1,218,693	605,726
Deferred third-party reimbursement	150,013	180,266
Advances from third party payors	515,340	480,060
Due to donor-restricted funds, net	699,275	591,312
Total current liabilities	*12,068,658*	*9,187,680*
Deferred third-party reimbursement	480,000	570,000
Estimated malpractice costs	2,396,495	1,296,495
Long-term debt, excluding current installments	26,624,320	17,709,861
Fund balance	61,273,527	53,255,964
Commitments and contingent liabilities (notes omitted)		
Total liabilities and fund balance	*$102,843,000*	*$82,020,000*

Assets	19X2	19X1
Donor-Restricted Funds		
Specific-purpose funds:		
Cash	$ 128,712	$ 95,406

Continued

Exhibit 2.3 Continued

Assets	19X2	19X1
Investments, at cost that		
approximates market	2,664,164	2,350,875
Due from general funds	205,233	174,310
Total assets	$ 2,998,109	$ 2,620,591
Liabilities and Fund Balances	**19X2**	**19X1**
Donor-Restricted Funds		
Specific-purpose funds:		
Fund balance	$ 2,998,109	$ 2,620,591
Total liabilities and fund balance	$ 2,998,109	$ 2,620,591
Assets	**19X2**	**19X1**
Donor-Restricted Funds		
Plant replacement and expansion funds:		
Cash	$ 136,371	$ 145,306
Investments, at cost that		
approximates market	2,469,715	2,135,480
Pledges receivable, net of estimated		
uncollectibles of $139,445 in		
19X2 and $65,000 in 19X1	1,816,620	890,475
Due from general funds	494,042	417,002
Total assets	$ 4,916,748	$ 3,588,263
Liabilities and Fund Balances	**19X2**	**19X1**
Donor-Restricted Funds		
Plant replacement and expansion funds:		
Fund balance	$ 4,916,748	$ 3,588,263
Total liabilities and fund balance	$ 4,916,748	$ 3,588,263

those properties consisting of cash or items that will be converted into cash or consumed or used within one year. The general funds current assets for Wilmette Community Hospital in 19X2 are shown in Exhibit 2.3.

These current assets illustrate the four components in this definition. The *cash* component is represented by the $450,794 in the cash account; the *converted into cash* component is represented by the net accounts receivable balance of $11,500,603 (gross receivables of $11,904,411, less the estimate for contractual allowances and provision for uncollectibles of $403,808, gives $11,500,603 as expected cash receipts); and the *consumed* or *used* components are represented by the $1,195,339 in inventories and the $478,427 in prepaid expenses and other current assets.

Investments may be classified as current assets if it is the intention of administration to convert these items into cash within one year and where there is a well-developed market for the investments. When investments are classified as current assets, they are referred to as *marketable securities.* Administrators often hold securities, bonds, and investments under flexible conditions in order to change their portfolios to suit the market outlook. These securities may be held for more than a year or for less than a year, depending on future conditions, and they are classified as *investments.*

Some securities and investments within the general funds may not be equally available to meet expenditure obligations. These properties or investments in the general funds may have limitations imposed on their use by the governing board; some investments are set aside in accordance with agreements with third party payors and some investments are held by trustees under indenture agreements and self-insurance trust arrangements. This limited use by indenture agreement is related to the bond indenture where the bond covenants limit the use of those funds. In Exhibit 2.3, Wilmette Community Hospital reports four categories of *assets whose use is limited* for 19X2. If it were not for the limitations on assets use, the $26,838,904 would be reported as investments.

Property and equipment include those physical properties, other than *land,* that are consumed or used in the creation of economic activity. The historical costs of these properties are allocated against revenues generated from using these fixed assets. The time period used for this allocation is a minimum number of years determined by the various regulatory agencies. Remember that historical costs represent the original acquisition cost and that no price level adjustment is permitted by the health care regulatory authorities. Thus, using the minimum number of years reduces the impact of matching cost dollars from past accounting periods with current revenue dollars. Appraised values were used to reflect some of the land, buildings, and equipment donated to Wilmette Community Hospital from the local government.

The historical cost of plant and equipment is $68,993,364, and the construction in progress is $14,222,842; thus, the combined value of fixed assets is $83,216,206. The cumulative depreciation (allowance for depreciation), which has been matched against revenues, is $22,603,972, giving a net plant and equipment balance of $60,612,234. The typical general funds balance sheet has a single line for the net balance of $60,612,234 and reports the detail items by notes to the financial statement. Exhibit 2.3 has this information in the balance sheet itself for convenience purposes.

Other assets include investments in other health care entities, deferred organization costs, and deferred financing costs. Many health care organizations have recorded a deferred pension asset that is included in other noncurrent assets. Wilmette Community Hospital does not have a major investment in another health care entity. Its only account in the "other assets" category is deferred financing costs for long-term debt.

Current liabilities represent obligations that must be paid to others within a 12-month period. The general funds have current liabilities of $12,068,658, including the current portion of the long-term debt totalling $1,416,240. Note in Exhibit 2.3 that the indenture requires $1,416,240 of assets to be transferred to the "current assets" group from the investments for matching with this current installment of the long-term debt.

Deferred revenues and *estimated liabilities* are disclosed separately from current and long-term liabilities. Deferred revenues are timing differences between the cash receipts and the delivery of health care services. Estimated liabilities arise from the matching of costs with revenue in the period when the malpractice events occurred rather than waiting for a claim or legal dispute. For cosmetic reasons, some hospitals prefer the term "accrued professional liability" rather than "estimated malpractice costs."

Long-term liabilities are obligations that do not have to be retired during the current 12-month period. The general funds have long-term debt of $26,624,320.

Fund balances represent the residual equities or the residual claims against total assets after all liabilities have been satisfied. The "general" versus "donor-restricted" partitions of fund balances are based on legal factors. Any donation, gift, or bequest to a hospital not accompanied by a written legal document constraining the use of the funds must be classified as general funds. A hospital administrator might suggest to a prospective donor that a restricted gift for a specific purpose would be helpful in carrying out the program of the health care facility. If the donor includes this type of specification in the letter of transmittal for a gift, then such funds are classified as donor-restricted. Once a gift to the general fund has been received and accepted by a hospital, any future specifications by the original donor have no legal bearing on the unrestricted classification of the funds.

Donor-restricted funds are often classified according to the use of the principal. If the restricted donations are for new facilities, these resources are recorded in the plant replacement and expansion fund, and often legal restrictions accompanying the donation specify that investment income is to be added to the plant replacement and expansion donor-restricted fund. Donor-restricted gifts to support specific medical and health services are classified as specific-purpose funds. Investment income from donor-restricted funds is accounted for in accordance with the written specifications imposed by the donor: sometimes the funds stay in the specific-purpose donor-restricted fund; in other cases the investment income goes to the general fund.

Assets donated for endowment are accounted for in accordance with the written instructions accompanying the gift. A regular endowment establishes a perpetual source of income where the principal is kept intact. The inability of the hospital's governing board to spend the principal is what differentiates an endowment fund from other types of donor-restricted funds. The income from the endowment fund is disbursed in accordance with the written specifications of the donor. In the case of a term endowment, the principal cannot be expended until after some time period has elapsed, or certain actions or activities have been accomplished. Regular endowments and term endowments are accounted for as donor-restricted funds.

Financial Reporting Practices

Major differences in financial reporting practices for health care entities have been reduced in many areas over the past 20 years. The new *Audit and Accounting Guide: Audits of Providers of Health Care Services* consolidated many of these changes. But there are still multiple audit guides directing reporting practices of health care entities.

Governmental health care entities

There are some significant differences in nonprofit accounting reporting practices between FASB and GASB, especially for fixed assets and depreciation. Health care entities are almost excluded from this dispute because of the governmental reporting arrangements under Medicare. Community hospitals, beginning in the late 1960s, have been permitted to record donated fixed assets on their books and receive reimbursement under Medicare for depreciation.[4] Many hospitals did not elect to participate in Medicare in 1965, but by 1970 most community hospitals were active participants. Thus, most hospitals have been following FASB rules for 20 years with respect to donated assets.

Hospitals operated by a governmental unit were subject to the AICPA's *Audits of State and Local Governmental Units* (1974); however, in an AICPA position paper, this was changed for fiscal years beginning after 30 June 1979.[5] The old *Hospital Audit Guide* applied to all nonfederal governmental community hospitals by 1980.

GASB has issued official opinions covering special problems in financial reporting by state and local governments, including some overlap with FASB's positions. For example, GASB "Statement No. 7: Advance Refunding Resulting in Defeasance of Debt" states the following:

> The disclosure guidance in paragraphs 11–14 is applicable to advance refundings of all entities and funds of those entities including state and local governments, public benefit corporations and authorities, public employee retirement systems, and governmental utilities, hospitals, colleges, and universities.[6]

The overlap between GASB and FASB had been formally addressed by the Financial Accounting Foundation, and GASB was given a larger mission in 1989.[7] It will take time for some of these issues to be resolved because of the diverse interests that are involved.[8]

Investor-owned health care entities

The movement from the retrospective cost reimbursement system for Medicare in 1983 to the prospective payment system began to remove some of the financial reporting differences between nonprofit health care entities and investor-owned facilities.[9] With the annual updates in the accounting under the prospective payment system, other differences in practice between nonprofit and investor-owned entities began to be eliminated.[10] While the old *Hospital Audit Guide* excluded investor-owned hospitals, investor-owned entities are fully included in the new *Audit and Accounting Guide: Audits of Providers of Health Care Services.*[11]

Private university hospitals

There are still major reporting differences for the health care entity that is a "department" in a private university. The university-based nongovernment not-for-profit community hospital that is a separate corporation is subject to AICPA's *Audit and Accounting Guide: Audits of Providers of Health Care Services*. If the university-based community hospital is not a separate corporation but part of a private university, then the AICPA's *Audits of Colleges and Universities* will have a significant impact on special reports related to the hospital. Those funds that are completely within the hospital's entity can follow the *Audit and Accounting Guide: Audits of Providers of Health Care Services*, but shared funds are under the reporting requirements of *Audits of Colleges and Universities*.

Exhibit 2.4 shows the balance sheet of Alpha Memorial Hospital—a division of the University of Alpha, a private institution—following AICPA's *Audits of Colleges and Universities*. The total assets in these five unrestricted funds is $121,926,001; however, there is some double accounting in the "due from" and "due to" transactions, which affects total assets and total liabilities. Note the separate funds and their balances within the unrestricted fund:

Undesignated current fund balance	$ 47,916
Designated for plant replacement fund	2,446,376
Designated for debt retirement fund	11,532,698
Designated for other fund balance	480,305
Designated for total building and equipment fund	30,438,974
Total unrestricted fund	*$44,946,269*

The aggregate unrestricted fund balance of $44,946,269 is not influenced by these double accounting entries.

State university hospitals

The state university–based community hospital that is not a separate corporation is in a similar position to the state governmental accounting procedures as is the private university hospital to *Audits of Colleges and Universities*. The state university hospital may be part of an integrated set of fund accounts used by the state government. Some of these fund accounts may be identical with those used by Alpha Memorial Hospital in Exhibit 2.4. GASB, FASB, and AICPA have rules that the state university–based community hospital must follow.

Exhibit 2.4 Alpha Memorial Hospital (A Division of the University of Alpha): Balance Sheet, 31 December 19X1

Assets		Liabilities and Fund Balances	
Unrestricted Fund			
Undesignated current:		Undesignated current:	
Cash—imprest funds	$ 45,814	Current portion of long-term debt	$ 3,594,246
Due from designated funds	3,850,772	Accounts payable	1,800,378
Patient accounts receivable	14,948,466	Accrued expenses	630,455
Allowance for doubtful accounts	(2,040,990)	Accrued salaries and taxes	3,450,203
Inventories	2,507,648	Accrued vacation	1,819,070
Deferred charges	1,052,174	Estimated third-party settlements	1,460,800
		Total current liabilities	$ 12,755,152
		Working capital advances payable due to unrestricted designated fund	7,560,816
		Fund balance	47,916
Total current assets	$ 20,363,884	Total current fund liabilities and fund balance	$ 20,363,884
Designated for specific purposes:		Designated for specific purposes:	
Plant replacement		Plant replacement	
Cash (university pool)	$ 82,892	Due to undesignated current fund	$ 2,400,772
Trustee-held funds	12,286,692	Due to debt retirement fund	3,500,898
Due from undesignated current fund	5,279,816	Long-term debt, net of current installments	9,416,354
Grant receivable	115,000	Total plant replacement liabilities	$ 15,318,024

Continued

Exhibit 2.4 Continued

Assets		Liabilities and Fund Balances	
Total plant replacement assets	$ 17,764,400	Fund balance	2,446,376
		Total plant replacement liabilities and fund balance	$ 17,764,400
Debt retirement:		Debt retirement:	
Cash (university pool)	$ 300,600	Due to current fund	$ 1,450,000
Investments	6,900,200		
Due from undesignated current fund	2,281,000	Fund balance	11,532,698
Due from plant replacement fund	3,500,898		
Total debt retirement assets	$ 12,982,698	Total debt retirement liabilities and fund balance	$ 12,982,698
Other:		Other:	
Cash (university pool)	$ 5,610	Fund balance	$ 480,305
Investments at market value (cost $648,320)	474,695		
Total other assets	$ 480,305	Total other fund balance	$ 480,305
Building and equipment:		Building and equipment:	
Buildings and improvements	$ 82,676,679	Long-term debt, net of current installments	$39,895,740
Equipment	33,182,123	Building and equipment net of long term debt	30,438,974
	$115,858,802		
Less accumulated depreciation	(48,489,591)		
	$ 67,369,211		

Construction in progress	2,965,503		
Net buildings and equipment	$ 70,334,714	Total building and equipment fund	$ 70,334,714
Total unrestricted fund	$121,926,001	Total unrestricted fund	$121,926,001

Restricted Fund

Specific-purpose funds:		Specific-purpose funds:	
Cash (university pool)	$ 24,380	Fund balance	$ 695,791
Investments at market value	671,411		
Total specific-purpose funds	$ 695,791	Total specific-purpose funds	$ 695,791
Endowment funds:		Endowment funds:	
Investments at market value	$ 5,741,560	Fund balance	$ 5,741,560
Total endowment funds	$ 5,741,560	Total endowment funds	$ 5,741,560

Depreciation, for example, is not required by governmental accounting or by *Audits of Colleges and Universities*; however, the cost-based reimbursement system in the past encouraged hospitals to use depreciation accounting.[12] Many potential differences in fixed asset reporting between health care entities following different audit guides do not really exist because of payment rules under Medicare.

Nonprofit health and welfare facilities

Financial reporting for the nonprofit clinics, medical and health services, mental health institutes, and community health and welfare facilities is specified by AICPA's *Audits of Voluntary Health and Welfare Organizations*. Other nonprofit entities are subject to AICPA's *Audits of Certain Nonprofit Organizations*.

Summary

The Social Security Amendments of 1965 (P. L. 89–97) created a national pressure on the accounting profession for financial statements for hospitals participating in Medicare and Medicaid. AHA issued the 1966 edition of *Chart of Accounts for Hospitals*. AICPA issued the *Medicare Audit Guide: An AICPA Industry Audit Guide* (1969), followed by the *Hospital Audit Guide* (1972). The states administered Medicaid, and state legislatures began to ask the state departments of public health for additional information when considering appropriations for matching funds.

Financial reporting and accounting practices for health care facilities changed significantly over the past two decades as the federal programs imposed reimbursement rules on the "cottage industry." P. L. 95–142 gave the authority to the secretary of the Department of Health and Human Services (DHHS) to mandate a uniform accounting system for each type of health care facility. Various rules have been published in the *Federal Register* in the interest of uniform accounting; however, each of these efforts has been delayed. Other developments have changed the need for uniform accounting.

The fixed-fee payment system under the prospective payment system for Medicare patients removed the need for cost comparisons in reimbursement; it was also the stimulus for many operational changes in a highly competitive health care environment. Some differences between investor-owned health care entities and nonprofit entities were eliminated under the annual revisions in the payment arrangement for Medicare patients.

Property, plant, and equipment funds were merged with the hospital's operating fund (now general funds) in 1976, and board-designated funds were reclassified as segment reports of the accounting entity for the basic hospital. The 1990 audit guide changed board-designated assets to "assets whose use is limited" within the general funds. There are still some differences when the health care unit is part of a university, a government, or a corporation and does not issue separate certified reports. Other AICPA audit guides may govern such activities, which have different reporting requirements than the *Audit and Accounting Guide: Audits of Providers of Health Care Services.*

Balance sheets report the assets, liabilities, and fund balances for nonprofit health care entities; the fund balance section of the balance sheet is replaced by a capital section when the statement is for an investor-owned facility. There are separate balance sheets for each fund, such as general funds, donor-restricted specific-purpose funds, plant replacement and expansion funds, and endowment funds.

Appendix: Reporting Guidelines for Health Care Entities

Current reporting practices of health care entities were formed in large part by responses of hospital administrators to regulatory, economic, and environmental factors. AICPA's *Hospital Audit Guide* was initially issued in 1972; the only previous AICPA industry guide was the *Medicare Audit Guide* in 1969. AHA was the dominant force in providing reporting guidelines from 1922 to the late 1960s.

AHA prepared its *Chart of Accounts for Hospitals* in 1966, which was a complete revision of its 1922 manual *Uniform Chart of Accounts and Definitions for Hospitals.* The foreword in the 1966 *Chart of Accounts for Hospitals* expresses the magnitude of the changes during this 44-year period:

> Recognizing the need for accounting data and information essential to effective financial management, the American Hospital Association has developed various materials on accounting since its publication of the first chart of accounts in 1922. This complete revision of the previous manual is the result of the many changes and modifications that have been necessitated by innovations in the accounting field, as well as by changes in the hospital field.[13]

Existing textbooks and references were the guides that new hospitals used in creating their unique chart of accounts and accounting procedures.[14] The impact of these unique general chart of accounts by hospitals (especially for the 1,292 nonfederal short-term general hospitals established between 1946 and 1965) can be seen in actions taken by the federal government in 1977 in the name of uniform reporting (P. L. 95–142).

Health care cost became a national political issue as national health expenditures rose from 8.3 percent of GNP in 1975 to 10.2 percent of GNP in 1982. As this rise in health expenditures occurred, critics searched for someone to blame. Hospital expenses—which represented about 47 percent of national health expenditures and had almost doubled between 1975 and 1980, from $52.4 billion in 1975 to $101.6 billion in 1980[15]—were selected by political leaders as the focus for major criticism. Hospitals were identified as a professional institution that could serve as an enemy.

Some government officials responded to a request for donations from a children's hospital with accompanying financial statements that looked like the hospital might discontinue operations unless contributions were immediately given. Further reflections upon this "marketing document" and an investigation by concerned government officials revealed that the children's hospital had raised several million dollars in the "board-designated unrestricted fund," which were not reported with the "operating fund." Since the children's hospital statements were certified financial reports, the accounting profession became the focus of criticism for misleading the public. Some government officials saw these financial statements of children's hospitals as encouraging changes in national health expenditures without informed consent by the responding public.

After the political debate had focused on the accounting practice that permitted contributions and donations to be excluded from the hospital's operating fund, regulatory officials urged members of the U.S. Congress to do something about the lack of uniform reporting by hospitals. Congressional hearings included presentations by regulatory personnel with experience in trying to compare hospital cost by department between similar bed-size institutions within the same service area who had discovered that variations in accounting practice often made such reports of questionable value. The absence of any "standards" on how hospital costs were to be measured by department left regulatory personnel in an uncomfortable position when there were objections to a given hospital's reporting procedure. Regulatory bodies asked Congress to establish a uniform hospital accounting system so meaningful comparisons can be made among hospitals in a given service area or across service areas.

As health expenditures became a national political issue, members of the U.S. Congress felt compelled to do something about these rising costs. They gave the authority to the secretary of DHHS to mandate a uniform accounting system for each type of health care facility. The Medicare-Medicaid Anti-Fraud and Abuse Amendments, P. L. 95–142 (dated 25 October 1977), Section 19 states:

> For the purposes of reporting the cost of services provided by, of planning, and of measuring and comparing the efficiency of and effective use of services in, hospitals, skilled nursing facilities, intermediate care facilities, home health agencies, health maintenance organizations, and other types of health services facilities and organizations to which payment may be made under this Act, the Secretary shall establish by regulation, for each such type of health services facility or organization, a *uniform system for the reporting* by a facility or organization of that type of the following information . . . . [16] [emphasis added]

Health Care Financing Administration (HCFA) became the regulatory unit to implement new procedures for the secretary of DHHS. The initial draft of the government's proposed system was called *System for Hospital Uniform Accounting* (SHUA) but some members of Congress objected to the federal government mandating "uniform accounting" for hospitals. In response to this criticism, the revised drafts of the government's proposed system substituted "Reporting" for "Accounting" as the fifth word in the title. *System for Hospital Uniform Reporting* (SHUR) was published on 29 September 1978 as a draft document and distributed to all short-term hospitals in the United States.[17] The notice of proposed rulemaking (NPRM) for SHUR was published in the *Federal Register* on 23 January 1979.

There were many excellent ideas in the reporting procedures in SHUR; however, there were a few requirements that were not reasonable and could not be justified on a cost-benefit basis. For example, when a nurse was delivering a tray to a patient, that time had to be separately measured and not reported as nursing care. There was no consideration of what else the nurse did when presenting the tray to a patient.

HCFA made changes that significantly reduced the cost and burden of the original SHUR proposal and called the modified version the *Annual Hospital Report*.[18] The NPRM appeared 29 days later, but the implementation was delayed by a series of legal and administrative activities from the health care industry.[19]

The accounting profession assumed a more active role in the health care industry during 1976–1982. The reporting of fixed-asset accounting by hospitals was changed in 1976, from being in a separate "plant fund" to being part of the "operating fund."[20] This meant that a significant number of donated facilities that had been placed on the books for purpose of cost-based reimbursement under Medicare and Medicaid were now part of the hospital's regular operating fund (which later became the general funds).

The fund development practices of selected nonprofit institutions were recognized by the accounting profession as not satisfying the full disclosure requirements. What is the accounting entity for the basic hospital? Can there be a certified set of financial statements for only a component of the basic hospital? The AICPA's 1990 *Audit and Accounting Guide: Audits of Providers of Health Care Services* eliminates segmented reports and shows board-designated assets as part of the general funds. Other issues related to investor-owned health care entities versus nonprofit entities were also addressed by the 1990 audit guide.

Notes

1. This nonprofit clinic was really established with donations from five foundations, including the building. After it was in operation, then the federal government made an award to the facility.
2. Some writers prefer to use a broad definition of equity that includes all claims against assets—for example, (C. P. Stickney, R. L. Weil, and S. Davidson, *Financial Accounting: An Introduction to Concepts, Methods, and Uses*, 6th ed., (New York: Harcourt Brace Jovanovich, Inc., 1991), 771. FASB's definition of the "residual interest in assets of an entity after deducting its liabilities" is followed in the current volume.
3. AICPA, *Audit and Accounting Guide*, 152.
4. AICPA, Committee on Health Care Institutions, *Medicare Audit Guide: An AICPA Industry Audit Guide* (New York: AICPA, 1969), 18: "With respect to all assets acquired before 1966, a provider may have chosen the optional allowance for depreciation based on a percentage of operating costs. The independent auditor should review the computation of the allowance and its limitations for propriety and conformance to the applicable regulations."
5. AICPA, "Statement of Position 78-7: Financial Accounting and Reporting by Hospitals Operated by a Governmental Unit" (New York: AICPA, 1978): "Hospitals that are operated by governmental units should follow the requirements of the AICPA's *Hospital Audit Guide*. Since the accounting

recommended in that guide can best be accommodated in the enterprise funds, such funds should be used in accounting for governmental hospitals."

6. Government Accounting Standards Board (GASB), "Statement No. 7: Advance Refundings Resulting in Defeasance of Debt" (Stamford, CT: GASB, 1987), paragraph 7.

7. "FAF Alters Position on FASB-GASB Jurisdiction," *Journal of Accountancy* 169 (January 1990): 13.

8. In 1991, GASB issued Statement No. 14, "The Financial Reporting Entity," which is effective for financial statements for periods beginning after 15 December 1992. Statement No. 14 (paragraph 127–8) takes exception with the AICPA use of the equity method for certain types of joint ventures. Financial-reporting entity and related issues are still under study by FASB, which issued a discussion memorandum, "Consolidation Policy and Procedures," with a comment period ending 15 July 1992.

9. The shift from cost-based reimbursement to the prospective payment system over a four-year phased implementation was authorized on 20 April 1983 by the Social Security Amendments of 1983, P. L. 98–21.

10. FASB, "Statement of Financial Accounting Concepts No. 6; Elements of Financial Statements, A Replacement of FASB Concepts Statement No. 3"; and AICPA, "Statement of Position 90-8: Financial Accounting and Reporting by Continuing Care Retirement Communities."

11. AICPA, Committee on Health Care Institutions, *Hospital Audit Guide* (New York: AICPA, 1972), 39: "Illustrative statements for investor-owned (proprietary) hospitals are not included since they should follow reporting requirements of other investor-owned business."

12. AICPA, Committee on College and University Accounting and Auditing, *Audits of Colleges and Universities* (New York: AICPA, 1973), 9.

13. AHA, *Chart of Accounts for Hospitals: Financial Management Series* (Chicago: AHA, 1966), iii.

14. Textbooks included L. E. Hay, *Budgeting and Cost Analysis for Hospital Management*, 2d ed. (Bloomington, IN: Pressler Publications, 1963); T. L. Martin, *Hospital Accounting: Principles and Practice* (Chicago: Physicians' Record Co., 1951); C. G. Roswell, *Accounting, Statistics and Business Office Procedures for Hospitals* (New York: United Hospital Fund of New York, 1946); L. Vann Seawell, *Principles of Hospital Accounting* (Chicago: Physicians' Record Co., 1960) and *Hospital Accounting and Financial Management* (Chicago: Physicians' Record Co., 1964); and P. J. Taylor and B. O. Nelson, *Management Accounting for Hospitals* (Philadelphia: W. B. Saunders Company, 1964).

15. D. R. Waldo, K. R. Levit, and H. Lazenby, "National Health Expenditures, 1985," *Health Care Financing Review* 8 (Fall 1986): 10.

16. 42 USC 1320a(a).

17. Office of Policy, Planning, and Research, HCFA, U.S. Department of Health, Education, and Welfare (DHEW), *System for Hospital Uniform Reporting* (29 September 1978).

18. HCFA, DHEW, *Annual Hospital Report: Draft for Discussion Only* (20 February 1980).
19. *Federal Register* 45(55): 17894–17911 (19 March 1980).
20. For example, the November 1977 Uniform CPA Examination included a problem called "Dexter Hospital," in which there were accounting transactions between the operating fund and the plant fund. The existence of this plant fund on the 1977 examination generated an explanatory footnote in *Uniform CPA Examination: May 1976 to November 1977: Unofficial Answers* (New York: AICPA, 1978), 96, indicating the change in accounting practice for fixed assets in 1976.

Additional Readings

Cleverley, W. O. "Strategic Financial Planning: A Balance Sheet Perspective," *Hospital & Health Services Administration* 32 (February 1987): 1–20.
Friedman, B., and S. Shortell. "The Financial Performance of Selected Investor-Owned and Not-for-Profit System Hospitals Before and After Medicare Prospective Payment," *Health Services Research* 23 (June 1988): 237–67.
Kane, N. M., and P. D. Manoukian. "The Effect of the Medicare Prospective Payment System on the Adoption of New Technology," *New England Journal of Medicine* 321 (16 November 1989): 1378–83.
Kleiner, R. G., M. Garner, and R. G. Colbert. "A Preview of the New Healthcare Audit Guide," *Journal of Accountancy* 168 (September 1989): 32–44.
McLean, R. A. "Outside Directors: Stakeholder Representation in Investor-Owned Health Care Organizations," *Hospital & Health Services Administration* 34 (Summer 1989): 255–68.

Discussion Questions

2.1. Explain the "self-contained" feature of a fund.

2.2. What are the names of the three most common funds in a not-for-profit community hospital?

2.3. What accounts replace the "fund balance" account in an investor-owned health care entity?

2.4. You are performing an analysis of Rose Nursing Home, Inc., and have received the following incomplete information:

Common stock	$ 80,000
Long-term debt, less current maturities	1,900,000
Paid-in surplus	65,000
Property and equipment, net	1,800,000 4th
Retained earnings	235,000

1st Total all assets up   2,600,000

Total assets whose use is limited	200,000 2nd
Total current assets	550,000 1st
Total other asset	50,000 3rd

Determine the total current liabilities at Rose Nursing Home, Inc.

2.5. You are performing an analysis of Green Home Health Agency and have received the following incomplete information:

Fund balance	$ 480,000
Long-term debt, less current maturities	90,000
Property and equipment, net	100,000
Total assets whose use is limited	120,000
Total current assets	950,000
Total other asset	20,000

Determine the total current liabilities at Green Home Health Agency.

2.6. Investor-owned hospitals were not governed by AICPA's old *Hospital Audit Guide*, but they are under the new *Audit and Accounting Guide: Audits of Providers of Health Care Services*. Explain the major events in the 1980s that eliminated these differences in reporting practices.

2.7 Explain the impact that reporting procedures under Medicare in the 1960s and 1970s have on the position in 1990 of nonprofit health care entities in the disputes between FASB and GASB.

2.8 The secretary of DHHS has the authority to mandate uniform accounting for each type of health care facility. Explain why the federal government is not attempting to mandate uniform accounting for community hospitals.

2.9 Explain the difference in focus between a *cost-based reimbursement system* and a *prospective payment system* for a community hospital.

2.10 List the accounting and reporting guides that may govern the financial statements of a community hospital at a private university.

2.11 List the accounting and reporting guides that may govern the financial statements of a community hospital at a state university.

2.12 List the accounting organizations that have jurisdiction over the financial statements of local and state government community hospitals.

2.13 Prepare Jones Community Hospital's balance sheet of general funds as of 31 December 19X1 from the following account information:

Accrued expenses	$ 5,000,000
Accounts payable	5,300,000
Accumulated depreciation and amortization	24,000,000
Advances from third party payors	600,000

Assets whose use is limited and that are required for current liabilities	1,500,000
Assets whose use is limited by agreements with third party payors for funded depreciation	12,000,000
Assets whose use is limited by board for capital improvements	16,400,000
Assets whose use is limited under indenture agreement—held by trustee	5,100,000
Assets whose use is limited under malpractice funding arrangement—held by trustee	2,000,000
Buildings and improvements	51,300,000
Cash and short-term investments, at cost that approximates market	400,000
Current installments of long-term debt	1,000,000
Deferred financing costs	1,200,000
Due to donor-restricted funds, net	700,000
Equipment	23,200,000
Estimated malpractice costs	3,000,000
Estimated third party payor settlement—Medicaid	1,400,000
Estimated third party payor settlement—Medicare	300,000
Fund balance	65,000,000
Inventory of supplies at lower of cost (first-in, first-out) or market	1,400,000
Land	4,000,000
Land improvements	500,000
Long-term debt, excluding current installments	25,000,000
Other current assets	200,000
Patient accounts receivable, net of estimated uncollectibles of $403,808 in 19X1	13,000,000

2.14 Alpha Memorial Hospital (Exhibit 2.4) reported "total unrestricted fund" of $121,926,001. Assume that Alpha Memorial Hospital became a separate not-for-profit corporation subject to the AICPA's *Audit and Accounting Guide: Audits of Providers of Health Care Services*. Using Exhibit 2.3 as a guide, determine the balance of the unrestricted fund. Hint: Eliminate the "Due To" and "Due From" references in Exhibit 2.4, such as the following:

	Debit	Credit
Due to undesignated current fund (plant replacement fund)	$2,400,772	
Due to current fund (debt retirement fund)	1,450,000	
Due from designated fund (undesignated current fund)		$3,850,772

2.15 Prepare hospital and donor-restricted funds balance sheets for Alpha Memorial Hospital under the assumptions of Question 2.14. This can be in the format of Exhibit 2.3 with multiple columns or a single set of columns with multiple pages.

2.16 Beta Memorial Hospital had the following fund balances at the end of the current fiscal year:

General funds	$26,000,000
Specific-purpose donor-restricted fund	8,000,000
Research foundation donor-restricted fund	9,000,000
Education foundation donor-restricted fund	7,000,000

Determine the consolidated balance of funds at Beta Memorial Hospital that are available to meet long-term obligations.

2.17 An employee at Beta Memorial Hospital (see Question 2.16) was injured by an accident while working in the Radiology Department. Which hospital assets are available for use in settling the case against this employee? Explain your position.

2.18 Beta Memorial Hospital incurred a $1,500,000 loss from operations during the current year according to the preliminary financial reports. A hospital trustee questioned why the $2,100,000 of investment income from the three donor-restricted funds was not transferred to general funds. If this had been done, the current year operations would have reflected a $600,000 profit. From the discussion, it appears as though the Fund Development Office prefers to have a loss reported for the year and keep the investment income in the donor-restricted funds. Explain the proper accounting and reporting of these events.

3

Statement of Revenue and Expenses

Introduction

Aggregate revenue, gains, and incomes from a health care entity's activities are matched against expired costs, expenses, and losses in the statement of revenue and expenses. Certified financial statements based on generally accepted accounting principles (GAAP) after the 1990 *Audit and Accounting Guide* provide uniform disclosure of these items across various types of health care entities. Ambulatory care clinics, home health agencies, nursing homes, HMOs, and community hospitals have suggested financial reports in the same AICPA guide.

This similarity in current reporting practice of GAAP statements is not applicable to reports accepted by Medicare, Medicaid, and other governmental agencies. The statement of revenue and expenses is the report with the *most* significant variation in contents and format among the diverse parties who act upon financial statements from health care entities. Some of this variation in reporting practice for community hospitals is illustrated in this discussion, based on an analysis of certified financial statements for more than 1,500 health care entities.

The statement of revenue and expenses is currently the most significant report for assessing the financial and operational performance of a health care entity. The 1990 audit guide requires a statement of cash flows for health care entities. The first of the three sections in the statement of cash flows contains a summary of the results from the statement of revenue and expenses. After the standard report of cash flows has been used for several years, then that report will become more important in assessing the financial and operational performance of health care facilities. Before addressing these refinements, the basic relationship of the statement of revenue and expenses to the balance sheet is examined in this chapter.

Relation of Income to Balance Sheet

The fundamental accounting equation expresses the equality of assets versus liabilities and net fund balance in nonprofit health care entities. Stockholders' equity is the same as net fund balance in investor-owned facilities, and this category contains three principal accounts: capital stock, paid-in surplus, and retained earnings. The accounts in the balance sheet equation are permanent accounts—they tend to last for many years.

Revenue, income, and expenses are temporary accounts that serve to accumulate certain types of transactions for a given period of time, such as a year. At the end of the year, the temporary accounts are matched against each other for purpose of determining "revenue and gains in excess of expenses and losses." A statement of revenue and expenses is prepared showing the aggregate amounts of revenue, income, expired costs, and expenses within categories. The net results from the statement of revenue and expenses is transferred to the net fund balance account in nonprofit entities, or to the retained earnings in investor-owned facilities. As part of the transfer transaction, all temporary accounts are set equal to zero for the past period.

Metropolitan Health Care Clinic with its balance after seven transactions (Exhibit 2.1), may be used to illustrate the integration of temporary and permanent accounts in the fundamental equation:

Permanent Accounts	*Temporary Accounts*

$$\text{Assets} = \text{Liabilities} + \text{Fund balance} + \text{Income} - \text{Expenses}$$

The 1 June 19X1 balance (Exhibit 2.2) is updated by the transactions for the first year of operation, ending on 31 May 19X2. The eight transactions plus the closing entries are reported in Exhibit 3.1.

Transaction (8). Gross charges of $160,000 are recorded for patient services rendered. This transaction increases the temporary income account by $160,000 and increases an asset account by $160,000. At the end of the period, the temporary income account is closed into the permanent account, net fund balance.

Transaction (9). Patients paid $16,000 to the cashier for the services received. An internal control procedure separates gross charge entry from the cashier function. This transaction reduces an asset

Exhibit 3.1 Metropolitan Health Care Clinic: Transactions 8–15

Transactions	Assets	=	Liabilities	+	Fund Balance	+	Income	−	Expense
Balance*	$580,000	=	$120,000	+	$460,000	+	0	−	0
(8)	+160,000	=				+	160,000		
(9)	+ 16,000								
	(16,000)								
(10)	(34,000)	=					(34,000)		
(11)			+ 80,000						(80,000)
(12)			+ 25,000						(25,000)
(13)	(3,000)	=							(3,000)
(14)	(70,000)	=	(70,000)						
(15)	(2,500)	=							(2,500)
End of period				+	15,500		(126,000)	+	110,500
Balance	$630,500	=	$155,000	+	$475,500	+	0	−	0

*See Exhibit 2.1 for information on the seven transactions summarized by the initial balance.

account (accounts receivable) and increases an asset account (cash) by $16,000.

Transaction (10). Gross charges include rates for services that are in excess of agreements with Medicare, Medicaid, various insurance companies, and HMOs. It is estimated that these contractual agreements total $34,000. The clinic is not entitled to collect from the patients for the $34,000. The $34,000 is really not an asset and is not revenue; it is a billing adjustment. The transaction reduces revenue by $34,000 (estimated difference between gross charges and net patient revenue) and reduces an asset account (accounts receivable) by $34,000.

Transaction (11). Salaries of $80,000 were incurred by the clinic. The transaction is recorded as $80,000 of expenses and an increase of $80,000 to liabilities. Expenses are temporary accounts that are closed into net fund balance at the end of the period along with the revenues. Expenses are negative accounts in the fundamental accounting equation because expenses reduce the net fund balance account.

Transaction (12). Supplies and professional services of $25,000 were incurred by the clinic. The transaction is recorded as $25,000 of expenses and an increase of $25,000 to liabilities.

Transaction (13). The medical equipment and office equipment purchased by Transactions (4) and (5) (see Exhibit 2.1) were used in generating revenue. The cost of this equipment is matched against the revenue over the useful life of the equipment. This assignment of cost, or depreciation, against revenue is recognized by an expense of $3,000 and an increase in a contra asset account (accumulated depreciation) for $3,000.

Transaction (14). Checks were issued for the payroll and for some of the vendors providing supplies and services. Note the aggregate amount of the disbursement is less than salaries expense. There is a delay between providing the services and the timing of the payment for those salaries. The transaction is a reduction in liabilities for $70,000 and a reduction in an asset account (cash) for $70,000.

Transaction (15). Many health care plans require the patient or the party responsible for the patient (in the case of a child) to pay a portion of the bill for services. The portion charged to the patient is usually between 10 to 20 percent of the total bill after some aggregate minimum payment for the year has been reached. There are also self-insured patients who are directly billed for services. It is estimated that $2,500 of the net patient revenues for the period will not be collected. This transaction is a bad debt expense of $2,500 and reduces an asset account (net patient receivables) by $2,500.

Transaction (16) or end of period. The temporary revenue and expense accounts are closed into the net fund balance account. The $126,000 of revenues are matched against the $110,500 of expenses, resulting in an increase of $15,500 in net fund balance. The details of this matching operation of cost and expenses against revenue are contained in the statement of revenue and expenses of general funds (Exhibit 3.2).

Special Financial Reporting Practice

Financial statements of health care entities are based on some unusual industry practices that arose from the responses of financial managers to various governmental regulations and administrative procedures in the absence of any contrary AICPA positions on these matters. The 1990 *Audit and Accounting Guide: Audits of Providers of Health Care Services* includes seven major changes in financial reporting practice with an effective date of 15 July 1990. The 1988 draft of the audit guide contained some unique health care reporting arrangements that were subsequently rejected. Some certified financial statements from 1988

Exhibit 3.2   Metropolitan Health Care Clinic: Statement of Revenue and Expenses of General Funds for Year Ended 31 May 19X2

Net patient service revenue	*$126,000*
Expenses:	
Salaries, wages, and employee benefits	$ 80,000
Supplies	10,000
Professional fees	15,000
Bad debts expense	2,500
Depreciation	3,000
Total expenses	*$110,500*
Revenue in excess of expenses	*$ 15,500*

to 1990 reflect these "new" industry practices that were discontinued by the final draft of audit guide. It will probably be several years before governmental regulations and administrative procedures are modified to reflect all of the 1990 audit guide changes.

Gross patient revenue

The health care industry has traditionally reported a gross patient revenue amount on a statement of revenue and expenses that is more than the legal amount that the health care entity is entitled to receive. Gross patient revenue may include charges for charity care for which patients are not billed and there is no basis for collection. This practice is stopped by the 1990 audit guide for certified reports, but some governmental agencies currently require this traditional information.

It is common practice in the health care industry to bill all patients the same amount for a test, procedure, or service, regardless of the special arrangement with different insurance carriers and providers. This billing procedure is related to the concept of equal access to health care without regard to the financial status of the patient.[1] Public policy considerations pertaining to the treatment of different financial classes of patients encourages a reporting of gross revenues or gross charges instead of using a "net invoice" approach that typically dominates business practice. Any difference between the "standard" billing rate and the "legal" rate per the agreement with a given insurance carrier is called *contractual allowances*. Patients covered by Medicare (Title XVIII of the federal statutes), Medicaid (Title XIX of the federal statutes), and Blue Cross–Blue Shield all cause the creation of contractual allowances and adjustments.

To illustrate this concept of contractual allowance, assume that Hospital A has a $30 laboratory test with a reasonable cost of $18. Direct labor, laboratory supplies, equipment rental, and other expenditures accepted by third party payors as being associated with this test equal $18. This $30 laboratory test is performed in 1982 (before the 1983 prospective payment system and its phased implementation) on four patients:

1. A self-pay patient who pays $30 in cash *Made .00*
$12.

2. A commercial insurance patient (with a signed agreement with the hospital specifying a $27 payment)

3. A Medicare patient who has no other insurance coverage (the hospital has signed an agreement to accept the Medicare payment as payment in full)

4. A Blue Cross patient (the hospital has signed an agreement of acceptance as payment in full).

Although gross charges are $30 for each of the four patients, the net patient revenue is different for each patient, as shown in Table 3.1.

The first patient pays in cash, and the net patient revenue is $30, the cost is $18, and the hospital's profit contribution is $12.

Table 3.1 Illustration of Accounting for Laboratory Test for Four Hospital Patients

	Patient 1 Cash Customer	Patient 2 Commercial Insurance	Patient 3 Medicare Program	Patient 4 Blue Cross– Blue Shield	Total
Gross patient revenue	$30.00	$30.00	$30.00	$30.00	$120.00
Adjustments and contractual adjustments	0.00	3.00	12.00	11.10	26.10
Net patient revenue	$30.00	$27.00	$18.00	$18.90	$ 93.90
Expenses	18.00	18.00	18.00	18.00	72.00
Profits	$12.00	$ 9.00	$ 0.00	$ 0.90	$ 21.90

The second patient's commercial insurance agreement means that the net patient revenue is $27 (gross charges of $30 less $3 contractual adjustment), the cost is $18, and the hospital's profit contribution is $9. The Medicare patient under the 1982 federal program only paid "reasonable cost" or $18; gross charge is $30, contractual adjustment is $12, net patient revenue is $18, cost is $18, and there is no contribution to the hospital's profit. The fourth patient covered by the Blue Cross plan paid "reasonable cost" plus 5 percent; gross charge is $30, contractual adjustment $11.10, net patient revenue is $18.90, cost is $18, and the hospital's profit contribution is $0.90. The four patients have gross charges of $120.00, contractual adjustment of $26.10, net patient revenue of $93.90, cost of $72.00, and hospital's profit contribution of $21.10.

Once the hospital has performed the $30 laboratory test for the four patients, does the hospital have a legal right to collect $120? The answer is, no. If the hospital has signed an agreement with a commercial insurance carrier to pay the prevailing rate (as with the second patient), then the $27 is the extent of the hospital's right to collect. If the hospital has signed agreements with Medicare and Blue Cross, then the hospital in 1982 cannot bill the patients for these allowances. It is important for this discussion that none of the patients has a second insurance carrier; otherwise, the answer might be different.

What is the meaning of the $120 of gross patient revenue in Table 3.1? It is merely the aggregation of patient charges from the hospital's internal records. The $26.10 of contractual allowance is obtained by aggregating adjustments in billing commercial insurance carriers and other payors. Hospitals' internal records do not customarily map the adjustments to insurance carriers and other payors to patient bills. Therefore, net patient revenue for the laboratory department consists of aggregating patient bills for laboratory services less an estimate for contractual allowances. If the report is net patient revenues for the laboratory department by financial class of patient, the same procedure is followed in aggregating the sorted patient bills for laboratory services less an estimate for contractual allowances.

In the situation illustrated in Table 3.1, the hospital's legal right for funds is $120 less the $26.10 of contractual allowances, or $93.90. The typical business organization might have only booked net invoices at $93.90 for "gross revenues" before deducting an allowance for uncollectibles. Net patient revenues and net sales are common concepts for hospitals and business firms, and net patient revenues should be used as the primary measure of economic activity for health care institutions.

Gross charges by patient category

Regulatory agencies may impose detailed reporting requirements on health care entities that are not compatible with those by the AICPA. Several agencies currently require data on gross patient charges by revenue area for certain types of health care entities. A few agencies may have more demanding reporting requirements in which gross patient charges by revenue area are separately disclosed for various categories of patients. In contrast, the AICPA reports emphasize expected cash receipts on balance sheets and statements of revenues and expenses; information on gross charges—when deemed necessary to report—is included in the notes to financial statements.

Payment for Medicare inpatients on a rate per case basis began in 1983 with a four-year implementation period, but this predetermined rate arrangement has not been mandated for Medicare outpatients. Although various federal projects are trying to establish outpatient, clinic, nursing home, and extended care diagnostic codes and reimbursement rates for Medicare patients, these efforts are still under development.

The state-administered Medicaid programs may continue using cost-based systems in reimbursement for inpatient, outpatient, and clinic services, but there are many combinations of payment arrangements currently being used by some states with Medicaid recipients. Some states require all recipients in certain geographical areas to belong to an HMO; others use predetermined rates per case or per person for inpatient care, with various methods for outpatient and clinic services. Nursing homes, freestanding clinics, and other health facilities may receive payment from federal program patients using cost-based reports.

These cost-based regulatory reports begin with gross patient charges by revenue department. These reports, at a minimum, might look as follows for all types of medical and health services to patients:

	Inpatient	*Outpatient*
Hospital routine care service	xxx	
Intensive care unit	xxx	
Coronary care unit	xxx	
Ancillary service	xxx	
Outpatient service	xxx	xxx
Home health agency	xxx	xxx
Same-day surgery clinic		xxx

. . .

If the regulatory agency does not require this separation of gross patient service revenue between inpatient and outpatient, then the data are aggregated in a single column. Other aspects of regulatory disclosure requirements are examined in Chapter 4.

Operating Revenue

The primary business of entities providing health care services to individuals is to provide patient service; all other activities are secondary to this fundamental purpose. Thus, the major heading of *net patient service revenue* in Exhibit 3.3 is to report the primary business of Wilmette Community Hospital. Patient service revenue is reported net of provisions for contractual allowances and other adjustments, but there is no deduction for bad debts. Instead, provision for bad debts is included as an operating expense.[2] Net patient service revenue excludes charity care because it is provided on a free basis without any expectation of direct payment for those health care services. This nongovernment not-for-profit corporation is organized under Section 501(c)(3) of the Internal Revenue Code, and the note to financial statements in Exhibit 3.3 is an AICPA type of disclosure on gross patient charges and contractual allowances.

The *other operating revenue* must be directly related to the primary business of the health care entity and arises from the normal day-to-day activities of the facility. A transfer of funds from a donor-restricted specific-purpose fund to the general funds in accordance with donors' written specifications is part of other operating revenue (such as gifts to finance charity care). Other operating revenue is not limited to patients; it encompasses revenues arising from non–health care sales and services provided to residents and from sales and services provided to nonpatients.

Each type of health care entity may identify its principal revenue sources with different labels that are representative of its mission. The freestanding ambulatory care unit uses "emergency patient service revenue," "referred outpatients patient service revenue," and "other operating revenue." An HMO uses revenue labels like "premiums earned," "reinsurance recoveries," "coinsurance," and "interest and other income" to represent its primary mission. A continuing-care retirement community (CCRC) facility has "revenues from amortization of advance fees," "resident service revenue," "patient revenues from nonresidents," and "other operating revenues." The HMO and

Exhibit 3.3   Wilmette Community Hospital: Statements of Revenues and Expenses of General Funds for Years Ended 31 December 19X2 and 19X1

	19X2	19X1
Net patient service revenue (note 1)	$80,539,794	$72,841,353
Other operating revenue	1,459,356	1,142,607
Total operating revenues	81,999,150	73,983,960
Operating expenses:		
Salaries and professional fees	38,248,849	35,488,941
Employee benefits	4,424,630	4,114,906
Supplies and other	16,705,814	15,803,465
Purchased services	8,909,768	8,419,731
Medical malpractice costs	1,100,000	750,000
Depreciation	3,931,051	3,845,970
Interest expense	1,963,984	1,416,845
Provision for bad debts	505,835	465,450
Total operating expenses	75,789,931	70,305,308
Income from operations	6,209,219	3,678,652
Nonoperating gains (losses):		
Unrestricted gifts and donations	90,793	26,350
Income on investments:		
Unrestricted	283,343	251,406
Whose use is limited under indenture agreement	22,240	20,300
Gain on sale of investments	980,698	830,704
Loss on sale of properties	(81,964)	0
Nonoperating gains, net	1,295,110	1,128,760
Excess of revenue over expenses	$ 7,504,329	$ 4,807,412

Note to Financial Statements

1. *Net patient service revenue*

The payment received by Wilmette Community Hospital for Medicare inpatient services is a stipulated amount per discharge plus an amount based on the cost of capital-related items. The reimbursement for Medicare outpatients is based on the actual cost of providing service, subject to certain limitations and ultimately determined by government examination of cost reports. Approximately 40 percent of patient revenue was derived from the Medicare program in 19X2; Medicare volume (calculated as a percentage of gross patient revenue) was approximately 42 percent.

Continued

Exhibit 3.3 Continued

Medicaid payments for inpatient service are on a contracted per diem basis, and Medicaid outpatient service is paid on the basis of a fee schedule. Approximately 3 percent of patient revenue was derived from the Medicaid program in 19X2.

Blue Cross payments for inpatient service are on an all-inclusive per diem rate. The prospectively determined per diem rates are not subject to retroactive adjustment. Outpatient service is paid on the basis of a fee schedule. Approximately 15 percent of patient revenue was obtained from Blue Cross in 19X2.

Wilmette Community Hospital has also entered into reimbursement agreements with certain commercial insurance carriers, corporations, health maintenance organizations, and preferred provider organizations. The basis for reimbursement under these agreements includes prospectively determined rates per discharge, discounts from established charges, and prospectively determined per diem rates.

A summary of gross and net patient service revenue for the years ended 31 December 19X2 and 19X1 follows:

Gross patient service revenue	$86,513,103	$78,411,154
Less provisions for:		
Medicare & Medicaid contractual adjustment	4,968,361	4,645,091
Blue Cross contractual adjustment	370,418	340,860
Other allowances	415,074	381,940
Charity	219,456	201,910
Total deductions	*5,973,309*	*5,569,801*
Net patient service revenue	*$80,539,794*	*$72,841,353*

The definition of net patient service revenue is in accordance with the American Institute of Certified Public Accountants' *Audit and Accounting Guide: Audits of Providers of Health Care Services,* New York, 1990. The information for 19X1 is restated to exclude the provision for bad debts, which is now reported as operating expenses. If the old definition of net patient service revenue were used, the following amounts would be obtained:

Net patient service revenue	*$80,539,794*	*$72,841,353*
Less provision for bad debts	505,835	465,450
	$80,033,959	*$72,375,903*

Continued

Exhibit 3.3   Continued

Some of the regulatory reports use the old definition of net patient service revenue that excludes provision for bad debts.

Wilmette Community Hospital provides charity care to individuals who meet certain financial criteria. The gross paitent charges for such free services are reported above for information purposes. The actual amount of charity care in 19X1 and 19X2 is believed to be larger than reported. Additional controls over units of service were recently implemented, primarily to capture free (charity) services that were often intentionally excluded in the past from the measurement process. Future financial statements will not include charity care as a component of gross patient service revenue, but charity care will be reported as a separate note in the financial statements explaining the estimation process used in measuring free care.

---

the CCRC report investment income as operating revenue; investment income for most other health care entities is nonoperating revenue. If the investment income is to be matched with an operating expense, then it is classified as operating revenue.

A university teaching hospital's other operating revenue includes tuition for schools (such as nursing) and revenue from educational programs and laboratory and x-ray technology. The medical school–affiliated community hospital's other operating revenue is similar to that of the university teaching hospital, but with a smaller proportion from educational programs. Both types of institutions may have other operating revenue from research and other gifts and grants, either unrestricted or for a specific purpose.

Other operating revenue is accounted for separately from net patient service revenue. The AICPA's 1990 audit guide contains the following list of revenue from miscellaneous sources that are included as other operating revenue:[3]

- Rental of health care facility space
- Sales of medical and pharmacy supplies to employees, physicians, and others
- Fees charged for transcripts for attorneys, insurance companies, and others
- Proceeds from sale of cafeteria meals and guest trays to employees, medical staff, and visitors
- Proceeds from sale of scrap, used x-ray film, etc.

- Proceeds from sales at gift shops, snack bars, newsstands, parking lots, vending machines, and other service facilities operated by the health care entity

Unrestricted investment income may be considered other operating revenue when the investment income is deemed to be central to the ongoing major operations of the hospital. Trustee-held bond fund income and investment income related to a malpractice trust are reported as other operating revenue. Investment income that is debt related and is derived from bond proceeds is reported as other operating revenue; investment income from all other general fund investments and investment income of endowment funds are reported as nonoperating gains.

Other operating revenue of $1,459,356 in Exhibit 3.3 is an aggregation of many diverse revenue sources at Wilmette Community Hospital. If Wilmette Community Hospital were a major teaching hospital, then the other operating revenue would be higher than $1,459,356. A teaching hospital has more volume in each of the above items and in the sale of medical records and abstracts; in fact, $3 million of other operating revenue is not unusual for a community hospital with $80 million of net patient service revenue.

Exhibit 3.4 shows the statements of revenues and expenses for Richmond Care Nursing Home, a nongovernment not-for-profit corporation organized under Section 501(c)(3) of the Internal Revenue Code. Under total operating revenues of $2,698,000 for Richmond Care Nursing Home in 19X2 are contained labels comparable to those used for hospitals. Total operating revenues are a significant measure of financial performance, used in comparison with operating expenses for budgeting purposes and also in forecasting funds flow for the nursing home.

Operating Expenses

Reporting guidelines give health care entities a choice of format in presenting operating expenses. One choice is to follow the natural classification of expenses, which emphasizes the dominant nature of expenditures. The operating expenses of $75,789,931 in Exhibit 3.3 for Wilmette Community Hospital are indicative of the natural classification structure, with salaries and professional fees, employee benefits, supplies, purchased services, medical malpractice costs, depreciation, interest expense, and provision for bad debts.

Exhibit 3.4   Richmond Care Nursing Home: Statements of Revenues and Expenses of General Funds for Years Ended 31 December 19X2 and 19X1

	19X2	19X1
Patient service revenue	$2,613,000	$2,353,000
Other operating revenue	85,000	28,000
Total operating revenues	2,698,000	2,381,000
Operating expenses:		
Nursing services	1,308,000	1,215,000
Dietary services	274,000	268,000
General services	264,000	255,000
Administrative services	208,000	179,000
Interest	195,000	201,000
Depreciation	83,000	68,000
Provision for bad debts	107,000	96,000
Total operating expenses	2,439,000	2,282,000
Income from operations	259,000	99,000
Nonoperating gains—interest and dividends	25,000	9,000
Excess of revenue over expenses	$ 284,000	$ 108,000

The first item—salaries and professional fees—is separated by some professional accountants into two components: (1) salaries and wages and (2) professional fees. Salaries and wages, with the associated employee benefits, typically represents more than 50 percent of the total operating expenses of a health care entity. Some professional accountants advocate disclosures of operating expenses that include salaries and wages plus the other natural classification of expense. Contract nursing is not part of salaries and wages. A relatively large amount of contract nursing costs for a hospital can significantly distort interhospital comparisons. If the amount of contract nursing is large, it is preferable to report these costs as a separate component.

A second choice in reporting operating expenses is to follow the organizational structure approach. This arrangement emphasizes the organizational structure or the responsibility center where the expenditures are incurred as the primary basis for reports. The operating expenses in Exhibit 3.4 for Richmond Care Nursing Home are representative of the organizational structure approach, with nursing services, dietary services, general services, administrative services, interest, depreciation, and provision for bad debts. Both Exhibits 3.3 and 3.4 are compatible with the suggested format in the AICPA's *Audit and Accounting Guide* for these respective health care entities.

If the organizational structure approach in Exhibit 3.4 were used at Wilmette Community Hospital, the operating expenses in 19X2 might appear as follows:

Daily hospital services	$15,109,429
Ancillary services	27,137,000
General services	13,159,867
Fiscal services	5,317,784
Administrative services	7,564,981
Medical malpractice costs	1,100,000
Depreciation	3,931,051
Interest expense	1,963,984
Provision for bad debts	505,835
Total Operating Expenses	*$75,789,931*

The AICPA's suggested format for operating expenses in a CCRC is also oriented toward the departments where the expenditures occur. This type of health care entity might have the following eight accounts: resident care, dietary, housekeeping, plant, general and administrative, depreciation, interest, and provision for uncollectible accounts. The provision for uncollectible accounts is an operating expense.[4]

Nonoperating Gains and Losses

A health care entity's nonoperating gains and losses in the general funds represent an assortment of other income and expense items that are unrelated to the primary purpose of the facility. The reporting of investment income varies by type of health care entity. Investment income of an HMO or a CCRC is directly related to the primary purpose and is therefore classified as operating revenue. If investment income is deemed to be central to the ongoing operation of the hospital, there is some flexibility in the classification between nonoperating gains and other operating revenue.

Unrestricted income from an endowment fund is classified as nonoperating gains. Investment income and gains (losses) on investments of donor-restricted funds are added to (deducted from) the appropriate donor-restricted fund balance. Investment income on a malpractice trust fund is included in the general funds' other operating revenue. General funds' nonoperating revenue may include gifts, grants, and bequests with no donor-imposed restrictions.

The nonoperating gains for Wilmette Community Hospital in 19X2 consisted of five items (Exhibit 3.3):

Unrestricted gifts and donations	$ 90,793
Income on investments:	
Unrestricted	283,343
Whose use is limited under	
indenture agreement	22,240
Gain on sale of investments	980,698
Loss on sale of properties	(81,964)
Nonoperating gains, net	$1,295,110

As previously explained, the classification of investment income may shift between operating income and nonoperating income depending on the type of health care entity.

Excess of Revenue over Expenses

The excess of revenues over expenses of $7,504,329 for Wilmette Community Hospital in 19X2 (Exhibit 3.3) is the result of combining $6,209,219 of income from operations with $1,295,110 of nonoperating revenue. Wilmette Community Hospital is a nonprofit corporation; therefore, the statement does not include any provision for income taxes. The excess of revenues over expenses of $284,000 for Richmond Care Nursing Home in 19X2 (Exhibit 3.4) is based on $259,000 of income from operations combined with $25,000 of nonoperating revenue.

The matching of revenue, income, gains, expired costs, operating expenses, and losses for diverse health care entities is aggregated in the bottom-line measure called "excess of revenue over expenses." It can be argued that nonoperating gains and losses are not part of the central mission of a health care entity (by definition); thus, the principal focus of analysis should be on operating income. The AICPA's 1988 *Proposed Audit Guide* took that position on operating income for community hospitals and nursing homes. But this distinction was eliminated in the 1990 *Audit and Accounting Guide.* Within the three-dimensional framework of ownership, control, and type of facility of Exhibit 1.1, comparisons of operating income across health care entities may be meaningless because of known differences in institutions.

Donations and contributions to a health care entity with restricted funds can be transferred under certain conditions and included as part of other operating revenue in the general funds. General gifts to a health care entity without restricted funds are part of the current year's nonoperating gains. Investment income may be part of other operating revenue or part of nonoperating gains, depending on certain conditions. The financial reporting of investment income is not consistent for health care entities within the three-dimensional framework of ownership, control, and type of facility.

Governmental bodies make grants to health care entities that are not directly related to patient services provided. Although some health care entities receive annual grants, it is risky for the certified public accountant to anticipate the receipt of such an award. If the accountant were to anticipate such an award by reporting it as other operating revenue and the grant did not occur for that exact amount, then the accounting firm may have a professional liability for the difference to outside creditors who have relied upon such financial statements.

Certified financial statements for a sample of 1,482 not-for-profit (NFP) community hospitals in 1988 reported $1.1 billion of tax support awards that were unrelated to patient services (Exhibit 3.5). This amount had increased from $0.9 billion in 1986. These 1988 tax support awards are twice as large as the $0.5 billion of income from operations for this national sample of hospitals.[5]

Revenue and gains in excess of expenses and losses are $3.6 billion for the national sample of NFP community hospitals in 1988, almost seven times the $0.5 billion of income from operations. The importance of nonoperating gains and tax support awards to the bottom line for these community hospitals is illustrated by the financial data in Exhibit 3.5. While income from operations decreased significantly between 1986 and 1988, there was a slight increase in nonoperating gains for the period.

The national sample of 1,482 NFP community hospitals is a small proportion of the 5,500 community hospitals, and it is not a random sample. Each of the 50 states and the District of Columbia are represented in the selected facilities, but all investor-owned community hospitals, children's hospitals, and women's hospitals are excluded. The credit-rating data source used in the study tends to exclude any freestanding community hospital with less than 60 beds. Twenty-one percent of NFP community hospitals had less than 50 beds in 1985, and 45 percent were under 100 beds.[6] Some small hospitals are included in the NFP sample if they are members of a system. But this NFP

Exhibit 3.5   Statements of Revenues and Expenses for 1,482 Not-for-Profit Community Hospitals (amounts in thousands)

	1986	1987	1988
Net patient service revenue	$75,911,977	$82,037,300	$90,400,427
Other operating revenue	3,179,320	3,704,174	4,122,124
Total revenue	79,091,297	85,741,474	94,522,551
Operating expenses	76,717,949	84,464,648	94,002,980
Income from operations	2,373,348	1,276,826	519,571
Nonoperating gains	1,862,664	1,917,789	1,986,338
Tax support awards	905,147	1,019,123	1,125,463
Taxes paid	(5,573)	(3,237)	(4,953)
Revenue and gains in excess of expenses and losses	$ 5,135,586	$ 4,210,501	$ 3,626,419

Source: The specific information on individual hospitals is from The Merritt System®, the product of Van Kampen Merritt Investment Advisory Corp. (VKM Advisory), a Xerox Financial Services Company, located in Lisle, Illinois. Copyright 1990 by Van Kampen Merritt Investment Advisory Corp. All rights reserved.

Note: Over 2,000 hospitals and 130 hospital systems are included as separate records in The Merritt System®, a credit analysis and database management system (DBMS) supporting comparative financial, operational, and bond issue data on not-for-profit hospitals. This DBMS runs on a personal computer and efficiently uses about 6 million characters of storage for the more than 2,150 health care entities within the database.

sample represents over 55 percent of net patient revenue and over 62 percent of excess of revenue over expenses for the 5,500 AHA hospitals (Table 3.2).

Summary

Health care entities typically use an accrual method of accounting in which gross patient charges are recorded at established rates when the services are provided. This unique approach in the health care industry is different from the expected cash receipts method mandated by the AICPA for most other industries. Although the gross patient method is used in internal accounting and regulatory reports, external financial statements for health care entities following AICPA guidelines begin with net patient service revenue. Contractual allowances, adjustments, and deductions to gross patient charges are only shown as notes to the financial statements.

Table 3.2   Selected Revenue and Expense Comparisons for
1,482 NFP Community Hospitals with AHA Data
(amounts in millions)

	1986	1987	1988
Net Patient Revenue			
All community hospitals*	$137,939	$147,326	$161,082
Sample of 1,482 NFP community hospitals	$ 75,912	$ 82,037	$ 90,400
Percent of AHA total	55.03%	55.68%	56.12%
Excess of Revenue over Expenses			
Net total revenue and nonoperating gains†	$148,549	$159,309	$174,558
Total expenses	140,655	152,585	168,723
Excess of revenue over expenses for over 5,500 hospitals	$ 7,894	$ 6,724	$ 5,835
Sample of 1,482 NFP community hospitals (Exhibit 3.5)	5,136	4,211	3,626
Percent of AHA total	65.06%	62.63%	62.14%

Sources: The data on all community hospitals are from Table 5A (p. 21) and Table
11 (p. 204) of 1987, 1988, and 1989–90 editions of AHA's *Hospital Statistics.* The
information on the sample of 1,482 NFP community hospitals is from The Merritt
System®.
*All community hospitals: 5,678 hospitals in 1986; 5,611 hospitals in 1987; 5,533
hospitals in 1988.
†Includes contributions, endowment revenue, government grants, and all other
payments not made on behalf of individual patients.

Statements of revenues and expenses are closely examined by
state regulatory agencies, administrators of federal health care programs, third party payors, and competitors—special reports filed with
regulatory bodies are often available to competitors and others through
the Freedom of Information Act.[7] Many health care entities have significantly reduced the amount and level of detail included in regulatory
reports because of competitive considerations and other marketing
issues. Revenue departments may be aggregated into a few groups
before cost, charge, and statistical information are prepared for a
regulatory agency. Most health care entities do not want to disclose
to regulatory agencies and their competitors departmental data by
financial class of the patient.

The statements of revenue and expenses of general funds for health care entities handle investment income in different ways, depending on the type of entity and the origin of the investment. Investment income directly related to the primary purpose of the organization, such as with an HMO or a continuing-care retirement community, is shown as operating revenue; otherwise, investment income is nonoperating gains. Transfers of donor-restricted funds may be shown as operating income in the general funds.

Intermediate measures, such as operating margins or operating income, are meaningless yardsticks for comparison across health care entities because of the unique characteristics within the three-dimensional framework of ownership, control, and type of facility. Donations, contributions, restricted funds, investment income, and governmental awards unrelated to patient services are some of the factors that make intermediate measures meaningless. The bottom line of excess of revenue over expenses is the appropriate measure for financial assessment of health care entities.

Appendix: Revenue Movements in Community Hospitals for 1981 to 1989

Table 3.3 is a statement of selected revenues and expenses for community hospitals in 1981 to 1989 using AHA's annual survey reports. The number of community hospitals decreased from 5,813 in 1981 to 5,455 in 1989. The excess of revenue and gains over expenses and losses for all community hospitals peaked at $8.4 billion in 1985 and then declined, as presented in Table 3.3.

The federal government implemented a prospective payment system (PPS) for Medicare under a phased approach, with 25 percent coverage in 1984, 50 percent coverage in 1985, and 75 percent coverage in 1986. Subsequently, the phased period was extended to four years. PPS replaced the retrospective cost-based payment system, under which Medicare paid "reasonable cost" for health services. Knowledge about PPS and the old Medicare program is required to appreciate fully the gross patient revenue and contractual allowance data for 1984 to 1989.

Many commercial insurance carriers and corporate agreements with hospitals began to use many of the features of the PPS in their 1985 contracts with health care providers. Billing by diagnostic category replaced billing by test, procedure, or service under some of these agreements. Some commercial insurance carriers negotiated with

Table 3.3 Selected Revenues and Expenses for Community Hospitals for 1981 to 1989 (amounts in millions)

	1981	1983	1985	1986	1987	1988	1989
Gross Revenues:							
Inpatient	$ 92,459	$125,925	$136,893	$146,704	$160,171	$179,065	$203,038
Outpatient	13,944	19,216	26,359	31,698	37,928	45,769	54,878
Total	106,403	145,141	163,252	178,402	198,099	224,834	257,916
Deductions and contractual adjustments	19,251	31,687	33,531	40,463	50,773	63,752	81,014
Net patient revenues	87,152	113,454	129,721	137,939	147,326	161,082	176,902
Contributions, endowment revenues, grants and other payments	6,815	8,044	9,160	10,610	11,983	13,476	14,461
Net total revenues	93,967	121,498	138,881	148,549	159,309	174,558	191,363
Expenses:							
Payroll	44,042	55,525	60,361	63,773	68,306	75,234	81,975
Employee benefits	7,253	10,199	11,640	11,998	12,686	14,068	16,069
Total labor	51,295	65,724	72,001	75,771	80,992	89,302	98,044
Other than labor	39,277	50,714	58,498	64,884	71,593	79,421	86,854
Total expenses	90,572	116,438	130,499	140,655	152,585	168,723	184,898
Profits	$ 3,395	$ 5,060	$ 8,382	$ 7,894	$ 6,724	$ 5,835	$ 6,465

Source: AHA's *Hospital Statistics,* annual volumes, Tables 5A and 11.

hospitals for contracts containing a contractual allowance on all patient services and with second opinions on surgery and monitoring
of health care costs. A few insurance carriers participated in the creation of their own HMOs, which have traditionally contracted with
hospitals under significant contractual allowances for HMO patients.
HMOs were also established by hospitals, alliances, and associations
to cope with the changes in health care delivery after PPS. Several
of the existing HMOs began to aggressively market services in new
geographical areas. Fiscal considerations in many states have resulted
in significant reductions in the payment level for Medicaid patients
with high contractual allowances; as other states have adopted some of
these new arrangements, high contractual allowances for these state-
administered Medicaid patients are becoming a common situation.

   The $7 billion increase in contractual adjustments in Table 3.3,
from $33.5 billion in 1985 to $40.5 billion in 1986, is a measure of
the impact of these layers of new contracts with hospitals. Net patient
revenues only increased $8 billion during this same 1985–1986 period,
from $129.7 billion in 1985 to $137.9 billion in 1986. This change
in billing practice became more prevalent in 1987 to 1989, when the
increases in contractual allowances were occurring at a higher rate
than the increases in gross hospital revenues. Contractual allowances
increased from 22.7 percent of gross revenue in 1986 to 31.4 percent
in 1989.[8]

   In reviewing the statement of selected revenues and expenses for
1981 to 1989, one of the most significant developments was the change
in outpatient revenue. Outpatient gross revenues increased by 294
percent, from $13.9 billion in 1981 to $54.9 billion in 1989, while the
medical care consumer price index increased by 80.1 percent between
1981 and 1989 (Table 3.4). If the 1981 gross outpatient revenues of
$13.9 billion are adjusted by the medical care consumer price index,
the adjusted value of $25.1 billion for 1989 ($13.9 x 180.1% = $25.1) is
$29.8 billion short of the $54.9 billion actual gross outpatient revenues
for 1989. This 294 percent increase in outpatient gross revenues represents many new services even if charges increased by 80.1 percent
for the medical care index.

   The change in gross inpatient revenues for 1981 to 1989 is a
different picture. Inpatient gross revenues increased by 119.6 percent,
from $92.5 billion in 1981 to $203.0 billion in 1989, while the 80.1
percent increase from the medical care consumer price index would
have priced the $92.5 billion in 1981 at $166.5 billion for 1989. The
$36.5 billion difference between adjusted and actual ($166.5 versus

Table 3.4   Computation of Changes in Purchasing Power:
Community Hospitals for 1981 to 1989

Year	Actual Profits (in millions)	Medical Care Index	Adjusted Index Using 1981 as Base	Profits Stated in 1981 Purchasing Power (in millions)
1981	$3,395	82.9	100.0%	$3,395
1982	4,582	92.5	111.6*	4,106†
1983	5,060	100.6	121.4	4,170
1984	6,616	106.8	128.8	5,135
1985	8,382	113.5	136.9	6,122
1986	7,894	122.0	147.2	5,364
1987	6,724	130.1	156.9	4,285
1988	5,835	138.6	167.2	3,490
1989	6,465	149.3	180.1	3,590

* 92.5/82.9 = 111.580%; 100.6/82.9 = 121.351% ...
† $4,582/111.580% = $4,106; $5,060/121.351 = $4,170 ...

$203.0) for 1989 is about a 39.5 percent increase (4.9 percent per
year) in health care services for all inpatients over eight years. Thus,
there was a modest increase in gross inpatient revenues for 1981 to
1989, while there was a dynamic change in gross outpatient revenues
for the same period.

Compare net patient revenues with total expenses in Table 3.3
for 1981 to 1989. In each year the total expenses are more than net
patient revenues, and this is not a recent event. Total expenses include
a calculation for depreciation of fixed assets based on the original cost
or purchase price and not on current market values; thus, a small
return is needed for an economic break-even position. Community
hospitals, in general, have always depended on donations, contributions, endowment income, grants, and other payments for financial
viability. Replacement of equipment, construction of new facilities, and
special initiatives are primarily financed by contributions, donations,
trustee-held income, and endowment income.

Profits for community hospitals increased, from $3.4 billion in
1981 to $8.4 billion in 1985, before decreasing to $5.8 billion in 1988.
Table 3.4 shows the annual data for 1981 to 1989 adjusted by the
medical care index. The 1989 adjusted position of $3.6 billion in Table
3.4 is slightly larger than the 1981 base. Many community hospitals
did not respond quickly to the change in economic events from 1985

to 1986. There was a $1.7 billion increase in 1985 profits over 1984, followed by a $0.5 billion decline in 1986 profits over 1985. AHA annual survey data reported only slight changes in occupancy rate, average length of stay, and admissions per bed for community hospitals in 1985 versus 1986. Many patient episodes in 1986 resulted in lower net patient revenues because of a PPS payment from Medicare or a similar payment from third party payors under new contracts. The decline in profits did not stop with 1986, but there was an additional $2 billion reduction in profits for 1987 and 1988. There was a slight improvement between 1988 and 1989.

The AHA data in Table 3.3 emphasize the role of contributions, donations, and other grants to community hospitals. New investments in medical technology, support for changes in medical practice, and additional health care services depend, to a large extent, on revenue sources external to the community hospital.

Notes

1. The billing procedures are also related to Medicare's uniform charging rules and the reimbursement reporting mechanism.
2. AICPA's 1990 *Audits of Providers of Health Care Services* contains a change in reporting practice for bad debts expense. Former financial statements reported "net patient service revenue" after deducting a provision for bad debts expense. Most regulatory reports continue to use the old disclosure arrangement, but it is expected that this will change after more experience is gained from using certified financial statements based on the 1990 audit guidelines.
3. AICPA, *Audit and Accounting Guide*, 111.
4. AICPA's *Audit and Accounting Guide* (p. xv) states: "Bad debts are to be reported as expenses in accordance with generally accepted accounting principles." This executive summary position is not compatible with the illustrated notes to financial statements (p. 205) in which net patient service revenue is reported at the estimated net realizable amounts. AICPA's *Proposed Audit and Accounting Guide* illustrates optional methods of disclosing provision for bad debts (paragraph 2.8 and reports on p. 119 and p. 133). Paragraph 2.8 in the proposed guide was deleted and the reports were modified in accordance with the revised position in the *Audit and Accounting Guide.*
5. The Merritt System® is the source of all data on selected NFP community hospitals reported in Exhibit 3.5. The Merritt System® is the product of Van Kampen Merritt Investment Advisory Corp. (VKM Advisory), a Xerox Financial Services Company, located in Lisle, Illinois. Copyright 1990 by Van Kampen Merritt Investment Advisory Corp. All rights reserved.

6. T. R. Prince, "Community Hospital Statistics by Ownership and Bed-Size Group: 1962–1984," *Journal of Health Administration Education* 6 (Winter 1988): 85–108.
7. For example, the Medicare cost reports that show detailed departmental information are available under the Freedom of Information Act.
8. Table 3.3 shows $40.5 billion in contractual allowances for 1986 versus $178.4 billion in gross revenue, for a relationship of 22.7 percent. The $81.0 billion in contractual allowances for 1989 versus $257.9 billion in gross revenue is 31.4 percent for this relationship.

Additional Readings

Butler, P. A., and R. E. Schlenker, "Case-Mix Reimbursement for Nursing Homes: Objectives and Achievements," *Milbank Quarterly* 67 (1989): 103–36.
Cohen, J. W., and L. C. Dubay, "The Effects of Medicaid Reimbursement Method and Ownership on Nursing Home Costs, Case Mix, and Staffing," *Inquiry* 27 (Summer 1990): 183–200.
Ginzberg, E., "Philanthropy and Nonprofit Organizations in U.S. Health Care: A Personal Retrospective," *Inquiry* 28 (Summer 1991): 179–86.
Kovener, R. R., "Reporting Method Can Meet New AICPA Guidelines," *Healthcare Financial Management* 45 (March 1991): 74–82.
Wickizer, T. M., J. R. C. Wheeler, and P. J. Feldstein, "Have Hospital Inpatient Cost Containment Programs Contributed to the Growth in Outpatient Expenditures?" *Medical Care* 29 (May 1991): 442–51.

Discussion Questions

3.1. Explain the meaning of "contractual allowances" as used with financial statements for health care entities.

3.2. AICPA's 1990 *Audit and Accounting Guide* moves information on gross charges *when deemed necessary to report* to notes to the financial statement. Under these conditions, explain why health care entities might continue to report information on gross charges in annual financial statements.

3.3. Explain the difference between net patient service revenue and other operating revenue.

3.4. Differentiate between other operating revenue and nonoperating gains.

3.5. Explain the natural classification structure of expenses versus an organizational structure.

3.6. Explain the measurement problems in using operating income as a yardstick for comparing financial feasibility of health care entities.

3.7. The sample of 1,482 NFP community hospitals reported $1.1 billion of government grants under nonoperating gains in 1988 (Exhibit 3.5). Why did the certified public accountants not include these awards under other operating revenue?

3.8. "Forecasting net patient service revenue in a federal hospital is an impossible task." Explain this statement.

3.9. Contractual allowances in community hospitals increased by more than 20 percent between 1985 and 1986, from $33.5 billion in 1985 to $40.5 billion in 1986, while gross patient charges went from $163.3 billion in 1985 to $178.4 billion in 1986 (Table 3.3). Explain the measurement issues confronting regulatory agencies monitoring the 1986 hospital data and why these same issues are not a problem with financial statements using the AICPA guidelines.

3.10. Some professional accountants advocate measuring revenue on the basis of expected cash receipts. Indicate the major issues encountered in applying this perspective to regulatory reports in the health care industry.

3.11. Explain why self-pay hospital patients represent a higher percent of net patient revenues than of gross patient revenues.

3.12. Why are donations, contributions, and endowment incomes so important to hospitals?

3.13. The data on selected revenue and expenses for community hospitals for 1981 to 1989 are presented in Table 3.3, and the annual community hospital profits for 1981 to 1989 are expressed in Table 3.4 in terms of the 1981 purchasing power based on the medical care component of the consumer price index (CPI).

  A. Using the 1981 medical care component of the CPI as the base (as in Table 3.4), restate the contributions, endowment revenues, grants, and other payments (Table 3.3) for 1985 to 1989 in terms of the 1981 purchasing power.

  B. Prepare an analysis of the overall movement of community hospital profits for 1981 to 1989.

3.14. Using the 1986 medical care component of the consumer price index as a base, there was a $1.19 billion decline in purchasing power of the net income between 1986 and 1988 for the 1,482 NFP community hospitals presented in Exhibit 3.5. This decline in purchasing power is computed in Table 3.5. From the information presented in Exhibit 3.5, determine if donations, contributions, and investment income (reported as nonoperating gains) for 1986 to 1988 kept pace with the change in purchasing power based on the medical care component of the consumer price index.

Table 3.5   Purchasing Power for 1,482 NFP Community Hospitals (1986–1988)

	Revenue over Expenses (in thousands)	Medical Care Index	Adjusted Amounts Using 1986 Base (in thousands)	Decline in Purchasing Power (in thousands)
1986	$5,135,586	122.0	base* $5,135,586	
1987	$4,210,501	130.1	106.6 $3,949,813	($1,185,773)
1988	$3,626,419	138.6	113.6 $3,192,270	($ 757,543)
Total				($1,943,316)

*130.1 medical care index for 1987 divided by 122.0 in 1986 gives the 106.6 value for 1987 expressed in terms of 1986 purchasing power. The $4,210,510,000 revenue over expenses for 1987 divided by 106.6 value equals $3,949,813,000 as the 1986 purchasing-power measure of this excess of revenue and gains over expenses and losses.

3.15.   Prepare in good format a statement of revenue and expenses for the year ended 31 December 19X2 using the following information provided by the internal records at Carle Community Hospital:

Ancillary services—inpatients revenues	$41,009,050
Ancillary services—outpatients revenues	9,625,166
Blue Cross contractual adjustment	1,095,275
Charity and other adjustments	2,545,978
Daily hospital services revenues	35,671,783
Depreciation	3,635,835
Employee benefits expense	6,607,351
Food expense	1,463,497
Housekeeping, maintenance, and office supplies	4,442,706
Interest expense	3,513,362
Investment income—assets limited to use	28,380
Investment income—unrestricted	215,579
Medicare and Medicaid contractual adjustment	4,669,329
Medical and surgical supplies	2,651,478
Medical malpractice costs	900,000
Other operating expenses	3,631,007
Other operating revenue	2,596,457
Pharmaceuticals	1,906,410
Provision for bad debts	1,000,000
Purchased services	5,026,355
Salaries and professional fees expense	37,719,291

Table 3.6 Distribution of Hospital Care Expenditures by Source of Funds

	1980 Amount (in billions)	Percent	1985 Amount (in billions)	Percent	1986 Amount (in billions)	Percent
Total expenditures	$101.6		$167.2		$179.6	
Direct patient payments	7.9	7.78%	14.5	8.67%	16.8	9.35%
All third parties	93.7	92.22	152.7	91.33	162.8	90.65
Private health insurance	38.7	38.09	60.5	36.18	64.9	36.14
Other private funds	1.1	1.08	2.0	1.20	2.2	1.22
Total government	53.9	53.05	90.2	53.95	95.7	53.29
Federal government	41.1	40.45	72.0	43.06	76.5	42.60
State and local goverment	12.8	12.60	18.2	10.89	19.2	10.69
Medicare	25.9	25.49	48.9	29.25	51.7	28.79
Medicaid	9.6	9.45	14.9	8.91	15.8	8.80

Source: Division of National Cost Estimates, Office of the Actuary, Health Care Financing Administration, "National Health Expenditures, 1986–2000," *Health Care Financing Review* 8 (Summer 1987): 1–36.

Unrestricted gifts and donations	2,088,032
Utilities and telephone expense	1,652,120

3.16. Prepare in good format a statement of revenues and expenses for the year ended 31 December 19X2 using the following information provided by the internal records at Clark Community Hospital:

Blue Cross contractual adjustment	$ 799,188
Charity and other adjustments	2,944,254
Daily hospital services revenues	36,340,043
Departmental services revenues	57,549,055
Depreciation expense	3,988,144
Employee benefits expense	6,146,275
Food expense	1,627,134
Housekeeping, maintenance, and office supplies	5,891,992
Interest expense	5,332,377
Investment income—assets limited to use	27,405
Investment income—unrestricted	922,964

Table 3.7 Distribution of Physician Care Expenditures by Source of Funds

| | 1980 | | 1985 | | 1986 | |
	Amount (in billions)	*Percent*	*Amount (in billions)*	*Percent*	*Amount (in billions)*	*Percent*
Total expenditures	$46.8		$82.8		$92.0	
Direct patient payments	14.2	30.34%	23.1	27.90%	26.2	28.48%
All third parties	32.6	69.66	59.7	72.10	65.8	71.52
Private health insurance	20.0	42.74	35.5	42.87	38.7	42.06
Other private funds	0.0	0.00	0.0	0.00	0.1	0.11
Total government	12.6	26.92	24.2	29.23	27.0	29.35
Federal government	9.6	20.51	19.7	23.79	22.0	23.91
State and local government	3.0	6.41	4.5	5.44	5.0	5.44
Medicare	7.9	16.88	16.9	20.41	19.0	20.65
Medicaid	2.4	5.13	3.5	4.23	3.9	4.24

Source: Division of National Cost Estimates, Office of the Actuary, Health Care Financing Administration, "National Health Expenditures, 1986–2000," *Health Care Financing Review* 8 (Summer 1987): 1–36.

Loss on sale of fixed assets	(98,000)
Medicare and Medicaid contractual adjustment	3,407,067
Medical malpractice costs	750,000
Other operating expenses	3,938,418
Other operating revenues	2,849,305
Pharmaceutical and medical supplies	5,184,663
Provision for bad debts	1,200,000
Purchased services	5,519,531
Salaries and professional fees expense	39,910,302
Unrestricted gifts and donations	3,464,463
Utilities and telephone expense	1,780,009

3.17. The chief financial officer at Wilmette Community Hospital examined the national health expenditures payment behavior for hospitals as presented in Table 3.6. The Medicaid program is Title XIX of the Social

Security Act and is jointly financed by the states and the federal government. The Medicare program is Title XVIII of the Social Security Act and is fully financed by the federal government. There are other social programs, such as Title V, that are financed by the federal government.

A. Determine the percent of hospital expenditures in 1986 that are paid by the federal, state, and local government, excluding the Medicare and Medicaid programs.

B. Compare the rate of increase of hospital expenditures in 1986 with those in Table 3.7 for physician expenditures.

C. Have Medicare payments to physicians increased faster in 1986 than Medicare payments for hospital services? Explain your position.

4

Statement of Changes in Fund Balances and Regulatory Disclosures

Introduction

The flexibility surrounding financial disclosure of nonoperating activities in health care entities was reduced by AICPA's 1990 *Audit and Accounting Guide*. Gains and losses are now required disclosures on a certified statement of revenue and expenses. These transactions were sometimes recorded directly in the fund balance account by many health care entities and were not reported on the statement of revenue and expenses. This industry practice may have occurred as a result of required reports for Medicare, which primarily focused on "operating income" with minimal disclosures for nonoperating gains.

An analysis of changes in financial disclosure for nonoperating gains is possible through the certified financial statements of health care entities in The Merritt System®. The Merritt System® is a credit analysis and database management system (DBMS) that contains comparative financial, operational, and bond issue data on not-for-profit hospitals. The 2,100 health care entities in the DBMS include over 1,000 facilities with complete financial data since 1985, and several hundred since 1984. Exhibit 3.5 presented a subset of this database, with aggregate statements of revenue and expenses for 1,482 community hospitals for 1986 to 1989.

Health care entities seeking new financial sources of funds must prepare financial statements for a three-to-five year period, depending on the type and nature of the long-term capital being requested. As these certified financial statements are prepared after the 1990 *Audit*

Guide, financial information for prior year reports are restated. Several community hospitals in the database for The Merritt System® were recently changed to reflect nonoperating gains and restricted funds. Many of these revisions were for fiscal years 1986 and 1987.[1]

Reporting under the new statement of changes in fund balances provides disclosure on fund transfers, restricted donations, and other extraordinary financial events. The statement of changes in fund balance reports a reconciliation of the fund balance between the current and prior balance sheets with net information on the excess of revenue and gains over expenses and losses. Tracing of changes in the overall fund balance is now a required disclosure for health care entities.

Closing and Fund Transfer Transactions

The basic accounting equation of assets equals liabilities plus equities is often expressed by T-accounts with left-side and right-side entries. An entry on the left side is called a *debit,* and an entry on the right side is called a *credit.* The terms *debit* and *credit* do not signal "good" or "bad" messages, but merely indicate the side where the transaction or balance is located.

Assets are on the left side of the accounting equation and are designated as debit accounts. Liabilities and equities are on the right side of the accounting equation and are specified as credit accounts. The balance in an account is increased by recording a transaction on the same side as the account balance. A decrease in an account is accomplished by a transaction on the opposite side to the usual balance of the account.

Exhibit 4.1 illustrates the balance of accounts for Metropolitan Health Care Clinic at the end of the period shown in Exhibit 3.1. Total assets of $630,500 are separated between cash and noncash in general funds for illustration purposes only. The beginning balance of the restricted fund is $350,000 and it is all in long-term investments (not the cash account).

Transaction (17). Patient service revenue of $300,000 and other operating revenue of $25,000 are recorded to the noncash account. Noncash assets are increased by $325,000 (a debit), and patient revenue is increased by $300,000 (a credit) and other operating revenue is increased by $25,000 (a credit).

Transaction (18). Operating expenses of $280,000 were incurred. Operating expenses are increased by $280,000 (a debit), and liabilities are increased by $280,000 (a credit).

Exhibit 4.1   Metropolitan Health Care Clinic: Balance of Accounts

General Funds *Cash Assets*		
Debit account Balance $130,500 T(20) $290,000 T(21) $ 70,000	T(24) $265,000	

Noncash Assets		
Debit account Balance $500,000 T(17) $325,000	T(19) $ 30,000 T(20) $290,000	

Patient Service Revenue		
T(25) $300,000	Credit account T(17) $300,000	

Operating Expenses		
Debit account T(18) $280,000	T(25) $280,000	

Due from Restricted Funds		
Debit account T(23) $ 12,000		

General Funds *Liabilities*		
T(24) $265,000	Credit account Balance $155,000 T(18) $280,000	

General Fund Balance		
	Credit account Balance $475,500 T(25) $ 97,000	

Other Operating Revenue		
T(25) $37,000	Credit account T(17) $ 25,000 T(23) $ 12,000	

Nonoperating Losses		
Debit account T(19) $ 30,000	T(25) $ 30,000	

Nonoperating Gains		
T(25) $ 70,000	Credit account T(21) $ 70,000	

Restricted Funds *Noncash Assets*		
Debit account Balance $350,000		

Restricted Funds *Due to General Funds*		
	Credit account T(22) $ 12,000	

Restricted Fund Balance		
T(22) $ 12,000	Credit account Balance $350,000	

Transaction (19). Nonoperating losses of $30,000 were sustained. Noncash assets are decreased by $30,000 (a credit), and nonoperating losses are increased by $30,000 (a debit).

Transaction (20). Collections of $290,000 were made on patient and accounts receivable. Cash account is increased by $290,000 (a debit), and noncash assets are decreased by $290,000 (a credit).

Transaction (21). A contribution of $70,000 for general support was received from a foundation. Nonoperating gains is increased by

$70,000 (a credit), and the cash account is increased by $70,000 (a debit).

Transactions (22) and (23). The general funds acknowledged that $12,000 of the operating expenses incurred in Transaction (18) are appropriate to charge to the restricted funds. The restricted noncash asset account is invested and cannot be immediately used to pay $12,000. Thus, the restricted fund balance is decreased by $12,000 (a debit), and a liability account due to general funds is increased by $12,000 (a credit). In the general fund, other operating revenue is increased by $12,000 (a credit), and due from restricted funds (an asset account) is increased by $12,000 (a debit).

Transaction (24). Liabilities of $265,000 were paid in the general fund. Liabilities are decreased by $265,000 (a debit), and the cash account is decreased by $265,000 (a credit).

Transaction (25). Revenue and gains are matched with expenses and losses in the general funds for the purpose of computing excess of revenue over expenses. This matching is accomplished by closing all accounts from the statement of revenue and expenses as follows:

	Debit	Credit
Patient service revenue	$300,000	
Other operating revenue	37,000	
Nonoperating gains	70,000	
Operating expenses		$280,000
Nonoperating losses		30,000
General fund balance		97,000

After the closing entries are recorded, the accounting equation is in balance, with $742,500 of assets versus $170,000 of liabilities plus $572,500 of equity in the general funds. These accounts, with their debit and credit balances, are as follows:

	Debit	Credit
Cash assets (general funds)	$225,500	
Noncash assets	505,000	
Due from restricted funds	12,000	
Liabilities		$170,000
General fund balance		572,500
Total	$742,500	$742,500

Exhibit 4.2 presents the statements of changes in fund balances for Metropolitan Health Care Clinic for years ended 31 December 19X2 and 19X1. The $12,000 transfer in Transactions (22) and (23)

is disclosed in Exhibit 4.2 by a reduction in the donor-restricted fund. There is no notation for the transfer under general funds because the transfer was classified as other operating revenue and included in the statement of revenue and expenses for general funds. If the transfer had been for equipment purchases, then there would have been an entry in the general funds column of Exhibit 4.2.

Exhibit 4.2   Metropolitan Health Care Clinic: Statements of Changes in Fund Balances for Years Ended 31 December 19X2 and 19X1

	19X2		19X1	
	General Funds	*Donor-Restricted Funds*	*General Funds*	*Donor-Restricted Funds*
Balances at beginning of year	*$475,500*	*$350,000*	*$460,000*	*$200,000*
Additions:				
Revenue and gains in excess of expenses and losses	97,000	—	15,500	—
Gifts and bequests	—	—	—	150,000
Transfers to other revenue	—	(12,000)	—	—
Balance at end of year	*$572,500*	*$338,000*	*$475,500*	*$350,000*

Note: Exhibit 3.1 reports the general fund transactions for 19X1; $150,000 was received in the restricted funds during 19X1.

Reporting Requirements

Certified financial statements for health care entities based on GAAP must include a statement of changes in fund balance. Under the new *Audit and Accounting Guide,* transactions omitted from the statement of revenue and expenses are highlighted in the statement of changes in fund balance. Flexibility in transaction reporting has been eliminated by the AICPA's new guidelines, which include mandated disclosures for many types of professional adjustments with health care entities.

Prior-period third-party adjustments

Review and audit of claims from third party payors typically extend from 15 to 18 months after the date of service. If Medicare is understaffed in an area, then a 24-month delay before the start of an audit is not unusual. Thus, balance sheets of health care entities may include a series of receivables and payables based on estimated collections from pending reviews and audits. Balances due from final settlements and appeals are reported separately from other current claims.

The 1990 *Audit and Accounting Guide* considers all third-party adjustments and final collections as normal operations, regardless of the delays. There are several other major decisions in this new policy.[2] First, net patient revenue is the new reporting format; gross charges are relegated on a need-to-know basis to the financial statement notes. In other words, gross charges and contractual allowances are not to appear on the statement of revenue and expenses. Second, any differences between estimates originally reported in the financial statements and the final settlements are "included in the statement of revenue and expenses in the period the settlements are made."[3] Third, bad debts expense is not to be included in the contractual allowances and adjustment computation, but bad debt expense is to be reported as a financial (operating) expense.

These new reporting guidelines for transactions with third-party payors are having a significant impact on current financial reports as prior-year adjustments are moved to the statement of revenue and expenses. AHA's data in Table 3.3 reported contractual allowances of 31.4 percent in 1989 for the 5,455 community hospitals. The magnitude of the allowances for various third party payors is of sufficient size that material measurement issues may be encompassed in some of the estimated receipts. Some final settlements may generate more income than what was originally reported as excess of revenue over expenses in the year the services were provided.

The measurement issues in final settlements can be seen in the certified financial statements for community hospitals in two eastern states that implemented an "all-payor rate plan" in the late 1980s. Final settlement adjustments for 1988 were of sufficient magnitudes in more than 25 community hospitals in the database in The Merritt System® that the contractual allowance measurement was negative. In each of these hospitals the actual and expected collections (net patient revenue) were larger than the annual gross charges for the year. Seven community hospitals had negative contractual allowances for two or more consecutive years.

Transfers and donations

Unrestricted donations are nonoperating revenue in general funds, and donor-restricted donations are recorded in the specific-purpose funds. A transfer from specific-purpose funds to general funds is reported as other operating revenue, and *this type of transaction can only be traced on the statement of changes in fund balances.* There is no required disclosure of these transfers on the statement of revenue and expenses of general funds. Many restricted donations to specific-purpose funds are transferred to general funds in the same fiscal year in which they are received.

Charity care

There are three distinct issues involving financial statement disclosures of charity care. First is the status of uncompensated services to people unable to pay under the Hill-Burton grants. Second is the separate reporting of charity care amounts in the notes, so potential donors and other readers of the financial statements are not misled. Third is full disclosure of investment income and grants that are restricted to support charity care.

The reporting of charity care is a critical problem for health care entities. Charity care represents health care services provided where there was never any expectation of cash collection; thus, charity care is not reported in the certified financial statements according to GAAP.

If the not-for-profit hospital received federal funds through the Hill-Burton Act for construction projects, the institution is required to render uncompensated services to persons unable to pay.[4] These individuals are identified as "charity cases" at the time the health care services are provided, and they are not billed for the services. The failure of a reimbursement system to fully cover services rendered to a welfare patient does not constitute a "charity case." The failure to collect from an individual for services rendered is not a sufficient condition to meet the charity-case grouping.

Donated services and donated properties

Participation of volunteers in philanthropic activities is usually not recorded in the financial statements of not-for-profit health care entities. Donated services are recorded only when there is an effective employer-employee relationship. If the donated services are not performed by a volunteer, a salaried employee must be required to perform these services because of the essential nature of the activities. Furthermore, the entity must exercise control over the time, location, nature, and performance of service provided by the volunteer. Finally, the entity must have a measurable basis for determining the amount to be recorded for the donated services. All three requirements must be present before the donated services are recorded as an expense with a corresponding amount as a contribution according to the AICPA's *Audit and Accounting Guide.*[5]

Health care entities are accustomed to recording donated services and donated property. Medicare has recognized donated services and depreciation on donated property as "regular expenses" since the late 1960s. Donated property is reported at its fair market value in the statement of revenue and expenses of general funds if unrestricted, or as additions to the appropriate fund balance if restricted.[6] Unrestricted donated assets are reported as other operating revenue if they are related to the primary mission of the health care entity. Unrestricted donated assets that are peripheral and incidental to the health care entity's mission are classified as nonoperating gains.[7]

Pledges

An unrestricted pledge is reported during the period in which it is made to the health care entity as revenue on the statement of revenue and expenses for general funds. The amount reported is net of an allowance for uncollectibles. Restricted pledges are reported on the statement of changes in fund balance as a transaction for the period that increases a donor-restricted fund balance.

Illustrative Statements

Wilmette Community Hospital's balance sheets for general funds and donor-restricted funds were previously discussed and were presented in Exhibit 2.3, but they are repeated in Exhibit 4.3 with the customary format and a note to the statements for fixed assets. There are transactions between the general funds and the donor-restricted funds; the statements of changes in fund balances provide an overview of movements among funds as well as within each fund. In the case of the general funds, the excess of revenue over expenses from the statements of revenue and expenses represents a major factor in the changes in the general fund balance.

Exhibit 4.3   Wilmette Community Hospital: Balance Sheets for 31 December 19X2 and 19X1

Assets	19X2	19X1
General Funds		
Current assets:		
Cash and cash equivalents	$ 450,794	$ 744,406
Assets whose use is limited and are required for current liabilities (note omitted)	1,416,240	1,370,880
Patient accounts receivable, net of estimated uncollectibles of $403,808 in 19X2 and $397,162 in 19X1	11,500,603	9,731,390
Estimated third party payor settlements— Medicare	390,000	470,000
Inventory of supplies at lower of cost (first in, first out) or market	1,195,339	1,025,281
Other current assets	478,427	380,874
Total current assets	*15,431,403*	*13,722,831*
Assets whose use is limited (notes omitted):		
By board for capital improvements	11,950,687	7,452,490
By agreements with third party payors for funded depreciation	7,791,722	5,681,609
Under malpractice funding arrangement —held by trustee	1,996,495	1,296,495
Under indenture agreement—held by trustee	5,100,000	4,300,000
Total assets whose use is limited	*26,838,904*	*18,730,594*
Less assets whose use is limited and that are required for current liabilities	1,416,240	1,370,880
Noncurrent assets whose use is limited	*25,422,664*	*17,359,714*
Property and equipment, net (note 2)	*60,612,234*	*50,019,350*
Other assets:		
Deferred financing costs	1,376,699	918,105
Total assets	*$102,843,000*	*$82,020,000*
Liabilities and Fund Balances	**19X2**	**19X1**
General Funds		
Current liabilities:		
Current installments of long-term debt	$ 1,416,240	$ 1,370,880

Continued

Exhibit 4.3 Continued

Liabilities and Fund Balances	19X2	19X1
Accounts payable	2,547,243	2,387,653
Accrued expenses	4,631,354	3,500,283
Retainage and construction accounts payable	890,500	71,500
Estimated third party payor settlement— Medicaid	1,218,693	605,726
Deferred third-party reimbursement	150,013	180,266
Advances from third party payors	515,340	480,060
Due to donor-restricted funds, net	699,275	591,312
Total current liabilities	12,068,658	9,187,680
Deferred third-party reimbursement	480,000	570,000
Estimated malpractice costs	2,396,495	1,296,495
Long-term debt, excluding current installments	26,624,320	17,709,861
Fund balance	61,273,527	53,255,964
Commitments and contingent liabilities (notes omitted)		
Total liabilities and fund balance	$102,843,000	$82,020,000

Note to Financial Statements

2. *Property and equipment*

A summary of property and equipment at 31 December 19X2 and 19X1 follows:

Land	$ 2,112,274	$ 2,112,274
Land improvements	284,317	284,317
Buildings and improvements	44,839,982	45,641,540
Equipment	21,756,791	20,181,080
	68,993,364	68,219,211
Less accumulated depreciation and amortization	22,603,972	19,881,699
	46,389,392	48,337,512
Construction in progress	14,222,842	1,681,838
Property and equipment, net	$ 60,612,234	$50,019,350

Continued

Exhibit 4.3   Continued

Construction contracts of approximately $18,450,000 exist for remodeling and expansion of hospital facilities. At 31 December 19X2, the remaining commitment on these contracts approximated $4,530,000.

Assets	19X2	19X1
Donor-Restricted Funds		
Special purpose funds:		
Cash	$ 128,712	$ 95,406
Investments, at cost that approximates market	2,664,164	2,350,875
Due from general funds	205,233	174,310
Total assets	2,998,109	2,620,591

Liabilities and Fund Balances	19X2	19X1
Donor-Restricted Funds		
Specific-purpose funds:		
Fund balance	$ 2,998,109	$ 2,620,591
Total liabilities and fund balance	$ 2,998,109	$ 2,620,591

Assets	19X2	19X1
Donor-Restricted Funds		
Plant replacement and expansion funds:		
Cash	$ 136,371	$ 145,306
Investments, at cost that approximates market	2,469,715	2,135,480
Pledges receivable, net of estimated uncollectibles of $139,445 in 19X2 and $65,000 in 19X1	1,816,620	890,475
Due from general funds	494,042	417,002
Total assets	$ 4,916,748	$ 3,588,263

Liabilities and Fund Balances	19X2	19X1
Donor-Restricted Funds		
Plant replacement and expansion funds:		
Fund balance	$ 4,916,748	$ 3,588,263
Total liabilities and fund balance	$ 4,916,748	$ 3,588,263

Exhibit 4.4 Wilmette Community Hospital: Statements of Changes in Fund Balances for Years Ended 31 December 19X2 and 19X1

	19X2			19X1		
		Donor-Restricted Funds			Donor-Restricted Funds	
	General Funds	Specific-Purpose Funds	Plant Replacement & Expansion Funds	General Funds	Specific-Purpose Funds	Plant Replacement & Expansion Funds
Balance at beginning of year	$53,255,964	$2,620,591	$3,588,263	$48,162,494	$2,341,674	$2,860,214
Additions:						
Excess of revenue over expenses	7,504,329			4,807,412		
Gifts and pledges		345,000	1,752,782		260,000	890,416
Investment income		220,409	201,576		190,312	170,094
Gain on sale of investments		23,952	35,740		12,507	22,954
Transfers to finance property and equipment additions	513,234		(513,234)	286,058		(286,058)
	8,017,563	589,361	1,476,864	5,093,470	462,819	797,406
Deductions:						
Provision for uncollectible pledges			(139,445)			(65,000)
Realized loss on sale of investments		(10,897)	(8,934)		(8,502)	(4,357)
Transfer to other operating revenue		(200,946)			(175,400)	
	0	(211,843)	(148,379)	0	(183,902)	(69,357)
Balance at end of year	$61,273,527	$2,998,109	$4,916,748	$53,255,964	$2,620,591	$3,588,263

Exhibit 4.4 presents the statements of changes in fund balances for Wilmette Community Hospital for years ended 31 December 19X2 and 19X1. Note that $513,234 was transferred from the plant replacement and expansion fund to the general funds in 19X2 to finance property and equipment additions. There is also a transfer in 19X2 in Exhibit 4.4 of $200,946 from specific-purpose funds to the general funds. But, note there is no entry in the general funds column for the $200,946 because it was included as other operating revenue in the statements of revenues and expenses (Exhibit 3.3) and is part of the $7,504,329 excess of revenues over expenses in the general funds column of Exhibit 4.4. The information in the statements of changes in fund balances permits the tracing of transactions among funds and within each fund.

Statements of revenue and expenses are not prepared for donor-restricted funds, but the detailed information on the statements of changes in fund balances encompasses all types of increases and decreases for the donor-restricted funds. The plant replacement and expansion funds for 19X2 received gifts and pledges of $1,752,782, against which $139,445 was estimated to be uncollectible; investment income of $201,576 was received; $35,740 was the gain on sale of investments; $8,934 was the loss on sale of investments; and a direct transfer of $513,234 was made to the general funds for property and equipment per donor specifications. These additions and deductions explain how the plant replacement and expansion fund went from $3,588,263 at the end of 19X1 to $4,916,748 at the end of 19X2, as follows:

Balance at end of 19X1	$3,588,263
Direct transfer to general funds to finance property and equipment additions	(513,234)
Receipt of gifts and pledges	1,752,782
Receipt of investment income	201,576
Receipt as gain on sale of investments	35,740
Decrease as loss on sale of investments	(8,934)
Provision for uncollectible pledges	(139,445)
Balance at end of 19X2	*$4,916,748*

The receipts and disbursements in the specific-purpose funds for 19X2 in Exhibit 4.4 are similar to the above, except for the transfer of $200,946 to other operating revenue of the general fund in accordance with the written instructions from donors.

The format and contents of balance sheets and statements of changes in fund balances are different depending on the ownership and type of health care entity. The Richmond Care Nursing Home follows the AICPA proposed format for financial statements, and the balance sheets for general funds and donor-restricted funds are combined on the same statement (Exhibit 4.5). The $12,000 of donor-restricted investments in 19X2 are shown in Exhibit 4.5 and in the fund balance as assets whose use is limited or restricted.[8] While these dollar amounts are not significant relative to the total assets of $3,164,000, Exhibit 4.5 is a report for two accounting entities: (1) general funds and (2) donor-restricted funds. These separate accounting entities are emphasized in the statements of changes in fund balances for Richmond Care Nursing Home (Exhibit 4.6).

The nursing home received $12,000 of donated equipment in 19X2, and $26,000 of donated equipment in 19X1; the assigned values for these donations are based on market value. Since in Exhibit 4.6 the donations are separate lines from the excess of revenues over expenses, the market value of these donations were not included in the statements of revenues and expenses (Exhibit 3.4). The nursing home's property and equipment in the general funds are increased by the market value of these donations. The statements of changes in fund balances also report restricted donations for the nursing home. Exhibit 4.6 provides insights into the changes in fund balances not revealed by the statements of revenues and expenses. In fact, the statement of changes in fund balances serves as the connecting link between balance sheets and shows the status of all transactions with the statements of revenues and expenses.

Impact of New Reporting Requirements

Health care entities with restricted funds must disclose transactions and transfers in the statement of changes in fund balances. Any certified financial statements based on GAAP for a health care entity for periods beginning on or after 15 July 1990 contain aggregate information on restricted donations and grants that was often not previously available. These disclosures will assist financial analysts in assessing the operational performance and financial viability of health care entities.

A sample of 990 NFP community hospitals that AHA designates by classification code 23 for "other nongovernment NFP" and code 10 for "general medical and surgical services" was taken from the database in The Merritt System®. Two panels were created from the sample based on the existence of restricted funds in the certified financial

Exhibit 4.5 Richmond Care Nursing Home: Balance Sheets for 31 December 19X2 and 19X1

Assets	19X2	19X1
Current assets:		
Cash	$ 72,000	$ 68,000
Investments, at cost that approximates market	200,000	91,000
Assets whose use is limited and are required for current liabilities	125,000	125,000
Patient accounts receivable less allowance for doubtful accounts:		
19X2—$8,100; 19X1—$6,400	307,000	276,000
Estimated third party payor settlements	62,000	51,000
Interest receivable	6,000	2,000
Supplies	65,000	60,000
Prepaid expenses	5,000	3,000
Total current assets	*842,000*	*676,000*
Assets whose use is limited or restricted:		
Under indenture agreement—held by trustee	235,000	195,000
By board for capital improvements	65,000	65,000
Donor-restricted investments	12,000	10,000
Total assets whose use is limited	*312,000*	*270,000*
Less assets whose use is limited and that are required for current liabilities	125,000	125,000
Noncurrent assets whose use is limited	*187,000*	*145,000*
Property and equipment:		
Land	300,000	300,000
Land improvements	46,000	46,000
Buildings	1,685,000	1,685,000
Major movable equipment	128,000	96,000
Furniture and fixtures	98,000	93,000
Automotive equipment	14,000	14,000
	2,271,000	*2,234,000*
Less accumulated depreciation	265,000	197,000
	2,006,000	*2,037,000*
Other assets:		
Notes receivable	75,000	70,000
Unamortized bond issuance cost	42,000	45,000

Continued

Exhibit 4.5 Continued

Assets	19X2	19X1
Other	12,000	9,000
	129,000	124,000
Total assets	$3,164,000	$2,982,000

Liabilities and Fund Balance	19X2	19X1
Current liabilities:		
Current maturities of long-term debt	$ 125,000	$ 125,000
Accounts payable	76,000	62,000
Accrued expenses	236,000	241,000
Total current liabilities	437,000	428,000
Long-term debt, less current maturities	1,750,000	1,875,000
Fund balance:		
General	965,000	669,000
Donor-restricted	12,000	10,000
Total fund balance	977,000	679,000
Total liabilities and fund balance	$3,164,000	$2,982,000

statements. Panel 1 consists of 283 hospitals without restricted funds, and Panel 2 represents 707 hospitals with restricted funds.

Table 4.1 shows that Panel 2 hospitals are significantly larger in net patient revenue, new investments in fixed assets, and net fixed assets. Panel 1 hospitals have a significantly larger percent of long-term debt to total unrestricted assets than the Panel 2 hospitals. More of the Panel 2 hospitals belong to the Council of Teaching Hospitals, have medical school affiliations, and are located in metropolitan statistical areas.

Four performance measures reported in Table 4.1 are adjusted for size differences. The Panel 1 hospitals are smaller in terms of average net patient revenue, but the excess of revenue and gains over expenses and losses to this smaller base is 4.32 percent on average—not significantly different from the 4.66 percent for the larger Panel 2 hospitals. Revenue over expenses to net fixed assets, revenue over expenses to total unrestricted assets, and net investment to net fixed assets are not significantly different for the two panels.

Some health care entities without restricted funds may have an affiliation with a medical foundation. The only disclosure in the certified

Exhibit 4.6   Richmond Care Nursing Home: Statements of Changes in Fund Balances for Years Ended 31 December 19X2 and 19X1

	19X2	19X1
General Funds		
Fund balance at beginning of year	$669,000	$535,000
Excess of revenues over expenses	284,000	108,000
Donations of equipment	12,000	26,000
Fund balance at end of year	$965,000	$669,000
Donor-Restricted Funds		
Fund balance at beginning of year	$ 10,000	$ 7,000
Donor-restricted gifts	2,000	3,000
Fund balance at end of year	$ 12,000	$ 10,000

financial statement is that of a related party. A note to the financial statement would indicate that there is a medical foundation, but it would not report the financial transactions of the foundation with the health care entity for the period.

Although the statement of changes in fund balances is very helpful in tracking transfers from restricted funds, the more important benefit of the new reporting requirements concerns changes within a fund. In the past, there was not full disclosure of how the general fund balance changed from one year to the next. The difference in the general fund balance was not equal to the bottom line of the statement of revenue over expenses. Was the unexplained difference because of prior-period third-party adjustments, or some special donation that was not reported on the statement of revenue and expenses? The new set of disclosures will permit a level of financial assessment of health care entities that was not previously possible from certified financial statements.

Regulatory Disclosures

Many health care entities are located in states where Medicaid requires detailed financial and departmental data that are in marked contrast to the AICPA reporting guidelines. Children's hospitals and rehabilitation hospitals are not under the 1983 prospective payment system for inpatients. Inpatient hospital capital–related costs for all hospitals

Table 4.1   Other Not-for-Profit Community Hospitals (Codes 10 and 23) Profile Comparison Based on Existence of Restricted Funds

	No Restricted Funds Panel 1 (283)		Restricted Funds Panel 2 (707)		Two-Sample t-Stat
	Mean	*Std Dev.*	*Mean*	*Std Dev.*	
Status					
1986–1989 Average net patient revenue (in thousands)	$47,709	$52,831	$64,632	$67,454	4.19***
1987–1988 Net fixed asset investment (in thousands)	$ 9,634	$12,375	$13,676	$23,638	3.50***
1988 Net fixed assets (in thousands)	$30,876	$33,664	$42,868	$53,347	4.23***
Long-term debt to total unrestricted assets	40.5%	19.8	37.6%	16.9	−2.16**
Performance Measures					
1986–1989 Revenue over expenses to net patient revenue	4.32%	5.30	4.66%	4.71	0.94
1986–1989 Revenue over expenses to net fixed assets	7.51%	9.77	7.63%	8.01	0.19
1986–1989 Revenue over expenses to total unrestricted assets	2.94%	4.61	2.80%	4.62	−0.42
Net investment to net patient revenue	9.54%	6.90	9.96%	9.23	0.78
Classification					
Member of the Council of Teaching Hospitals	6.4%		16.3%		
Medical school affiliation	18.7%		32.0%		
Metropolitan statistical area (MSA) location	73.1%		75.8%		

Source: The specific data on hospitals are from The Merritt System®.
  *Significant at 10% level.
  **Significant at 5% level.
  ***Significant at 1% level.

under the prospective payment system require computations at a lower level than the AICPA reporting guidelines.

Health care entities have regulatory reporting disclosures that are at a lower level than the AICPA guidelines. Some reporting requirements by regulatory agencies and governmental bodies may be in conflict with the AICPA guidelines. Ownership, control, type of facility, and geographical location are some of the factors that limit the applicability of a generalized statement on conflict between AICPA and regulatory disclosures.

Revenue by type

Health care entities often must prepare financial reports for regulatory bodies that separate gross revenue between inpatient and outpatient and the contractual allowances in total. Gross revenue, in this context, may include charity care. The financial data for Wilmette Community Hospital is used to illustrate these reporting requirements; however, Wilmette's contractual allowance is only 7.5 percent, while the national average of contractual allowances is 31.5 percent in 1989 (Table 3.3).

Exhibit 4.7 illustrates that some routine and special services at Wilmette Community Hospital are performed only on an inpatient basis, but most ancillary services are provided to both inpatients and outpatients. Note that clinic revenues include $855,461 of service charges for inpatients. After information on the 22 major patient services in Exhibit 4.7 for Wilmette Community Hospital has been filed with a regulatory agency, competitors of the health care entity may be able to gain access to this data through the Freedom of Information Act. Some health care entities elect to emphasize the major patient services in their annual reports, and other entities have special fund development reports that contain selected data on the various patient services. Other health care entities are concerned with competition and do not want to disclose any extra information; these entities may consolidate selected patient services before submitting a report in the format of Exhibit 4.7 to a regulatory agency.

Certificate of need

Some state agencies hold public hearings on proposed new health care facilities, modernization of departments and services, major equipment acquisitions, and changes in numbers of licensed beds within categories. After the hearings, the appropriate state agency can issue an approved certificate of need (CON) to the health care entity,

Exhibit 4.7   Wilmette Community Hospital: Schedule of Inpatient and Outpatient Revenues for Year Ended 31 December 19X2

	Total Revenue	Inpatient Revenue	Outpatient Revenue
Routine Care	$29,365,251	$29,365,251	$ 0
Intensive Care Unit	4,744,498	4,744,498	0
Diabetes Center	1,159,654	289,914	869,740
Operating Room	8,551,821	8,551,821	0
Recovery Room	879,301	879,301	0
Anesthesiology	2,023,295	2,023,295	0
Radiology—Diagnostic	7,191,095	4,838,379	2,352,716
CT Scanner	823,685	781,456	42,229
Laboratory	9,181,062	7,335,894	1,845,168
Blood Bank	1,154,735	1,063,821	90,914
Inhalation Therapy	1,644,560	1,372,283	272,277
Physical Therapy	2,664,733	1,443,289	1,221,444
Occupational Therapy	662,328	245,937	416,391
Speech Therapy	64,380	51,379	13,001
Electrocardiology	938,015	854,671	83,344
Electroencephalography	69,973	61,346	8,627
Medical Supplies—Patients	2,335,276	1,952,163	383,113
Drugs Charged to Patients	6,328,007	5,206,686	1,121,321
Pulmonary Rehabilitation	284,404	213,584	70,820
Clinic	2,376,283	855,461	1,520,822
Emergency	2,422,555	0	2,422,555
Day Surgery	1,648,192	0	1,648,192
Total patient revenues	*$86,513,103*	*$72,130,429*	*$14,382,674*

which, among other things, means that the depreciation for the new capability is an accepted cost for Medicare reimbursement purposes. The prospective payment system (PPS) has changed the method of payment for Medicare inpatients; however, many Medicare outpatients still follow a cost-based reimbursement system. There is a capital cost payment under Medicare that is separate from the rates per episode under PPS. A ten-year phased implementation of a new rate structure that replaces the current reasonable cost–based payment methodology was announced in the *Federal Register*.[9]

A bank or financial institution will require a copy of the approved CON as documentation in support of a loan, a line of credit, or other financial resources. An approved CON is an important asset to the health care entity; it is a state license to provide certain types of *new* services in a competitive environment. Some types of approved CONs may be sold in the marketplace; others are used for expansion of a facility into a major joint venture between several entities.

In processing the CON application, the public members on the health care regulatory boards often apply financial statement analysis from a business perspective to special reports by an applicant. Not all business ratios apply to the health care field. There are layers of added cost to facilities, equipment, and fixtures in most health care entities because of building code, fire, environment, and life-support requirements. When there is a closure of a facility, these added layers of cost may not have any value if the assets are being acquired for use in a non–health care field.

Summary

The statement of changes in fund balances must be closely examined for purposes of identifying movements between donor-restricted funds and general funds, and the movements within each fund. It would be of interest to reflect a fund balance transfer out of "start-up capital funds of a related entity" or a "donation" to the related foundation. There are alternative ways that health care entities might handle a financial transaction; the data in the statement of changes in fund balances indicate how a given transaction was actually processed. For some types of transfers and donations, the statement of changes in fund balances is the only disclosure of certain types of financial transactions in health care entities.

AICPA's current reporting guidelines require all prior-period transactions and adjustments with third party payors be reflected in the statement of revenue and expenses. The final settlements are often material amounts that increase or decrease the current period's results. This is a significant change in financial reporting practice for many health care entities.

Certified financial statements based on GAAP include a statement of revenue and expenses that begins with net patient revenue. Gross charges and contractual adjustments do not appear on the financial statement and are reported as a note *when it is deemed necessary.* Information on charity care should be included in a note to the financial statements so foundations and other interested parties are aware of the free care given to indigents. The not-for-profit status of health care entities is currently being questioned by proposed legislation pending in Congress; data on charity care would be helpful in this debate.

The aggregate level of AICPA reports is in marked contrast to regulatory reports with inpatient and outpatient data by department. Regulatory reports may be obtained by a health care entity's competitor under the Freedom of Information Act; thus, minimum discretionary disclosures are suggested.

Appendix: Disclosures of Competitive Environment to Regulatory Agencies

Some community hospitals respond to their competitive environments by changing the format of Exhibit 4.7 and eliminating the departmental level disclosures on inpatient versus outpatient revenues. This revised format contains a single column of amounts, total revenue, and has a note with two lines for gross patient services revenue:

Inpatient revenue	$72,130,429
Outpatient revenue	14,382,674
Gross revenues from patient service	*$86,513,103*

Various regulatory reports do permit hospitals to gain insights into other hospitals' patient revenues by major financial class of patient. Wilmette Community Hospital's $86,513,103 of patient revenues, for example, was from the major sources shown in Table 4.2.

Social policy requires a uniform billing rate for patient services regardless of the financial class of the patient; therefore, most of the "deductions from revenues" on the statement of revenues and expenses are contractual allowances, as illustrated in Exhibit 3.3. Five types of deductions for contractual allowances and adjustments reduces net patient service revenue to $80,033,959, as follows:

Gross patient service revenue	*$86,513,103*
Less provisions for:	
Medicare and Medicaid contractual adjustment	4,968,361
Blue Cross contractual adjustment	370,418
Provision for bad debts	505,835
Other allowances	415,074

Table 4.2 Major Sources of Patient Revenues for Wilmette Community Hospital

	Amount	Percent
Medicare	$36,337,807	42.00%
Blue Cross	12,157,522	14.05
Medicaid	2,842,038	3.29
Commercial insurance	14,626,252	16.91
Corporate arrangements	4,642,527	5.37
Health maintenance organizations	6,318,445	7.30
Self-pay	7,397,356	8.55
Charity	219,456	.25
Others	1,971,700	2.28
Total revenue	*$86,513,103*	*100.00%*

Charity	219,456
Total deductions	*6,479,144*
Net patient service revenue	*$80,033,959*

The method of accounting used in these regulatory reports reflects the application of a social belief. All patients are charged (thus, "gross charges") at the same rate for specific health care services regardless of the method of payment. Thus, the charity of $219,456 included in the deductions from revenue was also fully reflected in the gross charges called "total patient services revenues." The certified financial statement (Exhibit 3.3) reports net patient service revenue of $80,539,794 because the provision for bad debts ($505,835) is included as operating expenses in the statement of revenue and expenses.

Hill-Burton reporting

Wilmette Community Hospital received federal funds under the Hill-Burton Act in the 1970s to partially finance the expansion of the physical plant. As a requirement for these funds, a certain amount of uncompensated services is annually provided to the community. These uncompensated services are reported by Wilmette Community Hospital as patient services revenues of $219,456 for charity patients, offset by a contractual allowance for the same amount. Hill-Burton grants were used by other hospitals for the purchase of equipment.

Regulatory hospital reports must usually disclose contractual allowances for Medicare and Medicaid patients; however, many hospital reports may aggregate the other allowances for third party payors into a single line. Under this type of disclosure, a competing hospital may not know the expected cash receipts from, for example, commercial insurance versus corporate arrangements. There are many marketing and other considerations that encourage hospitals to limit the disclosures on contractual allowances; otherwise, the net patient revenue by financial class of patient can be determined as shown in Table 4.3.

Table 4.3   Net Patient Revenue by Financial Class of Patient for Wilmette Community Hospital

	Total Revenues	*Contractual Allowances and Adjustments*	*Net Patient Revenues*	*Percent*
Medicare	$36,337,807	$4,429,222	$31,908,585	39.87%
Blue Cross	12,157,522	370,418	11,787,104	14.73
Medicaid	2,842,038	539,139	2,302,899	2.88
Commercial insurance	14,626,252	286,107	14,340,145	17.92
Corporate arrangements	4,642,527	35,849	4,606,678	5.75
HMOs	6,318,445	93,118	6,225,327	7.78
Self-pay	7,397,356	505,835	6,891,521	8.61
Charity	219,456	219,456	—	—
Others	1,971,700	—	1,971,700	2.46
Total revenue	*$86,513,103*	*$6,479,144*	*$80,033,959*	*100.00%*

When that much detailed information is known, it is then possible to determine the relative importance of specific sources of net patient revenues as shown in Table 4.4. Net patient revenue from Medicare is 39.9 percent of the total, not 42.0 percent as suggested by gross charge data. Commercial insurance represents 17.9 percent of the total volume, 1 percent higher than the indications from gross charge data. Blue Cross and HMOs are much more important to the net patient services revenue than suggested by gross charges. But, again, the supporting schedules and notes in published annual hospital reports do not typically include sufficient information to determine the net patient revenues by major financial class, as illustrated above.

Table 4.4   Relative Importance of Sources of Net Patient Revenue
for Wilmette Community Hospital

	Total Patient Revenues	Net Patient Revenues	Difference
Medicare	42.00%	39.87%	−2.13%
Blue Cross	14.05	14.73	0.68
Medicaid	3.29	2.88	−0.41
Commercial insurance	16.91	17.92	1.01
Corporate arrangements	5.37	5.75	0.38
HMOs	7.30	7.78	0.48
Self-pay	8.55	8.61	0.06
Charity	0.25	0.00	−0.25
Others	2.28	2.46	0.18
Total revenues	*100.00%*	*100.00%*	*0.00%*

Departmental revenues and costs

Some regulatory reports require disclosure at the same organizational level for revenues and costs. Revenues for the 22 major patient services at Wilmette Community Hospital, totaling $86,513,103 for 19X2, were presented in Exhibit 4.7, and direct and assigned costs must be matched to these same 22 revenue centers in these regulatory reports. This matching is performed in Exhibit 4.8, where it is reported that the 22 major patient services incurred costs of $42,246,429 while generating $86,513,103 of revenues. There are 17 general service accounts in Exhibit 4.8, with $33,037,667 of aggregate costs, and these overhead and support costs must be assigned, based on utilization statistics, to the 22 revenue centers. The computations of this assignment are discussed in Chapter 10, but the impact of these computations are shown in the third column, where the $33,037,667 of support and overhead costs are assigned to the revenue centers. The last column contains the total costs of $75,284,096, matched against revenues of $86,513,103 for the 22 patient service accounts.

Operating expenses

A comparison of the data in Exhibit 4.8 for direct costs and assigned costs at the departmental level for Wilmette Community Hospital with the overall institutional data in Exhibit 3.3 brings into focus the

Exhibit 4.8   Wilmette Community Hospital: Schedule of Departmental Revenues and Costs for Year Ended 31 December 19X2

Cost Centers	Total Revenue	Direct Cost	Assigned Cost	Total Cost
Ancillary Service				
Diabetes Center	$ 1,159,654	$ 631,504	$ 490,894	$ 1,122,398
Operating Room	8,551,821	4,962,994	2,625,097	7,588,091
Recovery Room	879,301	444,615	240,517	685,132
Anesthesiology	2,023,295	986,502	313,564	1,300,066
Radiology—Diagnostic	7,191,095	4,136,600	2,028,196	6,164,796
CT Scanner	823,685	589,935	168,772	758,707
Laboratory	9,181,062	4,358,316	2,233,963	6,592,279
Blood Bank	1,154,735	822,607	229,715	1,052,322
Inhalation Therapy	1,644,560	945,671	340,766	1,286,437
Physical Therapy	2,664,733	1,362,615	1,113,663	2,476,278
Occupational Therapy	662,328	283,024	125,302	408,326
Speech Therapy	64,380	27,900	12,950	40,850
Electrocardiology	938,015	306,412	166,820	473,232
Electroencephalography	69,973	22,994	20,596	43,590
Medical Supplies	2,335,276	825,887	1,273,834	2,099,721
Drugs Charged to Patients	6,328,007	2,683,952	3,093,605	5,777,557
Pulmonary Rehabilitation	284,404	187,102	69,272	256,374
Inpatient Routine Service				
Routine Care	29,365,251	12,122,717	15,071,941	27,194,658
Intensive Care Unit	4,744,498	2,986,712	1,562,160	4,548,872
Outpatient Service				
Clinic	2,376,283	1,439,371	324,204	1,763,575
Emergency	2,422,555	1,269,520	972,320	2,241,840
Day Surgery	1,648,192	849,479	559,516	1,408,995
Subtotal	*86,513,103*	*42,246,429*	*33,037,667*	*75,284,096*
General Service				
Depreciation	0	3,931,051	0	0
Employee Health & Welfare	0	4,424,630	0	0
Administrative & General	0	6,989,635	0	0

Continued

Exhibit 4.8   Continued

Cost Centers	Total Revenue	Direct Cost	Assigned Cost	Total Cost
Plant Operations	0	2,663,345	0	0
Maintenance & Repairs	0	1,235,129	0	0
Laundry & Linen Service	0	936,880	0	0
Environmental	0	1,943,728	0	0
Dietary	0	2,211,284	0	0
Cafeteria	0	652,174	0	0
Nursing Administration	0	1,190,970	0	0
Central Services & Supply	0	696,703	0	0
Pharmacy	0	1,629,654	0	0
Medical Records	0	893,154	0	0
Social Service	0	230,850	0	0
Medical Malpractice Costs	0	1,100,000	0	0
Interest Expense	0	1,963,984	0	0
Intern-Resident Service	0	344,496	0	0
Total	$86,513,103	$75,284,096	$33,037,667	$75,284,096

magnitude of the difference between regulatory reports and AICPA statements. Exhibit 4.8 shows some of the detailed data included in the former Medicare cost reports for Wilmette Community Hospital. The 22 revenue cost centers appear at the top and show that a direct cost of $42,246,429 was charged during year 19X2 to these revenue centers, while they generated $86,513,103 of total patient service revenue. The third column reports the results of matching the 17 general service cost centers, with combined costs of $33,037,667, to these 22 revenue centers. After this matching of costs with revenue centers, the fourth column reveals that the $75,284,096 is assigned to the 22 revenue centers.

Certified financial statements based on GAAP begin with net patient revenue, and all gross charge and contractual allowance data are relegated to notes to the financial statements. Regulatory reports, on the other hand, often have required disclosures that permit an analysis of contractual allowance for each major third party payor.

Notes

1. The AICPA's *Exposure Draft; Proposed Audit and Accounting Guide: Audits of Providers of Health Care Services,* issued on 15 March 1988, appears to have been followed in certified financial statements issued in 1988 to 1990. This comment is based on an examination of over 1,800 financial statements in The Merritt System®.
2. AICPA's *Audit and Accounting Guide* encompasses many diverse types of health care entities with a new common level of required reporting. The new policy was already being followed by some types of health care entities.
3. AICPA, *Audit and Accounting Guide,* 55.
4. The Hospital Survey and Construction Act of 1946 (P. L. 79–725), often referred to as the "Hill-Burton Act," provided grants for construction, renovation, and modernization of not-for-profit hospitals. Facilities that received these funds must annually report to a regulatory agency the amount of uncompensated care provided in accordance with the requirements of these grants.
5. AICPA, *Audit and Accounting Guide,* 15.
6. AICPA, *Audit and Accounting Guide,* 14–15.
7. AICPA, *Audit and Accounting Guide,* 15 and 110. The notes to the financial statements for property and equipment illustrate one type of treatment (p. 158).
8. The format of the aggregated balance sheet was changed between the proposed audit guide and the one released. Donor-restricted investments were included as other assets in the proposed audit guide (p. 105) but under assets whose use is limited or restricted in *Audit and Accounting Guide* (pp. 168–69).
9. *Federal Register* 56 (40) (28 February 1991).

Additional Readings

Hillman, B. J. "Government Health Policy and the Diffusion of New Medical Devices," *Health Services Research* 21 (December 1986): 681–11.

Rosko, M. D. "All-Payer Rate-Setting and the Provision of Hospital Care to the Uninsured: The New Jersey Experience," *Journal of Health Politics, Policy and Law* 15 (Winter 1990): 815–31.

Sloan, F. A., M. A. Morrisey, and J. Valvona. "Effects of the Medicare Prospective Payment System on Hospital Cost Containment: An Early Appraisal," *Milbank Quarterly* 66 (1988): 191–220.

Tuckman, H. P., and C. F. Chang. "A Proposal to Redistribute the Cost of Hospital Charity Care," *Milbank Quarterly* 69 (1991): 113–42.

Wilkinson, R. "New Technology That Will Change Key Services," *Hospitals* 62 (20 May 1988): 56–61.

Discussion Questions

4.1. Explain the relationship of debits and credits to the basic accounting equation.

4.2. Explain why patient service revenue is a credit account and operating expenses is a debit account. Hint: Study T-accounts in Exhibit 4.1 and map the flow to the general fund balance account.

4.3. Give examples of how flexibility in reporting by health care entities was removed by the AICPA's 1990 *Audit and Accounting Guide.*

4.4. Metropolitan Health Care Clinic's statement of changes in fund balance for 19X2 (Exhibit 4.2) indicated that $12,000 was transferred from the donor-restricted fund to the general fund. Why is the amount not included on the last line in the first column of Exhibit 4.2 for general funds?

4.5. How is charity care disclosed under the 1990 *Audit and Accounting Guide?*

4.6. Is it possible for the statement of revenue and expenses to report more net patient revenue than gross charges?

4.7. Explain the major benefits of the statement of changes in fund balances.

4.8. Certified financial statements for health care entities based on GAAP now begin with net patient revenue. Gross charges and contractual allowances are reported as a note to the financial statement, if deemed necessary. Bad debts expense must now be recognized as an operating expense; previously bad debts were aggregated with contractual allowances and adjustments. Explain the measurement problem in reporting bad debts expense for health care entities.

4.9. Transfer of donor-restricted funds to general funds may go directly to the general funds account or it may be in operating revenue. What financial statements permit the tracing of these transfers?

4.10. Donation of property to the general funds might be reported as nonoperating revenue or as a direct charge to the general fund account. What financial statements permit the tracing of this donation?

4.11. A health maintenance organization receives $50,000 for investment income. It is recorded as

   a. operating revenues on statements of revenues and expenses of general funds

   b. nonoperating revenues on statements of revenues and expenses of general funds

   c. addition to general funds on statements of changes in fund balances

   d. transfer to general funds on statements of changes in fund balances

4.12. A nongovernment not-for-profit community hospital receives $50,000 for investment income. It is recorded as

　　a. operating revenues on statements of revenues and expenses of general funds

　　b. nonoperating revenues on statements of revenues and expenses of general funds

　　c. addition to general funds on statements of changes in fund balances

　　d. transfer to general funds on statements of changes in fund balances

4.13. A nongovernment not-for-profit continuing-care retirement community facility receives $50,000 for investment income. It is recorded as

　　a. operating revenues on statements of revenues and expenses of general funds

　　b. nonoperating revenues on statements of revenues and expenses of general funds

　　c. addition to general funds on statements of changes in fund balances

　　d. transfer to general funds on statements of changes in fund balances

4.14. A nongovernment not-for-profit skilled nursing facility receives $50,000 for investment income. It is recorded as

　　a. operating revenues on statements of revenues and expenses of general funds

　　b. nonoperating revenues on statements of revenues and expenses of general funds

　　c. addition to general funds on statements of changes in fund balances

　　d. transfer to general funds on statements of changes in fund balances

4.15. A nongovernment not-for-profit community hospital receives $50,000 as a donor-restricted specific-purpose contribution, which is immediately transferred to the general funds. It is recorded as

　　a. operating revenues on statements of revenues and expenses of general funds

　　b. nonoperating revenues on statements of revenues and expenses of general funds

　　c. addition to general funds on statements of changes in fund balances

　　d. transfer to general funds on statements of changes in fund balances

4.16. A nongovernment not-for-profit community hospital receives $50,000 as a plant replacement and expansion contribution, which is immediately transferred to the general funds. It is recorded as

　　a. operating revenues on statements of revenues and expenses of general funds

b. nonoperating revenues on statements of revenues and expenses of general funds

c. addition to general funds on statements of changes in fund balances

d. transfer to general funds on statements of changes in fund balances

4.17. A for-profit health care corporation owned several community hospitals within a given state, including several hospitals in rural areas and in medium-size cities, but it did not own a facility in the state's major metropolitan area. The for-profit corporation applied for a certificate of need to build a 300-plus-bed community hospital in the major metropolitan area that, among other functions, would be a referral institution for its own hospitals within the state. The state health facility planning board rejected the CON application from the for-profit health care entity.

At a subsequent meeting, the state health facility planning board approved a CON application for a nonprofit health care entity to build a 300-plus-bed community hospital in this same major metropolitan area. The approved location was within ten blocks of the site proposed by the for-profit chain. The nonprofit health care entity's existing facility was to be converted into a nursing home and extended-care facility after the new community hospital was opened; this arrangement was formally approved by the board with written concurrence from the nursing home licensure group and the state department of public health that handles licensure for extended-care facilities.

During the next 60 days, the for-profit health care corporation acquired the nonprofit health care entity and immediately began to construct the new community hospital. Explain the assets that were acquired by the for-profit corporation.

5

Statement of Cash Flows

Introduction

The statement of cash flows of general funds highlights the health care entity's annual changes in operating activities, investing activities, and financing activities. There is no other required financial statement that discloses this much information about the health care entity. The matching of revenue and gains with expenses and losses is reported in the statement of income and expenses, but this aggregate information is captured as part of the operating activities in the first part of the statement of cash flows. Certified financial statements of not-for-profit nongovernmental health care entities did not include the statement of cash flow until July 1990.

Investor-owned health care entities have had required cash flow statements since 1 July 1988, but not-for-profit health care entities were excluded by FASB Statement No. 95, "Statement of Cash Flows," from the scope of this reporting requirement.[1] GASB Statement No. 9, "Reporting Cash Flows of Proprietary and Nonexpendable Trust Funds and Governmental Entities That Use Proprietary Fund Accounting," covered governmental entities and specified cash flow statements for both general and restricted funds. AICPA's 1988 *Proposed Audit and Accounting Guide* contained a statement of changes in financial position that was different from the statement of cash flows.[2] Operating income, rather than excess of revenue and gains over expenses and losses was the beginning point in the statement of changes in financial position for nursing homes and hospitals. AICPA's 1990 *Audit and Accounting Guide* states: "Not-for-profit health care entities should apply the provisions of FASB Statement No. 95 to ensure that their financial statements are comparable with those of investor-owned entities."[3]

The suggested format of the statement of cash flows in the 1990 reporting guidelines contains several unique disclosures for health care entities. Donations and fund transfers, for example, may involve diverse cash flows depending on the purpose and source. Assets whose use is limited may comprise a significant portion of the health care entity's total assets. Transactions with third party payors may include current and noncurrent assets and liabilities. The annual change in net patient accounts receivable is separated in the suggested reports between provision for bad debts and other changes.

The statement of cash flows captures the overall movement of net assets between two balance sheets, and the movement (or flow) is expressed in terms of the cash account. The three required parts of the statement of cash flows separate the normal, day-to-day events of the health care entity (operating activities) from one-time events in the investing and financing areas. The resulting aggregate amounts from these three partitions represent new financial measures for explaining a health care entity's annual performance.

Operating Activities and Gains and Losses

The term "cash flows from operating activities" is from FASB Statement No. 95 for corporate enterprise and investor-owned facilities. The origin of the term is important because it does not imply an intermediate measure from the statement of revenue and expenses for health care entities. Operating activities include all transactions and events generally associated with producing and delivering services. This financial measure of performance is interpreted as a regular flow that will occur year after year. The collection of patient accounts and payment of vendors are as important components of operating activities as the bottom line from the statement of revenue and expenses.

The definition of "operating activities and gains and losses" in the reporting guidelines is equivalent to "other" or "residual." Operating activities include all transactions and events that are not mandated to be reported as investing activities or financing activities. Exhibit 5.1 shows that the 19X2 statement of revenue and expenses only accounted for $7,504,329 of the $12,550,345 in net cash provided by operating activities and gains and losses. The remaining $5 million is based on several asset movements between the two balance sheets.

Exhibit 5.1 Wilmette Community Hospital: Statements of Cash Flows of General Funds for Years Ended 31 December 19X2 and 19X1 (Indirect computations)

	19X2	*19X1*
Cash flows from operating activities and gains and losses:		
Revenue and gains in excess of expenses and losses	$ 7,504,329	$ 4,807,412
Adjustments to reconcile revenue and gains in excess of expenses and losses to net cash provided by operating activities and gains in losses:		
Depreciation and amortization	3,931,051	3,845,970
Provision for bad debts	505,835	465,450
Amortization of deferred financing costs	71,170	69,100
Loss on disposal of property	81,964	—
Increase in net amounts due to third party payors	607,994	114,000
Increase in liability for estimated malpractice costs	1,100,000	750,000
Increase in patient accounts receivable	(2,275,048)	(1,415,750)
Increase in supplies and other current assets	(267,611)	(2,000)
Increase in accounts payable and accrued expenses	1,290,661	77,000
Net cash provided by operating activities and gains and losses	*12,550,345*	*8,711,182*
Cash flows from investing activities:		
Purchase of property and equipment	(15,105,899)	(1,500,000)
Transfer from donor-restricted fund for purchase of property and equipment	513,234	286,058
Sale of property and equipment	500,000	—
Cash invested in assets whose use is limited	(8,108,310)	(6,030,594)
Net cash used by investing activities	*(22,200,975)*	*(7,244,536)*
Cash flow from financing activities:		
Increase in retainage and construction accounts payable	819,000	51,500
Repayment of long-term debt	(1,370,880)	(1,400,000)

Continued

Exhibit 5.1   Continued

	19X2	19X1
Proceeds from issuance of long-term debt	9,800,935	—
Temporary loans from donor-restricted funds	107,963	42,712
Net cash from (used by) financing activities	9,357,018	(1,305,788)
Net increase (decrease) in cash and cash equivalents	(293,612)	160,858
Cash and cash equivalents at beginning of year	744,406	583,548
Cash and cash equivalents at end of year	$ 450,794	$ 744,406

Depreciation, amortization, and provisions

The statement of revenue and expenses includes several expenses that do not require cash outlays during the current period. Since these noncash expenses are deducted in computing the bottom line, they must be added back to the excess of revenue over expenses in determining the cash flows from operating activities.

Depreciation is an allocation of historical cost of property and equipment to expense that does not require any current outlay. Thus, the $3,931,051 depreciation expense in 19X2 in Exhibit 3.3 is unlike most of the other cost elements in the $75,789,931 operating expenses. There were cash payments in 19X2 for all or most of these other items: salaries and professional fees, employee benefits, supplies, purchased services, medical malpractice costs, and interests. If there was not a cash payment in 19X2, the outstanding liability is recognized and will be paid in 19X3. But this is not the case with depreciation. The capital expenditures associated with the $3,931,051 of depreciation expense were made in prior years when the fixed assets were purchased, such as the $15,105,899 in Exhibit 5.1; the cash flow associated with the acquisition is reported as an investing activity.

Property and equipment in many health care entities were donated, and depreciation is recorded on these donated assets using appraised values. Overall, the depreciation expense is based on the matching of expired costs with revenue (Exhibit 3.3), and it is a noncash transaction appearing on the statement of revenue and expenses during the same time period in which these fixed-asset services are provided. If there were no other transactions, the net cash flow from operations in 19X2 in Exhibit 5.1 would be $11,435,380, as follows:

Revenue and gains in excess of expenses and losses	$ 7,504,329
Depreciation and amortization	3,931,051
Net cash provided	$11,435,380

Because of the relative magnitude of depreciation expense, cash flows from operating activities are significantly influenced by this account in most health care entities.

A new noncash item was created by the AICPA's 1990 reporting guidelines for separating the net changes in patient accounts receivable between provision for bad debts and other movements on the statement of cash flows. The $505,835 provision for bad debts in 19X2 in Exhibit 3.3 is a noncash deduction influencing the bottom line. This amount is added to the excess of revenue over expenses in determining cash flows from operating activities.

Wilmette Community Hospital had an amortization of deferred financing costs of $71,170, included in interest expense in Exhibit 3.3. This noncash amortization is added to the bottom line in calculating cash flows from operating activities.

Excluded gains and losses

The statement of revenue and expenses contains gains and losses from transactions and events classified as investing and financing activities. The net cash flows for these investing and financing activities must be separated from the other transactions on the statement of revenue and expenses.

Wilmette Community Hospital experienced a loss of $81,964 on the disposal of properties (Exhibit 3.3). The overall changes in the property and equipment accounts for 19X2, including a $500,000 receipt for the sale of equipment with a book value of $581,964, are summarized in Exhibit 5.2. The loss of $81,964 is not a recurring type of activity for this hospital; therefore, it should not be included in the computation of cash flows from operating activities. Instead, the $500,000 is reported in Exhibit 5.1 as the cash received from the sale of property and equipment. The loss on sale of equipment is added to the bottom line in computing cash flows from operating activities. If there had been a gain on the sale of equipment, then the gain would have been subtracted from the bottom line in calculating the recurring cash flows from operating activities.

Exhibit 5.2   Wilmette Community Hospital: Analysis of Property and Equipment Accounts for Year Ended 31 December 19X2

	Asset Accounts	Accumulated Depreciation
Balance at beginning of year in regular accounts (Exhibit 2.3)	$68,219,211	$19,881,699
Construction in progress	1,681,838	—
Total	$69,901,049	$19,881,699
Dispositions for $500,000 with book value of $581,964 for loss of $81,964:		
Cost $1,790,742		
Accum dep 1,208,778		
Book value 581,964		
Cash received 500,000		
Loss 81,964	(1,790,742)	(1,208,778)
New additions:		
General funds	14,592,665	
Donor-restricted fund transfers (Exhibit 4.4)	513,234	
Total additions	$15,105,899	
Depreciation expense for 19X2	—	3,931,051
Balance at end of year	$83,216,206	$22,603,972
Less accumulated depreciation	22,603,972	
Net balance (Exhibit 2.3)	$60,612,234	

The following fixed asset cash items for 19X2 in Exhibit 5.1 are illustrated above:

Depreciation and amortization for 19X2	$ 3,931,051
Loss on disposal of property	81,964
Purchase of property and equipment	(15,105,899)
Transfer from donor-restricted fund for purchase of property and equipment	513,234
Sale of property and equipment	500,000

Changes in net assets per accrual accounting

Revenue and income are reported on the statement of revenue and expenses when the services are provided and the products are sold. Expenses follow the revenue and income, so there is a matching of benefits and effort. This overall process, called "accrual accounting," is required for certified financial statements based on GAAP for health care entities.

The statement of revenue and expenses is accrual accounting. The bottom line from this accrual accounting report must be adjusted for those changes in assets and liabilities caused by noncash events. The five events for imputing cash flows in operating activities in Exhibit 5.1 are as follows:

Increase in net amounts due to third party payors	$ 607,994
Increase in liability for estimated malpractice costs	1,100,000
Increase in patient accounts receivable	(2,275,048)
Increase in supplies and other current assets	(267,611)
Increase in accounts payable and accrued expenses	1,290,661

The net cash provided by operating activities and gains and losses of $12,550,345 in Exhibit 5.1 is a measure of performance expected to occur year after year. The health care entity should have $12.6 million of new cash funds each year that can be assessed along with investing and financing activities. There are some limits to this recurring theme for "cash provided by operating activities." If there are no new investments in medical technology and equipment, then the patient service revenue will probably drop, since physicians tend to refer their patients to facilities with modern equipment.

Investing Activities

Cash flows from investing in property and equipment and cash from sales of fixed assets are one-time events, distinct from recurring transactions included in operating activities and gains and losses. There may be transfers from donor-restricted funds for the purchase of property and equipment. Many health care entities have investments in affiliated companies (examined in Chapter 6), reported on the statement of cash flows under investing activities.

The other general type of investing activity for health care entities is for assets whose use is limited. Wilmette Community Hospital had four examples of assets whose use is limited (Exhibit 4.3):

By board for capital improvements	$11,950,687
By agreements with third party payors for funded depreciation	7,791,722
Under malpractice funding arrangement—held by trustee	1,996,495
Under indenture agreement—held by trustee	5,100,000
Total assets whose use is limited	26,838,904
Less assets whose use is limited and that are required for current liabilities	1,416,240
Noncurrent assets whose use is limited	25,422,664

Financial transactions for assets whose use is limited are not part of recurring events included in operating activities and gains and losses, but they are mandated to be reported as investing activities.

Exhibit 5.1 reported $22,200,975 of net cash used by investing activities in 19X2, consisting of the following:

Purchase of property and equipment	(15,105,899)
Transfer from donor-restricted fund for purchase of property and equipment	513,234
Sale of property and equipment	500,000
Cash invested in assets whose use is limited	(8,108,310)

Changes in medical practice, medical technology, and competitive market factors tend to impose some minimum levels of required annual investing activities on health care entities. The minimum levels vary by ownership, control, and type of facility. This issue is examined in Chapter 7.

Financing Activities

Cash flows from financing activities are a major concern in almost all health care entities, except those with very large endowments or those that are annual recipients of major awards from governmental bodies. Community hospitals, for example, annually receive more donations and grants than the aggregate amount of revenue and gains over expenses and losses (Table 3.3). Many other types of health care facilities tend to depend on contributions and awards for financing major components of operations, such as indigent care, and acquisition of equipment. Third party payors are able to delay payment to health care entities for patient services because of a series of rules covering processing, reviewing, and validating of patient claims. This payment delay adds additional financial pressures on health care entities for funds for working capital.

Health care entities need long-term sources of funds rather than waiting for annual contributions and donations. Investor-owned facilities can issue equity instruments as a major source of cash inflows from financing activities. Nonprofit health care entities must depend on bonds, mortgages, notes, and other instruments. The tax-exempt status of nonprofit health care entities creates an opportunity for some facilities to manage the spread between the going rate of interest and the tax-exempt rate. They can borrow at tax-exempt interest rates and make investments in commercial securities at taxable rates.[4]

Cash flows from financing activities of health care entities in the 1990s are much more complex than during the early 1980s. The Federal Housing Administration (FHA) and the Government National Mortgage Association (GNMA) provided funding to hospitals and other entities in the 1970s and early 1980s. Long term financing was primarily a "political issue" of being on the approved list for funds. The FHA and GNMA programs are gone, and commercial financing arrangements are now the major sources.

Concurrently with the phasing out of FHA and GNMA programs, the Tax Equity and Fiscal Responsibility Act of 1982 (P. L. 97–248) was passed. Financial institutions and bond-rating services continue to refer to P. L. 97–248 as the major legislation on health care entities.[5] While the prospective payment provisions of P. L. 97–248 have had a major impact on many community hospitals, the other provisions of the act created some alarm in the industry. The secretary of Health and Human Services can enter into risk-based contracts with HMOs and competitive medical plans for providing comprehensive medical care to Medicare beneficiaries. Because of these concerns, commercial bond issue insurance became a requirement for many health care entities before these facilities could sell securities. California created a government-owned insurance group to cover health care facilities that had difficulty in obtaining commercial bond issue insurance.

The reporting of cash flow from financing activities under the 1990 audit guidelines contains unique features for health care entities.

Transfers from restricted funds and construction accounts are illustrated by Wilmette Community Hospital's financing events in 19X2 for $9,357,018:

Increase in retainage and construction accounts payable	$ 819,000
Repayment of long-term debt	(1,370,880)
Proceeds from issuance of long-term debt	9,800,935
Temporary loans from donor-restricted funds	107,963

There was a $10,330,699 increase in debt, of which $529,764 was financing charges; thus, the net cash from the debt was $10,330,699 less $529,764, or $9,800,935. Cash was used in 19X2 to pay an installment of $1,370,880 on existing long-term debt.

Direct Method for Operating Activities

The format followed in Exhibit 5.1 for cash flows from operating activities and gains and losses is representative of the *indirect method* for operating activities. The cash flows of $12,550,345 from operating activities in 19X2 are computed based on accrual accounting changes in various asset and liability accounts; the computations based on accrual accounting impute the cash movement—thus, the "indirect method." Alternatively, the actual changes in the cash account for revenue and expenses can be used in *directly* determining cash flows from operating activities. These direct computations are illustrated in Exhibit 5.3.

The direct method created by FASB Statement No. 95 is recommended by FASB because it focuses on the major uses and sources of cash in ordinary terms. The major uses of cash are for salaries, supplies, services, and so on, and the major sources of cash are from patients and third party payors. Cash receipts from other operating revenue ($1,459,356 in Exhibit 5.3) are separated from cash receipts from investment gains ($1,286,281 in Exhibit 5.3). Cash receipts for unrestricted gifts and bequests are a fourth type of inflow ($90,793) under the direct method for health care entities.

The computation of the direct method for cash flows from operating activities and gains and losses is an involved process because of the number of accruals included in each item. As an illustration of the process, the $78,872,740 in 19X2 for cash received from patients and third party payors in Exhibit 5.3 is the summation of the following net changes:

Exhibit 5.3   Wilmette Community Hospital: Statements of Cash Flows of General Funds for Years Ended 31 December 19X2 and 19X1 (Direct computations)

	19X2	*19X1*
Cash flows from operating activities and gains and losses:		
Cash received from patients and third party payors	78,872,740	72,357,603
Cash paid to employees and suppliers	(67,266,011)	(64,570,043)
Other receipts from operations	1,459,356	1,142,607
Receipts from unrestricted gifts and bequests	90,793	26,350
Interest and dividends received	1,286,281	1,102,410
Interest paid (net of amount capitalized)	(1,892,814)	(1,347,745)
Net cash provided by operating activities and gains and losses	*12,550,345*	*8,711,182*
Cash flows from investing activities:		
Purchase of property and equipment	(15,105,899)	(1,500,000)
Transfer from donor-restricted fund for purchase of property and equipment	513,234	286,058
Sale of property and equipment	500,000	—
Cash invested in assets whose use is limited	(8,108,310)	(6,030,594)
Net cash used by investing activities	*(22,200,975)*	*(7,244,536)*
Cash flow from financing activities:		
Increase in retainage and construction accounts payable	819,000	51,500
Repayment of long-term debt	(1,370,880)	(1,400,000)
Proceeds from issuance of long-term debt	9,800,935	—
Temporary loans from donor-restricted funds	107,963	42,712
Net cash from (used by) financing activities	*9,357,018*	*(1,305,788)*
Net increase (decrease) in cash and cash equivalents	(293,612)	160,858
Cash and cash equivalents at beginning of year	744,406	583,548
Cash and cash equivalents at end of year	$ *450,794*	$ *744,406*

Continued

Exhibit 5.3 Continued

Reconciliation of Revenue and Gains in Excess of Expenses and Losses to Net Cash Provided by Operating Activities and Gains and Losses	*19X2*	*19X1*
Revenue and gains in excess of expenses and losses	$ 7,504,329	$ 4,807,412
Adjustments to reconcile revenue and gains in excess of expenses and losses to net cash provided by operating activities and gains and losses:		
Depreciation and amortization	3,931,051	3,845,970
Provision for bad debts	505,835	465,450
Amortization of deferred financing costs	71,170	69,100
Loss on disposal of property	81,964	—
Increase in net amounts due to third party payors	607,994	114,000
Increase in liability for estimated malpractice costs	1,100,000	750,000
Increase in patient accounts receivable	(2,275,048)	(1,415,750)
Increase in supplies and other current assets	(267,611)	(2,000)
Increase in accounts payable and accrued expenses	1,290,661	77,000
Net cash provided by operating activities and gains and losses	$12,550,345	$ 8,711,182

Net patient service revenue (Exhibit 3.3)	$80,539,794
Less provision for bad debts (Exhibit 3.3)	(505,835)
Less increase in patient accounts receivable, net (Exhibit 2.3)	(1,769,213)
Add decrease in estimated third-party settlements—Medicare (asset; Exhibit 2.3)	80,000
Add increase in estimated third-party settlements—Medicaid (liability)	612,967
Less decrease in deferred third-party reimbursement (current liability)	(30,253)
Add increases in advances from third party payors	35,280
Less decrease in deferred third-party reimbursement (deferred liability)	(90,000)
Cash received from patients and third party payors	$78,872,740

It is difficult to predict what will be the response by nonprofit health care entities to the new AICPA requirement for cash flow statements in choosing between the direct method versus the indirect method for operating activities. However, less than 5 percent of the major industrial firms have adopted the direct method during the first four years of its existence.

If the direct method is followed, then a special schedule based on the indirect method must be attached. This schedule is called the "reconciliation of revenue and gains in excess of expenses and losses to net cash provided by operating activities and gains and losses" and is illustrated in Exhibit 5.3. The direct method does give a picture of aggregate cash receipts for four or five categories and the aggregate cash payments for expenses and interest. Although there is more disclosure with two reports than one (direct method and reconciliation), the additional accounting costs can be avoided by following the indirect method, as illustrated in Exhibit 5.1.

Illustrative Statements

Richmond Care Nursing Home's statements of cash flows of general funds are presented in Exhibit 5.4. Operating activities generated $328,000 of cash flows in 19X2; these funds were used for $199,000 in investing activities and $125,000 in repayment of long-term debt. Overall, there was an increase of $4,000 in Richmond Care Nursing Home's cash account for 19X2.

The direct method is used in reporting cash flows from operating activities; therefore, Exhibit 5.4 also contains the reconciliation of revenue and gains in excess of expenses and losses to net cash provided by operating activities and gains and losses. The bottom line of the statement of revenue and expenses in 19X2 is $284,000, which included some noncash expenses (such as depreciation and amortization) having a net impact of $44,000; thus, cash from operations in 19X2 is $328,000. The direct method in the initial part of Exhibit 5.4 shows receipts of $2,464,000 from residents and third party payors, payments to employees and suppliers of $2,050,000, receipts of $85,000 from other operating income, receipts of $21,000 from investment income, and cash payments for interest expense of $192,000. The direct method with the reconciliation in Exhibit 5.4 provides more information on the cash flows from operating activities and gains and losses.

Exhibit 5.4   Richmond Care Nursing Home: Statements of Cash Flows of General Funds for Years Ended 31 December 19X2 and 19X1

	19X2	19X1
Cash flows from operating activities and gains and losses:		
Cash received from residents and third party payors	2,464,000	2,237,000
Cash received from others	85,000	28,000
Cash paid to employees and suppliers	(2,050,000)	(1,915,000)
Interest and dividends received	21,000	10,000
Interest paid (net of amount capitalized)	(192,000)	(198,000)
Net cash provided by operating activities and gains and losses	*328,000*	*162,000*
Cash flows from investing activities:		
Purchase of property and equipment	(57,000)	(29,000)
Purchase of investments	(109,000)	(11,000)
Sale of property and equipment	3,000	5,000
Increase in notes receivable	(5,000)	(4,000)
Addition of other assets	(3,000)	(1,000)
Donation of equipment	12,000	26,000
Cash invested in assets whose use is limited	(40,000)	(10,000)
Net cash used by investing activities	*(199,000)*	*(24,000)*
Cash flow from financing activities:		
Repayment of long-term debt	(125,000)	(125,000)
Net cash used by financing activities	*(125,000)*	*(125,000)*
Net increase in cash and cash equivalents	4,000	13,000
Cash and cash equivalents at beginning of year	68,000	55,000
Cash and cash equivalents at end of year	$ 72,000	$ 68,000

Continued

The 19X2 cash flow movements in Exhibit 5.4 explain how Richmond Care Nursing Home's balance sheet (Exhibit 4.5) changed from 19X1 to 19X2. The actual preparation of a cash flow statement requires an analysis of the net change in each balance sheet account. The assets from the two balance sheets are listed in the first and second columns of Exhibit 5.5 as positive amounts; the liabilities and equities are reported in these columns as negative amounts. Since assets

Exhibit 5.4 Continued

Reconciliation of Revenue and Gains in Excess of Expenses and Losses to Net Cash Provided by Operating Activities and Gains and Losses	*19X2*	*19X1*
Revenue and gains in excess of expenses and losses	$284,000	$108,000
Adjustments to reconcile revenue and gains in excess of expenses and losses to net cash provided by operating activities and gains and losses:		
Depreciation and amortization	83,000	68,000
Provision for bad debts	107,000	96,000
Amortization of deferred financing costs	3,000	3,000
Loss on disposal of property	2,000	6,000
Increase in net amounts due from third party payors	(11,000)	(7,000)
Increase in patient accounts receivable	(138,000)	(110,000)
Increase in supplies and other current assets	(11,000)	(8,000)
Increase in accounts payable and accrued expenses	9,000	6,000
Net cash provided by operating activities and gains and losses	$ 328,000	$ 162,000

equals liabilities plus equities, the debits less the credits in the first two columns have a zero net balance.

The net change from 19X1 to 19X2 is expressed in the third and fourth columns of Exhibit 5.5, depending on whether the amount is a debit or a credit for that particular account. The unamortized bond issuance cost, for example, is an asset with debit amounts in the first and second columns of Exhibit 5.5. There is a reduction from $45,000 to $42,000 in the account balance; thus, the net change of $3,000 is the opposite (credit amount) of the normal asset account balance (a debit account). The net change in accounts receivable is after adjusting for bad debts expense. The total net change of $383,000 in the third and fourth columns is merely for control. The amount does not have any significance in the context of the statements of cash flow, except for a general comment that Exhibit 5.4 explains the $383,000 of net changes in the net asset accounts between 19X1 and 19X2.

The preparation of the statements of cash flows (Exhibit 5.4) is guided by the statement of change in account balances (Exhibit 5.5)

Exhibit 5.5   Richmond Care Nursing Home: Statement of Changes in Account Balances for Year Ended 31 December 19X2

			Net Change	
	19X2	*19X1*	*Debit*	*Credit*
Cash	$ 72,000	$ 68,000	4,000	—
Investments	200,000	91,000	109,000	—
Assets whose use is limited and are required for current liabilities	125,000	125,000	—	—
Patient accounts receivable, net	307,000	276,000	31,000	—
Estimated third party payor settlements	62,000	51,000	11,000	—
Interest receivable	6,000	2,000	4,000	—
Supplies	65,000	60,000	5,000	—
Prepaid expenses	5,000	3,000	2,000	—
Assets whose use is limited or restricted:				
Under indenture agreement	235,000	195,000	40,000	—
By board	65,000	65,000	—	—
Donor-restricted investments	12,000	10,000	2,000	—
Transferred to C assets	(125,000)	(125,000)	—	—
Property and equipment	2,271,000	2,234,000	37,000	—
Accumulated depreciation	(265,000)	(197,000)	—	68,000
Notes receivable	75,000	70,000	5,000	—
Unamortized bond issuance cost	42,000	45,000	—	3,000
Other assets	12,000	9,000	3,000	—
Current maturities of long-term debt	(125,000)	(125,000)	—	—
Accounts payable	(76,000)	(62,000)	—	14,000
Accrued expenses	(236,000)	(241,000)	5,000	—
Long-term debt, less current maturities	(1,750,000)	(1,875,000)	125,000	—
General fund balance	(965,000)	(669,000)	—	296,000
Donor-restricted	(12,000)	(10,000)	—	2,000
Total	0	0	$383,000	$383,000

Note: Exhibit 4.5 contains the detailed balance sheets for Richmond Care Nursing Home, Inc. Debit amounts in 19X2 and 19X1 are shown above as positive values in the first and second columns; credit amounts are reported as negative values in these columns.

Exhibit 5.6   Richmond Care Nursing Home: Cash Received from Residents and Third Party Payors

	19X2	19X1
Patient service revenue (Exhibit 3.4)	$2,613,000	$2,353,000
Less provision for bad debts (Exhibit 3.4)	(107,000)	(96,000)
Less increase in patient accounts receivable, net (Exhibit 5.5)	(31,000)	(16,000)
Less increase in estimated third party payor settlements	(11,000)	(4,000)
Cash received from residents and third party payors	$2,464,000	$2,237,000

and supported by the statements of revenue and expenses (Exhibit 3.4) and the statements of changes in fund balance (Exhibit 4.6). The cash received from residents and third party payors, for example, demonstrates this type of integration (Exhibit 5.6). The property and equipment accounts must be examined for dispositions, acquisitions, and donations; Exhibit 5.7 presents this analysis for Richmond Care Nursing Home.

Individuals familiar with FASB Statement No. 95 should note that the statements of cash flows (both Exhibits 5.1 and 5.4) contain some accommodations for the unique features of the health care industry following the illustrated reports in the 1990 audit guidelines. The reporting of transactions between funds are fully documented in the new guidelines for various types of facilities, but some combinations of transactions are not.

Summary

The statement of cash flows discloses more information than any other certified financial statement based on GAAP. Cash flow statements explain how the net assets of the health care entity changed from one year to the next, with emphasis on operating activities, investing activities, and financing activities. The term "operating activities" is more restricted in meaning within the health care industry than within business generally. In the 1990 *Audit and Accounting Guide*, AICPA modified the suggested heading in FASB Statement No. 95 for health care entities so the label more clearly designates the bottom line of

Exhibit 5.7   Richmond Care Nursing Home: Analysis of Property and Equipment Accounts for Year Ended 31 December 19X2

	Asset Accounts	*Accumulated Depreciation*
Balance at beginning of year in regular accounts (Exhibit 5.5)	$2,234,000	$197,000
Dispositions for $3,000 with book value of $5,000 for loss of $2,000	(20,000)	(15,000)
New additions:		
General funds	45,000	—
Direct donations (Exhibit 4.6)	12,000	—
Total additions	57,000	—
Depreciation expense for 19X2	—	83,000
Balance at end of year	*$2,271,000*	*$ 265,000*
Less accumulated depreciation	265,000	
Net balance (Exhibit 2.3)	*$2,006,000*	

The following fixed asset items for 19X2 in Exhibit 5.4 are illustrated above:

Depreciation and amortization for 19X2	$ 83,000
Loss on disposal of property	2,000
Additions of property and equipment	(57,000)
Donations of property and equipment	12,000
Sale of property and equipment	3,000

the statement of revenue and expenses: "cash flows from operating activities and gains and losses."

Each of the three aggregate measures on the cash flow statement is important in assessing health care entities. New investments are required to support changes in medical practice, medical technology, and competitive forces in the health care entity's service area. Relative amounts of investing activities versus operating activities in health care entities are carefully considered by financial analysts and bond rating services. Changes in the major external sources of long-term funds are expressed by cash flows from financing activities.

The statement of cash flows and the statement of changes in fund balances must be closely examined for purposes of tracking movements between donor-restricted funds and general funds, and the movements within each fund. There are alternative ways that health care entities might have handled a transaction. The data in these statements required by GAAP indicate how a given transaction was actually processed and disclose other information not previously available on fund transfers, donations, contributions, income on restricted funds, and unrealized losses and gains on investments.

Appendix: Illustration for Investor-Owned Facility

Woodstock Ambulatory Care, Inc., is an investor-owned health care entity with 26,000 shares of stock issued and outstanding in 19X1 (Exhibit 5.8). The $15 par value per share multiplied by the 26,000 shares outstanding at the end of 19X1 represents the $390,000 account balance in the common stock account. The difference between par value and market value of issued shares is recorded in the paid-in capital account. The aggregate earnings that have not been distributed to shareholders as dividends are represented by the ending balance in the retained earnings account.

Toward the end of 19X2, 3,000 shares of stock were issued and outstanding, with aggregate proceeds of $330,000. The common stock account is increased by $45,000, based on par value of $15 multiplied by the 3,000 shares. The paid-in capital account is increased by $285,000; the net proceeds of $330,000 less par value of $45,000 equals $285,000. Note the balance sheet must disclose the number of shares authorized, number of shares issued, and number of shares outstanding for investor-owned facilities. These new resources were placed in an investment account and reported as assets whose use is limited (Exhibit 5.8).

The balance in the retained earnings account decreased from $1,233,000 at the end of 19X1 to $1,123,000 at the end of 19X2. Statements of income and retained earnings show that this decline of $110,000 for 19X2 is due to a net loss (Exhibit 5.9). There were no other transactions beyond those summarized in the statement of income for 19X2.

The indirect method for operating activities is followed in the statement of cash flows in Exhibit 5.10. The unusual items in the statement of cash flows include two transactions with Medical Affiliates for 19X2, which explains how the other assets decreased from $240,000

Exhibit 5.8   Woodstock Ambulatory Care: Balance Sheets for 31
December 19X2 and 19X1

Assets	19X2	19X1
Current assets:		
Cash	$ 90,000	$ 60,000
Patient accounts receivable, net of estimated uncollectible of $20,000 in 19X2 and $14,000 in 19X1	340,000	310,000
Estimated retroactive adjustments—third party payors	15,000	20,000
Accounts receivable—other	10,000	6,000
Inventories of supplies	25,000	22,000
Prepaid expenses and deposits	6,000	8,000
Total current assets	*486,000*	*426,000*
Assets whose use is limited:		
By board for capital improvements	*330,000*	*0*
Property and equipment, at cost:		
Land	150,000	150,000
Land improvements	350,000	350,000
Buildings	750,000	750,000
Equipment	1,285,000	1,200,000
	2,535,000	*2,450,000*
Less accumulated depreciation and amortization	253,000	138,000
Net property and equipment	*2,282,000*	*2,312,000*
Other assets:		
Advances receivable	170,000	240,000
Total assets	*$3,268,000*	*$2,978,000*
Liabilities and Shareholders' Equity	**19X2**	**19X1**
Current liabilities:		
Notes payable	$ 85,000	$ 0
Accounts payable	60,000	65,000
Accrued expenses	35,000	28,000
Estimated retroactive adjustment—third party payors	20,000	17,000
Deferred revenue	25,000	45,000
Total current liabilities	*225,000*	*155,000*

Continued

Exhibit 5.8 Continued

Liabilities and Shareholders' Equity	19X2	19X1
Shareholders' equity:		
Common stock, $15 par value; authorized 40,000 shares; 26,000 in 19X1 and 29,000 in 19X2 issued and outstanding	435,000	390,000
Paid in capital	1,485,000	1,200,000
Retained earnings	1,123,000	1,233,000
Total shareholders' equity	3,043,000	2,823,000
Total liabilities and shareholders' equity	$3,268,000	$2,978,000

to $170,000. As stated in the note to the financial statement, $80,000 was written off based on anticipated advances recoverable, and $10,000 was advanced to Medical Affiliates under the guarantee arrangement. The $80,000 write-off is a noncash item that increases cash flows from operating activities and gains. The $10,000 advance under the guarantee arrangement is part of the cash used by investing activities.

The $330,000 proceeds from the issuance of 3,000 shares in 19X2 are reported as cash flow from financing activities in Exhibit 5.10. These funds were placed in an investment account and reported as cash invested in assets whose use is limited (Exhibit 5.10). Proceeds of $85,000 from short-term notes payable are an increase in cash from financing activities for 19X2.

Woodstock Ambulatory Care's total assets increased from $2,978,000 in 19X1 to $3,268,000 in 19X2 (Exhibit 5.8). The overall movement of net assets between these two balance sheets is captured by the three sections of the statement of cash flows in Exhibit 5.10:

Net cash provided by operating activities and gains	$ 40,000
Net cash used by investing activities	(425,000)
Net cash from financing activities	415,000
Net increase in cash	30,000
Beginning cash balance	60,000
Ending cash balance	$ 90,000

Cash of $455,000 was provided, and cash of $425,000 was used, for a net change of $30,000 at Woodstock Ambulatory Care, in 19X2.

Exhibit 5.9   Woodstock Ambulatory Care: Statements of Income and
Retained Earnings for Year Ended 31 December 19X2

Patient service revenue, net (notes 1 and 2)	$ 900,000
Other operating revenue	60,000
Total revenue	*960,000*
Operating expenses:	
Salaries and wages	462,000
Employee benefits	81,000
Supplies	125,000
Purchased services	194,000
Insurance	45,000
Professional fees	30,000
Interest	17,000
Depreciation	115,000
Provision for bad debts	18,000
Total expenses	*1,087,000*
Loss from operations	*(127,000)*
Nonoperating gain:	
Interest income	1,000
Contributions and donations	16,000
Total nonoperating gains	*17,000*
Net loss	*($110,000)*
Retained earnings at beginning of year	1,233,000
Retained earnings at end of year	*$1,123,000*

Notes to Financial Statements

1. *Net patient service revenue*

Patient service revenues are recorded at established rates, and a provision
is recorded for contractual adjustments, uncollectible accounts, and policy
adjustments. The established rates are reduced or increased by these adjustments in arriving at net patient service revenue. Two of the third party payors
reimburse Woodstock Ambulatory Care at tentative payment rates, which are
adjusted after the annual cost reports have been submitted and audited by
the third party payor.

2. *Advances receivable*

Woodstock Ambulatory Care has guaranteed that Medical Affiliates (MA) will
collect at least $60,000 per month from the direct billing MA does for services
rendered. Such advances are to be repaid to the extent MA's net cash collections exceed the minimum guarantee amount. In 19X2, $80,000 was written
off based on anticipated advances recoverable, and $10,000 was advanced by
Woodstock Ambulatory Care to MA under the guaranteed arrangement.

Exhibit 5.10   Woodstock Ambulatory Care: Statement of Cash Flows for Year Ended 31 December 19X2

Cash flows from operating activities and gains:	
Net loss	($110,000)
Adjustments to reconcile net income to net cash provided by operating activities and gains:	
Depreciation	115,000
Provision for bad debts	18,000
Write-down of receivables from Medical Affiliates	80,000
Increase in net amounts due to third party payors	8,000
Increase in patient accounts receivable	(48,000)
Increase in supplies and other current assets	(5,000)
Increase in accounts payable and accrued expenses	2,000
Decrease in deferred revenue	(20,000)
Net cash provided by operating activities and gains	*40,000*
Cash flow used for investing activities:	
Acquisitions of property and equipment	(85,000)
Cash invested in assets whose use is limited	(330,000)
Advance to Medical Affiliates	(10,000)
Net cash used by investing activities	*(425,000)*
Cash flows from financing activities:	
Issuance of stock	330,000
Proceeds from notes payable	85,000
Net cash from financing activities	*415,000*
Net increase in cash	*30,000*
Beginning cash balance	60,000
Ending cash balance	*$ 90,000*

Notes

1. Financial Accounting Standards Board (FASB) of the Financial Accounting Foundation, "Statement of Financial Accounting Standards No. 95, Statement of Cash Flows" (Stamford, CT: FASB, November 1987), 26: "The Exposure Draft did not include not-for-profit organizations within its scope. A few respondents to that document said that a statement of cash flows is also useful for not-for-profit organizations and suggested that those organizations be included in the scope of the final Statement."
2. AICPA, *Proposed Audit and Accounting Guide*, 91.
3. AICPA, *Audits and Accounting Guide*, 23.

4. Internal Revenue Service, Department of the Treasury, "Arbitrage Restrictions on Tax Exempt Bonds: Temporary Regulations," *Federal Register* 56 (25 April 1991): 19023–38, and "Proceeds of Bonds Used for Reimbursement: Notice of Proposed Rulemaking and Notice of Public Hearing," *Federal Register* 56 (25 April 1991): 19046–60.
5. R. Lamb and S. P. Rappaport, *Municipal Bonds*, 2d ed. (New York: McGraw-Hill Book Company, 1987), 127.

Additional Readings

Carslaw, C. A., J. R. Mills. "Developing Ratios for Effective Cash Flow Statement Analysis," *Journal of Accountancy* 172 (November 1991): 63–70.
Hauser, R. C., D. E. Edwards, and J. T. Edwards. "Cash Budgeting: An Underutilized Resource Management Tool in Not-for-Profit Health Care Entities," *Hospital & Health Services Administration* 36 (Fall 1991): 439–46.
Kronquist, S. L., N. Newman-Limata. "Reporting Corporate Cash Flows," *Management Accounting* 72 (July 1990): 31–36.
McCue, M. J., "The Use of Cash Flow to Analyze Financial Distress in California Hospitals," *Hospital & Health Services Administration* 36 (Summer 1991): 223–41.

Discussion Questions

5.1. Explain the purpose of the statement of cash flows of general funds.

5.2. Explain the relationship of the statement of cash flows of general funds to the statement of revenue and expenses for nonprofit health care entities.

5.3. Describe the three parts of the statement of cash flows of general funds in nonprofit health care entities.

5.4. Are cash flow statements prepared by investor-owned health care facilities different from those prepared by nonprofit health care entities? Explain your answer.

5.5. "Net patient revenue" on a certified financial statement based on GAAP is different from "net patient revenue" on most 1991 regulatory reports. Explain how this new definition of "net patient revenue" created a new noncash item for the statement of cash flows.

5.6. Why are investing activities so important in assessing performance of health care entities?

5.7. Explain four common types of "assets whose use is limited" that are reported as investing activities.

5.8. A "long-term debt to total unrestricted assets" ratio of 40 percent is typical of many health care entities. Briefly indicate reasons for long-term debt by health care entities, and explain how these transactions are reported in the statement of cash flows.

5.9. Explain the difference between the direct method and indirect method for operating activities.

5.10. Exhibit 5.5 is a statement of changes in account balances for Richmond Care Nursing Home, Inc. Explain the relationship of Exhibit 5.5 to the cash flow statement in Exhibit 5.4.

5.11. Explain the unique aspects of the health care industry, in contrast with business practice, that are identified in the preparation of cash flow statements.

5.12. There are four exhibits for Rose Ambulatory Care, Inc:

- Exhibit 5.11: statement of changes in account balances
- Exhibit 5.12: statement of revenue and expenses

Exhibit 5.11 Rose Ambulatory Care: Statement of Changes in Account Balances for Year Ended 30 June 19X2

	19X2	19X1	Net Change Debit	Net Change Credit
Cash	$ 70,000	$100,000	—	$ 30,000
Patient accounts receivable	456,000	481,000	—	25,000
Estimated retroactive adjust-ments—third party payors	24,000	30,000	—	6,000
Accounts receivable—other	26,000	10,000	$ 16,000	—
Supplies	75,000	50,000	25,000	—
Prepaid expenses	17,000	10,000	7,000	—
Property and equipment	640,000	564,000	76,000	—
Accumulated depreciation	(260,000)	(315,000)	55,000	—
Other assets	11,000	18,000	—	7,000
Notes payable—current	(25,000)	(25,000)	—	—
Accounts payable	(57,000)	(73,000)	16,000	—
Accrued payroll, benefits, and taxes	(34,000)	(40,000)	6,000	—
Estimated retroactive adjust-ment—third party payors	(36,000)	(50,000)	14,000	—
Long-term notes payable	(200,000)	(225,000)	25,000	—
Fund balance	(707,000)	(535,000)	—	172,000
Total	0	0	$240,000	$240,000

Exhibit 5.12   Rose Ambulatory Care: Statement of Revenue and Expenses for Year Ended 30 June 19X2

Patient service revenue, net	$1,285,000
Other operating revenue	84,000
Total revenue	*1,369,000*
Operating expenses:	
Salaries and wages	583,000
Employee benefits	94,000
Supplies	147,000
Purchased services	221,000
Insurance	42,000
Professional fees	65,000
Interest	18,000
Depreciation	51,000
Provision for bad debts	26,000
Total expenses	*1,247,000*
Income from operations	*122,000*
Nonoperating gains:	
Contributions and donations	24,000
Loss on sale of equipment	(9,000)
Nonoperating gains	*15,000*
Excess of revenue over expenses	$ *137,000*

- Exhibit 5.13: selected account information
- Exhibit 5.14: statement of cash flows of general funds

The direct method for operating activities is followed in Exhibit 5.14. After studying these materials, prepare the statement for the indirect method, or the "reconciliation of revenue and gains in excess of expenses and losses to net cash provided by operating activities and gains and losses" for the year ended 30 June 19X2.

5.13. Exhibit 5.14 reports $1,276,000 as the cash received from residents and third party payors. Using the information in Exhibits 5.11 to 5.14, show the computation of the $1,276,000 in cash receipts.

5.14. Exhibit 5.14 reports $1,206,000 as the cash paid to employees and suppliers. Using the information in Exhibits 5.11 to 5.14, show the computation of the $1,206,000 in cash payments.

5.15. Exhibit 5.14 reports $40,000 as the cash received from sale of property and equipment. Using the information in Exhibits 5.11 to 5.14, show the computation of the $40,000 in cash receipts.

Exhibit 5.13   Rose Ambulatory Care: Selected Account Information for Year Ended 30 June 19X2

General Funds
Property and Equipment

Debit account			
Balance	$564,000	Sale	$125,000
Purchase	$231,000	Write-off*	$ 30,000
$640,000			

General Funds
Accumulated Depreciation

		Credit account	
Sale	$76,000	Balance	$315,000
Write-off	$30,000	Deprecation	$ 51,000
		$260,000	

General Fund Balance

	Credit account	
	Balance	$535,000
	Income	$137,000
	Transfer†	$ 35,000
	$707,000	

*The write-off of fully depreciated assets did not generate any gain or loss.
†The transfer of $35,000 from restricted funds is for purchase of equipment.

Exhibit 5.14   Rose Ambulatory Care: Statement of Cash Flows of General
Funds for Year Ended 30 June 19X2

Cash flows from operating activities and gains and losses:	
Cash received from residents and third party payors	$1,276,000
Cash received from others	68,000
Cash paid to employees and suppliers	(1,206,000)
Nonoperating receipts	24,000
Interest paid (net of amount capitalized)	(18,000)
Net cash provided by operating activities and gains and losses	*144,000*
Cash flows from investing activities:	
Purchase of property and equipment	(231,000)
Sale of property and equipment	40,000
Reduction of other assets	7,000
Transfer from donor-restricted funds for purchase of equipment	35,000
Net cash used by investing activities	*(149,000)*
Cash flow from financing activities:	
Repayment of long-term debt	(25,000)
Net cash used by financing activities	*(25,000)*
Net decrease in cash and cash equivalents	*(30,000)*
Cash and cash equivalents at beginning of year	100,000
Cash and cash equivalents at end of year	$ *70,000*

5.16. Exhibit 5.14 reports $68,000 as the cash received from others. Using
the information in Exhibits 5.11 to 5.14, show the computation of the
$68,000 of cash receipts.

5.17. Bob Major, employed as a junior with a certified public accounting firm,
had his initial exposure to the health care industry when he was assigned
on an engagement at South Shore Community Hospital. Major was given
a copy of an old statement of cash flows in the unrestricted fund for
South Shore Community Hospital (see Exhibit 5.15) and was asked to
convert this old report to the new AICPA format. Assist Bob in performing this assignment using the indirect method for operating activities.

Exhibit 5.15   South Shore Community Hospital: Statement of Cash Flows in Unrestricted Fund for Year Ended 30 June 19X1

Cash beginning of year	*$2,640,881*
Sources of funds:	
Operations	
Operating income	$1,405,803
Nonoperating gains	2,100,000
Noncash charges against net income: Depreciation	3,668,045
Total provided from operations	*$7,173,848*
Increase in current liabilities	563,972
Property and equipment financed by donor-restricted assets	104,188
Increase in estimated malpractice costs	192,673
Total sources of funds	*$8,034,681*
Use of funds:	
Additions to property and equipment	$3,785,809
Increase in assets whose use is limited	2,066,559
Reduction of long-term debt and capital lease obligation	555,997
Increase in current assets with the exception of cash	316,317
Increase in due from restricted fund	289,171
Total uses of funds	*$7,013,853*
Cash end of year	*$3,661,709*

6

Financial Accounting Issues

Introduction

An analysis of unmet needs for health care services in a geographical or service area may identify requirements that cannot be responded to by expansion of existing facilities without possibly jeopardizing the health care entity's financial future. Responding to some unmet needs may involve substantial risk from adverse outcomes, and malpractice insurance may only provide partial coverage against some extreme outcomes. Furthermore, the more pressing unsatisfied needs may relate to health services for people who cannot afford charges for optimal service; more specifically, the population has major unmet requirements with economic resources for minimal service. Responding to this situation may endanger the future of a health care entity.

Investments in new legal entities, affiliates, and joint ventures are often required by health care entities as part of this response to unmet needs. These separate structures, combined with malpractice insurance, can provide the required financial protection so various new initiatives can be undertaken by the parent organization.

The fundamental nature of the patient services performed by health care entities puts the facilities always at risk for errors, carelessness, misjudgments, and incompetence by one or more employees. Isolated employees may not follow a physician's orders, with adverse consequences to patients. Where economic factors necessitate limited staffing (such as in an extended-care facility or a residential home), there may not be the opportunity for other employees to take corrective actions to negate inappropriate services performed by isolated employees.

The health care entity's mission is to respond to these unmet needs in the service area. Two or more community hospitals may agree

147

to jointly support a new health care facility (such as an ambulatory care clinic) to satisfy these unmet needs without any financial risk beyond their initial investments. If the new facility is a separate 501(c)(3) corporation and there has been no misleading advertisement or other misrepresentation, then the potential malpractice claim against the other hospitals is limited to their monetary investment in the new entity. After this concept of limiting the recovery from the founding hospitals to their initial investments was upheld in court, many new freestanding facilities were established under joint-venture financial arrangements.

Investments in Other Health Care Entities

External financial reporting of a proprietary health care entity investing in another for-profit health care entity follows the same AICPA procedures as other business firms. An investment in another investor-owned corporation of less than 20 percent of the outstanding common stock is reported according to the cost method, and an investment of 20 to 50 percent of outstanding stock is reported following the equity method.[1] Investment of more than 50 percent of the voting stock can no longer be reported by the equity method but is disclosed by a consolidated statement.[2] A corporation with a majority-owned subsidiary constitutes a "reporting entity," which is different from the legal entity and is accounted for by a consolidated statement.[3]

The absence of stock ownership in the 501(c)(3) corporation by another not-for-profit (NFP) health care entity requires a different set of criteria for determining if one NFP health care entity is controlled by another NFP entity. The NFP case is further complicated by the fact that one NFP entity can control another entity without any financial investment in the second entity. Where there is a financial investment, professional practice tends to follow the same "percent of ownership" rules with NFP as are used in investor-owned entities. Financial disclosure has varied because practitioners were waiting for additional guidance from both FASB and GASB, who were studying the concept of a reporting entity and its financial disclosure.[4]

GASB issued in 1991 Statement No. 14, "The Financial Reporting Entity," which resolves many of the reporting issues regarding what constitutes an equity interest in a joint venture. This statement is effective for financial statements for periods beginning after 15 December 1992.[5] FASB issued a discussion memorandum, "Consolidation Policy and Procedures," in 1991 with a comment period ending 15 July 1992.

When there is no financial investment of one NFP health care entity in another NFP entity, the first entity may be able to significantly influence the management or operating policies of the other. Control or significant influence can be achieved in different ways. If there is a common governing board for both health care entities, it obviously has effective control. If the governing board of one entity appoints a majority of the board members for the other entity, it too has effective control. This type of relationship is most common when there is a foundation as a separate legal entity that raises funds for another NFP entity, such as a hospital.[6] GASB's reporting entity statement expresses this situation as follows: "If a primary government appoints a voting majority of an organization's officials and has the ability to impose its will on the organization, the primary government is financially accountable for that organization."[7]

Foundations are a special problem in financial disclosure because new health care NFP entities are created around AICPA guidelines so they may be exempt from consolidation.[8] An early rule pertained to the health care entity benefiting from the foundation's activities; thus new NFP foundations were to raise a minor amount of funds for public services, with a majority of the funds for a single health care entity. Furthermore, these new foundations do not have any contracts or other legal documents that place them under the control of another health care entity. If these two conditions are closely followed, the foundation can be reported as a related organization and included in notes to financial statements without being in a consolidated report.

Three methods are currently practiced in disclosing the relationship between two NFP health care entities where there is no financial investment. The first method is a consolidated statement. The second method is a combined statement.[9] The third method is a related-organization disclosure by note to the financial statements containing a summary of the other entity's assets, liabilities, changes in fund balances, total revenue, total expenses, and amount of transactions between the two entities.[10]

Cost method

Investments in a freestanding clinic organized as a 501(c)(3) corporation are recorded by the cost method if the investor does not exert a significant influence over the operating and financial policies of an investee. Adjustments are made to the original investment under the cost method of accounting upon the receipt of cash; there is no accrual entry for anticipated cash based on the freestanding clinic's

Exhibit 6.1 Illustration of Cost Method

Community Hospital	*Debit*	*Credit*
Investment in affiliated company	$500,000	
Cash		$500,000
No entry under cost method		
Cash	$ 30,000	
Investment income		$ 30,000

Freestanding Clinic	*Debit*	*Credit*
Cash	$3,000,000	
Fund balance		$3,000,000
Cash & other assets	$ 300,000	
Fund balance		$ 300,000
Fund balance	$ 180,000	
Cash		$ 180,000

Exhibit 6.2 Illustration of Equity Method

Community Hospital	*Debit*	*Credit*
Investment in affiliated company	$1,000,000	
Cash		$1,000,000
Investment in affiliated company	$ 100,000	
Investment income		$ 100,000
Cash	$ 60,000	
Investment in affiliated company		$ 60,000

Freestanding Clinic	*Debit*	*Credit*
Cash	$3,000,000	
Fund balance		$3,000,000
Cash & other assets	$ 300,000	
Fund balance		$ 300,000
Fund balance	$ 180,000	
Cash		$ 180,000

earnings. Professional practice follows a 20 percent rule as a guideline for applying the cost method. If the investment in the clinic is less than 20 percent of the fund balance, then the cost method is followed. If the investment is between 20 and 50 percent, the equity method is followed. For investments that are over 50 percent, consolidated financial statements are prepared.

To illustrate the cost method, assume that $3,000,000 is the total fund balance for the new freestanding clinic. Six nongovernment not-for-profit community hospitals invested $500,000 each in the clinic; so each hospital has a one-sixth interest, or 16.7 percent of the fund balance. The clinic earned $300,000 in the first year of operation, but elected to pay $180,000 to the six investors during the early part of the second year. Selected entries for these transactions are shown in Exhibit 6.1. As indicated in the year-end transaction, no adjustment is made to the investment accounts under the cost method until cash is received.

Equity method

Investments where there is a 20 to 50 percent level of control over the operating and financial policies of the clinic are recorded by the equity method. GASB in Statement No. 14 on reporting entity states that if joint venture agreements are silent as to the relative equity of the participants, then the agreements should be modified. An equity interest under GASB only exists when it is both explicit and measurable.[11] The investor has significant influence over the clinic, and therefore an accrual procedure must be followed so adjustments are made in the investment accounts as soon as income is earned by the clinic.

Assume the same clinic with a $3,000,000 fund balance is established by three nongovernment not-for-profit community hospitals with equal investments. The clinic earns $300,000 in the first year and pays $180,000 to the three hospitals early in the second year. Selected entries for these transactions are shown in Exhibit 6.2. The equity method recognizes the $100,000 increase in the investment accounts as soon as it is earned by the freestanding clinic. The accrual entry for the income increases the investment in an affiliated company account as if it were a receivable. The investment account is then reduced with the cash receipt of $60,000.

There are many joint ventures among community hospitals for supporting freestanding clinics where no given hospital has more than a 50 percent investment. Thus, the equity method is widely used in external financial statements for health care entities.

Consolidated financial statements

Expansion of health care services by establishing a separate 501(c)(3) corporation for the new set of activities is a common approach in the industry. A major medical center may want to open a clinic in an underserved and financially depressed area where the population cannot fully afford all the health care services and where even a simple medical condition can become very complex because of contributing factors. The new clinic will incur an annual loss, which can be projected by the medical center and reflected in the medical center's consolidated financial statements. But by organizing the clinic as a separate corporation without any misrepresentations or misleading advertisement, the medical center's financial exposure is limited to the initial investment in the 501(c)(3) corporation plus any subsequent payments made to the clinic.

Assume the medical center (parent) invested $2,000,000 in creating the clinic, and the clinic incurs an annual loss of $300,000, which includes a depreciation charge of $75,000. A consolidated worksheet prepared after this loss is illustrated by Exhibit 6.3, showing the reduction in the medical center's fund balance.

The medical center has assets of $47 million, including the $2 million investment in the clinic. The clinic has assets of $2.1 million because liabilities of $400,000 have not been paid. The reporting entity for the medical center and consolidated subsidiaries is different from

Exhibit 6.3   Medical Center and Subsidiary Consolidation Worksheet 1

	Medical Center	Clinic	Intercompany Eliminations	Consolidated Statements
Investment in clinic	$ 2,000,000	—	($2,000,000)	—
Cash plus other assets	45,000,000	$2,100,000	—	$47,100,000
Liabilities	16,000,000	400,000	—	16,400,000
Fund balance—center	31,000,000	—	(300,000)	30,700,000
Fund balance—clinic	—	1,700,000	(1,700,000)	—

the summation of these two accounting entities. The fund balance in the reporting entity consists of the medical center's balance before consolidation, adjusted by the impact of eliminating intercompany transactions.

The worksheet prepared in support of the consolidated financial statements has the following entry for eliminating the medical center's investment, the clinic's fund balance, and the clinic's loss from operations:

	Debit	Credit
Clinic's fund balance	$1,700,000	
Medical center's fund balance	300,000	
Medical center's investment in clinic		$2,000,000

The medical center's consolidated statement of revenue and expenses will report a $300,000 loss on operation of the clinic, and the total assets on the consolidated statements are $47.1 million.

Assume the medical center transfers $225,000 to the clinic after the end of each fiscal year to maintain the clinic's working capital. The commitment of $225,000 to the clinic after the end of the fiscal year might be disclosed as a note to the financial statements on the consolidated reports, especially if the transaction occurs before the consolidated financial statements are issued. But, even if the cash has been transferred, there are legal reasons not to disclose the facts in the notes; otherwise, there is the possibility of future liability to the medical center.

The reporting entity is not the same as the legal entity in consolidated financial statements. In the above example, there are two legal entities, both of which are 501(c)(3) corporations. The separate corporation for the clinic was established to limit the liability of the medical center in providing services to an underserved and financially depressed area. Preparing consolidated financial statements for the reporting entity does not modify the situation. These consolidated financial statements are only for external reporting requirements. The example given included a parent and one subsidiary. It is not unusual for a community hospital or medical center to have multiple subsidiaries.

Consolidated financial statements are required when the health care entity's financial interest is above 50 percent. A clinic established as a joint venture by two hospitals can have both entities reporting by the equity method if it is exactly a 50 percent interest, or by consolidated statements and the equity method if it is a 60:40 relation. If the dominant hospital has more than an 80 percent interest, the other hospital will use the cost method.

If one health care entity is not the sole investor in a subsidiary, then the rights of the other investors must be reported in the con-solidated financial statements as *minority interests.* A medical center's consolidated financial statements may have the equity account title "minority interest in subsidiaries" to show the aggregate interest of all other legal entities in the consolidated assets of the reporting entity.

Assume the medical center (parent) invested $1,600,000 for an 80 percent interest in a new clinic, and the clinic incurs an annual loss of $300,000, which includes a depreciation charge of $75,000. A consolidated worksheet prepared after this loss is illustrated by Exhibit 6.4, showing the reduction in the medical center's fund balance and the recognition of minority interests for 20 percent, or $340,000 (20 percent of the clinic's fund balance). The other intercompany elimi-nation items are similar to the previous entry, as follows:

	Debit	Credit
Clinic's fund balance	$1,700,000	
Medical center's fund balance	240,000	
Medical center's investment in clinic		$1,600,000
Minority interest		340,000

The medical center and the other investor transfer $225,000 to the clinic after the end of each fiscal year to maintain the clinic's

Exhibit 6.4   Medical Center and Subsidiary Consolidation Worksheet 2

	Medical Center	Clinic	Intercompany Eliminations	Consolidated Statements
Investment in clinic	$ 1,600,000	—	($1,600,000)	—
Cash plus other assets	45,400,000	$2,100,000	—	$47,500,000
Liabilities	16,000,000	400,000	—	16,400,000
Minority interest	—	—	340,000	340,000
Fund balance— center	31,000,000	—	(240,000)	30,760,000
Fund balance—clinic	—	1,700,000	(1,700,000)	—

working capital; the medical center transfers $180,000 for its part, and the minority interest transfer $45,000. There is no disclosure of this general understanding in Exhibit 6.4; otherwise, external creditors for the clinic may be able to obtain payment from the medical center and minority interest in the future if the clinic is unable to make payment to them.

If a consolidated balance sheet were to be prepared after this transfer of $225,000, there would be clinic assets of $2,325,000 and a fund balance of $1,925,000 ($1,700,000 + $225,000), as depicted in Exhibit 6.5. The medical center's investment increases by the $180,000 transferred to the clinic, and the minority interest increases by the additional investment to $385,000. Note the total assets of the consolidated entity increased by $45,000, to $47,545,000, as a result of these minority investments.

Exhibit 6.5 Medical Center and Subsidiary Consolidation Worksheet 3

	Medical Center	Clinic	Intercompany Eliminations	Consolidated Statements
Investment in clinic	$ 1,780,000	—	($1,780,000)	—
Cash plus other assets	45,220,000	$2,325,000	—	$47,545,000
Liabilities	16,000,000	400,000	—	16,400,000
Minority interest	—	—	385,000	385,000
Fund balance—center	31,000,000	—	(240,000)	30,760,000
Fund balance—clinic	—	1,925,000	(1,925,000)	—

Advances and other support

The impact of professional and medical malpractice liabilities can be seen in legal documents in which a principal health care entity guarantees specific actions for a subsidiary without assuming any overall responsibility. The principal may agree to provide the monthly cash difference between a given amount and the actual collections on patient accounts. For example, if the guarantee was $50,000, and $35,000 was collected, the principal would pay $15,000 to the subsidiary. The $15,000 payment may or may not be considered a loan; it depends on the legal document. It may be an expense the principal is willing to incur on behalf of the continued activities by the subsidiary.

The minimum guarantee amount may have a front-end requirement for the principal health care entity to provide the initial working capital for the new entity. In other cases there are annual provisions for working capital support over a specified period. This type of advance payment is classified as an "other asset" on the financial statements of the principal health care entity because the entity does not expect to collect the advance receivable within the near future. Notes to the financial statements for major health care entities often include some conditions and terms that seem unusual to readers not familiar with the industry.

Related Organizations and Related-Party Transactions

Foundations, auxiliaries, guilds, and similar organizations often exist as entities for the purpose of assisting one or more health care entities. The not-for-profit health care entity does not have any stock or investment in the foundation, auxiliary, guild, or related organization, but does exercise control over the entity's activities, management, and policies. The health care foundation is, of course, the prime example of a related organization.

The role of a separate legal structure is important in distinguishing between being a related organization versus being part of the existing health care entity. Fund development activities are often conducted for a donor-restricted specific-purpose effort where there is not a separate legal entity, such as a 501(c)(3) organization for a foundation. These fund development activities are part of the regular health care entity's donor-restricted operations and are reported in the statements of changes in fund balances. Information on a related organization is reported either by consolidated financial statements or by notes to the financial statements of the benefiting health care entity.

This separate legal structure is a tax-exempt corporation; thus, there is no stock ownership by the principal health care entity that may benefit from the tax-exempt corporation's activities. If the tax-exempt corporation is related to the principal health care entity, there must be a contract or legal documents providing the authority for the principal health care entity to direct the separate organization's activities, management, and policies. Under the AICPA guidelines for related organizations, the principal health care entity must have the above documents of authority plus receive one of the following three benefits from the tax-exempt corporation:

1. The organization has solicited funds in the name of the health care entity and with the expressed or implied approval of the health care entity, and substantially all the funds solicited by the organization were intended by the contributor, or were otherwise required, to be transferred to the health care entity or used at its discretion or direction.

2. The health care entity has transferred some of its resources to the organization, and substantially all of the organization's resources are held for the benefit of the health care entity.

3. The health care entity has assigned certain of its functions (such as the operation of a dormitory) to the organization, which is operating primarily for the benefit of the health care entity.[12]

If one of the above three conditions exist, then the tax-exempt corporation is a related organization to the health care entity.

The issue of required disclosure for related organizations is currently being studied by the AICPA. If the tax-exempt corporation is not included in the consolidated financial statement of the principal health care entity, detailed data on the tax-exempt corporation must be included in notes to the financial statements. The minimum disclosure includes the assets, liabilities, fund balance, and transactions between the tax-exempt organization and the health care entity. The related organization's ending balance may be $250,000 in cash and $250,000 in the fund balance because there are no liabilities, even if, during the period, $5 million was raised and transferred to the health care entity. The specifics of activities by related organizations are important for proper interpretation of the financial statements of the benefiting health care entity.

A related organization is usually a foundation or other tax-exempt corporation; a related party may be a proprietary corporation or a not-for-profit corporation. If one health care entity has at least a 20 percent investment in another health care entity, the second entity is a related party.[13] Thus, all investments reported by the equity method or by consolidated statements are related parties, and the notes to financial statements must include information on this relationship and the transactions between these entities.

The concept of a related party is applicable to a separate corporation where there is no financial investment but where one entity exercises significant influence over the management or operating activities of a separate organization. One organization may be economically dependent on another organization, but that does not constitute a related party unless the "significant influence" condition is also present. A certified financial statement will include a disclosure on an entity that is economically dependent on another, but the reason for this information is "fair presentation" and not the requirements for a related party. Some hospital financial statements include, as related-party disclosure, information on proprietary clinical laboratories, proprietary diagnostic treatment centers, and physician-group facilities.[14]

Many related-party disclosures in financial statements of health care entities are for organizations where there is also a financial investment and other agreements between the two entities. The concept of control is exercised through these agreements and other legal documents.

Marketable Equity Securities

The AICPA reporting procedures for short-term *equity* securities and short-term *debt* securities are inconsistent. The lower-of-cost-or-market method is applied to short-term equity securities, but it is not used with short-term debt securities. Debt instruments are reported at amortized cost, and the investment income from the debt securities is adjusted by the amortized cost. Financial accounting reporting procedures for short-term debt securities in health care entities are the same as those followed in other industries, but there are special issues in health care with the financial reporting of marketable equity securities in not-for-profit entities.

Investment pools and portfolios

Not-for-profit health care entities may combine assets from various funds into a single investment pool, or some assets may be combined while other assets are maintained as separate investments. Financial accounting procedures do not limit the most effective management of investments for a health care entity, but these investment pools must be separated into portfolios before balance sheets can be prepared, and the market-value method is used in partitioning the pool.

At the time the investment pool is established, each participating fund is assigned a number of *units* based on the current market value of investments placed in the pool by each fund. This same approach is used in measuring units added to or withdrawn from the pool during the year. Income from investments and gains or losses of the pool are allocated to the participating funds in accordance with each fund's portion of the total units.

Assume, for example, that on 1 January 19X2 an investment pool of $1 million is established by a $500,000 transfer from noncurrent assets in the general funds, a $300,000 transfer from specific-purpose donor-restricted funds, and a $200,000 transfer from plant replacement and expansion funds. Values of 5, 3, and 2 units are assigned, respectively, to the three funds. On 1 July 19X2 the market price of the investment pool was identical to the 1 January 19X2 position, and a $400,000 addition to the pool is made from the specific-purpose funds. A value of 4 units is assigned for this investment, but these 4 units do not participate in earnings for the first half of the year.

The investment pool earned $180,000 for the year—$90,000 in the first half of the year and $90,000 in the second half. These earnings are assigned as follows:

General funds	5 units	$ 75,000
Specific purpose	3 units initial	45,000
Specific purpose	4 units ($\frac{1}{2}$ year), or 2 units	30,000
Plant replacement	2 units	30,000
		$180,000

The market value of the investment pool was $1,680,000 at the end of the year, and it is assigned to the three funds based on units as follows:

General fund	5 units	$ 600,000
Specific purpose	7 units	840,000
Plant replacement	2 units	240,000
	14 units	$1,680,000

Commercial banks and financial institutions that handle investment pools for health care entities may prepare special monthly reports that provide information on units for investments, earnings, additions, and withdrawals. Some special reports include monthly comparisons of cost and market value of securities. Exhibit 6.6 is an annual summary from a commercial bank of an investment pool with three portfolios. The bank was given the labels for the three portfolios, which permitted the identification by fund of the quarterly distribution of $37,500 in investment income on 31 March 19X2. Observe that this annual report shows the change from $50,000 per unit on 1 January 19X2, to $62,500 per unit on 1 July 19X2, when there was an additional investment, and to $55,000 per unit on 31 December 19X2, in support of external financial statements.

Marketable equity securities in not-for-profit health care entities must be separated into groups or portfolios; the investment portfolio of current assets in the general funds must be separate from the investment portfolio of noncurrent assets in the general funds. Donor-restricted securities must be separate from those in the general funds; however, the current assets versus noncurrent assets partitioning is not required in donor-restricted funds, as is depicted by the single portfolio for specific-purpose donor-restricted funds in Exhibit 6.6. Marketable equity securities in different types of specific-purpose donor-restricted funds can be aggregated into a single portfolio, but marketable equity securities in specific-purpose funds cannot be combined with those in endowment funds.

Lower-of-cost-or-market method

A valuation account is used to record the excess of aggregate cost of a portfolio over the market value of that portfolio. The valuation account has a zero balance if market value is equal to or greater than aggregate cost. The valuation account is a contra asset, called "allowance to reduce marketable security investments." No entries in the valuation account are made during the fiscal period. When the valuation account is initially established, there must be an unrealized loss on marketable security investments. In subsequent years the valuation account may increase or decrease depending on market price, with the transaction showing an unrealized loss or an unrealized gain on marketable security investments.

Exhibit 6.6 presents the data on three portfolios, established on 1 January 19X2, and with an additional investment on 1 July 19X2. The 31 December 19X2 portfolio balance for the current assets in general funds is $350,000 for cost and $330,000 for market value, so the following valuation adjustment is required:

	Debit	Credit
Unrealized loss on marketable security investment portfolio	$20,000	
Allowance to reduce marketable security investment		$20,000
This contra asset reduces the portfolio by $20,000 from $350,000 to $330,000.		

Exhibit 6.6   Not-for-Profit Health Care Entity Investment Pool with Three Portfolios ($50,000 unit value)

1 January 19X2 initial investment pool		$1,000,000
(Unit is valued at $50,000 on 1 January 19X2)		
Current assets in general funds	2 units	100,000
Noncurrent assets in general funds	8 units	400,000
Specific-purpose donor-restricted funds	10 units	500,000
31 March 19X2 investment income		$37,500
Current assets in general funds	2 units	3,750
Noncurrent assets in general funds	8 units	15,000
Specific-purpose donor-restricted funds	10 units	18,750
30 June 19X2 Investment Income		$38,000
Current assets in general funds	2 units	3,800
Noncurrent assets in general funds	8 units	15,200
Specific-purpose donor-restricted funds	10 units	19,000
1 July 19X2 investment pool (20 units) market value		$1,250,000
(Unit is valued at $62,500 on 1 July 19X2)		
Additional investment:		
Current assets in general funds	4 units	250,000
Net investment pool balance (24 units)		$1,500,000
30 September 19X2 investment income		$46,800
Current assets in general funds	6 units	11,700
Noncurrent assets in general funds	8 units	15,600
Specific-purpose donor-restricted funds	10 units	19,500
31 December 19X2 investment income		$47,040
Current assets in general funds	6 units	11,760
Noncurrent assets in general funds	8 units	15,680
Specific-purpose donor-restricted funds	10 units	19,600
31 December 19X2 investment pool (24 units) market value		$1,320,000
(Unit is valued at $55,000 on 31 December 19X2)		
Current assets in general funds	6 units	330,000
Noncurrent assets in general funds	8 units	440,000
Specific-purpose donor-restricted funds	10 units	550,000
31 December 19X2 assigned cost of three portfolios		$1,250,000
Current assets in general funds	6 units	350,000*
Noncurrent assets in general funds	8 units	400,000
Specific-purpose donor-restricted funds	10 units	500,000

*$100,000 + $250,000 = $350,000.

After this entry is recorded, the balance sheet, as of 31 December 19X2, shows $330,000 for the current assets portfolio, and the unrealized loss of $20,000 for the current assets is reported in the nonoperating revenue section of statements of revenue and expenses of general funds.

The 31 December 19X2 portfolio balance for the noncurrent assets in general funds is $400,000 for cost and $440,000 for market value, so no valuation adjustment is required under lower-of-cost-or-market method. The 31 December 19X2 portfolio balance for the specific-purpose donor-restricted funds is $500,000 for cost and $550,000 for market value, so no valuation adjustment is required.

Assume, for example, a new portfolio of $200,000 was established as current assets in the general funds of a nongovernment not-for-profit community hospital; $18,000 of investment income was received by 31 December 19X2; and the market value of the portfolio was $195,000 on 31 December 19X2. These transactions are as follows:

	Debit	Credit
Marketable equity security investments	$200,000	
Cash		$200,000
To establish the new portfolio, which is a current asset.		
Cash	$ 18,000	
Investment income		$ 18,000
Nonoperating revenues for the hospital.		
Unrealized loss on marketable security investment portfolio	$ 5,000	
Allowance to reduce marketable security investment		$ 5,000
This contra asset reduces the portfolio by $5,000, from $200,000 to $195,000.		

The term *unrealized* indicates there is not a final transaction with external parties that satisfies the revenue recognition concept in financial accounting. Revenue is realized when there is an arm's length transaction with an external party (such as the passage of legal title to goods).

To further illustrate the application of lower-of-cost-or-market to marketable equity securities, assume a nongovernment not-for-profit community hospital has four portfolios: current asset portfolio in general funds, noncurrent asset portfolio in general funds, specific-purpose donor-restricted funds portfolio, and endowment donor-restricted funds portfolio. These four portfolios have been in existence for a few years, and the contra asset or valuation accounts had the following respective balances on 31 December 19X1: $20,000, $35,000, $20,000, and $30,000. There have been purchases and sales of investments in each portfolio during 19X2, and the current status of these four portfolios immediately before making the 31 December 19X2 adjustment to the valuation accounts is shown in Table 6.1. The current assets portfolio in the general funds currently has a net balance of $130,000 ($150,000 cost less $20,000 valuation), which should be increased by $15,000 to market value of $145,000. The increase cannot be made to the asset account; adjustments can only be made to the valuation account, as represented by the following transaction:

	Debit	Credit
Allowance to reduce marketable security investment	$15,000	
Unrealized gain on marketable security investment portfolio		$15,000
To modify the valuation account to $5,000 difference between cost of $150,000 and market value of $145,000.		

Table 6.1 Illustration of the Application of Lower-Cost-or-Market Method to Marketable Equity Securities

	General Fund		Donor-Restricted	
	Current Assets Portfolio	Noncurrent Assets Portfolio	Specific-Purpose Funds Portfolio	Endowment Funds Portfolio
Balance 31 December 19X2 valuation allowance	$ 20,000	$ 35,000	$ 20,000	$ 30,000
Cost of equity securities	$150,000	$290,000	$300,000	$240,000
Market value of securities	$145,000	$280,000	$305,000	$200,000

The unrealized gain on marketable security investment portfolio of $15,000 is reported in the nonoperating revenue section of statements of revenue and expenses for the hospital. This reporting location for the unrealized gain or loss on short-term investment portfolio is only applicable to current assets in the general funds. Unrealized gain or loss for all other portfolios is reported on the statements of changes in fund balances.

The noncurrent assets portfolio in the general funds currently has a net balance of $255,000 ($290,000 cost less $35,000 valuation), which should be increased by $25,000 to market value of $280,000. An adjusting entry is made to the valuation, or contra asset, account as follows:

	Debit	Credit
Allowance to reduce marketable security investment	$25,000	
Unrealized gain on marketable security investment portfolio		$25,000
To modify the valuation account to $10,000 difference between cost of $290,000 and market value $280,000.		

The unrealized gain on marketable security investment portfolio of $25,000 is reported on the statement of changes in fund balances because it captures the change in noncurrent assets in general funds.

The specific-purpose donor-restricted funds portfolio shows cost of $300,000 and market value of $305,000. The financial statement reports the lower-of-cost-or-market ($300,000), and the existing valuation account is set equal to zero, as follows:

	Debit	Credit
Allowance to reduce marketable security investment	$20,000	
Specific-purpose fund balance		$20,000

The unrealized gain on marketable security investment portfolio is recorded directly in the specific-purpose fund account; however, it is reported on the statements of changes in fund balances.

Assume that investment income on the endowment funds is restricted. The endowment portfolio has a net balance of $210,000 ($240,000 cost less $30,000 valuation), which must be reduced by $10,000 to market value of $200,000 as follows:

	Debit	Credit
Endowment fund	$10,000	
Allowance to reduce marketable security investment		$10,000

The unrealized loss on marketable security investment portfolio for endowment funds is recorded directly in the endowment fund balance account, and it is reported on the statements of changes in fund balances.

Where consolidated financial statements are to be prepared, the portfolio for current assets in general funds of the parent is combined with the portfolios for current assets in general funds of the various subsidiaries, and these aggregated investments are treated as a single portfolio for financial reports. The portfolios for noncurrent assets in general funds of the parent and the subsidiaries are combined and treated as a single portfolio for consolidated financial statements. Similar donor-restricted fund portfolios of entities included in the consolidated financial statements are also treated as a single portfolio.

Other issues

Donations may have written conditions that limit investment options and require separate accounting for principal and income transactions. Marketable equity securities in current assets in general funds must be viewed as distinct from those in noncurrent assets in general funds. If there is any change in a marketable security's classification between current and noncurrent assets in general funds, the transfer is handled as if it were an outside transaction. The lower-of-cost-or-market becomes the new assigned cost of the transferred equity security, and the difference is accounted for as if it were a *realized* loss.

Advance Fees for Future Services

Financial reporting and disclosure requirements for current liabilities and long-term obligations of health care entities are the same as those for corporate enterprise and other business organizations. There are special disclosure requirements for continuing-care retirement community (CCRC) entities regarding the method of accounting for advance fees, the method of calculating the obligation to provide future services, and the refund policy for refundable fees. In addition to the notes to financial statements, refundable fees to CCRC residents or their estate on death are a liability based on the contractual and statutory requirements.[15] The AICPA is studying the issue of reporting refundable fees under a moral obligation as a liability. Nonrefundable fees to CCRC residents are accounted for as deferred revenues and amortized to income on a straight-line basis over the term of the obligation.

Assume that the CCRC facility receives $10,500,000 in nonrefundable fees, increasing the balance in deferred revenues to $15,000,000. The amortization for the current year is $4,900,000 in fees. These two transactions are as follows:

	Debit	*Credit*
Cash	$10,500,000	
Deferred revenue from advanced fees		$10,500,000
Deferred revenue from advanced fees	$ 4,900,000	
Resident service revenue		$ 4,900,000

On 1 January 19X2, the deferred revenue from advanced fees had a balance of $4,500,000, and the estimated obligation to provide future service was $4,560,000. Thus, an estimated liability of $60,000 was recognized in the balance sheet on 31 December 19X1. On 31 December 19X2, the deferred revenue from advanced fees has a balance of $10,100,000 ($4,500,000 + $10,500,000 − $4,900,000 = $10,100,000), and the estimated obligation to provide future service was $10,240,000. The estimated liability must be increased from $60,000 to $140,000 as follows:

	Debit	*Credit*
Loss on obligation to provide future services	$80,000	
Estimated obligation to provide future services		$80,000

The $80,000 loss on obligation to provide future services appears on the CCRC's statement of revenue and expenses after operating expenses and before the computation of "income (loss) from operations." The balance sheet for 31 December 19X2 contains two measures of these future services:

Estimated obligation to provide future services, in excess of amounts received or to be received	$ 140,000
Deferred revenue from advanced fees	$10,100,000

Residents in a CCRC facility may be charged in various ways for service. Some contracts specify an advance fee with no additional bills—the resident receives services free for his or her life. Other contracts may be similar, but the duration is for a fixed time period. Terms and conditions for terminating a CCRC contract may relate to the resident's permanent requirement for life support facilities that are only available as a hospital inpatient. Other CCRC facility contracts are for an advance fee with periodic fees, and these periodic fees may be fixed or may be subject to increases in operating costs, inflation adjustments, or other economic factors. There are contracts where there is no advance fee, but the resident pays monthly, quarterly, or semiannually for the use of all services and facilities in the CCRC.

Financial analysis of a CCRC for some purposes may require more information on obligations to provide future services, refundable fees, and advance fees than is readily available in the financial statements, including the notes to statements. The life expectancy of current residents is the critical measure in projecting future services, not the national average. Careful study of various contracts that may apply to current residents, rather than only reviewing the latest policy, is important. Some exceptional cases may have a significant impact on the financial future of the CCRC.

There are different types of risk contracts in the arrangements between health care entities, such as hospitals, physicians, health maintenance organizations, clinics, and therapy facilities, to provide services to individuals enrolled in a health care plan. The central feature of the risk contract is that payment is determined on a capitated basis, and the various providers covered by the contract are at risk for health care costs in excess of the capitation revenue. Information on the contingent liability related to risk contracts are included in notes to the financial statements.

Other Reporting Issues

Pension plans and postretirement health care coverage are two financial reporting issues that affect many health care entities.[16] If the health care entity has a defined-contribution pension plan, there is no obligation to employees beyond the specified amounts of annual contributions to the pension fund. If the health care entity has a defined-benefit pension plan, there may be an obligation that must be recognized in the financial statements.

There are two components of a defined-benefit pension plan—service cost and prior service cost. The actuarial present value of benefits attributed by the pension benefit formula to employee service during that period represents service cost. Pension expense and a pension liability are recorded for this actuarial amount of benefits based on current services. The prior service cost may result from a plan amendment or from the initiation of a pension plan. Prior service cost is the actuarial present value of retroactive benefits of current employees. The complete liability for retroactive benefits does not have to be recognized in the initial year of reporting under FASB Statement No. 87. This reporting arrangement may result in an understatement of the pension liability on the balance sheet.

Commitments by health care entities to employees on postretirement benefits other than pensions (primarily health care coverage) must be disclosed in the financial statements. FASB Statement No. 106, "Employers' Accounting for Postretirement Benefits Other Than Pensions," is implemented for public enterprises for fiscal years beginning after 15 December 1992 and for nonpublic enterprises for fiscal years beginning after 15 December 1994.[17] The current pay-as-you-go (cash) method for recognizing postretirement benefits is replaced by actuarial present value of benefits attributed by the plan to current employees and retired employees. This accrual method results in a substantial transition obligation that can be recognized in a given year or over a number of years.

Summary

Medical centers and community hospitals are very concerned over the malpractice risk from a clinic, nursing home, CCRC, ambulatory surgical center, rehabilitation facility, or other outpatient clinic. A separate 501(c)(3) corporate structure permits the establishment of a needed service while limiting the risk of the parent to the initial investment plus any subsequent financial support. Many freestanding facilities are wholly owned subsidiaries and included in the consolidated financial statements of the parent. Other freestanding facilities are joint ventures by two or more health care entities. These investments may be handled by the cost method or the equity method, depending on the percent of interest. If the investment is less than 20 percent, the cost method is used; no adjustment is made to the investment in the affiliated company account until cash is received. When the investment is between

20 and 50 percent, the equity method is followed, which immediately records any change in the status of the affiliated company. The equity method is the same as accrual accounting, in contrast with the cash method of accounting. An investment above a 50 percent interest results in a parent-subsidiary relationship that must be reported with a consolidated financial statement.

Medical centers and large community hospitals are complex organizational structures. It is not uncommon to have a consolidated financial statement with three or four subsidiaries and with investments in the consolidated statements using both the cost method and the equity method for five or six affiliated companies. Notes to the consolidated financial statements contain disclosures on the related-party activities of all these subsidiaries and affiliated companies. One indication of this complexity is that the notes may require more written space than that taken by all formal statements.

The consolidated financial statement is for the reporting entity, which may not be identical with any legal entity. The reporting entity is a summation of information from subsidiary and parent corporations. If the subsidiaries are wholly owned, the reporting entity is a summation of legal entities after eliminating investments and subsidiary fund balances. The adjusted parent's fund balance becomes the net equity for the reporting entity. The only difference for partially owned subsidiaries is that the residual balance of outsiders is included in the net equity for the reporting entity as minority interests.

Joint ventures with members of the medical staff and other professionals frequently result in cash advances, collection guarantees on patient billings, and loans. These payments become account receivable under other assets of general funds. There are usually disclosures in notes of financial statements explaining the joint venture.

A situation where a separate organization performs fund-raising activities for another health care entity and where the benefiting entity has the authority to control the activities, management, and policies of the separate organization is referred to as a *related organization*. A tax-exempt foundation is the usual organizational structure of a related organization. A related party may be a proprietary corporation or a not-for-profit entity. All investments in affiliated companies that are reported by the equity method are related parties; all subsidiaries are related parties to the parent. There is a difference between economic dependency and a related party. Fair financial presentation may require disclosure of economic dependency, even though there is no control over the other party. A related party is a situation where the parent exercises control over activities, policies, or management of another entity.

The investment portfolio of current assets of general funds must be separate from the investment portfolio of noncurrent assets of general funds. The investment portfolio of donor-restricted specific-purpose funds must be separate from general funds and from endowment funds. It is not necessary to have separate portfolios for current versus noncurrent assets within donor-restricted funds. The lower-of-cost-or-market method is applied with each portfolio. Various portfolios can be combined into an investment pool where a unit method is followed in tracking each portfolio based on market value at the time of a transaction (both investments or withdrawals).

The financial reporting of investment income may vary by type of health care entity as well as by type of fund within a not-for-profit entity. Investment income of HMOs and CCRCs is considered to be directly related to the ongoing principal operations, and the AICPA permits the entity to classify investment income as operating income on the statement of revenue and expenses of general funds. Investment income for other types of health care entities is considered to be nonoperating revenue. Investment income for an endowment fund can be unrestricted or restricted. If it is unrestricted, it is reported as nonoperating revenue on the statement of revenue and expenses of general funds. If it is restricted, it is shown as an addition to the endowment fund on the statements of changes in fund balances.

With hospitals and nursing homes, the unrealized gains or losses from investment portfolios of current assets of general funds are reported in the nonoperating revenue section of the statement of revenue and expenses. The statement of changes in fund balances shows the unrealized gains or losses for noncurrent assets of general funds for hospitals and nursing homes. Unrealized gains and losses for donor-restricted specific-purpose funds and for plant replacement and expansion funds are reported on the statement of changes in fund balances.

Appendix: Multientity Health Care Structures

Many not-for-profit hospitals and other health care entities have been restructured over the past decade for a variety of purposes, resulting in the requirement for consolidated financial statements and a close monitoring of income-tax regulations. Protection from malpractice claims was previously discussed as one of the reasons for creating freestanding health care entities to provide for unmet needs in an underserved area or adding new health services without risking the assets of the principal entity. Retention of existing medical staff and recruitment of physicians in some specialties may be facilitated through multientity structures; however, the Tax Reform Act of 1986, the Revenue Act of 1987, and several general counsel memorandums (GCM) by the Internal Revenue Service (IRS) have imposed more structure on terms, conditions, and arrangements that are acceptable to the IRS without violating the tax-exempt status of the parent entity.

There are different arrangements for multientity health care structures, but they tend to have a board of trustees; an exempt holding company; a series of hospitals, nursing homes, and retirement homes that are 501(c)(3) corporations; and a real estate or professional-building 501(c)(2) corporation. Figure 6.1 is a simple form of multientity health care structure in which there are no taxable entities.

Figure 6.1   Multientity Health Care Structure with No Taxable Entities

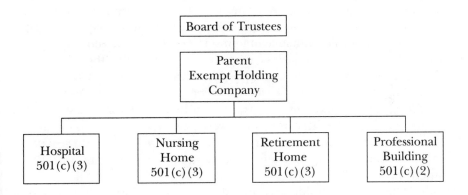

The current organizational and legal structures are influenced by income-tax and regulatory efforts in the 1970s for promoting cooperative activities among not-for-profit hospitals as a cost-containment measure. Cooperative hospital service organizations that perform data processing, purchasing, or clinical services for two or more tax-exempt hospitals can obtain an exempt charitable status under IRS regulations. If one of the hospitals performed these same services (such as data processing) for the other not-for-profit hospitals, and if there are more than 100 inpatients in the hospital that is receiving services, then the

IRS rules call that unrelated business income.[18] There are other IRS rules that have influenced these organizational and legal structures, such as classifying laundry services as a commercial activity and subject to unrelated business income tax if performed for another health care entity.

The *parent exempt holding company* (see Figure 6.1) has often been created as a nonprofit corporation organized for charitable, training, and educational purposes as well as other health care–related activities. A public charity status of the parent company in a multientity health care structure is desirable, but the IRS code does not use the term "public charity status."[19] Instead, the term "private foundation" includes all 501(c)(3) organizations other than those in four distinct categories.[20] The parent company can achieve a public charity status through these exceptions in the IRS code.

The most onerous public charity status requirement for health care entities is that they must receive more than one-third of their annual support from members and the public and not more than one-third from investment income and unrelated business income. A general guide is to demonstrate that at least 10 percent of the parent's support over a four-year period has come from general public contributions. In addition to these major fund-raising requirements, there are limitations on management services that the parent company can render to its subsidiaries. Another category under the IRS rules for a public charity status is supporting organizations. The IRS GCM of 28 May 1986 requires a certain type of structure, where a majority of the parent's board must serve on the boards of each tax-exempt subsidiary. Many health care entities were not organized in this manner when the 1986 IRS rules were received, and these entities are seeking more guidance on options and arrangements for complying with the intent of the IRS.[21]

If the parent holding company is a public charity, it can have taxable or for-profit subsidiaries, such as a clinical laboratory, a nuclear magnetic resonance imaging company, and a management services company. A taxable subsidiary holding company is often established to facilitate the accounting process so all for-profit companies are under this taxable subsidiary. Figure 6.2 illustrates a multientity health care structure with taxable companies.

The status of a private foundation is an alternative to the public charity status for a holding company. If the parent holding company is a private foundation, it cannot have a wholly owned for-profit subsidiary; its investment in any for-profit corporation cannot be more

Figure 6.2   Multientity Health Care Structure with Taxable Entities

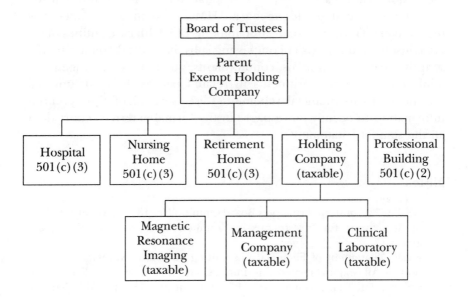

than 20 percent. The multientity health care structure in Figure 6.1 might be for a holding company with a private foundation status. There are also excise taxes on income for the private foundation, with major penalties for failure to give a certain amount to charity. Some not-for-profit entities directed by a religious body may not have any problems with most of the provisions of being a private foundation, although the fund-raising or board membership requirements of the public charity may not be compatible with the religious body's other plans.

There are many legal issues not cited in the above remarks on multientity health care structures. Each tax-exempt organization is now required to annually file with the IRS Form 990 for maintaining tax-exempt status. There are unrelated business income issues that exist whether the parent holding company is a public charity or a private foundation. In many competitive health care environments, joint ventures with physicians require careful legal assistance to maintain the principal entity's tax-exempt status.

The typical financial statement for a major health care entity may include information on four or five subsidiaries, two or three related parties, and a related organization—a foundation. Even if the number of subsidiaries is increased to eight or ten, the frequency of financial statements under these conditions is not exceptional. If the major health care entity is a hospital, then it is not unusual for one of the related parties to be an HMO, and in some states it is highly likely. Thus, the financial statements of health care entities often are consolidated reports encompassing subsidiaries and containing descriptive materials on loans, commitments, guarantees, contingencies, joint ventures, and investments in related parties. It is not unusual for the notes to financial statements disclosing all of this required information to occupy more pages in the formal external report than all the standard statements.

Notes

1. AICPA, "Accounting Principles Board Opinion No. 18: The Equity Method of Accounting for Investments in Common Stock, March 1971," paragraph 17.
2. FASB, "Statement of Financial Accounting Standards No. 94: Consolidation of All Majority-owned Subsidiaries, an amendment of ARB No. 51, which related amendments of APB Opinion No. 18, and ARB No. 43, Chapter 12, October 1987," paragraph 15.
3. AICPA, "Accounting Research Bulletin No. 51: Consolidated Financial Statements, August 1959," paragraph 1.
4. AICPA, *Audit and Accounting Guide*, 127.
5. GASB, "Statement No. 14 of the Governmental Accounting Standards Board—The Financial Reporting Entity," paragraph 82.
6. AICPA, *Audit and Accounting Guide*, 134–35.
7. GASB, "The Financial Reporting Entity," paragraph 25.
8. For example, AICPA, "Statement of Position 81-2, Reporting Practices Concerning Hospital-Related Organizations, August 1, 1981," paragraph 9.
9. AICPA, "Accounting Research Bulletin No. 51: Consolidated Financial Statements, August 1959," paragraph 22.
10. FASB, "Statement of Financial Accounting Standards No. 57: Related Party Disclosures, March 1982," paragraph 2.
11. GASB, "The Financial Reporting Entity," paragraphs 127–28.
12. AICPA, *Audit and Accounting Guide*, 128.
13. The 20 percent investment may require the equity method of reporting. "Entities for which investments are accounted for by the equity method" is part of the definition of "related parties" in FASB Statement No. 57, "Related Party Disclosures," paragraph 24.
14. Related-party transactions encompass "significant relationships and transactions not in the ordinary course of business with directors, management, medical staff or other related parties." AICPA, *Audit and Accounting Guide*, paragraph 13.8.

15. AICPA, "Statement of Position 90-8; Financial Accounting and Reporting by Continuing Care Retirement Communities, November 28, 1990"; Amendment to AICPA, *Audit and Accounting Guide.*
16. FASB, "Statement of Financial Accounting Standards No. 87: Employers' Accounting for Pensions, December 1985" and "Statement of Financial Accounting Standards No. 106: Employers' Accounting for Postretirement Benefits Other Than Pensions, December 1990."
17. FASB, "Statement of Financial Accounting Standards No. 106: Employers' Accounting for Postretirement Benefits Other Than Pensions, December 1990," paragraph 108.
18. CCH Tax Law Editors, *U.S. Master Tax Guide, 1991* (Chicago: Commerce Clearing House, 1990), paragraph 631.
19. K. H. Silverberg, "Obtaining and Maintaining Exempt Status," *Topics in Health Care Financing* 14 (Summer 1988): 9–14.
20. CCH Tax Law Editors, *Federal Tax Guide, 1992* (Chicago: Commerce Clearing House, 1991), paragraph 4527A.
21. D. Taylor, "The Tax Environment: Changes and Challenges," *Topics in Health Care Financing* 14 (Summer 1988), 1–7.

Additional Readings

Alexander, J. A., "Diversification Behavior of Multihospital Systems: Patterns of Change, 1983–1985," *Hospital & Health Services Administration* 35 (Spring 1990): 83–102.
Bromberg, R. S., "Can a Joint Venture Threaten the Hospital's Tax-Exempt Status?" *Healthcare Financial Management* 40 (December 1986): 76–86.
Custis, T. K., "Coping with Retiree Health Benefits," *Management Accounting* 72 (April 1991): 22–26.
Finkler, S. A., "Accounting Issues: Should the Merger Be Treated as Purchase or Pooling?" *Healthcare Financial Management* 39 (May 1985): 90–100.
Seidner, A. G., "Pension Funds Warrant a Financial Manager's Review," *Healthcare Financial Management* 44 (October 1990): 42–47.
Tracy, K. L., "Know the Effects of Not-for-Profit Conversions," *Healthcare Financial Management* 45 (March 1991): 56–66.
Wilbert, J. R., and K. E. Dakdduk, "The New FASB 106: How to Account for Postretirement Benefits," *Journal of Accountancy* 172 (August 1991): 36–41.

Discussion Questions

6.1. If a major medical center were concerned with unmet needs in a service area, explain reasons why the medical center might establish two separate 501(c)(3) corporations for a new nursing home and for a new outpatient clinic. Assume both new corporations are in this defined service area.

6.2. Explain the difference between the reporting entity and legal entities in consolidated financial statements. In your answer assume there is a tax-exempt holding company and nine subsidiary 501(c)(3) corporations.

6.3. Assume that an outpatient clinic is totally dependent on the nearby medical center for referrals. Does information on the outpatient clinic have to be disclosed on the medical center's financial statement under the requirements of a related party? Explain your answer.

6.4. Ashland Memorial Hospital invests $250,000 for a one-sixth interest in Southside Diagnostic and Health Service, a 501(c)(3) corporation, which is also supported by five other health care entities. Both Ashland and Southside use the calendar year as their fiscal period. Record the transaction for Ashland Memorial Hospital when Southside earns $90,000 from its first year of operation:

	Debit	Credit
a. Cash	$15,000	
Investment income		$15,000
b. Investment in affiliated company	$15,000	
Investment income		$15,000
c. Accounts receivable	$15,000	
Investment income		$15,000
d. No entry		

6.5. (See Question 6.4). Southside Diagnostic and Health Service pays $60,000 out of its first-year earnings to the six investing entities, including $10,000 to Ashland Memorial Hospital. Record the transaction for Ashland Memorial Hospital when Southside pays $60,000:

	Debit	Credit
a. Cash	$10,000	
Investment income		$10,000
b. Investment in affiliated company	$10,000	
Investment income		$10,000
c. Cash	$10,000	
Investment in affiliated company		$10,000
d. No entry		

6.6. Alexander Community Hospital invests $400,000 for a 40 percent interest in Westside Home Health Agency, a 501(c)(3) corporation, which is also supported by two other health care entities. Both Alexander and Westside use the calendar year as their fiscal period. Record the transaction for Alexander Community Hospital when Westside earns $90,000 from its first year of operation:

	Debit	Credit
a. Cash	$36,000	
Investment income		$36,000
b. Investment in affiliated company	$36,000	
Investment income		$36,000
c. Accounts receivable	$36,000	
Investment income		$36,000
d. No entry		

6.7. (See Question 6.6). Westside Home Health Agency pays $60,000 out of its first-year earnings to the three investing entities, including $24,000 to Alexander Community Hospital. Record the transaction for Alexander Community Hospital when Westside pays $60,000:

	Debit	Credit
a. Cash	$24,000	
Investment income		$24,000
b. Investment in affiliated company	$24,000	
Investment income		$24,000
c. Cash	$24,000	
Investment in affiliated company		$24,000
d. No entry		

6.8. A medical center invested $3,000,000 to establish a freestanding health care entity as a 501(c)(3) corporation. The new facility lost $145,000 from its first year of operations, and the balance sheets for the two separate accounting entities were as follows:

	Medical Center	Separate Facility
Investment in affiliated company	$ 3,000,000	—
Cash and other assets	46,000,000	$3,160,000
Liabilities and deferred revenue	18,000,000	305,000
General funds balance	31,000,000	2,855,000

The total assets on the medical center's consolidated financial statement are:

a. $52,160,000

b. $49,305,000

c. $49,160,000

d. None of the above

6.9. Explain the difference between a related organization and a related party.

6.10. A not-for-profit health care entity has $12,700,000 of investments in the following accounts:

Current assets in general funds	$ 300,000
Noncurrent assets in general funds	3,800,000
Current assets in donor-restricted specific-purpose funds	1,500,000
Noncurrent assets in donor-restricted specific-purpose funds	2,000,000
Noncurrent assets in endowment funds	5,100,000

In an investment pool, how many separate portfolios must be established? Explain your answer.

6.11. Exhibit 6.7 is a report from a commercial bank on the investment pool for a not-for-profit hospital. The gross investment income that will be reported in the nonoperating revenue section of the statement of revenue and expenses of general funds is

a. $134,670

b. $ 83,340

c. $ 51,330

d. $208,750

6.12. (See Question 6.11 and Exhibit 6.7.) The gross investment income that is directly reported on statements of changes in fund balances is

a. $208,750

b. $ 74,080

c. $125,410

d. $157,420

6.13. Exhibit 6.7 is a report from a commercial bank on the investment pool for a not-for-profit hospital. The portfolio valuation adjustment that is required on 31 December 19X2 for current assets in general funds is

	Debit	*Credit*
a. Unrealized loss on marketable security investment portfolio	$325,000	
Allowance to reduce marketable security investment		$325,000
b. Unrealized loss on marketable security investment portfolio	$205,000	
Allowance to reduce marketable security investment		$205,000

Exhibit 6.7   Not-for-Profit Health Care Entity Investment Pool with Three Portfolios ($75,000 unit value)

1 January 19X2 initial investment pool		$1,500,000
(Unit is valued at $75,000 on 1 January 19X2)		
Current assets in general funds	3 units	225,000
Noncurrent assets in general funds	9 units	675,000
Specific-purpose donor-restricted funds	8 units	600,000
31 March 19X2 investment income		$45,000
Current assets in general funds	3 units	6,750
Noncurrent assets in general funds	9 units	20,250
Specific-purpose donor-restricted funds	8 units	18,000
30 June 19X2 investment income		$46,000
Current assets in general funds	3 units	6,900
Noncurrent assets in general funds	9 units	20,700
Specific-purpose donor-restricted funds	8 units	18,400
1 July 19X2 investment pool (20 units) market value		$1,300,000
(Unit is valued at $65,000 on 1 July 19X2)		
Additional investment:		
Current assets in general funds	5 units	325,000
Net investment pool balance (25 units)		$1,625,000
30 September 19X2 investment income		$58,750
Current assets in general funds	8 units	18,800
Noncurrent assets in general funds	9 units	21,150
Specific-purpose donor-restricted funds	8 units	18,800
31 December 19X2 investment income		$59,000
Current assets in general funds	8 units	18,880
Noncurrent assets in general funds	9 units	21,240
Specific-purpose donor-restricted funds	8 units	18,880
31 December 19X2 investment pool (25 units) market value		$1,500,000
(Unit is valued at $60,000 on 31 December 19X2)		
Current assets in general funds	8 units	480,000
Noncurrent assets in general funds	9 units	540,000
Specific-purpose donor-restricted funds	8 units	480,000
31 December 19X2 assigned cost of three portfolios		$1,825,000
Current assets in general funds	8 units	550,000*
Noncurrent assets in general funds	9 units	675,000
Specific-purpose donor-restricted funds	8 units	600,000

*$225,000 + $325,000 = $550,000.

c. Unrealized loss on marketable
security investment portfolio — $135,000
   Allowance to reduce marketable
   security investment — — $135,000
d. Unrealized loss on marketable
security investment portfolio — $ 70,000
   Allowance to reduce marketable
   security investment — — $ 70,000

6.14. Exhibit 6.7 is a report from a commercial bank on the investment pool for a not-for-profit hospital. The portfolio valuation adjustment that is required on 31 December 19X2 for noncurrent assets in general funds is

	Debit	Credit
a. Unrealized loss on marketable security investment portfolio	$325,000	
Allowance to reduce marketable security investment		$325,000
b. Unrealized loss on marketable security investment portfolio	$205,000	
Allowance to reduce marketable security investment		$205,000
c. Unrealized loss on marketable security investment portfolio	$135,000	
Allowance to reduce marketable security investment		$135,000
d. Unrealized loss on marketable security investment portfolio	$ 70,000	
Allowance to reduce marketable security investment		$ 70,000

6.15. Exhibit 6.7 is a report from a commercial bank on the investment pool for a not-for-profit hospital. The portfolio valuation adjustment that is required on 31 December 19X2 for donor-restricted specific-purpose funds is

	Debit	Credit
a. Specific-purpose funds	$325,000	
Allowance to reduce marketable security investment		$325,000
b. Specific-purpose funds	$190,000	
Allowance to reduce marketable security investment		$190,000

c. Specific-purpose funds $255,000
    Allowance to reduce marketable
    security investment $255,000
d. Specific-purpose funds $120,000
    Allowance to reduce marketable
    security investment $120,000

6.16. Assume a continuing-care retirement community accepts an advance fee with no additional bills that provides the resident with services for his or her life. Explain the measurement problems in matching the revenue from these advance fees with services to the residents and indicate the required disclosures for financial statements.

6.17. Assume that income from operations of general funds is the critical factor for a community hospital in a proposed major redevelopment. A friend of the hospital is planning on donating $500,000 to the institution; from the position of "income from operations," which is preferred: (a) an unrestricted contribution or (b) a donor-restricted specific-purpose contribution. Explain your answer.

6.18. Assume a CCRC is a separate 501(c)(3) corporation, and its 31 December 19X1 balance sheet included the following accounts:

Deferred revenue from advanced fees $10,500,000
Estimated obligation to provide future services, in
    excess of amounts received or to be received   200,000

In 19X2 the CCRC received $6,000,000 in nonrefundable fees, and the amortization for 19X2 is $5,300,000. These two transactions are

	Debit	Credit
a. Cash	$4,500,000	
Deferred revenue from advanced fees		$4,500,000
Deferred revenue from advanced fees	$4,300,000	
Resident service revenue		$4,300,000
b. Cash	$6,000,000	
Deferred revenue from advanced fees		$6,000,000
Deferred revenue from advanced fees	$5,300,000	
Resident service revenue		$5,300,000
c. Cash	$4,500,000	
Deferred revenue from advanced fees		$4,500,000
Deferred revenue from advanced fees	$5,300,000	
Resident service revenue		$5,300,000
d. Cash	$5,800,000	
Deferred revenue from advanced fees		$5,800,000
Deferred revenue from advanced fees	$4,500,000	
Resident service revenue		$4,500,000

6.19. (See Question 6.18.) On 31 December 19X2 the estimated obligation
to provide future service was $11,350,000. The required transaction is

	Debit	Credit
a. Estimated obligation to provide future service	$150,000	
Gain on obligation to provide future service		$150,000
b. Loss on obligation to provide future service	$150,000	
Estimated obligation to provide future service		$150,000
c. Estimated obligation to provide future service	$ 50,000	
Gain on obligation to provide future service		$ 50,000
d. Loss on obligation to provide future service	$ 50,000	
Estimated obligation to provide future service		$ 50,000

7

Financial Statement Analysis

Introduction

Financial ratios are useful measures of transactions and events that facilitate the assessment of a health care entity's performance. Some standard financial ratios are an integral part of the performance assessment of a health care entity and are part of the common, professional vocabulary. But there are many other ratios where some of the components in the calculation may vary among financial analysts and the ratios may be applied in different ways for specific groups of health care entities. The debt-to-equity ratio, for example, may be based on three different definitions of the term "debt." The factors included in each financial ratio should be understood by an analyst so inappropriate comparisons are not made.

The three-dimensional framework of ownership, control, and type of facility in Exhibit 1.1 partitions health care entities into broad categories that may still have significant variation in common characteristics between entities. Some critical characteristics in comparisons of community hospitals within the three-dimensional framework are as follows:

1. Medical school affiliation

2. Membership in the Council of Teaching Hospitals (COTH)

3. Location in a standard metropolitan statistical area (MSA)

4. Case-mix index for Medicare patients

5. Complexity of outpatient services performed based on volume, surgical codes, and procedures

6. Existence of donor-restricted funds

University teaching hospitals that are not state controlled tend to have similar specifications for these critical characteristics.

Financial ratio analysis of health care entities must be performed in a context where the legal status, ownership, control, type of facilities, various funds (if applicable), related entities, affiliated organizations, and other arrangements are known. After Medicare began the certification of freestanding clinics and outpatient facilities in the mid 1980s, financial ratio analysis of investor-owned health care entities became more complex. The traditional role of the community hospital changed, and physician-controlled for-profit health care entities often obtained major cash advances from community hospitals as a condition for their affiliation with the new freestanding facilities. These cash advances may be a long-term source of funds to the for-profit health care entities. Alternative health care delivery systems may negate the relevance of certain types of ratio analysis for a given health care entity, but the facts and the context are prerequisites for this assessment. The notes to the health care entity's certified financial statements must be carefully studied in establishing the appropriate context for that unique entity *before* performing ratio analysis.

Regulatory agencies, licensure groups, accreditation bodies, bond-rating services, commercial banks, and financial institutions are some of the external parties that perform financial ratio analysis of health care entities. Financial analysts for each external party may have a different orientation and purpose in applying ratio analysis to a health care entity. The sections on ratios in this chapter discuss the relevant external parties using the financial ratio and include some guidelines on how the ratio is interpreted.

Performance Measures

Net patient revenue is a significant factor used in many performance measures for health care entities. With a new definition for net patient revenue in the 1990 AICPA reporting guidelines, some traditional performance measures must be recalculated for the prior year before comparisons are made with certified financial statements based on GAAP. Provision for bad debts is now reported as operating expenses (either as a separate line or as part of administrative expenses), instead of being deducted from gross patient revenue in computing net patient revenue. The total amount of operating expenses is increased by this new reporting guideline versus the prior practice.

Excess of revenue over expenses

The bottom line of the statement of revenue and expenses is the most important financial measure of the health care entity's performance. The label for the bottom line varies from "net income" in investor-owned facilities to "excess of revenue and gains over expenses and losses" in some types of nonprofit health care entities. The term "excess of revenue over expenses" is used in this chapter to refer to the bottom line of each health care entity's statement of revenue and expenses.

There are four common ratios featuring excess of revenue over expenses as the numerator, with the following denominators:

1. Net patient revenue
2. Total revenue
3. Net fixed assets
4. Total unrestricted assets

Exhibit 7.1 illustrates the four ratios, using data in previous chapters for Wilmette Community Hospital. The choice of denominator depends on selected characteristics of the health care entity and the purpose. If the objective is to measure return per dollar of revenue, then one of the first two ratios from the statement of revenue and expenses is used. If the objective is to measure return per dollar of assets employed, then one of the last two ratios from the balance sheet is used. When comparisons are made across health care entities, all four of the ratios are frequently used.

Ratios 1 and 2 in Exhibit 7.1 are based on the statement of revenue and expenses. The difference between the two ratios is the importance of other operating revenue in the health care entity. Other operating revenue is not a significant component of total revenue in many health care entities; some entities depend on the transfer of restricted contributions for uninsured care as a major part of other operating revenue. Several entities have increased their sale volumes of products to patients, residents, and nonpatients so these components of other operating revenue are material amounts in the statement of income and expenses.

Some health care entities with long-term bonds have significant amounts of "assets whose use is limited" represented by deposits in investments accounts that will eventually be used to retire the bonds. Because term rather than serial bonds were issued, the trustee can take advantage of differences between the interest rates of the bonds and

Exhibit 7.1   Selected Performance Ratios for Wilmette Community
Hospital for Year Ended 31 December 19X2

Ratio 1: $\dfrac{\text{Excess of revenue over expenses}}{\text{Net patient revenue}} = \dfrac{7{,}504{,}329 \times 100}{80{,}539{,}794} = 9.318\%$

Ratio 2: $\dfrac{\text{Excess of revenue over expenses}}{\text{Total operating revenue}} = \dfrac{7{,}504{,}329 \times 100}{81{,}999{,}150} = 9.152\%$

Ratio 3: $\dfrac{\text{Excess of revenue over expenses}}{\text{Average net fixed assets}} = \dfrac{7{,}504{,}329 \times 100}{(50{,}019{,}350 + 60{,}612{,}234)/2}$

$= 13.57\%$

Ratio 4: $\dfrac{\text{Excess of revenue over expenses}}{\text{Average total unrestricted assets}} = \dfrac{7{,}504{,}329 \times 100}{(82{,}020{,}000 = 102{,}843{,}000)/2}$

$= 8.12\%$

Source: Selected information is from Exhibit 2.3 (balance sheet) and Exhibit 3.3 (statement of revenue and expenses).

the prime rate. Term bonds provide the opportunity to invest in the taxable market with a cost of capital in the tax-exempt market. There are major restrictions on the type of investments the trustee can make. If the noncurrent assets are board designated, then the investments can be made in opportunities with higher potential returns.

There are four major types of noncurrent assets included in "assets whose use is limited," and the investment opportunities vary by the nature of the noncurrent asset. Certified financial statements for community hospitals report significant amounts of these noncurrent assets. For example, a health care entity may have $180 million of unrestricted assets, consisting of the following:

Total current assets	$ 42 million
Noncurrent assets whose use is limited	70 million
Net property, plant, and equipment	60 million
Total other assets	8 million
Total unrestricted assets	*$180 million*

For some types of comparisons, the $60 million of net property and equipment may be the relevant denominator for expressing the excess of revenue over expenses. But, investment income from the noncurrent assets whose use is limited is included in the statement of revenue and expenses; this situation supports using the $180 million of total unrestricted assets as the denominator (Ratio 4 in Exhibit 7.1). Consideration must be given to the restrictions placed on investments from the noncurrent assets as far as returns versus the situation for the remainder of the health care entity's assets.

When there are major differences in the age of property and equipment, then the net fixed assets may not be a relevant measure (Ratio 3 in Exhibit 7.1). Since net fixed assets is included in total unrestricted assets, the selection of a denominator quickly moves to either net patient revenue or total revenue. The shift in health care services toward outpatient care, combined with the acquisition of medical equipment through short-term rental arrangements, also tends to reduce the relative importance of using either of the assets as the denominator in the ratio with excess of revenue over expenses. Applying all four ratios in comparisons across health care entities will highlight exceptional situations involving noncurrent assets, old property and equipment, and large volumes of other operating revenue.

Operating margin

A common ratio in the analysis of performance in a given health care entity is the operating margin, which compares income from operations to total operating revenues. At Wilmette Community Hospital, this is computed as

$$\frac{\text{Income from operations}}{\text{Total operating revenues}} = \frac{\$6,209,219 \times 100}{\$81,999,150} = 7.57\%$$

The operating margin may be useful in assessing how a given health care entity performed in the current year versus the prior year. There are major problems in comparing operating margins across entities.

The operating margin is an intermediate measure of activity on the statement of revenue and expenses. Health care entities partitioned by ownership, control, and type of facility still have a wide range of financial activities that may not be appropriately assessed by cross comparisons of intermediate measures. For example, several community hospitals report over $50 million each year in grants as nonoperating gains; these grants are unrelated to patient services and cannot be anticipated from governmental bodies. Since the grants are nonoperating gains, these funds are not part of the intermediate measure of operating margin. There are other matching problems in the computation of operating margin; for example, interest expense is included, but interest income is excluded. The operating margin is frequently negative in health care entities that expect to receive grants and awards for uninsured care and indigent services. There are other types of general support donations classified as nonoperating gains. Uninsured and indigent care are often factors influencing general contributions reported as nonoperating gains.

Operating margin is an important intermediate measure of a health care entity's activities versus prior-year performance. It may be inappropriate to compare various health care entities—even within the same ownership, control, and type of facility—by this intermediate measure. The four measures of revenue over expenses are preferred over the operating margin.

Component analysis

Revenue and expenses are often separated by functions, departments, and services, and then subjected to financial analysis. Exhibit 7.2 illustrates the statement of revenue and expenses for Wilmette Community Hospital where each item is expressed as a percent of net patient revenue. Some analysts may use total operating revenue instead of net patient revenue as the basis for these comparisons. The choice will vary by selected characteristics of the health care entity.

Some analysts prefer to focus on expenses rather than revenue. Consistent with this approach, salaries and professional fees, for example, are expressed as a percent of total operating expenses and then compared across health care entities. Depreciation and interest are matched against operating revenues, but they are viewed differently than salaries and the remaining expense items. Therefore, depreciation and interest are aggregated and expressed as a percent of the total operating expenses.

Component analysis is helpful in comparing a health care entity with its prior-year performance and in comparing two similar health care entities in the same service area. This analysis may indicate differences in practice that can be adopted by the other entity.

Days in accounts receivable

Analysts calculate the average number of patient revenue days that are contained in net patient receivables. This number of days is compared with the data for another health care entity of the same type with a similar financial class of patients. The patient days in accounts receivable is a measure of the hospital's liquidity and shows the effectiveness of the institution's credit and collection efforts. The ratio is also an indirect measure of coordination and administrative effectiveness.

Exhibit 7.2   Wilmette Community Hospital: Statement of Revenue and Expenses of General Funds for Years Ended 31 December 19X2 and 19X1

	In Thousands		Expressed as Percent of Net Patient Services Revenues	
	19X2	*19X1*	*19X2*	*19X1*
Net patient service revenue (note 1)	$80,540	$72,841	100.00%	100.00%
Other operating revenue	1,459	1,142	1.81	1.57
Total operating revenues	*81,999*	*73,983*	*101.81*	*101.57*
Operating expenses:				
Salaries and professional fees	38,249	35,489	47.49	48.72
Employee benefits	4,424	4,115	5.49	5.65
Supplies and other	16,706	15,803	20.74	21.69
Purchased services	8,910	8,420	11.06	11.56
Medical malpractice costs	1,100	750	1.37	1.03
Depreciation	3,931	3,846	4.88	5.28
Interest expense	1,964	1,417	2.44	1.95
Provision for bad debts	506	465	0.63	0.64
Total operating expenses	*75,790*	*70,305*	*94.10*	*96.52*
Income from operations	*6,209*	*3,678*	*7.71*	*5.05*
Nonoperating revenue:				
Unrestricted gifts and donations	91	26	0.11	0.03
Income on investments:				
Unrestricted	283	252	0.35	0.35
Whose use is limited under indenture agreement	22	20	0.03	0.03
Gain on sale of investments	981	831	1.22	1.14
Loss on sale of properties	(82)	0	−0.10	0.00
Total nonoperating revenue	*1,295*	*1,129*	*1.61*	*1.55*
Excess of revenue over expenses	$ 7,504	$ 4,807	9.32%	6.60%

Note to Financial Statements

1. *Net patient service revenue*

Gross patient service revenue	*$86,513*	*$78,411*	*107.42%*	*107.65%*
Less provisions for:				
Medicare & Medicaid contractual adjustment	4,968	4,645	6.17	6.38

Continued

Exhibit 7.2   Continued

Blue Cross contractual				
adjustment	370	341	0.46	0.47
Other allowances	415	382	0.52	0.52
Charity	220	202	0.27	0.28
Total deductions	*5,973*	*5,570*	*7.42*	*7.65*
Net patient service revenue	*$80,540*	*$72,841*	*100.00%*	*100.00%*

In calculating this ratio, first determine the average net patient revenue per day by dividing the total operating revenues by 365 days. Then, divide the net accounts receivable by this average net patient revenue per day to compute the patient days in accounts receivable, as shown in Exhibit 7.3 for Wilmette Community Hospital. This method of computing patient days in accounts receivable is not ideal. Net patient service revenue should be used in place of operating revenues as the numerator in Exhibit 7.2. Net accounts receivable in many certified financial statements includes both net patient service revenue and other operating revenue. The suggested formula is a pragmatic approach to current professional practice.

The days in accounts receivable is related to the mix of patients by financial class. The state in which the entity is located is an important factor because of the role of the insurance director in regulating payment arrangements with insurance carriers.[1] Medicare and Blue

Exhibit 7.3   Wilmette Community Hospital: Days in Accounts Receivable for 19X2

Average net patient revenue per day	$= \dfrac{\text{Total operating revenues}}{365 \text{ days}}$
Patient days in accounts receivable	$= \dfrac{\text{Net accounts receivable}}{\text{Average net patient revenue per day}}$
Net patient revenue per day	$= \$81,999,150/365 \text{ days} = \$224,655$
Days in accounts receivable	$= \$11,500,603/\$224,655 = 51.2 \text{ days*}$

Source: Selected information is from Exhibit 2.3 (balance sheet) and Exhibit 3.3 (statement of revenue and expenses).

*The AICPA change in the definition of "net patient revenue" regarding provision for bad debts deceased this ratio from 51.5 to 51.2 days.

Cross make prompt payments on claims. In some states there may be a four- to six-week delay before an approved claim is paid by some commercial insurance carriers (in accordance with the insurance rules for that state). Payment under Medicaid may occur in a few states before approved claims are paid by selected third party payors.[2]

Cash flows and delays in collections from third party payors are an integral part of the day-to-day management of health care entities. Medicare, Medicaid, Blue Cross, commercial insurance carriers, health maintenance organizations, preferred-provider groups, corporate alliances, and governmental agencies may represent over 85 percent of the annual cash collections of a health care entity. The health care entity's claims with this network of third party payors must be carefully monitored to insure prompt collection.

Days in accounts receivable provides more than just an assessment of the performance of the collection effort. It may provide signals that new medical services are not fully approved by all agencies, that claims are not fully documented by physicians and health care professionals, or that there has been a shift in payor mix for the patient base. This performance measure is widely used by financial analysts, bond-rating services, regulatory agencies, and other interested parties. The interpretation given to days in accounts receivable may vary by user.

Cash flows from operating activities

Cash flows from operating activities is an extension of the four ratios for excess of revenue over expenses. Cash flows from operating activities is the first section of the statement of cash flows and represents what the health care entity generated (in terms of cash) by regular day-to-day events and transactions. This decision-making capability may be related to each of the four ratios in Exhibit 7.1.

Cash flows from operating activities is compared to net patient service revenue for Wilmette Community Hospital in Exhibit 7.4. This measure shows the net cash flow created on each dollar of patient service revenue (0.1558 in Exhibit 7.4). This amount is expected to be a recurring cash flow for future periods. For every dollar of net patient service revenue, Wilmette Community Hospital might plan on $0.15 of cash, which can be invested in medical technology, support changes in medical practice, or be invested in new initiatives. Implicit in this interpretation is that all other factors will remain constant.

A different dimension of cash flows from operating activities as related to revenue activities is to focus on total operating revenue rather

Exhibit 7.4   Wilmette Community Hospital: Cash Flows from
Operating Activities and Gains and Losses

$$\frac{\text{Cash flows from operating activities}}{\text{Net patient revenue}} = \frac{12,550,345 \times 100}{80,539,794} = 15.58\%$$

$$\frac{\text{Cash flows from operating activities}}{\text{Net fixed assets}} = \frac{12,550,345 \times 100}{68,993,364} = 18.19\%$$

$$\begin{aligned}\text{Operating cash flow growth ratio} &= \frac{\text{Change in cash flows from operating activities}}{\text{Change in total operating revenue}}\\[6pt] &= \frac{(12,550,345 - 8,711,182) \times 100}{(81,999,150 - 73,983,960)} = 47.90\%\end{aligned}$$

Source: Selected information is from Exhibit 2.3 (balance sheet), Exhibit 3.3 (statement of revenue and expenses), and Exhibit 5.1 (statement of cash flows of general funds).

than net patient service revenue. The third formula in Exhibit 7.4 illustrates this, with the numerator and denominator showing annual change in the two measures. The annual growth rate in this cash flow measure at Wilmette Community Hospital is 47.90 percent for 19X2.

Cash flows from operating activities is expressed to net fixed assets as the second ratio in Exhibit 7.4. This ratio shows the net cash flows generated on each dollar of net fixed asset employed (0.1819 in Exhibit 7.4). If Wilmette Community Hospital can maintain its current situation in the marketplace, the measure suggests a $0.18 cash increase for each dollar of net fixed assets employed in future fiscal periods. This cash flow capability is anticipated to occur in the near future because it is based on the regular, day-to-day events and transactions of the health care entity.

Liquidity

Financial viability of health care entities is captured by several ratios that focus on the ability of facilities to meet current obligations and current debt payments. The term "cash flows" is used in some liquidity ratios, but its meaning is not the same as in the statement of cash flows and the above ratios of cash flows from operating activities. In this special use of the term "cash flows," and in all other liquidity ratios, the focus is very short term. Liquidity ratios address the question, Does the entity have sufficient short-term cash-generating capabilities for paying salaries, vendors, interest payments, final settlements with third party payors, and current installments on long-term instruments.

Debt-service coverage

This financial ratio measures the ability of the health care entity to meet current obligations of interest expense and the current portion of long-term debt. The debt-service coverage ratio is widely used by bond-rating services and other financial institutions. Investors are concerned with the ability of the health care entity to make the maximum annual payment under the provisions of a long-term debt. If there is a balloon payment, then the total principal and interest payments for that period are used in the computation.

The formula is the excess of revenue over expenses plus depreciation plus amortization plus interest expense divided by the maximum annual payment. Part of this numerator is called "cash flow" by some financial analysts, where "cash flow" means the excess of revenue over expenses plus depreciation and amortization expense. Wilmette Community Hospital does not have any balloon payments within its retirement plan for the long-term debt, and its debt-service coverage is 3.96 (Exhibit 7.5).

Financial analysts for bond-rating services and financial institutions give more emphasis to the debt-service coverage than to the operating margin or the revenue over expenses ratios. Many analysts have relied on a debt-service coverage of *three times* as a yardstick. Several community hospitals in 1989–1990 had a drop in debt-service

Exhibit 7.5   Wilmette Community Hospital: Debt-Service Coverage for 19X2

$$\text{Debt-service coverage} = \frac{\text{Excess of revenue over expenses} + \text{Depreciation} + \text{Amortization} + \text{Interest expense}}{\text{Maximum annual payment*}}$$

$$= \frac{7,504,329 + 3,931,051 + 1,963,984}{1,416,240 + 1,963,984} = 3.96$$

Source: Selected information is from Exhibit 2.3 (balance sheet) and Exhibit 3.3 (statement of revenue and expenses).

*Maximum annual payment equals current installment or actual paid on cash flow on long-term debt ($1,416,240) plus interest expense ($1,963,984). It is the largest amount in any future year.

coverage to 2.8 times. This historical drop forced financial analysts to examine alternative measures of performance because Standard & Poor's Corporation and Moody's Investors Service, Inc., continued to classify many community hospital's securities as investment-grade bonds even though the debt-service coverage was below the three-times yardstick.

Fixed-charge coverage

Leasing and using long-term contracts to provide equipment, fixtures, and facilities are approaches that some health care entities follow in coping with technology and changes in medical practice. The debt-service coverage ratio does not apply to these entities, but lenders are very interested in the ability of the health care entity to pay fixed charges. Fixed charges are interest expense plus fixed annual payments on leases plus other annual contractual payments. The fixed-charge coverage ratio expresses the excess of revenue over expenses plus annual fixed charges divided by fixed charges; this measure indicates the number of times that the health care entity could have paid those fixed charges. At Wilmette Community Hospital the fixed-charge coverage for 19X2 is 4.82 times (Exhibit 7.6).

The adjusted version of the fixed-charge coverage ratio uses income from operations rather than the excess of revenue over expenses

Exhibit 7.6   Wilmette Community Hospital: Fixed-Charge Coverage for 19X2

$$\text{Fixed-charge coverage} = \frac{\text{Excess of revenue over expenses} + \text{Fixed charges}}{\text{Fixed charges}}$$

$$= \frac{7,504,329 + 1,963,984}{1,963,984} = \frac{9,468,313}{1,963,984} = 4.82$$

$$\text{Adjusted fixed-charge coverage} = \frac{\text{Income from operations} + \text{Fixed charges}}{\text{Fixed charges}}$$

$$= \frac{6,209,219 + 1,963,984}{1,963,984} = 4.16 \ times$$

Source: Selected information is from Exhibit 2.3 (balance sheet), Exhibit 3.3 (statement of revenue and expenses), and Exhibit 5.1 (statement of cash flows of general funds).

Note: The above computations are included for purposes of illustrating the ratio; the debt-service coverage ratio is more applicable to Wilmette Community Hospital.

(Exhibit 7.6). Does the clinic, outpatient facility, or other health care entity generate sufficient cash from regular activities, excluding gains, to handle fixed charges with a margin of safety? This is really what the adjusted version of the ratio is expressing.[3]

Other ratios

Health care entities may have unique sets of current and noncurrent assets. A liquid funds ratio is computed for purposes of separating cash and cash-equivalent items from other items. It is the ratio of the summation of cash and cash equivalents for both current assets and noncurrent assets to total unrestricted assets. Another dimension of liquidity is the ratio of total current liabilities to total unrestricted assets.

Some analysts look at liquidity from a long-term perspective and focus on how long it will take for the regular activities to meet current liabilities plus other liabilities plus long-term debt. Cash from regular activities is viewed as excess of revenue over expenses plus depreciation and amortization expenses. The formula is as follows:

$$\frac{\text{Total debt}}{\text{to cash flow}} = \frac{\begin{array}{c}\text{Current} \\ \text{liabilities}\end{array} + \begin{array}{c}\text{Other} \\ \text{liabilities}\end{array} + \text{Long-term debt}}{\text{Excess of revenue over expenses} + \text{Depreciation}}$$

Ratios for total liabilities to cash flow in a recent study of community hospitals ranged from 3 to 15 years.[4]

Cash plus cash equivalents from the current assets section and the board-designated funds section are often expressed to the maximum annual debt service and to daily operating expenses. These other ratios are as follows:

$$\text{Cushion ratio} = \frac{\text{Cash plus cash equivalents}}{\text{Maximum annual debt service}}$$

$$\frac{\text{Days of operating}}{\text{cash on hand}} = \frac{\text{Cash plus cash equivalents}}{\text{Daily operating expense}}$$

Inclusion of board-designated cash items expresses what can be made available under certain circumstances.

Financial Status and Leverage

Assessments of performance and financial status of health care entities are overlapping evaluations, but the reasons for performing the assessments are different. Financial analysts have different implicit benchmarks for assessing performance and evaluating returns for new investments. Many health care entities have recently experienced a decrease in their returns because of (1) changes in payment arrangements, (2) pricing pressures from managed-care groups and other third party payors, (3) added costs from changes in medical practice, (4) increased costs from technology, (5) price competition from other health care providers. Some health care entities have coped with these opportunities and achieved increased returns.

Return on investment

There are a series of ratios that financial analysts call "return on investment" with different meanings for the term "investment." "Return" usually means the excess of revenue and gains over expenses and losses. Two common definitions of "investments" are net fixed assets and total unrestricted assets. Ratios 3 and 4 in Exhibit 7.1 illustrated these two denominators, with excess of revenue over expenses as the numerator. A third definition of "investments" is the average general funds; revenue over expenses to general funds is 13.10 percent in 19X2 (Exhibit 7.7). A fourth definition of "investments" uses the summation of average long-term debt plus the average capitalized leases plus the average fund balance; the return on this denominator is 9.45 percent in 19X2 (Exhibit 7.7).

Debt-to-equity ratios

There are several ratios that measure the relative position of creditors to the health care entity, and all of these ratios are loosely called "debt" to "equity" with different meanings of each term. Four of the more frequently used ratios for health care institutions are listed below:

1. Current debt to equity
2. Total debt to equity
3. Total debt to total assets
4. Total long-term debt to equity

These four ratios are illustrated for Wilmette Community Hospital in Exhibit 7.7.

Capitalized leases are included as part of long-term debt under current reporting guidelines. Some financial analysts prefer to compare long-term debt without including capitalized leases. Other

Exhibit 7.7   Selected Financial Ratios for Wilmette Community
Hospital for 19X2

---

*Return on Investments:**

Revenue over expenses to general funds

$$= \frac{\text{Revenue over expenses}}{\text{Average general fund balance}}$$

$$= \frac{\$7,504,329 \times 100}{\$57,264,745} = 13.10\%$$

Revenue over expenses to long-term debt + General funds

$$= \frac{\text{Revenue over expenses}}{\text{Average long-term debt} + \text{Average general fund balance}}$$

$$= \frac{\$7,504,329 \times 100}{\$22,167,090 + \$57,264,745} = 9.45\%$$

Debt to Equity:

Current debt to equity

$$= \frac{\text{Average current liabilities}}{\text{Average general fund balance}}$$

$$= \frac{\$10,628,169 \times 100}{\$57,264,745} = 18.56\%$$

Total debt to equity

$$= \frac{\text{Average total liabilities}}{\text{Average general fund balance}}$$

$$= \frac{\$35,166,755 \times 100}{\$57,264,745} = 61.41\%$$

Total debt to total assets

$$= \frac{\text{Average total liabilities}}{\text{Average total assets}}$$

$$= \frac{\$35,166,755 \times 100}{\$92,431,500} = 38.05\%$$

Total long-term debt to equity

$$= \frac{\text{Average long-term debt}}{\text{Average general fund balance}}$$

$$= \frac{\$22,167,090 \times 100}{\$57,264,745} = 38.71\%$$

Continued

Exhibit 7.7 Continued

Averages for 19X2:

Current liabilities $\quad = \quad \dfrac{\$9,187,680 + \$12,068,658}{2} \quad = \quad \mathit{\$10,628,169}$

General fund balance $\quad = \quad \dfrac{\$53,255,964 + \$61,273,527}{2} \quad = \quad \mathit{\$57,264,745}$

Long-term debt $\quad = \quad \dfrac{\$17,709,861 + \$26,624,320}{2} \quad = \quad \mathit{\$22,167,090}$

Total liabilities $\quad = \quad \dfrac{\$28,764,036 + \$41,569,473}{2} \quad = \quad \mathit{\$35,166,755}$

Total assets $\quad = \quad \dfrac{\$82,020,000 + \$102,843,000}{2} \quad = \quad \mathit{\$92,431,500}$

Source: Selected information is from Exhibit 2.3 (balance sheet) and Exhibit 3.4 (statement of revenue and expenses).

*Revenue over expenses to net fixed assets and revenue over expenses to total unrestricted assets are illustrated in Exhibit 7.1.

analysts focus on each major component in these four ratios with additional measures. Many analysts use year-end balances, rather than the averages for the year illustrated in Exhibit 7.7.

Financial analysts for bond-rating services and financial institutions use the debt-to-equity ratios as measures of risk. The general guideline for long-term debt to equity is 55 percent; then there is sufficient balance in general funds to absorb a write-down or reduction in the market value of assets that must be disposed of because of technology, changes in medical practice, shift in demographics, revised economic conditions, new governmental policies on health care reimbursement, changes in coverage by third party payors, closing of industrial plants, and other factors that may be beyond the control of the health care entity. While 55 percent is the guideline for new bond issues, a 70 percent ratio is common for many old bond issues.

Leverage

Long-term debt to total unrestricted assets is the standard measure of leverage for health care entities. The general guideline for leverage is 40 percent because of the risk for major write-downs of assets. The special life-support and building code requirements for health care entities are not appreciated by other purchasers of these assets.

Current obligations

The solvency of health care entities under current reimbursement and payment arrangements is an important matter not taken for granted. There has been frequent media coverage since the mid 1980s on financially distressed health care institutions and bankruptcy procedures for hospitals, HMOs, outpatient clinics, nursing homes, CCRC facilities, rehabilitation facilities, and hospital management corporations. Some proprietary health care entities have sold facilities to their employees' pension plans and performed other major restructuring because of survival considerations. Long delays in collection from state-administered Medicaid and other welfare programs have heightened the cash crunch for many institutions. The ability to meet current obligations is a major concern for all types of health care entities, and creditors are learning that contributions from a community do not necessarily keep the health care entity from closing its doors.

Financial statements of health care entities are beginning to show extensive disclosures required by external funding parties. In coping with this environment, the indentures for bonds and notes are placing limitations on the health care entity's assets in general funds. These limitations on assets in general funds may significantly change the level of risk for unsecured creditors and place more emphasis on the ability of the health care entity to satisfy current reimbursement and payment arrangements. Financial disclosure under the current rules for Medicare may influence items reported as board-designated funds rather than as current assets. Hence, the cushion ratio, previously described, uses both current assets and board-designated funds.

The current ratio is the standard financial ratio showing number of dollars (represented by total current assets) available to pay the current obligations (Exhibit 7.8). Individuals can easily manipulate the current ratio by paying off current liabilities, given that the current assets are greater than the current liabilities. After each payment, the residual current assets will have a higher ratio to the residual current liabilities. A second comparison is made with a focus on an amount, working capital; working capital is equal to current assets less current liabilities.

The current ratio at Wilmette Community Hospital for the general funds in 19X2 is 1.28 times; working capital is $3,362,745 (Exhibit 7.8). Since the inventory and prepaid expense items included in

Exhibit 7.8   Other Financial Ratios

Health Care Entities:

Long-term debt to net property, plant, and equipment	=	$\dfrac{\text{Long-term debt}}{\text{Net property, plant, and equipment}}$
Average age of facility	=	$\dfrac{\text{Accumulated depreciation}}{\text{Depreciation expense}}$
Remaining average life of facility	=	$\dfrac{\text{Net property, plant, and equipment}}{\text{Depreciation expense}}$
Long-term debt to depreciation	=	$\dfrac{\text{Long-term debt}}{\text{Depreciation expense}}$

Community Hospital–Specific Ratios:

Net property, plant, and equipment per bed	=	$\dfrac{\text{Net property, plant, and equipment}}{\text{Available beds}}$
Total assets per bed	=	$\dfrac{\text{Total assets}}{\text{Available beds}}$
Net patient revenues per bed	=	$\dfrac{\text{Net patient service revenue}}{\text{Available beds}}$
Working capital per bed	=	$\dfrac{\text{Working capital}}{\text{Available beds}}$
Discharges per bed	=	$\dfrac{\text{Discharges for year}}{\text{Available beds}}$
Current ratio	=	$\dfrac{\text{Current assets}}{\text{Current liabilities}}$
Working capital	=	Current assets − Current liabilities

Application to Wilmette Community Hospital:

Current ratio	=	$\dfrac{\$15,431,403}{\$12,068,658}$	= *1.28 times*
Working capital	=	$\$15,431,403 - \$12,068,658 = \$3,362,745$	

current assets cannot be converted into cash, it is traditional to use a current ratio of 2 as a guide in business; however, it is not unusual in the health care industry to have a current ratio of 1.2 to 1.4.

The evaluation of a health care entity's current ratio must recognize the financial class of patients for that entity. The assessment of patient days in accounts receivable is an integral part of determining the financial ability of the health care entity to meet current obligations.

Other ratios

Some financial analysts representing investors prefer to look at risk by the ratio of long-term debt to net property, plant, and equipment (PP&E). The formulas for this and other selected financial ratios are shown in Exhibit 7.8. Rigid financial guidelines for financial ratios in health care entities were revised in 1989–1990 and were replaced by new approaches implemented by bond-rating services for assessing the health entity, the administrative team, management development, and the entity's competitive environment. The ability of the administrative team to manage change became a key factor; financial ratios were assessed as supporting evidence rather than being the prime consideration, as was the case in the 1970s.

Summary

Regulatory agencies, licensure groups, accreditation bodies, bond-rating services, commercial banks, financial institutions, and other creditors are some of the external parties performing ratio analysis of health care entities. The reasons for these assessments vary from determining financial viability to solvency to measuring performance. Financial analysts representing external parties new to the health care field often get excited over some ratio that may not be applicable to a given entity. A health care entity's financial class of patients, for example, may significantly influence the results of two organizations of similar size, type, ownership, control, and structure so that the two entities ratios are not comparable. The notes to the financial statements are the key source of information for establishing the context in which financial statement analysis can be accomplished.

The excess of revenue and gains over expenses and losses is the most important financial measure of a health care entity. Financial analysts refer to this measure as the health care entity's *return*. Performance is assessed by relating the return to total patient service revenue, total revenue, net fixed assets, and total unrestricted assets. The choice of denominator used in these comparisons is based on the characteristics of the health care entity and the purpose of the analysis.

Operating margin is an intermediate measure of performance and is primarily useful for evaluating an entity with its prior-year activities. Nonoperating gains are excluded from the computation of operating margin and can result in misleading assessments in comparisons across health care entities.

Days in accounts receivable is more than just a measure of the health care entity's credit and collection efforts. Knowledge of the type of facility and the mix of patients is required as a context in which to assess collection operations. The number of days may suggest that the health care entity has a lack of coordination between departments and a failure to document claims of services provided to patients.

Debt-service coverage measures the ability of the health care entity to meet current obligations of interest expense and current portion of long-term debt from returns (excess of revenue over expenses) plus depreciation expense (noncash). An index of less than 1.6 times implies the health care entity is in a critical status, 1.6 to 2.0 is a warning zone, and 3.0 or larger is a comfort zone.

Return on investment and debt-to-equity measures have multiple meanings; it is necessary to confirm how each formula is being used *before* assessments are performed. Financial analysts seek a margin of safety in dealing with health care entities because of special building codes, life-support capabilities, fire protection, and environmental requirements that add to the cost of buildings and equipment. Dispositions may be in a different market, where these added features are not appreciated by prospective purchasers. Assessments of return on investments and debt-to-equity ratios are guided by benchmarks that consider these possible write-downs on dispositions of assets.

Current ratio and working capital measures are closely monitored by some uninsured creditors because they may not have a claim to noncurrent assets whose use is limited. Cash flows from operating activities is a new measure for nonprofit health care entities to use in evaluating cash movements. The recurring nature of events and transactions supporting these cash flows permits projects for the near future.

Financial analysts have new opportunities for assessment with full disclosures from the certified statements of cash flows. The single-period reports from cash used (provided) by investing activities and financing activities can be considered with return on investment, debt to equity, and leverage measures, resulting in new types of financial comparisons.

Appendix: Analysis of Not-for-Profit Community Hospitals Based on Medical School Affiliation for 1986–1989

Are there differences in the financial profile of community hospitals affiliated with medical schools versus other hospitals? A sample of 1,227 nongovernment not-for-profit (NFP) community hospitals was examined for 1986–1989 based on data from certified financial statements and operational reports contained in The Merritt System®.[5] Application of the three-dimensional framework from Exhibit 1.1 separated the NFP community hospitals into 968 independent hospitals and 259 church-operated hospitals.[6]

Community hospitals range from 6 beds to over 2,000 beds. These size differences are accommodated by using ratios rather than numeric values. For many community hospitals, outpatient services generate more than 35 percent of their revenue. Thus, a ratio of net patient revenue per bed is not a relevant measure for general comparisons across NFP community hospitals.

Geographical location

Community hospitals with a medical school affiliation are almost entirely located in standard metropolitan statistical areas (MSAs). Table 7.1 reports that 97 percent of medical school–affiliated independent community hospitals are located in MSAs, and Table 7.2 shows 96 percent of medical school–affiliated church-operated community hospitals are located in MSAs. There are differences in MSA status for independent versus church-operated hospitals without a medical school affiliation: 67 percent of the independent hospitals were located in MSAs versus 80 percent for church-operated hospitals.

Outpatient revenue as percent of total

Medical school–affiliated community hospitals have significantly lower proportions of their total revenue coming from outpatient services than other hospitals. The proportion is 18.07 percent for medical school–affiliated independent hospitals versus 23.11 percent for other independent hospitals (Table 7.1). The proportion is 16.48 percent for medical school–affiliated church-operated hospitals versus 21.51 percent for other church-operated hospitals (Table 7.2).

Although medical school–affiliated community hospitals have lower proportions of gross patient revenue coming from outpatient

Table 7.1 Selected Comparisons between NFP Independent Community Hospitals Based on Medical School Affiliation

| | *Medical School Affiliation* | | | | |
| | *No* (696 Hospitals) | | *Yes* (272 Hospitals) | | *Two-Sample t-Stat* |
	Mean	Std Dev.	Mean	Std Dev.	
Debt-service coverage	3.02 times	3.52	3.54 times	4.58	−1.66*
Case-mix index for Medicare	1.21	0.13	1.36	0.19	−11.70***
New asset investment to total unrestricted assets for 1987–1988	14.24%	9.76	15.68%	8.45	−2.29**
New asset investment to net fixed assets for 1987–1988	27.4%	35.5	32.0%	14.6	−2.84***
New asset investment to total net patient revenue for 1987–1988	18.7%	18.5	19.7%	11.5	−0.97
Age property, plant & equipment	7.05 years	1.90	7.22 years	1.73	−1.26
Contractual allowances	25.8%	9.73	25.6%	11.3	−1.29
Revenue over expenses to net patient revenue	4.45%	5.08	4.88%	4.69	−1.23
Revenue over expenses to unrestricted assets	3.47%	3.76	3.88%	3.59	−1.57
Revenue over expenses to total fixed assets	6.5%	10.8	6.49%	9.56	−0.05
Outpatient revenue as percent of total	23.11%	7.87	18.07%	5.64	10.08***
Long-term debt to total assets	40.2%	17.0	35.9%	14.6	3.91***
Total liabilities to total assets	55.9%	18.0	55.5%	15.5	0.35
Located in metropolitan statistical area	67%	0.47	97%	0.18	−14.12***

Source: The specific data on hospitals are from The Merritt System®.
 *Significant at 10% level.
 **Significant at 5% level.
 ***Significant at 1% level.

Table 7.2 Selected Comparisons between NFP Church-Operated Community Hospitals Based on Medical School Affiliation

	Medical School Affiliation				
	No (181 Hospitals)		Yes (78 Hospitals)		Two-Sample t-Stat
	Mean	Std Dev.	Mean	Std Dev.	
Debt-service coverage	2.90 times	2.88	3.41 times	3.40	−1.16
Case-mix index for Medicare	1.27	0.15	1.34	0.15	−3.65***
New asset investment to total unrestricted assets for 1987–1988	14.20%	9.22	13.20%	7.40	0.92
New asset investment to net fixed assets for 1987–1988	27.7%	17.2	27.6%	15.7	0.04
New asset investment to total net patient revenue for 1987–1988	18.0%	12.7	16.9%	9.3	0.79
Age property, plant & equipment	7.46 years	1.75	7.45 years	1.51	0.01
Contractual allowances	25.81%	9.50	25.7%	10.0	0.10
Revenue over expenses to net patient revenue	4.15%	5.42	5.42%	4.51	−1.94**
Revenue over expenses to unrestricted assets	3.19%	4.14	4.14%	3.22	−2.00**
Revenue over expenses to total fixed assets	5.6%	13.4	7.29%	8.04	−1.22
Outpatient revenue as percent of total	21.51%	6.81	16.48%	4.61	6.49***
Long-term debt to total assets	41.7%	16.8	38.2%	14.7	1.67*
Total liabilities to total assets	57.4%	17.9	55.5%	16.5	0.83
Located in metropolitan statistical area	80%	0.40	96%	0.19	−4.34***

Source: The specific data on hospitals are from The Merritt System®.
*Significant at 10% level.
**Significant at 5% level.
***Significant at 1% level.

services, their average charge per visit is much higher than for other hospitals. These tables do not reflect the information, but the database shows large numbers of outpatient surgical operations and procedures performed by the medical school–affiliated hospitals versus small numbers for the other community hospitals. Thus, the other community hospitals tend to have large dollar volumes of outpatient revenue based on simple documentation of cases that qualify for minimum payment levels from third party payors.

Case-mix index for Medicare patients

The 272 medical school–affiliated independent hospitals and the 78 medical school–affiliated church-operated hospitals have significantly higher case-mix indexes for Medicare patients than the respective other hospitals. There is a high correlation between medical school affiliation, case-mix index for Medicare patients, and a relatively high volume of complex outpatient surgical procedures per dollar volume of outpatient revenue.

Membership in COTH

Medical school affiliation is the first step toward classification as a member of the Council of Teaching Hospitals (COTH). Of the 272 medical school–affiliated independent hospitals, 44 percent are members of COTH, but only 33 percent of the 78 medical school–affiliated church-operated hospitals are.

Equity to total unrestricted assets

The average independent NFP community hospital is represented by a 44 percent ratio of equity to total unrestricted assets. There is no difference in this ratio based on medical school affiliation (Table 7.1). Some community hospitals in the study have negative equity balances; therefore, the ratio of total liabilities to total unrestricted assets is used in this computation. Total liabilities plus equity equals total unrestricted assets; thus, the 44 percent equity amount is calculated by deducting 56 percent from total assets. The 78 church-operated hospitals with medical school affiliation also have a 44 percent ratio of equity to total assets (Table 7.2); the 181 other church-operated hospitals are at 43 percent for equity to total assets.

New fixed-asset investments

There are three measures of new investments in medical technology and facilities in Tables 7.1 and 7.2. Both groups of church-operated hospitals are in a similar position of not investing as much in fixed assets as do the 272 medical school–affiliated independent hospitals (Table 7.1). Note that the 272 medical school–affiliated independent hospitals differ significantly from the 696 other independent hospitals in only two of the three ratios for new fixed-asset investments. The third ratio, of new fixed assets to net patient revenue, is influenced by some extreme values in both distributions. The first-quartile, median, and third-quartile measures all favor a strong finding for the 272 medical school–affiliated hospitals over the 696 other hospitals in the ratio of new fixed-asset investments to net patient revenue.

Long-term debt

Medical school–affiliated hospitals in both groups have significantly smaller percentages of long-term debt to total unrestricted assets than the other hospitals. Since the equity is at 44 percent of total assets, on the average, for all hospitals, medical school–affiliated hospitals are able to do more short-term financing with current liabilities and other deferred revenues than the hospitals without medical school affiliation.

Revenue over expenses

The 272 medical school–affiliated independent hospitals do not have any higher returns (revenue over expenses) to net patient revenue or assets than the 696 other independent hospitals (Table 7.1). The 272 medical school–affiliated independent hospitals have higher dollar volumes of net patient revenues to fixed assets than the other 696 hospitals; however, the bottom line is not significantly different from that of the other 696 hospitals. Contractual allowances to gross patient revenue is not significantly different among any of the groups. The payor mix is different for the medical school–affiliated hospitals than for the other hospitals.[7]

The 78 medical school–affiliated church-operated hospitals have significantly higher returns to net patient revenue and returns to total unrestricted assets than the 181 other church-operated hospitals (Table 7.2).

Summary

A medical school–affiliated NFP community hospital tends to have a different profile of operating performance, serving a broad range of patients from many more financial payor classes, than the NFP hospital without medical school affiliation. Church-operated medical school–affiliated hospitals do not have the same profile as independent community hospitals with medical school affiliations. A similar conclusion is reached if medical school–affiliated governmental community hospitals are compared to the 272 medical school–affiliated independent hospitals in Table 7.1.

Notes

1. T. R. Prince and R. Ramanan, "Collection Performance: An Empirical Analysis of Not-for-Profit Community Hospitals," *Hospital & Health Services Administration* (forthcoming).
2. See the findings in Prince and Ramanan, "Collection Performance."
3. A different approach is to show interest expense as a percent of net patient services revenue, which at Wilmette Community Hospital is 2.44 percent in 19X2 and 1.95 percent in 19X1 (Exhibit 7.2). This change in interest between 19X1 and 19X2 is because of an increase in long-term debt (Exhibit 2.3).
4. T. R. Prince, "Assessing Financial Outcomes of Not-for-Profit Community Hospitals," *Hospital & Health Services Administration* 36 (Fall 1991): 331–49.
5. See Chapter 4 for information on The Merritt System® and a description of the database.
6. The church-operated NFP hospitals versus independent NFP hospitals are based on AHA control codes 21 and 23 in the *Guide to the Health Care Field*. More than 100 hospitals in this sample of 968 independent hospitals with a code of 23 in the AHA guide are members of the Catholic Health Association. As previously explained, there is a difference between church-operated (AHA guide definition) and church-affiliated (formal relationship of the health care entity to another legal entity).
7. For more information on payor-mix issues see Prince and Ramanan, "Collection Performance."

Additional Readings

Cleverley, W. O. "Improving Financial Performance: A Study of 50 Hospitals," *Hospital & Health Services Administration* 35 (Summer 1990): 173–87.
Fonner, E., Jr., and L. Hammond. "Financial Trends for Urban Catholic Hospitals," *Health Progress* 72 (November 1991): 57–64.

Kwon, I., S. R. Safranski, D. G. Martin, and W. R. Walker. "Cause of Financial Difficulty in Catholic Hospitals," *Health Care Management Review* 13 (Winter 1988): 29–37.

McCue, M. J. "Financial Leases in the Hospital Industry: An Analysis of California Hospitals," *Medical Care* 28 (August 1990): 672–80.

Pauly, M. V. "Returns on Equity for Not-for-Profit Hospitals," *Health Services Research* 21 (April 1986): 1–16.

Wedig, G. J., M. Hassan, and F. A. Sloan. "Hospital Investment Decisions and the Cost of Capital," *Journal of Business* 62 (October 1989): 517–37.

Discussion Questions

7.1. Explain why standard financial ratios cannot be applied to all health care entities and used in comparisons across entities.

7.2. Briefly explain the problems in using operating margin for cross comparisons of health care entities.

7.3. List the four common denominators for comparing revenue over expenses in health care entities and indicate the type of situations that support selecting each of the four denominators.

7.4. Why is days in accounts receivable so important in assessing a health care entity's ability to meet current obligations?

7.5. Explain why a debt-service coverage of less than 1.6 times signals that the health care entity is in a critical status.

7.6. Explain why financial analysts desire a long-term debt to general fund balance of less than 55 percent.

7.7. Explain the following ratio: cash provided by operating activities and gains and losses to net patient service revenue.

7.8. Medical school–affiliated community hospitals have significantly lower proportions of outpatient revenue to gross revenue than other community hospitals. But, in comparing two similar-size hospitals (one is medical school affiliated, the other is not), the medical school–affiliated community hospital may have more "net income" from the lower quantity of outpatient services than the other hospital. Explain how this is possible.

7.9. The 696 independent hospitals in Table 7.1 without any medical school affiliation are partitioned into four panels (A through D) based on the return on net patient revenue. Panel A, with returns of 6.51 percent or higher, contains 227 hospitals. Panel D, with returns of 1.21 percent or less, contains 205 hospitals. Table 7.3 presents the same type of profile comparisons for Panel A and Panel D hospitals as Table 7.1. After studying Tables 7.1 and 7.3, determine if you would recommend

Table 7.3 Profile Comparisons of NFP Independent Community Hospitals without Medical School Affiliation

| | Return on Net Patient Revenue | | | | |
| | High (Panel A, 227) | | Low (Panel D, 205) | | Two-Sample t-Stat |
	Mean	Std Dev.	Mean	Std Dev.	
By Construction					
Revenue over expenses to net patient revenue	9.40%	2.49	−1.07%	4.61	28.89***
Selected Comparisons					
Debt-service coverage	4.43 times	3.01	1.38 times	2.71	11.04***
Case-mix index for Medicare	1.24	0.14	1.18	0.13	4.34***
New asset investment to total unrestricted assets for 1987–1988	15.06%	9.29	13.3%	11.8	1.75*
New asset investment to net fixed assets for 1987–1988	32.2%	16.3	21.5%	60.6	2.45***
New asset investment to total net patient revenue for 1987–1988	21.5%	15.4	17.2%	27.0	1.98**
Age property, plant & equipment	6.86 years	1.60	7.16 years	2.13	−1.63*
Contractual allowances	24.79%	9.18	27.6%	10.7	−2.90***
Revenue over expenses to unrestricted assets	6.88%	2.08	−0.64%	3.34	27.71***
Revenue over expenses to total fixed assets	14.72%	7.60	−3.2%	10.3	20.28***
Outpatient revenue as percent of total	23.08%	8.04	22.91%	8.85	0.19
Long-term debt to total assets	35.3%	15.4	45.5%	20.1	−5.87***
Total liabilities to total assets	46.9%	14.6	67.1%	19.6	−12.04***
Located in metropolitan statistical area	63%	0.48	71%	0.45	−1.92**

Source: The specific data on hospitals are from The Merritt System®.
*Significant at 10% level.   **Significant at 5% level.   ***Significant at 1% level.

additional payment to rural community hospitals that are not medical school affiliated.

7.10. (See Question 7.9.) Compute the ratio of equity to total assets for Panel A hospitals versus Panel D hospitals in Table 7.3. Interpret your findings.

7.11. (See Question 7.9.) Interpret the findings for the three ratios for new fixed-asset investments and the age of property, plant, and equipment in Table 7.3.

7.12. (See Question 7.9.) The debt-service coverage for the average Panel D hospital is 1.38 times (Table 7.3), while the average return (revenue over expenses) is a loss of 1.07 percent. Explain the positive findings for debt-service coverage in this context.

7.13. (See Question 7.9.) A consultant to the average Panel D hospital in Table 7.3 has recommended that the facility should expand its outpatient activities as a method of improving the overall net patient revenue. What guidance is suggested by the profile data in Tables 7.1 and 7.3 for expanding outpatient activities?

7.14. The 272 independent hospitals with medical school affiliation in Table 7.1 are partitioned into four panels (E through H) based on the return on net patient revenue. Panel E, with returns of 6.51 percent or higher, contains 91 hospitals. Panel H, with returns of 1.21 percent or less, contains 86 hospitals. Table 7.4 presents the same type of profile comparisons for Panel E and Panel H hospitals as Table 7.1. Interpret the findings for the three ratios for new fixed-asset investments and the age of property, plant, and equipment in Table 7.4.

7.15. (See Question 7.14.) Compute the ratio of equity to total assets for Panel E hospitals versus Panel H hospitals in Table 7.4. Interpret your findings.

7.16. (See Question 7.14.) Interpret the significant findings for the case-mix index for Medicare patients in Panel E hospitals versus Panel H hospitals in Table 7.4.

7.17. Exhibit 7.9 contains segments of Caldwell Community Hospital's statement of revenue and expenses of general funds for year ended 31 December 19X2, and Exhibit 7.10 presents the results from the Doctors' Office Building. Exhibit 7.11 contains selected balance sheet accounts as of 31 December 19X2. Compute the following ratios for Caldwell Community Hospital:

A. Excess of revenue over expenses to net patient revenue

B. Excess of revenue over expenses to net fixed assets

C. Excess of revenue over expenses to total assets

D. Operating margin

E. Fixed-charge coverage

Table 7.4 Profile Comparisons of NFP Independent Community Hospitals with Medical School Affiliation

| | Return on Net Patient Revenue | | | | |
| | High (Panel E, 91) | | Low (Panel H, 86) | | Two-Sample t-Stat |
	Mean	Std Dev.	Mean	Std Dev.	
By Construction					
Revenue over expenses to net patient revenue	9.81%	2.93	−0.003%	3.03	21.96***
Selected Comparisons					
Debt-service coverage	5.42 times	7.11	1.78 times	1.67	4.74***
Case-mix index for Medicare	1.40	0.20	1.34	0.17	2.16**
New asset investment to total unrestricted assets for 1987–1988	14.91%	6.69	15.9%	11.5	−0.72
New asset investment to net fixed assets for 1987–1988	32.7%	14.1	29.7%	16.3	1.33
New asset investment to total net patient revenue for 1987–1988	20.7%	10.3	19.3%	15.4	0.71
Age property, plant & equipment	6.82 years	1.44	7.59 years	1.88	−3.05***
Contractual allowances	25.4%	10.3	27.5%	12.3	−1.20
Revenue over expenses to unrestricted assets	7.29%	2.65	0.19%	2.44	18.53***
Revenue over expenses to total fixed assets	14.47%	8.17	−2.06%	7.41	14.07***
Outpatient revenue as percent of total	17.36%	6.14	18.10%	5.30	−0.77
Long-term debt to total assets	33.2%	12.9	39.3%	16.9	−2.71***
Total liabilities to total assets	47.4%	12.7	66.6%	15.3	−9.06***
Located in metropolitan statistical area	97.8%	0.15	96.5%	0.18	0.51**

Source: The specific data on hospitals are from The Merritt System®.
*Significant at 10% level.   **Significant at 5% level.   ***Significant at 1% level.

Exhibit 7.9   Caldwell Community Hospital: Statement of Revenue
and Expenses of General Funds for Year Ended
31 December 19X2

Net patient service revenue (note 1)	$78,267,810
Other operating revenue	3,107,114
Total operating revenues	*81,374,924*
Operating expenses:	
Salaries and professional fees	36,517,926
Employee benefits	5,623,842
. . .	. . .
Depreciation	3,649,152
Interest expense	3,342,300
Provision for bad debts	800,000
Total operating expenses	*75,262,994*
Income from operations	*6,111,930*
Nonoperating gains (losses):	
Unrestricted gifts and bequests	2,669,984
Income on investments:	
Unrestricted	893,108
Whose use is limited under indenture agreement	46,317
Net deficit of the Doctors' Office Building	
(Exhibit 7.10; note 2)	(58,596)
Nonoperating gains, net	*3,550,813*
Excess of revenues over expenses	$ *9,662,743*

Notes to Financial Statements

1. *Net patient service revenue*

Gross patient service revenue:	
Daily hospital services	$33,251,139
Departmental services	52,657,386
Total gross patient service revenue	*85,908,525*
. . .	. . .
Net patient service revenue	*$78,267,810*

2. *Doctors' Office Building*

Caldwell Community Hospital opened the Doctors' Office Building in 19X0
for the purpose of retaining the existing medical staff and for assistance in
physician recruitment. The Doctors' Office Building is not a separate corporation, but is part of the hospital complex.

F. Debt-service coverage

G. Return on investment/equity (use 19X2 data only)

H. Current debt to equity (use 19X2 data only)

I. Total debt to equity (use 19X2 data only)

J. Total liabilities to total assets (use 19X2 data only)

K. Long-term debt to total assets (use 19X2 data only)

L. Total long-term debt to equity (use 19X2 data only)

M. Current ratio

N. Working capital

7.18. Caldwell Community Hospital's net accounts receivable on 31 December 19X2 was $11,716,261. Using information in Exhibit 7.9 compute patient days in accounts receivable.

7.19. A member of Wilmette Community Hospital's administrative team attended a seminar on measures of performance and the investment of current resources in support of patient care. It was stated that a 490-bed community hospital with less than 20 percent of its gross revenues from outpatient services should have approximately $2,100 inventory per bed. Using the average inventory information in Exhibit 2.3, determine the inventory per bed using the following additional data. Wilmette Community Hospital has 490 beds with four types of services:

General medical and surgical services	406 beds
Intensive care unit	24 beds
Coronary care unit	12 beds
Intermediate care unit	48 beds
Total hospital beds	*490 beds*

Exhibit 7.10 Caldwell Community Hospital: Statement of Revenue and Expenses for Doctors' Office Building for Year Ended 31 December 19X2

Revenue	
Rental income	*$1,097,200*
Expenses	
Interest	415,820
. . .	. . .
Depreciation	365,900
Total operating expenses	*1,155,796*
Loss from operations	*$ 58,596*

Exhibit 7.11 Selected Balance Sheet Accounts for Caldwell
Community Hospital as of 31 December 19X2

Total assets	*$121,362,158*
Total current assets	$ 15,628,513
Property and equipment, net	$ 39,271,311
Assets whose use is limited	$ 31,575,045
Current installment on long-term debt	$ 2,345,474
Total current liabilities	$ 14,139,271
Long-term debt (19 years)	$ 44,564,000
Total liabilities	*$ 58,703,271*
General funds balance	$ 62,658,887
Total liabilities and general funds	*$121,362,158*

Part II

Internal Accounting and Management Control Procedures

8

Cost-Accounting Procedures for Health Care Entities

Introduction

Cost accounting is relating expenditures to a statistical measure of performance and performing an assessment for some purpose, such as management control, pricing, planning, marginal analysis, or operational strategy. The fundamental theory of cost accounting is that there are different costs for various purposes. The same database of expenditures and performance information can support a wide range of calculated "costs," depending on the purpose of the analysis. There are acceptable analytical models, presented in this and subsequent chapters, for assessing costs for different purposes.

Cost management for health care entities includes additional features in the analytical models for assessment that are not applicable to other industries. The provision of patient care to individuals is different from other personal services. The analytical models for cost management encompass the standard assessments from industrial engineering and managerial economics, plus features for patient care services to individuals. Frequent changes in medical practice and medical technology affect the statistical methods included in analytical cost models for health care entities.

Another major dimension of unique features in health care relates to fixed costs that support the delivery of patient services. Medical and surgical services require staffing of certain types of professionals in ancillary and support departments. But, the concern does not stop with the staffing; there must be monitoring to see if minimum volumes of specific tests, procedures, and activities are performed by these professionals to maintain their technical competence in critical supporting areas. There are, for example, critical tests and procedures in blood bank, laboratory, and pulmonary function that a cardiologist expects to be available, if required, before complex surgery is even scheduled. The nature of these fixed costs and the type of monitoring are unique to health care.

Cost-accounting transactions in health care entities are recorded in cost accounts that designate the organization unit and the nature of the expenditure being charged. There were efforts in the late 1970s and early 1980s to have a uniform coding structure for all health care entities, but the shift to a prospective payment arrangement in 1983 removed the need for uniform reporting by community hospitals.[1] The impact of these proposed changes, however, can be seen in many computer packages, designed by vendors during 1978–1983, that had to accommodate the proposed uniform coding structure. Overall, there was a significant movement toward more uniform recording of transactions by health care entities as vendor packages for personal computers became a common feature in the finance and administrative offices of health care entities.

Cost Pools

A *cost pool* is an organizational unit or subunit in a health care entity where expenditure data are desired for some decision-making purpose, such as expenditure monitoring, performance evaluation, pricing, departmental assessment, planning, or external reporting. This defined cost pool may be located *at any level* within the health care entity and must be identified by a unique code within the data structure. A given cost pool may be where transaction data are initially captured; or it may be an aggregation account that summarizes transaction data from other cost pools; or it may be a special account whose defined data are extracted, processed, and summarized from other cost pools. The specification of this organizational unit or subunit within the health care entity may be for a group, a division, a department, a clinic, a center, a section, or a given type of practice.

Regular cost account

A *regular cost account* is an organizational unit where initial expenditure data can be recorded by the natural classification of expense and compared with the approved annual budget amount for that category.

Many complex health care entities have six or seven organizational levels, and there are usually regular cost accounts at all of them. A health care entity's approved annual budget is really by regular cost account because that is the organizational unit where expenditures occur.

Major cost center

A *major cost center* is not used to initially record any transaction, but its values are derived by aggregation of selected data from regular cost accounts. The reported budget data for a major cost center or for a special cost pool are obtained by aggregating selected transaction information on the expenditure, utilization, and budget amounts from the detailed recordings by regular cost account captured in the database management system (DBMS).

It is important to remember that a major cost center can never initially incur an expenditure; regular cost accounts are the only organizational units where initial transaction data are recorded. There may be regular cost accounts and major cost centers at each and every organizational level of the health care entity. Figure 8.1 illustrates nine regular cost accounts and nine major cost centers at the first and second organizational levels of Demonstration Memorial Hospital.

A job title indicates a position that is normally associated with an organizational level and a certain salary range within a complex health care entity. For example, a department chair or center director is typically at organizational level 3. Physicians coordinating the activities of a medical specialty at organizational level 4 are frequently given the title of director. A physician serving as a department chair may elect to have a nonphysician serve as director, resulting in two positions in the same department at organizational level 3. Assistant directors and managers are often at organizational level 4; assistant managers, level 5; supervisors, level 6; and section heads, level 7.

All organizational levels are not necessarily represented in each area of a complex health care entity. There may be a center director at organizational level 3, two managers at level 4, and five or six supervisors at level 6, without having any assistant managers at level 5. Figure 8.2 shows a missing organizational level 5 for the Department of Physical Medicine and Rehabilitation Services. The absence of an organizational level, however, causes no problems with the aggregation process of cost data because the application computer programs for the DBMS permit mappings of regular cost accounts and major cost centers so as to accommodate any missing levels.

Figure 8.1   Demonstration Memorial Hospital: First and Second
Organizational Levels—Major Cost Centers and Regular
Cost Accounts

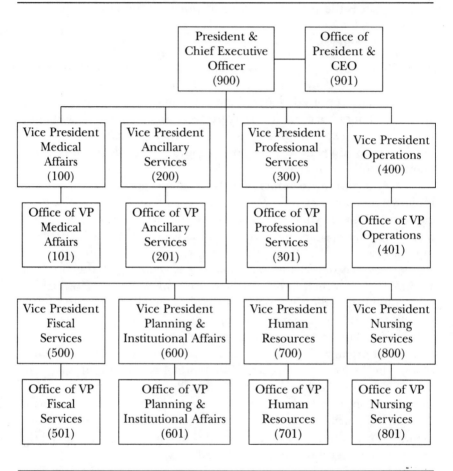

Major Cost Center	Regular Cost Account	
900 Level 1	901	Office of president and chief executive officer
100 Level 2	101	Office of vice president, Medical Affairs
200 Level 2	201	Office of vice president, Ancillary Services
300 Level 2	301	Office of vice president, Professional Services
400 Level 2	401	Office of vice president, Operations

Continued

Figure 8.1 Continued

500 Level 2	501	Office of vice president, Fiscal Services
600 Level 2	601	Office of vice president, Planning & Institutional Affairs
700 Level 2	701	Office of vice president, Human Resources
800 Level 2	801	Office of vice president, Nursing Services

Figure 8.2 also depicted the five major cost centers (codes 270, 272, 274, 276, and 278) and the respective five regular cost accounts (codes 271, 273, 275, 277, and 279). The actual salaries for physical therapist, occupational therapist, and speech therapist are charged to the regular cost accounts with a title beginning with "office of supervisor." Master cost center 272 (manager of Physical Medicine) consists of the aggregation of one regular cost account (273) and three major cost centers (274 + 276 + 278), as noted in Figure 8.2. In this example, all the three-digit cost center codes in the hospital's therapy area have been assigned to regular cost accounts and major cost centers. Many health care facilities have expanded to a four-digit cost center code, which permits more cost center codes for management planning and control purposes.

The major organizational units under the vice president of Ancillary Services (cost code 200 in Figure 8.1) further illustrate the distinction between regular cost accounts and major cost centers. There are seven major cost centers in the ancillary area at organizational level 3 that are aggregated into major cost center 200 for the vice president of Ancillary Services:

210	Level 3	Chair, Department of Pathology
250	Level 3	Chair, Department of Radiology
260	Level 3	Director, Diabetes Center
265	Level 3	Director, Evaluation Center
270	Level 3	Director, Physical Medicine & Rehabilitation Services
280	Level 3	Director, Respiratory Physiology
290	Level 3	Director, Pharmacy

The regular cost account 201 for the office of vice president, Ancillary Services, at organizational level 2 is also aggregated into the reporting cost center 200.

Figure 8.2   Demonstration Memorial Hospital: Department of
Physical Medicine & Rehabilitation Services—Major Cost
Centers and Regular Cost Accounts

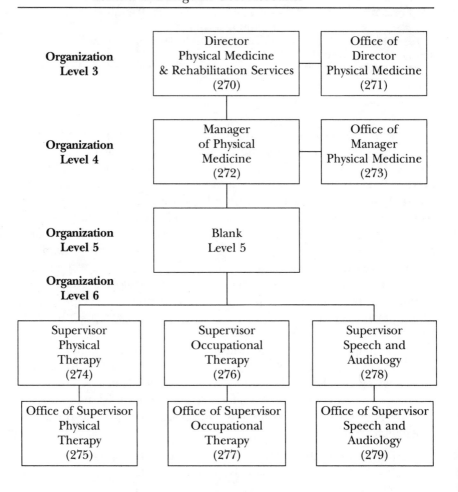

Each of the seven major cost centers in the ancillary department aggregated into code 200 is supported by a regular cost account and one or more major cost centers. For example, major cost center 210 for the chair, Department of Pathology, consists of the regular cost account 211 for office of the chair, Department of Pathology, plus two organizational level 4 major cost centers: 212 (manager of Laboratories) and 244 (manager of Blood Center).

Exhibit 8.1 shows these seven major cost centers in ancillary services that are aggregated into organizational level 2's major cost center 200. The major cost centers and regular cost accounts that are aggregated into these level 3 cost centers in ancillary services are also presented in Exhibit 8.1. Thus, regular cost accounts are summarized into major cost centers at each and every level of the organizational structure, with the detailed data stored in the DBMS for purposes of capturing the overall expenditures for a period.

Direct Cost of a Patient Service

Measuring the direct cost of a patient service is not a simple process because multiple regular cost accounts participate in admitting or registering a patient, scheduling the patient services, providing the patient services, and accounting and collecting for those services. The major cost center, or group of major cost centers, providing the patient services recognizes all the revenues from the episode, and all of the other major cost centers are classified as *support cost centers.* At the end of the fiscal period, the combined cost of the support cost centers are assigned and matched with the *revenue cost centers* in determining operating income from these patient services.

The cost-accounting procedures followed with revenue and support cost centers have been well developed in industrial enterprise for more than 40 years; however, because of the reimbursement arrangements under Medicare, standard cost-accounting procedures were not followed in hospitals from 1965 to 1984. With the full implementation of the prospective payment system for Medicare inpatients, the full gamut of cost-accounting procedures are now being applied to health care facilities for management planning and control purposes.

Many individuals are surprised in their initial exposure to cost accounting because of misconceptions about the term "cost." Some individuals expect the cost of patient service to be the same regardless of whether the computation is to support a marginal decision, a short-term pricing decision, or a long-term contract. But such uniformity of computations is not possible for different decision-making purposes. The relevant definition of health care costs is specified by the context and the environment, and any precise statement of health care costs must include a statement of the framework or environment associated with this measurement of expenditures for some defined purpose. A

Exhibit 8.1   Demonstration Memorial Hospital: Seven Major Cost Centers in Ancillary Services, Organizational Level 3

---

210   Chair, Department of Pathology
    211* Level 3 Office of the chair, Department of Pathology
    212   Level 4 Manager of Laboratories
    244   Level 4 Manager of Blood Center

250   Chair, Department of Radiology
    251* Level 3 Office of the chair, Department of Radiology
    252   Level 4 Supervisor, Diagnostic Radiology
    254   Level 4 Supervisor, Radiation Therapy
    256   Level 4 Supervisor, Nuclear Medicine

260   Director, Diabetes Center
    261* Level 3 Office of the director, Diabetes Center
    262   Level 4 Manager, Diabetes Center

265   Director, Evaluation Center
    266* Level 3 Office of the director, Evaluation Center
    267   Level 4 Manager, Evaluation Center

270   Director, Physical Medicine and Rehabilitation Services
    271* Level 3 Office of the director, Physical Medicine &
                      Rehabilitation Services
    272   Level 4 Manager, Physical Medicine
    273* Level 4 Office, manager of Physical Medicine
    274   Level 6 Supervisor, Physical Therapy
    276   Level 6 Supervisor, Occupational Therapy
    278   Level 6 Supervisor, Speech and Audiology

280   Director, Respiratory Physiology
    281* Level 3 Office of the director, Respiratory Physiology
    282   Level 4 Manager, Respiratory Physiology
    284   Level 6 Supervisor, Respiratory Therapy

290   Director, Pharmacy
    291* Level 3 Office of the director, Pharmacy
    292   Level 4 Manager, Pharmacy
    294   Level 4 Manager, Purchasing and Inventory Control

---

*Indicates a regular cost account.

fundamental concept of cost accounting is that *there are different costs, using the same database, for various management planning and control purposes.*

In looking at the cost of the delivery of a health care service, the term "cost" constitutes a measurement of expenditure directly associated with providing a given health care service. This expenditure may have been paid in a previous period, paid in the current period, or estimated to be paid in a future period, but the cost of an item always constitutes a measurement of an expenditure. Saying that the cost of a health care service is a measurement of an expenditure is not a complete definition; there are four specific assumptions that must be addressed in a framework of determining the cost of a health care service:

- What is the time period associated with this cost measure?
- What are the capacity assumptions of fixed assets and the expected utilization range of resources employed in creating the unit?
- What are the volume assumptions associated with the unit? Is it an average cost for some assumed relevant range of output? Or is it a marginal cost for moving from one level of output to the next level?
- What is the management or administrative purpose for which this cost per unit is to be determined? Within each cost element (such as direct labor, direct materials, indirect labor, contracted services, overhead, etc.), the planning, control, and administrative purpose will be identified with different applicable measures.

The cost per service for pricing purposes is different from the cost per service for management control purposes. The cost per service for long-range planning purposes may be different from the cost per service for short-term pricing purposes. Different costs may be determined for the various objectives or purposes for which the health care entity's administration desires to measure activity.

This same multidimensional issue can be expressed as a requirement for specifying parameters (such as time period, capacity, volume, and management purpose) *before* a frame of reference can be associated with the process of determining the assigned cost of a unit produced or a health care service provided. Alternatively, it can be stated that the assigned cost of a patient service or a product is a construct that assumes its meaning from the administrative purpose and specified parameters identified with a given analysis.

Cost measurement framework

This framework of cost is applicable to all cost determination efforts: What is the purpose? What is the capacity? What is the volume? What is the time period? Other parameters are added to this framework in more complex patient care settings.

Demonstration Memorial Hospital is considering establishing a screening and testing clinic in a nearby shopping center. A local real-estate broker has proposed that the hospital rent a recently closed medical office facility that has appropriate waiting room and office furniture.

The annual rent for the facility, including utilities, is $24,000. Salaries of a nurse and an assistant are $43,600 per year, and the fringe benefits are $7,400 per year. The screening and testing equipment costs $300,000 and has an engineering life of fifteen years, but it is estimated to have a six-year technological life. With annual depreciation of $60,000 for the equipment, the annual support costs are $135,000 (Table 8.1).

There are two types of variable costs that will be incurred with each patient at the screening and testing clinic. First, there are supplies, costing $2 per patient, that are used with each set of tests. Second, the physician review of the results by a medical group is $7 per patient.

Advocates of the proposed screening and testing facility believe that 24 patients can be processed each day (one shift) and that after

Table 8.1 Demonstration Memorial Hospital: Proposed Screening and Testing Clinic—Annual Cost per Service

| | *Annual Volume* | | | | | |
	4,800	*4,000*	*3,600*	*3,000*	*2,000*	*1,500*
Medical review	$ 33,600	$ 28,000	$ 25,200	$ 21,000	$ 14,000	$ 10,500
Supplies	9,600	8,000	7,200	6,000	4,000	3,000
Total variable	*$ 43,200*	*$ 36,000*	*$ 32,400*	*$ 27,000*	*$ 18,000*	*$ 13,500*
Annual rent	$ 24,000	$ 24,000	$ 24,000	$ 24,000	$ 24,000	$ 24,000
Salaries	43,600	43,600	43,600	43,600	43,600	43,600
Fringe benefits	7,400	7,400	7,400	7,400	7,400	7,400
Depreciation	60,000	60,000	60,000	60,000	60,000	60,000
Total support	*$135,000*	*$135,000*	*$135,000*	*$135,000*	*$135,000*	*$135,000*
Total cost	*$178,200*	*$171,000*	*$167,400*	*$162,000*	*$153,000*	*$148,500*
Average cost	*$37.13*	*$42.75*	*$46.50*	*$54.00*	*$76.50*	*$99.00*

adjusting for holidays, vacations, and maintenance of the equipment, the facility will be open for 200 days per year and process 4,800 patients. If the volume of 4,800 patients is reached, the variable cost is $43,200, which combined with the support cost of $135,000 gives a total direct cost of $178,200 that is traced to this cost center, or an average cost of $37.13 per patient (see Table 8.1).

Critics of the proposed screening and testing facility accept the 200 days per year as a base, but do not believe that appropriate adjustments have been made in the number of tests per day for late arrivals and patients failing to show on the scheduled day; some patients may elect to go to a competing clinic after tentatively scheduling to use the hospital's facility. Some critics feel that a 200-day average of 15 tests, or 3,000 per year, is an optimistic goal. The last line in Table 8.1 shows the average annual cost per patient service under a range of volumes (from $37.13 to $99.00 per patient service).

What is the average cost per patient service? If advancements in technology were to require the equipment to be replaced in 36 months in order to stay competitive, would that affect the average cost per patient service? If a health maintenance organization agrees to send 500 patients a year to the screening and testing facility, would that affect the average cost per patient service?

The six average annual costs per service in Table 8.1 are each correct computations for a set of assumptions. The economic life of the medical equipment and its technology certainly affects the average cost; this investment must be recovered as it is matched with the patient service revenues from using the equipment. Capacity, volume, and time period in the cost framework are addressed by these comments; the purpose of the cost is the other dimension. The average cost for regular pricing considerations is different from the position taken with the HMO with a proposed contract for 500 patients per year.

Costs follows revenue

The cost framework affects the statement of revenue and expenses only when the expired costs are associated with the generation of revenue. A realization concept is followed that revenue is recognized under accrual-accounting procedures when the patient services are provided. The timing of the cash payment for those services is not relevant in determining when the patient service revenue is to be reported. Thus, if the patient services have been rendered, they are reported as patient service revenues in that same fiscal period. Once the realization concept has been satisfied, then all expired costs and expenses associated with the creation of those revenues are matched against these returns and reported on the same statement of revenue and expenses. There is no general theory of cost accounting, but there is a general theory of revenue recognition with the follow-up specification that costs follow revenue.

The application of this framework and the general theory to a health care entity can be seen in the cost accounting for a laboratory test performed by an automatic chemical analyzer (Exhibit 8.2). This sophisticated clinical laboratory equipment contains a small computer with a printer and is capable of performing a wide range of chemical analyses in a timely manner.

The automatic chemical analyzer may have an engineering life of twelve years, but technological changes are occurring at such a rapid rate that the expected life during which the hospital can economically use the equipment under competitive conditions may be only six years or less. The published depreciation schedules by the federal government permit a life of five years for this type of laboratory equipment in determining income tax (if applicable) or in determining reimbursement from a federal program (such as the non-DRG part of Medicare). The professional accountant will then use the five-year life as the time period over which to match the depreciation expense against revenue in preparing external financial statements.

There are 9,000 nonbilled tests in Exhibit 8.2 that are not included in the denominator for computing depreciation expense per test. Since costs follow revenue, it is inappropriate to assign any expense to the 9,000 nonbilled tests for certified financial statement purposes. However, the health care entity may want to measure opportunity costs and quality control expenses; in these cases, the 9,000 tests are important factors.

The average cost of salaries per test for technologists and laboratory assistants and supplies required for using the clinical equipment is determined in the same manner, with the 91,000 billed tests serving as the denominator in each calculation. The technologists and laboratory assistants will perform other tests in the laboratory not associated with the automatic chemical analyzer; thus, in computing the numerator in the measurement of average salaries per test, it is necessary to separate efforts associated with the 91,000 billed tests versus efforts associated with all other tests and activities.

[handwritten annotation: Denominator for each equation]

Exhibit 8.2   Cost of Service from Automatic Chemical Analyzer

Assume the following about the automatic chemical analyzer:

- Purchase price, including installation services, is $45,500.

- Estimated salvage value of the equipment at the end of the five year life will exactly offset the cost of removing the automatic chemical analyzer from the laboratory.

- The estimated time period is five years.

- The engineering capacity of the automatic chemical analyzer is 1,000,000 tests per year; however, the health care entity does not have the demand for that volume of test within its service area.

- The health care entity expects 100,000 tests to be physically performed on the automatic chemical analyzer during the first year, including 91,000 billed to patients. Details are as follows:

	Tests
Quality control tests for the equipment	4,000
Repeat tests using same specimen	2,500
Environmental control tests performed for the health care entity	500
Courtesy and administrative tests	2,000
Patient-billed tests	91,000
Estimated annual tests for year one	*100,000*

With these facts, the historical or acquisition cost of the asset less salvage value is depreciated over the five-year life. Thus, the cost of $45,500 divided by five years gives an annual depreciation expense under the straight-line depreciation method of $9,100 ($45,500/5 = $9,100 per year).

Using the accounting concept that costs follow revenue, the 91,000 tests estimated to be performed and billed to patients during year 19X2 will serve as the *denominator* in determining the average cost of a test for cost assignment purposes. Since the annual depreciation expense is $9,100 and there are 91,000 billed tests, the assigned depreciation charge per billed test is $0.10 ($9,100/91,000 billed tests = $0.10 per test).

In this example, consideration has been given to the direct labor, supplies, and assigned cost of equipment in computing the average cost of a test performed on an automatic chemical analyzer. In addition to these direct costs, the salaries of supervisory personnel and fees of pathologists must be included with other indirect costs and matched with benefits for most management purposes. Depending on the management purpose, a portion of the general and administrative overhead for the health care entity may be appropriate to include in this analysis. As the relevant expenditures included in the numerator are changed for different management purposes, a different value will be calculated for the average cost of a laboratory test.

Classification of Costs

Many adjectives are used with the term "cost" to designate some generally accepted assumptions regarding the four dimensions of the specified framework—time period, capacity assumptions, volume assumptions, and management or administrative purpose. Some adjectives used with the term "cost" have conflicting meanings, depending on the user group. Brief attention is given to some of these generally accepted meanings in the context of health care entities.

Direct costs versus indirect costs

Those expenditures that can be traced to a specific organizational unit or to a specific health care service are designated as *direct costs* of that unit or service. A cost is traceable to a regular cost center if the expenditure is incurred entirely to support one or more activities in that cost center. The adjective "direct" in reference to cost means that there is an obvious matching of the expenditure with some event or activity. Although all four dimensions in the above framework provide structure to the measurement of direct cost, the relevant range of the volume assumptions in this framework must be explicitly known before the measurement of direct costs can begin. Those expenditures or cost equivalents that are loosely associated (as distinct from precisely matched) with the occurrence of an event or activity are designated as *indirect costs* of that unit or service.

All the cost data in Table 8.1 are classified as direct because these expenditures were incurred entirely to support the cost center for the screening and testing facility. In the case of the automatic chemical analyzer, the labor of the technologist and the laboratory assistant who perform a test, along with the supplies required for conducting the test, are direct costs of that test. Supervisory and clerical support for the test are indirect costs under the usual conditions in which these overhead services are performed in health care entities.

Fixed costs versus variable costs

Some expenditures are directly associated with a period of time or with a specified volume of services; other expenditures increase proportionally with changes in the volume of services. Those expenditures that are constant for a period of time or for a relevant range of services are designated as *fixed costs.* Those expenditures that directly respond to the units of health care service are designated as *variable costs.* As will be discussed in the next section, many expenditures are semifixed or semivariable in their behavior over a relevant range of activity, and this complexity is especially applicable to expenditures in health care entities.

Marginal costs versus average costs

The term "marginal" implies an incremental analysis: What is the impact of one additional service or health care activity? The *marginal cost* is that incremental expenditure required at a given moment in time for one additional service or unit. Whether the marginal cost is relatively high or low is a function of the status of utilization of fixed cost at a given moment in time when an incremental assessment is performed. An average is the opposite of incremental analysis: What expenditures on a per unit basis will support the occurrence of a specified aggregation of services? The measurement of an *average cost* requires specifications in all four dimensions of the cost framework: time period, capacity assumptions, volume assumptions, and management or administrative purpose.

In the case of the laboratory where 91,000 chargeable tests are performed on an annual basis and where the equipment is capable of handling a multiple of that volume (Exhibit 8.2), the marginal cost of that increment of going from 91,000 to 91,001 tests is extremely low. In fact, the direct labor may not even be sensitive to such a small increment, and the direct supplies may be the only marginal expenditure. The critical question in the use of marginal cost is, What is the purpose of this analysis or calculation? Marginal cost considerations are only valid in very short-term situations where there are no known long-term repercussions from using incremental analyses.

Controllable costs versus noncontrollable costs

Expenditures that are under the jurisdiction of a decision maker are designated as *controllable costs* if the individual has the choice whether to incur the said expenditures. Delegation of authority, with the incumbent reporting requirements of responsibility accounting, is often associated with formal arrangements for handling controllable costs. If the decision maker does not have the authority to incur an expenditure associated with a given service or organizational unit, then that expenditure is a *noncontrollable cost.* A higher organizational level may have mandated short-term staffing is not compatible with the actual volume requirements of a responsibility unit. The expenditures associated with this excess staffing are a noncontrollable cost from the standpoint of that organizational unit.

Assigned costs versus allocated costs

Expenditures that are traced in an explicit manner to an organizational unit or health care service were designated as direct costs. If the traced expenditures are mapped with benefits based on utilization experience, then these direct costs are also designated as *assigned costs.* In the case of indirect costs, the expenditures could only be loosely mapped against benefits in an organizational unit or health care service. If utilization statistics were accumulated for handling the mapping of these indirect costs, then these expenditures are referred to as assigned costs. On the other hand, if estimated data are used to support this mapping process, then such expenditures are designated as *allocated costs.* From a conceptual standpoint, it is clear whether or not a health care organization has accumulated utilization statistics for performing a mapping of costs with benefits; such distinctions are not always followed in health care practice. It is not uncommon to find reported assigned costs, upon further scrutiny, to really be allocated costs.

Common costs versus joint costs

There are many situations in health care institutions where it is economically preferable to share secretarial, clerical, administrative, and technical services among two or more departments rather than having full support services within each department. These administratively created organizational units for sharing of support services can be a *common cost center* if all the expenditures charged to that center are for these support services. A single information desk in a health care institution may support inpatients, outpatients, scheduled patients, and visitors; the expenses associated with staffing this information desk are designated as *common costs.*

Within a health care entity there are often administrative modules or cost centers that provide common support to two or more departments. If all the administrative efforts within a cost center are directly associated with providing these common support services, then the total costs of that center are referred to as common costs. From an accounting standpoint, it is easier to handle expenditures that are designated as common costs by specifying a separate cost center for this single purpose.

A common cost, in the context of a health care organization, is usually associated with an administratively created cost-accounting unit that accumulates expenditures associated with support services benefiting two or more departments. A distinction is made between common costs that are created for management control purposes versus common costs that are incurred by regular support centers (explained in Chapters 10 and 12).   *They ÷ cost out.*

Joint costs are common costs that support two or more revenue centers. A small hospital might have an administrative support center that provides secretarial and clerical assistance to the hematology section of a laboratory and to the blood bank at the hospital. There are regulatory requirements for separating laboratory operations from blood bank processing operations; therefore, the blood bank and the laboratory are separate revenue centers, even if they are located in the same physical area. Thus, expenditures for these common support services are joint costs.

In many health care entities there is a sharing of services between the blood-gas section of the laboratory and the related activities in the pulmonary function area. If extensive sharing of services is going to occur, then it is easier from a cost-accounting standpoint to establish a separate cost center for these joint costs.

A medical clinic where all new patients are examined by a physician represents a joint cost center that supports the five or six therapy centers in the clinic. The registration and administrative cost incurred by the new patient's initial visit with a physician should be shared with each of the therapy revenue centers that will be treating the patient.

Patterns of Cost Behavior

Fixed costs were defined as expenditures traceable to a given organizational unit or service that are constant for a period of time or for a relevant range of service. Implicit within this definition of fixed costs are some assumptions about the expected use of long-term resources in the health care institution. Specifically, the fixed costs represent the systematic assignment of part of a major expenditure to a time period for the purpose of matching the utilization of the services provided by the major expenditure against the benefits received during the period. Limiting the fixed costs in a period to part of a major expenditure is based on the assumption that the health care entity's administration has a long-term commitment to employ this major resource in generating revenue for the organization. Depreciation expense and a long-term lease agreement are examples of fixed costs. Figure 8.3 presents the cost curve for a fixed cost constant in dollar amount within some relevant range of activity, regardless of any change in volume.

Figure 8.3   Fixed Cost Curve: An Annual Fixed Cost of $120,000

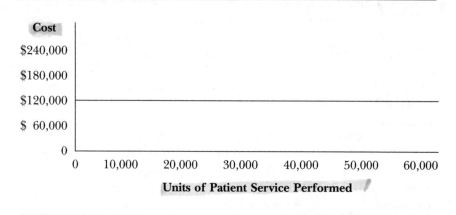

Note: The annual depreciation charge is constant at $120,000 in the relevant range of patient services performed.

Variable costs are expenditures that increase proportionally with changes in volume of services or level of activity. Unlike fixed costs, there are no long-term resource utilization assumptions implicit within the concept of variable costs. Direct labor (especially where the employment is part-time and on an hourly basis) can be an example of a variable cost under given conditions. Figure 8.4 presents the cost curve for a variable cost.

Figure 8.4   Variable Cost Curve: An Annual Variable Cost of $4 per Service

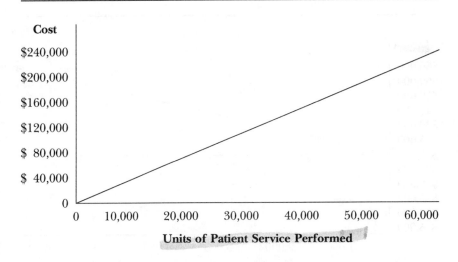

Note: If the cost and service units are on the same proportional scale, then the $4 variable cost line will be a 45° angle.

Fixed costs and variable costs are the two end positions on a continuum; many health care expenditures fall between these end-points. Two intermediate locations on this continuum are described as semivariable costs and semifixed costs.

A *semivariable cost* is an assigned value that has the combined characteristics of a variable component and a fixed component. Once a full-time employee is hired, there is the fixed cost of that staff member. If a second employee is hired on a part-time basis, as required, then the labor cost of the second employee will vary proportionally with needs, requirements, or volume. Figure 8.5 presents a semivariable cost curve expressing the combination of these two employees; there is a fixed component or base (for the first employee) and a variable component that increases in activity (for the second employee).

A *semifixed cost* is an assigned value that is constant for some intermediate range of activity, but then increases by a step or layer for the next intermediate range of activity. If there is a small staff and only full-time personnel are employed, then the total personnel cost may tend to be indicative of a semifixed cost. Figure 8.6 shows a

Figure 8.5   Semivariable Cost Curve: First Employee's Annual Salary
Is $30,000; Second Employee Is Paid $5 per Service
Performed

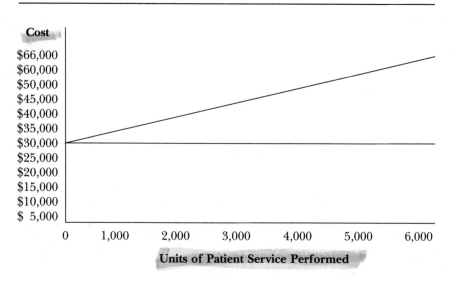

semifixed cost where each full-time employee can handle 15,000 units
of service; a second employee must be hired for the range of 15,001
to 30,000; a third employee must be hired for the range of 30,001 to
45,000; and so on.

A flexible budgeting model supported by a computer-based system can quickly present detailed assigned costs applicable to a given
volume of health care service. Layers of semifixed costs can be incorporated into the flexible budgeting model so that the pattern of fixed
cost increase is like Figure 8.6. But in this type of setting, it is more
common to have some semivariable cost (such as labor) occurring at
the same time there is a semifixed cost curve (such as equipment).
The combined cost curve (Figure 8.7) is more indicative of the typical
hospital's cost for routine care, where semifixed costs represent the
opening of wards or wings in the hospital and where the semivariable costs represent the nursing component (both part-time and full-
time personnel).

The medical and health care services provided to a given inpatient vary depending on many factors (for example, the medical
reason for admission to the hospital, the type of treatment given,

Figure 8.6 Semifixed Cost Curve: Annual Salary of Each Employee
Is \$30,000; Each Employee Can Handle 15,000 Services
on New Equipment

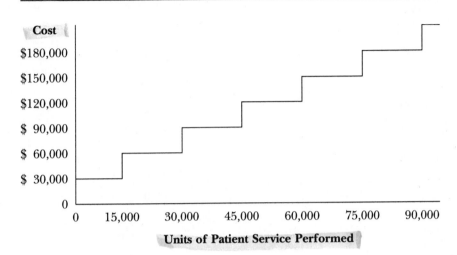

which physician is providing the treatment, the age of the patient, the
sex of the patient, whether there are complications in the patient's
condition). All of these factors (examined in subsequent analyses)
influence the number of days of care provided to inpatients over a
year. There are frequent shifts in some of these factors over time;
other factors appear to have had a constant influence during the past
few years.

The flexible budgeting model must have the capability to determine the estimated cost under a variety of conditions and changes
in patient profiles if it is to be helpful to hospital administrators.
Other aspects of the cost curves in these flexible budgeting models will
be deferred until *after* the cost accumulation procedures for external
reports and cost accounting for management control are considered
in Chapters 10 and 12.

Equivalent Units of Service

Each regular cost center may incur direct labor, professional fees,
contractual services, supplies, and other expenses, depending on the

Figure 8.7   Combined Cost Curve: Routine Care Cost with Semifixed
Cost of Wings and with Semivariable Cost of Nursing

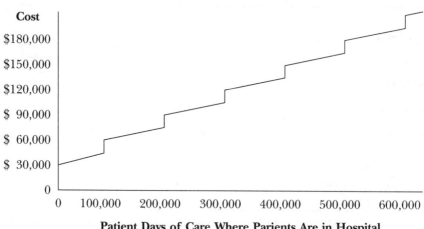

**Patient Days of Care Where Parients Are in Hospital
for a Specified Length of Stay for a Common Treatment**

budget approvals. These aggregate expenditures incurred by a regular cost center during a fiscal period permit some activities or services to be accomplished in accordance with the annual plan. But many activities or services may be only partially performed, and possibly never completed. A cost center that provides a treatment requiring four patient visits may have only 90 percent of its patients making all four visits, and the other patients discontinuing the treatment at different points in the program. The measurement of cost per service or per activity requires a determination of how many defined services are not completed and how much effort was extended to those uncompleted units.

Figure 8.8 presents two regular cost centers that jointly support a five-part treatment program where $164,000 of combined costs were incurred. The five-part treatment is typically performed on two successive days; the first three parts are performed on the first day in cost center A, and the fourth and fifth parts of the treatment are performed on the second day in cost center B. The treatment is a medical necessity for patients with a given diagnosis, and some patients needing this treatment will use false names and depart during the five-part treatment without paying for any services. There are other hospitals in

Figure 8.8 Five-Part Treatment Program by Two Related Cost Centers: Patient Visits and Cost Data

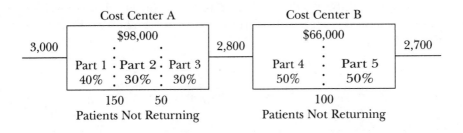

this metropolitan area that are experiencing this loss of revenue from patients providing false information when receiving this treatment.

There were 3,000 patients who began the treatment program in cost center A, but 150 patients departed before the start of the second part of the treatment program. After completing the second part of the program, 50 of the patients departed without participating in the third part of the treatment in cost center A. All the patients who completed the third part of the treatment returned on the next day for the fourth part of the program, but 100 patients departed before the start of the final part in cost center B. In summary, 2,700 of the 3,000 patients who began the two-day treatment completed the program; no revenues are ever received from departing patients in this hospital's service area.

The three parts of the treatment in cost center A use equal amounts of health care services after administrative efforts representing 10 percent of the total were spent in the first part; thus, the distribution for the three parts in cost center A was 40, 30, and 30 percent. There was an equal division of effort between the two parts in cost center B. Assume that all expenses are consumed proportionally among parts within cost centers A and B.

Equivalent unit

The concept of an "equivalent unit" in cost accounting implies an output orientation for the health care entity in terms of good units. The inputs to an organizational unit are important only to the extent that there is a requirement of accountability. Cost center A in Figure 8.8 had 3,000 patients who began the treatment program (or 3,000 inputs); there were no patients in progress at the beginning or end of the fiscal period. There were 2,800 patients who completed the three parts of treatment on the first day, and there were 200 "lost units," or patients who departed during the first day of the program in cost center A. In Exhibit 8.3 these 200 lost units are converted to equivalent units based on the degree of effort extended to each before the patient decided to depart.

Exhibit 8.3   Treatment Program by Two Related Cost Centers: Equivalent Unit Calculations

	Cost Center A	Cost Center B
Units started, completed, and transferred out	2,800	2,700
Lost units after Part 1	60 (150 × 40%)	
Lost units after Part 2	35 (50 × 70%)	
Lost units after Part 4		50 (100 × 50%)
Total equivalent units	*2,895*	*2,750*

Lost unit

In calculating the lost-unit costs in cost center A, the 150 patients who departed after receiving 40 percent of the composite effort are considered to be 60 (150 × 40 percent) equivalent units with a total assigned cost of $2,031.00 (see Exhibit 8.4 for computations). The 50 patients not returning after the second part of the treatment are the same as 35 (50 × 70 percent) equivalent units with an assigned cost of $1,184.75.

The cost accounting for the lost units in cost center A is influenced by the 10 percent administrative efforts within the cost center. If the registration of patients were in a different cost center, the 200 lost units in cost center A, with an assigned cost of $3,215.75, would be charged to the cost center handling the registration. The 100 lost units in cost center B have a higher per unit assigned cost because of the transfer-in cost of $35.00 from cost center B; the total assigned cost for the 100 units is $4,700 (Exhibit 8.4).

Where the cost center handles the patient registration, the hospital follows the policy of charging all the lost unit costs to that area. As indicated in Exhibit 8.4, the $164,000 incurred during the fiscal period

Exhibit 8.4   Treatment Program by Two Related Cost Centers: Lost-Unit Cost Calculations

---

Average cost of services performed in cost center A per equivalent unit is $98,000 divided by 2,895 equivalent units, or *$33.85* per patient.

Average prior–cost center costs equals $98,000 divided by 2,800 patients who participated in the fourth part, or *$35.00* per patient.

Average cost of services performed in cost center B per equivalent unit is $66,000 divided by 2,750 equivalent units, or *$24.00* per patient.

Average cost of services performed in cost center B plus transferred in cost is $35.00 plus $24.00, equals *$59.00* per equivalent unit.

Average cost per complete treatment equals $164,000 ($98,000 plus $66,000) divided by 2,700 patients, gives *$60.74* per treatment.

Lost-unit cost in cost center A:
150 units × 40% × $33.85	$2,031.00
50 units × 70% × $33.85	1,184.75
Total assigned cost of 200 lost units	*$3,215.75*

Average lost unit cost for each good unit
2,800 good units: $3,215.75/2,800 = $1.14848, or	*$1.15 per good unit*
Proof: $35.00 − $33.85 = $1.15	

Lost-unit cost in cost center B:
100 lost units × $35.00 prior–cost center cost ×100%	$3,500.00
100 units × 50% × $24.00	1,200.00
Total assigned cost of 100 lost units	*$4,700.00*

Average lost-unit for each good unit:
2,700 good units: $4,700.00/2,700 = $1.7407407, or	*$1.74 per good unit*
Proof: $60.74 − $59.00 = $1.74	

---

is assigned to the 2,700 good units, with an average cost of $60.74 per patient completing the treatment program.

Summary

A cost pool is any organizational unit or subunit within the health care entity for which detailed expenditure, utilization, and budget data are required for some decision-making purpose. Each cost pool is identified by a unique code that is compatible with the code structure for the cost accumulation system. Regular cost accounts are the cost pools that are used for expenditure control purposes. After expenditure monitoring and management control have been achieved, then expenditure, utilization, and budget data in regular cost accounts are transferred and assigned to major cost centers—a second type of cost pool. The third type of cost pool is for those organizational units performing special analyses that require retrieval of diverse information from various regular cost accounts and major cost centers.

What is the cost of a given health care service? There are many "correct" answers to this question, depending on the management purpose and the context (time period, capacity, and volume). Without knowing the purpose and context, it is not proper to attempt to measure the cost of a given health care service. This is the meaning of a fundamental concept of cost accounting—there are different costs, using the same database, for various management planning and control purposes.

The cost accumulation system captures transaction data by the natural classification of accounts for each regular cost account, and these transaction data are specified by the organizational unit with the initial responsibility for incurring the expenditure, the nature of the accounting entry, and the periodicity of the data. Major cost centers are organizational units that cannot initially incur any expenditures, but these organizational units may receive cost transfers, cost assignments, and cost allocations from other cost accounts and cost centers. A major cost center may be at one or more organizational levels above the regular cost accounts that are assigned to it; the major exception to this organizational level statement is the regular cost account for the office of the manager or administrator of the major cost center.

The boundaries of a regular cost account should be specified so that it fully captures some activity, operation, product, or service. In those cases where the regular cost account is less than the boundaries of the patient service, the matching of costs and revenues will occur at a higher organizational level created by combining the regular cost accounts that comprise the components of that patient service.

The typical patient receives medical and health care services from professional and technical personnel representing several regular cost centers. Therefore, it is a complex effort to determine the direct cost of providing a patient service. Advancements in medical practice and technology may affect the cost accumulation to such an extent that major revisions are required in the specification of regular cost accounts within the health care entity from the traditional structure primarily followed for Medicare cost reimbursement reports. There must be a way of matching the regular cost accounts to the typical mix of patient services, including using common support costs and joint cost centers. The need for this matching capability of patient services with regular cost accounts is the focus of this chapter.

An equivalent unit is an output orientation of services provided by a cost center that should be matched with revenues. A fundamental concept of cost accounting is that costs follow revenue—what the matching process is all about. Equivalent units are required in the measurement efforts for relating bundles or sets of services to the revenue flow. A laboratory test to calibrate equipment before processing a large set of patient tests is not included in the base of equivalent units. There is no revenue associated with the calibration efforts; thus, only the billable tests are aggregated in the equivalent units of output.

Appendix: Selecting the Equivalent Unit

Each cost center provides a service or activity central to the organizational unit's objective, and there are alternative ways to measure volumes of services or activities. Specifying one alternative method versus another for expressing the common dimensions of those services does not change the overall results in assigning costs to bundles of activities based on a calculation of equivalent units and relating the total expenses to those equivalent units. It is important, however, that there has been sufficient analysis to determine the common dimensions of those services; otherwise, erroneous results can be calculated. If components of a treatment program are unequal, then the complete program must be the equivalent unit unless the components can be subdivided into a homogenous measure such as tests, procedures, operations, or time.

The specification of an equivalent unit is by organizational unit, and the selection of a meaningful measure is entirely from the context of that cost center's activities or services. If a treatment requires services from two or more cost centers, the definition of an equivalent unit can be different in each cost center, but a bridge is required for relating the output from one cost center to the inputs for the next cost center within the treatment program for overall analysis.

Figure 8.9 illustrates a treatment program requiring two visits; a two-step procedure is applied in each of the two related cost centers. Patients are billed at the beginning of each visit, and an adjustment is made if the patient departs before completing each phase of the treatment. In this example there are no lost units since patients are

Figure 8.9   Four-Part Treatment Program by Two Related Cost
Centers: Patient Visits and Cost Data

	Cost Center A				Cost Center B		
4,000	$167,450 • Part 1 : Part 2 60% : 40%		3,850	3,725	$192,920 • Part 3 : Part 4 70% : 30%		3,675
	150 patients		125 patients		50 patients		

Cost to be explained in cost center A	*$167,450.00*
Equivalent units in cost center A:	
3,850 units plus 60% of 150 units not continuing (60% × 150 = 90), or *3,940 EUs* (3,850 + 90 = 3,940)	
Assigned cost per equivalent unit in cost center A:	
$167,450/3,940 EUs = *$42.50*	
The 3,725 units who continued in Part 3	$158,312.50
The 125 units who did not continue in Part 3	5,312.50
The 150 units who stopped after Part 1 and are representative of 90 equivalent units (60% × 150)	3,825.00
Total cost in cost center A	*$167,450.00*
Cost to be explained in cost center B	*$192,920.00*
Equivalent units in cost center B:	
3,675 units plus 70% of 50 units not continuing (70% × 50 = 35), or *3,710 EUs* (3,675 + 35 = 3,710)	
Assigned cost per equivalent unit in cost center B:	
$192,920/3,710 EUs = *$52.00*	
The 3,675 units who completed the treatment program	$191,100.00
The 50 units who stopped after Part 3 and are representative of 35 equivalent units (70% × 50)	1,820.00
Total cost in cost center B	*$192,920.00*

billed proportionally for each part of the treatment; however, there are lost charges or bad debts because of stolen credit cards or other false documents used in the payment process.

The defined set of procedures for each patient within a cost center is an equivalent unit. Thus, in cost center A of Figure 8.9, an equivalent unit is completing both part 1 and part 2 in the treatment program. Part 1 represents 60 percent of the effort, and part 2 is the remaining 40 percent of the service. If a patient does not continue in the program after completing part 1, then the services to that patient constitute 60 percent of an equivalent unit for cost center A.

The treatment program continues in cost center B; part 3 represents 70 percent of the effort, and part 4 is the remaining 30 percent of the service. If a patient does not continue in the program after completing part 3, then the services to that patient constitute 70 percent of an equivalent unit for cost center B.

During the current fiscal period, $167,450 of costs is incurred in cost center A, and $192,920 is incurred in cost center B. Figure 8.9 shows that 4,000 patients received part 1 of the treatment, but only 3,850 patients received part 2. The 150 patients who did not continue with part 2 are the same as 90 equivalent units (60% × 150 = 90 equivalent units). The total cost incurred in cost center A ($167,450) divided by the total equivalent units receiving these services (3,940 equivalent units) gives an assigned cost of $42.50 per unit. Using this $42.50 as the basis, the total assigned cost in cost center A is partitioned into the three groups of patients as follows:

3,725 patients who continued with treatment in part 3	$158,312.50
150 patients who discontinued treatment after completing part 1 (90 EUs)	3,825.00
125 patients who completed treatment in part 2 but elected not to continue in cost center B	5,312.50
Total cost incurred in cost center A	$167,450.00

The 3,725 patients who received part 3 of the treatment in cost center B included 50 patients who did not continue after part 3. The 3,675 patients who completed part 4 plus the 50 patients who stopped after part 3 represent 3,710 equivalent units (70% × 50 = 35 equivalent units). The total cost incurred in cost center B ($192,920) divided by the total equivalent units receiving these services (3,710 equivalent units) gives an assigned cost of $52.00 per unit. Using this $52.00 as the basis, the total assigned cost in cost center B is partitioned into the two groups of patients as follows:

3,675 patients who completed the treatment program	$191,100.00
50 patients who discontinued treatment after completing part 3 (35 EUs)	1,820.00
Total cost incurred in cost center B	$192,920.00

The measure of activity that is envisioned as an equivalent unit can be for example, a visit, a treatment, a patient episode, a test, or a procedure. *The measure that is selected as an equivalent unit must totally represent the services within the cost center under scrutiny.* Analysts may use different concepts of equivalent units for a cost center, but their findings should be compatible regardless of the equivalent unit definition being used. For example, assume there are three identical procedures within a given treatment and that 900 procedures were performed this month for 300 patients at a cost of $4,500. One analyst using "procedure" as the equivalent unit would determine that the cost per procedure was $5 and the cost per patient was $15. Another analyst using "treatment" as the equivalent unit would convert the 900 procedures into 300 treatments and determine the cost per treatment as $15.

Patients begin treatment programs on the date specified by their physicians, which may not coincide with the fiscal period. Thus, on the start of a fiscal period, there are usually some patients who are in progress in a given treatment program, and the prior period's cost must be matched against those in-progress efforts. After confronting large amounts of uncollectible accounts for outpatient services, many health care facilities attempt to collect before the services are rendered. The actual amount billed for a segment of service (especially the first segment) may include an overhead factor and a provision for bad debts. Billing by segments of a treatment program provides options for matching costs with revenues that are not available in billing by procedure or test.

Note

1. P. L. 95–142 (dated 25 October 1977) mandated a uniform accounting system for each type of health care facility. The Health Care Financing Administration issued the *System for Hospital Uniform Reporting* (29 September 1978) and the *Annual Hospital Report* (20 February 1980), in which detailed cost codes were prescribed. Implementation procedures for the *Annual Hospital Report* had been listed in the *Federal Register*, but the adoption of the prospective payment system for Medicare inpatients in 1983 coincided with the dropping of the uniform reporting requirements.

Additional Readings

Cleverly, W. O. "Product Costing for Health Care Firms," *Health Care Management Review* 12 (Fall 1987): 39–48.

Coddington, D. C., D. J. Keen, K. D. Moore, and R. L. Clarke. "Factors Driving Costs Must Figure into Reform," *Healthcare Financial Management* 45 (July 1991): 44–62.

Counte, M. A., and G. L. Glandon. "Managerial Innovation in the Hospital: An Analysis of the Diffusion of Hospital Cost-Accounting Systems," *Hospital & Health Services Administration* 33 (Fall 1988): 371–84.

Hogan, A. J., and R. Marshall. "How to Improve Allocation of Support Service Costs," *Healthcare Financial Management* 44 (February 1990): 42–52.

Kaskiw, E. A., P. Hanlon, and P. Wulf. "Cost Accounting in Health Care: Fad or Fundamental?" *Hospital & Health Services Administration* 32 (November 1987): 457–74.

Serway, G. D., D. W. Strum, and W. F. Haug. "Alternative Indicators for Measuring Hospital Productivity," *Hospital & Health Services Administration* 32 (August 1987): 379–98.

Discussion Questions

8.1.   What rules determine if costs of a service are to appear in a given year's statement of revenue and expenses or on the balance sheet?

8.2.   Explain the key dimensions of the cost measurement framework.

8.3.   Some cost pools are identified as "regular cost accounts"; others are called "major cost centers." Explain the difference between a regular cost account and a major cost center.

8.4.   Explain the difference between a marginal cost and an average cost of a health care service.

8.5.   Can a joint cost also be a common cost? Explain your answer.

8.6.   What is an equivalent unit in the context of cost accounting?

8.7.   Explain the importance of the statement "costs follow revenue" in preparing financial statements for health care institutions where there are support departments and revenue departments.

8.8.   Explain the statement "different costs for different decision-making purposes."

8.9.   Why would members of the health care entity's administrative team want to have a database of all cost-accounting entries rather than being restricted to the ending balances in general ledger accounts?

8.10. Major cost center 200 (vice president, Ancillary Services) in Figure 8.1 and Exhibit 8.1 is equal to

    a. summation of cost codes 201 + 301 + 401 + 211 + 251 + 260 + 270 + 280 + 290

    b. summation of cost codes 201 + 501 + 210 + 250 + 260 + 265 + 270 + 280 + 290

    c. summation of cost codes 201 + 210 + 250 + 260 + 265 + 270 + 280 + 290

    d. summation of cost codes 201 + 211 + 251 + 261 + 266 + 271 + 273 + 281 + 291

8.11. Major cost center 290 (director, Pharmacy) in Exhibit 8.1 is equal to

    a. summation of cost codes 291 + 292 + 294

    b. summation of cost codes 291 + 293 + 295

    c. summation of cost codes 291 + 292

    d. summation of cost codes 292 + 294

8.12. From the facts in Exhibit 8.5, suggest the regular cost accounts and the major cost centers that are required for each of Evansville Clinic's three locations. Explain the reasons for your specifications.

8.13. Indicate the activities at Evansville Clinic in Exhibit 8.5 that are common costs.

8.14. Indicate the activities at Evansville Clinic in Exhibit 8.5 that are joint costs.

Exhibit 8.5   The Evansville Clinic

The Evansville Clinic was established by two physicians to conveniently support the rehabilitation and physical therapy requirements of outpatients in the metropolitan area. The clinic has three locations within the metropolitan area (North Park, West Point, and Eastbrook) that offer a full range of services for occupational therapy, physical therapy, and speech therapy. The two physicians examine each new patient to the clinic, and they monitor the patient care services provided by twenty-one professional therapists. Each clinic has seven therapists, including one speech therapist. North Park has three occupational therapists and three physical therapists. West Point has two occupational therapists and four physical therapists. Eastbrook has one occupational therapist and five physical therapists.

    A clinic manager is responsible for the administrative, support, patient-scheduling, billing, and accounting activities at all three locations, and she is assisted by an office supervisor at each location who directs five clerical and support personnel. In total there are forty-two personnel at the Evansville Clinic: two physicians, six occupational therapists, twelve physical therapists, three speech therapists, one clinic manager, three office supervisors, and fifteen clerical and support staff.

8.15. The distribution of therapists by location in Exhibit 8.5 relates to the usual mix of patients. Assume that a retirement village is opened near Eastbrook and additional occupational therapists are required to support the expanded caseload. Until new personnel can be hired, occupational therapists from the other two locations perform overtime services at Eastbrook. Explain how the data on these overtime services should be recorded in the cost centers.

8.16. Figure 8.10 contains a segment of the second and third organizational levels for the vice president, Fiscal Services. The total cost for the vice president of Fiscal Services, (major cost center 500) is

   a. summation of cost codes 501 + 511 + 521 + 531 + 541 + 561 + 571 + 581 + 591

   b. summation of cost codes 500 + 501 + 511 + 521 + 531 + 541 + 561 + 571 + 581 + 591

   c. summation of cost codes 501 + 510 + 520 + 530 + 540 + 560 + 570 + 580 + 590

   d. summation of cost codes 500 + 510 + 520 + 530 + 540 + 560 + 570 + 580 + 590

8.17. The monthly salary of the director of patient accounting at Demonstration Memorial Hospital (Figure 8.10) is $3,600. Indicate the cost account to which the $3,600 is charged.

8.18. Demonstration Memorial Hospital's director of Information Systems spent $600 to attend a computer conference. Indicate the cost account in Figure 8.10 to which the $600 is charged.

8.19. Demonstration Memorial Hospital's director of Utilization Review incurred $400 for a statistical package to run on her personal computer. Indicate the cost account in Figure 8.10 to which the $400 is charged.

8.20. Study Exhibit 8.6 and determine the out-of-pocket incremental expenses for performing a single test at the Eastside Medical and Screening Clinic.

8.21. (See Question 8.20 and Exhibit 8.6.) Assume a third employee is added at an annual cost of $34,000 as the volume increased from 7,200 screens to 10,800 screens. Determine the return before income tax at 10,800 screens. Fixed stay the same - redo variables

8.22. (See Question 8.20 and Exhibit 8.6.) Assume 7,200 screens were performed in year 1 and that 10,800 screens were annually performed in years 2, 3, and 4. New technology was introduced at the end of year 4, which meant that the old screening system could no longer be used and there was no market value for the old equipment. To continue in operations, $400,000 was spent at the beginning of year 5 for a new screening system estimated to have a four-year life. Determine the return before income tax for years 4 and 5 if 10,800 screens were processed

Figure 8.10   Demonstration Memorial Hospital: Segment of Second and
Third Organizational Levels—Major Cost Centers
and Regular Cost Accounts

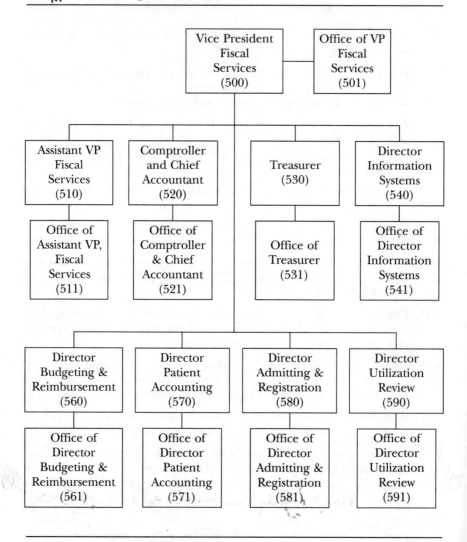

Note: Each account ending with the digit 0 is a major cost center; those account
codes ending with the digit 1 are regular cost accounts.

Exhibit 8.6   Eastside Medical and Screening Clinic

The Eastside Medical and Screening Clinic consists of a waiting area and a screening area. The two employees handle the registration, scheduling, billing, and screening operations, using a $300,000 screening system. Consulting physicians are paid $10 per chart to review the results and dictate a statement sent by the two employees to the patient. The following is other information on activities for the past year:

Revenues ($45 per screen × 7,200 screens)	$324,000
Less: contractual allowance (4%) ~~add~~	12,960
Net revenues	$311,040
Operating expenses:	
Salaries and benefits (12-month contract)	$ 62,000 × 34,000
Rent and utilities (rent is an annual lease)	24,000
Maintenance fee for equipment (per contract)	14,000
Depreciation (six-year life)	50,000
Supplies ($2 per test × 7,200 screens)	14,400
Medical review ($10 per chart × 7,200 screens)	72,000
Financial expense (1%) ~~of Revenue~~	3,240
Total operating expenses ~~- net. Rev~~	$239,640
Return before income tax ~~↗~~	$ 71,400

each year with the three employees and the annual maintenance on the new equipment was $15,000.

8.23. Assume that 45 independent, nonprofit hospitals have elected to join in the formation of an "alliance" that will perform some cooperative procurement and other shared services for these institutions. Reflecting upon the financial-accounting and managerial-accounting materials in this text, explain the major problems in making financial ratio and managerial cost comparisons among the 45 hospitals. Indicate the types of comparisons that would be most meaningful for specific purposes.

9

Cost Measurement and Matching Issues in Health Care Entities

Introduction

Organizations that provide health care services to individuals tend to be different from many other legal entities. There are significant components of supporting services associated with each major cost/ revenue (MC/R) center. The aggregate expenditures in supporting major cost centers may exceed the direct expenditures incurred in MC/R centers, but a 40:60 expenditure ratio for supporting centers to revenue centers is more common.

The organizational differences in health care entities versus many other legal entities do not stop with a consideration of support versus revenue centers. The delivery of health care often requires many highly trained professionals with narrow areas of specialty that may be clustered within the same MC/R center or major support center. A given MC/R center in medium-size health care entities often encompasses an administrative support unit within the center that handles professionals from three or four subspecialties.

Regular cost accounts are aggregated into major cost centers and into MC/R centers. Some cost pools in health care entities are often created at a lower level than regular cost accounts for special monitoring purposes. These cost pools are referred to as *temporary cost accounts*. The organizational existence of these temporary cost accounts is related to the complexity of health care entities and the diverse group of subspecialties within a given MC/R center.

In matching costs with revenue for pricing and planning purposes, the analysis may focus on tests, procedures, and operations performed by a subspecialty. The support services, especially from ancillary departments in hospitals, may come from regular cost accounts encompassing diverse activities that can be separated, to some extent, by principal clusters of activities.

Matching of costs with revenue in health care entities requires coding of transactions that identify the detailed cost unit providing the service and the detailed cost unit receiving the service. The detailed cost unit may be a temporary cost account, associated with a regular cost account, that facilitates the matching of costs and revenue by clusters of tests and procedures.

Cost Transactions

The coding of a cost transaction must include the designation of (1) the organizational unit initiating the event, (2) the organizational unit receiving the benefit of the service, and (3) the natural classification of expenses or revenue. A fourth requirement is imposed by regulatory agencies that seek information on cost transactions by department and by other specific types of events. A general ledger chart of accounts (GLCA) must be implemented in each health care entity that accommodates these four general requirements. For illustration purposes these four components are referred to as follows:

- *FinStat:*   Financial statements for external and regulatory agencies
- *Cost To:*   Cost code of unit receiving the benefit or sustaining the charge from the transaction
- *Cost From:* Cost code of unit initiating the transaction
- *Nature:*   Natural classification of the transaction by operating expenses, revenue, and nonoperating gains and losses

In the Department of Physical Medicine and Rehabilitation Services in Figure 8.2, the $4,000 salary for the supervisor of Physical Therapy can be coded as follows:

FinStat	Cost To	Cost From	Nature	Amount
PhyMed & Rehab	275	275	Salaries	$4,000

The transaction reflects the regular cost code 275 in place of the major cost center 274 (Figure 8.2).

For a second example, assume the manager of Physical Medicine spends $125 for supplies. This transaction is coded as follows:

FinStat	Cost To	Cost From	Nature	Amount
PhyMed & Rehab	273	273	Supplies	$125

The regular cost code 273 (see Figure 8.2) initially captures the expenditure before it is aggregated into major cost center 272.

The director of Physical Medicine incurs $1,500 in professional fees for consultation services on review of departmental operations. This transaction is coded as follows:

FinStat	Cost To	Cost From	Nature	Amount
PhyMed & Rehab	271	271	Professional fees	$1,500

The regular cost code 271 (see Figure 8.2) initially captures the expenditure before it is aggregated into major cost center 270.

Assume that the $1,500 in professional fees for cost code 271 is for the benefit of Physical Therapy, Occupational Therapy, and Speech and Audiology. Expenditures and transfers are always charged to a regular cost account (such as code 271); assignments and allocations are always charged to major cost centers.[1] Under these guidelines, codes 274, 276, and 278 (major cost centers) contain the assigned professional fees from the regular cost account 271 (where the expenditure occurred). The assignment of benefit on $450, $675, and $375 basis is captured as follows:

FinStat	Cost To	Cost From	Nature	Amount
PhyMed & Rehab	274	271	Assigned prof fees	$450
PhyMed & Rehab	276	271	Assigned prof fees	$675
PhyMed & Rehab	278	271	Assigned prof fees	$375
PhyMed & Rehab	271	271	Total assigned fees	($1,500)

The last entry is a credit amount (negative) to an expense account (normal balance debit).

Temporary Cost Accounts

Changes in medical practice may significantly affect the designation of organizational units providing direct and support services for key clusters of tests, procedures, and operations. The existing regular cost accounts may not be compatible with the most recent changes in medical practice that were supported by new equipment. While these changes are being fully implemented in the health care entity, other extensions from this medical technology may occur that will affect additional regular cost accounts.

Cost pools are specified in the form of temporary cost accounts that capture information required for matching costs and revenue under these changes in medical practice and medical technology. The aggregate data in a temporary cost account are transferred to regular cost accounts by the computer system so that the data from regular cost accounts can flow normally to MC/R centers for standard reports.

Accounting for Joint Costs

The concept of a joint cost has meaning only in the accounting context of matching costs with revenues; after the management control process is completed, then joint cost issues can emerge in assigning costs to a product or service. Furthermore, the concept of joint costing has nothing to do with the reporting arrangement for regular cost accounts or with the mapping of a common cost account into other regular cost accounts performed by computer programs. Joint costs, as explained in Chapter 8, are common cost areas that support two or more major revenue centers.

The complexity of health care entities, in combination with the clusters of medical practice within a specialty, may result in multiple product areas within the same department or division. In the matching of costs with revenue for each of these products, there may not be ideal measures of effort for partitioning support costs to facilitate the matching process. Even when there are excellent measures of effort, administrative personnel may elect to emphasize the joint cost issue because of contract terms with some third party payors. In the matching of costs with revenues in health care facilities, a common cost area may support two or more major revenue centers, and "good" work measurement units that can be used in cost assignment may not be available. Such common cost areas were previously described as joint costs, and these common costs can be assigned to the revenue centers following any one of several alternative methods used in this matching process.

The alternative methods either focus on utilization statistics for the joint costs or "net sales" from the revenue centers that are used in matching the joint costs to the revenue centers. The net sales may be gross revenue less the direct costs in the revenue areas. A different method is to subtract contractual allowances and estimated bad debts from gross sales before deducting the direct costs in the revenue areas. The traditional approach in accounting is to follow the *net realizable value method*, which attempts to precisely measure the cash flow in each revenue center.

To illustrate the net realizable value method, assume the Garfield Medical Clinic had three revenue departments, and that common costs of $120,000 are incurred in support of these three revenue departments. Additional direct costs for labor and services are incurred in each of the three revenue departments. This situation is depicted in Figure 9.1.

According to the net realizable value method, the $500,000 of net cash flows (net revenues of $645,000 less expenses of $145,000) resulting from each revenue stream subsequent to the point of incurring the $120,000 of common costs is the basis for assigning joint costs. Thus, 34 percent of the joint costs are assigned to Revenue Area 1; 44 percent to Revenue Area 2; and 22 percent to Revenue Area 3. Exhibit 9.1 shows these assignments of joint costs at Garfield Medical Clinic by the net realizable value method.

One definition of the net sales method ignores the $32,800 of contractual allowances and provision for bad debts in the measurement of net revenue flows at Garfield Medical Center. The joint cost assignments under this definition of net sales are $41,058 to Area 1,

Figure 9.1 Garfield Medical Clinic: Joint Cost Assignment Problem

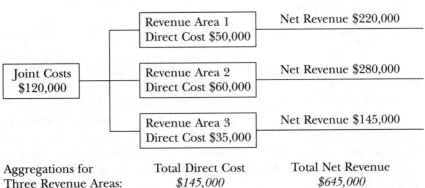

	Revenue Area 1 Direct Cost $50,000	Net Revenue $220,000
Joint Costs $120,000	Revenue Area 2 Direct Cost $60,000	Net Revenue $280,000
	Revenue Area 3 Direct Cost $35,000	Net Revenue $145,000
Aggregations for Three Revenue Areas:	Total Direct Cost *$145,000*	Total Net Revenue *$645,000*

Exhibit 9.1   Garfield Medical Clinic: Assignment of Joint Cost

	Area 1	Area 2	Area 3	Total
Assignment of Joint Cost by Net Realizable Value Method				
Average billing rate per visit	$ 20	$ 50	$ 40	$ 31.85
Number of visits	11,615	5,890	3,775	21,280
Gross revenues	*$232,300*	*$294,500*	*$151,000*	*$677,800*
Contractual allowances & bad debts	12,300	14,500	6,000	32,800
Net revenues	*$220,000*	*$280,000*	*$145,000*	*$645,000*
Less direct costs	50,000	60,000	35,000	145,000
Return	*$170,000*	*$220,000*	*$110,000*	*$500,000*
Percent for joint cost	34%	44%	22%	100%
Application to $120,000 of joint costs	$ 40,800	$ 52,800	$ 26,400	*$120,000*
Assignment of Joint Cost by Net Sales Method (Return ignoring contractual allowances and bad debts in this case)				
Return	*$182,300*	*$234,500*	*$116,000*	*$532,800*
Percent for joint cost	34.215%	44.013%	21.772%	100%
Application to $120,000 of joint costs	$ 41,058	$ 52,816	$ 26,126	*$120,000*
Assignment of Joint Cost by Number-of-Visits Method				
Number of visits	11,615	5,890	3,775	21,280
Percent for joint cost	54.582%	27.679%	17.739%	100%
Application to $120,000 of joint costs	$ 65,498	$ 33,215	$ 21,287	*$120,000*

$52,816 to Area 2, and $26,126 to Area 3. Another definition of the net sales method may include contractual allowances but ignore provision for bad debts in the measurement of net revenue flows. Depending upon which combination of factors are included, there can be several different joint cost assignments under the net sales method for the same situation. When a health care facility indicates that the net sales method is being used for matching joint costs with revenue centers, additional specifications are required before there is any understanding of the details of how this matching is to occur.

Using the number of visits as the physical measure of service for the joint costs will produce significantly different answers because of the variation in average billing rate per visit of $20, $50, and $40, respectively, in the three areas. Area 1 has the most volume, based on number of visits, and is assigned 54.6 percent of joint cost, or $65,498. Area 2 has 27.7 percent of visits and is assigned $33,215 of joint cost; Area 3 has 17.7 percent of visits and is assigned $21,287 of joint cost. Area 1 really shows the impact of using number of visits rather than the net realizable value method. There is a $24,698 difference between the $40,800 under net realizable value method and the $65,498 under number-of-visits method (Exhibit 9.1).

What is the *correct* answer for Garfield Medical Clinic? Should Area 1 have 34 percent of joint cost or 54.6 percent? The answer to these questions centers on the organizational area incurring the $120,000 of expenditures. If this organizational area is a common cost unit that is totally providing standard support services to patients for the three areas of the clinic with the objective of minimizing the total cost of the administrative effort, then the clinic is a joint cost location where there can be no correct answer.

A joint cost location exists where a common cost center provides support services to two or more major revenue centers. By definition, there is no one way of measuring these services that is accepted by all parties. Although there is statistical precision in using, for example, time, number of procedures, documents processed, key strokes entered, or number of registration items verified, none of these quantitative measures captures the essence of the support services provided in a joint cost setting. Therefore, there can be no correct answer on the assignment of joint cost to the revenue centers.

Some professional accountants have real problems in coping with joint cost issues. They are familiar with one way of approaching a problem and are unable to view situations from alternative perspectives. The conceptual foundation of a joint cost is based on the premise of a setting providing common services to two or more major revenue centers. Although various alternative methods can be used in quantifying these common services, there is no universal answer, even in economic utility theory, as to the precise measure of the joint cost provided to patients.

There are some accounting disclosure issues regarding joint costing in price contracts. The net realizable value method has been the historical approach to the problem, and in some situations there are requirements to document that the net realizable value method was considered and rejected.[2] These steps do not limit the administrator's choice in selecting the method for assigning joint cost; they are merely disclosure and documentation requirements for binding contracts so that there are no open issues on the price to be paid by third party payors.

Statistical Measures in Service Areas

The Medicare cost-based reimbursement arrangement that was phased out in 1987 by the prospective payment system (PPS) made extensive use of statistical measures of performance at the departmental level. The reimbursement advantage from statistical measures of performance encouraged many community hospitals with 300 or more beds to employ one or more management engineers. These health care "industrial" engineers designed work-load measurement units for selected cost centers, and these statistical measures were used in the hospital's Medicare worksheet for computing reimbursement.

Managers and directors of ancillary departments in hospitals began to look to their respective professional associations to develop unique work-load measurement units that could be used in place of the management engineering "standards" derived at a single facility. Professional association–directed work-load measurements are based on an understanding of the unique health care practices performed in that ancillary area and the related staffing and support equipment. If the hospital's management engineering team devoted sufficient time to the analytical efforts in a given ancillary unit, the resulting work-load measurements might be similar to those from the professional association. Selected statistical measures of work load are presented in Exhibit 9.2.

Some procedures and tests may be required by an emergency at the hospital 24-hours-a-day, seven-days-a-week. Other procedures and tests performed in the same revenue centers may be deferred until a certain minimum volume is reached. These patient orders may then be performed with different equipment on an automated basis. Laboratory is a good example of where many manual tests may be performed during the evening and early morning hours, but where a different approach is followed in handling patient orders with automated equipment for two shifts a day. Some radiology equipment is

Exhibit 9.2   Selected Statistical Measures by Service
Area

Number of procedures
- Anesthesia
- Electrocardiograph
- Electroencephalograph
- Nuclear medicine
- Radiology
- Ultrasound

Number of tests with a loading factor
- Laboratory
- Pharmacy

Number of treatments
- Occupational therapy
- Physical therapy
- Speech therapy

Number of visits
- Dental clinic
- Diabetes center
- Emergency room
- Orthopedic services
- Outpatient Clinic

Number of cases
- Same day surgery

---

only operated for two shifts a day; a different procedure is available for the evening and early morning hours. Blood bank operations are in a different category—the same level of service is performed 24-hours-a-day. Occupational, speech, and physical therapy are at the other end of the continuum from blood bank; these therapy services may be performed only on a scheduled basis during regular working hours. But to add to the complexity and requirements for institutional knowledge, some tests, treatments, and procedures may be shifted to other equipment depending on the mix and volume of patient orders at a given point in time.

With the shift to PPS, work-load measurements developed by professional associations are replacing local performance statistics that were primarily used for reimbursement purposes. The unit of analysis may be a procedure, test, treatment, visit, or case, depending on the ancillary department or service. The work-load measures and other performance data are captured for each regular cost account in the health care entity. Performance can be assessed only when expenditures and statistical measures (including revenue) are compared for the cost pool.

Net Revenues by Financial Class of Patients

A three-year comparison of gross revenue for a given department in a health care facility may be of limited value because of the potential variation in contractual allowances and adjustments between years. Net patient revenue is a more appropriate benchmark for study. Concurrent with the full implementation of PPS, there has been a significant increase in the number and types of health care service contracts with hospitals. Each contract may create a new financial class of patient for that hospital. Because of this fluctuating set of contractual allowances and adjustments in patient billing, any major analysis must be based on net revenues by financial class of patients.

There are two dimensions to this last statement. First, all major analysis of revenue centers is by net revenue. Contractual allowances and other adjustments are subtracted from gross revenue to arrive at net revenue. When there are significant delays before payment occurs, then a discounting factor is computed, resulting in net cash revenue. Second, the financial class of the patient is important, and the set of potential financial classes of patients has significantly increased over the past few years. The number of HMOs in a service area may have increased from 3 to 35 in the past four years. Blue Cross and commercial insurance policies are being replaced by hospital agreements directly with corporations for their employees and dependents.

It is not unusual for a retired patient over 65 to be covered by Medicare, Blue Cross, and commercial insurance, especially when the retired person has continued a company policy that may only have limited coverage and has not been kept up-to-date with the changes in Medicare. In this situation, the retired person has knowingly purchased another policy for those conditions excluded from full coverage by the other two policies. In these examples we are omitting any fraudulent cases where a patient has been sold duplicate "Medicare supplement" policies that do not change the coverage.

Some persons with special health care conditions may have a separate policy for an excluded coverage from their employer's policy.

Employed spouses with dependent coverage is another example of three types of coverage beyond cash payments for deductibles. But, three sources of payment may represent less than 10 percent of all inpatients. Part of the problem is that the hospital's admitting group may not have obtained complete information from the patient on insurance coverage. Except for hospitals whose service areas include large pockets of poverty, Medicare patients will typically have either Blue Cross or commercial insurance coverage. For couples where both are employed with dependent coverages, two sources of payments are common.

Cost-Volume Analysis by Revenue Center

A fundamental concept of cost accounting is that costs follow revenue; the matching of costs with revenue is an application of this concept. Revenues are recognized when the health care services are provided, including preparing interim (current) bills for those inpatients who have not been discharged as of the last day of the accounting period. For example, a health care service might be a treatment that requires two or more patient visits, and the patient is not billed until the treatment is finished. If the fiscal year were to end between these patient visits, the health care institution can have estimated revenues from unbilled patient services. But this is not a common situation. Many health care institutions require the billing to be based on an outpatient visit, as distinct from the treatment; in this case, aggregate billings for the period are identical with services provided for the period. In those outpatient facilities where payment occurs before services are provided, there can be unearned income if the patient elects to defer a test or treatment after the advance payment for such services has been made to the cashier.

Interim billing for inpatients and billing per visit (if not cash) for outpatient and clinic services makes gross revenues almost equal to total services provided by the health care facility. Contractual allowances and other adjustments must be determined by revenue center so that net revenue is known for purposes of cost-volume analysis.

Fixed and variable costs

The costs that are matched with the net revenue must be separated into fixed costs and variable costs. The fixed costs are those expenditures associated with the revenue center that are constant in amount for a defined period. The variable costs are expenditures that change in direct proportion to number of tests, services, operations, treatments, or activities performed. The cost behavior of an account may indicate both a fixed and a variable component, and for purposes of cost-volume analysis, these expenditures are partitioned into the respective fixed and variable components.

It is important to specify the context in which the separation of fixed costs versus variable costs is valid using the four factors in a cost framework: (1) time period, (2) capacity assumption, (3) volume assumption, and (4) management or administrative purpose. The fixed costs are constant for a defined period and for a relevant range of volume; the behavior of variable costs is also dependent upon these same factors. A change in either the time period or the relevant range of volume may totally negate any insights resulting from cost-volume analysis based on these prior assumptions.

Contribution margin

The excess of net revenues over variable costs is the *contribution margin*, or the return available for supporting fixed costs and other investment requirements. The net revenues and variable costs are expressed in terms of expected cash receipts and expected cash outflows; thus, the contribution margin is a measure of the expected cash to be gained from a specified volume of services in a revenue center. If the contribution margin in dollars is divided by the specified volume, then the contribution margin per unit of service is obtained.

Work-load measurement units for a revenue center are accumulated in a responsibility accounting system for management control and are useful in evaluating performance, staffing, and planning next period's requirements. But, a revenue center may not be able to price exactly based on work-load measurement units. Market conditions, existing contracts with third party payors and corporate groups, regulatory considerations, competitors, and environmental factors all influence the price of a service. Therefore, work-load measurement units are typically not used in cost-volume analysis.

A measure of the revenue function that drives volume in the contribution margin is required for break-even analysis. This measure or index selected for volume is related to the general activity of a billed test, procedure, operation, or treatment and where there is an adjustment among areas within a revenue center for the fluctuations in price. The process of identifying the volume measure for break-even analysis is beneficial for subsequent consideration of future pricing of services within the revenue center.

The calculation of break-even point is a simple computation after the contribution margin per unit of service has been determined. The revenue center's fixed costs, divided by the contribution margin per unit of service, equals the break-even point in number of services. If the objective is to have a desired return, then this dollar amount is added to the fixed costs, and the aggregate amount, divided by the contribution margin per unit of service, gives the volume of services that will equal the desired return.

Break-even example

Revenue and expenses at Gary Memorial Hospital were examined for inpatients. The 18,000 patient days in 19X1 resulted in $10,800,000 of charges, $5,148,000 of variable expenses, and $4,752,000 of contribution margin (Exhibit 9.3). The average charge per patient day is $600, but this is not the expected "cash flow" from revenue. Contractual allowances and other adjustments are $900,000, or $50 per patient day ($900,000/18,000 = $50). Cost-volume analysis is based on $550 of expected cash flows. Variable expenses divided by patient days ($5,148,000/18,000 = $286) shows $286 as the cash payment for expenses per patient day. The contribution margin per patient day is $264 ($550 − $286 = $264), which, divided into fixed expenses of $3,100,000, equals a break-even point of 11,743 patient days ($3,100,000/$264 = 11,742.42 patient days).

In Exhibit 9.3, patient day served as the volume measure, and the management control reports probably also used patient days as the work-load measurement units. But environmental factors, marketing considerations, and contractual relations with third party payors may not permit a pricing strategy that is based on work-load statistics for each test, procedure, or treatment provided by the same revenue center. For example, a laboratory typically charges more per work-load statistic for tests in hematology and chemistry and charges less per work-load measure for tests in microbiology and pathology. The variation between the pricing function and the service function is not limited to the organizational units where the tests are performed. Within hematology or chemistry, for example, there are numerous tests, each with its own work-load measurement units, and the pricing function within the organizational unit is not proportional to the service function.

Exhibit 9.3   Gary Memorial Hospital: Cost-Volume Analysis of
Inpatients for Year Ended 31 December 19X2

Gross revenue (18,000 patient days @ $600)	$10,800,000
Contractual allowances and other adjustments	900,000
Net patient revenue	*$9,900,000*
Variable expenses (per detailed study)	5,148,000
Contribution margin	*4,752,000*
Fixed expenses	3,100,000
Return	*$ 1,652,000*
Gross revenue (18,000 patient days @ $600)	$10,800,000
Net revenue per patient day ($9,900,000/18,000)	$ 550
Variable expenses ($5,148,000/18,000)	286
Contribution margin ($4,752,000/18,000)	*$ 264*
Break-even point in patient days (fixed expenses/ contribution margin = $3,100,000/$264 = 11,742.42)	*11,743 patient days*
Proof: 11,743 patient days @ $550 = net revenues	$ 6,458,650
11,743 variable expenses @ $286 = $3,358,498	
fixed expenses = 3,100,000	
	6,458,498
Variance 11,742.42 and 11,743 patient days	*$ 152*

Case-mix assumptions

For purposes of cost-volume analysis, some assumptions are made for coping with variation between the service function and the pricing function. It is first assumed that within an organizational area the distribution or mix of tests is constant for the relevant range of analysis. If there is a 10 percent change in volume for that organizational unit, each type of test is changed by 10 percent. After cost-volume analysis is performed under this constant case-mix assumption, then consideration can be given to "what if" questions for changes in marketing and pricing.

In applying cost-volume analysis to a revenue center containing two or more organizational units, it is assumed that the mix of tests across organizational units is constant. There are established relationships among tests performed in hematology, for example, with those in chemistry and microbiology. When there is a 10 percent change in volume in one organizational unit, there is a proportional change in activities in the other units. The findings from cost-volume analysis must be qualified by this significant assumption on constant mix before the health care facility's management can consider "what if" questions for changes in marketing, competition, and pricing.

The impact of these two case-mix assumptions is illustrated by the experience of Glenfield Medical Clinic, which has three organizational units (see Exhibit 9.4). The price range of the 14,640 tests in Area 1 was \$18 to \$39 for the year, with an average of \$25. Under the constant case-mix assumption for Area 1, the \$366,000 of net revenues, divided by the 14,640 tests, gives \$25 (\$366,000/14,640 = \$25) as the expected cash receipts, which versus variable expenses of \$175,680, or \$12 (\$175,680/14,640 = \$12) as expected cash outflows, results in a contribution margin per test of \$13 (\$25 − \$12 = \$13). The separable fixed costs of \$96,000, divided by \$13 contribution margin per test, gives a break-even point for Area 1 at 7,385 tests (\$96,000/\$13 = 7,384.62).

The price range of the 10,875 tests in Area 2 was \$27 to \$41, with \$32 as the average; the price range for the 10,725 tests in Area 3 was \$30 to \$65, with \$40 as the average (Exhibit 9.4). Under the constant case-mix assumption for each area, the contribution margins were \$21 and \$27, respectively, and the break-even points were 6,096 and 6,519 tests.

The \$400,000 of separable fixed costs in Exhibit 9.4 was segmented by the three areas; however, the \$130,000 of general fixed costs is not directly related to any one of the areas. The assumption of constant case-mix across the three areas permits the calculation of the break-even point for the Glenfield Medical Clinic. The \$1,143,000 of net revenues, divided by the 36,240 tests, gives a net price of \$31.54 per test (\$1,143,000/36,240 = \$31.54). The \$434,730 variable expenses, divided by 36,240 tests, gives an expected cash outlay of \$12.00 per test (\$434,730/36,240 = \$12.00). The clinic's contribution margin is \$19.54 per test (\$31.54 − \$12.00 = \$19.54). The composite fixed costs of \$530,000, divided by the contribution margin of \$19.54, gives a break-even point of 27,124 tests for the clinic (\$530,000/\$19.54 = 27,123.85). This computation of a break-even point of 27,124 tests for the clinic is dependent upon the assumptions of constant case-mix within each area and constant case-mix across areas.

A break-even computation by area for the separable fixed costs is helpful in pricing strategies for the coming period; these calculations are presented in Exhibit 9.4. Some managers of health care facilities

Exhibit 9.4   Glenfield Medical Clinic: Cost-Volume Analysis for Year
Ended 31 December 19X2

	Area 1	Area 2	Area 3	Total
Gross revenues	$385,000	$365,000	$450,000	$1,200,000
Contractual allowances &				
other adjustments	19,000	17,000	21,000	57,000
Net revenues	*$366,000*	*$348,000*	*$429,000*	*$1,143,000*
Less variable costs	175,680	119,625	139,425	434,730
Contribution margin	*$190,320*	*$228,375*	*$289,575*	*$ 708,270*
Separable fixed costs	96,000	128,000	176,000	400,000
Return	*$ 94,320*	*$100,375*	*$113,575*	*$ 308,270*
General fixed costs				130,000
Operating income				*$ 178,270*
Volume of tests	14,640	10,875	10,725	36,240
Price range per test	$18–39	$27–41	$30–65	
Net revenue per test	$25	$32	$40	$31.54
Variable costs per test	12	11	13	12.00
Contribution margin	*$13*	*$21*	*$27*	*$19.54*
Break-even point				
$96,000/$13	7,385			
$128,000/$21		6,096		
$176,000/$27			6,519	
$530,000/$19.54				27,124
Work-load				
measurement units	161,040	174,000	235,950	570,990
Average work-load units				
per test				
161,040/14,640	11			
174,000/10,875		16		
235,950/10,725			22	
Average net revenue per				
workload unit	$2.27	$2.00	$1.82	

specify a fixed return for each area and then compute the volume required for supporting that return. These various computations provide
insights into the contribution margin per unit by area, the work-load
distributions, and the net revenue per work-load unit. With these cash

flow measures, the manager of the health care facility is in a stronger position for assessing marketing conditions and competitors.

Exhibit 9.4 shows that 36,240 medical clinic tests consisted of 570,990 work-load measurement units, where the average net revenue per work-load statistic was $2.27 in Area 1, $2.00 in Area 2, and $1.82 in Area 3. Should Glenfield Medical Clinic move toward a more uniform pricing arrangement per work-load statistic, or does the competitive market require this general type of structure? Cost-volume analysis does not give answers to these issues, but it does provide a framework for directly addressing them. Informed assessment and interpretation must be performed with full recognition of the impact of assumptions regarding time period, capacity, volume, management or administrative purpose, constant case-mix of tests within an area, and constant case-mix of tests across areas within the clinic.

Summary

A cost transaction is coded to show the cost account initiating the event, the cost account receiving the benefit of the service, the natural classification of expenses or revenue, and financial statement and regulatory agency data. Expenditures incurred by a regular cost account may be assigned to one or more other cost areas that received the benefit of the expenditures. For illustration purposes, all assignments and allocations are recorded in major cost centers. Expenditures and transfers are recorded in regular cost accounts.

Temporary cost accounts are cost pools created to capture transactions for some specific purpose. Changes in medical practice and implementation of medical technology may affect the relevance of traditional costs-revenue comparisons. Temporary cost accounts permit new accumulations of data for matching costs and revenue without upsetting traditional cost flows from regular cost accounts to major cost/revenue centers.

Some common cost accounts or common cost areas that exclusively support two or more major revenue centers are called *joint cost centers*. Where health care utilization statistics are accumulated for joint cost centers, the common costs are assigned in the same manner as other common cost areas. But there are joint cost centers in health care organizations where there are no good measures of utilization because of the diversity and complexity of services provided to the receiving revenue centers. The latter type of joint cost center is more representative of the situation in other industries where the net realizable value method is used in assigning common costs to the major revenue centers. Contractual allowances and other adjustments are factors that must be determined for each receiving revenue center under the net realizable value method. If these factors are not to be measured, then the net sales method can be used in assigning the joint costs to the respective revenue centers. A wide variation by revenue center in the average price of a visit or service may produce a significantly different assignment of joint costs under physical unit methods. Other statistical measures of service by the joint cost center can also be used as an alternative method for assigning these common costs to the revenue centers.

Work-load measurement units for tests, procedures, operations, and treatments are specified by various health care professional associations identified with the ancillary department or medical specialty. Performance statistics are accumulated for each regular cost account as an essential part of the management control system. These work-load and statistical measures (including revenue) are subsequently used for all types of decision-making activities in pricing, planning, and strategic assessments.

Gross revenue data for a health care facility are often misleading because of the tremendous variation that may occur in contractual allowances and other adjustments with third party payors. Some third party payors may use one health care facility for some services and another facility for other related services. Therefore, the distribution of health care services by third party payor (such as an HMO) may be very restricted and not the normal array of services. Because of the variation in contract terms and distribution of services, informed analyses of revenue centers are based on net revenue by financial class of patients.

Cost-volume analysis provides a framework in which to assess the contribution margin from selected operations, to determine the break-even point for those operations, and to calculate the level of services that produce a given financial return. For health care settings, net revenues must be used in expressing the net cash flow to be realized from the sale of services. All costs must be partitioned between variable costs and fixed or period costs. The net revenues less these variable costs equal the contribution margin in dollars. Pricing for health care services is not proportional with work-load measurement units; therefore, the relevant volume measure for expressing the contribution margin is based on the pricing function and not on performance statistics. Variations between the pricing function and performance statistics occur within a revenue center and among revenue centers. Case-mix assumptions are made regarding a constant distribution of tests or services both within and among revenue centers so that the linear calculations can be performed for cost-volume analysis. With the insights provided from the cost-volume assessment, considerations can then be given to the possible impact of shifts in case mix.

Appendix: Cost Assignments in a Hospital Laboratory Department

Demonstration Memorial Hospital's Department of Pathology contains 17 regular cost accounts, which accumulate transaction data in an appropriate manner for aggregation in various ways for diverse reporting requirements (see Figure 9.2). Some external reports focus on three areas: laboratory services—clinical; laboratory services—pathological; and blood and blood processing. Other external reports disclose data on two areas: laboratory (clinical and pathological) and blood and blood processing. Internal assessments are either by area, (for example, hematology, chemistry, immunology) or by groups of tests within an area.

Many internal evaluations of transaction data depend on transaction data from organizational level 7 within the laboratory department. But, for illustration purposes, regular cost accounts at level 7 are omitted in Figure 9.2. Hematology, for example, contains an automated section with a computer-based blood-analysis instrument and a bench section where manual assessments are performed, using a variety of instruments and procedures. The separation of activities within hematology between the two sections is really at organization level 7.

Joint cost accounts

Clinical laboratory services are coordinated by an assistant manager (regular cost code 215) for five master cost/revenue centers. Cost code 215 is a joint cost account, and the aggregated data in this account are assigned to the five MC/R centers, based on work-load measurements accumulated in the hospital laboratory computer system. The work-load measurement units are from the College of American Pathologists

Figure 9.2 Demonstration Memorial Hospital: Department of Pathology—Major Cost/Revenue Centers and Regular Cost Accounts (Level 7 regular cost accounts omitted)

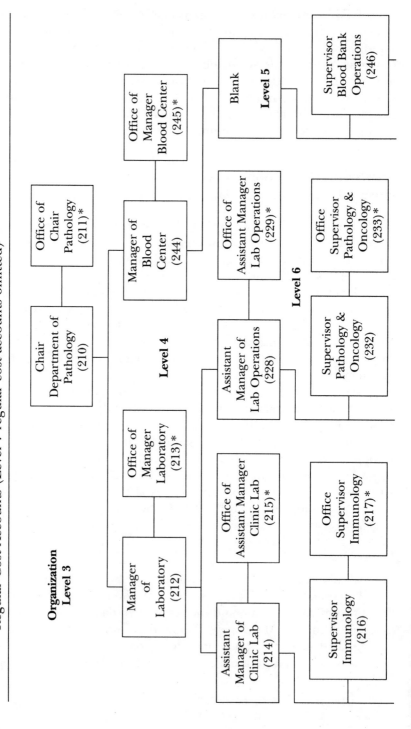

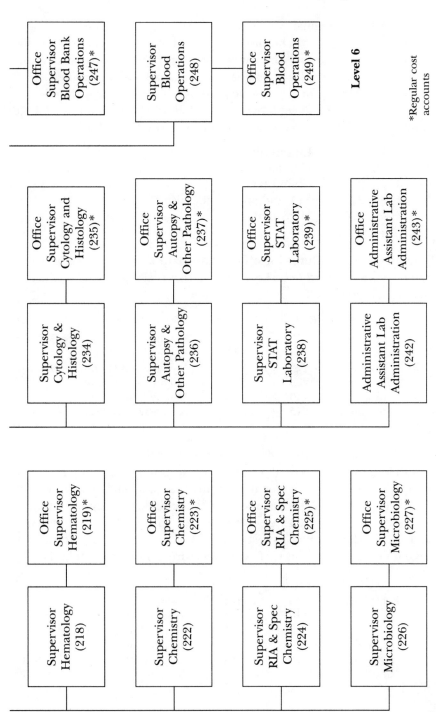

Office Supervisor Blood Bank Operations (247)*

Supervisor Blood Operations (248)

Office Supervisor Blood Operations (249)*

Level 6

*Regular cost accounts

Office Supervisor Cytology and Histology (235)*

Supervisor Cytology & Histology (234)

Office Supervisor Autopsy & Other Pathology (237)*

Supervisor Autopsy & Other Pathology (236)

Office Supervisor STAT Laboratory (239)*

Supervisor STAT Laboratory (238)

Office Administrative Assistant Lab Administration (243)*

Administrative Assistant Lab Administration (242)

Office Supervisor Hematology (219)*

Supervisor Hematology (218)

Office Supervisor Chemistry (223)*

Supervisor Chemistry (222)

Office Supervisor RIA & Spec Chemistry (225)*

Supervisor RIA & Spec Chemistry (224)

Office Supervisor Microbiology (227)*

Supervisor Microbiology (226)

(CAP) and are primarily based on the direct labor associated with each laboratory. The laboratory computer system contains over 800 test codes, in which the same laboratory tests may be listed twice. Some tests can be ordered as a manual test or as an instrument test. CAP units are different for the test depending on how it was ordered.

The five MC/R centers had the following distribution of CAP units, expressed as percentages for the period ended 19X2:

Code 216	Immunology	15%
Code 218	Hematology	25%
Code 222	Chemistry	30%
Code 224	RIA and special chemistry	10%
Code 226	Microbiology	20%
Total		*100%*

The direct expenditures for office of assistant manager, Clinical Laboratory (code 215), were $83,837. This direct cost is assigned to the five MC/R centers as follows:

FinStat	*Cost To*	*Cost From*	*Nature*	*Amount*
LabClinical	216	215	Assigned direct cost	$12,576
LabClinical	218	215	Assigned direct cost	$20,959
LabClinical	222	215	Assigned direct cost	$25,151
LabClinical	224	215	Assigned direct cost	$ 8,384
LabClinical	226	215	Assigned direct cost	$16,767
LabClinical	215	215	Total assigned direct	($83,837)

Note the five MC/R codes are used rather than the respective regular cost codes for the "office of..." associated with each of the five areas.

Utilities are assigned to key cost accounts based on statistical sampling techniques performed by the hospital staff. Three regular cost accounts in the Department of Pathology are assigned utilities: codes 214, 228, and 244 (see Figure 9.2). The $1,240 of utility costs charged by the hospital to cost code 214 is further assigned to the five MC/R centers based on CAP work measurement units as follows:

FinStat	*Cost To*	*Cost From*	*Nature*	*Amount*
LabClinical	216	214	Assigned utility cost	$186
LabClinical	218	214	Assigned utility cost	$310
LabClinical	222	214	Assigned utility cost	$372
LabClinical	224	214	Assigned utility cost	$124
LabClinical	226	214	Assigned utility cost	$248
LabClinical	214	214	Total assigned utility	($1,240)

Note in the above six entries, only MC/R codes are used for transfer-ring of assigned amounts.

Housekeeping costs are allocated to key cost centers within the hospital. Three regular cost accounts in the Department of Pathol-ogy are allocated housekeeping costs: codes 214, 228, and 244. The $1,341 of housekeeping costs allocated by the hospital to cost code 214 is further allocated to the five MC/R centers based on CAP work measurement units as follows:

FinStat	Cost To	Cost From	Nature	Amount
LabClinical	216	214	Allocated housekeeping	$201
LabClinical	218	214	Allocated housekeeping	$335
LabClinical	222	214	Allocated housekeeping	$403
LabClinical	224	214	Allocated housekeeping	$134
LabClinical	226	214	Allocated housekeeping	$268
LabClinical	214	214	Total housekeeping	($1,341)

Note in the above six entries, only MC/R codes are used for transfer-ring of allocated amounts.

Each of these entries for joint cost accounts 214 and 215 must be repeated for joint cost accounts 228 and 229 and for accounts 244 and 245. The office of assistant manager, Laboratory Operations (code 229), is assigned to five MC/R accounts: 232, 234, 236, 238, and 242. The office of manager, Blood Center, is assigned to two MC/R accounts: 246 and 248.

Layers of administrative support

Joint cost accounts 215, 229, and 245 in Demonstration Memorial Hospital's Department of Pathology represent one layer of adminis-trative support to the MC/R centers. The office of manager of Labo-ratory (code 213) is a second layer of direct support for clinical and pathological laboratory services. The office of chair, Pathology (code 211), is a third layer of support for clinical laboratory, pathological laboratory, and blood and blood processing. Figure 8.1 shows the office of vice president of Ancillary Services (201), another layer of support to laboratory and blood processing operations.

In addition to the layers of administrative support along orga-nizational levels, there are specific units that provide administrative services to all hospital departments. There are several support units in human resources and fiscal services that constitute another layer of administrative support to laboratory and blood operations.

Notes

1. A sophisticated computer program can handle different types of transactions in an account without requiring special codes. These types include (1) direct expenditure, (2) transfer of an expenditure, (3) assigned costs, and (4) allocated costs. But for illustration purposes, regular cost accounts are only designed to record direct expenditures and transfers. The major cost center contains the aggregation from the related regular cost account(s) and assigned costs and allocated costs.
2. The cost-or-market rule for valuation dates back to some books from 1404–1406 [L. L. Vance, *Accounting Review* 18: (July 1943) 218]. Many professionals cite the Ordinance of 1673 (Jacques Savary) in France as the origin of the lower-cost-or-market rule. Others refer its origin to the Accounting Rules of the Commercial Code of 1807 (also called the Napoleonic Code), which substituted a period of forced labor for the death penalty associated with a fraudulent bankruptcy when the accountant valued inventory items on financial statements at amounts in excess of their net realizable value. The lower-cost-or-market rule was specified in a law enacted by the state of Prussia in 1794 and in the uniform commercial code for the German states in 1857.

Additional Readings

Long, M. J., J. D. Chesney, and S. T. Fleming. "Were Hospitals Selective in Their Product and Productivity Changes? The Top 50 DRGs after PPS," *Health Services Research* 24 (December 1989): 615–41.

Munoz, E., D. Chalfin, H. Johnson, and L. Wise. "Hospital Costs, Resource Characteristics, and the Dynamics of Death for Surgical Patients," *Hospital & Health Services Administration* 34 (Spring 1989): 71–83.

Smith, D. B., and J. L. Larsson. "The Impact of Learning on Cost: The Case of Heart Transplantation," *Hospital & Health Services Administration* 34 (Spring 1989): 85–97.

Stier, M. M., and A. H. Rostenstein, "Scrutiny of Resource Use Can Increase Efficiency," *Healthcare Financial Management* 44 (November 1990): 26–34.

Discussion Questions

9.1. Explain the purpose of temporary cost accounts.

9.2. There are two cost codes included in each entry for a transaction. Explain the function performed by each cost code.

9.3. Explain the difference between "an appropriate application of statistical methods to the assignment of joint cost" and "a correct answer to the assignment of joint cost."

9.4. In the context of matching costs with revenue for an ancillary service, explain the concept of contribution margin.

9.5. Explain why a health care entity might elect to use the number-of-visits method in place of the net realizable value method for assigning joint cost to three major revenue centers.

9.6. Differentiate between the net realizable value method for handling a joint cost center and the net sales method.

9.7. For Figure 9.2, the transaction for salaries directly incurred by Immunology in Department of Pathology is

FinStat	Cost To	Cost From	Nature	Amount
a. LabClinical	216	216	Salaries & wages	$76,887
b. LabClinical	216	218	Salaries & wages	$76,887
c. LabClinical	217	217	Salaries & wages	$76,887
d. LabClinical	217	216	Salaries & wages	$76,887

9.8. For Figure 9.2, the transaction for salaries directly incurred by Cytology and Histology in Department of Pathology is

FinStat	Cost To	Cost From	Nature	Amount
a. LabClinical	235	234	Salaries & wages	$194,432
b. LabClinical	234	235	Salaries & wages	$194,432
c. LabClinical	234	234	Salaries & wages	$194,432
d. LabClinical	235	235	Salaries & wages	$194,432

9.9. For Figure 9.2, the transaction for allocated housekeeping costs for Immunology in Department of Pathology from the assistant manager, Clinical Laboratories, is:

FinStat	Cost To	Cost From	Nature	Amount
a. LabClinical	217	215	Allocated housekeeping	$2,682
b. LabClinical	216	214	Allocated housekeeping	$2,682
c. LabClinical	217	214	Allocated housekeeping	$2,682
d. LabClinical	216	215	Allocated housekeeping	$2,682

9.10. For Figure 9.2, the transaction for allocated housekeeping costs for Hematology in Department of Pathology from the assistant manager, Clinical Laboratories, is:

FinStat	Cost To	Cost From	Nature	Amount
a. LabClinical	218	214	Allocated housekeeping	$16,092
b. LabClinical	218	215	Allocated housekeeping	$16,092
c. LabClinical	219	214	Allocated housekeeping	$16,092
d. LabClinical	219	215	Allocated housekeeping	$16,092

9.11. For Figure 9.2, the transaction for salaries directly incurred by Microbiology in Department of Pathology is:

FinStat	Cost To	Cost From	Nature	Amount
a. LabClinical	226	226	Salaries & wages	$344,590
b. LabClinical	227	226	Salaries & wages	$344,590
c. LabClinical	226	227	Salaries & wages	$344,590
d. LabClinical	227	227	Salaries & wages	$344,590

9.12. Security and Parking is collectively viewed as a support area containing four regular cost accounts (442, 445, 447, and 449) at Demonstration Memorial Hospital, as represented by Exhibit 9.5. Other health care facilities have different arrangements for Security and Parking. Explain the organizational location in another health care facility if Security and Parking was:

a. A regular cost account

b. A major cost center

c. A common cost account

d. A support cost area

9.13. For Exhibit 9.5, the transaction for salaries directly incurred by the Chief of Security is

FinStat	Cost To	Cost From	Nature	Amount
a. SecParking	444	444	Salaries & wages	$216,000
b. SecParking	445	444	Salaries & wages	$216,000
c. SecParking	445	445	Salaries & wages	$216,000
d. SecParking	444	445	Salaries & wages	$216,000

9.14. For Exhibit 9.5, the transaction for salaries directly incurred by the Department of Parking is

FinStat	Cost To	Cost From	Nature	Amount
a. SecParking	447	446	Salaries & wages	$198,000
b. SecParking	446	446	Salaries & wages	$198,000
c. SecParking	446	447	Salaries & wages	$198,000
d. SecParking	447	447	Salaries & wages	$198,000

9.15. For Exhibit 9.5, the transaction for assigning costs from the office of the director, Security and Parking, to Central Transportation is

FinStat	Cost To	Cost From	Nature	Amount
a. SecParking	448	440	Salaries & wages	$32,000
b. SecParking	448	442	Salaries & wages	$32,000
c. SecParking	449	440	Salaries & wages	$32,000
d. SecParking	449	442	Salaries & wages	$32,000

Exhibit 9.5   Demonstration Memorial Hospital: Department of
Security and Parking—Major Cost Centers and Regular Cost
Accounts

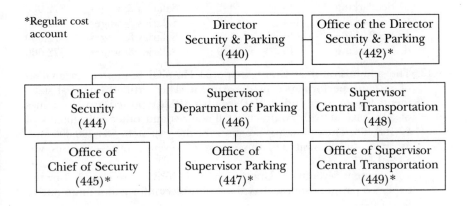

Part I management control report for period:

Cost Account	Title	Direct Expenditures
SecParking 440	Director, Security and Parking	$ 0
SecParking 442	Office of the director	160,000
SecParking 445	Chief of Security	216,000
SecParking 447	Supervisor, Parking	198,000
SecParking 449	Supervisor, Central Transportation	156,000
	Total direct costs	$730,000

For simplification purposes, salaries are used to represent all "direct expenditures."

Statistical measures indicate that regular cost account 442's services are consumed as follows:

Account	Services Consumed Units	Percent
444 Chief of Security	225	45
446 Supervisor, Parking	175	35
448 Supervisor, Central Transportation	100	20
Total services from common cost account	500	100

9.16. For Exhibit 9.5, the transaction for assigning costs from the office of the director, Security and Parking, to the chief of Security is

FinStat	Cost To	Cost From	Nature	Amount
a. SecParking	445	442	Salaries & wages	$72,000
b. SecParking	444	442	Salaries & wages	$72,000
c. SecParking	444	440	Salaries & wages	$72,000
d. SecParking	445	440	Salaries & wages	$72,000

9.17. The administrator at Grant Memorial Hospital requested an analysis of revenue performance by department. The certified financial statements for the year ended 31 December 19X2 reported gross revenues of $46,700,000, with contractual allowances and other adjustments of $7,198,493. The operating expenses for the year were $34,700,000 and, as shown in Exhibit 9.6, the excess of revenue over expenses was $4,801,507.

Patient revenues at Grant Memorial Hospital are classified by the expected payment source, based on admission information, into one of four categories:

- Federal program patients
- HMOs (participate in 12 different HMOs)
- Commercial insurance
- Private (includes free care)

The deductibles charged to the patients are reported in the same category. Furthermore, the initial admission data serve as the source for classification, and there is no adjustment for those charges that are rejected by third party payors and billed to the patients. Exhibit 9.7 contains the departmental revenue data, based on aggregating the information on patient bills. Exhibit 9.8 shows the departmental revenue data by the four categories of payments. (The actual hospital data have been consolidated into only four categories and nine departments for illustration purposes and to facilitate various analyses.)

From discussions with finance department personnel, you determine the $7,198,493 of allowances and adjustments has the distribution shown in Exhibit 9.9. The departmental cost data are reported in Exhibit 9.10, using information from the certified financial statements. The assigned and allocated costs are combined in a single column for purposes of this analysis.

The contractual allowances and adjustments at Grant Memorial Hospital are equally distributed by category within the nine departments on a dollar basis. For example, the $1,143,125 of operating room and recovery room revenue from federal program patients reflects 5.71213 percent ($1,143,125 revenue/$20,012,208 total revenue = 0.0571213) of the total federal program adjustment, or $179,938 ($3,150,109 × 0.0571213 = $179,938).

Exhibit 9.6   Grant Memorial Hospital: Statement of Revenue and Expenses for Year Ended 31 December 19X2

Net patient service revenue (note 1)	*$39,501,507*
Operating expenses:	
Salaries, wages, and benefits	19,070,125
Professional fees	3,516,449
Insurance	1,048,387
Food	836,279
Fuel, electricity, and gas	744,370
Drugs and pharmaceutical supplies	742,455
Other supplies and expenses	4,549,512
Repairs and maintenance	375,775
Depreciation and amortization	1,780,000
Interest expense	1,336,648
Provision for bad debts	700,000
Total operating expenses	*$34,700,000*
Income from operations	*$ 4,801,507*

Note to Financial Statement

1. *Net patient service revenue*

Gross patient service revenue:	
Inpatient routine care	$17,680,000
Inpatient ancillary care	25,320,000
Outpatient services	3,700,000
Total gross patient service revenue	*$46,700,000*
Less provisions for:	
Contractual allowances for federal program patients	$ 3,150,109
Other adjustments and free care	4,048,384
Total allowances	*$ 7,198,493*
Net patient service revenue	*$39,501,507*

    A. Determine the return by department (excess of revenue over expenses).

    B. Prepare a schedule of net revenue by department.

    C. Prepare a schedule of net return by department.

    D. Compute the net contribution margin for the nine departments.

9.18. The Gold Medical Clinic incurred $200,000 of administrative and support costs for the year ended 30 September 19X2 for the three medical

Exhibit 9.7   Grant Memorial Hospital: Statement of Revenue by
Department for Year Ended 31 December 19X2
(Simplified for illustration purposes)

Department	Gross Revenues
Operating Room & Recovery Room	$ 2,950,000
Delivery Room	750,000
Radiology	4,820,000
Laboratory	7,940,000
EKG & Cardiology	2,040,000
EEG & Other Ancillary Units	2,220,000
Respiratory Therapy	4,600,000
Routine Care	17,680,000
Outpatient Service	3,700,000
Total	$46,700,000

Exhibit 9.8   Grant Memorial Hospital: Statement of Revenue by
Department for Year Ended 31 December 19X2

Department	Federal Patients	12 HMOs	Commercial Insurance	Private Patients
Operating Room & Recovery Room	$ 1,143,125	$ 576,430	$ 649,887	$ 580,558
Delivery Room	174,395	183,485	202,509	189,611
Radiology	2,496,676	689,578	987,283	646,463
Laboratory	3,471,644	1,386,617	1,742,706	1,339,033
EKG & Cardiology	1,139,544	291,786	403,521	205,149
EEG & Other Ancillary	1,114,662	346,804	465,008	293,526
Respiratory Therapy	2,202,440	780,026	1,026,359	591,175
Routine Care	7,288,242	3,260,080	3,828,452	3,303,226
Outpatient Service	981,480	1,040,453	972,069	705,998
Total	$20,012,208	$8,555,259	$10,277,794	$7,854,739

Exhibit 9.9 Grant Memorial Hospital: Distribution of Allowances and Adjustments

	Revenues	Adjustments	Net Revenues
Federal program patients	$20,012,208	$3,150,109	$16,862,099
12 HMOs	8,555,259	1,673,405	6,881,854
Blue Cross & commercial insurance	10,277,794	1,449,233	8,828,561
Private patients	7,854,739	925,746	6,928,993
Total revenue	$46,700,000	$7,198,493	$39,501,507

Exhibit 9.10 Grant Memorial Hospital: Statement of Expenses by Department for Year Ended 31 December 19X2

Department	Total Expenses	Direct Cost	Assigned and Allocated
Operating Room & Recovery Room	$ 2,578,000	$ 1,660,582	$ 917,418
Delivery Room	722,000	497,458	224,542
Radiology	3,372,000	2,147,290	1,224,710
Laboratory	3,108,000	2,054,698	1,053,302
EKG & Cardiology	1,820,000	1,176,994	643,006
EEG & Other Ancillary Units	2,186,000	1,146,775	1,039,225
Respiratory Therapy	2,150,000	1,182,476	967,524
Routine Care	16,302,000	7,402,901	8,899,099
Outpatient Service	2,462,000	2,009,481	452,519
Total	$34,700,000	$19,278,655	$15,421,345

offices in its facility. Patient billing, collection, and direct support resulted in the data presented in Exhibit 9.11 for the year ended

A. Determine the assigned joint costs to the three offices by the net realizable value method.

B. Explain how you would assign joint costs by the net sales method.

C. Determine the assigned joint costs to the three offices by the number-of-visits method.

9.19. Grace Community Hospital had 16,500 patient days for the year ended 31 October 19X2, with gross revenues of $9,487,500. From the patient accounting records it is determined that contractual allowances and

Exhibit 9.11   Gold Medal Clinic: Billing, Collection, and Direct
Support

	Office A	*Office B*	*Office C*	*Total*
Average billing rate	$ 25	$ 20	$ 40	$ 25.95
Number of visits	9,800	16,850	7,800	34,450
Gross revenue	$245,000	$337,000	$312,000	$894,000
Contractual allowances & other adjustments	$ 5,000	$ 7,000	$ 12,000	$ 24,000
Direct costs	$ 44,000	$ 57,000	$ 69,000	$170,000

other adjustments were $247,500 for the year ended. The $6,960,000 of inpatient costs is partitioned into variable costs of $3,960,000 and fixed costs of $3,000,000.

A. Determine the break-even point in patient days.

B. In planning for 19X3 it is expected that patient days will increase by 10 percent; there will be a 5 percent increase in gross charges per inpatient day and a corresponding 5 percent increase in contractual allowances; variable expenses will increase by 3 percent; and fixed expenses will increase by $100,000, to $3,100,000. Determine the break-even point in patient days for 19X3.

9.20. The director of Glenfield Medical Clinic has reached an agreement with third party payors for gross billing at $2.24 per work-load measurement unit for the year ended 31 December 19X3. From studying historical experience (Exhibit 9.4) and data for prior years, it is expected that contractual allowances and other adjustments will average $0.11 per work-load measurement unit in 19X3. Variable costs, separable fixed costs, general fixed costs, test volume, and distribution of tests are expected to be the same in 19X3 as they were in 19X2.

A. Using the data in Exhibit 9.4 with the above adjustments for pricing, determine the contribution margins, by area and in total, for the year ended 31 December 19X3.

B. Determine the break-even point for Glenfield Medical Clinic for the year ended 31 December 19X3.

9.21. An ancillary department at Goodwin Community Hospital performed 12 tests for the year ended 31 December 19X2, which had a total volume of 48,490 tests, representing $2,081,000 of gross patient bills. An analysis of patient records and payment behavior indicated contractual allowances and other adjustments of $374,152. The variable costs for

Exhibit 9.12   Distribution of Work-Load Statistics for Goodwin
Community Hospital

Tests	Work-Load Statistic per Test	Number of Units	Total Work-Load Statistics	Price per Test	Gross Revenues	Price per Work-Load Statistic
Test 1	2.34	4,510	10,553.40	$20.00	$ 90,200.00	$8.547
Test 2	2.89	6,520	18,842.80	24.00	156,480.00	8.304
Test 3	3.76	3,250	12,220.00	30.00	97,500.00	7.979
Test 4	4.86	4,210	20,460.60	35.00	147,350.00	7.202
Test 5	5.73	2,870	16,445.10	36.00	103,320.00	6.283
Test 6	12.04	3,910	47,076.40	60.00	234,600.00	4.983
Test 7	3.40	5,240	17,816.00	25.00	131,000.00	7.353
Test 8	9.65	4,760	45,934.00	65.00	309,400.00	6.736
Test 9	8.47	2,480	21,005.60	70.00	173,600.00	8.264
Test 10	7.21	2,950	21,269.50	50.00	147,500.00	6.935
Test 11	6.50	3,140	20,410.00	45.00	141,300.00	6.923
Test 12	11.92	4,650	55,428.00	75.00	348,750.00	6.292
		48,490	307,461.40		$2,081,000.00	

the ancillary department were $630,370 and the fixed costs for the year
were $350,000. The distribution of work-load statistics among the tests
and the price per work-load statistic are presented in Exhibit 9.12.

A. Determine the contribution margin for this ancillary department for
the year ended 31 December 19X2.

B. Determine the break-even point.

C. Explain the assumptions that are required for performing the above
break-even analysis.

D. The director of Goodwin Community Hospital was surprised at the
distribution of price per work-load statistic in 19X2 and has reached
an agreement with third party payors for 19X3 as follows: price of
Test 6, $65.00; price of Test 12, $80.00. The gross charges for all
other tests are $8.20 per work-load statistic, rounded to the nearest
amount divisible by 5. (For example, Test 8 has 9.65 units @ $8.20
= $79.13, or $79.15; Test 10 has 7.21 units @ $8.20 = $59.122, or
$59.10.) Under the assumption of the same volume and distribution
of tests for 19X3 as for 19X2, and without any change in variable and
fixed costs or in the billing arrangement, compute the contribution
margin for the year ended 31 December 19X3.

E. Under the same conditions as *D* above, compute the break-even
point for 19X3.

Exhibit 9.13   Data for Garrison Medical Clinic

	Area 1	Area 2	Area 3	Total
Gross revenues	$649,000	$443,000	$467,000	$1,559,000
Contractual allowances & adjustments	$ 41,750	$ 25,850	$ 30,200	$ 97,800
Variable costs	$242,900	$185,400	$145,600	$573,900
Separable fixed costs	$154,350	$ 91,750	$101,200	$347,300
General fixed costs				$140,000
Volume of tests	17,350	15,450	20,800	53,600

9.22. The Garrison Medical Clinic has three areas, with gross revenues of $1,559,000, contractual allowances of $97,800, variable expenses of $573,900, and fixed costs of $487,300. The annual volume of tests for the year ended 31 December 19X2 was 53,600. Other data for 19X2 are shown in Exhibit 9.13.

A. Compute the contribution margin for each area.

B. Compute the overall break-even point for Garrison Medical Clinic for the year ended 31 December 19X2.

10

Cost-Assignment Methods with Single and Multiple Supporting Units

Introduction

Health care entities are often very complex organizations with many layers of support units and administrative services assisting in the delivery of services to patients. Some support units are dedicated cost areas that provide exclusive services to a few major cost areas. There are other interactive support units that both receive and provide services to other support units. It is not unusual for a health care entity to incur more than 40 percent of total expenditures in support units. Cost assignments and cost allocations with single and multiple supporting units are central issues in financial management of most health care entities.

Health care entities are also unique in the amount and depth of information required to be maintained on each patient and on the services provided to each patient. The registration or admission of a patient is documented in a chart or medical record. The order-entry and result-reporting module in the computer system contains information on the various ancillary services provided to the patient. A summary statement of all tests, procedures, services, and operations is prepared at the end of the episode of care. The summary statement must also contain clinical codes on the reasons for the admission or registration, date and time information on each test or service, and signature of physician responsible for the care, and it must comply with other documentation requirements.

The registration and reporting requirements for each episode of care represent an outstanding database for assessing the delivery of services to patients. From the context of financial management, the matching of costs and revenue in many major cost/revenue (MC/R) centers can be accomplished with a choice of statistical measures of service. The database for a typical regular cost account in a health care entity contains two or three excellent measures of activity for evaluating the performance of that cost unit. The overall quality of the statistical database of patient services is so good that detailed cost assignments can be accomplished on an automatic basis by the health care entity's computer system.

There are two phases to this computer processing. First is the management control phase. Each expenditure or revenue transaction is subjected to a series of checks and balances, screens, filters, cross-comparisons of data elements, and internal control procedures as the event is captured in the computer-based system. After each transaction is processed, a comparison of actual with budget is performed, with exception reporting of results. At the end of the month, management reviews detailed data (expenditure, revenue, and statistical measures) for each regular cost account, monitors performance, and implements various management control processes. All of these steps are part of the management control phase, discussed in Chapter 12.

Second is the reporting and decision-making phase. Some regular cost accounts are only for expenditure control and revenue-monitoring purposes. After the month-end management control processing and reviews are completed, these regular cost accounts are assigned to other MC/R centers. The statistical database from services to patients and registration information can be used by the computer-based system in automatically assigning regular cost accounts to other MC/R centers that benefitted from the expenditures. This chapter examines four categories of cost assignments and allocations for both single and multiple supporting units.

Assigned and Allocated Costs to Organizational Units

There are many organizational and administrative reasons to establish specific clusters of activities, designated as cost pools, for management control and monitoring purposes. Some cost pools are temporary cost accounts rather than regular cost accounts because of, for example, changes in medical practice and medical technology (Chapter 9).

Transfers from a temporary cost account to a regular cost account are handled in the management control reporting arrangement as if the transaction occurred in a regular cost account. Although transactions to transfer data are the exception in many health care entities, cost assignment and cost allocation entries are typical transactions in health care entities.

Common costs, as explained in Chapter 8, are cost pools that accumulate expenditures associated with support services benefiting two or more departments. Organizationally, common costs can exist at much lower levels than departments. Common costs may support two or more major cost centers at organizational level 6 in a health care entity.

This discussion of assigning and allocating costs to organizational units separates common costs into three categories, based on the distance between the cost pool incurring the expenditures and the cost pools benefiting from the services. These three categories are (1) common direct costs, (2) common assigned support costs, and (3) common allocated overhead costs. A fourth category, which excludes common costs, is general allocated overhead costs.

Some professional accountants restrict the use of the term "common cost account" to aggregations of regular cost accounts that provide services to other organizational units, from which the common cost area receives its meaning. The more general usage of "common cost account," used in this discussion, denotes an organizational unit used for management control purposes that is directly assigned by application computer programs to the benefiting regular cost accounts and major cost centers.

Common direct costs

Expenditures are initially captured in cost pools, designated as temporary cost accounts or as regular cost accounts. After the management control processes and reviews are completed, all expenditure and performance data in some designated cost accounts are moved to specified MC/R centers that directly benefit from that cost pool.

Physician salaries are a typical example of this type of transaction. In a department or organizational unit where the number of employed physicians is between one and three, a separate cost pool located at a high organizational level is established for physician salaries. This arrangement protects inquiries by staff professionals into the specific payment terms of a given physician. Any analysis for planning, pricing, and assessment purposes needs the information on physician salaries.

After the management control review process is finished, then the computer system automatically assigns the applicable physician salary costs to the benefiting MC/R centers.

A regular cost account with the title "office of. . ." is another example of this type of transaction. The regular cost account for the office of manager, Physical Medicine (code 273 in Figure 8.2) is representative of common costs that are assigned as soon as the management control processes are completed. The three MC/R centers (codes 274, 276, and 278) receive all of the benefit from code 273. All management planning, pricing, and strategic decisions for MC/R centers 274 (Physical Therapy), 276 (Occupational Therapy), and 278 (Speech and Audiology) must consider the applicable expenditures incurred in code 273 that benefitted them.

Assume that $8,000 was incurred by office of manager, Physical Medicine, for the period and that the work-load units in the computer-based system indicate a 40 percent, 35 percent, and 25 percent distribution of services to Physical Therapy, Occupational Therapy, and Speech and Audiology, respectively. These common costs are assigned as follows:

FinStat	Cost To	Cost From	Nature	Amount
PhyMed & Rehab	274	273	Assigned direct costs	$3,200
PhyMed & Rehab	276	273	Assigned direct costs	$2,800
PhyMed & Rehab	278	273	Assigned direct costs	$2,000
PhyMed & Rehab	273	273	Total assigned costs	($8,000)

After the computer processes this assignment, regular cost account 273, with a zero balance, is eliminated from any further assessment.

A dedicated support area is a third example of common direct costs. Demonstration Memorial Hospital's Department of Pathology contains an administrative assistant, Laboratory Administration (regular cost code 243 in Figure 9.2. Pathological laboratory services at organizational level 6 contains four MC/R centers and one major cost center (242). Code 242 is primarily for human resource requirements, and after the management control review is completed, regular cost account 243 is assigned to the four MC/R centers receiving the benefit: 232 (Pathology and Oncology), 234 (Cytology and Histology), 236 (Autopsy and Other Pathology), and 238 (STAT Laboratory).

Common assigned support costs

The second category of common costs, common assigned support costs, is where there is an organizational distance (two or three levels) between the cost pool incurring the expenditures and the benefiting

MC/R centers. Another requirement is that the computer-based system must accumulate work load units that can be used in matching costs with the benefiting MC/R centers.

The Department of Pathology (illustrated by Figure 9.2) contains both of the first two categories of common costs. Common cost account 243 is explained above as a joint cost that benefits four MC/R centers (232, 234, 236, and 238). The appendix to Chapter 9 shows the transfer of the direct expenditures in common cost account 215 to the five MC/R centers (216, 218, 222, 224, and 226). There are two other common cost accounts in Figure 9.2 that are representative of the first category: codes 229 and 245.

The office of the manager, Laboratory (code 213), and the office of chair, Pathology (code 211), are examples of the second category. The matching of costs with revenue demands that codes 213 and 211 are assigned to the 11 MC/R centers that directly benefit from these administrative services:

216 Supervisor, Immunology
218 Supervisor, Hematology
222 Supervisor, Chemistry
224 Supervisor, RIA and Special Chemistry
226 Supervisor, Microbiology
232 Supervisor, Pathology and Oncology
234 Supervisor, Cytology and Histology
236 Supervisor, Autopsy and Other Pathology
238 Supervisor, STAT Laboratory (Emergency Laboratory Unit)
242 Supervisor, Blood Bank and Operations
248 Supervisor, Blood Operations

There are over 800 tests distributed among these 11 MC/R centers.

Common allocated overhead costs

The third category, common allocated overhead costs, is similar to the second category regarding the organizational distance between the cost pool where the expenditure is incurred and the location of the benefiting MC/R centers. The other attribute of the second category, however, is not present; the computer-based system does not contain work-load units for assigning the benefits. When work-load measures are present, common costs are assigned to MC/R centers; when surrogate amounts and statistical data are used in estimating benefit, common costs are allocated to MC/R centers.

General allocated overhead costs

The fourth category, general allocated overhead costs, is for general administrative services and facility support. These expenditures are not common costs that primarily support two or more MC/R centers, but are indirect support services required by all MC/R centers. Human resources, fiscal services, housekeeping, and general maintenance are representative of this fourth category of indirect support services.

The fourth category differs from the three categories of common costs automatically assigned by the computer-based system to the benefiting MC/R centers. General overhead encompasses multiple supporting units with interactions among units. Because of this interaction, assessment and review are required before any general overhead transactions are actually entered into the DBMS. Some general overhead allocations are for a special report or a regulatory statement. Transactions for this type of general overhead allocation are not recorded in the health care entity's computer-based system.

Selection of Method and Utilization Statistics

Cost accounting is a very unusual area of study—the more an individual understands about cost-accounting procedures, the more choices are available to the individual in the matching of costs with revenues. The fundamental concept of "different costs for various decision-making purposes" applies to all aspects of the matching of support and overhead costs with revenue. The selection of a cost-assignment method is in the same context. After reviewing the three common approaches for matching support and overhead costs with revenue, the individual must specify which of the alternative sets of utilization statistics in the DBMS are to be used with each method.

The three common approaches for matching support and overhead costs with revenue are (1) the direct method, (2) the step-down method, and (3) the reciprocal method. The selection of a cost-assignment method, combined with the specification of the utilization statistics to be employed, may significantly affect payments for patient services under a third-party contract. Each third-party contract with a health care entity must be reviewed because the terms and conditions are frequently not compatible. Administrative personnel must carefully examine the distribution of patient services by financial class and study the impact of various contracts with third party payors *before* agreeing to enter the results of a method in the DBMS. There are several legal reasons not to always enter the support assignments and overhead allocations in the DBMS; however, keep documentation of these transactions to support reports prepared under each matching of costs with revenue.

Direct Method

The direct method of cost assignment for overhead or support units to revenue centers is based on mapping of utilization statistics from each overhead cost center to the various revenue centers, and all services provided by the cost center to nonrevenue centers are ignored. The aggregate costs for each overhead cost center are prorated among the revenue centers in proportion to the utilization statistics of that revenue center to the aggregate statistics for all revenue centers. The direct method is a simple way of assigning these overhead costs; however, it completely ignores all interaction among supporting costing centers.

Some types of health care entities cannot use the direct method of cost assignment on financial statements to regulatory agencies because the approach does not calculate services provided among support cost centers. In the case of community hospitals, these multiple layers of support, excluding common cost centers, may represent more than 25 percent of operating expenses; therefore, with this magnitude of effort classified as overhead, it is not surprising that a regulatory agency does not accept the direct method in determining reimbursement for outpatient services when utilization data of services provided to other support centers are ignored.

To compare the three cost assignment methods, consider the example of Elmwood Medical Services Clinic. Elmwood Medical Services Clinic is a single facility containing (1) physician offices for group practice services, (2) rehabilitation services, and (3) mental health services. There are three support departments for these three service groups:

- Administration
- Business office
- Housekeeping/maintenance

During the year, overhead cost is charged directly to a cost center when the benefit is specifically identified. Otherwise, the overhead expenditure is reflected in one of the three support cost centers.

Elmwood Medical Services Clinic incurred $2,600,000 of operating expenses for the year ended 31 December 19X2, including

$1,170,000 of overhead expenditures (Exhibit 10.1). The three revenue centers were charged with $290,000 of these overhead expenditures; the remainder, or $880,000, was reported by the three support departments. The results of the cost-accounting entries at the end of the current fiscal year before any support departments are allocated to revenue departments is shown by the distribution of operating expenses in Exhibit 10.1.

Elmwood Medical Services Clinic has a management control system, including a full reporting of statistical measures of performance

Exhibit 10.1   Elmwood Medical Services Clinic: Schedule of Overhead and Support Services for Year Ended 31 December 19X2

Overhead Costs and Total Costs for Year

	Overhead Costs	Direct Costs	Total Costs
Revenue Departments			
Physician group practice	$ 141,500	$ 650,000	$ 791,500
Rehabilitation services	86,500	480,000	566,500
Mental health services	62,000	300,000	362,000
Support Departments			
Administration	320,000	—	320,000
Business office	410,000	—	410,000
Housekeeping/maintenance	150,000	—	150,000
Total operating expenses	$1,170,000	$1,430,000	$2,600,000

Support Services for Year

	Services Provided		
	Administration	Business Office	Housekeeping/ Maintenance
Users			
Physician group practice	25%	35%	20%
Rehabilitation services	30	10	10
Mental health services	20	20	25
Administration	—	15	20
Business office	10	—	25
Housekeeping/maintenance	15	20	—
Total	100%	100%	100%

by department. These same statistical measures in the database are used to map the activities provided by one department to another. Administration, for example, consumes 15 percent of the total services provided by the business office and 20 percent of the total services provided by housekeeping/maintenance (Exhibit 10.1). The business office consumes 10 percent of administration's services and 25 percent of housekeeping/maintenance's services. Housekeeping/maintenance consumes 15 percent of administration's services and 20 percent of business office's services. But, under the direct method, these services consumed by the various support departments are ignored in the overall assignment of $880,000 of support department costs to the three revenue departments.

Under the direct method, the $320,000 of administration costs is assigned to the three revenue centers based on the utilization rate per revenue department to the aggregate for the three revenue centers. Physician group practice consumed 25 percent of administration's services, one-third of the net (25 percent of the 75 percent total for the three revenue departments); thus, the physician group practice is assigned $106,667 of the administration's cost (Exhibit 10.2).

Rehabilitation consumed 30 percent of administration's services and is assigned 30/75 of the $320,000, or $128,000 (Exhibit 10.2). Mental health services consumed 20 percent of administrations's services and is assigned 20/75 of the $320,000, or $85,333 (Exhibit 10.2). A similar type of calculation is performed with the matching of the business office and housekeeping/maintenance costs to the three revenue departments. After the matching of the $880,000 of support and overhead services with revenues, the three revenue centers reflect the full $2,600,000 of costs ($1,720,000 initial expenses plus $880,000 of overhead).

The direct method ignores the interaction among support departments. In Exhibit 10.2 for Elmwood Medical Services Clinic, no attention was given to the consumption of services by the three support departments in calculating the overhead assignments to the three revenue departments. If this interaction is fairly constant among all support departments, then the results from cost assignments to the remaining revenue departments under the direct method may be similar to those from the reciprocal method. If the interaction is not steady among support departments, then the results under the direct method can be significantly different from the reciprocal method.

The more fundamental problem with the direct method is the absence of a foundation for interpreting the results. Although a cost analyst knows that the consumption of overhead services by the various

Exhibit 10.2   Elmwood Medical Services Clinic: Support Services
Assigned by Direct Method for Year Ended
31 December 19X2

Direct Method Cost Assignment

Revenue Departments	Administration	Business Office	Housekeeping/ Maintenance
Physician group practice	$106,667	$220,769	$ 54,545
(Utilization rate)	(25/75 = 1/3)	(35/65 = 7/13)	(20/55 = 4/11)
Rehabilitation services	128,000	63,077	27,273
(Utilization rate)	(30/75 = 2/5)	(10/65 = 2/13)	(10/55 = 2/11)
Mental health services	85,333	126,154	68,182
(Utilization rate)	(20/75 = 4/15)	(20/65 = 4/13)	(25/55 = 5/11)
Total assignment	*$320,000*	*$410,000*	*$150,000*

Operating Expenses after Overhead Assignment

Revenue Departments	Initial Cost	Assigned Cost	Total Cost
Physician group practice	$ 791,500	$381,981	$1,173,481
Rehabilitation services	566,500	218,350	784,850
Mental health services	362,000	279,669	641,669
Total costs	*$1,720,000*	*$880,000*	*$2,600,000*

support departments has been ignored with the direct method, the analyst does not know the impact of excluding this interaction. If the reciprocal cost method is applied to capture the interaction, then the analyst can decide if the matching of costs with revenue under the direct method is advantageous to the health care entity under certain contract terms.

Step-Down Method

The step-down method does consider the consumption of services by all open support departments in the proration of costs according to measures of utilization. The label "step-down" refers to the general appearance of an assignment worksheet: departments are listed in the order in which they will be closed. After a support department or area is closed, that unit does not participate in any subsequent cost assignments regardless of the amount of services utilized by the closed support unit from the remaining open departments.

Regulatory agencies in the health care industry tend to prescribe the order in which general service cost centers are closed or matched against the remaining accounts. There are certain types of specialty hospitals and clinics that are exempt from the usual rules for community hospitals. In the absence of regulations to the contrary, the sequence for applying the step-down method is based on the support center that renders service to the greatest number of other service departments. This suggested sequence for financial statements is a change from the previous position which, sequenced cost centers by dollar volume of direct cost without regard to services.

The order in which cost accounts are closed in the step-down method is critical to the results in the final matching of costs with revenue centers. The most important support cost centers are closed first. The least important support cost center is matched with the revenue centers in the last step according to some utilization criteria; however, this least important cost center has been magnified in importance by the assignment to it of costs from each of the other support cost centers. In a typical community hospital with many support cost centers, the last three or four cost centers closed against the remaining open cost centers under the step-down method may significantly affect the overall process and the final matching of costs to the revenue centers.

The step-down method was the principal approach followed by most community hospitals in the preparation of Medicare cost reports under the retrospective cost-based reimbursement system. The double apportionment and reciprocal cost methods were approved by the Medicare regulations, but they were seldom used because the sequence mandated by Medicare for closing support areas under the step-down method tended to provide an economic advantage to community hospitals. When a community hospital used the reciprocal cost method because of its precision for long-range planning, the step-down method was still used for reimbursement purposes; otherwise, there would have been a reduction in the amount of payment to the hospital from the federal programs and other third party payors.

Medicare inpatients are now paid according to a fee structure for the diagnosis-related group (DRG) under the prospective payment system (PPS); several other third party payors have also implemented a fee per DRG as a basis for payment. A fee-for-service payment system for clinic and outpatient visits is being developed. But, some administrative personnel in community hospitals have not been able to remove

Exhibit 10.3 Elmwood Medical Services Clinic: Support Services Assigned by Step-Down Method for Year Ended 31 December 19X2

Support Departments	Initial Cost	Administration	Business Office	Housekeeping/ Maintenance	Total Cost
Administration	$ 320,000	($320,000)			
Business office	410,000	32,000	($442,000)		
(Utilization rate)		(10%)			
Housekeeping/maintenance	150,000	48,000	104,000	($302,000)	
(Utilization rate)		(15%)	(20/85 = 4/17)		
Physician group practice	791,500	80,000	182,000	109,818	$1,163,318
(Utilization rate)		(25%)	(35/85 = 7/17)	(20/55 = 4/11)	
Rehabilitation services	566,500	96,000	52,000	54,909	769,409
(Utilization rate)		(30%)	(10/85 = 2/17)	(10/55 = 2/11)	
Mental health servies	362,000	64,000	104,000	137,273	667,273
(Utilization rate)		(20%)	(20/85 = 4/17)	(25/55 = 5/11)	
Total operating expenses	$2,600,000	0	0	0	$2,600,000

Operating Expenses after Overhead Assignments

Revenue Departments	Direct Method	Step-Down Method	Variance in Methods
Physician group practice	$1,173,481	$1,163,318	($10,163)
Rehabilitation services	784,850	769,409	(15,441)
Mental health services	641,669	667,273	25,604
Total cost	$2,600,000	$2,600,000	0

themselves from the retrospective cost-based reimbursement system in place before PPS. These individuals often confuse cost behavior with traditional methods for increasing third-party payments under the old retrospective cost-based reimbursement system.

In illustrating the step-down method, assume that Elmwood Medical Services Clinic is told by a regulatory body which sequence to follow in applying this approach:

1. Administration
2. Business office
3. Housekeeping/maintenance

Using the same overhead costs for the year and utilization statistics on services consumed by department in Exhibit 10.1, the step-down worksheet is illustrated in Exhibit 10.3. Note the three support departments are listed in the order in which they are closed.

The administration support unit consumed 15 percent of the business office's services and 20 percent of housekeeping/maintenance's services; yet, no cost from the business office or housekeeping/maintenance is assigned to administration because the unit is closed. After a cost unit is closed in the step-down method, it cannot be reopened to receive any assigned cost for that period. But, the step-down method does permit assigning costs to all open service departments, resulting in a different mix of cost assignments among the revenue accounts than what was produced by the direct method (Exhibit 10.3).

The direct costs in the business office for assignment are $442,000: the initial expenditures incurred of $410,000 plus the $32,000 of cost transferred in from administration. The term "direct cost" is used in regulatory reports in the health care industry for these combined amounts because the transfer was based on utilization statistics. The proration of the $442,000 of direct costs for the business office is based on 85 percent of utilization, since the administration unit, which is closed at this point in the step-down, had consumed 15 percent. The prorations to housekeeping/maintenance and to the three revenue departments are illustrated in Exhibit 10.3.

The direct costs in housekeeping/maintenance are $302,000: the initial expenditures incurred of $150,000 plus $48,000 transferred in from administration and $104,000 transferred in from business office. In Exhibit 10.3, the administration and business office are closed; thus, the prorations for housekeeping/maintenance are the same ratios as for the direct method in Exhibit 10.2.

Exhibit 10.4 Elmwood Medical Services Clinic: Business Office Services Assigned by Total Cost Incurred for Year Ended 31 December 19X2

Departments	Initial Cost	Administration	Balance of Cost Incurred	Business Office	Total Cost
Administration	$ 320,000	($320,000)			
Business office	410,000	32,000	$ 442,000	($442,000)	
(Utilization rate)		(10%)			
Housekeeping/maintenance	150,000	48,000	198,000	40,554	$ 238,554
(Utilization rate)		(15%)		(198,000/2,158,000)	
Physician group practice	791,500	80,000	871,500	178,500	1,050,000
(Utilization rate)		(25%)		(871,500/2,158,000)	
Rehabilitation services	566,500	96,000	662,500	135,693	798,193
(Utilization rate)		(30%)		(662,500/2,158,000)	
Mental health services	362,000	64,000	426,000	87,253	513,253
(Utilization rate)		(20%)		(426,000/2,158,000)	
Total operating expenses	$2,600,000	0	$2,600,000	0	$2,600,000

Elmwood Medical Services Clinic has only three support depart-ments—a helpful characteristic for illustrating the reciprocal cost method later. But in comparing the direct method and the step-down method, there is only a $25,604 variance in the overhead balance for the mental health services revenue center under the two methods. If there were more support departments, the interactive services could cause a more drastic shift in the residual balances in the revenue centers. Even a small community hospital will have at least 25 sup-port departments used in regulatory reports, and the potential for differences between the two methods is much greater with the inter-action of 25 support units. The mental health services direct costs of $362,000 in Exhibit 10.3 is before overhead assignments; thus, $305,273 is overhead, and the $25,604 variance in overhead assignments is more than an 8 percent change ($25,604 divided by $305,273). The variance cannot be ignored even for three simple cost centers.

Regulatory agencies not only mandate the order in which support centers are closed in the step-down, but these agencies may prescribe the statistical basis of utilization for a given support center. Assume, for example, that the business office must be assigned based on total costs incurred (illustrated in Exhibit 10.4). In applying the total-cost-incurred approach, it is necessary to know how the total operating expenses are distributed immediately prior to the point of this as-signment. The third column in Exhibit 10.4 shows the $2,600,000 of operating expenses immediately prior to the assignment of the business office by the total-cost-incurred approach. Subtract the direct cost of the support area to be assigned ($442,000 in this example) from the total operating expenses ($2,600,000) to obtain the denominator for the proration ($2,600,000 − $442,000 = $2,158,000).

The housekeeping/maintenance department had direct expenses of $198,000 ($150,000 of initial cost incurred plus $48,000 of assigned administrative cost). The fourth column shows $40,554 of business office cost being assigned to housekeeping/maintenance based on $442,000 multiplied by 198,000/2,158,000 (the fraction of the receiving unit's cost to the denominator for proration). This same type of calcu-lation is performed for the three revenue centers in Exhibit 10.4. Note from the last column, containing aggregate cost by open department, the total operating expenses remain at $2,600,000 for the reduced set of cost accounts.

Compare the business office assignments in Exhibit 10.3 with those in Exhibit 10.4. There is a $83,693 difference in the assignment for rehabilitation services and a $63,446 difference in the assignment for housekeeping/maintenance under the two approaches. The magnitude of these variances causes administrative personnel to pause and reflect on the reasons for this matching. Should the health care entity use the mandated approach by the regulatory agency in place of actual utilization data in pricing decisions? There are different costs for various management purposes, and no one approach is "correct."

Reciprocal Cost Method

Another approach to cost assignments of administrative overhead and support expenditures, the reciprocal cost method, fully captures the interaction of all participating cost centers within the methodology. The algorithm simultaneously closes all support cost areas to revenue centers so that the interaction among overhead cost centers is fully expressed in the calculations. A linear-programming package on a personal computer can efficiently perform these simultaneous assignments rather than using mathematical equations.

The reciprocal method can properly address complex organizations with many layers of support units and administrative services assisting in the delivery of services to patients. Although the step-down method may be used by a community hospital, for example, for purposes of obtaining the maximum reimbursement from Medicare outpatients, the reciprocal method is the only approach that focuses on the complete set of relations that provided those services to patients. The community hospital, in this example, will use both methods without posting either to the DBMS; instead, a report file containing the posting for the reciprocal method may be created by extracting data from the DBMS. Various decision makers at the community hospital accessing the report file (a separate DBMS with static information for the period that has just ended) can retrieve the proper overhead and support allocations to a revenue center when those factors are relevant. Supporting documentation for both the step-down and reciprocal cost method are maintained by the health care entity.

The linear-programming algorithm concurrently closes all service support areas to revenue centers; thus, all overhead and support areas are open to receive transfer costs from other service departments based on utilization factors. From a conceptual standpoint, the reciprocal method is superior to either the direct method or the step-down method in proper matching of cost and benefit. The limitation in the past has been the difficulty in applying the reciprocal method for the health care entity with numerous service departments and without access to a linear-programming algorithm on a large computer system for its administrative team. But, the availability of linear-programming application packages on the personal computer is significantly changing the frequency with which the reciprocal method is being used for budgeting in health care institutions.

Since the Elmwood Medical Services Clinic has three service departments, these cost centers can be represented by three equations with three unknowns, and the reciprocal cost assignments can be determined by algebraic calculations. Using algebraic procedures will illustrate the impact of reciprocal cost assignments on the gross assignments from service departments.

Under the reciprocal method, the cost in the administration department is $320,000 plus 15 percent of the cost in the business office department plus 20 percent of the cost in the housekeeping/maintenance department (Exhibit 10.1). If the administration department is represented by X, the business office department by Y, and housekeeping/maintenance by Z, this equation is

$$X = \$320,000 + 0.15Y + 0.20Z$$

A review of the services-provided data in Exhibit 10.1 dictates the following two equations for the other support departments:

$$Y = \$410,000 + 0.10X + 0.25Z$$

$$Z = \$150,000 + 0.15X + 0.20Y$$

The revenue centers do not provide any services to the support units; the above equations do not include any notation for the three revenue centers.

The three equations representing Elmwood Medical Services Clinic's support units can be solved by algebra as follows:

$$
\begin{aligned}
X &= \$320,000 && + 0.15Y + 0.20Z && \text{(Eq. 1)} \\
Y &= \$410,000 + 0.10X && + 0.25Z && \text{(Eq. 2)} \\
Z &= \$150,000 + 0.15X + 0.20Y && && \text{(Eq. 3)}
\end{aligned}
$$

$$
\begin{aligned}
5X - 0.75Y - 1.00Z &= 1{,}600{,}000 && \text{(Eq. 1*; Eq. 1 times five)} \\
-0.15X - 0.20Y + 1.00Z &= 150{,}000 && \text{(Eq. 3)} \\
4.85X - 0.95Y &= 1{,}750{,}000 && \text{(Eq. 4; adding Eq. 1* plus Eq. 3)}
\end{aligned}
$$

$$-0.40X + 4.00Y - 1.00Z = 1,640,000 \quad \text{(Eq. 2*; Eq. 2 times four)}$$
$$-0.15X - 0.20Y + 1.00Z = 150,000 \quad \text{(Eq. 3)}$$
$$-0.55X + 3.80Y = 1,790,000 \quad \text{(Eq. 5; adding Eq. 2* plus Eq. 3)}$$

$$19.40X - 3.80Y = 7,000,000 \quad \text{(Eq. 4*; Eq. 4 times four)}$$
$$-0.55X + 3.80Y = 1,790,000 \quad \text{(Eq. 5)}$$
$$18.85X = 8,790,000 \quad \text{(Eq. 6; adding Eq. 4* plus Eq. 5)}$$

$$X = \$466,313$$
$$Y = \$538,545$$
$$Z = \$327,656$$

If a linear-programming application package is used to solve these transfer cost determinations, then the inputs to the package are as follows:

```
MIN       X + Y + Z
SUBJECT TO
    2)      X    - 0.15Y - 0.2Z  ≥ 320,000
    3)  -0.1X  +    Y    - 0.25Z ≥ 410,000
    4)  -0.15X - 0.2Y  +    Z    ≥ 150,000
END
```

The linear-programming application package will indicate a solution is found in the third step with the following values for variables:

Variable	Value
X	466,313.00
Y	538,545.30
Z	327,656.00

These values for support departments are used in matching costs with benefits at Elmwood Medical Services Clinic. Inserting these values, as shown in Exhibit 10.5, illustrates the reciprocal cost process. Note that X includes $146,313 that has been concurrently assigned from Y ($80,782) and Z ($65,531) in Exhibit 10.5. Likewise, Y includes $128,545 that has been concurrently assigned from X ($46,631) and Z ($81,914), and Z includes $177,656 that has been concurrently assigned from X ($69,947) and Y ($107,709). After the assignment process, the total costs of the three revenue centers in Exhibit 10.5 is equal to the full $2,600,000 of operating expenses.

The linear-programming application package indicates that the objective function value is $1,332,514—the combined cost of X plus Y plus Z ($466,313 + $538,545 + $327,656)—more than the $880,000 of overhead cost that was to be assigned to the revenue centers. Do

Exhibit 10.5 Elmwood Medical Services Clinic: Support Services Assigned by Reciprocal Method for Year Ended 31 December 19X2

Part I. Initial Cost and Support Services for Year

Departments		Initial Cost	Services Provided		
			Administration X	Business Office Y	Housekeeping/ Maintenance Z
Physician group practice	A	$ 791,500	25%	35%	20%
Rehabilitation services	B	566,500	30	10	10
Mental health services	C	362,000	20	20	25
Administration	X	320,000	—	15	20
Business office	Y	410,000	10	—	20
Housekeeping/maintenance	Z	150,000	15	20	—
Total cost		$2,600,000			

Part II. Algorithm's Computed Values

Cost	X	Y	Z	Total
Reciprocal cost	$466,313	$538,545	$327,656	$1,332,514

Continued

Exhibit 10.5   Continued

Part III.   Support Cost Assignments

Departments	Initial Cost	Services Provided			Total Cost
		Administration X	Business Office Y	Housekeeping/ Maintenance Z	
Physician group practice A (Utilization rate)	$ 791,500	$ 116,578 (25%)	$ 188,491 (35%)	$ 65,531 (20%)	$1,162,100
Rehabilitation services B (Utilization rate)	566,500	139,894 (30%)	53,854 (10%)	32,766 (10%)	793,014
Mental health services C (Utilization rate)	362,000	93,263 (20%)	107,709 (20%)	81,914 (25%)	644,886
Administration X (Utilization rate)	320,000	(466,313)	80,782 (15%)	65,531 (20%)	0
Business office Y (Utilization rate)	410,000	46,631 (10%)	(538,545)	81,914 (25%)	0
Housekeeping/maintenance Z (Utilization rate)	150,000	69,947 (15%)	107,709 (20%)	(327,656)	0
Total cost	$2,600,000	0	0	0	$2,600,000

not be concerned about the inflated value of the objective function. There are double cost assignments within the reciprocal method that can be viewed as "weights" (as in a weighted-average cost), but the algorithm then assigns these inflated values to the respective revenue accounts. Thus, the step-by-step mathematical procedure within the reciprocal method offsets any inflation of cost values so that the final cost assignments are compatible with the $880,000 of cost that was to be allocated.

The general format of the information in Exhibit 10.5 is compatible with the arrangement when there are numerous support departments. The first part, showing initial cost and support services, is the critical section for health care administrative personnel; the second part is merely where the algebraic results from the algorithm are entered; the third part is the location of the assignments. The use of electronic spreadsheets to perform the calculations in the third part is discussed later in this chapter.

There are only three support departments in the example of Elmwood Medical Services Clinic to facilitate illustrating the concurrent assignment of support departments by simultaneous equations that were solved algebraically. If there were several departments in which to capture the interactions among cost pools under the reciprocal cost method, then there would be more differences in the final overhead costs assigned to the respective revenue centers than represented by this simple case in Table 10.1.

At Elmwood Medical Services Clinic, concerns have been expressed by the physician groups over the increases in the total overhead cost, and the clinic's administrator has initiated a review of all costing.

Table 10.1   Elmwood Medical Services Clinic: Support Services Assigned by Three Methods for Year Ended 31 December 19X2

Revenue Departments	Direct Method	Step-Down Method	Reciprocal Cost Method
Physician group practice	$1,173,481	$1,163,318	$1,162,100
Rehabilitation services	784,850	769,409	793,014
Mental health services	641,669	667,273	644,886
Total cost	$2,600,000	$2,600,000	$2,600,000

Table 10.2 Elmwood Medical Services Clinic: Operating Expenses by Expanded Set of Cost Centers for Year Ended 31 December 19X2

	Unit Label	Total Cost
Revenue Departments		
Physician group practice	A	$ 791,500
Rehabilitation services	B	566,500
Mental health services	C	362,000
Support Departments		
Administrative activities	T	80,000
Operations manager	U	165,000
Cashier and financial manager	V	135,000
Registration and medical records	W	185,000
Patient accounting	X	145,000
Housekeeping	Y	90,000
Maintenance	Z	80,000
Total operating expenses		$2,600,000

Although the organizational structure with six departments (three revenue departments and three support departments) was not changed, additional cost centers were created, which are mapped into the support departments for some decision-making purposes. As a result of these efforts, the operating expenses of $2,600,000 are represented in an expanded set of cost centers in Table 10.2. The utilization of services from the support departments was reviewed concurrently with the partitioning of the overhead expenditures into the cost centers. Table 10.3 shows the revised utilization of services encompassing all new cost centers.

The inputs to the linear-programming algorithm under the expanded set of cost centers are as follows:

MIN $T + U + V + W + X + Y + Z$
SUBJECT TO

2) $T - 0.01U - 0.05V - 0.1W - 0.11X - 0.06Y - 0.13Z \geq 80,000$

3) $-0.01T + U - 0.08V - 0.04W - 0.05X - 0.04Y - 0.14Z \geq 165,000$

4) $-0.02T - 0.037U + V - 0.01W - 0.01X - 0.05Y - 0.1Z \geq 135,000$

5) $-0.045T - 0.034U - 0.04V + W - 0.01X - 0.06Y - 0.07Z \geq 185,000$

6) $-0.03T - 0.042U - 0.02V - 0.01W + X - 0.05Y - 0.06Z \geq 145,000$

Table 10.3 Elmwood Medical Services Clinic: Utilization of Support Services by Department

| | Support Services Provided | | | | | | |
Users	Admin Support T	Opr Mgr U	Cashier Fin Mgr V	Reg M R W	Pat Acct X	House-keeping Y	Maint Z
Physician group practice	0.230	0.265	0.340	0.360	0.350	0.250	0.150
Rehabilitation services	0.340	0.250	0.140	0.080	0.090	0.150	0.080
Mental health services	0.190	0.205	0.180	0.190	0.210	0.290	0.230
Administrative support	—	0.010	0.050	0.100	0.110	0.060	0.130
Operations manager	0.010	—	0.080	0.040	0.050	0.040	0.140
Cashier & financial manager	0.020	0.037	—	0.010	0.010	0.050	0.100
Registration & medical records	0.045	0.034	0.040	—	0.010	0.060	0.070
Patient accounting	0.030	0.042	0.020	0.010	—	0.050	0.060
Housekeeping	0.055	0.087	0.030	0.110	0.060	—	0.040
Maintenance	0.080	0.070	0.120	0.100	0.110	0.050	—
Total overhead cost	*1.000*	*1.000*	*1.000*	*1.000*	*1.000*	*1.000*	*1.000*

7) $-0.055T - 0.087U - 0.03V - 0.11W - 0.06X + Y - 0.04Z \geq 90{,}000$

8) $-0.08T - 0.07U - 0.12V - 0.1W - 0.11X - 0.05Y + Z \geq 80{,}000$

END

The linear-programming algorithm indicates that the solution is at step 7 with an objective value of $1,347,873 and with the following values for variables:

T	$168,745.00	Administrative activities
U	$231,856.10	Operations manager
V	$177,879.10	Cashier and financial manager
W	$232,387.90	Registration and medical records
X	$185,107.80	Patient accounting
Y	$168,782.50	Housekeeping
Z	$183,114.80	Maintenance

Note that the weighting factors have increased the objective value from $1,332,514 in Exhibit 10.5 to $1,347,873—more than the $880,000 of overhead costs to be assigned. However, these inflated values from double accounting are eliminated within the methodology for matching costs with the revenue centers.

The three parts in the reciprocal cost statement presented in Exhibit 10.5 are repeated with the expanded cost centers in Exhibit 10.6. Study the overall cost data in Exhibit 10.6, observing that the initial cost incurred was $2,600,000 and the matching of costs to the three revenue cost centers in Lines 26 to 28 also equals $2,600,000. There can be no change in total cost incurred in the proper application of the reciprocal cost method.

In examining the cost assignment for the administrative activities (T), note the initial cost incurred was $80,000, but $168,745 was assigned to the other nine consuming units in Part III. This $88,745 additional cost is a double accounting from Line 29 as follows:

Operations manager	$ 2,318.56
Cashier and financial manager	8,893.96
Registration and medical records	23,238.79
Patient accounting	20,361.86
Housekeeping	10,126.95
Maintenance	23,804.92
Total costs from double accounting	$88,745.04

Each of these assignments is based on simultaneous equations for the initial cost incurred in the support unit plus the interactive cost assignments from the other six support units. The operations manager (U) had an initial cost of $165,000, but $231,856 was assigned to the consuming units in Part III. This $66,856 additional cost is a double accounting from Line 30 as follows:

Administrative activities	$ 1,687.45
Cashier and financial manager	14,230.33
Registration and medical records	9,295.52
Patient accounting	9,255.39
Housekeeping	6,751.30
Maintenance	25,636.07
Total costs from double accounting	$66,856.06

After costs by the double-accounting process have been matched with all consuming units, the final assigned costs for the open revenue centers are the $2,600,000 of operating expenses incurred for the period.

The clinic's administrator had partitioned the three support departments into seven support cost units to enhance the mapping of

Exhibit 10.6 Elmwood Medical Services Clinic: Assignment of Support Services by Reciprocal Method

Part I. Initial Cost and Support Services for Year (Matrix A3...I16)

Column	A	B	C	D	E	F	G	H	I	J	
		Initial Cost	Admin T	Oper U	Cashier V	Reg & MR W	Pat Acct X	Housek Y	Maint Z	Total Cost	3 / 4 / 5
Phys G	A	$ 791,500	0.230	0.265	0.340	0.360	0.350	0.250	0.150		6
Rehab	B	566,500	0.340	0.250	0.140	0.080	0.090	0.150	0.080		7
Mental	C	362,000	0.190	0.205	0.180	0.190	0.210	0.290	0.230		8
Admin	T	80,000	(1.000)	0.010	0.050	0.100	0.110	0.060	0.130		9
Oper	U	165,000	0.010	(1.000)	0.080	0.040	0.050	0.040	0.140		10
Cashier	V	135,000	0.020	0.037	(1.000)	0.010	0.010	0.050	0.100		11
Reg & MR	W	185,000	0.045	0.034	0.040	(1.000)	0.010	0.060	0.070		12
Pat Acct	X	145,000	0.030	0.042	0.020	0.010	(1.000)	0.050	0.060		13
Housek	Y	90,000	0.055	0.087	0.030	0.110	0.060	(1.000)	0.040		14
Maint	Z	80,000	0.080	0.070	0.120	0.100	0.110	0.050	(1.000)		15
Total		$2,600,000	0.000	0.000	0.000	0.000	0.000	0.000	0.000		16

Part II. Algorithm's Computed Values (Matrix A19...J20)

Column	A	B	C	D	E	F	G	H	I	J	
Reciprocal cost			$168,745	$231,856	$177,879	$232,388	$185,108	$168,783	$183,115	$1,347,873	19 / 20 / 21

Continued

Exhibit 10.6   Continued

Part III.   Support Cost Assignments and Total Cost (Matrix A23...J36)

Column	A	B	C	D	E	F	G	H	I	J
		Initial Cost	Admin T	Oper U	Cashier V	Reg & MR W	Pat Acct X	Housek Y	Maint Z	Total Cost
Phys G	A	$ 791,500	$ 38,811	$ 61,441	$ 60,479	$ 83,660	$ 64,788	$ 42,196	$ 27,467	$1,170,342
Rehab	B	566,500	57,373	57,964	24,904	18,591	16,660	25,317	14,649	781,958
Mental	C	362,000	32,062	47,531	32,018	44,154	38,872	48,947	42,116	647,700
Admin	T	80,000	(168,745)	2,319	8,894	23,239	20,362	10,127	23,804	0
Oper	U	165,000	1,687	(231,856)	14,230	9,296	9,256	6,751	25,636	0
Cashier	V	135,000	3,375	8,579	(177,879)	2,324	1,851	8,439	18,311	0
Reg & MR	W	185,000	7,594	7,883	7,115	(232,388)	1,851	10,127	12,818	0
Pat Acct	X	145,000	5,062	9,738	3,558	2,324	(185,108)	8,439	10,987	0
Housek	Y	90,000	9,281	20,171	5,336	25,563	11,106	(168,783)	7,326	0
Maint	Z	80,000	13,500	16,230	21,345	23,239	20,362	8,439	(183,115)	0
Total		$2,600,000	0	0	0	0	0	0	0	$2,600,000

Notes: Phys G   = Physician Group Practice
Rehab   = Rehabilitation Services
Mental = Mental Health Services
Admin   = Administrative Activities
Oper   = Operations Manager

Cashier   = Cashier and Financial Manager
Reg & MR = Registration and Medical Records
Pat Acct = Patient Accounting
Housek   = Housekeeping
Maint   = Maintenance

utilization to the benefiting areas in response to concerns from the physician group. Utilization statistics in Part I of Exhibit 10.6 are similar to those in Exhibit 10.5, except that one support department in the former exhibit is composed of two or three cost units in the expanded presentation. The utilization by department in Exhibit 10.5 is compatible with the average utilization of related cost units in Exhibit 10.6. The result is an increase in total costs from $1,162,100 to $1,170,342 for the physician group under the expanded mapping of utilization statistics.

Summary

"Costs follow revenue" is a basic concept of financial accounting and the driver for matching expenditures with revenue. The matching process is performed at different levels—from matching marginal cost and marginal revenue to the full costing of a patient service; the latter includes assigning to patient revenue the cost of all administrative and support activities associated with providing that patient service. Some of the layers of support services are represented by common cost accounts where application computer programs can match (assign) the expenditures to the benefiting MC/R centers.

The statistical, clinical, and financial database in a health care entity can provide quality data for automatic assignment of common costs to specified MC/R centers. General overhead costs are not automatically recorded to MC/R centers. Instead, the proposed allocations of general overhead are examined, with emphasis given to the interactions among the multiple support units. Transactions capturing the allocation of these general overhead costs may or may not be recorded in the DBMS. Many general overhead allocations are for a limited number of users, such as a given regulatory agency. When there is limited use of such general allocations, the transactions are often not stored in the DBMS.

Various revenue centers in health care entities can be described as the hub of patient services surrounded by a layer of common cost areas and dedicated support units, which are surrounded by one or more layers of support services, which in turn are surrounded by an outer layer of general and administrative expenditures. The cost-assignment methods in this chapter address the matching of the layers of support services and the outer layer of general and administrative expenditures to the benefiting revenue centers.

There are three common methods for matching overhead or support costs with revenues: the direct method, the step-down method, and the reciprocal cost method. The direct method prorates support costs to each revenue center in proportion to the utilization statistics for that center over the aggregate utilization statistics for all revenue centers. Under the direct method, there is no recognition of the interaction of one support area with another support area; the only utilization statistics included in the denominator are for revenue centers. Because these utilization data for support units are excluded, some regulatory agencies do not permit the direct method to be used by selected health care entities, such as community hospitals.

The step-down method was very popular under Medicare cost-based reimbursement because the order in which cost center accounts were mandated to be closed tended to benefit the typical community hospital more than the reimbursement under other approved methods. After a cost center is closed under the step-down procedure, that center no longer participates in further cost-matching processes. Thus, the order in which cost accounts are closed in the step-down method is critical to the results in the final matching of costs to the revenue centers. In the process of closing, the least important support cost center, which is closed in the last step, becomes significant to the final results because its impact has been expanded by assigned values from other closed accounts.

The reciprocal cost method captures the interaction among all support cost centers and simultaneously assigns overhead cost based on total utilization of services in the process of matching all operating expenses from these units with the revenue centers. Statistical measures and performance data in the DBMS from Part III of the responsibility accounting reports are the source of most utilization data for the reciprocal cost method. Except for the small clinic, most ambulatory care and community hospital facilities contain numerous support and overhead cost centers that must be included in the application of the reciprocal cost method. Linear-programming algorithms on personal computers can perform the reciprocal cost assignments on a timely basis, and application packages on the personal computer can accommodate the matching of 200-plus cost centers to revenue centers.

The appendix to this chapter suggests that the reciprocal cost method should be viewed as a set of three matrices:

1. Matrix A contains direct cost plus utilization data on the consumption of services for each support and overhead account.

2. Matrix B contains the reciprocal cost values for the support departments from the linear-programming algorithm.

3. Matrix C is a computational unit in which cells are individually cross-referenced to the multiplication of a specific cell in Matrix A (containing a utilization percent) by a cell in Matrix B (with reciprocal cost values).

Administrative personnel in health care entities are primarily concerned with Matrix A; however, many of the cells in this matrix are constant from one period to the next. The entries in Matrix A are utilization percents, not absolute amounts; thus, proportional changes with volume are represented by the same percents without any new input requirements. The reciprocal cost values for each support account must be entered in Matrix B. Entries are made in Matrix C only for the addition or deletion of cost accounts.

Long-term contracts, pricing arrangements, and strategic assessments require the full matching of all overhead and support costs with revenue centers. The reciprocal cost method is the only conceptual approach that encompasses the interaction of all support centers. With the availability of linear-programming application packages on personal computers, it is expected that the reciprocal cost method will become the dominant approach for matching costs with revenues in health care entities. Long-term pricing and contractual decisions must be based on full knowledge of the impact of interaction among all support cost centers.

Appendix: Linear-Programming Considerations with Reciprocal Cost Method

Individuals with experience in linear programming may question why Parts III of Exhibits 10.5 and 10.6 were not encompassed in the specification of the problem. Exhibit 10.7 illustrates this point by displaying the answer to Elmwood Medical Services Clinic's expanded set of cost centers in place of the specifics in Exhibit 10.6. The reciprocal cost method may be applied 10 or 12 times at the end of the fiscal period using alternative utilization statistics. For multiple applications of the reciprocal method, it is helpful to have an electronic spreadsheet in the format of Part III of Exhibit 10.6. This procedure facilitates interpretation of the results where the focus is only on the support cost units. Including revenue centers in the specification of the problem produces an answer without providing a framework that is useful for assessment in many health care entities.

A designated general ledger chart of account (GLCA) number is used in most health care entities to identify depreciation expense. This specification permits a partitioning of depreciation expense by major

Exhibit 10.7   Elmwood Medical Services Clinic: Assignment of Support Services by Reciprocal Method (Expanded specification)

Expanded Specification of Support Cost Units

MIN $T + U + V + W + X + Y + Z + A + B + C$
SUBJECT TO

2) $T - 0.01U - 0.05V - 0.1W - 0.11X - 0.06Y - 0.13Z \geq 80,000$
3) $-0.01T + U - 0.08V - 0.04W - 0.05X - 0.04Y - 0.14Z \geq 165,000$
4) $-0.02T - 0.037U + V - 0.01W - 0.01X - 0.05Y - 0.1Z \geq 135,000$
5) $-0.045T - 0.034U - 0.04V + W - 0.01X - 0.06Y - 0.07Z \geq 185,000$
6) $-0.03T - 0.042U - 0.02V - 0.01W + X - 0.05Y - 0.06Z \geq 145,000$
7) $-0.055T - 0.087U - 0.03V - 0.11W - 0.06X + Y - 0.04Z \geq 90,000$
8) $-0.08T - 0.07U - 0.12V - 0.1W - 0.11X - 0.05Y + Z \geq 80,000$
9) $-0.23T - 0.265U - 0.34V - 0.36W - 0.35X - 0.25Y - 0.15Z + A \geq 791,500$
10) $-0.34T - 0.25U - 0.14V - 0.08W - 0.09X - 0.15Y - 0.08Z + B \geq 566,500$
11) $-0.19T - 0.205U - 0.18V - 0.19W - 0.21X - 0.29Y - 0.23Z + C \geq 362,000$
END

Solution from Linear-Programming Algorithm (LINDO)

LP optimum found at step 10

	Objective function value	
1)	3,947,872.90	

Variable	*Value*	
T	$ 168,745.00	Administrative activities
U	$ 231,856.10	Operations manager
V	$ 177,879.20	Cashier and financial manager
W	$ 232,387.80	Registration and medical records
X	$ 185,107.80	Patient accounting
Y	$ 168,782.60	Housekeeping
Z	$ 183,114.80	Maintenance
A	$1,170,342.00	Physician group practice
B	$ 781,957.70	Rehabilitation services
C	$ 647,699.90	Mental health services

categories within the health care entity. The matching of depreciation expense to the benefiting regular cost account is accomplished by a set of assignment entries in the application program processed at the end of the period. In retrieving data for use in the reciprocal cost method, the initial cost for a support or revenue-cost center includes depreciation expense. It also includes the assigned costs for physician salaries, common cost centers, and dedicated support centers.

Using electronic spreadsheets

Health care facilities may add a few cost centers during the year, and some cost centers may be deleted. But, overall these are minor changes in comparison with the dominant group of cost centers that continue from period to period. With shifts in patient loads, case-mix profiles, acuity of patients, and treatment programs, there are changes in the distribution of services provided by one support department to another support department. As the volume of patients changes, there may not be an exact one-to-one response in the utilization of support services because of other factors (such as acuity level of patient upon admission). While the utilization behavior of some cost centers may be highly related to these shifts in volumes and patient profiles, other support cost centers may have semifixed patterns of consumption.

These generalizations about health care facilities suggest that if there were 200 cost centers last period, then probably about 195 of those cost centers have continued. There may be 10 new cost centers, and 5 former cost centers may be dropped; thus, there are now 205 cost centers. Thus, 10 new columns will be added to the electronic spreadsheet; however, 195 columns from last period can be used again this period.[1] The utilization percentage in about 140 of the 195 columns may be the same for this period as for the prior period; thus, adjustments must be made to the 55 cost centers with changes in utilization. Because utilization is expressed as a percent and not as an absolute amount, there are frequently fewer changes required than might be expected even when there are major shifts in the health care entity's volume.

The electronic spreadsheet should be specified to make use of this degree of continuity in identification of cost centers and in the amount of support service utilization. The reciprocal method can be viewed as containing three matrices; seen from this perspective, the Elmwood Medical Services Clinic can be described as a master matrix A3 . . . K36 with three parts, as illustrated in Exhibit 10.6. These three matrices are as follows:

Matrix A (A3 . . . K17):   direct cost plus utilization for each support cost center

Matrix B (A19 . . . K20):   results from linear programming for support cost centers

Matrix C (A23 . . . K36):   calculations of cells in Matrix A times column data in Matrix B

Viewing the reciprocal cost method in a health care setting as three matrices in the context of an electronic spreadsheet encourages the classification of Matrix C as computational. The only changes that should be made in Matrix C are to add or delete a cost center; otherwise, the formula in each cell within Matrix C is the same from period to period. To illustrate this approach, note that physician-group practice is on Line 6 in Matrix A and on Line 26 in Matrix C in Exhibit 10.6 and that the reciprocal cost values are on Line 20. Column C in Exhibit 10.6 is for the support cost unit administrative activities. Thus, the $38,811 assigned cost in Cell C26 is obtained by the formula C6 × C20: the percent of cost consumed by physician-group practice and entered in Cell C6 (23% in Exhibit 10.6) is multiplied by the reciprocal cost amount in Cell C20 for administrative activities ($168,745) giving $38,811 for Cell C26. Since Cell C26 is a formula and not an amount, a change in either the percent consumed (Cell C6) or the reciprocal cost value (Cell C20) will change the assigned cost for the physician group. Some problems at the end of the chapter are based on this approach to Matrix C.

Exhibit 10.8 shows a segment of Matrix C where the formulas in the various cells are illustrated for purposes of showing their pattern in the context of an electronic spreadsheet. After the formulas have been entered in matrix C26 . . . C36 of an electronic spreadsheet, matrix D26 . . . F36 can be created by a simple copy command, which will automatically index each cell correctly. The copy command can be extended to as many cells as there are support cost centers. Thus, only one column of computational cells must be entered in Matrix C; the remaining support cost units are created and appropriately indexed by the copy command.

Decision-making context

Health care entities are often involved in contract conditions related to the total operating expenses for a segment of activity because of the problems involved with gross patient revenues and calculating net cash

Exhibit 10.8 A Segment of Matrix C with Formulas

Part III. Support Cost Assignments and Total Cost (Matrix A23. .J36)

		Total Cost	(Column C) Admin T	(Column D) Oper U	(Column E) Cashier V	(Column F) Reg & MR W	
							23
							24
							25
Phys G	A	$ 791,500	(C6*C20)	(D6*D20)	(E6*E20)	(F6*F20)	26
Rehab	B	566,500	(C7*C20)	(D7*D20)	(E7*E20)	(F7*F20)	27
Mental	C	362,000	(C8*C20)	(D8*D20)	(E8*E20)	(F8*F20)	28
Admin	T	80,000	(C9*C20)	(D9*D20)	(E9*E20)	(F9*F20)	29
Oper	U	165,000	(C10*C20)	(D10*D20)	(E10*E20)	(F10*F20)	30
Cashier	V	135,000	(C11*C20)	(D11*D20)	(E11*E20)	(F11*F20)	31
Reg & MR	W	185,000	(C12*C20)	(D12*D20)	(E12*E20)	(F12*F20)	32
Pat Acct	X	145,000	(C13*C20)	(D13*D20)	(E13*E20)	(F13*F20)	33
Housek	Y	90,000	(C14*C20)	(D14*D20)	(E14*E20)	(F14*F20)	34
Maint	Z	80,000	(C15*C20)	(D15*D20)	(E15*E20)	(F15*F20)	35
Total		$2,600,000	@SUM(C26…C35)	@SUM(D26…D35)	…		36

Notes:

Phys G	= Physician Group Practice		Cashier	= Cashier and Financial Manager
Rehab	= Rehabilitation Services		Reg & MR	= Registration and Medical Records
Mental	= Mental Health Services		Pat Acct	= Patient Accounting
Admin	= Administrative Activities		Housek	= Housekeeping
Oper	= Operations Manager		Maint	= Maintenance

flows, especially when there are 20 or more financial classes of patients. Financial institutions working with health care entities are accustomed to examining selected revenue centers that may be unique to each entity and then using the results of those centers as a barometer for the overall entity's financial health. Contract terms often select one or more of these key revenue centers as the basis for monitoring the health care entity's progress and as a signal that additional corrective actions may be required.

Approximately 65 percent of a health care entity's operating expenses are identified with direct labor and fringe benefits; supplies account for about 10 percent of operating expenses. Management control procedures appropriately focus on monitoring and verifying direct labor expenses, including a mapping of approved position codes to the regular cost account and to its budget. There are also special operating control procedures for supplies because of their use in supporting services to patients; the costing of the supplies builds upon these other control procedures.

Application computer programs working with the DBMSs in health care entities provide excellent management control over the majority of the operating expenses, such as direct labor, fringe benefits, and supplies. Consulting expense, professional services, and special project expenses are often recorded in regular cost accounts under the direction of the administrator of the health care entity and where there is sufficient balance in the board-approved budget to support the expenditures. These major items of expense do not surface as exceptions in the management control reports since they are within the cost center's overall budget. But when the reciprocal cost method is applied to the period's ending status, one or more revenue centers may have cost in excess of a guideline or a contract term for that revenue center. The above sequence of events has been observed in several community hospitals and in a few clinics.

In the case of the physician group at Elmwood Medical Services Clinic, represented by the special partitioning of support departments in Exhibit 10.6, it is highly likely that some of the $791,500 of direct expenses may include a special charge to that account. Alternatively, the initial expenditures in each of the seven support cost accounts must be analyzed for special charges to those regular cost units that may need to be reclassified.

Professional consultants in health care are often engaged to review selected revenue centers where there are problems with contracts or regulatory agencies. In most cases the problems have nothing to do with direct labor, fringe benefits, or supplies, but are the results of "special costing" under the approval of the administrator that have been forgotten because of their small dollar amount relative to the total revenues for the health care entity. Once these items are identified, they are quickly reclassified and are often directly charged to nonsupport cost centers so that they are outside the reciprocal cost calculations.

Federal program inpatients in community hospitals are subject to PPS with payment per fee schedule by DRG. Federal program outpatients in community hospitals are still under a retrospective cost-based reimbursement system, except where there is a demonstration project. There are other types of health care entities where federal program patients and selected third party payors also follow a retrospective cost-based reimbursement system. The mandated sequence by a regulatory agency for closing support cost centers continues to support the use of the step-down method. The calculation of contractual allowances for federal program outpatients in this decision-making context must be reviewed, and any irregular entries identified. There may be a need for some reclassification of entries of the type previously described.

Assume that Woodstock Community Hospital had operating expenses of $33 million for the year ended 31 December 19X2 and that 40 percent of gross charges to ancillary departments were for outpatients. Federal program and third party payors following a retrospective cost-based reimbursement arrangement comprised between 50 to 65 percent of these outpatient services, depending on the revenue center. Exhibit 10.9 shows the gross charges and assigned cost balances for the revenue centers. Costs are matched with revenues on a proportional basis for those outpatient ancillary services; thus, 40 percent of the ancillary gross charges ($8,400,000) are matched against the 40 percent of the assigned cost ($5,560,000) giving a "return" of $2,840,000. The term "return" is before contractual adjustments; these adjustments are based on the utilization percentage in each revenue center by the cost-based users. The initial situation reports contractual adjustments of $1,638,000 in Exhibit 10.9.

After reviewing the results for Woodstock Community Hospital, it was discovered that a $200,000 expenditure charged to the radiology cost area could have been charged to the laboratory cost area. This transaction has no impact on either gross patient charges or the $33 million in operating expenses for the year; there is the potential for reclassification of the $200,000 from radiology to laboratory. If the proposed transaction is recorded, it will have no impact on outpatient

Exhibit 10.9 Computing Contractual Adjustments for Federal Program Outpatients at Woodstock Community Hospital for the Year Ended 31 December 19X2

	Gross Patient Charges	Assigned Cost	Ratio Cost/ Charges
Routine care	$20,000,000	$19,100,000	0.955
Laboratory department	7,000,000	4,200,000	0.60
Radiology	9,000,000	6,300,000	0.70
Respiratory therapy	5,000,000	3,400,000	0.68
Totals	*$41,000,000*	*$33,000,000*	

Partitioning of Gross Revenue:

Inpatient ($20,000,000 + 60% of $21,000,000)	$32,600,000
Outpatient (40% of $21,000,000)	8,400,000
Total gross patient revenues	*$41,000,000*

In the matching of cost to 40 percent of ancillary revenues, this can be accomplished by taking 40 percent of each department's cost or by applying the ratio of cost/charges times the outpatient revenues.

Ancillary Depts (40% of Gross)	Outpatient Revenues	Assigned Costs by Ratio	Net for All Outpatients	Cost-based Users	Contractual Adjustments
Laboratory	$2,800,000	$1,680,000	$1,120,000	0.55	$ 616,000
Radiology	3,600,000	2,520,000	1,080,000	0.65	702,000
Respiratory	2,000,000	1,360,000	640,000	0.50	320,000
Totals	*$8,400,000*	*$5,560,000*	*$2,840,000*		*$1,638,000*

Assume $200,000 of cost initially charged to radiology can be reclassified to laboratory; thus, the adjusted cost for laboratory is $4,400,000, and radiology is $6,100,000. The total cost is still $33,000,000, and the assigned cost for outpatient ancillary is the same as before, or $5,560,000. However, there is a difference in contractual adjustments because of the percent of utilization by cost-based users in the revenue centers.

Ancillary Depts (40% of Gross)	Outpatient Revenues	Assigned Costs by Ratio	Net for All Outpatients	Cost-based Users	Contractual Adjustments
Laboratory	$2,800,000	$1,760,000	$1,040,000	0.55	$ 572,000
Radiology	3,600,000	2,440,000	1,160,000	0.65	754,000
Respiratory	2,000,000	1,360,000	640,000	0.50	320,000
Totals	*$8,400,000*	*$5,560,000*	*$2,840,000*		*$1,646,000*

Because there is a loss of $8,000 from contractual adjustments, the reclassificaiton of $200,000 is rejected.

Note: For illustration purposes, only three ancillary departments are shown.

revenues; the total outpatient assigned costs are the same in aggregate as before.

The assigned cost for laboratory under the proposed transaction would be $80,000 more (40 percent of $200,000), with a reduction of $80,000 in the assigned cost for radiology. Because of differences in the rate of utilization of services by cost-based users, there would be a loss of $8,000 if the proposed transaction is recorded. Unless there are other factors not cited, the reclassification entry is not recorded.

Note

1. The term "electronic spreadsheets" is intentionally used to indicate that students have responded to the assigned problems with different brands of electronic worksheets. Northwestern University now has multiple types of worksheets for all students.

Additional Readings

Baptist, A. J., J. Saylor, and J. Zerwekh. "Developing A Solid Base for a Cost Accounting System," *Healthcare Financial Management* 41 (January 1987): 42–48.

Goldschmidt, Y., and A. Gafni. "A Managerial Approach to Allocating Indirect Fixed Costs in Health Care Organizations," *Health Care Management Review* 15 (Spring 1990): 43–51.

McFadden, D. W. "The Legacy of the $7 Aspirin," *Management Accounting* 71 (April 1990): 38–41.

Schlenker, R. E., and P. W. Shaughnessy. "Swing-Bed Hospital Cost and Reimbursement," *Inquiry* 26 (Winter 1989): 508–21.

Discussion Questions

10.1. A regular cost account containing salaries of two physicians is treated as

   a. allocated general overhead costs to MC/R centers

   b. common allocated overhead costs to MC/R centers

   c. common assigned support costs to MC/R centers

   d. common direct costs to MC/R centers

10.2. In an organizational area where there are four related regular cost accounts for Security and Parking, a regular cost account for the "office of director, Security and Parking" is treated as

    a. allocated general overhead costs to MC/R centers

    b. common allocated overhead costs to MC/R centers

    c. common assigned support costs to MC/R centers

    d. common direct costs to MC/R centers

10.3. A regular cost account containing expenditures for housekeeping expense is treated as

    a. allocated general overhead costs to MC/R centers

    b. common allocated overhead costs to MC/R centers

    c. common assigned support costs to MC/R centers

    d. common direct costs to MC/R centers

10.4. In a health care entity's Department of Pathology with many MC/R centers at organizational level 6, a regular cost account for the office of chair, Pathology (organizational level 3) is treated as

    a. allocated general overhead costs to MC/R centers

    b. common allocated overhead costs to MC/R centers

    c. common assigned support costs to MC/R centers

    d. common direct costs to MC/R centers

10.5. The manager of Physical Medicine directs three areas: Physical Therapy, Occupational Therapy, and Speech and Audiology. A regular cost account for the office of manager of Physical Medicine is treated as

    a. allocated general overhead costs to MC/R centers

    b. common allocated overhead costs to MC/R centers

    c. common assigned support costs to MC/R centers

    d. common direct costs to MC/R centers

10.6. A regular cost account containing salaries of the CEO and administrative assistants is treated as

    a. allocated general overhead costs to MC/R centers

    b. common allocated overhead costs to MC/R centers

    c. common assigned support costs to MC/R centers

    d. common direct costs to MC/R centers

10.7. Considering the excellent databases in many health care entities, explain why general overhead costs are not automatically allocated by application computer programs to MC/R centers.

10.8. Some regulatory agencies do not accept financial statements for health care entities where the direct method of cost assignment for overhead and support centers has been used. Explain the conceptual problem with the direct method for health care entities.

10.9.   The step-down method begins with utilization data on consumption of support services for all cost centers. How does the methodology in the step-down approach not capture the full interaction of these support departments?

10.10. Explain why the sequence to be followed in applying the step-down method to support cost centers is critical in the final matching of costs with MC/R centers.

10.11. How can the least important support cost center, which is closed in the final process of the step-down method, significantly affect the final assignment of costs to MC/R centers?

10.12. Prior to the prospective payment system, some community hospitals used the reciprocal cost method for long-range planning but filed their Medicare cost reports with the step-down method. What was the reason for this choice of methods in reporting to regulatory agencies?

10.13. How does the reciprocal cost method capture the interaction of all support departments in the process of assigning costs to the MC/R centers?

10.14. Some contracts, loan agreements, and other financial instruments may have terms and conditions that use total costs of specific revenue centers in the health care entity as the basis for various courses of action. Explain the measurement problems in some health care entities for expressing (A) net income for the total entity and (B) net return for specific MC/R centers.

10.15. Professional consultants assisting a health care entity where the assigned costs to a MC/R center are in excess of a contract condition often discover an accounting transaction that must be reclassified. Explain why this transaction was not reported on an exception basis by the management control system.

10.16. Selected income and cost information for the Eastwood Community Hospital for the year ended 31 December 19X2 are shown in Exhibit 10.10. The step-down approach at Eastwood Community Hospital is based on the aggregation shown in Exhibit 10.11. A regulatory agency has specified that Eastwood Community Hospital's support departments are allocated to the remaining departments in the following order: (1) depreciation (on the basis of square feet), (2) employee health and welfare (on the basis of gross salaries), (3) administration (on the basis of accumulated cost at that point in the step-down method), (4) operation of plant (on the basis of square feet), and (5) dietary and cafeteria (on the basis of meals served).

   A. Determine the total assigned cost for each revenue department at the Eastwood Community Hospital. In your computations, assume

Exhibit 10.10   Selected Income and Cost Information for the Year Ended 31 December 19X2 for Eastwood Community Hospital

FinStat	Amount
Income	
Routine Care Daily Hospital Service	
11301 Medical/surgical routine care services	$18,000,000
Revenue Departments	
11421 Laboratory services—clinical	2,300,000
11423 Laboratory services—pathological	2,100,000
11432 Diagnostic radiology	1,200,000
11434 CT scanner	1,000,000
11436 Therapeutic radiology	900,000
11438 Nuclear medicine	700,000
11439 Ultrasound	800,000
11442 Respiratory therapy	2,100,000
Total revenue for year	$29,100,000
Cost	
Routine Care Daily Hospital Service	
11601 Medical/surgical routine care services	$ 9,920,000
Revenue Departments	
11721 Laboratory services—clinical	800,000
11723 Laboratory services—pathological	1,000,000
11732 Diagnostic radiology	373,100
11734 CT scanner	330,050
11736 Therapeutic radiology	301,200
11738 Nuclear medicine	215,250
11739 Ultrasound	215,400
11742 Respiratory therapy	950,000
11831 Dietary services	1,700,000
11841 Plant operations and maintenance	1,645,000
11861 Hospital administration	4,620,000
11881 Depreciation—fixed assets	1,400,000
11883 Employee benefits	1,530,000
Total cost	$25,000,000

Exhibit 10.11   Aggregation upon Which the Step-Down Method for
Eastwood Community Hospital Is Based

FinStat		Amount
	Laboratory department	$1,800,000
11721	Laboratory services—clinical	800,000
11723	Laboratory services—pathological	1,000,000
	Radiology department	$1,435,000
11732	Diagnostic radiology	373,100
11734	CT scanner	330,050
11736	Therapeutic radiology	301,200
11738	Nuclear medicine	215,250
11739	Ultrasound	215,400

Statistical Basis for Allocation of Departmental Cost

	Square Feet	Total Salaries	No. Meals Served
1. Depreciation	0	0	
2. Employee benefits	16,000	$ 800,000	10,000
3. Administration	32,000	2,250,000	30,000
4. Operation of plant	72,000	1,500,000	15,000
5. Dietary	32,000	1,500,000	20,000
Routine care	96,000	6,750,000	180,000
Laboratory department	32,000	1,500,000	22,500
Radiology	24,000	750,000	11,250
Respiratory therapy	16,000	750,000	11,250
Total	320,000	$15,800,000	300,000

the hospital aggregates all radiology activities into a single "department" and aggregates all laboratory activities into another single "department." Show your computations with appropriate labels.

B. Map the assigned cost for the aggregate radiology area to the revenue departments in that group based on *revenue*. Use the same approach with the two areas in the laboratory.

C. Map the assigned cost for the aggregate radiology area to the revenue departments in that group based on *cost*. Use the same approach with the two areas in the laboratory.

D. Assume that 35 percent of gross patient revenues in ancillary departments are for outpatients and that 60 percent of the services for outpatients are for federal program patients covered by a cost-based reimbursement arrangement. Calculate the contractual allowance for these federal program outpatients in these three ancillary departments under the assumption that the assigned cost is approved for payment by the fiscal intermediary for the federal program.

10.17. Selected income and cost information for the Eaton Memorial Hospital for the year ended 31 December 19X2 are shown in Exhibit 10.12. The allocated cost approach at Eaton Memorial Hospital is based on the aggregation shown in Exhibit 10.13. A regulatory agency has specified that Eaton Memorial Hospital's support departments are allocated to the remaining departments in the following order: (1) depreciation (on the basis of square feet), (2) employee health and welfare (on the basis of gross salaries), (3) administration (on the basis of accumulated cost at that point in the step-down method), (4) operation of plant (on the basis of square feet), (5) housekeeping (on the basis of hours worked), (6) dietary and cafeteria (on the basis of meals served).

A. Determine the total assigned cost for each revenue department at the Eaton Memorial Hospital. In your computations, assume the hospital aggregates all radiology activities into a single "department" and aggregates all laboratory activities into another single "department." Show your computations with appropriate labels.

B. Map the assigned cost for the aggregate radiology area to the revenue departments in that group based on *revenue*. Use the same approach with the two areas in the laboratory.

C. Map the assigned cost for the aggregate radiology area to the revenue departments in that group based on *cost*. Use the same approach with the two areas in the laboratory.

D. Assume that 40 percent of gross patient revenues in ancillary departments are for outpatients and that 55 percent of the services for outpatients are for federal program patients covered by a cost-based reimbursement arrangement. Calculate the contractual allowance for these federal program outpatients in these three ancillary departments under the assumption that the assigned cost is approved for payment by the fiscal intermediary for the federal program.

10.18. (See Question 10.17.) Exhibit 10.14 presents the $20,800,000 of total cost for Eaton Memorial Hospital at the start of the application of the reciprocal cost method. Routine care's cost is $5,299,500 (in place of $4,800,000 in Question 10.17) because of

a. assignment of estimated income tax expense

b. assignment of interest expense

c. assignment of depreciation expense

d. assignment of physician salaries

Exhibit 10.12   Selected Income and Cost Information for the Year Ended
31 December 19X2 for Eaton Memorial
Hospital

FinStat		Amount
Income		
Routine Care Daily Hospital Service		
11301	Medical/surgical routine care services	$15,800,000
Revenue Departments		
11421	Laboratory services—clinical	2,400,000
11423	Laboratory services—pathological	2,200,000
11432	Diagnostic radiology	1,350,000
11434	CT scanner	1,150,000
11436	Therapeutic radiology	1,000,000
11438	Nuclear medicine	800,000
11439	Ultrasound	900,000
11442	Respiratory therapy	2,400,000
	Total revenue	$28,000,000
Cost		
Routine Care Daily Hospital Service		
11601	Medical/surgical routine care services	$ 4,800,000
Revenue Departments		
11721	Laboratory services—clinical	700,000
11723	Laboratory services—pathological	1,200,000
11732	Diagnostic radiology	390,000
11734	CT scanner	360,000
11736	Therapeutic radiology	290,000
11738	Nuclear medicine	240,000
11739	Ultrasound	220,000
11742	Respiratory therapy	1,140,000
11831	Dietary services	1,400,000
11841	Plant operations and maintenance	2,800,000
11851	Housekeeping	1,600,000
11861	Hospital administration	3,200,000
11881	Depreciation—fixed assets	900,000
11883	Employee benefits	1,560,000
	Total cost	$20,800,000

Exhibit 10.13   Aggregation upon Which the Allocated Cost Approach for Eaton Memorial Hospital Is Based

FinStat		Amount
	Laboratory department	*$1,900,000*
11721	Laboratory services—clinical	700,000
11723	Laboratory services—pathological	1,200,000
	Radiology department	*$1,500,000*
11732	Diagnostic radiology	390,000
11734	CT scanner	360,000
11736	Therapeutic radiology	290,000
11738	Nuclear medicine	240,000
11739	Ultrasound	220,000

Statistical Basis for Allocation of Departmental Cost

| | | | Housekeeping | |
	Square Feet	Direct Salaries	Hours Worked	Meals Served
Employee benefits	10,800	$ 139,500	2,000	4,080
Hospital administration	14,400	1,539,500	2,000	18,000
Plant operations and maintenance	9,000	1,560,500	2,000	25,200
Housekeeping	7,200	799,000	2,200	27,000
Dietary services	18,000	918,000	3,000	31,400
Routine care services	199,800	2,709,000	76,000	124,320
Laboratory services	39,600	1,035,000	6,000	16,200
Radiology	32,400	819,000	5,000	14,400
Respiratory therapy	28,800	620,000	4,000	10,800
Totals	*360,000*	*$10,139,500*	*102,200*	*271,400*

10.19. (See Question 10.17.) Utilization statistics are the basis in Exhibit 10.14 for the usage factors specified for assigning the administration support account (W) in Column D of the electronic worksheet. The problem in using the accumulated cost at that point in the assignment (as in Question 10.17) is

a. rounding issues in projecting cost at the third step in the reciprocal method

b. the simultaneous assignment of all cost centers in the reciprocal method

Exhibit 10.14 Eaton Memorial Hospital: Assignment of Support Services by Reciprocal Method

Matrix A

Column A	B	C	D	E	F	G	H	
	Initial Cost	Employee Benefits V	Administrative W	Operation of Plant X	Housekeeping Y	Dietary Z	Total Cost	6 / 7 / 8
Routine care	$ 5,299,500	0.27090	0.30496	0.56923	0.76000	0.51800		9
Laboratory	1,999,000	0.10350	0.12071	0.11282	0.06000	0.06750		10
Radiology	1,581,000	0.08190	0.09530	0.09231	0.05000	0.06000		11
Respiratory therapy	1,212,000	0.06200	0.07243	0.08205	0.04000	0.04500		12
Employee benefits V	1,587,000	(1.00000)	0.07624	0.03077	0.02000	0.01700		13
Administrative W	3,236,000	0.15395	(1.00000)	0.04103	0.02000	0.07500		14
Operation of plant X	2,822,500	0.15605	0.17789	(1.00000)	0.02000	0.10500		15
Housekeeping Y	1,618,000	0.07990	0.06353	0.02051	(1.00000)	0.11250		16
Dietary Z	1,445,000	0.09180	0.08894	0.05128	0.03000	1.00000		17
Total	$20,800,000	0.00000	0.00000	0.00000	0.00000	0.00000		18 / 19 / 20

Matrix B

Column A	B	C	D	E	F	G	H	
Reciprocal cost		$2,101,472	$3,947,322	$4,138,785	$2,377,229	$2,272,544	$14,837,352	21 / 22

Continued

Exhibit 10.14 Continued

Matrix C

Column A		Initial Cost	Employee Benefits V	Administrative W	Operation of Plant X	Housekeeping Y	Dietary Z	Total Cost	
		B	C	D	E	F	G	H	
Routine care		$ 5,299,500	$569,289	$1,203,775	$2,355,921	$1,806,694	$1,177,178	$12,412,356	26
Laboratory		1,999,000	217,502	476,481	466,938	142,634	153,397	3,455,952	27
Radiology		1,581,000	172,110	376,180	382,051	118,861	136,353	2,766,555	28
Respiratory therapy		1,212,000	130,291	285,905	339,587	95,089	102,264	2,165,137	29
Employee benefits	V	1,587,000	(2,101,472)	300,944	127,350	47,545	38,633	0	30
Administrative	W	3,236,000	323,522	(3,947,322)	169,814	47,545	170,441	0	31
Operation of plant	X	2,822,500	327,935	702,189	(4,138,785)	47,544	238,617	0	32
Housekeeping	Y	1,618,000	167,908	250,773	84,887	(2,377,229)	255,661	0	33
Dietary	Z	1,445,000	192,915	351,075	212,237	71,317	(2,272,544)	0	34
Total		$20,800,000	0	0	0	0	0	$20,800,000	35

c. determining the sequence to close the accounts in the reciprocal method

d. the adjustment of accumulated cost for rounding errors in the reciprocal method

10.20. In Exhibit 10.14 the equation used to calculate the reciprocal cost for the employee benefits (V) support cost center is

a. $V - 0.07624W - 0.03077X - 0.02Y - 0.17Z \geq \$1,587,000$

b. $V - 0.15395W - 0.15605X - 0.0799Y - 0.0918Z \geq \$1,587,000$

c. $V - 0.15395W - 0.03077X - 0.0799Y - 0.0918Z \geq \$2,101,472$

d. $V - 0.07624W - 0.04103X - 0.02Y - 0.1125Z \geq \$1,587,000$

10.21. In Exhibit 10.14 the equation used to calculate the reciprocal cost for the housekeeping (Y) support cost center is

a. $-0.76A - 0.06B - 0.05C - 0.04D - 0.02V - 0.02W - 0.02X + Y - 0.03Z \geq \$2,377,229$

b. $-0.02V - 0.02W - 0.02X + Y - 0.03Z \geq \$1,618,000$

c. $-0.0799V - 0.06353W - 0.02051X + Y - 0.03Z \geq \$2,377,229$

d. $-0.0799V - 0.06353W - 0.02051X + Y - 0.1125Z \geq \$1,618,000$

10.22. In Exhibit 10.14 the equation used to calculate the reciprocal cost for the dietary (Z) support cost center is

a. $-0.017V - 0.075W - 0.105X - 0.1125Y + Z \geq \$1,445,000$

b. $-0.017V - 0.075W - 0.105X - 0.1125Y + Z \geq \$2,272,544$

c. $-0.0918V - 0.08894W - 0.05128X - 0.03Y + Z \geq \$1,445,000$

d. $-0.0918V - 0.08894W - 0.05128X - 0.03Y + Z \geq \$2,272,544$

10.23. In Exhibit 10.14 the employee benefits support account (V) is in Column C. Assume that Matrix C is a computational matrix. The content of Cell C27, showing the assignment of employee benefits support cost to laboratory, is

a. $217,502

b. C9 × C21

c. C10 × C21

d. C10 × B27

10.24. In Exhibit 10.14 the administration support account (W) is in Column D. Assume that Matrix C is a computational matrix. The content of Cell D26, showing the assignment of administration support cost to routine care, is

a. $1,203,775

b. B26 × D9

c. (0.30496 × 3,947,322)

d. D9 × D21

10.25. In Exhibit 10.14 the administration support account (W) is in Column D. Assume that Matrix C is a computational matrix. The content of Cell D31, showing the assignment of administration support cost to administration cost center, is

a. B31 + C31 + E31 + F31 + G31

b. D14 × D21

c. B31 × D14

d. D14 × (–3,947,322)

10.26. In Exhibit 10.14 the administration support account (W) is in Column D. Assume that Matrix C is a computational matrix. The content of Cell D28, showing the assignment of administration support cost to radiology cost center, is

a. B28 × D21

b. D11 × D21

c. B28 × D11

d. B28 + C28 + E28 + F28 + G28

10.27. In Exhibit 10.1 operation of plant support account (X) is in Column E of this electronic spreadsheet and assume that Matrix C is a computational matrix. The absolute value of Cell E32 is equal to

a. B32 + C32 + D32 + F32 + G32

b. initial cost incurred + net transfer-ins + depreciation expense

c. B32 + C32 + net transfer-ins + depreciation expense

d. B32 + C32 + D32 + net transfer-ins + depreciation expense

10.28. Compare the cost data in Exhibit 10.15 for Elmwood Medical Services Clinic with the data in Exhibit 10.6. You will note there are no changes in the initial cost data by account, but the utilization factors in Column C for administrative support (T) are different. There are also two changes in utilization factors in Column D for operations manager (U). The utilization data in the other five columns within Matrix A are identical in the two exhibits.

    Given this situation, and observing that Line 9 in Matrix A in the two exhibits is identical for the administrative activities cost center, explain why the reciprocal cost value increased from $168,745 to $171,341.

10.29. (See Question 10.28.) The reciprocal cost values are different on Line 20 of Matrix B in Exhibits 10.6 and 10.15. Explain why all the values

Exhibit 10.15 Elmwood Medical Services Clinic: Assignment of Support Services by Reciprocal Method

Matrix A

Part I. Initial Cost and Support Services for Year (Matrix A3 . . . I16)

Column		A	B	C	D	E	F	G	H	I	J	
			Initial Cost	Admin T	Oper U	Cashier V	Reg & MR W	Pat Acct X	Housek Y	Maint Z	Total Cost	3
Phys G	A	$	791,500	0.210	0.265	0.340	0.360	0.350	0.250	0.150		6
Rehab	B		566,500	0.320	0.250	0.140	0.080	0.090	0.150	0.080		7
Mental	C		362,000	0.110	0.185	0.180	0.190	0.210	0.290	0.230		8
Admin	T		80,000	(1.000)	0.010	0.050	0.100	0.110	0.060	0.130		9
Oper	U		165,000	0.035	(1.000)	0.080	0.040	0.050	0.040	0.140		10
Cashier	V		135,000	0.040	0.057	(1.000)	0.010	0.010	0.050	0.100		11
Reg & MR	W		185,000	0.065	0.034	0.040	(1.000)	0.010	0.060	0.070		12
Pat Acct	X		145,000	0.050	0.042	0.020	0.010	(1.000)	0.050	0.060		13
Housek	Y		90,000	0.075	0.087	0.030	0.110	0.060	(1.000)	0.040		14
Maint	Z		80,000	0.095	0.070	0.120	0.100	0.110	0.050	(1.000)		15
Total			$2,600,000	0.000	0.000	0.000	0.000	0.000	0.000	0.000		16
												17
												18

Continued

Exhibit 10.15 Continued

Matrix B

Part II. Algorithm's Computed Values (Matrix A19...J20)

Column	A	B	C	D	E	F	G	H	I	J	
											19
Reciprocal cost			$171,341	$238,354	$187,297	$237,298	$189,734	$174,243	$188,751	$1,387,018	20
											21
											22

Matrix C

Part III. Support Cost Assignments and Total Cost (Matrix A23...J36)

Column	A	B	C	D	E	F	G	H	I	J	
		Initial Cost	Admin T	Oper U	Cashier V	Reg & MR W	Pat Acct X	Housek Y	Maint Z	Total Cost	23
											24
											25
Phys G	A	$ 791,500	$ 35,982	$ 63,164	$ 63,681	$ 85,427	$ 66,407	$ 43,561	$ 28,312	$1,178,034	26
Rehab	B	566,500	54,829	59,589	26,222	18,984	17,076	26,136	15,100	784,436	27
Mental	C	362,000	18,848	44,096	33,713	45,086	39,844	50,530	43,413	637,530	28
Admin	T	80,000	(171,341)	2,383	9,365	23,730	20,871	10,455	24,538	0	29
Oper	U	165,000	5,997	(238,354)	14,984	9,492	9,487	6,970	26,425	0	30
Cashier	V	135,000	6,854	13,586	(187,297)	2,373	1,897	8,712	18,875	0	31
Reg & MR	W	185,000	11,137	8,104	7,492	(237,298)	1,897	10,455	13,213	0	32
Pat Acct	X	145,000	8,567	10,011	3,746	2,373	(189,734)	8,712	11,325	0	33
Housek	Y	90,000	12,850	20,737	5,619	26,103	11,384	(174,243)	7,550	0	34
Maint	Z	80,000	16,277	16,684	22,475	23,730	20,871	8,712	188,751	0	35
Total		$2,600,000	0	0	0	0	0	0	0	$2,600,000	36

Exhibit 10.15 Continued

Notes: Phys G   = Physician Group Practice
       Rehab   = Rehabilitation Services
       Mental   = Mental Health Services
       Admin   = Administrative Activities
       Oper   = Operations Manager
       Cashier   = Cashier and Financial Manager
       Reg & MR = Registration and Medical Records
       Pat Acct   = Patient Accounting
       Housek   = Housekeeping
       Maint   = Maintenance

are different when there were no changes in direct cost for any of the accounts and the utilization factors in five of the seven cost centers were the same in the two exhibits.

10.30. (See Question 10.28.) Assume that Exhibit 10.15 is an electronic spreadsheet and that Matrix C is a computational matrix. The number of entries that must be made in matrix A23 . . .J36 for the revised utilization and new reciprocal cost values is

    a. 18 entries under the assumption the total is by a formula

    b. 14 entries under the assumption the total is by a formula

    c. 4 entries under the assumption the total is by a formula

    d. 0 entries

10.31. (See Question 10.28.) Assume that Exhibit 10.15 is an electronic spreadsheet and that Matrix C is a computational matrix. The number of entries that must be made in matrix A3 . . .J16 for the revised utilization and new reciprocal cost values is

    a. 18 entries under the assumption the total is by a formula

    b. 14 entries under the assumption the total is by a formula

    c. 11 entries under the assumption the total is by a formula

    d. 8 entries under the assumption the total is by a formula

10.32. Explain why the use of the reciprocal cost method is more critical in the health care industry than in the corporate business sector.

11

Different Costs for Various Purposes: A Review

Introduction

This optional chapter is a review of cost-accumulation, cost-assignment, cost-allocation, and cost matching procedures previously discussed. The materials in this optional chapter were initially used as computer exercises that illustrated how the same set of cost data can serve diverse purposes. Management control and departmental assessments are only briefly examined in this case example; the primary emphasis is given to planning, pricing, and strategic operations. The case example is intentionally presented before the management control steps in Chapter 12; this review highlights the uses of cost data by various decision-making activities.

The coding structure for the transactions is simplified for illustration purposes. A given type of transaction (such as overhead) is represented by a single entry rather than multiple accounts. The workload measurement units are from the College of American Pathologists and are presented as averages for groups of tests. A few tests are covered in each revenue area, so there is a difference between analysis by test versus by revenue area.

Organization

Glenwood Laboratories, Inc., is a wholly owned division of QWE, Inc., a provider of laboratory services to the adjacent Medical Center Hospital, to two community hospitals, and to clinics in the service area.

Most (80 percent) of the revenue comes from the Medical Center Hospital and the two community hospitals. The remainder (20 percent) is derived from the clinics.

Glenwood Laboratories contains 21 regular cost accounts. Employees are assigned to 18 of the accounts. Three regular cost accounts (codes 303, 304, and 305) do not have any assigned employees, but these cost pools are for the purpose of monitoring contracts and agreements. The number of employees assigned to each regular cost account is specified in Figure 11.1. Overall, there are 39 employees at Glenwood, with the following organizational distribution:

Office of the Director	3
Finance and Operations	8
Clinical Laboratories	16
Pathology and Microbiology	12
Total employees	39

Glenwood's computer coding structure permits the same three-digit cost code to serve as both the regular cost account and the MC/R center. An additional digit in the coding structure specifies how a transaction is recorded. There are eight MC/R centers serving in this dual role as regular cost accounts:

Code	Name
432	Hematology—A
433	Hematology—B
462	Chemistry—A
463	Chemistry—B
532	Pathology and Cytology—A
533	Pathology and Cytology—B
562	Microbiology—A
563	Microbiology—B

The dual role of these eight cost codes eliminates the aggregation transactions from the regular cost account to the MC/R center in this case example.

Glenwood has eight MC/R centers in which the dual coding arrangement is not followed:

Code	Name
200	Director, Glenwood Laboratories, Inc.
300	Manager of Finance and Operations
400	Manager of Clinical Laboratories
500	Manager of Pathology and Microbiology

430	Supervisor, Hematology
460	Supervisor, Chemistry
530	Supervisor, Pathology and Cytology
560	Supervisor, Microbiology

Finance and Operations

The Finance and Operations Department (codes 300–306 in Figure 11.1) is a support area for the two revenue departments: (1) Clinical Laboratories and (2) Pathology and Microbiology. QWE, Inc. (the parent corporation) provides maintenance services (code 303), housekeeping services (code 304), and general accounting services (code 305) under contracts and agreements administered by the office of Finance and Operations (code 301). There is a contract (parent corporation) for custodial services with a commercial service company; the bill for these services is sent by the parent corporation to Glenwood for payment to the commercial service company. The maintenance services are partially performed by employees of QWE, Inc., and by outside specialists for laboratory equipment. The parent sends Glenwood a monthly bill for the total maintenance services and the accounting services.

The manager of Finance and Operations (code 301) also supervises the business office (code 302) and the waiting room (code 306). The three employees in the business office handle the patient accounting and cashier activities. The four employees in the waiting area perform the patient registration, when a patient comes to Glenwood Laboratories, and test recording, when a specimen is sent to the lab from the hospital or clinic.

Clinical Laboratories

The Clinical Laboratories Department (codes 400–463) consists of Hematology and Chemistry, and most of the tests performed in these two sections make extensive use of automated equipment. The office of manager of Clinical Laboratories (code 401) has an assistant and a secretary. There are supervisors in Hematology (code 431) and Chemistry (code 461). The activities within each of these sections are partitioned into two areas where patient revenues are accumulated. Thus, there are four MC/R areas within the Clinical Laboratories Department: codes 432, 433, 462, and 463.

Figure 11.1 Glenwood Laboratories: Major Cost/Revenue Centers and Regular Cost Accounts

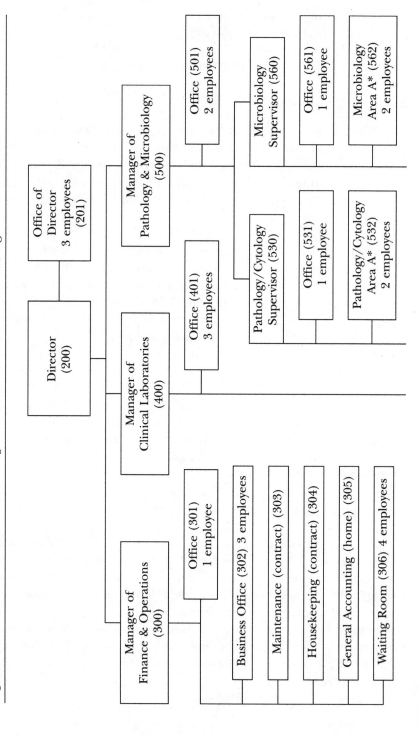

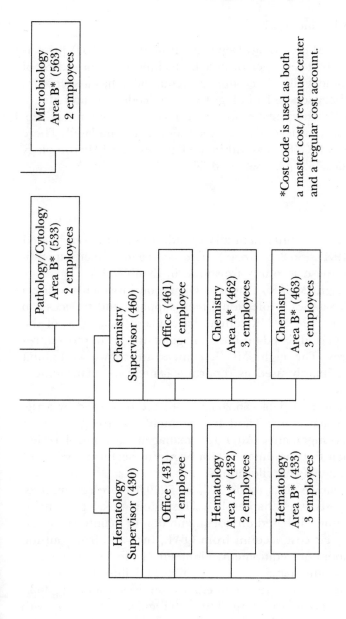

Microbiology
Area B* (563)
2 employees

Pathology/Cytology
Area B* (533)
2 employees

Chemistry
Supervisor (460)

Office (461)
1 employee

Chemistry
Area A* (462)
3 employees

Chemistry
Area B* (463)
3 employees

Hematology
Supervisor (430)

Office (431)
1 employee

Hematology
Area A* (432)
2 employees

Hematology
Area B* (433)
3 employees

*Cost code is used as both
a master cost/revenue center
and a regular cost account.

Pathology and Microbiology

The Pathology and Microbiology Department (codes 500–563) primarily represents manual tests performed by technicians. The office of manager of Pathology and Microbiology (code 501) has a secretary, and there are supervisors in Pathology-Cytology (code 531) and Microbiology (code 561). The activities within each of these sections are separated into two areas where patient revenues are accumulated. There are, therefore, four MC/R areas within the Pathology and Microbiology Department: codes 532, 533, 562, and 563.

Cost Transactions

The 21 regular cost accounts incur all expenditures for the year ended 30 September 19X1 ($6,286,578.48). The aggregate direct expenditures for each of these accounts are shown in Exhibit 11.1.

There are eight MC/R centers at Glenwood in which no direct expenditures for salaries, professional fees, supplies, and services can be entered. These eight MC/R centers have a zero balance as of the end of the fiscal period based on the management control procedures over expenditures. The eight MC/R centers are shown in Exhibit 11.2. They are primarily used as reporting centers for management control purposes.

The aggregate cost data ($6,286,578.48) are processed by a rigorous set of internal control and management control procedures and reporting arrangements. After the management control review is completed, then the computer system begins to perform a series of automatic assignments and allocations.

The maintenance costs (code 303) of $250,000 are common assigned support costs (see Chapter 10). The automatic assignment by Glenwood's computer is based on documentation of maintenance services to each regular cost account from QWE, Inc., and from outside specialists for laboratory equipment. Eighteen of the 21 regular cost accounts receive maintenance services. Exhibit 11.3 illustrates the common assigned support costs for maintenance services from code 303.

Housekeeping costs are charged to each regular cost account with an employee. In Glenwood Laboratories' experience (although the experiences of other entities may differ), housekeeping is a common allocated overhead cost (Chapter 10). A transaction similar to that for the 18 regular cost accounts in Exhibit 11.3 is made, but with code 304

Exhibit 11.1 Glenwood Laboratories: Direct Expenditures for Year Ended 30 September 19X1

Code	Name	Amount
201	Office of director, Glenwood	$ 216,148.00
301	Office of manager of Finance & Operations	42,740.00
302	Business Office	74,972.00
303	Maintenance (contract & agreement)	250,000.00
304	Housekeeping (contract)	50,000.00
305	General Accounting Service (agreement)	25,000.00
306	Waiting Room	98,216.00
401	Office of manager of Clinical Laboratories	84,020.00
431	Office of supervisor of Hematology	26,422.00
432*	Hematology area A	652,099.38
433*	Hematology area B	812,004.09
461	Office of supervisor of Chemistry	28,641.00
462*	Chemistry area A	917,426.84
463*	Chemistry area B	1,067,501.64
501	Office of manager of Pathology and Microbiology	58,929.00
531	Office of supervisor of Pathology/Cytology	29,044.00
532*	Pathology/Cytology area A	560,674.38
533*	Pathology/Cytology area B	389,534.73
561	Office of supervisor of Microbiology	29,402.00
562*	Microbiology area A	426,627.96
563*	Microbiology area B	447,175.46
	Total	$6,286,578.48

*These eight codes are both regular cost accounts and MC/R centers.

instead of code 303. The aggregate common allocated overhead cost for the period is $50,000 for housekeeping Exhibit 11.1.

A third transaction automatically processed by Glenwood's computer system is for general accounting (code 305), a common assigned support cost. The entry is similar to Exhibit 11.3 except that code 305 (general accounting) is used, and the total amount is $25,000 (Exhibit 11.1).

After these three transactions are automatically processed by Glenwood's computer, there are a total of 204 entries in the financial database for the period. Individual payments and receipts are consolidated as if they were single entries. There are five products (tests) in each of the eight MC/R areas with separate reporting of revenue

Exhibit 11.2 Eight MC/R Centers at Glenwood Laboratories with Zero Balances

Code	Name	Amount
200	Director, Glenwood Laboratories	0
300	Manager, Finance and Operations	0
400	Manager, Clinical Laboratories	0
500	Manager, Pathology and Microbiology	0
430	Supervisor, Hematology	0
460	Supervisor, Chemistry	0
530	Supervisor, Pathology and Cytology	0
560	Supervisor, Microbiology	0

and direct material costs. Exhibit 11.4 contains these 204 entries for the period ended 30 September 19X1.

Management Control and Departmental Assessments

Assume the 204 entries in Exhibit 11.4 are in a database management system in which data can be retrieved by cost code, element, account, nature, description, and amount. If all costs are retrieved, then they must equal $6,286,578.48 (Exhibit 11.1). If all revenues from the eight MC/R areas are retrieved, they must equal $7,166,122.00 (Exhibit 11.5).

Glenwood's computer system is current with processing transactions. All laboratory tests that are completed by midnight on the last day of the fiscal period are included as revenue. Pending tests in pathology and microbiology are not reported as revenue until they are completed. Some cultures may require several days for growth, and the exact tests that are eventually performed (and the revenue) may not be known until the microbiologists have assessed the growths.

Management control reports are prepared early in the morning on the first day of each month. These reports contain current month's actual compared with budget and the cumulative year-to-date data compared with budget. The management control reports are based on an R status in column E of the database, per the note in Exhibit 11.3 designating the nature of the transaction to be the cost pool's direct responsibility. Transactions on lines 24, 26, and 28 in Exhibit 11.4 contain the R status for the initial expenditures supporting the common

Text continues on page 356

Exhibit 11.3 Glenwood Laboratories: Common Assigned Support Costs for Maintenance

A	B	C	D	E	F	G
			FinStat*			
Cost To	Cost From	Element	Acc	Nat	Description	Amount
201	303	MAINT	E	A	Assigned maintenance costs	$ 1,000.00
301	303	MAINT	E	A	Assigned maintenance costs	1,500.00
302	303	MAINT	E	A	Assigned maintenance costs	1,900.00
306	303	MAINT	E	A	Assigned maintenance costs	4,500.00
401	303	MAINT	E	A	Assigned maintenance costs	1,700.00
431	303	MAINT	E	A	Assigned maintenance costs	2,500.00
432	303	MAINT	E	A	Assigned maintenance costs	30,100.00
433	303	MAINT	E	A	Assigned maintenance costs	27,000.00
461	303	MAINT	E	A	Assigned maintenance costs	2,400.00
462	303	MAINT	E	A	Assigned maintenance costs	24,000.00
463	303	MAINT	E	A	Assigned maintenance costs	21,000.00
501	303	MAINT	E	A	Assigned maintenance costs	1,400.00
531	303	MAINT	E	A	Assigned maintenance costs	3,000.00
532	303	MAINT	E	A	Assigned maintenance costs	28,000.00
533	303	MAINT	E	A	Assigned maintenance costs	29,000.00
561	303	MAINT	E	A	Assigned maintenance costs	2,000.00
562	303	MAINT	E	A	Assigned maintenance costs	38,000.00
563	303	MAINT	E	A	Assigned maintenance costs	31,000.00
303	303	TASSIGN	E	A	Assigned maintenance costs	(250,000.00)

*There are three components of FinStat:
1. Element—Glenwood's computer system contains 13 codes for elements:

DTREVE	Direct revenue
DLABOR	Direct labor
DLFBEN	Direct labor fringe benefits
DIRMAT	Direct materials
DRSUPP	Direct supplies and other indirect costs
DCONTR	Contractual services
MAINT	Dedicated maintenance assigned costs
HOUSEK	Dedicated housekeeping assigned costs
GENACCT	Dedicated general & accounting assigned costs
DCOST	Assigned joint costs—direct
SUPPORT	Assigned joint costs—dedicated
OVERHEAD	Reciprocal cost assignments
TASSIGN	Total assigned

2. Acc—Expense (E) or revenue (R) designation for the account code.
3. Nat—Nature of transaction: direct responsibility (R), assigned or allocated (A), and summary (S).

Exhibit 11.4   Glenwood Laboratories: Cost Data for Year Ended 30
September 19X1

A	B	C	D	E	F	G	H
			FinStat				*Line*
Cost To	*Cost From*	*Element*	*Acc*	*Nat*	*Description*	*Amount*	*No.*
201	201	DLABOR	E	R	Director	$ 95,000.00	2
201	201	DLABOR	E	R	Assoc. director	80,000.00	3
201	201	DLABOR	E	R	Admin. assistant	19,000.00	4
201	201	DLFBEN	E	R	Director	9,630.00	5
201	201	DLFBEN	E	R	Assoc. director	9,418.00	6
201	201	DLFBEN	E	R	Admin. assistant	2,100.00	7
201	201	DRSUPP	E	R	Indirect costs	1,000.00	8
201	303	MAINT	E	A	Maintenance contract	1,000.00	9
201	304	HOUSEK	E	A	Housekeeping contract	700.00	10
201	305	GENACCT	E	A	General accounting fee	2,300.00	11
301	301	DLABOR	E	R	Manager, Finance & Operations	38,000.00	12
301	301	DLFBEN	E	R	Manager, Finance & Operations	3,540.00	13
301	301	DRSUPP	E	R	Indirect costs	1,200.00	14
301	303	MAINT	E	A	Maintenance contract	1,500.00	15
301	304	HOUSEK	E	A	Housekeeping contract	500.00	16
301	305	GENACCT	E	A	General accounting fee	1,100.00	17
302	302	DLABOR	E	R	Business office	66,000.00	18
302	302	DLFBEN	E	R	Business office	7,272.00	19
302	302	DRSUPP	E	R	Indirect costs	1,700.00	20
302	303	MAINT	E	A	Maintenance contract	1,900.00	21
302	304	HOUSEK	E	A	Housekeeping contract	800.00	22
302	305	GENACCT	E	A	General accounting fee	2,800.00	23
303	303	DCONTR	E	R	Maintenance contract	250,000.00	24
303	303	TASSIGN	E	S	Maintenance assignment	(250,000.00)	25
304	304	DCONTR	E	R	Housekeeping contract	50,000.00	26
304	304	TASSIGN	E	S	Housekeeping assignment	(50,000.00)	27
305	305	DCONTR	E	R	General accounting fee	25,000.00	28
305	305	TASSIGN	E	S	General accounting assign	(25,000.00)	29
306	306	DLABOR	E	R	Waiting area	88,000.00	30
306	306	DLFBEN	E	R	Waiting area	8,316.00	31
306	306	DRSUPP	E	R	Indirect costs	1,900.00	32

Continued

Exhibit 11.4 Continued

A	B	C	D	E	F	G	H
			FinStat				*Line*
Cost To	*Cost From*	*Element*	*Acc*	*Nat*	*Description*	*Amount*	*No.*
306	303	MAINT	E	A	Maintenance contract	4,500.00	33
306	304	HOUSEK	E	A	Housekeeping contract	900.00	34
306	305	GENACCT	E	A	General accounting fee	400.00	35
401	401	DLABOR	E	R	Secretary, Clinical Lab	14,000.00	36
401	401	DLABOR	E	R	Mgr., Clinical Lab	35,000.00	37
401	401	DLABOR	E	R	Assistant mgr., Clinical Lab	26,000.00	38
401	401	DLFBEN	E	R	Secretary, Clinical Lab	1,540.00	39
401	401	DLFBEN	E	R	Mgr., Clinical Lab	3,147.00	40
401	401	DLFBEN	E	R	Assistant mgr., Clinical Lab	2,933.00	41
401	401	DRSUPP	E	R	Indirect costs	1,400.00	42
401	303	MAINT	E	A	Maintenance contract	1,700.00	43
401	304	HOUSEK	E	A	Housekeeping contract	500.00	44
401	305	GENACCT	E	A	General accounting fee	1,300.00	45
431	431	DLABOR	E	R	Supervisor, Hematology	23,000.00	46
431	431	DLFBEN	E	R	Supervisor, Hematology	1,922.00	47
431	431	DRSUPP	E	R	Indirect costs	1,500.00	48
431	303	MAINT	E	A	Maintenance contract	2,500.00	49
431	304	HOUSEK	E	A	Housekeeping contract	400.00	50
431	305	GENACCT	E	A	General accounting fee	400.00	51
432	432	DIRMAT	E	R	Test #85610	109,911.46	52
432	432	DIRMAT	E	R	Test #89051	180,022.04	53
432	432	DIRMAT	E	R	Test #85055	88,481.42	54
432	432	DIRMAT	E	R	Test #85050	77,026.93	55
432	432	DIRMAT	E	R	Test #85580	150,931.53	56
432	432	DRSUPP	E	R	Indirect costs	5,700.00	57
432	432	DLABOR	E	R	Hematologists	37,000.00	58
432	432	DLFBEN	E	R	Hematologists	3,026.00	59
432	432	DTREVE	R	R	Test #85055	(127,336.80)	60
432	432	DTREVE	R	R	Test #85050	(111,952.50)	61
432	432	DTREVE	R	R	Test #85610	(146,278.40)	62
432	432	DTREVE	R	R	Test #89051	(251,078.40)	63
432	432	DTREVE	R	R	Test #85580	(186,099.20)	64
432	303	MAINT	E	A	Maintenance contract	30,100.00	65
432	304	HOUSEK	E	A	Housekeeping contract	6,100.00	66
432	305	GENACCT	E	A	General accounting fee	1,400.00	67

Continued

Exhibit 11.4   Continued

A	B	C	D	E	F	G	H
		FinStat					Line
Cost To	Cost From	Element	Acc	Nat	Description	Amount	No.
433	433	DIRMAT	E	R	Test #85660	147,792.51	68
433	433	DIRMAT	E	R	Test #85030	113,681.69	69
433	433	DIRMAT	E	R	Test #85640	181,084.08	70
433	433	DIRMAT	E	R	Test #85020	196,439.36	71
433	433	DIRMAT	E	R	Test #85730	106,667.45	72
433	433	DLABOR	E	R	Hematologists	55,500.00	73
433	433	DLFBEN	E	R	Hematologists	4,539.00	74
433	433	DRSUPP	E	R	Indirect costs	6,300.00	75
433	433	DTREVE	R	R	Test #85660	(232,110.00)	76
433	433	DTREVE	R	R	Test #85020	(304,752.00)	77
433	433	DTREVE	R	R	Test #85640	(311,542.40)	78
433	433	DTREVE	R	R	Test #85730	(172,068.80)	79
433	433	DTREVE	R	R	Test #85030	(181,286.40)	80
433	303	MAINT	E	A	Maintenance contract	27,000.00	81
433	304	HOUSEK	E	A	Housekeeping contract	6,300.00	82
433	305	GENACCT	E	A	General accounting fee	1,700.00	83
461	461	DLABOR	E	R	Supervisor, Chemistry	23,800.00	84
461	461	DLFBEN	E	R	Supervisor, Chemistry	2,741.00	85
461	461	DRSUPP	E	R	Indirect costs	2,100.00	86
461	303	MAINT	E	A	Maintenance contract	2,400.00	87
461	304	HOUSEK	E	A	Housekeeping contract	450.00	88
461	305	GENACCT	E	A	General accounting fee	350.00	89
462	462	DIRMAT	E	R	Test #82310	153,604.80	90
462	462	DIRMAT	E	R	Test #82251	162,072.27	91
462	462	DIRMAT	E	R	Test #82465	173,594.82	92
462	462	DIRMAT	E	R	Test #82890	182,453.31	93
462	462	DIRMAT	E	R	Test #82565	173,654.64	94
462	462	DLABOR	E	R	Technician, Chemistry	57,000.00	95
462	462	DLFBEN	E	R	Technician, Chemistry	4,947.00	96
462	462	DRSUPP	E	R	Indirect costs	10,100.00	97
462	462	DTREVE	R	R	Test #82251	(339,372.00)	98
462	462	DTREVE	R	R	Test #82890	(295,198.20)	99
462	462	DTREVE	R	R	Test #82310	(268,808.40)	100
462	462	DTREVE	R	R	Test #82465	(229,495.90)	101
462	462	DTREVE	R	R	Test #82565	(244,584.00)	102
462	303	MAINT	E	A	Maintenance contract	24,000.00	103

Continued

Exhibit 11.4   Continued

A	B	C	D	E	F	G	H
			FinStat				*Line*
Cost	*Cost*						
To	*From*	*Element*	*Acc*	*Nat*	*Description*	*Amount*	*No.*
462	304	HOUSEK	E	A	Housekeeping contract	5,700.00	104
462	305	GENACCT	E	A	General accounting fee	2,000.00	105
463	463	DIRMAT	E	R	Test #84520	261,611.27	106
463	463	DIRMAT	E	R	Test #84140	217,705.90	107
463	463	DIRMAT	E	R	Test #83020	198,345.60	108
463	463	DIRMAT	E	R	Test #83420	131,595.93	109
463	463	DIRMAT	E	R	Test #84295	187,095.94	110
463	463	DLABOR	E	R	Technician, Chemistry	57,000.00	111
463	463	DLFBEN	E	R	Technician, Chemistry	4,947.00	112
463	463	DRSUPP	E	R	Indirect costs	9,200.00	113
463	463	DTREVE	R	R	Test #83420	(171,055.20)	114
463	463	DTREVE	R	R	Test #84295	(296,176.50)	115
463	463	DTREVE	R	R	Test #84140	(297,518.40)	116
463	463	DTREVE	R	R	Test #84520	(359,971.20)	117
463	463	DTREVE	R	R	Test #83020	(285,127.80)	118
463	303	MAINT	E	A	Maintenance contract	21,000.00	119
463	304	HOUSEK	E	A	Housekeeping contract	5,600.00	120
463	305	GENACCT	E	A	General accounting fee	1,800.00	121
501	501	DLABOR	E	R	Mgr., Pathology & Microbiology	39,000.00	122
501	501	DLABOR	E	R	Secretary, Pathology & Microbiology	14,000.00	123
501	501	DLFBEN	E	R	Secretary, Pathology & Microbiology	1,135.00	124
501	501	DLFBEN	E	R	Mgr., Pathology & Microbiology	3,194.00	125
501	501	DRSUPP	E	R	Indirect costs	1,600.00	126
501	303	MAINT	E	A	Maintenance contract	1,400.00	127
501	304	HOUSEK	E	A	Housekeeping contract	500.00	128
501	305	GENACCT	E	A	General accounting fee	1,200.00	129
531	531	DLABOR	E	R	Supervisor, Pathology Cytology	25,000.00	130
531	531	DLFBEN	E	R	Supervisor, Pathology- Cytology	2,744.00	131
531	531	DRSUPP	E	R	Indirect costs	1,300.00	132
531	303	MAINT	E	A	Maintenance contract	3,000.00	133
531	304	HOUSEK	E	A	Housekeeping contract	400.00	134

Continued

Exhibit 11.4   Continued

A	B	C	D	E	F	G	H
		FinStat					
Cost	*Cost*						*Line*
To	*From*	*Element*	*Acc*	*Nat*	*Description*	*Amount*	*No.*
531	305	GENACCT	E	A	General accounting fee	300.00	135
532	532	DIRMAT	E	R	Test #88410	104,871.71	136
532	532	DIRMAT	E	R	Test #88340	110,090.23	137
532	532	DIRMAT	E	R	Test #88370	103,155.37	138
532	532	DIRMAT	E	R	Test #88146	63,978.64	139
532	532	DIRMAT	E	R	Test #88350	125,784.43	140
532	532	DLABOR	E	R	Pathology-Cytology Technicians	40,000.00	141
532	532	DLFBEN	E	R	Pathology-Cytology Technicians	4,594.00	142
532	532	DRSUPP	E	R	Indirect costs	8,200.00	143
532	532	DTREVE	R	R	Test #88350	(186,588.00)	144
532	532	DTREVE	R	R	Test #88410	(154,836.00)	145
532	532	DTREVE	R	R	Test #88370	(144,462.60)	146
532	532	DTREVE	R	R	Test #88340	(168,708.00)	147
532	532	DTREVE	R	R	Test #88146	(100,533.20)	148
532	303	MAINT	E	A	Maintenance contract	28,000.00	149
532	304	HOUSEK	E	A	Housekeeping contract	3,900.00	150
532	305	GENACCT	E	A	General accounting fee	1,900.00	151
533	533	DIRMAT	E	R	Test #88150	64,737.28	152
533	533	DIRMAT	E	R	Test #88175	56,636.82	153
533	533	DIRMAT	E	R	Test #88155	42,660.44	154
533	533	DIRMAT	E	R	Test #88300	62,051.11	155
533	533	DIRMAT	E	R	Test #88305	112,055.08	156
533	533	DLABOR	E	R	Pathology-Cytology Technicians	40,000.00	157
533	533	DLFBEN	E	R	Pathology-Cytology Technicians	4,594.00	158
533	533	DRSUPP	E	R	Indirect costs	6,800.00	159
533	533	DTREVE	R	R	Test #88175	(75,888.00)	160
533	533	DTREVE	R	R	Test #88305	(157,533.90)	161
533	533	DTREVE	R	R	Test #88150	(109,548.00)	162
533	533	DTREVE	R	R	Test #88300	(98,899.20)	163
533	533	DTREVE	R	R	Test #88155	(66,830.40)	164
533	304	HOUSEK	E	A	Housekeeping contract	5,400.00	165
533	303	MAINT	E	A	Maintenance contract	29,000.00	166
533	305	GENACCT	E	A	General accounting fee	2,200.00	167

Continued

Exhibit 11.4 Continued

A	B	C	D	E	F	G	H
Cost To	Cost From	FinStat Element	Acc	Nat	Description	Amount	Line No.
561	561	DLABOR	E	R	Supervisor, Micro-biology	25,700.00	168
561	561	DLFBEN	E	R	Supervisor, Micro-biology	2,602.00	169
561	561	DRSUPP	E	R	Indirect costs	1,100.00	170
561	303	MAINT	E	A	Maintenance contract	2,000.00	171
561	304	HOUSEK	E	A	Housekeeping contract	450.00	172
561	305	GENACCT	E	A	General accounting fee	250.00	173
562	562	DIRMAT	E	R	Test #87092	108,036.24	174
562	562	DIRMAT	E	R	Test #87095	77,105.26	175
562	562	DIRMAT	E	R	Test #87094	41,610.05	176
562	562	DIRMAT	E	R	Test #87093	101,488.76	177
562	562	DIRMAT	E	R	Test #87091	48,073.65	178
562	562	DLABOR	E	R	Microbiologists	41,000.00	179
562	562	DLFBEN	E	R	Microbiologists	4,814.00	180
562	562	DRSUPP	E	R	Indirect costs	4,500.00	181
562	562	DTREVE	R	R	Test #87091	(76,128.00)	182
562	562	DTREVE	R	R	Test #87094	(59,536.00)	183
562	562	DTREVE	R	R	Test #87092	(158,288.90)	184
562	562	DTREVE	R	R	Test #87093	(173,716.00)	185
562	562	DTREVE	R	R	Test #87095	(128,609.40)	186
562	303	MAINT	E	A	Maintenance contract	38,000.00	187
562	304	HOUSEK	E	A	Housekeeping contract	5,900.00	188
562	305	GENACCT	E	A	General accounting fee	1,500.00	189
563	563	DIRMAT	E	R	Test #87190	64,439.48	190
563	563	DIRMAT	E	R	Test #87350	109,139.24	191
563	563	DIRMAT	E	R	Test #87000	43,808.12	192
563	563	DIRMAT	E	R	Test #87096	79,157.75	193
563	563	DIRMAT	E	R	Test #87025	100,116.87	194
563	563	DLABOR	E	R	Microbiologists	41,000.00	195
563	563	DLFBEN	E	R	Microbiologists	4,814.00	196
563	563	DRSUPP	E	R	Indirect costs	4,700.00	197
563	563	DTREVE	R	R	Test #87025	(116,032.00)	198
563	563	DTREVE	R	R	Test #87190	(80,418.80)	199
563	563	DTREVE	R	R	Test #87000	(63,714.40)	200
563	563	DTREVE	R	R	Test #87350	(129,234.60)	201
563	563	DTREVE	R	R	Test #87096	(104,804.10)	202

Continued

Exhibit 11.4   Continued

A	B	C	D	E	F	G	H
		FinStat					
Cost	*Cost*						*Line*
To	*From*	*Element*	*Acc*	*Nat*	*Description*	*Amount*	*No.*
563	303	MAINT	E	A	Maintenance contract	31,000.00	203
563	304	HOUSEK	E	A	Housekeeping contract	5,500.00	204
563	305	GENACCT	E	A	General accounting fee	2,100.00	205
					Total items	($879,543.52)	206

cost assignment entries in codes 303–305 (maintenance, housekeeping, and general accounting).

Eight MC/R centers are primarily used in Glenwood's management control reports. These eight MC/R centers representing the hierarchical reporting structure are codes 200, 300, 400, 500, 430, 460, 530, and 560 (see Figure 11.1). Glenwood's computer system contains the mapping of regular cost accounts and MC/R centers into these eight reporting cost centers. But there are no entries in the database (Exhibit 11.4) for the special aggregations for these eight reporting cost centers.

Departmental assessments require mapping of various cost accounts in Exhibit 11.4 to internal activity measures. The comparisons for departmental assessment are different from the expenditure analysis performed for management control. There are minimum volumes

Exhibit 11.5   Glenwood Laboratories: Total Revenue for Year Ended 30 September 19X1

Code	Name	Amount*
432	Hematology area A	(822,745.30)
433	Hematology area B	(1,201,759.60)
462	Chemistry area A	(1,377,458.50)
463	Chemistry area B	(1,409,849.10)
532	Pathology/Cytology area A	(755,127.80)
533	Pathology/Cytology area B	(508,699.50)
562	Microbiology area A	(596,278.30)
563	Microbiology area B	(494,203.90)
	Total	($7,166,122.00)

*Revenue is a credit account. Since a single column is used in this case example, credit amounts are displayed as negative amounts; debit amounts are positive.

of certain types of complex laboratory tests that must be performed each fiscal period to maintain professional competence. The departmental assessments primarily focus on the mix and distribution of tests, and this information in used in conjunction with the expenditure and revenue data from Exhibit 11.4.

The retrievals from the DBMS for departmental assessment vary by area. Finance and Operations is concerned with direct expenditures (excluding assigned common costs) by the initial elements; this aggregate information is given in the first part of Exhibit 11.6. Note that the total expenditures are the same as in Exhibit 11.1. Clinical Laboratories is concerned with expenses (including assigned common costs) and revenue by area—information that can be extracted directly from Exhibit 11.4. The second part of Exhibit 11.6 shows revenue of $822,745.30 and expenses of $689,699.38 for Hematology, area A (code 432), for a net return of $133,045.92. The Hematology data are extracted from Lines 52 to 67 from Exhibit 11.4.

Other Common Cost Entries

There are four "office of supervisor. . . " accounts in clinical and pathological laboratories, which are dedicated cost areas to their respective MC/R centers. These four accounts are joint cost areas (Chapter 9), and utilization experience in Glenwood's computer system for the MC/R centers is used in assigning the common costs.

Exhibit 11.7 illustrates these joint cost assignments for Hematology (code 431), Chemistry (461), Pathology-Cytology (531), and Microbiology (561). These transactions are stored in Glenwood's DBMS because the assigned costs are used in many decision-making activities. It is suggested that readers trace the aggregate data for direct costs and support costs in these four cost accounts to the detailed entries in the database in Exhibit 11.4. The direct costs of Hematology (431), for example, are contained on Lines 46–48, and support costs are on Lines 49–51 of Exhibit 11.4. For illustration purposes there are a minimum number of lines containing the direct costs and support costs for each of the accounts.

Some readers may question the support service assignments on Lines 252–263 of Exhibit 11.7. The joint cost transactions for support costs can be eliminated, and these amounts consolidated in the joint cost assignments on Lines 240–251. This handling will not alter the cost account balances for any of the eight MC/R centers. This arrangement, however, can result in the failure to provide full information for certain

Exhibit 11.6   Selected Retrievals for Glenwood Laboratories for Year Ended 30 September 19X1

Total Direct Costs by Element

Code	Name	Amount
DLABOR	Direct labor	$ 980,000.00
DIRMAT	Direct materials	4,812,769.48
DCONTR	Contractual services	325,000.00
DLFBEN	Direct labor fringe benefits	98,509.00
DRSUPP	Direct supplies and other costs	70,300.00
	Total direct costs	$6,286,578.48

Total Management Control Items in Hematology (432) Area A

A	B	C	D	E	F	G	H
		FinStat					*Line*
Cost To	*Cost From*	*Element*	*Acc*	*Nat*	*Description*	*Amount*	*No.*
432	432	DIRMAT	E	R	Test #85610	109,911.46	52
432	432	DIRMAT	E	R	Test #89051	180,022.04	53
432	432	DIRMAT	E	R	Test #85055	88,481.42	54
432	432	DIRMAT	E	R	Test #85050	77,026.93	55
432	432	DIRMAT	E	R	Test #85580	150,931.53	56
432	432	DRSUPP	E	R	Indirect costs	5,700.00	57
432	432	DLABOR	E	R	Hematologists	37,000.00	58
432	432	DLFBEN	E	R	Hematologists	3,026.00	59
432	432	DTREVE	R	R	Test #85055	(127,336.80)	60
432	432	DTREVE	R	R	Test #85050	(111,952.50)	61
432	432	DTREVE	R	R	Test #85610	(146,278.40)	62
432	432	DTREVE	R	R	Test #89051	(251,078.40)	63
432	432	DTREVE	R	R	Test #85580	(186,099.20)	64
432	303	MAINT	E	A	Maintenance contract	30,100.00	65
432	304	HOUSEK	E	A	Housekeeping contract	6,100.00	66
432	305	GENACCT	E	A	General accounting fee	1,400.00	67

Recap:

432					Total revenue Hematology area A	(822,745.30)	
432					Total costs	689,699.38	
					Net	(133,045.92)	

Exhibit 11.7   Glenwood Laboratories: Joint Cost Transactions for Dedicated Cost Areas

A	B	C	D	E	F	G	H
			FinStat				*Line*
Cost	*Cost*						
To	*From*	*Element*	*Acc*	*Nat*	*Description*	*Amount*	*No.*
432	431	DCOST	E	A	Joint cost (45% experience)	11,889.90	240
433	431	DCOST	E	A	Joint cost (55% experience)	14,532.10	241
431	431	DCOST	E	S	Joint cost (total direct costs)	(26,422.00)	242
432	431	SUPPORT	E	A	Support services (45% experience)	1,485.00	252
433	431	SUPPORT	E	A	Support services (55% experience)	1,815.00	253
431	431	SUPPORT	E	S	Support services (total support)	(3,300.00)	254
462	461	DCOST	E	A	Joint cost (52% experience)	14,893.32	243
463	461	DCOST	E	A	Joint cost (48% experience)	13,747.68	244
461	461	DCOST	E	S	Joint cost (total direct costs)	(28,641.00)	245
462	461	SUPPORT	E	A	Support services (52% experience)	1,664.00	255
463	461	SUPPORT	E	A	Support services (48% experience)	1,536.00	256
461	461	SUPPORT	E	S	Support services (total support)	(3,200.00)	257
532	531	DCOST	E	A	Joint cost (43% experience)	12,488.92	246
533	531	DCOST	E	A	Joint cost (57% experience)	16,555.08	247
531	531	DCOST	E	S	Joint cost (total direct costs)	(29,044.00)	248
532	531	SUPPORT	E	A	Support services (43% experience)	1,591.00	258
533	531	SUPPORT	E	A	Support services (57% experience)	2,109.00	259
531	531	SUPPORT	E	S	Support services (total support)	(3,700.00)	260
562	561	DCOST	E	A	Joint cost (60% experience)	17,641.20	249
563	561	DCOST	E	A	Joint cost (40% experience)	11,760.80	250

Continued

Exhibit 11.7   Continued

A	B	C	D	E	F	G	H
			FinStat				
Cost	Cost						Line
To	From	Element	Acc	Nat	Description	Amount	No.
561	561	DCOST	E	S	Joint cost (total direct costs)	(29,402.00)	251
562	561	SUPPORT	E	A	Support services (60% experience)	1,620.00	261
563	561	SUPPORT	E	A	Support services (40% experience)	1,080.00	262
561	561	SUPPORT	E	S	Support services (total support)	(2,700.00)	263

Note: The cost assignments on lines 207–39 are not illustrated in the text.

types of marginal and short-term pricing decisions. The merging of the contents Lines 252–263 with Lines 240–251 will limit proper traceability from the final MC/R center's costs back to the origin of each transaction flowing into that composite amount.

Reciprocal Cost Entries

After the joint costing entries for the four common cost accounts in Exhibit 11.7 are processed, Glenwood's total costs and total revenue are encompassed in 14 cost codes. Thus, 15 cost codes depicted in Figure 11.1 have zero balances: the eight reporting cost centers (codes 200, 300, 400, 500, 430, 460, 530, and 560) used for management control and departmental assessments, the three accounts for handling contracts and agreements (codes 303, 304, and 305), and the four common cost accounts (codes 431, 461, 531, and 561).

The 14 active cost codes (see Exhibit 11.8) consist of six support regular cost accounts (codes 201, 301, 302, 306, 401, and 501) and eight MC/R centers (codes 432, 433, 462, 463, 532, 533, 562, and 563). The utilization experiences of the closed joint cost accounts (codes 431, 461, 531, and 561) have been factored into the measures of services received by the eight MC/R accounts for use in the reciprocal cost assignments. Exhibit 11.8 shows the reciprocal cost assignment where the six support cost accounts are closed into the eight MC/R centers. Note that the total cost ($6,286,578) is the same as in Exhibit 11.1.

Exhibit 11.8 Glenwood Laboratories: Assignment of Support Services by Reciprocal Method

Matrix A

	Cost Centers	201	301	302	306	401	501		
Column A	B	C	D	E	F	G	H	I	
Account	Cost	Dept R	Dept S	Dept T	Dept U	Dept V	Dept W	Total	
432	$ 703,074	0.06	0.03	0.03	0.04	0.18	0.00	Hematology A	6
433	863,351	0.08	0.04	0.04	0.02	0.17	0.00	Hematology B	7
462	965,684	0.04	0.02	0.03	0.05	0.21	0.00	Chemistry A	8
463	1,111,186	0.07	0.03	0.04	0.06	0.20	0.00	Chemistry B	9
532	608,554	0.08	0.04	0.03	0.07	0.00	0.19	Pathology A	10
533	444,799	0.04	0.02	0.04	0.05	0.00	0.17	Pathology B	11
562	491,289	0.07	0.03	0.02	0.09	0.00	0.21	Microbiology A	12
563	498,616	0.06	0.02	0.03	0.09	0.00	0.18	Microbiology B	13
201	220,148	(1.00)	0.04	0.18	0.07	0.10	0.09	Director	14
301	45,840	0.16	(1.00)	0.07	0.08	0.09	0.10	Finance and Operations	15
302	80,472	0.06	0.39	(1.00)	0.31	0.05	0.06	Business Office	16
306	104,016	0.02	0.25	0.09	(1.00)	0.00	0.00	Waiting Room	17
401	87,520	0.14	0.05	0.22	0.03	(1.00)	0.00	Clinical Laboratory	18
501	62,029	0.12	0.04	0.18	0.04	0.00	(1.00)	Pathology and Microbiology L	19
Total	$6,286,578	0.00	0.00	0.00	0.00	0.00	0.00		20

Matrix B

Column A	B	C	D	E	F	G	H	I	
Reciprocal cost		$314,090	$159,273	$233,584	$171,139	$195,979	$154,981	$1,229,046	22

Continued

Exhibit 11.8 Continued

Matrix C

Column A	B	C	D	E	F	G	H	I	23
Account	*Cost*	*Dept R*	*Dept S*	*Dept T*	*Dept U*	*Dept V*	*Dept W*	*Total*	24
432	$ 703,074	$ 18,845	$ 4,778	$ 7,008	$ 6,846	$ 35,276	$ 0	$ 775,827	25
433	863,351	25,127	6,371	9,343	3,423	33,317	0	940,932	26
462	965,684	12,564	3,186	7,007	8,557	41,155	0	1,038,153	27
463	1,111,186	21,986	4,778	9,343	10,268	39,196	0	1,196,757	28
532	608,554	25,127	6,371	7,008	11,980		29,446	688,486	29
533	444,799	12,564	3,185	9,343	8,557		26,347	504,795	30
562	491,289	21,986	4,778	4,672	15,403		32,546	570,674	31
563	498,616	18,845	3,186	7,008	15,402		27,897	570,954	32
201	220,148	(314,090)	6,371	42,045	11,980	19,598	13,948	0	33
301	45,840	50,255	(159,273)	16,351	13,691	17,638	15,498	0	34
302	80,472	18,845	62,116	(233,584)	53,053	9,799	9,299	0	35
306	104,016	6,282	39,818	21,023	(171,139)	0	0	0	36
401	87,520	43,973	7,964	51,388	5,134	(195,979)	0	0	37
501	62,029	37,691	6,371	42,045	6,845	0	(154,981)	0	38
Total	$6,286,578	0	0	0	0	0	0	$6,286,578	39

After the reciprocal cost assignments have been determined (Exhibit 11.8), the transactions are entered in Glenwood's DBMS because full costing information is used in several decision-making activities. Exhibit 11.9 shows the entry for closing the six support cost accounts into the eight MC/R centers.

For illustration purposes, the direct and support services for reciprocal costing assignments were combined into single recordings on Lines 264–277 in Exhibit 11.9. There was also a merger at a different level: the six support cost accounts were part of a single reciprocal cost assignment. For various decision-making purposes, layers of overhead assignments to the revenue centers will provide more information to management; thus, there are usually a series of reciprocal cost assignments for support and administrative cost centers.

For example, assume there are two reciprocal cost assignments. The first assignment might capture the full interaction of all six support cost accounts, but only show the closing of three centers—the waiting room (306), the office of manager of Clinical Laboratories (401), and the office of manager of Pathology and Microbiology (501)—for an

Exhibit 11.9   Glenwood Laboratories: General Overhead Support Assignments

A	B	C	D	E	F	G	H
		FinStat					
Cost To	Cost From	Element	Acc	Nat	Description	Amount	Line No.
432	201	OVERHEAD	E	A	Overhead services	72,752.89	264
433	201	OVERHEAD	E	A	Overhead services	77,580.70	265
462	201	OVERHEAD	E	A	Overhead services	72,469.11	266
463	201	OVERHEAD	E	A	Overhead services	85,571.93	267
532	201	OVERHEAD	E	A	Overhead services	79,931.84	268
533	201	OVERHEAD	E	A	Overhead services	59,996.22	269
562	201	OVERHEAD	E	A	Overhead services	79,384.77	270
563	201	OVERHEAD	E	A	Overhead services	72,337.54	271
201	201	OVERHEAD	E	S	Overhead services	(220,148.00)	272
301	301	OVERHEAD	E	S	Overhead services	(45,840.00)	273
302	302	OVERHEAD	E	S	Overhead services	(80,472.00)	274
306	306	OVERHEAD	E	S	Overhead services	(104,016.00)	275
401	401	OVERHEAD	E	S	Overhead services	(87,520.00)	276
501	501	OVERHEAD	E	S	Overhead services	(62,029.00)	277

aggregate transfer of $345,615.31, as in Exhibit 11.10. The second assignment will then handle the business office (302), the office of the manager, Finance and Operations (301), and the office of the director (201), for an aggregate transfer of $254,409.69 (Exhibit 11.10).

In a more complex organizational setting, each layer of support and administrative activities may have limited direct interactions with other layers. Each layer may be addressed by reciprocal cost assignment without directly linking services to another support or overhead layer. The only common accounts across layers might be the MC/R centers, which will appear in each of the reciprocal cost matrices.

Analysis of Revenue and Costs

After general overhead services are allocated to the eight MC/R centers, then aggregate costs of $6,286,578 (Exhibit 11.1) and aggregate revenue of $7,166,122 (Exhibit 11.5) are matched in these eight centers. Exhibit 11.11 shows the return (loss) for each of the eight MC/R centers. The direct costs from the database in Exhibit 11.4 are repeated in Exhibit 11.11, so the costs and revenue in each of the eight MC/R areas are representative of what a user might retrieve from Glenwood's computer system. The line numbers in Exhibit 11.11 permit immediate

Exhibit 11.10   Illustration of Two Reciprocal Cost Assignments for Glenwood Laboratories

Revenue Center	Initial Combined Cost	Assigned Reciprocal Cost #1	Assigned Reciprocal Cost #2	Total Cost
Hematology A (432)	$ 703,074.28	$ 42,121.76	$ 30,631.13	$ 775,827.17
Hematology A (433)	863,351.19	36,739.20	40,841.50	940,931.89
Chemistry A (462)	965,684.16	49,712.52	22,756.59	1,038,153.27
Chemistry B (463)	1,111,185.32	49,464.12	36,107.81	1,196,757.25
Pathology A (532)	608,554.30	41,426.19	38,505.65	688,486.14
Pathology B (533)	444,798.81	34,903.79	25,092.43	504,795.03
Microbiology A (562)	491,289.16	47,948.59	31,436.18	570,673.93
Microbiology B (563)	498,616.26	43,299.14	29,038.40	570,953.80
Total	$5,686,553.48	$345,615.31	$254,409.69	$6,286,578.48

identification of the entry from one of the three prior exhibits: Exhibit 11.4 (Lines 2–205), Exhibit 11.7 (Lines 240–263), and Exhibit 11.9 (Lines 264–277).

Summary

Glenwood Laboratories is a case example of how different costs are used for various decision-making purposes. The materials in this chapter emphasize the data flows through the network of organization codes at Glenwood. Discussion questions at the end of the case focus on the interpretation of these data for various purposes.

Transaction data recorded for expenditure and management control purposes flow through the network of cost codes within Glenwood's computer system. An organization chart with 29 cost codes is presented so the flow through the network can be easily traced. Eight of the cost codes are used as reporting centers for management control and departmental assessment purposes. Glenwood's computer system provides the mapping of cost codes to these eight reporting centers, but there is no stored aggregation for these reporting centers in the DBMS (Exhibits 11.4 and 11.1).

This case example illustrates the joint cost assignment of dedicated support areas for both direct expenditures and support services. General overhead and administrative support services are allocated by the reciprocal cost method to the eight MC/R centers. Revenue and expenses are matched in the computation of returns and losses for the eight centers.

Appendix: Traceability of Transaction Data

Directors, managers, and supervisors in health care entities are very much aware that financial and operational data are used in assessing performance. Any cost allocation, assignment, or transfer appearing in a MC/R center is subject to close scrutiny. The MC/R center's coordinator must be able to trace the reverse flow of each cost allocation, assignment, or transfer. The analysis is from the matching of costs and revenue in a MC/R center back through the flow network to the origin of the transaction. Often, reverse cost-flow analysis will span three or four organizational levels.

Text continues on page 371

Exhibit 11.11   Glenwood Laboratories: Cost Data for Year Ended 30
September 19X1

A	B	C	D	E	F	G	H
			FinStat				
Cost	*Cost*						*Line*
To	*From*	*Element*	*Acc*	*Nat*	*Description*	*Amount*	*No.*
432					*Hematology Area A*	*($ 46,918.13)*	
					Return		
432	432	DIRMAT	E	R	Test #85610	109,911.46	52
432	432	DIRMAT	E	R	Test #89051	180,022.04	53
432	432	DIRMAT	E	R	Test #85055	88,481.42	54
432	432	DIRMAT	E	R	Test #85050	77,026.93	55
432	432	DIRMAT	E	R	Test #85580	150,931.53	56
432	432	DRSUPP	E	R	Indirect costs	5,700.00	57
432	432	DLABOR	E	R	Hematologists	37,000.00	58
432	432	DLFBEN	E	R	Hematologists	3,026.00	59
432	432	DTREVE	R	R	Test #85055	(127,336.80)	60
432	432	DTREVE	R	R	Test #85050	(111,952.50)	61
432	432	DTREVE	R	R	Test #85610	(146,278.40)	62
432	432	DTREVE	R	R	Test #89051	(251,078.40)	63
432	432	DTREVE	R	R	Test #85580	(186,099.20)	64
432	303	MAINT	E	A	Maintenance contract	30,100.00	65
432	304	HOUSEK	E	A	Housekeeping contract	6,100.00	66
432	305	GENACCT	E	A	General accounting fee	1,400.00	67
432	431	DCOST	E	A	Joint cost (45% experience)	11,889.90	240
432	431	SUPPORT	E	A	Support services (45% experience)	1,485.00	252
432	201	OVERHEAD	E	A	Overhead services	72,752.89	264
433					*Hematology Area B*	*($260,827.71)*	
					Return		
433	433	DIRMAT	E	R	Test #85660	147,792.51	68
433	433	DIRMAT	E	R	Test #85030	113,681.69	69
433	433	DIRMAT	E	R	Test #85640	181,084.08	70
433	433	DIRMAT	E	R	Test #85020	196,439.36	71
433	433	DIRMAT	E	R	Test #85730	106,667.45	72
433	433	DLABOR	E	R	Hematologists	55,500.00	73
433	433	DLFBEN	E	R	Hematologists	4,539.00	74
433	433	DRSUPP	E	R	Indirect costs	6,300.00	75
433	433	DTREVE	R	R	Test #85660	(232,110.00)	76
433	433	DTREVE	R	R	Test #85020	(304,752.00)	77
433	433	DTREVE	R	R	Test #85640	(311,542.40)	78

Continued

Exhibit 11.11   Continued

A	B	C	D	E	F	G	H
		FinStat					*Line*
Cost To	*Cost From*	*Element*	*Acc*	*Nat*	*Description*	*Amount*	*No.*
433	433	DTREVE	R	R	Test #85730	(172,068.80)	79
433	433	DTREVE	R	R	Test #85030	(181,286.40)	80
433	303	MAINT	E	A	Maintenance contract	27,000.00	81
433	304	HOUSEK	E	A	Housekeeping contract	6,300.00	82
433	305	GENACCT	E	A	General accounting fee	1,700.00	83
433	431	DCOST	E	A	Joint cost (55% experience)	14,532.10	241
433	431	SUPPORT	E	A	Support services (55% experience)	1,815.00	253
433	201	OVERHEAD	E	A	Overhead services	77,580.70	265
462					*Chemistry Area A Return*	*($339,305.23)*	
462	462	DIRMAT	E	R	Test #82310	153,604.80	90
462	462	DIRMAT	E	R	Test #82251	162,072.27	91
462	462	DIRMAT	E	R	Test #82465	173,594.82	92
462	462	DIRMAT	E	R	Test #82890	182,453.31	93
462	462	DIRMAT	E	R	Test #82565	173,654.64	94
462	462	DLABOR	E	R	Technician, Chemistry	57,000.00	95
462	462	DLFBEN	E	R	Technician, Chemistry	4,947.00	96
462	462	DRSUPP	E	R	Indirect costs	10,100.00	97
462	462	DTREVE	R	R	Test #82251	(339,372.00)	98
462	462	DTREVE	R	R	Test #82890	(295,198.20)	99
462	462	DTREVE	R	R	Test #82310	(268,808.40)	100
462	462	DTREVE	R	R	Test #82465	(229,495.90)	101
462	462	DTREVE	R	R	Test #82565	(244,584.00)	102
462	303	MAINT	E	A	Maintenance contract	24,000.00	103
462	304	HOUSEK	E	A	Housekeeping contract	5,700.00	104
462	305	GENACCT	E	A	General accounting fee	2,000.00	105
462	461	DCOST	E	A	Joint cost (52% experience)	14,893.32	243
462	461	SUPPORT	E	A	Support services (52% experience)	1,664.00	255
462	201	OVERHEAD	E	A	Overhead services	72,469.11	266
463					*Chemistry Area B Return*	*($213,091.85)*	
463	463	DIRMAT	E	R	Test #84520	261,611.27	106
463	463	DIRMAT	E	R	Test #84140	217,705.90	107

Continued

Exhibit 11.11 Continued

A	B	C	D	E	F	G	H
		FinStat					
Cost	*Cost*						*Line*
To	*From*	*Element*	*Acc*	*Nat*	*Description*	*Amount*	*No.*
463	463	DIRMAT	E	R	Test #83020	198,345.60	**108**
463	463	DIRMAT	E	R	Test #83420	131,595.93	**109**
463	463	DIRMAT	E	R	Test #84295	187,095.94	**110**
463	463	DLABOR	E	R	Technician, Chemistry	57,000.00	**111**
463	463	DLFBEN	E	R	Technician, Chemistry	4,947.00	**112**
463	463	DRSUPP	E	R	Indirect costs	9,200.00	**113**
463	463	DTREVE	R	R	Test #83420	(171,055.20)	**114**
463	463	DTREVE	R	R	Test #84295	(296,176.50)	**115**
463	463	DTREVE	R	R	Test #84140	(297,518.40)	**116**
463	463	DTREVE	R	R	Test #84520	(359,971.20)	**117**
463	463	DTREVE	R	R	Test #83020	(285,127.80)	**118**
463	303	MAINT	E	A	Maintenance contract	21,000.00	**119**
463	304	HOUSEK	E	A	Housekeeping contract	5,600.00	**120**
463	305	GENACCT	E	A	General accounting fee	1,800.00	**121**
463	461	DCOST	E	A	Joint cost (48% experience)	13,747.68	**244**
463	461	SUPPORT	E	A	Support services (48% experience)	1,536.00	**256**
463	201	OVERHEAD	E	A	Overhead services	85,571.93	**267**
532					*Pathology-Cytology Area A ($ 66,641.66) Return*		
532	532	DIRMAT	E	R	Test #88410	104,871.71	**136**
532	532	DIRMAT	E	R	Test #88340	110,090.23	**137**
532	532	DIRMAT	E	R	Test #88370	103,155.37	**138**
532	532	DIRMAT	E	R	Test #88146	63,978.64	**139**
532	532	DIRMAT	E	R	Test #88350	125,784.43	**140**
532	532	DLABOR	E	R	Pathology-Cytology Technicians	40,000.00	**141**
532	532	DLFBEN	E	R	Pathology-Cytology Technicians	4,594.00	**142**
532	532	DRSUPP	E	R	Indirect costs	8,200.00	**143**
532	532	DTREVE	R	R	Test #88350	(186,588.00)	**144**
532	532	DTREVE	R	R	Test #88410	(154,836.00)	**145**
532	532	DTREVE	R	R	Test #88370	(144,462.60)	**146**
532	532	DTREVE	R	R	Test #88340	(168,708.00)	**147**

Continued

Exhibit 11.11   Continued

A	B	C	D	E	F	G	H
Cost To	Cost From	FinStat Element	Acc	Nat	Description	Amount	Line No.
532	532	DTREVE	R	R	Test #88146	(100,533.20)	148
532	303	MAINT	E	A	Maintenance contract	28,000.00	149
532	304	HOUSEK	E	A	Housekeeping contract	3,900.00	150
532	305	GENACCT	E	A	General accounting fee	1,900.00	151
532	531	DCOST	E	A	Joint cost (43% experience)	12,488.92	246
532	531	SUPPORT	E	A	Support services (43% experience)	1,591.00	258
532	201	OVERHEAD	E	A	Overhead services	79,931.84	268
533					*Pathology-Cytology Area B ($ 3,904.47) Return*		
533	533	DIRMAT	E	R	Test #88150	64,737.28	152
533	533	DIRMAT	E	R	Test #88175	56,636.82	153
533	533	DIRMAT	E	R	Test #88155	42,660.44	154
533	533	DIRMAT	E	R	Test #88300	62,051.11	155
533	533	DIRMAT	E	R	Test #88305	112,055.08	156
533	533	DLABOR	E	R	Pathology-Cytology Technicians	40,000.00	157
533	533	DLFBEN	E	R	Pathology-Cytology Technicians	4,594.00	158
533	533	DRSUPP	E	R	Indirect costs	6,800.00	159
533	533	DTREVE	R	R	Test #88175	(75,888.00)	160
533	533	DTREVE	R	R	Test #88305	(157,533.90)	161
533	533	DTREVE	R	R	Test #88150	(109,548.00)	162
533	533	DTREVE	R	R	Test #88300	(98,899.20)	163
533	533	DTREVE	R	R	Test #88155	(66,830.40)	164
533	304	HOUSEK	E	A	Housekeeping contract	5,400.00	165
533	303	MAINT	E	A	Maintenance contract	29,000.00	166
533	305	GENACCT	E	A	General accounting fee	2,200.00	167
533	531	DCOST	E	A	Joint cost (57% experience)	16,555.08	247
533	531	SUPPORT	E	A	Support services (57% experience)	2,109.00	259
533	201	OVERHEAD	E	A	Overhead services	59,996.22	269

Continued

Exhibit 11.11   Continued

A	B	C	D	E	F	G	H
		FinStat					
Cost	Cost						Line
To	From	Element	Acc	Nat	Description	Amount	No.
562					Microbiology Area A Return	($ 25,604.37)	
562	562	DIRMAT	E	R	Test #87092	108,036.24	174
562	562	DIRMAT	E	R	Test #87095	77,105.26	175
562	562	DIRMAT	E	R	Test #87094	41,610.05	176
562	562	DIRMAT	E	R	Test #87093	101,488.76	177
562	562	DIRMAT	E	R	Test #87091	48,073.65	178
562	562	DLABOR	E	R	Microbiologists	41,000.00	179
562	562	DLFBEN	E	R	Microbiologists	4,814.00	180
562	562	DRSUPP	E	R	Indirect costs	4,500.00	181
562	562	DTREVE	R	R	Test #87091	(76,128.00)	182
562	562	DTREVE	R	R	Test #87094	(59,536.00)	183
562	562	DTREVE	R	R	Test #87092	(158,288.90)	184
562	562	DTREVE	R	R	Test #87093	(173,716.00)	185
562	562	DTREVE	R	R	Test #87095	(128,609.40)	186
562	303	MAINT	E	A	Maintenance contract	38,000.00	187
562	304	HOUSEK	E	A	Housekeeping contract	5,900.00	188
562	305	GENACCT	E	A	General accounting fee	1,500.00	189
562	561	DCOST	E	A	Joint cost (60% experience)	17,641.20	249
562	561	SUPPORT	E	A	Support services (60% experience)	1,620.00	261
562	201	OVERHEAD	E	A	Overhead services	79,384.77	270
563					Microbiology Area B Loss	$ 76,749.90	
563	563	DIRMAT	E	R	Test #87190	64,439.48	190
563	563	DIRMAT	E	R	Test #87350	109,139.24	191
563	563	DIRMAT	E	R	Test #87000	43,808.12	192
563	563	DIRMAT	E	R	Test #87096	79,157.75	193
563	563	DIRMAT	E	R	Test #87025	100,116.87	194
563	563	DLABOR	E	R	Microbiologists	41,000.00	195
563	563	DLFBEN	E	R	Microbiologists	4,814.00	196
563	563	DRSUPP	E	R	Indirect costs	4,700.00	197
563	563	DTREVE	R	R	Test #87025	(116,032.00)	198
563	563	DTREVE	R	R	Test #87190	(80,418.80)	199
563	563	DTREVE	R	R	Test #87000	(63,714.40)	200

Continued

Exhibit 11.11 Continued

A	B	C	D	E	F	G	H
			FinStat				*Line*
Cost	*Cost*						
To	*From*	*Element*	*Acc*	*Nat*	*Description*	*Amount*	*No.*
563	563	DTREVE	R	R	Test #87350	(129,234.60)	**201**
563	563	DTREVE	R	R	Test #87096	(104,804.10)	**202**
563	303	MAINT	E	A	Maintenance contract	31,000.00	**203**
563	304	HOUSEK	E	A	Housekeeping contract	5,500.00	**204**
563	305	GENACCT	E	A	General accounting fee	2,100.00	**205**
563	561	DCOST	E	A	Joint cost (40% experience)	11,760.80	**250**
563	561	SUPPORT	E	A	Support services (40% experience)	1,080.00	**262**
563	201	OVERHEAD	E	A	Overhead services	72,337.54	**271**

Tracing an item to the initial set of expenditures or revenue for that event is dependent upon references in the data structure. Each component of a transaction in the DBMS contains an entry for "cost to" code, "cost from" code, element, account, and nature. The composite information provided by this reference material permits reverse tracing in Glenwood's network to the origin of a transaction.

Exhibit 11.12 is an extract of the 19 lines of information in Exhibit 11.11 for Hematology area A (432). The 19 lines are separated into eight parts for scrutiny: direct materials, other direct costs, revenue, assigned maintenance costs, housekeeping costs, general accounting fee, joint cost assignment, and general overhead allocation. An explanation is given in each part of Exhibit 11.12 about the tracing of that disclosure to the source of the information for that event. The abbreviations and symbols used in Glenwood's references are interpreted within the explanation for the eight categories of transactions in Exhibit 11.12. Specific lines in other exhibits are given to facilitate the reverse tracing through this example case.

Additional Readings

Herzlinger, R. E. "The Failed Revolution in Health Care—The Role of Management," *Harvard Business Review* 67 (March–April 1989): 95–103.

Exhibit 11.12   Hematology, Area A (432): Traceability of
Transaction Data

Cost To	Cost From	FinStat Element	Acc	Nat	Description	Amount	Line No.
432					*Hematology Area A Return*	*($46,918.13)*	

Part 1.   Direct Materials (Lines 52–56)

Cost To	Cost From	FinStat Element	Acc	Nat	Description	Amount	Line No.
432	432	DIRMAT	E	R	Test #85610	109,911.46	52
432	432	DIRMAT	E	R	Test #89051	180,022.04	53
432	432	DIRMAT	E	R	Test #85055	88,481.42	54
432	432	DIRMAT	E	R	Test #85050	77,026.93	55
432	432	DIRMAT	E	R	Test #85580	150,931.53	56

Direct materials (DIRMAT) for the five hematology tests were initially recorded as an expense (E for account code; see Exhibit 11.3) where the direct responsibility (R for nature of transaction; see Exhibit 11.3) is with Hematology area A (432 in Column B for "Cost From"). Information on Lines 52–56 from Exhibit 11.4 also appeared in the management control reports for the period, which were not illustrated in this case example.

Part 2.   Other Direct Costs (Lines 57–59)

Cost To	Cost From	FinStat Element	Acc	Nat	Description	Amount	Line No.
432	432	DRSUPP	E	R	Indirect costs	5,700.00	57
432	432	DLABOR	E	R	Hematologists	37,000.00	58
432	432	DLFBEN	E	R	Hematologists	3,026.00	59

Direct supplies and other indirect costs (DRSUPP), direct labor (DLABOR), and direct labor fringe benefits (DLFBEN) were initially recorded as an expense (E) where the direct responsibility (R) is with Hematology area A (432 in Column B). Information on Lines 57–59 appeared in the management control reports for the period.

Part 3.   Revenue (Lines 60–64)

Cost To	Cost From	FinStat Element	Acc	Nat	Description	Amount	Line No.
432	432	DTREVE	R	R	Test #85055	(127,336.80)	60
432	432	DTREVE	R	R	Test #85050	(111,952.50)	61
432	432	DTREVE	R	R	Test #85610	(146,278.40)	62
432	432	DTREVE	R	R	Test #89051	(251,078.40)	63
432	432	DTREVE	R	R	Test #85580	(186,099.20)	64

Direct revenue (DTREVE) for the five hematology tests were initially recorded as revenue (R for account code) where the direct responsibility (R for nature of transaction) is with Hematology area A (432 in Column B). Information on Lines 60–64 appeared in the management control reports for the period.

Continued

Exhibit 11.12   Continued

Cost To	Cost From	FinStat Element	Acc	Nat	Description	Amount	Line No.

Part 4. Assigned Maintenance Costs (Line 65)

| 432 | 303 | MAINT | E | A | Maintenance contract | 30,100.00 | 65 |

Maintenance costs (MAINT) are assigned (A for nature of transaction) by cost code 303 (maintenance contract label from Figure 11.1). The detailed costs for maintenance (code 303) can be traced to Line 24 in Exhibit 11.4. The aggregate common assignment entry for maintenance is illustrated in Exhibit 11.3.

Part 5. Housekeeping Costs (Line 66)

| 432 | 304 | HOUSEK | E | A | Housekeeping contract | 6,100.00 | 66 |

Housekeeping costs (HOUSEK) are assigned (A for nature of transaction) by cost code 304 (maintenance contract label from Figure 11.1). The detailed costs for housekeeping (code 304) can be traced to Line 26 in Exhibit 11.4.

Part 6. General Accounting Fee (Line 67)

| 432 | 305 | GENACCT | E | A | General accounting fee | 1,400.00 | 67 |

General accounting fee (GENACCT) is assigned (A for nature of transaction) by cost code 305 (general accounting fee label from Figure 11.1). The detailed costs for general accounting fee (code 305) can be traced to Line 28 in Exhibit 11.4.

Part 7. Joint Cost Assignment (Lines 240 and 252)

| 432 | 431 | DCOST | E | A | Joint cost (45% experience) | 11,889.90 | 240 |
| 432 | 431 | SUPPORT | E | A | Support services (45% experience) | 1,485.00 | 252 |

Assigned joint costs—direct (DCOST) and assigned joint costs—dedicated (SUPPORT) represent 45 percent of the office of supervisor, Hematology area A's (431) costs. Exhibit 11.7 shows the joint cost transactions for code 431. The initial expenditures and support costs for code 431 can be traced to Lines 46–51 of Exhibit 11.4.

Part 8. General Overhead Allocation (Line 264)

| 432 | 201 | OVERHEAD | E | A | Overhead services | 72,752.89 | 264 |

Reciprocal cost assignments (OVERHEAD) can be traced to Exhibit 11.9 for the entries and to Exhibit 11.8 for the computations.

Kis, G. M. J., and G. Bodenger. "Cost Management Information Improves Financial Performance," *Healthcare Financial Management* 43 (May 1989): 36–48.

Kovner, A. R. "The Case of the Unhealthy Hospital," *Harvard Business Review* 69 (September–October 1991): 12–26.

Discussion Questions

11.1. Eight of Glenwood's cost codes serve as both regular cost accounts and MC/R centers. Explain the benefit of this arrangement.

11.2. From the perspective of Hematology area B (code 433) in Figure 11.1, identify the layers of administrative support services to code 433.

11.3. From the perspective of Microbiology area B (code 563) in Figure 11.1, identify the layers of administrative support services to code 563.

11.4. After studying Figure 11.1, prepare a list of the 29 cost codes at Glenwood Laboratories and designate for each cost code whether it is a regular cost account, a major cost/revenue center, or a reporting cost center.

Hint: *Cost* *Code*	*Title*	*Regular* *Cost* *Account*	*Major* *Cost/Revenue* *Center*	*Reporting* *Cost* *Center*
200	Director, Glenwood			X
201	Office of Director	X		
. . .				
563	Microbiology, Area B	X	X	

11.5. Exhibit 11.1 reports direct expenditures for office of manager of Finance and Operations (code 301) as $42,740. This same cost code reports a balance of $45,840 in Column B, Line 15 of Exhibit 11.8. Explain the difference in these amounts for 301.

11.6. Explain the $159,273 of reciprocal cost for code 301 (office of manager of Finance and Operations) on Line 34 of Exhibit 11.8.

11.7. Explain the $154,981 of reciprocal cost for code 501 (office of manager of Pathology and Microbiology) on Line 38 of Exhibit 11.8.

11.8. List the transactions that compose the $62,029 balance in cost code 501 (office of manager of Pathology and Microbiology) in Column B, Line 19, of Exhibit 11.8.

11.9. Chemistry area B (code 463) reports direct expenditures in Exhibit 11.1 of $1,067,502. Column B, Line 9, of Exhibit 11.8 reports $1,111,186 for code 463. Explain the difference in these amounts for 463.

Exhibit 11.13 Profile Comparison of Eight MC/R Areas: Cost Elements as Percent of Total Cost

Elements	Hematology		Chemistry		Pathology		Microbiology		Averages for Eight Profit Centers
	A(432)	B(433)	A(462)	B(463)	A(532)	B(533)	A(562)	B(563)	
DLABOR	5.26%	6.43%	5.90%	5.13%	6.57%	8.99%	8.35%	8.22%	6.48%
DLFBEN	0.43	0.52	0.51	0.44	0.76	1.03	0.98	0.97	0.64
DIRMAT	86.25	86.37	87.54	89.67	83.46	76.02	76.60	79.55	84.63
DRSUPP	0.81	0.73	1.05	0.83	1.35	1.53	0.92	0.94	0.97
MAINT	4.28	3.13	2.49	1.89	4.60	6.52	7.73	6.22	4.01
HOUSEK	0.87	0.73	0.59	0.50	0.64	1.21	1.20	1.10	0.78
GENACCT	0.20	0.20	0.21	0.16	0.31	0.50	0.30	0.42	0.26
DCOST	1.69	1.68	1.54	1.24	2.05	3.72	3.59	2.36	2.00
SUPPORT	0.21	0.21	0.17	0.14	0.26	0.48	0.33	0.22	0.23
Total	100.00%	100.00%	100.00%	100.00%	100.00%	100.00%	100.00%	100.00%	100.00%

11.10. Compute the contribution margin for the eight MC/R centers according to the information in Exhibit 11.11.

11.11. Prepare a schedule showing the matching of total costs with revenue for Glenwood's eight MC/R centers according to the information in Exhibit 11.11. This statement is to be used in long-range planning.

11.12. Perform a profitability assessment of Hematology area A (432) versus Hematology area B (433) using the information in Exhibit 11.11 and 11.13.

11.13. Perform a profitability assessment of Chemistry area A (462) versus Chemistry area B (463) using the information in Exhibit 11.11 and 11.13.

11.14. Perform a profitability assessment of Pathology-Cytology area A (532) versus Pathology-Cytology area B (533) using the information in Exhibit 11.11 and 11.13.

11.15. Perform a profitability assessment of Microbiology area A (562) versus Microbiology area B (563) using the information in Exhibits 11.11 and 11.13.

11.16. Exhibit 11.14 shows the distribution of revenue for the eight MC/R centers by the Medical Center Hospital, Eastside Community Hospital, Carol Memorial Hospital, Clinic A, Clinic B, Clinic C, and Clinic D. What new insights are suggested by the data in Exhibit 11.14?

11.17. (See Question 11.16.) The third party payor mix is different for each of the facilities in Exhibit 11.14. Each facility contains an emergency laboratory where some hematology and chemistry tests are performed. What additional insights are suggested by shifts in payor mix and distribution of tests?

Exhibit 11.14   Distribution of Revenue by Source for Eight MC/R Centers

	Medical Center Hospital	Eastside Community Hospital	Carol Memorial Hospital	Clinic A	Clinic B	Clinic C	Clinic D
Total revenue	50.00%	20.00%	10.00%	6.00%	5.00%	5.00%	4.00%
Code							
432	56.00	16.16	10.10	6.24	5.50	4.00	2.00
433	48.10	23.52	10.70	6.00	5.00	4.18	2.50
462	55.80	12.91	11.00	7.00	5.59	5.10	2.60
463	48.00	24.20	9.50	6.00	5.30	4.00	3.00
532	49.00	19.90	9.60	5.70	4.60	5.20	6.00
533	48.00	20.80	9.70	5.50	4.50	5.50	6.00
562	44.00	24.09	8.91	5.00	4.00	7.00	7.00
563	45.00	20.00	9.00	5.00	4.00	8.00	9.00

Recap of Total Revenue

Medical Center Hospital	$3,583,061
Eastside Community Hospital	1,433,224
Carol Memorial Hospital	716,612
Clinic A	429,968
Clinic B	358,306
Clinic C	358,306
Clinic D	286,645
Total revenue	*$7,166,122*

12

Management Control for Health Care Entities

Introduction

Cost pools were emphasized in the previous chapters as the designated organizational units in a network of cost accumulations, cost transfers, common cost assignments, and joint cost assignments that match efforts with revenue. Cost pools also encompass performance measurements that are supported by the aggregation of activities, procedures, services, and work-load statistics. Some key cost pools contain revenue; others do not, but provide support services. All key cost pools are designated as major cost/revenue centers.

Profitability analysis and contribution margins by type of patient service were performed on some MC/R centers. Layers of support and administrative services are matched with benefits for pricing, contractual agreements, and decision-making activities. The reciprocal cost method integrates cost drivers of support services into a meaningful framework for cost assignments and cost allocations. General overhead allocations are performed by key cost pools for some types of financial statements and long-range planning activities.

The previous discussions of cost pools are all predicated on a foundation of transaction control, expenditure control, and management control. Figure 12.1 shows the locations of the previous discussions in conceptual levels 4 to 6 in a framework for cost and management control analysis. Different costs for various decision-making purposes are emphasized in levels 4 to 6, but the foundation for all cost analysis is the integrated nature of the initial two levels. The capture of transaction data by regular cost accounts is the initial process that permits everything else to happen.

Figure 12.1   Cost and Management Control Analysis for Health
Care Entities

Conceptual Level 6 Operational strategy and external reporting requirements by various clusters and organizational groups plus the total entity		
Conceptual Level 5 Pricing and contractual agreements by service or groups of service		*Conceptual Level 5* Pricing and contractual agreements by service or groups of service
Conceptual Level 4 Profitability analysis by major cost/revenue centers		*Conceptual Level 4* Profitability analysis by major cost/revenue centers
Conceptual Level 3 Departmental assessment by major cost/revenue centers		*Conceptual Level 3* Departmental assessment by major cost/revenue centers
Conceptual Level 2 Management control by regular cost account		*Conceptual Level 2* Management control by regular cost account
Conceptual Level 1 Expenditure control by regular cost account	*Conceptual Level 1* Expenditure control by temporary cost pool and regular cost account	*Conceptual Level 1* Expenditure control by regular cost account

Transaction Control

The delivery of health care services to individuals imposes professional
responsibilities on a health care entity's staff for monitoring patient
information. If the patient has received treatment from the health
care entity during the past seven years and has a documented medical
condition requiring special attention, then the staff has professional
and legal responsibilities to be aware of the situation. In the registration
or admission of a patient, a computer inquiry is made against a medical
record index for any prior episodes of care with that institution.

The health care entity's computer system must incorporate rigorous sets of editing procedures, screening of inputs, cross-verification
of patient identification information, and other internal controls for
monitoring of proposed transactions. The editing, screening, and verification module interacts with (1) the order entry module for tests,

procedures, and operations, (2) the scheduling module for services, (3) the result-reporting module for outcomes in tests, procedures, operations, services, and activities, and (4) the financial module for billing, reporting, and management.

These editing, monitoring, and internal control requirements result in four major advantages. First, transactions tend to be complete for all key data fields with a reasonable degree of confidence in the contents. Second, there are very few omitted transactions because of the checks and balances within and between the various computer system modules. Third, internal control procedures impose numbering, identification, and quantification requirements on the network of flows, which results in the creation of a statistical database of the health care entity's operations. Fourth, access and security controls to protect privileged patient information adds more verification and comparison procedures of regular cost account codes.

Management control is possible because of the foundation of internal controls that must exist in health care entities. Financial and operational transactions are edited, screened, filtered, and cross-referenced by the health care entity's computer system before they are accepted in cost pools. The health care entity must protect the privileged status of certain patient information by restricting the access to computer files and by electronic monitoring of retrievals. Some patient information (such as unusual medical problems and conditions) may be so sensitive that it cannot be stored in a computer system.[1] While initial checking, screening, and monitoring is beyond the scope of this book, it is important to know that this module exists and interacts with all transactions before the event is accepted into the entity's computer for storage in a cost pool.

Cost Pools for Management Control

Health care entities are often organized into several patient care groups, divisions, departments, and clinics, with many ancillary and support areas. Within each organizational unit, there may be several clusters of specialists, technicians, and support personnel whose actions are fairly independent of the other clusters. From a management control perspective, each cluster might be an appropriate segment for a regular cost account, but there is no desire to perform pricing, contract negotiation, or other decision-making activities by that segment beyond expenditure control.

The mapping of regular cost accounts into MC/R centers is illustrated in the previous chapters with transactions for cost transfers, cost assignments, common cost assignments, and reciprocal cost allocations. MC/R centers are the cost pools in most health care entities for activity-based costing. They are the organizational units that are the primary focus of profitability analysis, pricing, and other decision-making activities.

Expenditure control and other management control purposes are primarily achieved through regular cost accounts and master reporting centers. Master reporting centers are like temporary MC/R centers that only exist in the computer system for purposes of preparing management control reports and departmental assessments. These cost accounts have zero balances at all times in the health care entity's DBMS. Any balance ascribed to a master reporting center is a computational amount restricted to the computer-based application package and its outputs.

The organization chart for Demonstration Memorial Hospital's Department of Pathology is presented in Figure 9.2. The organizational level 7 regular cost accounts were omitted for illustration purposes. Exhibit 12.1 shows the separation of these cost codes among 17 regular cost accounts, 6 major reporting centers, and 11 MC/R centers. It is significant that the 11 MC/R centers in Exhibit 12.1 are all located at organizational level 6 in this department. Profitability analysis and activity-based costing will initially focus on these 11 MC/R centers. Special studies may then shift to the supporting regular cost accounts that map into these 11 MC/R centers.

Expenditure control is achieved through regular cost accounts with computer-based monitoring of transactions by element or natural classification of the event. The editing, screening, and verification module in the health care entity's computer system confirms that the type of expenditure or revenue is "acceptable" for a given regular cost account. An acceptable transaction is within the budget guidance by element for that cost account. The budget guidance for elements with variable volumes is based on flexible budgeting methods.

Changes in medical practice and implementation of medical technology affect the "traditional" regular cost accounts in a health care entity. Cost pools may be established as temporary cost accounts to support these developments. When this occurs, expenditure control is achieved by temporary cost accounts. The temporary cost accounts are mapped into regular cost accounts so the normal processing of cost flows can be achieved without modification.

Exhibit 12.1 Demonstration Memorial Hospital: Mapping of Cost Codes for Department of Pathology

Code		Regular Cost Account	Master Reporting Center	Master Cost/Revenue Center
210	Chair, Department of Pathology		X	
211	Office of chair, Pathology	X		
212	Manager of Laboratory		X	
213	Office of manager of Laboratory	X		
214	Assistant manager of Clinical Laboratories		X	
215	Office of assistant manager of Clinical Laboratories	X		
216	Supervisor, Immunology			X
217	Office of supervisor, Immunology	X		
218	Supervisor, Hematology			X
219	Office of supervisor, Hematology	X		
222	Supervisor, Chemistry			X
223	Office of supervisor, Chemistry	X		
224	Supervisor, RIA and Special Chemistry			X
225	Office of supervisor, RIA/Special Chemistry	X		
226	Supervisor, Microbiology			X
227	Office of supervisor, Microbiology	X		
228	Assistant manager of Laboratory Operations		X	
229	Office of assistant manager of Lab Operations	X		
232	Supervisor, Pathology and Oncology			X
233	Office of supervisor, Pathology and Oncology	X		
234	Supervisor, Cytology and Histology			X
235	Office of supervisor, Cytology and Histology	X		
236	Supervisor, Autopsy and Other Pathology			X
237	Office of supervisor, Autopsy & Other Pathology	X		
238	Supervisor, STAT Laboratory			X
239	Office of supervisor, STAT Laboratory	X		

Continued

Exhibit 12.1   Continued

Code		Regular Cost Account	Master Reporting Center	Master Cost/Revenue Center
242	Administrative assistant, Lab Administration		X	
243	Office of administrative assistant	X		
244	Manager of Blood Center		X	
245	Office of manager, Blood Center	X		
246	Supervisor, Blood Bank Operations			X
247	Office of supervisor, Blood Bank Operations	X		
248	Supervisor, Blood Operations			X
249	Office of supervisor, Blood Operations	X		
	Total	17	6	11

Regular cost accounts permit the orderly accumulation of expenditure, revenue, statistical, and utilization data in the health care entity's DBMS. The regular cost accounts serve as the defined cost pools around which alternative uses of the same database are accomplished. Figure 12.1 shows the cost pool and regular cost account as the foundation (level 1) for all financial decision-making activities.

The complexity of patient services often involves direct efforts by resources in several cost accounts where different professionals direct the management control function in each unit. The physician responsible for ordering patient services is usually not employed by any of the units in the health care entity that deliver the service. The pricing of patient services and contract negotiations covering price and volume of services are typically performed by administrative personnel from a different organizational area than those professionals in charge of delivering the patient services. The department head of a health care ancillary area may have limited involvement in influencing the demand for specific services from that department. This separation between management control function and other decision-making activities in health care entities often is related to the required professional education and experience of the individual performing the management control function. A pathologist, for example, is not the physician ordering laboratory tests for patients, but is the professional with a deep interest in quality control and expressing judgment on minimum volumes of tests in isolated categories before those services must be performed by reference laboratories. The pathologist has professional training for performing various operational control functions in the health care entity and also monitors the management control function in the department of pathology. Administrative personnel with a different type of professional education and experience are responsible for the management planning and decision-making activities.

The six levels in Figure 12.1 depict cost procedures, cost matching, cost assignments, cost allocations, and financial reporting that are associated with different types of decision-making purposes. The hierarchical flow is not along traditional organizational lines. There are multiple decision-making activities at each of the six conceptual levels in Figure 12.1.

Management Control Framework

Health care entities serving as early adopters of advancements in medical technology may discover that there are no reliable budget data on average cost per patient service for these new practices. The medical centers and research institutes where the new technology was implemented did not measure the efforts required for the new practice in a regular health care entity. These early adopters of the new practice can only monitor expenditures identified with patient service and observe if all efforts are being made to minimize total costs and to limit the disrupting effect on other areas in the health care entity. But, after a period of observation and monitoring, an estimate can be prepared for the new area, including expenses, volumes, activities, revenue, and services.

Management control is similar to the latter situation. The term "control" has no meaning in the absence of a plan, a standard, or a goal; control is an implied comparison with a benchmark. The concept of control is a framework where performance is measured against a standard, and it can be applied, for example, to laboratory tests, procedures, treatments, time, volume, expenditures, or activities. The adjective "management" with the term "control" relates to an administrative framework with the following features:

1. A defined mission
2. Delegation of authority

3. Budget resources
4. Specified activities to be accomplished
5. Identified operations to be performed for these activities
6. Measurement of efforts
7. Comparison of actual efforts with budgets
8. An exception reporting of results

Management control in a health care entity applies this eight-part administrative framework to a regular cost account. The contents of the measurement are broader than expenditures and revenue, and encompass various types of statistics and activities essential for performance assessment. The multidimensional set of events identified with the regular cost account are of equal importance with the budget-versus-actual comparisons of expenditures by natural element of cost. In many health care organizations the management control framework does not stop at the natural element of direct labor; instead, the comparing and monitoring process is followed with each category and type of direct labor.

Some products and services may dominate the outputs of health care entities in one month of a year and then have only nominal importance in another month. There are seasonal influences on some bundles of products and services that may be the major outputs of a period. These known shifts in outputs of health care entities are accommodated in the flexible budgeting calculations driven by monthly factors. Thus, year-to-date budget information for a health care institution is envisioned as an aggregation of monthly derived projections based on considerations of volume by categories of outputs.

Responsibility Accounting for Health Care Entities

Responsibility accounting is based on the management control framework, including the concept of comparing actual revenue, cost, and performance statistics with budget information by category or component within a regular cost account assigned to a given individual for monitoring purposes. The concept of responsibility accounting was presented in 1951 by John A. Higgins, a partner with Arthur Andersen & Co., as a way of shifting the focus of internal accounting procedures from product costing to the cost control aspects that are useful for operating management.[2] A manufacturing company was used in the initial example, where the suggested format of internal reports was based on "who did it" as far as incurring expenditures rather than on aggregation of items for product-costing purposes. The manually prepared reports contained three parts:

- Part I: Actual-versus-budget comparisons
- Part II: Transfer-ins and transfer-outs
- Part III: Performance evaluation

Several vendors have responsibility-accounting computer packages based on application programs with DBMSs that retrieve, edit, sort, process, and aggregate volumes of transactions and then generate reports with Mr. Higgins' three parts.

Roll-up reporting arrangement

Each responsibility-accounting application package contains a report generator and extracts transaction data by regular cost account from the DBMS.[3] This retrieval process includes all expenditures, revenue, utilization measures, services, activities, and transfers by regular cost account. The computer package does not extract the end-of-the-period assigned and allocated costs, nor does it retrieve the aggregate data in an MC/R center. The application module does contain a mapping of each regular cost account to a temporary reporting cost center that only exists in the context of the computer package. These temporary reporting cost centers approximate the hierarchical organizational structure of the health care entity. Some master reporting centers (see Exhibit 12.1) used for administrative and management control purposes are also included as temporary reporting cost centers in the responsibility-accounting application package.

Exhibit 12.2 presents the responsibility-accounting report for the vice president of ancillary services at Demonstration Memorial Hospital. The office of the vice president (code 201) incurred expenditures of $466,370 for the year (Exhibit 12.2). The Part I expenses for code 201 in the lower portion of the exhibit all show 201 as both the "cost to" and "cost from" plus the code *R* in the nature column. There were no transfers for code 201; total costs are the same direct expenditures from Part I. Each item in the lower section of the report is fully coded and is from a regular cost.

The top portion of Exhibit 12.2 illustrates the roll-up to the temporary reporting cost center 200. The account and nature columns are blank in the top portion; the term "SUM" as the element designates a temporary reporting cost center where the amount is calculated

Exhibit 12.2 Demonstration Memorial Hospital: Office of Vice President of Ancillary Services Responsibility-Accounting Report

Cost To	Cost From	FinStat Element	Acc Nat Labor			Description	Amount

Part I. *Actual-Versus-Budget Comparisons*

200						Vice president of Ancillary Services, total expenditures	$13,223,685
200	201	SUM				Vice president of Ancillary Services	466,370
200	210	SUM				Chair, Pathology	5,204,515
200	250	SUM				Chair, Radiology	3,028,900
200	270	SUM				Director, Physical Medicine/Rehabilitation	2,174,000
200	290	SUM				Director, Pharmacy	2,349,900

Part II. *Transfers In/Out*

| 210 | | | | | | Vice president of Ancillary Services, total costs | $13,223,685 |

Part I. *Actual Versus Budget Comparisons*

201						Vice president of Ancillary Services, total expenditures	$ 466,370
201	201	DLABOR	DE	R	12	Salaries & wages—regular	152,820
201	201	DLABOR	DE	R	16	Salaries & wages—regular	48,605
201	201	DLABOR	DE	R	56	Salaries & wages—regular	53,754
201	201	DLFBENF	DE	R		FICA (Social Security tax)	19,037
201	201	DLFBENG	DE	R		Group health insurance	24,354
201	201	DIRMAT	DE	R		Supplies (direct purchases)	25,000
201	201	DRSUPP	DE	R		Professional fees	142,800

Part II. *Transfers In/Out*

| 201 | | | | | | Vice president of Ancillary Services, total costs | $ 466,370 |

by the computer. Nothing in a temporary reporting cost center is retained in the health care entity's DBMS. The vice president of ancillary services' actual expenditures are $13,223,685 including $466,370 directly incurred by account 201 and $12,757,315 incurred by four departments under the vice president's control (Exhibit 12.2). One of these four departments is the Department of Pathology (210), which has expenditures of $5,204,515. The detailed flow supporting these costs for account 210 is presented in the appendix to this chapter, with a summary in Exhibit 12.10.

A vendor's standard package for responsibility-accounting systems may have to be modified to fully support the master reporting centers in some health care entities. These special requirements for the health care industry include physician salaries, pool nursing, clerical support, and shared services. The use of special cost accounts to accumulate physician salaries and the direct cost assignment of these salaries to regular cost accounts and MC/R centers were discussed in Chapter 10.

Pool nursing

A method for reducing health care costs is to have some employees who are not permanently assigned to a given ward or unit but are directed to work during a given shift where the current need is. The need is determined by nursing personnel analyzing patient loads by acuity level. The coordinator of pool nursing uses the acuity level information to determine where these nonpermanently assigned personnel work. Some individuals are employed on a part-time basis, which gives the coordinator more flexibility in responding to the patient-load requirements by ward or unit.

The regular cost account that supports pool nursing is a dummy organizational location. If the facility has six floors, for example, pool nursing personnel are assigned to the seventh floor. These personnel are identified with the dummy location for administrative purposes, and each person is assigned for each shift to a real or valid regular cost account based on patient load. The transfer-out expense for a day exactly equals the total expense of personnel assigned to the dummy organizational location. If the dummy cost center has a balance, it means that some individual is seeking payment for a shift when the person did not work. There is considerable movement of personnel from one work area to another in some health care entities; the pool nursing arrangement serves to provide control over these transfers.

In terms of the first and second parts of the standard responsibility-accounting reports, the total direct labor incurred for the dummy cost center in Part I should exactly equal the total transfer-out expense for direct labor in Part II. The monitoring of expenditures for management control purposes is accomplished through the administrative review of the dummy cost center and the transfer-out of the total salary expense based on payroll documents. The appendix illustrates these transfers.

Clerical support

The pool nursing concept has been very successful in balancing patient care requirements with staffing. This same approach is followed in staffing for clerical and administrative support. The personnel department is aware of the overall staffing requirements for the health care entity, and there is a monitoring of short-term staffing needs because of emergencies, hospitalization of employees, resignations, terminations, and leaves of absence. A coordinator in the personnel department typically handles a clerical support pool with a group of full-time and part-time employees.

The salary expense for the temporary staffing pool is charged to a dummy regular cost account in DBMS. The application package extracts these data for the dummy organizational unit, and a three-part responsibility accounting report is prepared for the coordinator of the temporary staffing pool. Transfer-outs in Part II can be compared with the direct cost in Part I for purposes of providing assurance that no person is paid for work not performed.

Shared services

A major cost-containment initiative by the federal government in the 1970s was shared services among health care providers. Regulatory agencies often required letters from various health care facilities confirming sharing of professional services with an applicant for new equipment or expansion of facilities. Once the concept of sharing was accepted by health care facilities, the object of the sharing shifted from equipment to procurement, collection efforts, continuing education, training, local transportation, legal services, and professional services. Joint ventures are also created for the purpose of shared services among health care entities.

A dummy cost center must be established for coordinating those expenses transferred to other health care entities. Part I and Part II of the responsibility-accounting reports are critical for bringing closure to the sharing arrangement. The dummy cost center has the flexibility to handle multientity constructs.

The common thread in physician salaries, pool nursing, clerical support, and shared services is the dummy cost center. The responsibility-accounting mechanism must not be limited to the confines of the existing organizational structure. The checks and balances in Part I expenses and Part II transfer-outs for the dummy cost accounts provide a management control foundation that would otherwise not be available. Physician salaries may be recorded in a dummy regular cost account, but these costs are handled by assignment rather than by transfer to maintain the privileged status of the information.

Special Controls for Salaries and Wages

More than 60 percent of the typical health care entity's expenses are for salaries, wages, and fringe benefits. Medical supplies, surgical supplies, and patient care supplies represent less than 15 percent of the total operating expenses. This 60 percent component receives special attention in expenditure controls and other management control activities.

Human resources departments in many health care entities maintain a position database by regular cost code. The entries in the position database are cross-referenced to the salaries and wages expense accounts and to the approved budget by cost center. The position database includes a position table for Demonstration Memorial Hospital containing seven digits (Exhibit 12.3). Cross-referencing the position table to the approved budget is a control procedure that precludes the unauthorized addition of personnel. The entries for the regular cost account (201) in Exhibit 12.2 included in the labor column position codes 12, 16, and 56 from Exhibit 12.3.

Departmental Management Control Assessments

Management planning and control in health care entities is a three-phase process. The responsibility-accounting system is the first phase in this process and provides expenditure control by regular cost accounts in a framework of delegation of responsibility and a reporting requirement of accountability.

The departmental management control system (DMCS) is the second phase in this process and supports management control of selected organizational units. The computer-based application package for DMCS extracts all transaction data from the health care entity's DBMS and aggregates the data based on tables of regular cost accounts and MC/R centers cross-referenced to temporary reporting centers. The organizational level at which this aggregation occurs is often classified as a department, and the unit is identified with a major cluster or group of services and products. The DMCS is for cost control and management assessment, not expenditure control, by major category of effort for each intermediate product. The emphasis, for example,

Exhibit 12.3   Demonstration Memorial Hospital: Position Database

---

Natural Classification of Salaries and Wages

11	Salaries and wages—regular
12	Salaries and wages—vacation
13	Salaries and wages—sick
14	Salaries and wages—holiday
15	Salaries and wages—overtime
16	Salaries and wages—on-call and standby
17	Salaries and wages—special

. . .

Job Titles for Salaries and Wages

03	Physicians
04	Dentists
05	Residents and fellows
06	Nonphysician medical practitioners
12	Management and supervision
13	Registered nurses
14	Licensed vocational (practical) nurses
15	Aides, orderlies, and attendants
16	Coordinators
17	Environment, hotel, and food service employees
32	Specialists
46	Technicians
56	Clerical and other administrative employees
59	Other employee classifications

. . .

Seven-Digit Position Table

```
       1 2 3  4 5  6 7
       XXX XX XX
```

1–3	XXX	Three-digit cost center code
4–5	XX	Two-digit natural classification of salaries and wages
6–7	XX	Two-digit job title

---

is on the laboratory and the aggregate tests performed by that unit, rather than on a specific set of tests for patients in a given DRG, treated by a certain physician.

Extracted data by the DMCS module are adjusted by transfers of labor and services for purposes of showing the matching of costs by natural element with benefits. The adjusted data also reflect the assigned common cost from dedicated cost centers to the benefiting cost accounts and cost centers (Chapter 10); the data also include assigned support and administrative costs based on utilization measures (Chapter 10). Some facilities extract the data for overhead allocation entries; other facilities do not include overhead allocation entries in the DMCS.

The DMCS is concerned with the overall mix and distribution of services or activities within the selected organizational unit. Expenditure control under responsibility accounting is at a lower organizational level than the DMCS and monitors actual disbursements against budget. The DMCS assesses the balance of activities that are within the organizational unit, regardless of which regular cost account initially incurred the expenditure. Special attention is given to fixed costs and minimum volumes of services that are required for supporting critical medical and surgical procedures. There are many quality-of-care considerations that depend on the DMCS.

The management of patient services is the third and final phase in this process. Patient-episodes-of-care management, case-mix management, and revenue center analysis are integral parts of this third phase, discussed in Chapters 15 and 16. Community hospitals, ambulatory surgical centers, and selected medical group management facilities are providers of patient services by a series of "departments" for given episodes of care. Continuing-care retirement communities, residential facilities, and some types of therapy clinics are providers of patient services by a given department. Skilled nursing facilities, intermediate care facilities, health maintenance organizations, and ambulatory care facilities are providers of patient services by a few departments for given episodes of care.

The patient care management system represented by the third phase in this process is essential for health care entities where multiple departments are directly involved in providing patient services for given episodes of care. DRGs under the prospective payment system serve as the designated categories of inpatient services for the Medicare program in community hospitals. Other patient classification systems currently provide the specification for hospital outpatients, clinic visits, therapy treatments, and nursing home stays.

The designated organizational unit for the DMCS and cost control may vary by type and size of the health care entity. The emphasis in the DMCS is on cost control and management assessment by key organizational units, including direct cost, assigned cost, support cost, and full (corporate) cost. The final outcome of the DMCS is to determine the average direct, assigned, and full cost of intermediate products in each of the revenue areas, such as a laboratory test, an x-ray, a treatment in a therapy unit, operating room time, and a nursing care hour.

The DMCS module, like the responsibility-accounting system, is an application computer program for extracting, processing, reporting, and analyzing data without initiating any entries in the financial DBMS. Transactions retrieved reflect the full range of information in the DBMS. The DMCS module also provides additional checks and balances against the mix and distribution of transaction data, which increases the confidence in the overall health care entity's DBMS.

Departmental Analysis

Cost control over intermediate products by department is based on a monitoring of the mix and distribution of activities within a relevant range using management-by-exception reporting capabilities in the DMCS module. Departmental analysis supports the administrative function of comparing actual with budget for direct cost, assigned cost, allocated cost, revenues, performance measures, patient order-entry profiles, and operational statistics. A regular cost center's expenditures and performance may be compatible with the responsibility-accounting budget; however, the mix and distribution of patient services from that cost center may not be compatible with the relevant range specifications for the department in the DMCS module. But, expenditure control through the responsibility-accounting system has provided the foundation for cost control in the DMCS.

Expenditure control is accomplished by the responsibility-accounting system at relatively low organizational levels; however, the individuals (such as supervisors) who can control expenditures at this low level probably have only limited impact on the mix and distribution of services provided by these regular cost accounts. Supervisors respond to the demand for services and monitor expenditures and services that are incurred in delivering the products; however, physicians are typically responsible for creating the request for services while caring for patients.

Wages paid versus hours worked

Holidays, special days, vacation days, and sick days are all factors in computing the number of days worked by an employee in a year. Although the labels differ from entity to entity, there are about 225 workdays in a year for full-time employees (365 days, less 104 Saturdays and Sundays, less 11 holidays and special days, less 15 vacation days, less 10 sick days). The salary payments must be based on the 261 weekdays for expenditure control in responsibility accounting, including the basis of the transfer entries.

To illustrate the problem, assume each workday is 7.5 hours and the hourly rate is $15, for an annual salary of $29,362.50. The expected annual distribution of this salary, and the related fringe benefits, by expense category is shown in Table 12.1. The time and attendance information processed by the payroll system will equal 1,957.5 hours in the year, with assigned salary of $29,362.50 and fringe benefits of $5,872.50. The seven types of salaries and wages in Exhibit 12.3 are used in Demonstration Memorial Hospital's responsibility-accounting reports.

Table 12.1 Expected Annual Distribution of Salary and Fringe Benefits by Expense Category for Demonstration Memorial Hospital

	Days	*Hours*	*Salary Expense*	*Fringe Benefits**
Holidays and special events	11	82.5	$ 1,237.50	$ 247.50
Vacation	15	112.5	1,687.50	337.50
Sick	10	75.0	1,125.00	225.00
Active work	225	1,687.5	25,312.50	5,062.50
Total (omits weekends)	*261*	*1,957.5*	*$29,362.50*	*$5,872.50*

*Assume 20% of salaries.

The mapped regular cost accounts that are aggregated for the department in DMCS will show, for example, total hours and total expense for each of the seven types of salaries and wages. The information in these seven accounts is helpful in understanding hours paid versus hours worked. There may be variances between budget and actual if an employee does not use the sick days, resulting in more active workdays.

Assume the $29,362.50 employee performs 200 hours of service for another department; a transfer of $3,000 salary (200 hours at $15 per hour) and $600 fringe benefits is made to that account by the responsibility-accounting system. The transfer of $3,600 for salary and fringe benefits for the 200 hours of service is correct for expenditure control, but not for matching costs with revenue. The salary and benefits of $35,235 related to the 1,687.5 hours gives an effective hourly rate of $20.88. Assuming the employee works 1,487.5 hours in the current department and 200 hours in the other department, the assigned annual cost is as follows:

Regular department	1,487.50 hours	$31,059.00
Other department	200.00 hours	4,176.00
Total cost		$35,235.00

Thus, the effective transfer should have been $4,176 for matching purposes, not $3,600—an adjustment of $576 is required. The adjusting entry for $576 is handled by the application program for payroll and is stored in the financial DBMS.

Fixed cost versus minimum volume

The flexible budgeting system used for expenditure control by regular cost account contains a calculator that is applicable to a relevant range of activities for that account. There may be several subareas within the cost account that are blended together for measuring volume (such as number of procedures, treatments, tests, or visits). Although cost behavior for purposes of expenditure control may be appropriately represented by this blend, it is not satisfactory for cost control in DMCS.

Departmental cost control is more than an aggregation of data from mapped regular cost accounts that have been analyzed by the responsibility-accounting reports. There is an overall set of planned services, with minimum and maximum points for each subset, and the maintenance of this relevant range for the period is critical to the delivery of quality care. The administrator for the department is concerned with the mix and distribution of the activities in each subset and with any shifts in utilization factors because of changes in staffing and modifications in demand. These composite movements may affect cost assignments, cost allocations, and progress of key elements used in third-party agreements. Cost control in the DMCS module serves as an alert for such courses of action.

Demonstration Memorial Hospital's Cytology and Histology area can be used to illustrate departmental cost control as distinct from expenditure control. The regular cost account for Cytology and Histology (code 235) incurred costs of $128,933. Assume that these expenditures and the laboratory tests performed are slightly above the minimal points within the tolerance range for the budget. This cost included $78,883 for direct labor. An analysis of the minimal effort for the relevant range indicated fixed labor of $72,000; however, the cost incurred for the period contained $60,000 for fixed labor cost. The variance of $12,000 in fixed labor is identified with two of the four subsets of data in Cytology and Histology being below the minimal points for the relevant range for the patient order-entry and result-reporting module. This $12,000 variance in fixed labor cost is also related to an exception for fixed fringe benefits.

The total direct labor cost for the two position codes in Cytology and Histology is within budget, and the responsibility-accounting statement for the supervisor of Cytology and Histology and the roll-up of data for the reporting cost centers do not include any exception notations. The fixed-versus-variable components in the DMCS module will identify the $12,000 variance in fixed labor cost, the related variance in fixed fringe benefits, and the two exceptions for achieving minimal volumes of services for the patient order-entry and result-reporting module. The department's efforts in responding to this situation are disclosed in each monthly report in the DMCS module. The application programs for these monthly disclosures may use additional data on services and resource utilization from the computer-based operational control packages in the department.

Operational control measures

The departmental cost in the DMCS module serves as the foundation for various decision-making activities; therefore, it is essential that this analysis is thorough and complete. The operational aspects of providing these intermediate products must be carefully analyzed by the application computer programs and reviewed by the department's administrative director. The failure to use scheduled automated equipment with some tests and treatments must be closely monitored so that unnecessary direct labor costs are not incurred. The relative-value units on manual tests and treatments are typically higher than from using automated equipment; thus, the completed service approach of analysis will not uncover this general problem.

The patient order-entry and result-reporting module, combined with the computer-based operational control module, contains the necessary information for comparing "ideal" delivery of services versus the actual. Scheduled equipment maintenance versus actual downtime for maintenance is important in financial management of fixed assets, evaluation of direct labor costs, and staff planning for the coming period. The departmental review of both modules should also include cancelled patient orders that are replaced by new orders initiated within the department. A cancelled order for services from automated equipment that is replaced by new orders for services from manual efforts is often not disclosed by the standard software for operational control. Technicians who are concerned about employment opportunities have been known to use the canceled order procedure for justifying more direct labor cost.

Summary

Management control in a health care entity is the application to a regular cost account of an administrative framework containing eight elements: (1) a defined mission, (2) delegation of authority, (3) budget resources, (4) specified activities to be accomplished, (5) identified operations to be performed for these activities, (6) measurement of efforts, (7) comparison of actual efforts with budgets, and (8) an exception reporting of results. The specification of the regular cost account may be identical with the organizational codes by unit, or a designated person may elect to have regular cost accounts by subunit so there is an aggregation of subunits into a reporting cost account for the same person. Management control only works through people; thus, there must be a mapping of each regular cost account to a person.

Responsibility-accounting systems are management control constructs for achieving expenditure monitoring and performance evaluation within an organization. After expenditure control has been achieved by regular cost account, then other types of monitoring and assessment decisions can be made. Transaction control is achieved by an editing, screening, and verification module that interacts with all other modules within the health care entity's computer system. The patient registration module, order entry module, result-reporting module, patient scheduling module, and financial module cannot process an event until the transaction is "accepted" by the editing, screening, and verification module.

Expenditure control is achieved by comparing actual with budget at the element level (natural classification of expense) within a regular cost account. Temporary cost pools may be used to capture data before the transaction flows through a regular cost account. Expenditure control by regular cost accounts is the foundation for all data in the DBMS. Figure 12.1 shows three levels of internal control, management control, and departmental assessment supporting profitability analysis by MC/R centers.

Internal controls and processing operations that are applied to the editing, screening, and verification module and the expenditure control module result in the creation of two DBMSs. The first DBMS is the financial database of expenditure and revenue data by regular cost account. The second DBMS is a statistical database encompassing work-load measures, activities, operations, procedures, tasks, and other performance statistics that are also captured by regular cost account. Both databases are used by application and analytical modules. The responsibility-accounting module is an application package that extracts expenditure, revenue, statistical, and performance data from the DBMS for expenditure control purposes. The integrated features of the responsibility-accounting module include expenditure control–reporting arrangements, transfer-in and transfer-out capabilities, and statistical measures for performance assessment and evaluation. A unique roll-up structure of cost reporting in the responsibility-accounting system facilitates expenditure control at all organizational levels. The special features in the responsibility-accounting system also support the proper matching of costs with the benefiting regular cost accounts for pool nursing, pool clerical and support personnel, and shared services. These transfer transactions, however, are for control aspects of expenditures and are not for matching costs with revenue centers. The comparison of hours transferred out to hours billed in a controlled setting, for example, gives additional assurance that expenditures for salaries relate to services provided to an identified regular cost account.

Salaries, wages, and fringe benefits represent about 60 percent of total expenses in many health care entities. A job and position table cross-referenced by regular cost account may be included in the transaction control module for special monitoring purposes. Exhibit 12.3 illustrates a position database.

Expenditures for individual regular cost accounts may be compatible with the budget, but the mix and distribution of activities performed may not be. Management control is accomplished by a departmental assessment module that focuses on the mix and distribution of activities. The DMCS module also focuses on fixed costs and performance against minimum volumes of required effort for key support functions to medical and surgical activities.

Expenditure control and the roll-up reporting arrangement are not duplicated by the DMCS module. The application program does extract data from the DBMS, aggregates according to cross-reference tables, assigns common costs according to instructions, and compares current period actual with budget against year-to-date information. There are no outputs from the DMCS to the DBMS, but insights from analysis of DMCS reports may significantly change the existing data structure and transactions in the DBMS.

There are internal control considerations in extracting data for the DMCS module. The Part I and Part II expenditures in the reporting cost center in responsibility accounting are reconciled with aggregated data for the department in the DMCS. After the net expenditures have been reconciled for all departments, then assignments, adjustments, and allocations are made in the separate database for DMCS.

Departmental cost control includes issues regarding the mix and distribution of services from the set of mapped regular cost accounts. There are fixed and variable dimensions of cost at the department level that are essential in management planning, pricing, and strategic assessment. Quality control, risk management, and malpractice insurance are other reasons for DMCS monitoring.

Flexible budgeting is required for meaningful expenditure control in most health care entities. The delegated responsibility for incurring expenditures in a regular cost account by a particular expense category is a functional relationship dependent upon certain conditions. The on-line calculator used in budgeting for each expense item provides this dynamic (or flexible) capability so that the level of the "approved" expenditure is responsive to the conditions. The budget for a given position code in a regular cost account may be constant; other position codes may be a combination of a constant and a variable element captured by the on-line calculator.

Appendix: Responsibility-Accounting Reports

The organization chart for Demonstration Memorial Hospital's Department of Pathology is presented in Figure 9.2. The cost codes for regular cost accounts and MC/R centers in Figure 9.2 are used in the responsibility-accounting reports contained in this appendix. The code structure is expanded from that illustrated in Chapter 9 for Demonstration Memorial Hospital and is compatible with that for Glenwood in Exhibit 11.3. The Human Resources Department added position and job codes to the basic code structure for transactions in the DBMS. These position and job codes are disclosed in the Part II transfers within a responsibility-accounting report. For illustration purposes, revenue, statistical, and operational data from Part III of the responsibility-accounting reports are omitted. The roll-up reports show costs for some of the accounts and centers from organizational level 6 to level 3.

Exhibit 12.4 illustrates the responsibility-accounting report for the supervisor of Blood Bank Operations (code 247), with direct expenditures of $233,504. Blood bank personnel provide services to Hematology (code 219) to maintain staff competence in certain types of blood analysis. The transfer-out costs of $10,239 is reported in Part II of Exhibit 12.4. Note that 14 of the 15 element codes in Exhibit 12.4

Exhibit 12.4   Demonstration Memorial Hospital: Supervisor of Blood Bank Operations Responsibility-Accounting Report

Cost To	Cost From	FinStat* Element	Acc	Nat	Labor†	Description	Amount
Part I.	*Actual-Versus-Budget Comparisons*						
247	Supervisor, Blood Bank Operations, total expenditures						$233,504
247	247	DLABOR	DE	R	12	Salaries & wages— regular	41,253
247	247	DLABOR	DE	R	16	Salaries & wages— regular	38,706
247	247	DLABOR	DE	R	46	Salaries & wages— regular	67,439
247	247	DLFBENF	DE	R		FICA (Social Security tax)	11,943
247	247	DLFBENG	DE	R		Group health insurance	14,103
247	247	DIRMAT	DE	R		Supplies (direct purchases)	30,450
247	247	DRSUPP	DE	R		Professional fees	29,610
Part II.	*Transfers In/Out*						
247	Supervisor, Blood Bank Operations, total transfers						($10,239)
247	219	DLABOR	DTOE	R	46	Salaries & wages— regular	(8,752)
247	219	DLFBENF	DTOE	R		FICA (Social Security tax)	(656)
247	219	DLFBENG	DTOE	R		Group health insurance	(831)
247	Supervisor, Blood Bank Operations, total costs						$223,265

Continued

Exhibit 12.4   Continued

---

*There are three components of FinStat:
1. Element—The hospital's computer system contains 15 codes:

DTREVE	Direct revenue
DLABOR	Direct labor
DLFBENF	Direct labor fringe benefits—FICA
DLFBENG	Direct labor fringe benefits—group health
DIRMAT	Direct materials
DRSUPP	Direct supplies and other indirect costs
DCONTR	Contractual services
SUM	Aggregations in responsibility-accounting module only—*not stored in permanent DBMS*
MAINT	Dedicated maintenance assigned costs
HOUSEK	Dedicated housekeeping assigned costs
GENACCT	Dedicated general & accounting assigned costs
DCOST	Assigned joint costs—direct
SUPPORT	Assigned joint costs—dedicated
OVERHEAD	Reciprocal cost assignments
TASSIGN	Total assigned

2. Acc—Expense (E) or revenue (R) designation for the account code with the following adjectives: direct (D), direct transfer in (DTI), direct transfer out (DTO).
3. Nat—Nature of transaction: direct responsibility (R), assigned or allocated (A), and summary (S).
†Labor—Position and job codes from the human resources department.

---

are recorded in the DBMS; the exception is the code "SUM," which designates aggregation for responsibility-accounting reports only. The matching of costs with revenue for Blood Bank Operations (code 247) will begin with direct costs of $223,265 retrieved from the DBMS. The summation of Parts I and II of responsibility-accounting reports is the starting point for additional common cost assignments, assigned direct costs, and layers of administrative overhead allocation.

Exhibit 12.5 shows the responsibility-accounting report for the supervisor of Hematology, with total direct expenditures of $676,634 and transfer-in costs of $10,239 for the direct labor services provided by blood bank personnel. The position and job codes are included in the Part II listing of transfers for full disclosure and analysis for management control purposes.

Exhibit 12.5   Demonstration Memorial Hospital: Supervisor of
Hematology Responsibility-Accounting Report

Cost To	Cost From	*FinStat* Element	Acc	Nat	Labor	Description	Amount

Part I.   Actual-Versus-Budget Comparisons

219		Supervisor, Hematology, total expenditures					*$676,634*
219	219	DLABOR	DE	R	12	Salaries & wages—regular	88,979
219	219	DLABOR	DE	R	16	Salaries & wages—regular	158,612
219	219	DLABOR	DE	R	46	Salaries & wages—regular	203,864
219	219	DLFBENF	DE	R		FICA (Social Security tax)	33,846
219	219	DLFBENG	DE	R		Group health insurance	43,898
219	219	DIRMAT	DE	R		Supplies (direct purchases)	64,075
219	219	DRSUPP	DE	R		Professional fees	83,360

Part II.   Transfers In/Out

219		Supervisor, Hematology, total transfers					*$ 10,239*
219	247	DLABOR	DTIE	R	46	Salaries & wages—regular	8,752
219	247	DLFBENF	DTIE	R		FICA (Social Security tax)	656
219	247	DLFBENG	DTIE	R		Group health insurance	831
219		Supervisor, Hematology, total costs					*$686,873*

There are five MC/R centers reporting to the assistant manager of
Clinical Laboratories at Demonstration Memorial Hospital (Figure 9.2
and Exhibit 12.1). For illustration purposes, the regular cost codes at
organizational level 7 are omitted; thus, only five regular cost accounts
for the "office of . . ." are included in the five MC/R centers at
organizational level 6.

The aggregation of cost data at organizational level 5 for the assistant manager of Clinical Laboratories (MC/R center 214) is the summation of the "office of . . ." account (215) plus the five MC/R centers
at level 6. Exhibit 12.6 shows the responsibility-accounting reports
for both the "office of. . ." account (215) and the major reporting

center (214). The aggregate direct expenditures that flow through the assistant manager of Clinical Laboratories is $2,775,537 (Exhibit 12.6). Hematology has transfer-ins of $10,239, and Chemistry has transfer-outs of $16,832.

The element "SUM" in the top section of Exhibit 12.6 indicates that these aggregate data are not stored in the DBMS. The total costs of $2,768,944 for account 214 only exist in the application package for

Exhibit 12.6 Demonstration Memorial Hospital: Assistant Manager, Clinical Laboratories, Responsibility-Accounting Report

Cost To	Cost From	FinStat Element	Acc	Nat	Labor	Description	Amount
Part I.	*Actual-Versus-Budget Comparisons*						
214		Assistant manager, Clinical Lab, total expenditures					*$2,775,537*
214	215	SUM				Assistant Manager, Clinical Lab	83,837
214	216	SUM				Supervisor, Immunology	143,200
214	218	SUM				Supervisor, Hematology	676,634
214	222	SUM				Supervisor, Chemistry	1,151,878
214	224	SUM				Supervisor, RIA/Special Chemistry	198,273
214	226	SUM				Supervisor, Microbiology	521,715
Part II.	*Transfers In/Out*						
214		Assistant manager, Clinical Lab, total transfers					($ 6,593)
214	218	SUM				Supervisor, Hematology	10,239
214	222	SUM				Supervisor, Chemistry	(16,832)
214		Assistant manager, Clinical Lab, total costs					*$2,768,944*
Part I.	*Actual-Versus-Budget Comparisons*						
215		Assistant manager, Clinical Lab, total expenditures					*$ 83,837*
215	215	DLABOR	DE	R	16	Salaries & wages—regular	46,100
215	215	DLFBENF	DE	R		FICA (Social Security tax)	4,379
215	215	DLFBENG	DE	R		Group health insurance	3,458
215	215	DIRMAT	DE	R		Supplies (direct purchases)	10,800
215	215	DRSUPP	DE	R		Professional fees	19,100
Part II.	*Transfers In/Out*						
215		Assistant manager, Clinical Lab, total costs					*$ 83,837*

Exhibit 12.7   Demonstration Memorial Hospital: Assistant Manager, Laboratory Operations, Responsibility-Accounting Report

Cost To	Cost From	Element	Acc	Nat	Labor	Description	Amount
		FinStat					

Part I.   Actual-Versus-Budget Comparisons

Cost To	Cost From	Element	Acc	Nat	Labor	Description	Amount
228						Assistant manager, Lab Operations, total expenditures	*$1,417,788*
228	229	SUM				Assistant Manager, Lab Operations	74,051
228	232	SUM				Supervisor, Pathology/Oncology	431,998
228	234	SUM				Supervisor, Cytology/Histology	128,933
228	236	SUM				Supervisor, Autopsy/Other Pathology	332,375
228	238	SUM				Supervisor, STAT Laboratory	305,009
228	242	SUM				Administrative assistant	145,422

Part II.   Transfers In/Out

Cost To	Cost From	Element	Acc	Nat	Labor	Description	Amount
228						Assistant manager, Lab Operations, total transfers	$ 16,832
228	234	SUM				Supervisor, Cytology/Histology	16,832
228						Assistant manager, Lab Operations, total costs	*$1,434,620*

Part I.   Actual-Versus-Budget Comparisons

Cost To	Cost From	Element	Acc	Nat	Labor	Description	Amount
229						Assistant manager, Lab Operations, total expenditures	$ 74,051
229	229	DLABOR	DE	R	16	Salaries & wages—regular	45,600
229	229	DLFBENF	DE	R		FICA (Social Security tax)	3,419
229	229	DLFBENG	DE	R		Group health insurance	4,332
229	229	DIRMAT	DE	R		Supplies (direct purchases)	9,000
229	229	DRSUPP	DE	R		Professional fees	11,700

Part II.   Transfers In/Out

Cost To	Cost From	Element	Acc	Nat	Labor	Description	Amount
229						Assistant manager, Lab Operations, total costs	$ 74,051

responsibility accounting. Account 214 is a master reporting center used for management control statements only, and no costs are assigned to code 214 in the DBMS.[4] The office of assistant manager of Clinical Laboratories (215) is a common cost account. Demonstration

Hospital's computer will automatically assign account 215's costs to the five MC/R centers that benefit from these administrative services. These five MC/R centers are identical to the five MC/R centers listed in the top section of Exhibit 12.6.

Exhibit 12.7 presents the responsibility-accounting report for assistant manager of Laboratory Operations (228). The lower section of the exhibit shows the direct expenditures for the regular cost account (229) "office of. . . " with a total of $74,051. The major reporting center (228) shows total costs of $1,434,620 in the responsibility-accounting statements. The regular cost accounts for the assistant manager (229) and for the administrative assistant (243) are common costs and are assigned to the four MC/R centers (232, 234, 236, and 238) by Demonstration Hospital's computer system after the responsibility-accounting reports are completed.

The information from master reporting center 228 in Exhibit 12.7 is aggregated by the responsibility-accounting package under master reporting center 212. Exhibit 12.8 shows the responsibility-accounting report for manager of Laboratory (212). Exhibit 12.9 reports aggregate data for the manager of Blood Center (244). The next roll-up is for the chair of the Department of Pathology (210), which is illustrated by Exhibit 12.10.

Notes

1. A computer failure during the early 1970s in a California hospital that was upgrading the mainframe resulted in confidential information on a socially prominent woman's prior "professional" activities being made available to a few interested parties. The legal outcome was multimillion dollar settlements by the hospital, the computer vendor, and the consulting firm installing the system. There was no judgment against the person who disseminated this unusual information.
2. J. A. Higgins, "Responsibility Accounting," *The Arthur Andersen Chronicle* 12 (April 1952): 93–113.
3. A report generator is a special class of application package for mainframe and personal computers. Computer programming knowledge is not required for a user to interact with a report generator and to produce special analytical reports from a DBMS. The report generator for responsibility accounting includes the following capabilities:

   • Extracts transaction data for a period

   • Aggregates this period's data in a prescribed manner

   • Stores the aggregated period's data in a predefined set of storage locations

Exhibit 12.8 Demonstration Memorial Hospital: Manager of
Laboratory Responsibility-Accounting Report

Cost To	Cost From	*FinStat* Element	Acc	Nat	Labor	Description	Amount
Part I.		*Actual-Versus-Budget Comparisons*					
212		Manager of Laboratory, total expenditures					*$4,320,691*
212	213	SUM				Manager of Laboratory	127,366
212	214	SUM				Assistant Manager, Clinical Lab	2,775,537
212	228	SUM				Assistant Manager, Lab Operations	1,417,788
Part II.		*Transfers In/Out*					
212		Manager of Laboratory, total transfers					$ 10,239
212	214	SUM				Assistant Manager, Clinical Lab	(6,593)
212	228	SUM				Assistant Manager, Lab Operations	16,832
212		Manager of Laboratory, total costs					*$4,330,930*
Part I.		*Actual-Versus-Budget Comparisons*					
213		Manager of Laboratory, total expenditures					$ 127,366
213	213	DLABOR	DE	R	12	Salaries & wages—regular	49,200
213	213	DLABOR	DE	R	46	Salaries & wages—regular	34,380
213	213	DLFBENF	DE	R		FICA (Social Security tax)	6,247
213	213	DLFBENG	DE	R		Group health insurance	7,939
213	213	DIRMAT	DE	R		Supplies (Direct purchases)	11,000
213	213	DRSUPP	DE	R		Professional fees	18,600
Part II.		*Transfers In/Out*					
213		Manager of Laboratory, total costs					$ 127,366

- Contains prior periods' experience and budget data stored in other locations that are mapped to this period's data
- Compares this period's data against budget and prior year's experience on both a monthly and year-to-date basis
- Generates comparative reports in accordance with parameter-driven selections
- Updates the stored information for corrections and adjustments, when required

Exhibit 12.9   Demonstration Memorial Hospital: Manager of Blood
Center Responsibility-Accounting Report

Cost To	Cost From	FinStat Element	Acc	Nat	Labor	Description	Amount
Part I.		*Actual-Versus-Budget Comparisons*					
244		Manager of Blood Center, total expenditures					*$651,590*
244	245	SUM				Manager of Blood Center	107,513
244	246	SUM				Supervisor, Blood Bank Operations	233,504
244	248	SUM				Supervisor, Blood Operations	310,573
Part II.		*Transfers In/Out*					
244		Manager of Blood Center, total transfers					*($ 10,239)*
244	248	SUM				Supervisor, Blood Operations	(10,239)
244		Manager of Blood Center, total costs					*$641,351*
Part I.		*Actual-Versus-Budget Comparisons*					
245		Manager of Blood Center, total expenditures,					*$107,513*
245	245	DLABOR	DE	R	12	Salaries & wages—regular	48,687
245	245	DLABOR	DE	R	46	Salaries & wages—regular	24,145
245	245	DLFBENF	DE	R		FICA (Social Security tax)	5,462
245	245	DLFBENG	DE	R		Group health insurance	6,919
245	245	DIRMAT	DE	R		Supplies (direct purchases)	10,000
245	245	DRSUPP	DE	R		Professional fees	12,300
Part II.		*Transfers In/Out*					
245		Manager of Blood Center, total costs					*$107,513*

There are no outputs from the management control application package
that must be recorded in the mainframe computer system. The DBMS used
by the application package retains extensive amounts of budget and actual
experience for, at least, the past 24 months.
4. There are eight MC/R centers in Glenwood Laboratories that were also for
reporting purposes only and had zero balances in the DBMS (see Chapter 11). Exhibit 12.1 shows six master reporting centers in Demonstration
Memorial Hospital's Department of Pathology.

Exhibit 12.10 Demonstration Memorial Hospital: Chair, Department of Pathology, Responsibility-Accounting Report

Cost To	Cost From	FinStat Element	Acc	Nat	Labor	Description	Amount
Part I. Actual-Versus-Budget Comparisons							
210						Chair, Department of Pathology, total expenditures	$5,204,515
210	211	SUM				Chair, Dept. of Pathology	232,234
210	212	SUM				Manager, Laboratory	4,320,691
210	244	SUM				Manager, Blood Center	651,590
Part II. Transfers In/Out							
210						Chair, Department of Pathology, total transfers	$ 0
210	212	SUM				Manager, Laboratory	10,239
210	244	SUM				Manager, Blood Center	(10,239)
210						Chair, Department of Pathology, total costs	$5,204,515
Part I. Actual-Versus-Budget Comparisons							
211						Chair, Department of Pathology, total expenditures	$ 232,234
211	211	DLABOR	DE	R	12	Salaries & wages—regular	67,850
211	211	DLABOR	DE	R	32	Salaries & wages—regular	38,600
211	211	DLABOR	DE	R	56	Salaries & wages—regular	52,126
211	211	DLFBENF	DE	R		FICA (Social Security tax)	11,893
211	211	DLFBENG	DE	R		Group health insurance	15,065
211	211	DIRMAT	DE	R		Supplies (direct purchases)	20,000
211	211	DRSUPP	DE	R		Professional fees	26,700
Part II. Transfers In/Out							
211						Chair, Department of Pathology, total costs	$ 232,234

Additional Readings

Alexander, J. A., and M. A. Morrisey. "Hospital-Physician Integration and Hospital Costs," *Inquiry* 25 (Fall 1988): 388–401.

Barnes, G., and J. J. Jurinski. "Strategic Management of Employee Health Care Costs," *Management Accounting* 71 (September 1989): 44–48.

Bowers, M. R. "Product Line Management in Hospitals: An Exploratory Study of Managing Change," *Hospital & Health Services Administration* 35 (Fall 1990): 365–75.

Griffith, J. R. "Principles of the Well-Managed Community Hospital," *Hospital & Health Services Administration* 34 (Winter 1989): 457–70.

Discussion Questions

12.1. Financial data stored in a health care entity's DBMS come from

    A. transactions by master reporting centers

    B. transactions by master cost/revenue centers

    C. transactions by regular cost accounts

    D. transactions from the department management control module

12.2. Explain why the management control function and other decision-making activities are often separated in health care entities.

12.3. In the final step, where does the traceability of profitability analysis by MC/R center lead to?

12.4. Exhibit 12.1 lists six master reporting centers within the Department of Pathology. Explain the amount of information stored in the DBMS for these six master reporting centers.

12.5. Explain the two databases within a health care entity's DBMS.

12.6. Explain the difference between the responsibility-accounting reporting system and the departmental management control system (DMCS).

12.7. Contrast intermediate products in the departmental management control system with the management of patient services.

12.8. The total direct cost of an ancillary department in the DMCS may be different from the aggregation of the reporting cost center's Part I and Part II responsibility-accounting statements because of

    A. addition of transfer-in costs for administrative pool

    B. subtraction of transfer-out costs for shared services

    C. transfer of assigned physician salaries

    D. addition of transfer-in costs for pool nursing

12.9. The total direct cost of an ancillary department in the DMCS may be different from the aggregation of the reporting cost center's Part I and Part II responsibility-accounting statements because of

    A. addition of transfer-in costs for administrative pool

    B. computer-assigned common costs

    C. allocated administrative support costs

    D. deduction of transfer-out costs for pool nursing

12.10. The total direct cost of an ancillary department in the DMCS may be different from the aggregation of the reporting cost center's Part I and Part II responsibility-accounting statements because of

   A. computer-assigned direct costs based on utilization

   B. allocated corporate support

   C. allocated administrative support costs

   D. deduction of transfer-out costs for salaries of personnel loaned to another department

12.11. The transfer-out cost in Part II of responsibility accounting is driven by the payroll application computer program and supports expenditure control; however, an adjusting entry is also processed by the payroll program and stored in the financial DBMS. This adjusting entry does not include

   A. vacation time

   B. estimated sick days

   C. holidays

   D. in-service training

12.12. Departmental cost control is more than an aggregation of data from mapped regular cost accounts that have been analyzed by the responsibility accounting system. This departmental monitoring of the mix and distribution of planned services is *not* important for

   A. quality control

   B. expenditure control

   C. malpractice insurance

   D. risk management

12.13. Explain the relationship between minimum volumes of laboratory and blood bank operations to a health care surgical unit. Why are these minimum volumes handled as fixed cost?

12.14. A clinic is open five days a week, except for holidays. Each technician at the clinic has a 7.5-hour day. Therefore, there are 261 paid days per year at 7.5 hours per day equals 1,957.5 hours per year (261 × 7.5 = 1,957.5). A technician's annual salary at the clinic is $27,405, based on $14 per hour for 1,957.5 hours per year. Each worker has 11 holidays and special days, 15 vacation days, and 10 sick days per year. There are 225 effective days, (261 − 11 − 15 − 10 = 225). The fringe benefits are $5,481 per year on the technician's salary ($27,405 × 20 percent = $5,481).

   The technician works 250 hours per year in another department, and the responsibility-accounting system shows the appropriate transfer cost of $3,500 for salary (250 hours at $14 per hour = $3,500) and $700 for fringe benefits. Calculate the appropriate adjustment so that the 250 hours are at the full cost for those services.

12.15. The technician in Question 12.14 must participate in 10 days of professional training per year, which has an assigned cost of 75 hours at $14 per hour, or $1,050, plus $210 for fringe benefits. How much of this $1,260 can be transferred to the department where the technician works 250 hours per year?

12.16. Explain the procedure you would follow in computing total hours worked versus total hours paid in salaries for a department at Demonstration Memorial Hospital.

13

Flexible Budgeting and Statistical Techniques for Health Care Entities

Introduction

The management control process includes an automatic comparison within the computer system of actual versus budget expenditures by element within a regular cost account. Salaries and wages are often compared at the job position level (see Exhibit 12.3) within a regular cost account. The budget component of this comparison is flexible budgeting that responds in a prescribed manner within a specified relevant range of activity.

Changes in medical practice, implementations of new medical equipment, and other new initiatives may affect selected regular cost accounts so that it is difficult to specify outcomes 12 months in advance. First, there is a minimal set of baseline data from which to project outcomes. Second, the actual outcomes during the initial implementation are usually much lower than the performance a few months later. There are statistical techniques for addressing each of these situations.

Long-term moving averages and standard cost measures for specific tasks are not statistically proper methods for some regular cost accounts in many health care entities. The dynamic changes in the delivery of health care services results in limited observation periods from which to project outcomes 12 months in advance for use in computer-based monitoring of results. There are statistical techniques for use with limited observation periods, which are examined in this chapter.

Flexible Budgeting

The third step within the administrative framework of management control presented in Chapter 12 is budget resources. This function can be based on a constant set of facts, giving a static budget value, or based on a variable set of conditions adjusted for changes in volume, giving a flexible budget value. Expenditure control and cost control need a dynamic basis of comparison for each category of expense and measure of performance within a regular cost account. The volume factor within the calculator of the application computer programs for each of these items provides this dynamic capability and is driven by the activity (statistical and performance measures) in the DBMS for a given component.

Different organizational locations within a health care entity may have unique variable functions or volume factors. Patient days, for example, might be the volume factor in one cost account, number of treatments in a second, number of procedures in a third, number of tests in a fourth, time in the operating room in a fifth, number of visits in a sixth, and number of relative-value units in a seventh. The variable function for each category of expense within a regular cost account may be different. Furthermore, there is a relevant range of activity in which the volume factor is applicable. The calculator stored in the application computer program for each category of expense and measure of performance within a regular cost account must be so specified that the variable factor and relevant-range conditions are automatically handled by the computer system. Any out-of-range condition will generate an exception report.

Relevant range

The calculator for projecting expenditures, services, and activities is valid for a defined range of effort. When the limits of the relevant range are violated, the calculator is void, and the projected response should not be accepted for any purpose. A well-defined calculator for inpatient services, for example, that is based on 71–75 percent occupancy is not applicable in the same community hospital if the occupancy level drops to 64 percent. But, it is important to know that current activities are outside the relevant range, and the health care entity's administration must prepare a new budget of resources.

For various patient services in health care entities there are minimal volumes of activities that must be maintained for quality-control reasons. There are minimal volumes of hematology and chemistry tests that should be performed by a laboratory unit before blood bank operations are undertaken in support of certain types of surgery. The state health departments may even restrict a teaching hospital from performing certain types of surgery because minimal volumes of activities have not been present over the previous 24 months. These quality-control issues in health care entities are very common and are important considerations in planning the implementation of new medical technologies and medical practices.

The volume factor begins with this minimal level of activity. To a large extent, all the cost associated with the minimal volume of effort are fixed for that time period. The minimal staffing of direct labor and fringe benefits, the supplies used by that staff in achieving the minimal volume, and the direct support services consumed in providing this goal are fixed costs. These minimal volumes relate to each month and the overall distribution for the 12 months, including seasonal adjustments from medical records data.

Constant items

There are minimal staffing levels of nurses and health care professionals associated with the licensure of certain types of facilities. The bed capacity of the institution may be such that the minimal staffing for 24 hours a day, seven days a week is also the maximum staffing under the current conditions. In other facilities, personnel in excess of the minimal staffing may be scheduled for work in other departments but respond on an alert basis to the critical area. This latter type of scheduling is a way of converting a fixed cost into a variable cost for the health care entity.

The flexible budget is for a 12-month period for expenditure control and cost control; there are many personnel positions in regular cost accounts that are constant for that period. The personnel-review actions may not exactly coincide with the 12-month period, and those approved changes are made in the budget when the salary adjustments are processed. Thus, the calculator for many categories of expense is a static set of facts for the relevant range of activity. The salary of the director, the manager, or the supervisor is a constant even in a flexible budgeting model. An annual employment contract for a health care professional results in a fixed cost to the entity for that period regardless of the level of activity.

But multiple personnel covered by the same position code within salaries-and-wages expense for a regular cost account removes the chains of a static set of facts and introduces some options. The actual behavior of the expense by the position code may resemble the semi-fixed cost curve or the combined cost curves (see Chapter 8), but either type of behavior can be specified in the calculator.

Quality-control considerations in health care, risk management, and malpractice insurance suggest that relevant range minimal levels of activity should be carefully studied when they are encountered. If the application programs must be adjusted to support expanded areas of fixed expenses for minimal volumes, the investment should be made in view of the possible loss by the health care entity from failure to properly respond to a crisis.

Statistical Techniques

The merging of patient order-entry and result-reporting data with the mapped regular cost accounts from the financial DBMS and activity DBMS for cost control of intermediate products often requires partitioning categories of expense between the fixed and variable components. The aggregate expenditures are known from the financial DBMS for the expense category, but the cost behavior of the item is not known. There are a series of observations for each expense category, but there are price, volume, and mix changes incorporated in each observation. Statistical techniques are useful in identifying the overall behavior of the item if there is both an expenditure and a performance measure for each observation.

High-low method

The high-low method is a statistical technique that uses only two observations for approximating cost behavior. If there are very few observations, then the high-low method at least provides a procedure for separating the fixed and variable components. Assume there are multiple observations with one outlier. In applying the high-low method, the outlier is excluded, and the lowest-cost point and the highest-cost point of the remaining observations are used for computing the fixed and variable components. The weakness in the high-low method is that the other observations are excluded.

Exhibit 13.1 presents nine observations for supplies and patient services. The difference between the lowest-cost point and the highest-cost point is $2,000 and 500 services; therefore, the variable factor is $4 per service. Either point can be used to determine the fixed cost of $900, as illustrated in Exhibit 13.1. There is no calculation of how the other seven observations relate to the high-low position. An informed assessment does require a plotting of the points for excluded observations to determine their relationship to a line connecting the lowest-cost point with the highest-cost point used in the high-low method.

Least-squares regression analysis

Making a scatter diagram of all observations and attempting to fit a line to the various data points is similar to the approach of least-squares regression analysis. Standard electronic worksheet packages for the personal computer can provide an answer by least-squares regression analysis with the same effort required to plot a scatter diagram. The regression analysis provides an answer for all points; the scatter diagram must be reviewed and a line fitted to the various data points before there is an answer.

The nine observations in Exhibit 13.2 are the same as in Exhibit 13.1, and the formula for the straight line is

$$y' = a + bx$$
$$= \$1,061.89 + \$3.97x$$

The constant a is the fixed cost, and the regression coefficient b is the variable cost ratio. Exhibit 13.2 shows the calculation for each

Exhibit 13.1 High-Low Method of Cost Behavior

Period	Supplies	Patient Services				
1	$4,500	900	Lowest	$4,500	900 —	Change
2	$5,560	1,100				$2,000
3	$5,790	1,200				
4	$5,070	1,000				500
5	$5,780	1,175				services
6	$6,250	1,300				or $4 per
7	$6,500	1,400	Highest	$6,500	1,400 —	service
8	$6,330	1,325				
9	$6,000	1,225				

Variable rate is $4 per patient service ($2,000/500 = $4).

Highest: 1,400 × $4 = $5,600 + $900 (fixed cost) = $6,500

Lowest: 900 × $4 = $3,600 + $900 (fixed cost) = $4,500

observation and the variance between actual and the regression line. The summations of the positive and negative variances for the nine observations are equal, as shown in Exhibit 13.2.

Exhibit 13.2   Least-Squares Regression Analysis

Period	Patient Services x	Supply Cost y'		
1	900	$4,500	*Regression Output:*	
2	1,100	$5,560	Constant (fixed cost)	$1,061.894
3	1,200	$5,790	Std error of y est.	93.77065
4	1,000	$5,070	R-squared	.981204
5	1,175	$5,780	No. of observations	9
6	1,300	$6,250	Degrees of freedom	7
7	1,400	$6,500		
8	1,325	$6,330	x Coefficient (variable cost)	$3.973924
9	1,225	$6,000	Std error of coefficient	0.207880

$y' = a + bx$ $y' = \$1,061.89 + \$3.97x$
Fixed cost + Variable cost × Services

y'	x	a + bx	Variance in Estimate	
$4,500	900	4,638.426	$138.43	
$5,560	1,100	5,433.210		−126.79
$5,790	1,200	5,830.603	40.60	
$5,070	1,000	5,035.818		−34.18
$5,780	1,175	5,731.255		−48.74
$6,250	1,300	6,227.995		−22.00
$6,500	1,400	6,625.388	125.39	
$6,330	1,325	6,327.343		−2.66
$6,000	1,225	5,929.951		−70.05
			$304.42	−304.42

A comparison of the results for these nine observations from the high-low method and the least-squares regression analysis reveals a $162 difference in fixed costs: $900 in Exhibit 13.1 versus $1,062 in Exhibit 13.2. There is not much difference in variable costs from the two methods in this simple case.

Other methods

Linear programming is used with the reciprocal cost method for assigning support costs to revenue centers, as illustrated in Chapter 10. If the reciprocal cost assignments are not in the financial DBMS, the linear-programming algorithm is used for the full costing requirements and the results are stored in the separate database for the DMCS module. Nonlinear methods, such as a center-moving average, may provide insight into the monthly movements of admission and registration efforts and the related corporate cost. From these insights, the initial department data may be adjusted and then subjected to regression analysis or linear programming.

The selection of the appropriate statistical techniques requires consideration of the many endogenous and exogenous factors that influence the health care entity and its intermediate products in the DMCS module. Organizational arrangements and delegation of authority for a department are not uniform between health care entities; there may even be major differences among departments in the same entity. General characteristics that separate departments are mix of patients by DRGs or other clinic groupings, type of medical practice, financial class of patients, status of medical technologies, simple versus complex patient cases, and status of patients on admissions or at time of initial visit. Some patient episodes of care are subject to seasonal fluctuations; others tend to occur around holidays and periods of increased patient stress. There is a direct relation between the patient mix and the distribution of physicians by specialties for the health care entity. If there is a change in medical specialties, there may be permanent shifts in the mix of patients for the health care entity.

Learning Curve

New medical technologies and medical practices are periodically being implemented in health care facilities, and in many situations there is an identified learning process, which results in a dramatic reduction in direct labor effort over time. Employees performing repetitive tests, procedures, and activities on behalf of patients use less time per item as increased experience is gained. With increased experience, individuals performing support and corporate overhead functions for health care entities use less time to accomplish the same set of services. Patients have their own learning curves as they respond to experienced therapists, affecting the number of sessions required for achieving certain objectives.

These reductions in labor hours by an individual from performing repetitive operations are statistically predictable and are expected. Significant variations from the expected improvement curve may be related to employee turnover, absenteeism, lack of motivation, interference by organized labor, change in procedures, or new equipment. Professional accountants use the learning curve as a benchmark; major deviation from expected behavior triggers an investigation or detailed audit. The behavior of the learning curve is so well established that it is not an acceptable excuse in federal court for cost-assignment problems in pricing litigation cases.

Origin of concept

Administrative and technical personnel observed the learning process of employees performing new operations in the aircraft-frame industry during World War II.[1] After the design features were accepted and the operations became stable, it was noted that the learning process continued over time with improvements in efficiency. The repetitive experience in the aircraft-frame industry permitted administrative and technical personnel to plot the statistical values of the learning process by employees. P. B. Crouse, in a 1943 professional paper, noted that the projected labor loads in aircraft production followed an 80 percent curve. This overall improvement in labor began to be referred to as the "Curtiss 80 Per Cent Curve," and the relevant range from these empirical studies of highly motivated American workers was between 80.00 and 80.02 percent without any reported outlier. The repercussions to a worker for performance outside that employee's learning curve were severe; however, it is difficult to accept these professional papers in which there are no outliers for numerous workers.

Observations about the learning process were not restricted to the aircraft-frame industry. Much of American business enterprise had shifted during the early 1940s to the production of military items. Some of the assembly-line operations included many repetitive steps performed by the same set of workers over successive weeks. As these repetitive activities were performed and the output measured according to the military monitoring requirements, the cost accountants began to observe a pattern of improvement. The required monitoring of the military effort in all industries resulted in extensive comparisons of worker productivity in the performance of existing tasks versus the performance of new tasks. When the same set of tasks or operations was performed on a repetitive basis, there was a measurable improvement in worker productivity.

One of the first managerial accounting articles on this type of labor improvement from repetitive work was written by Rolfe Wyer, who suggested the generic concept of the learning curve with a broader set of outcomes than the Curtiss 80 Per Cent Curve.[2] The theory of the learning curve suggests that there is a predictable pattern of improvement in worker efficiency when the same set of tasks is handled on a repetitive basis. The key point for measuring this improvement is with each doubling of the cumulative output from the repetitive set of tasks.

The theory of the learning curve states that the cumulative average time is reduced by the experience factor as the cumulative output is doubled. In the case of Exhibit 13.3, the first 20 units required an average of 2.0 minutes per test for a total time of 40 direct labor minutes. When the cumulative output reaches 40 units, the cumulative average time for all 40 units is reduced by the experience factor (which in this example is 0.8 × 2.0 minutes = 1.6 minutes), giving a cumulative total time of 64 direct labor minutes (40 units × 1.6 minutes). After the cumulative average time of 64 minutes is computed, then the incremental time of 24 direct labor minutes can be derived for the second layer of 20 units, with an incremental average time of 1.2 direct labor minutes. These four steps in creating a learning curve schedule are illustrated in Exhibit 13.4.

After the 1.20 minutes per incremental test is established for the second layer in Exhibit 13.3, the values for each subsequent marginal effort can be derived by the 80 percent learning curve (80 percent of 1.2 minutes = 0.96 minutes for the third layer, etc.).

Application

Computer-based systems captured the individual performance of workers, and an analysis of these empirical data permitted a refinement of the learning curve concept. Social scientists also studied the same phenomena and observed that an 80 percent improvement was a maximum level of achievement for a controlled experiment. If a faster level of improvement was reported than the 80 percent, then there must be another contributing factor. In Exhibit 13.3, if the curve were 70 percent, the cumulative time for the second layer would be 1.4 minutes on the average × 40 units, or 56 minutes in total. (A 70 percent curve

Exhibit 13.3   Minutes to Process a Test under an 80 Percent Learning Curve (One method)

Layer	Marginal or Incremental			Cumulative		
	Total Time	Units per Layer	Average Time	Total Time	Total Units	Average Time
1				40	20	2.00
2	24	20	1.20	64	40	1.60
3	38.4	40	0.96	102.4	80	1.28
4	61.44	80	0.768	163.84	160	1.024
5	98.304	160	0.6144	262.144	320	0.8192
6	157.2864	320	0.49152	419.4304	640	0.65536

Note: As the cumulative units double from 20 to 40 tests, the average time for all 40 units is 80 percent of the initial time (1.6 minutes is 80 percent of 2.0 minutes) per test. This 80 percent improvement occurs for each layer, including the last layer of 320 units, which went from 0.82 minutes per unit to 0.66 minutes. If this improvement had not occurred, the 640 units would have required 1,280 minutes instead of 419 minutes.

Exhibit 13.4   Illustration of Four Steps in Creating a Learning Curve Schedule

Layer	Marginal or Incremental			Cumulative		
	Total Time	Units per Layer	Average Time	Total Time	Total Units	Average Time
Step #1: Determine 40 DL minutes						
1				40	20	2.00
Step #2: 2.00 × 0.8 = 1.6 DL minutes						
2	24	20	1.20	64	40	1.60
Step #3: 1.6 × 40 units = 64 DL minutes						
Step #4: 64 DL minutes − 40 DL minutes = 24 DL minutes						
				24/20 units = 1.20 DL minutes per test		

is a faster improvement than an 80 percent curve; an 80 percent curve is faster than a 90 percent curve.) If 80 percent is the maximum, a 70 percent finding suggests either that the baseline is wrong or that there is a structural change (for example, new equipment, a new labor-saving procedure, addition of an experienced employee) that is responsible for a portion of this improvement.

Organized labor accepts the learning curve concept, but labor representatives typically restrict contracts to a 90 percent learning curve. Exhibit 13.5 presents the same situation as in Exhibit 13.3 but with a 90 percent curve. The cumulative total for the 640 tests under a 90 percent curve is 756 minutes (Exhibit 13.5) versus 419 minutes for the 80 percent curve (Exhibit 13.3). Note that the 320 units in Exhibit 13.5 are comparable in total time (420 minutes) to the 640 units in Exhibit 13.3 (419 minutes). The impact of the 80 percent versus the 90 percent learning curve is experienced at every layer; for example, 1,280 tests under the 80 percent learning curve would require 671 minutes, while 640 tests under the 90 percent learning curve in Exhibit 13.5 use 756 minutes. The magnitude increases at each subsequent layer of the 80 percent versus the 90 percent curve.

The cumulative columns of the learning curve are helpful in long-term pricing contracts and other agreements. The volume of these contracts may require the layers to be extended, which can

Exhibit 13.5 Minutes to Process a Test under a 90 Percent Learning Curve

| | Marginal or Incremental | | | Cumulative | | |
Layer	Total Time	Units per Layer	Average Time	Total Time	Total Units	Average Time
1				40	20	2.00
2	32	20	1.60	72	40	1.80
3	57.6	40	1.44	129.6	80	1.62
4	103.68	80	1.296	233.28	160	1.458
5	186.624	160	1.1664	419.904	320	1.3122
6	335.9232	320	1.04976	755.8272	640	1.18098

Note: As the cumulative units double from 20 to 40 tests, the average time for all 40 units is 90 percent of the initial time (1.8 minutes is 90 percent of 2.0 minutes) per test. This 90 percent improvement occurs for each layer, including the last layer of 320 units, which went from 1.31 minutes per unit to 1.18 minutes.

easily be accomplished with a calculator. The type of disclosure in Exhibits 13.3 and 13.5 permits assessment concerning the outcome if a layer of improvement did not occur for some exogenous reason. The marginal or incremental columns are used for management control and establishing the short-term performance budgets. If these layers on the margin are not accomplished, then the long-term projections cannot be obtained.

The learning curve can also be calculated by a formula; however, the results often must be disclosed in a format similar to Exhibit 13.3 so that all members of the health care entity's administrative team fully understand the layers of improvement. The formula for the learning curve is

$$Y = aX^b$$

where

Y = productivity expressed as the average time per unit.

a = parameter value expressing the total time for the first unit (a unit may be a single item or a group of items processed as a lot, depending on the economic specifications of start-up)

X = cumulative number of units processed or total output

b = parameter value expressing the index of the "learning improvement" (often expressed as $a - 0.322$ or $a - 0.3219$, depending on level of specification for the 80 percent learning curve)

Exhibit 13.6 illustrates the application of the formula in solving an 80 percent learning curve problem. The usual layer approach is also given in this exhibit.

Interpretation

As a construct, the learning curve is applicable to repetitive operations performed by the *same* employees. When new employees join a team, they have their own learning curves and cannot immediately assume the position of a prior employee. Therefore, when there is a turnover of personnel, the projected improvements from the learning curve based on previous employees will not be valid as a measure of performance for new employees.

The learning curve is applicable to the continuation of an existing test, procedure, product, process, or operation. Changes in the item (even minor modifications) may cause a shift in performance

Exhibit 13.6   Minutes to Process a Test under an 80 Percent
Learning Curve (Two methods)

Situation:

New medical practice and technological advancements permit 20 tests to be performed as a lot in 500 minutes, or an average of 25 minutes per test. All research efforts suggest there will be an 80 percent learning curve at least until the volume reaches 1,280 tests. Determine the average amount of time to perform a test if the total is 1,280 tests.

Solution Using Formula:

$$Y = aX^b$$
$$Y = (25.0) (64)^{-.3219}$$

where

Y = productivity expressed as the average time per unit

a = 25.0 direct labor minutes, the total time for the first unit to be created (500 minutes divided by 20 = 25.0)

X = 64 lots, the cumulative number of lots manufactured in order to create the 1,280 desired output (1,280/20 = 64 lots)

b = −0.3219, the 80 percent learning curve factor

$$
\begin{aligned}
Y &= (25.0)\ (64)^{-.3219} \\
\log Y &= \log 25 + (-0.3219)\ (\log 64) \\
&= 1.39794 - (.3219)\ (1.80618) \\
&= 1.39794 - 0.5814093 \\
&= 0.8165307 \\
Y &= 6.554 \text{ minutes}
\end{aligned}
$$

If Y equals 6.554, then X equals 64 multiples of 20-lot units times the derived average time, or

$$X = 64 \times 20 \times 6.554 = 8,389.12 \text{ direct labor hours}$$

Alternatively, the 80 percent learning curve example can be solved by incremental computations where *each layer* in a schedule represents the required number of lots to double the cumulative output, as follows:

Continued

and result in the establishment of a new learning curve. Employees' perceptions of the degree of change between a previous situation and the current situation, along with their attention to the nature of the

Exhibit 13.6   Continued

| Layer | Marginal or Incremental | | | Cumulative | | |
	Total Time	Units per Layer	Average Time	Total Time	Total Units	Average Time
1				500.00	20	25.00
2	300.00	20	15.00	800.00	40	20.00
3	480.00	40	12.00	1,280.00	80	16.00
4	768.00	80	9.60	2,048.00	160	12.80
5	1,228.80	160	7.68	3,276.80	320	10.24
6	1,996.08	320	6.144	5,242.88	640	8.192
7	3,145.728	640	4.9152	8,388.608	1,280	6.5536

Average time for 1,280 units is 6.554 minutes.

change, are more important in projecting the improvements from the learning curve than knowledge about the actual degree of change.

Although the statistical experience supporting the learning curve is based on the aircraft-frame industry, these statistical curves have been replicated many times in the analysis of information systems projects. The time required for new remote terminal users to fully accept computer-based systems that directly support the user can be estimated by applying the learning curve formula. If the remote terminal user's economic return (salary and bonus) is directly dependent upon using the computer-based application package, then even the experienced new employee will go through about the same length of learning curve as the inexperienced new employee, based on an analysis of investment account managers in major commercial banks in New York City and Chicago.

Some patient services are for a specific amount of time, such as a 25- or 55-minute physical therapy or occupational therapy session; the experienced therapist is able to accomplish more with the patient in the same time period. Overall, there may be a series of 12 sessions by an experienced therapist with a patient for a defined problem rather than the 16 or more sessions with an inexperienced therapist. The physician monitoring the patient care will adjust the number of therapy sessions based on the results.

The flexible budgeting system for expenditure control in health care entities by cost element within each regular cost account must include the impact of the learning curve on direct labor hours and related items. Thus, the marginal or incremental average times in the learning curve schedules of Exhibits 13.5 and 13.6 are of primary interest in both responsibility accounting modules and departmental management control modules. Supervisors, health care coordinators, and managers must carefully monitor the incremental progress along a learning curve schedule because any failure to achieve the expected reduction in direct labor effort will affect all future direct labor costs for those services. The reductions in direct labor hours through the learning curve schedule should not be part of the regular bonus to workers. Failure to achieve the learning curve projected reduction in direct labor hours indicates possible problems with absenteeism, employee turnover, poor motivation, or lack of coordination of efforts.

The learning curve is very important to all types of health care entities because direct labor is the dominant expense item. Direct labor and fringe benefits are often between 55 to 70 percent of total operating expenses in health care entities, and the flexible budgeting and incentive system should incorporate these expected improvements. Bonus and incentive programs should be based at least on a 90 percent learning curve for repetitive operations (organized labor officially accepts a 90 percent learning curve).

The learning curve has a major impact on utilization statistics for support and corporate overhead accounts. The contractual agreements with third party payors for certain types of entities are often based on overhead charges that are, in turn, based on direct labor. Failure to properly reflect the expected reduction in direct labor because of gains from repetitive operations can result in significant amounts of unassigned corporate overhead costs to external payors. The impact of the learning curve can also be seen in the utilization statistics for the reciprocal cost method in a health care entity where there is a stable set of employees with a significant amount of repetitive operations.

Summary

The high-low method is a useful technique for comparing expenses and statistical measures of service and computing the fixed and variable components when there are a limited number of observations. If there are more observations, then least-squares regression analysis is the preferred method for analyzing the fixed and variable components. The reciprocal cost method, using the linear-programming algorithm, is widely used in cost analysis and in assignment of support and overhead costs.

The introduction of new medical practices and changing procedures creates predictable problems with direct labor performance measures. These outliers in linear assessments are following the learning curve and its statistically predictable slope. There is a significant reduction in the cumulative average time to perform an operation with each doubling of the cumulative number of operations performed. Organized labor will accept a 90 percent learning curve in its contracts before any bonus or incentive program begins.

Appendix: Adjustments for Cost Control

The extracted expenditure, revenue, and performance data from the DBMSs serve as the foundation for the DMCS module; however, these mapped items within the regular cost accounts to the related department are adjusted for purposes of cost-control management. The patient order-entry and result-reporting module and computer-based operational control modules are important data sources for partitioning expenditure items into their fixed and variable components. Other order-entry data are extracted and summarized from these modules for use with revenue and performance assessments. The historical database for the DMCS module is really an integration of four sets of information:

1. Transaction data in the financial DBMS

2. Performance data in the activity DBMS

3. Tests and treatment data in the patient order-entry and result-reporting module

4. Departmental performance measures in the computer-based operational control module

Expenditure control of transactions in the financial DBMS is by each category of expense in a regular cost account. This delegation of authority and accountability-reporting requirement is for 100 percent of the expenditures. The recording, accumulation, and roll-up procedures for responsibility-accounting reports are based on complete coverage of all expenditures. The organizational level at which expenditures are controlled is typically at a much lower level than a department and is performed by individuals with limited areas of responsibility. Any efforts to initially record labor, supplies, professional fees, or other expenses by their fixed versus variable components would involve considerations that are external to these persons' areas of responsibility. However, expenditure control is ideally achieved at the lowest organizational level where there is a delegation of budget authority.

After the financial expenditure data have been adjusted for their fixed and variable components, exception reporting may be required at the department level because the mix of patient services or the mode of delivering the services is not compatible with the budget. The four sets of integrated information in the DMCS module support the multidimensional analysis by the designated organizational unit of a department.

Exhibit 13.7 shows the results from the DMCS module at Demonstration Memorial Hospital for the Department of Pathology. The $5,204,515 of direct costs is reported by the fixed and variable components for each item. The concept of a relevant range is central to the proper interpretation of Exhibit 13.7. The position codes (see Exhibit 12.3) are helpful in the aggregation of mapped regular cost accounts for the Department of Pathology in separating fixed and variable expenditures related to staffing. Position code 12, for management and supervision, shows that costs of $928,687 are required for the minimal staffing in the relevant range. Exhibit 13.7 reports the full $928,687 as fixed costs for the period. Some of the laboratory coordinators become part-time technicians at a minimal staffing volume; thus, $442,617 of costs for position code 16 is reported as variable expense in Exhibit 13.7.

A technician in Chemistry may not be qualified to immediately perform selective services in Oncology or in Cytology. There are limits to assignment of technicians from one section of the laboratory to another without providing time for special training and instruction.

Demonstration Memorial Hospital performed over 1 million tests in the Department of Pathology for the year ended 31 December 19X2. Some patient orders have a one-to-one relation to laboratory tests performed; others may require a battery of tests for a given order. The laboratory is in operation 24 hours a day, seven days a week, but not all equipment is utilized during slow periods. The STAT Laboratory (code 238) is only in operation when Hematology, Chemistry, and the regular sections of the laboratory are closed; thus, all staffing efforts

Exhibit 13.7 Demonstration Memorial Hospital: Department of
Pathology (Code 210) DMCS Cost Data for Year Ended
31 December 19X2

Total Cost Data for Department of Pathology

Total direct costs from Part I and Part II of responsibility-
accounting reports $5,204,515

	Variable Cost	Fixed Cost	Total Cost
Salaries and wages—regular			
Position 12—management and supervision	$ 0	$ 928,687	$ 928,687
Position 16—coordinators	442,617	598,063	1,040,680
Position 32—specialists	0	38,600	38,600
Position 46—technicians	681,383	552,670	1,234,053
Position 56—clerical and other administrative	71,182	58,240	129,422
Total salaries and wages	$1,195,182	$2,176,260	$3,371,442
FICA	89,622	163,188	252,810
Group health insurance	115,924	211,081	327,005
Professional fees	325,489	383,360	708,849
Supplies	313,225	231,184	544,409
Total direct cost	$2,039,442	$3,165,073	$5,204,515
Assigned utilities	74,000	45,040	119,040
Allocated housekeeping	0	119,349	119,349
Allocated costs, office, vice president, ancillary services	0	238,000	238,000
Allocated administrative overhead	0	1,400,000	1,400,000
Total	$2,113,442	$4,967,462	$7,080,904

Cost Categories for the Relevant Range

Variable labor	$1,195,182
Variable fringe benefits	205,546
Variable supplies	313,225
Variable professional fees	325,489
Variable utilities	74,000
Fixed direct labor	2,176,260
Fixed fringe benefits	374,269
Fixed supplies	231,184

Continued

Exhibit 13.7   Continued

Fixed professional fees	383,360
Fixed utilities	45,040
Fixed housekeeping	119,349
Fixed vice president	238,000
Fixed administrative overhead	1,400,000
Total	$7,080,904

in Demonstration Memorial Hospital's STAT Laboratory are identified with minimal level of patient services and are reported as fixed costs. There are start-up costs with most laboratory equipment to the extent that it is not economically feasible to perform individual tests on an automated basis during a slow period. Automated equipment may be down for repair or maintenance when patient orders are received in the laboratory, resulting in tests performed on a manual basis even during a peak period. The operational control module monitors scheduled equipment in use and provides summary exception reporting on down time at the end of the period.

Demonstration Memorial Hospital has 850 standard types of laboratory orders in the patient order-entry and result-reporting module. For each of these standard types, the computer-based operational control module provides data on the number of patient orders and where these tests were performed by equipment. It also reports the relative-value units by performance measures from the College of American Pathologists.

The statistical data on the mix and distribution of tests and location of laboratory services are used in partitioning three expenditure items in Exhibit 13.7 between fixed and variable costs: professional fees, supplies, and assigned utilities. Some professional fees are based on contracts in support of the minimum volume for the department, amounting to $383,360. Other professional fees that increased per service within the relevant range equaled $325,489 (Exhibit 13.7). Supplies, such as test tubes, that are consumed on a per-unit basis are partially reported as a fixed cost. The amount of the fixed cost is equal to the aggregate support required for the minimum volume in the relevant range. The same concept is applied to the partitioning of assigned utilities. Utilities costing $45,040 are required to support the minimum volume of effort; expansion within the relevant range used $74,000 of utilities.

Some health care accountants may not agree with the concept, applied in Exhibit 13.7, that the relevant range for the Department of Pathology is used as the basis for partitioning fixed versus variable costs; they argue for using the unique behavior of each cost element. Supplies that are consumed on a per-test basis, according to this group, should be entirely a variable expense since there is one test tube for each order. As an indication of the number of individuals following this position, there are application computer programs uniquely designed for the health care industry that do not support fixed supply expense as a standard feature. These programs only accommodate variable supply expense; however, other vendors have packages that do support both fixed and variable segments.

Notes

1. P. B. Crouse, "Projecting Labor Loads in Aircraft Production," *Aero Digest* 43 (October 1943): 216–18, 242–43.
2. R. Wyer, "Learning Curve Helps Figure Profits, Control Costs," *N.A.C.A. Bulletin* 35 (December 1953): 490–502.

Additional Readings

Abernathy, W. J., and K. Wayne. "Limits of the Learning Curve," *Harvard Business Review* 52 (September–October 1974): 109–19.
Broadston, J. A. "Learning Curve Wage Incentives," *Management Accounting* 49 (August 1968): 15–23.
Cromwell, J., and D. Puskin. "Hospital Productivity and Intensity Trends: 1980–87," *Inquiry* 26 (Fall 1989): 366–80.
Finkler, M. D., and D. D. Wirtschafter. "Cost-Effectiveness and Obstetric Services," *Medical Care* 29 (October 1991): 951–63.
Hirschmann, W. B. "Profit from the Learning Curve," *Harvard Business Review* 42 (January–February 1964): 125–39.

Discussion Questions

13.1. A 350-bed community hospital recently implemented a standard cost system for inpatients that is used in matching costs with revenue. Five years of financial and utilization experience were used in calculating the standard values when the average occupancy was 78 percent. The impact of the prospective payment system has finally been felt in this hospital's inpatient services and the occupancy has dropped to the

64–67 percent range for the past five months. How applicable is the standard cost system under these conditions? Explain your position.

13.2. A 450-bed community hospital recently signed agreements with eighteen new HMOs that have started to provide services in the metropolitan area. To what extent are the mix and distribution of services provided to three "old" HMOs applicable to the eighteen new agreements? Explain your position.

13.3. You are performing an activity-based costing of the patient-billing department in a community hospital. What is the relevant activity to use as a cost driver? Explain your choice. The alternatives you are considering include the following:

- Total number of patients billed
- Weighted number of patients billed, adjusted for mix using electronic billing to third party payors and those using manual billing
- Total number of third party payors
- Number and mix of third party payors with patient volumes for electronic billing versus manual billing

13.4. Explain why the high-low method is probably the most widely used budgeting technique in health care entities.

13.5. Assume a new therapy program has been implemented in two competing clinics (Clinic A and Clinic B). Assume the minimum volume for an "improvement" is accomplished within one month. Explain the long-term competitive issues if Clinic A maintains an 80 percent curve over the first 32 months and Clinic B maintains a 92 percent curve over the same period.

13.6. The on-line calculators performing flexible budgeting for each expense category in a regular cost account are driven by unique variable functions and volume factors. List six types of volume factors for health care entities.

13.7. It is estimated that patient services will be 2,200 in June 19X2. Using the high-low method, determine the fixed and variable costs for the first five months from the following data and then project total cost for June 19X2.

Month	Patient Service	Direct Cost
Jan 19X2	1,500	$ 8,400
Feb 19X2	1,800	9,400
Mar 19X2	1,750	9,500
Apr 19X2	2,000	10,200
May 19X2	2,300	11,600

13.8. With eight months of data for the new facility in Question 13.7, you elected to use the least-squares regression capability in an electronic spreadsheet on a personal computer. The regression output is $1,657.855 for the constant and 4.401036 for the *x*-coefficient from the following data:

Month	Patient Service	Direct Cost
Jan 19X2	1,500	$ 8,400
Feb 19X2	1,800	9,400
Mar 19X2	1,750	9,500
Apr 19X2	2,000	10,200
May 19X2	2,300	11,600
Jun 19X2	2,200	11,500
Jul 19X2	2,400	12,300
Aug 19X2	2,600	13,200

Calculate the estimated cost for the next four months using the following estimated patient services:

Sep 19X2	2,800
Oct 19X2	3,000
Nov 19X2	3,200
Dec 19X2	3,100

13.9. A new clinic has been in operation for nine months with the following cost and patient service data:

Month	Patient Service	Direct Cost
Jan 19X2	2,400	$18,000
Feb 19X2	2,200	16,700
Mar 19X2	2,500	18,400
Apr 19X2	3,000	21,700
May 19X2	2,900	20,400
Jun 19X2	3,400	24,500
Jul 19X2	3,700	26,400
Aug 19X2	3,900	27,500
Sep 19X2	4,100	28,100

The output from the least-squares regression capability in an electronic spreadsheet on a personal computer is $2,761.04 for the constant and 6.293618 for the *x*-coefficient. Determine the estimated cost for the next three months with the following estimated patient services:

Oct	4,200
Nov	4,600
Dec	4,500

13.10. The new health care facility has completed its first year of operations with the following results:

Month	Patient Service	Direct Cost
Jan 19X2	2,000	$20,000
Feb 19X2	2,200	21,700
Mar 19X2	2,400	23,900
Apr 19X2	2,900	27,500
May 19X2	3,500	31,250
Jun 19X2	3,700	32,900
Jul 19X2	3,900	36,000
Aug 19X2	4,200	39,000
Sep 19X2	4,300	40,000
Oct 19X2	4,250	39,500
Nov 19X2	4,300	40,000
Dec 19X2	4,400	42,000

The output from the least-squares regression capability in an electronic spreadsheet on a personal computer is $2,306.68 for the constant and 8.705584 for the x-coefficient. Determine the estimated cost for the next three months with the following estimated patient services:

Jan 19X3	4,500
Feb 19X3	4,600
Mar 19X3	4,800

13.11. Assume there is an 80 percent learning curve and that tests are performed in lots of 30 using a new medical technology with an average time per test of 20 minutes. The technicians are paid $18.50 per hour. Determine the total cost of performing 3,840 tests under the 80 percent learning curve.

13.12. Assume there is an 85 percent learning curve and that tests are performed in lots of 25 using a new medical technology with an average time per test of 30 minutes. The technologists are paid $19 per hour. Determine the total cost of performing 3,200 tests under the 85 percent learning curve.

13.13. The Jameson Jones Clinic opened in January 19X2 with a single physician, but there are facilities to support sixteen physicians. The inexperienced staff encountered many problems in responding to patients, which had been anticipated. A second physician began to practice at the clinic on 1 March 19X2. The third and fourth physicians joined the clinic on 1 April 19X2. There are twelve other physicians who are scheduled to join the Jameson Jones Clinic in May or June (four on 1 May 19X2, and eight on 1 June 19X2).

There is one full-time employee and several part-time employees; all of the workers began in January and have an average rate of $11 per hour. The January to March operations were as shown in Exhibit 13.8. The following volumes are estimated for April to June:

Apr 19X2   1,760 visits (4 physicians)
May 19X2   3,520 visits (8 physicians)
Jun 19X2   7,040 visits (16 physicians)

A. Determine the learning curve for January to March. *Hint:* Use Exhibit 13.3 as a guide for separating monthly from cumulative data.

B. Using the learning curve experience for January–March, project the monthly expenditures for April, May, and June 19X2.

C. Estimate the average cost for the 14,080 visits during January to June 19X2.

Exhibit 13.8   Jameson Jones Clinic: January to March Operations

	Visits	Hours	Average per Visit per Month	
Jan 19X2	440	264	0.6 hours	$6.60
Feb 19X2	440	179.52	0.408 hours	4.49
Mar 19X2	880	301.5936	0.34272 hours	3.77

14

Variance Analysis and Management Control

Introduction

The departmental management control system (DMCS) is a computer-based application package that extracts, processes, cross-references, reports, and retains key information on the health care entity. The DMCS module extracts transactions data and performance measures from the financial DBMS and the activity DBMS, respectively; it uses the mapped regular cost accounts to aggregate the information by department. The DMCS also extracts (1) service data from the patient order-entry and result-reporting module and (2) statistical data from the computer-based operational control module. Chapter 10 described the adjustments made to the departmental data so that fixed and variable components are emphasized. The previous chapter explained the departmental monitoring process over the mix and distribution of services and cost control over intermediate products.

There are no inputs from the DMCS to the financial DBMS; therefore, those additional cost assignments and cost allocations made in matching costs and revenue by department for monitoring interme-diate products are only retained in the separate database for the DMCS. The insights from these departmental assessments may necessitate that adjustments be made directly in the approved budgeting data stored in the financial DBMS. These new levels of assessment are possible be-cause of the management control activities in responsibility-accounting systems and in the DMCS. Variance analysis is a central feature in these management control activities.

Variance Analysis

Actual expenditures and performance are often different from bud-geted levels. The comparison of budget with actual data for each com-ponent of expense, revenue, and performance measure in a regular cost account was previously explained as a standard capability of the responsibility-accounting reporting system. This calculation of budget may include a volume factor from the activity DBMS so that a relevant yardstick of performance is used in comparing actual data with the plan. Major variances between budget and actual data are noted in the explanation column of the responsibility reports, and a series of internal actions are triggered by these notations.

Exception reporting in the responsibility-accounting system is lim-ited to expenditure control. Variances in revenues and performance measures are noted, and the applicability of the flexible budget data used in expenditure control is strengthened by the DBMSs containing revenues and performance measures. As explained in Chapter 12, the DMCS builds upon the foundation created by the responsibility-accounting system.

Variance analysis is a systematic examination of actual and budget results from a multidimensional perspective. Actual expenditures may be compatible with budget, but the expected performance may not have been achieved. There may be quality-of-care issues with regard to different performance levels. Because of patient care, variance analysis in health care entities at the department level is much more complex than in other industries. There must be constant monitoring of the mix and distribution of critical services for quality assurance.

Effective analysis of the difference between actual and budgeted values requires identifying the reasons for the difference and, to the extent possible, relating each component of the variance to a person. An increase in price of an input may be beyond the control of the health care entity. Technically, an agent of the health care entity must approve the price increase, but this action may be a recognition of external events that are beyond the entity's control. An examination of the reasons for the variance should result in separating the impact of external events from internal actions by employees.

The tracking of data in computer systems has permitted some new types of variances to be calculated for health care entities. There are problems with some new calculations. If the component related to internal events cannot be matched with a person because of mixed jur-isdictional issues, then it might not be feasible to correct the "interesting" findings. Effective variance analysis can only be performed in a health care entity when well-defined lines of responsibility and accountability exist. The perspective for examining these variances must be compatible with that area's delegation of responsibility.

The departmental framework for variance analysis must be compatible with the requirements of quality care and the minimum volumes of services in key areas. The fixed and variable components of expense elements in departments with intermediate products are recognized and are subjected to separate study. These expense items in comparison with budget often have a price or rate variance and a quantity or volume variance. If work measurement units are available for the department, the quantity variance can be partitioned between productivity or efficiency and other factors.

The concept of variance analysis is illustrated by a series of events in the Carrington Health Clinic, which has a group of physicians from various medical specialties who collectively handle about 3,150 patients per month. Direct labor hours for nursing care is the activity used in assigning costs and in contractual agreements. For illustration purposes the fringe benefits are combined with the salary as a single item, and there are a sufficient number of part-time employees to respond by shift to changes in demand. The budget is based on nursing care of $18 per hour, and the average nursing cost is $3.59 per patient visit. A flexible budget system is used, and the 3,150 expected patients for the month, at $3.59 per visit, gives a nursing budget of $11,308.50, which is 628.25 nursing hours at $18 per hour.

Price and efficiency variance

Competitive pressures forced an increase in nursing cost from $18 to $19.50 per hour, which went into effect on the first of the month. Actual nursing cost was $12,675 (650 hours at $19.50 per hour), and there were 3,200 patient visits. Exhibit 14.1 shows a total variance of $1,187, which includes a price variance of $975 and a quantity or efficiency variance of $212. The part-time nurses were closely monitored to changes in mix and distribution of patients, resulting in only 11.78 extra hours being incurred for the month (650 hours versus 638.22).

Supplies for patients at Carrington Health Clinic are prepackaged for the different types of medical specialties. The budget is based on one package per visit, at a cost of $1.10 per package. There was a 10 percent increase in price, from $1.10 to $1.21 per package, effective the first of the month, and 3,300 packages were used for the 3,200

Exhibit 14.1 Carrington Health Clinic: Nursing Care for the Month Ended 30 September 19X2

	Cost incurred actual inputs × Actual price	Flexible budget based on actual quantity × Budget prices	Flexible budget based on standard inputs allowed for actual outputs achieved × Budget prices
	(650 × $19.50)	(650 × $18.00)	(638.222 × $18.00)
Nursing salaries	$12,675	$11,700	$11,488

Price Variance $975 U	Efficiency Variance $212 U

Total Variance $1,187 U

Note: U indicates an unfavorable variance; *F* is a favorable variance.
The 3,200 visits × $3.59 = $11,488/18.00 = 638.222 nursing hours.
The efficiency variance is 11.778 hours × $18.00 = $212.00.
The price variance is 650 hours × $1.50 = $975.00.

Exhibit 14.2 Carrington Health Clinic: Patient Supplies for the Month Ended 30 September 19X2

	Cost incurred actual inputs × Actual price	Flexible budget based on actual quantity × Budget prices	Flexible budget based on standard inputs allowed for actual outputs achieved × Budget prices
	(3,300 × $1.21)	(3,300 × $1.10)	(3,200 × $1.10)
Supplies	$3,993	$3,630	$3,520

Price Variance $363 U	Efficiency Variance $110 U

Total Variance $473 U

Note: U indicates an unfavorable variance; *F* is a favorable variance.
The efficiency variance is 100 units × $1.10 = $110.00.
The price variance is 3,300 units × $0.11 = $363.00.

patients. Exhibit 14.2 reports the total variance of $473 for patient supplies, of which $363 is a price variance and $110 is a quantity or efficiency variance.

The pool of qualified personnel permitted the clinic to retain the rate of $12 per hour for clerical salaries; however, the hourly rate for technicians was increased from $20 to $21 as of the first of the month. Part-time personnel enable the staffing to fluctuate by volume of patient visits, but the change is by shift. Exhibit 14.3 reports 20.3 extra hours of clerical effort for an efficiency variance of $244 and 4.4 extra hours of technician effort for an efficiency variance of $88. The increase of $1 per hour in technician's salaries caused a rate or price variance of $390 for the month.

Departmental variance

Nursing hours, as previously stated, are used by Carrington Health Clinic for assigning costs and in contractual agreements. The flexible budget for variable and fixed support costs in the relevant range of 2,800 to 3,700 patient visits is presented in Exhibit 14.4; these amounts are compatible with the clinic's data in Exhibits 14.1 to 14.3.

The actual expenditures for the month are shown in Exhibit 14.5 for the 3,200 visits versus the expected volume of 3,150 patient visits. The 3,200 visits, at $12.48 variable support per visit, should have cost $39,936, but the actual cost was $42,318 for a total variable support variance of $2,382. The aggregation of the total variance for the individual items in Exhibits 14.1 to 14.3 must equal the overall support variance (Exhibit 14.6).

Variable support cost as an aggregate is applied based on nursing hours; and the results of using this single index are proper to the extent to which nursing hours are a surrogate for the total movement of variable support cost. At Carrington, the total variance of $2,382 is partitioned slightly differently, using nursing hours as the reference point instead of the respective hours or units for each expense item. The total in Exhibit 14.7 is the same $2,382, but the aggregate spending variance driven by nursing hours is $1,645 instead of $1,728, with the offsetting adjustments for $737 efficiency variance by nursing hours instead of $654 from Exhibits 14.1 to 14.3.

The fixed-support analysis in Exhibit 14.7 uses 3,150 patient visits as the denominator volume for fixed support of $15,581 and 628.25 nursing hours; the application rate per nursing hour is $24.80. The actual output of 3,200 patient visits was 50 visits more than expected, or

Exhibit 14.3   Carrington Health Clinic: Clerical Personnel and Technicians for the Month Ended 30 September 19X2

	Cost incurred actual inputs × Actual price	Flexible budget based on actual quantity × Budget prices	Flexible budget based on standard inputs allowed for actual outputs achieved × Budget prices
	(1,455 hours × $12)	(1,455 hours × $12)	(1,434.67 hours × $12)
Clerical salaries	$17,460	$17,460	$17,216

Price Variance $0	Efficiency Variance $244 U

Total Variance $244 U

	(390 hours × $21)	(390 hours × $20)	(385.6 hours × $20)
Technicians' salaries	$8,190	$7,800	$7,712

Price Variance $390 U	Efficiency Variance $88 U

Total Variance $478 U

Note: U indicates an unfavorable variance; F is a favorable variance.
For clerical salaries, the 3,200 visits × $5.38 = $17,216/$12 = 1,434.67 clerical hours. The efficiency variance is 20.333 hours × $12.00 = $244.00.
For technicians' salaries, the 3,200 visits × $2.41 = $7,712/$20 = 385.6 technician hours.
The efficiency variance is 4.4 hours × $20.00 = $88.00.
The price variance is 390 hours × $1.00 = $390.00.

638.222 nursing hours versus 628.25 nursing hours, for a favorable volume variance of $247 (Exhibit 14.7). The actual cost incurred for fixed support was $250 more than budget ($15,831 actual versus $15,581 budget); this unfavorable variance offsets the volume variance, giving an underapplied fixed-support cost of $3 for the month.

Three-way analysis

After separating the variable- and fixed-support cost for management control purposes, some health care entities combine these components

Exhibit 14.4 Carrington Health Clinic: Flexible Budget Data for the Month Ended 30 September 19X2

	Per Visit	Relevant Range of Activity (Patient Visits per Month)			
		2,800	3,100	3,400	3,700
Variable-support cost:					
Clerical	$ 5.38	$15,064	$16,678	$18,292	$19,906
Nursing*	3.59	10,052	11,129	12,206	13,283
Technicians	2.41	6,748	7,471	8,194	8,917
Supplies—patients	1.10	3,080	3,410	3,740	4,070
Total	$12.48	$34,944	$38,688	$42,432	$46,176
Fixed-support cost:					
Administration		$ 6,246	$ 6,246	$ 6,246	$ 6,246
Supplies—office		635	635	635	635
Utilities and rent		4,500	4,500	4,500	4,500
Medical equipment rental		2,500	2,500	2,500	2,500
Office equipment rental		500	500	500	500
Accounting and legal fees		1,200	1,200	1,200	1,200
Total		$15,581	$15,581	$15,581	$15,581

*The hourly rate for nursing salaries and fringe benefits is $18, which gives the following distribution for hours:
 2,800 visits is 558.44 hours
 3,100 visits is 618.28 hours
 3,400 visits is 678.11 hours
 3,700 visits is 737.94 hours

into a single rate for product-pricing purposes. The clinic uses nursing hours as the basis for some agreements, which in the context of Exhibit 14.7 means combining the $62.574 variable-support rate with the $24.80 fixed-support rate, giving a combined rate of $87.374 per nursing hour. The 3,200 visits at this combined rate of $87.374 equal $55,764 for the output in Exhibit 14.7 ($39,936 variable support + $15,828 fixed). Thus, the variable and fixed variances in Exhibit 14.7 are combined into a $1,895 unfavorable spending variance, a $737 unfavorable efficiency variance, and a $247 favorable volume variance, for a total unfavorable variance of $2,385.

Exhibit 14.8 presents the standard three-way analysis of support costs. Study the components in Exhibit 14.7 to see the variable and fixed segments that are aggregated in the three-way analysis. Some health care entities combine the spending and efficiency variance into

Exhibit 14.5 Carrington Health Clinic: Actual Data for the Month Ended 30 September 19X2

	Actual	*Expected*	*Variance*
Patient visits for month	3,200	3,150	50 visits
Nursing hours for month	650.00	628.25	21.75 hours

Variable-support cost:		Fixed-support cost:	
Clerical	$17,460	Administration	$ 6,246
Nursing	12,675	Supplies—office	635
Technicians	8,190	Utilities and rent	4,500
Supplies—patients	3,993	Medical equipment rental	2,700
Total	$42,318	Office equipment rental	550
		Accounting and legal fees	1,200
		Total	$15,831

Exhibit 14.6 Variances for Carrington Health Clinic for the Month Ended 30 September 19X2

	Spending Variance	*Efficiency Variance*	*Total*
Nursing care	$ 975 Unfavorable	$212 Unfavorable	$1,187
Supplies	363 Unfavorable	110 Unfavorable	473
Clerical salaries	0	244 Unfavorable	244
Technicians	390 Unfavorable	88 Unfavorable	478
Total	$1,728 Unfavorable	$654 Unfavorable	$2,382

a flexible budget variance; the volume variance remains as a separate item to measure the difference between expected and actual levels of operation. This approach is a two-way analysis and is depicted in Exhibit 14.8.

Operational Measures

The spending, efficiency, and volume variances can be augmented by work measurement data from computer-based operational control packages in a health care department for management control purposes. These work measurement units, as previously explained, tend

Exhibit 14.7 Carrington Health Clinic: Support Cost Analysis for the Month Ended 30 September 19X2

	Actual costs incurred	Flexible budget based on actual inputs	Flexible budget based on standard inputs allowed	Flexible budget applied standard inputs allowed for actual outputs
	(Given)	$(650 \times \$62.574)$	(638.222×62.574)	$(638.22 \times \$62.574)$
Variable support	$42,318	$40,673	$39,936	$39,936
		Spending Variance $1,645 U	Efficiency Variance $737 U	
		Underapplied Support Cost $2,382 U		
		$(628.25 \times \$24.80)$		$(638.222 \times \$24.80)$
Fixed support	$15,831	$15,581	$15,581	$15,828
		Spending Variance $250 U		Volume Variance $247 F
		Underapplied Fixed-Support Cost $3 U		

Note: U indicates an unfavorable variance; F is a favorable variance.
Denominator volume used to set fixed support is 628.25 nursing hours for 3,150 patient visits.
Budgeted fixed-support rate = $15,581/628.25 hours, or $24.80 per nursing hour.
Standard inputs allowed for 3,200 units is 638.222 hours, or $15,828 (638.222 hours × $24.80).

Exhibit 14.8 Carrington Health Clinic: Three-Way Support Cost Analysis for the Month Ended 30 September 19X2

	Actual costs incurred	Flexible budget based on actual inputs	Flexible budget based on standard inputs allowed	Flexible budget applied standard inputs allowed for actual outputs
	($42,318 + $15,831)	($40,673 + $15,581)	($39,936 + $15,581)	($39,936 + $15,828)
Total support	$58,149	$56,254	$55,517	$55,764

Three-way analysis

- Spending Variance $1,895 U
- Efficiency Variance $737 U
- Volume Variance $247 F

Two-way analysis

- Flexible Budget Variance $2,632 U
- Volume Variance $247 F

One-way analysis

- Total Variance (Underapplied Support Cost) $2,385 U

Note: U indicates an unfavorable variance; *F* is a favorable variance.
The data in this exhibit are based on aggregating items in Exhibit 14.7.

to emphasize the direct labor component in a given service. This orientation is compatible with the dominant role of direct labor expense in health care entities. A secondary objective of these work measurement units is to provide a foundation for monitoring compliance by departmental personnel with the minimum mix and distribution of services for quality care.

Relative-value units

The computer-based operational control packages for a health care department frequently contain work measurement units established by a professional association for monitoring and evaluating performance. Vendors begin to assist members of a professional association in establishing a classification system and an accumulation arrangement for specific health care activities as a way of increasing the vendor's market share. Eventually, members of the professional association adopt a nomenclature for identifying a test, treatment, procedure, or operation in this department. Various vendor packages are modified to comply with the adopted system, and data are accumulated and processed with these revised packages.

The professional association's committee uses the processed data to develop relative-value units (RVUs) for specific tasks. Where the labor effort changes in response to the equipment used, the assigned RVUs are identified with specific equipment. Some teaching and research facilities may develop institution-specific RVUs, but these efforts are usually supported by the accumulation of the standard work measurement units from the health care professional association.

There are problems in interpreting aggregate RVUs for a department because they are based on an assumed work flow in the organization with a certain mix and distribution of services using specified equipment. Operating automated equipment at less than its capacity permits increasing volume of tests with minor changes in direct labor effort beyond handling of the specimen; the impact on RVUs and productivity measures is significant. These work measurement units capture the direct labor effort in performing certain procedures or operations with specific equipment under general assumptions regarding the flow of work. If there is a substitution of equipment, the RVUs may increase to reflect more labor effort in performing the same set of tests or services.

The detailed data on RVUs from the operational control packages permit a very thorough analysis of departmental activities, work flow, substitution of equipment, scheduling, quality control, delays, and lost patient orders. Decisions on the minimum staffing or fixed cost for quality care are made based on these detailed data on RVUs for the department. By separating the RVUs for fixed cost from the remainder, the departmental RVUs for variable efforts are more applicable than would otherwise be the case. A management consultant analyzing unusual RVU variances for a department often discovers that the fixed and variable components have not been separated.

Nursing acuity system

In the 1960s and 1970s, inpatient facilities began to identify, by tasks, the hours required to provide care for the patients in each type of nursing unit per shift. Various types of patient acuity measures were established for required tasks in different inpatient locations, and they were assigned and assessed by patient for each shift. After the patient acuities were accumulated and analyzed, it became apparent that the type of admission, diagnostic category, age, and sex of patient are not necessarily associated with the requirements for nursing care over the inpatient stay.

An emergency admission with major surgery and recovery in the intensive care unit who is subsequently moved into a regular nursing area may require less nursing care than a medical admission in the same regular nursing area who needs assistance with eating, walking, and other basic functions. If the length of stay, for example, is ten days, then the ninth and tenth days may require relatively limited nursing care while extensive amounts of nursing care were needed in the first three days. Two patients admitted for the same medical problem and with similar profiles may respond differently to treatment and have unique distributions of nursing care requirements during the inpatient recovery. After further analysis, a different approach to patient acuity became the standard.

A point count by patient is recorded for each shift and is used to project requirements for the next shift. The point count over several days in the patient's recovery is used to estimate the patient's needs for the next few days. This information is aggregated and used in nurse scheduling. Nursing administration monitors the entries for each patient by shift and takes appropriate corrective action for erroneous assessments of patients' needs. The pool nursing and part-time arrangements provide the capabilities for matching the composite patient acuity requirements with personnel. Where there are shortages of nursing staff, acuity levels facilitate the best assignment of scarce nursing resources.

Patient acuity and nurse care management application packages have moved from the large mainframe computer to the personal computer. Some of the international public accounting firms began to implement in 1981–1983 patient acuity and nursing care management application packages on personal computers for a total investment of less than $12,000 (including the personal computer and printer). Health care consulting firms created their own versions that combine patient acuity, nurse scheduling, and variance analysis. These packages on personal computers are widely used today.

Variance analysis with patient acuity

The patient acuity index facilitates nurse scheduling and staffing, but it does not accommodate nursing requirements for a portion of a shift. The patient mix and composite patient status may change after scheduling nursing personnel for the next shift; some patients may be transferred, other patients' conditions may change adversely due to medication, complications, surgery, or internal problems. In spite of these measurement issues, the acuity index is the best approach for matching patient needs with nurse staffing by shift, and the monthly reports provide an assessment of nursing activities based on empirical data that otherwise would be available only by inferences and from the absence of complaints.

The aggregate patient acuity index can be related to the nursing hours for the period both as a measure of quality care and of efficiency. In fact, these acuity data permit a separation of nursing efficiency from nonacuity increase in quantity (nursing hours). Thus, the three-way analysis of price, efficiency, and volume variance is expanded to a four-way analysis with efficiency consisting of two components: (1) nurse staffing changes directly in response to aggregate shifts in patient acuity and (2) changes in nursing hours not related to shifts in patient acuity.

The variance analysis for nursing begins with comparing actual and budgeted direct labor expenditures from the mapped regular cost accounts, even though expenditure control was performed in the responsibility-accounting system. Cost control for a department requires explaining all variances with confidence that the study is complete; expenditure analysis is required for closure. Exhibit 14.9 presents a situation where actual nursing cost was $121,440 (10,120 hours at $12.00 per nursing hour) versus a budget of $89,700 (7,800

Exhibit 14.9   Nursing Department Direct Labor Variances

Situation:

The nursing department has a monthly budget of 1,200 patient days with average direct labor of $11.50 per hour and average acuity level of 6.5 nursing hours per patient, for a total direct labor budget of $89,700, or 7,800 hours at $11.50. In response to competitive pressures, salaries were increased to $12.00 per hour as of the beginning of the month. The actual patient load was 1,350 patient days, and the average acuity level was 7.4 hours per patient day. The actual nursing costs were $121,440 (10,120 hours at $12.00 per hour). Determine the volume, acuity, nonacuity quantity, and price nonacuity quantity variances.

Solution:

	Actual cost incurred (hours and rate)	Flexible Budget Based On			
		Actual nursing hours and budget rate	Actual inputs and actual acuity	Actual inputs and budget acuity	Budget inputs and budget acuity
	(10,120 × $12.00)	(10,120 × $11.50)	(1,350 × 7.4 × $11.50)	(1,350 × 6.5 × $11.50)	(1,200 × 6.5 × $11.50)
Nursing salaries	*$121,440*	*$116,380*	*$114,885*	*$100,912.50*	*$89,700*

Price Variance $5,060 U	Nonacuity Quantity Variance $1,495 U	Acuity Variance $13,972.50 U	Volume Variance $11,212.50 U

Total Nursing Variance $31,740 U

Note: U indicates an unfavorable variance; *F* is a favorable variance.
Price variance = 10,120 nursing hours at $0.50 increase per hour, or $5,060.00 U.
Nonacuity quantity variance = 130 hours at $11.50 budget rate, or $1,495.00 U.
Acuity variance = 1,350 patient days × 0.9 acuity increase × $11.50 budget rate, or $13,972.50 U.
Volume variance = 150 patient days × 6.5 budget acuity × $11.50 budget rate, or $11,212.50 U.

hours at $11.50 per nursing hour), for a total variance of $31,740. The complete variance for the department must be explained by the four-way analysis.

The price variance in the nursing department is the increase from $11.50 to $12.00 per nursing hour, or $0.50, multiplied by the actual number of nursing hours (10,120 hours), giving an unfavorable variance of $5,060 (Exhibit 14.9). The nonacuity quantity variance is the difference between the actual nursing hours at the budget rate and the actual inputs at the actual patient acuity level. The 1,350 patient days at actual acuity of 7.4 indicate 9,990 nursing hours versus 10,120 actual hours, giving 130 extra hours, which at the budget rate of $11.50 per nursing hour is a $1,495 unfavorable nonacuity quantity variance.

The acuity variance is the difference between the actual inputs at the actual patient acuity level versus the actual inputs at the budget patient acuity level. The budget acuity level is 6.5, the actual acuity level is 7.4—an increase of 0.9, which multiplied by the 1,350 actual patient days at the budget rate of $11.50 per nursing hour gives a $13,972.50 unfavorable acuity variance.

The volume variance is the difference between the actual inputs at the budget patient acuity level versus the budget inputs at the budget patient acuity level. The actual quantity of 1,350 patient days was 150 days greater than the budget of 1,200 patient days. The 150 days at 6.5 budget acuity hours give 975 hours at the budget rate of $11.50 per nursing hour—an unfavorable volume variance of $11,212.50 (Exhibit 14.9).

There is no set of uniform definitions for price, acuity, volume, and nonacuity quantity variance among health care accountants. The specifications given in Exhibit 14.9 have been applied to various settings and are compatible with the format subsequently followed in RVU analysis. The price variance may be zero in most months, but the other three variances are relevant. The forecasting of patient days and episodes of care is dependent upon many factors outside the control of the nursing department. The 10,120 actual nursing hours incurred is 130 hours more than the estimated staffing based on actual patient days and actual patient acuity levels; this small variance is typical. If you or a member of your family is an inpatient, you prefer that the health care entity has an unfavorable nonacuity quantity variance. Otherwise, the actual requirements for nursing care are greater than the ability of the staff to support that level of care during the shift.

Many health care entities do not follow the cost-accounting structure described in this book, and in those entities complications may arise because of mixed data within a given expense item. For example, Ashland Memorial Hospital's payroll system does not separate vacation, holidays, sick time, and special time from regular hours. All labor hours are charged to the designated regular cost account for each employee, and transfers of services are recorded in the financial DBMS and reported in the responsibility-accounting system. A full-time employee reports hours for 261 days a year (365 − 104 = 261), which are reduced by 36 days for vacation, holidays, and sick time, giving 225 regular days. Ashland charges a 16 percent overhead on each regular day, which, on the average, assigns the cost for the 261 days (225 regular days × 116% = 261).

Continuing with this example, Ashland's nursing area expects to have 7,500 patient days this month. The medical/surgical unit is expected to have 2,400 patient days and an average patient acuity of 7.5 hours of nursing care per patient day. The average nurse's salary, including fringe benefits, is $12.00 per hour; after adjusting for vacation, holidays, and sick time, the salary is increased by 16 percent to $13.92 per hour. The monthly budget for the medical/surgical unit is 18,000 hours at $13.92, or $250,560.

The departmental report indicated the medical/surgical unit had a cost of $336,284, based on 22,300 hours at $15.08 per hour. It was announced on the first of the month that nursing salaries, including fringe benefits, were increased from $12.00 to $13.00 per hour; thus, the effective rate was 116 percent of $13.00 or $15.08 per nursing hour. The actual monthly experience was 2,700 patient days, with an average patient acuity of 8.0 hours of nursing. In-service training required 380 hours; the remaining 320 hours were related to scheduling of a nurse for a shift. Exhibit 14.10 presents the price, volume, acuity, training, and scheduling variances for the month at Ashland Memorial.

The total variance of $85,724 in Exhibit 14.10 is presented in the same general format as that followed in Exhibit 14.9. The nonacuity quantity variance of $9,744 is separated between in-service training of $5,290 and scheduling of $4,454. Note that in Exhibit 14.10 the variance analysis focuses on the 225 working days and the hourly rates for those days, which are 116 percent of the normal rate. Thus, vacation, holidays, and sick time are monitored for expenditure control in the responsibility-accounting system but are omitted from the departmental variance analysis. If it is possible to charge in-service training to another cost account, the current hourly rate of $15.08 might be used in place of the budget rate of $13.92 per hour.

This discussion of variance analysis with patient acuity has focused on nursing salaries. There are other services and supplies related to the patient acuity index. The four-way analysis in Exhibits 14.9 and 14.10 can be performed at the department level for each of these items.

Exhibit 14.10 Ashland Memorial Hospital: Medical/Surgical Nursing Unit Direct Labor Variances

	Actual cost incurred (hours and rate)	Flexible Budget Based On			
		Actual nursing hours and budget rate	Actual inputs and actual acuity	Actual inputs and budget acuity	Budget inputs and budget acuity
	(22,300 × $15.08)	(22,300 × $13.92)	(2,700 × 8.0 × $13.92)	(2,700 × 7.5 × $13.92)	(2,400 × 7.5 × $13.92)
Nursing salaries	$336,284	$310,416	$300,672	$281,880	$250,560

Price Variance $25,868 U	Nonacuity Quantity Variance $9,744 U	Acuity Variance $18,792 U	Volume Variance $31,320 U

Total Nursing Variance $85,724 U

Note: U indicates an unfavorable variance; is a favorable variance.

Price variance = 22,300 nursing hours at $1.16 increase per hour, or $25,868.00 U.

Nonacuity quantity variance = 700 hours at $13.92 budget rate, or $9,744.00 U. (There were 22,300 actual hours less 21,600 scheduled hours per patient acuity, or 700 extra hours.) These 700 extra hours are divided between 380 hours for in-service training and 320 hours for scheduling; the cost separation is as follows:

In-service training 380 hours × $13.92 = $5,289.60
Scheduling   320 hours × $13.92 = 4,454.40
$9,744.00 U

Acuity variance = 2,700 patient days × 0.5 acuity increase × $13.92 budget rate, or $18,792.00 U.

Volume variance = 300 patient days × 7.5 budget acuity × $13.92 budget rate, or $31,320.00 U.

Analysis of intermediate products with RVUs

The RVUs provided by the computer-based operational control packages in departments permit a patient acuity type of analysis for intermediate products. The three-way analysis of price, efficiency, and volume is expanded to include a partitioning of efficiency or quantity into two segments: (1) those related to an increase in RVUs and (2) all others. The interpretation of non-RVU variance is difficult because of the absence of complete knowledge. If the non-RVU variance is positive, then workers might argue that it measures an increase in productivity; if the non-RVU variance is negative, it might be argued that factors external to the department caused the problem. The detailed data in the departmental operational control module contain information on services ordered, timing of flows, services performed, equipment and operations used, and results reported. Thus, in each department an analysis can be made of each non-RVU quantity variance so that it is appropriately interpreted.

It is important for health care entities to separate fixed and variable costs in a department before examining RVU variances; otherwise, an averaging of these components may suggest misleading results. Quality care requires compliance with all minimum staffing requirements that are represented by these fixed costs. Exhibit 14.11 presents a situation where RVUs are used in performing a four-way analysis of direct labor and where quality assurance and minimum staffing considerations are also included. In studying RVU variance, it is important that the example contain the other three types of variances; shortcuts taken with simple cases do not work for the complete case.

Exhibit 14.11   Pathology Department Direct Labor Variances

Situation:

The pathology department has a monthly budget of 67,000 tests representing 810,640 RVUs and a direct labor budget of $97,238. This budget is separated into a fixed-labor budget of $55,000 for 35,000 tests with 490,000 RVUs and a variable-labor budget estimated at $42,238 for 2,277 hours at $18.55 per hour for the remaining tests. The relevant range for the monthly variable budget is from 48,001 to 76,000 tests, with the fixed and variable computations being performed in each of the 14 mapped regular cost accounts. But, for illustration purposes, assume the average of $1.32 per test and 10.02 RVUs represent the variable direct labor expense in the relevant range.

The actual for the month is 69,000 tests, with 841,750 RVUs and total direct labor of $102,500. The variable-labor cost was $47,500 for 2,500 hours at $19.00 per hour. The direct fixed labor of $55,000 was incurred, but the minimum mix and distribution of tests did not occur; only 34,000 of the baseline tests representing 476,000 RVUs were performed. The variable tests were slightly more complex than expected, with an average of 10.45 RVUs per test. Determine the fixed and variable variances for the period.

Exhibit 14.11   Continued

Solution:

Fixed and Variable

Estimated		Actual
$97,238		$102,500

| | Total Variance $5,262 | |

The fixed budget of $55,000 was actually incurred; thus, no variance in expenditures. The prescribed mix and distribution of 35,000 tests in the fixed budget were not achieved; only 34,000 tests were performed. There is a performance variance of 1,000 tests, representing 14,000 RVUs, which might be costed at $1,571.43 (1/35th of the $55,000 fixed budget). The failure to perform these 1,000 tests is an important issue for quality assurance.

	Actual cost incurred (hours and rate)	Flexible Budget Based On			
		Actual laboratory hours and budget rate	Actual inputs and actual RVUs	Actual inputs and budget RVUs	Budget inputs and budget RVUs
	(2,500 × $19.00)	(2,500 × $18.55)	(35,000 × 10.45 × 0.1317365)	(35,000 × 10.02 × 0.1317365)	(32,000 × 10.02 × 0.1317365)
Variable laboratory salaries	*$47,500*	*$46,375*	*$48,182.62*	*$46,200*	*$42,238*

	Price Variance $1,125 U	Non-RVU Quantity Variance $1,807.62 F	RVUs Variance $1,982.62 U	Volume Variance $3,962 U

| | Total Laboratory Variance $5,262 U | |

Note: U indicates an unfavorable variance; *F* is a favorable variance.

Price variance = 2,500 laboratory hours at $0.45 increase per hour, or $1,125.00 U.

Non-RVU quantity variance indicates an increase in productivity for handling 5.483 more RVUs per direct labor hour, which extended for the 2,500 hours is 13,708 RVUs, which at the budget of 140.81686 RVUs per hour is 97.345 laboratory hours at $18.55, or $1,807.62 F. (There may be changes in mix and distribution of tests, work flow, or in available equipment that contribute to this non-RVU variance.)

RVU variance = 35,000 actual tests × 0.43 RVU per test increase × $0.1317365 budget rate, or $1,982.62 U.

Volume variance = 3,000 tests × 10.02 RVUs per test × $0.1317365 budget cost per RVU, or $3,962.00 U.

There is a fixed labor budget of $55,000, with a prescribed mix of 35,000 tests representing 490,000 RVUs, and a variable budget that is expected to be $42,238 for 32,000 tests. Note that the relevant range is from 48,001 to 76,000 tests while the fixed budget stops at 35,000 tests. Thus, quality assurance issues are satisfied at 35,000 tests, but the current staffing assignments do not consider the possibility of events from 35,001 to 48,000 tests.

The actual fixed cost incurred of $55,000 was the same as budgeted, but the minimum mix and distribution of 35,000 tests were not accomplished. The 35,000 tests that were budgeted represented 490,000 RVUs, or 14 RVUs per test; the 34,000 tests that were performed contained 476,000 RVUs, or the same average of 14 RVUs per test. The 1,000 tests that were not performed, representing 14,000 RVUs, are important for quality assurance and quality care. Various health care issues come into focus over the failure to perform these other 1,000 tests.

The budget hourly rate for variable direct labor was increased from $18.55 to $19.00, so there is a $0.45 per hour price variance for each of the 2,500 hours performed, or a $1,125 unfavorable price variance. The actual variable cost incurred increased from $46,375 to $47,500 because of this hourly rate change.

The 32,000 tests in the variable budget, representing 320,640 RVUs (810,640 − 490,000), had a labor budget of $42,238, or a budget cost of $0.13173 per RVU; each test had an average of 10.02 RVUs (320,640/32,000). But 35,000 tests were performed, and this volume increase of 3,000 tests under the budget 10.02 RVUs per test and budget rate of $0.13173 is $3,962 (there is a $2 rounding adjustment).

The 35,000 tests in the variable budget, containing 365,750 RVUs (841,750 − 476,000), is an average of 10.45 RVUs per test rather than the budget of 10.02 RVUs. This increase of 0.43 RVUs per test multiplied by the 35,000 actual tests at the budget rate of $0.13173 gives the unfavorable RVU variance of $1,982.62. Thus, the actual services performed were more labor intensive than expected, and the price of tests tends to be based, to some extent, on RVUs. Revenues probably increased $3,000 to $4,000, at least, if the cost of labor increased by $1,982.62 because of more RVUs.

The 32,000 tests with a budget of 320,640 RVUs and 2,277 direct labor hours were based on an average labor effort of 140.817 RVUs per hour (320,640/2,277). The 35,000 actual tests with 365,750 RVUs were accomplished in 2,500 hours, for an average of 146.3 RVUs per hour (365,750/2,500). This is a significant change of 5.483 RVUs per hour

(146.3 − 140.817), or 13,707.8 RVUs for the 2,500 hours. If the budget of 140.817 RVUs per hour were achieved, the 13,708 RVUs would have equaled 97.345 direct labor hours at the budget of $18.55 per hour, which would have equaled the $1,807.62 (after $2 rounding) non-RVU quantity variance in Exhibit 14.11.

Another way of showing this increase in RVUs per direct labor hour (DLH) over budget is

Budget 320,640 RVUs for 2,277 DLHs or 140.81686 RVUs per hour
= Actual DLHs × Budget RVUs per DLH × Budget cost per RVU
= 2,500 DLHs × 140.81686 × $0.1317365 = $46,375.00 ($2 rounding adjustment)

Actual 365,750 RVUs for 2,500 DLHs or 146.30 RVUs per hour
= Actual DLHs × Actual RVUs per DLH × Budget cost per RVU
= 2,500 DLHs × 146.30 × $0.1317365 = $48,182.62

$48,186.62 − $46,375.00 = $1,807.62

An alternative approach to the non-RVU quantity variance is to view the flexible budget without the $0.45 labor rate increase. The 2,500 DLHs at $18.55 would have been $46,375 for the 365,750 RVUs, or an adjusted cost of $0.1267942 per RVU. This approach to computing the non-RVU quantity variance is

Budget 35,000 tests for 365,750 actual RVUs at budget cost per RVU
= Actual tests × Actual RVUs per test × Budget cost per RVU
= 35,000 tests × 10.45 RVUs × $0.1317365 = $48,182.62

Actual 2,500 DLHs at prior budget cost of $18.55 or $0.1267942 per RVU
= Actual tests × Actual RVUs per test × Adjusted cost per RVU
= 35,000 tests × 10.45 RVUs × $0.1267942 = $46,375.00

$48,182.62 − $46,375.00 = $1,807.62

This gain of $1,807.62 in productivity may be based on individual labor efforts, or it may be the result of the time flow of tests and automated equipment was more fully utilized during normal periods. The answer to this issue can be determined by reviewing the outputs from the computer-based operational control package containing the detail data on tests ordered and where services were performed by equipment.

Compare the solutions for Exhibit 14.9 and 14.11. The most important difference is the fixed component in Exhibit 14.11; the variable frameworks are the same, with patient acuity in Exhibit 14.9 being replaced with RVUs in Exhibit 14.11. These exhibits are standard four-way analyses of direct labor in health care entities.

Other Variances

Quality assurance and quality care issues often impose a fixed and variable partitioning over departmental cost in a support area. In other organizational units that are not critical for quality care, there may be employment contracts that create a fixed-cost component in a general support or an overhead area. Thus, the fixed and variable analysis of cost behavior is very common in health care entities for management control purposes.

The three-phase approach to management control outlined at the beginning of Chapter 12 must be closely followed in variance analysis; otherwise, attention can inappropriately be directed toward the wrong issues. First, examine the aggregated results of expenditure control from the responsibility-accounting system. Second, study the DMCS outputs for intermediate products. Third, review the pricing per service and demand issues. After the DMCS study is completed, the fixed- and variable-cost components in an area (or in groups of areas) may be blended together for purposes of computing a rate that can be used as a guide in pricing of intermediate products. Careful attention must be given to separating the management control aspects of the second phase from these pricing dimensions.

The Springfield Memorial Hospital's housekeeping and general services department is used to illustrate the importance of this three-phase approach. This department aggregates patient days, outpatient registrations, and clinic visits and then uses conversion factors in creating work units of services that are expressed as an index. The aggregate departmental cost is compared against this benchmark.

The current month's budget is based on a 74 percent occupancy index, or 10,160 work units with a budget rate of $4.50, giving a total budget of $45,720. The three components of this rate are labor and fringe benefits for $3.00, supplies for $1.00, and "other" for $0.50 per work unit. The labor budget of $30,480 (10,160 × $3.00) is 3,048 hours at $10.00 per hour, which can also be separated into fixed and variable parts. There are 330 hours of fixed labor at $17.00 per hour, for a fixed-labor cost of $5,610. The variable budget consists of 2,718 hours at $9.15 per hour, for a variable-labor cost of $24,870. The standard inputs for the budget are 0.2675 hours (2,718 hours/10,160 units) with a variable budget rate of $14.757 ($40,110/2,718 hours) per variable-labor hour.

The monthly responsibility-accounting statement reported an increase in fixed-labor cost from $5,610 to $5,940, based on 330 hours at $18.00 per hour. Variable direct labor was increased from 2,718 to 2,820 hours, for a cost of $25,803. The total monthly cost of $48,151 included $10,900 for supplies and $5,508 for other. The occupancy index assessment was 10,800 work units. Exhibit 14.12 shows that the output for the month has a standard cost of $48,600, which is a $449 favorable variance over the $48,151 actual cost for the month. There is an unfavorable spending variance of $926, consisting of $330 for fixed housekeeping and $596 for variable housekeeping. There is a $1,022 favorable efficiency variance and a $353 favorable volume variance.

After studying the computations in Exhibit 14.12, a decision is made to examine the spending variance in housekeeping. There is a rate increase from $17 to $18 per hour for the 330 fixed labor hours, resulting in a $330 spending variance for fixed labor. If the cost of 2,820 hours of variable labor is $25,803, then the actual price per hour was $9.15—the same as budget. The responsibility-accounting statements do not report any price changes for variable labor, supplies, or other expenses. There is a $634 favorable efficiency variance for direct labor, a $100 unfavorable efficiency variance for supplies, and a $108 unfavorable efficiency variance for other expenses. The net of these three variances is $426, which equals the excess of the $1,022 favorable efficiency variance over the $596 unfavorable spending variance.

What does it mean for the expenditure control variances by item to be different from the aggregate movement of the department in Exhibit 14.12? The items of variable expense are not changing proportionally with direct labor hours. A possibility is that the current month's direct labor hours as related to work-load units is an outlier and should only be monitored. Otherwise, this measure contains mixed fixed and variable components that require further study. The results for variable housekeeping in Exhibit 14.12, combined with knowledge about expenditures from the responsibility-accounting system, alerts departmental personnel that there are some measurement problems in using direct labor hours in the current context as a basis for pricing.

Assume that the work units of service at Springfield Memorial Hospital have been correctly calculated. The approach presented in Exhibit 14.12 permits the matching of the total departmental effort on a monthly basis with outputs, and further study may suggest a

Exhibit 14.12   Springfield Memorial Hospital: Housekeeping and General Services Departmental Variances for the Month Ended 30 September 19X2

	Actual costs incurred	Flexible budget based on actual inputs	Flexible budget based on standard inputs allowed	Flexible budget applied based on standard inputs allowed for actual outputs
Total department	$48,151	$47,225	$48,247	$48,600

Spending Variance $926 U	Efficiency Variance $1,022 F	Volume Variance $353 F

Total Variance $449 F

	(Given)	(2,820 × $14.7572)	(2,889.2 × $14.7572)	
Variable housekeeping	$42,211	$41,615	$42,637	$42,637

Spending Variance $596 U	Efficiency Variance $1,022 F	

Overapplied Support Cost $426 F

		(330 × 18)	(330 × 17)	(2,889.2 × $2.064)
Fixed housekeeping	$5,940	$5,610	$5,610	$5,963

Spending Variance $330 U		Volume Variance $353 F

Overapplied Fixed Cost $23 F

Note: U indicates an unfavorable variance; F is a favorable variance.

Denominator volume used to set fixed support is 2,718 variable-labor hours for 10,160 work units.

Budgeted fixed-support rate = $5,610/2,718 hours, or $2.064 per variable-labor hour.
Standard inputs for budget = (2,718 hours/10,160 units) 0.26752 hours.

Budgeted variable-support rate = $40,110/2,718 hours, or $14.7572 per variable-labor hour.

Standard inputs allowed for 10,800 work units is 2,889 hours (10,800 × 0.26752, or $42,637 (2,889.2 × $14.7572).

different separation between fixed and variable direct labor. At the end of the year, reciprocal cost is applied for the final matching of expenses and revenues. An examination of various statistical bases used in the reciprocal cost assignment may indicate a better monthly index than direct labor hours for monthly guidance.

The minimum staffing arrangements for health care professionals are closely monitored for quality of care. A more expensive per-hour mix of professionals may be required because of unusual circumstances, and an adjustment can be made for this mix variance—the difference in cost for the actual mix of professionals versus the standard mix for a defined set of shifts or effort. The monthly calculation of a mix variance for direct labor is not compatible with minimum staffing for quality care in health care entities.

Summary

Variance analysis provides an explanation of why actual and budgeted expenditures are different. The focus of variance analysis is much broader than the limited perspective of expenditure control by regular cost account under responsibility accounting. Departmental variance analysis uses the mapped regular cost accounts plus two new databases in seeking answers. The patient order-entry and result-reporting module and the computer-based operating statistics module provide insights into various aspects of departmental performance that are essential for proper variance analysis.

The actual-versus-budget data for individual items of expense from the mapped regular cost accounts are analyzed for price and efficiency. Aggregate expenditure data from the financial DBMS and budget data from various sources are mapped into three amounts:

1. Actual cost incurred
2. Flexible budget based on actual inputs at budget prices
3. Flexible budget based on standard inputs allowed for actual outputs achieved at budget prices

After the differences between these three amounts have been identified as price and efficiency variances by the computer-based reports, an analysis of the reasons for significant changes begins. At the department level, variance analysis should start with the individual items of expense before examining groups of items.

The budget-versus-actual expenditures per position code within a regular cost account are part of the responsibility-accounting reports; the departmental mapping of elements in regular cost accounts is by the GLCA structure. There are separate aggregations and analyses for each of the seven types of salaries and wages, for example, so that direct labor—regular does not have to be adjusted for vacation time, sick leave, and other special situations. Volume, activity, and service data are retrieved for the department from the patient order-entry and result-reporting module and the computer-based operational control packages. The dominant role of direct labor is recognized in these departmental application packages for measuring performance and scheduling personnel.

Patient acuity measures are used in matching patient needs with assignment of nursing personnel. Standard software packages have been available for several years that assist in nurse scheduling and patient care management. The outputs from these packages are integrated with transactions data from the financial DBMS and other databases to permit a four-way analysis of direct labor: (1) price variance, (2) nonacuity quantity variance, (3) acuity variance, and (4) volume variance. The items included in the nonacuity quantity variance depend on the payroll procedure for handling days worked versus days paid and nonproductive time. Vacations, holidays, sick time, in-service training, and other events must be appropriately coded and excluded from the acuity analysis. In a simple health care entity, an average can be calculated to represent a standard blending of tasks, but in a more complex health care entity, there is too much variation around these tasks. As the variation increases, the averages in these acuity reports may become meaningless.

Patient acuity should relate tasks mapped to nursing requirements. In-service training, coordination, and special projects are examples of items that should be separate data elements from patient acuity measures. The proper accumulation of acuity and nonacuity information can provide an excellent foundation for quality care and assessment.

Relative-value units provide an index for support departments so that a four-way analysis can be performed by data element where the quantity or efficiency variance is partitioned into those related to RVUs and all others. RVUs primarily capture the direct labor effort in a service, operation, procedure, test, or treatment; potential problems arise when RVU data are used in contexts that are unrelated to labor effort.

The fixed and variable partitioning of expenditures may be required in a support department for quality care and in an overhead department for employment agreements. If the fixed and variable components exist, variance analysis must be compatible with the situation. The type of analysis that can be performed depends on whether or not there is an intermediate product for the area. In an overhead and general support area without an intermediate product, some type of surrogate of service or work unit measure may be established for management control purposes. If there is an output measure, then a standard three-way analysis of price, efficiency, and volume can be performed.

Additional Readings

Burik, D., and D. L. Marcellino. "Successfully Implementing a Multihospital Cost System," *Healthcare Financial Management* 41 (January 1987): 50–54.

Finkler, S. A. "Flexible Budget Variance Analysis Extended to Patient Acuity and DRGs," *Health Care Management Review* 10 (Fall 1985): 21–34.

Helmi, M. A., and S. Burton. "Cost Control under the DRG System," *Hospital & Health Services Administration* 33 (Summer 1988): 263–69.

Discussion Questions

14.1.   What data sources are available for departmental analysis?

14.2.   Explain the input/output relationship between the departmental management control system and the financial DBMS.

14.3.   Explain how a patient acuity system for nurse scheduling is different from using an average length of stay for a diagnosis-related group multiplied by the number of patients in that category.

14.4.   The Ferdinand Health Clinic uses a flexible budgeting system and expects to have 6,400 visits in May 19X2. The monthly labor budget is $18,700 for 1,100 hours at $17.00 per hour, including fringe benefits. The actual was 7,360 visits with a cost of $22,500, based on an increase to $18.00 per hour for labor. Compute the price and efficiency variance for May 19X2.

14.5.   The Farwell Health Clinic uses a flexible budgeting system and expects to have 8,000 visits in June 19X2. The monthly labor budget is $24,000 for 1,500 hours at $16.00 per hour, including fringe benefits. The actual was 7,850 visits with a cost of $25,900, based on an increase to

$17.50 per hour for labor. Compute the price and efficiency variance for June 19X2.

14.6.   The Fargo Health Clinic separates variable-support cost from fixed-support cost and uses direct labor hours of nursing care as the basis for applying these expenditures. The total budget for July 19X2 is $81,000, based on 4,500 patient visits, consisting of $54,000 variable-support cost and $27,000 fixed-support cost. The July budget was based on 1,600 direct labor hours of nursing care.

There were 4,800 patient visits in July 19X2, with a total cost of $92,700. The fixed-support cost increased because of price changes from $27,000 to $28,000. The direct labor hours of nursing care was 1,700. The price of items in variable-support cost increased by 12.5 percent for the month of July.

A. Compute the spending, efficiency, and volume variances for variable- and fixed-support cost.

B. Prepare a three-way support cost analysis. *Hint:* Use Exhibit 14.8 as a guide.

14.7.   The nursing department at Jackson Memorial Hospital has a monthly budget of 1,600 patient days with average direct labor of $12.50 per hour and an average acuity level of 6.7 nursing hours per patient, for a total direct labor budget of $134,000, or 10,720 hours at $12.50. In response to competitive pressures, salaries were increased to $12.80 per hour as of the beginning of the month. The actual patient load was 1,500 patient days, and the average acuity level was 7.6 hours per patient day. The actual nursing cost was $147,456 (11,520 hours at $12.80 per hour). Determine the volume, acuity, nonacuity quantity, and price variances.

14.8.   The nursing department at Jasper Community Hospital has a monthly budget of 1,350 patient days with average direct labor of $12.75 per hour and an average acuity level of 6.8 nursing hours per patient, for a total direct labor budget of $117,045, or 9,180 hours at $12.75. In response to competitive pressures, salaries were increased to $13.00 per hour as of the beginning of the month. The actual patient load was 1,500 patient days, and the average acuity level was 7.8 hours per patient day. The actual nursing cost was $155,350 (11,950 hours at $13.00 per hour). Determine the volume, acuity, nonacuity quantity, and price variances.

14.9.   The nursing department at Johnson Memorial Hospital has a monthly budget of 1,400 patient days with average direct labor of $12.25 per hour and an average acuity level of 7.1 nursing hours per patient, for a total direct labor budget of $121,765, or 9,940 hours at $12.25. In response to competitive pressures, salaries were increased to $12.75 per hour as of the beginning of the month. The actual patient load was 1,350 patient days, and the average acuity level was 8.0 hours per patient day. The actual nursing cost was $140,250 (11,000 hours at $12.75 per hour). Determine the volume, acuity, nonacuity quantity, and price variances.

14.10. The pathology department at Joel Katz Memorial Hospital has a monthly budget of 79,000 tests, representing 1,009,500 relative-value units, and a direct labor budget of $109,920. This budget is separated into a fixed-labor budget of $60,000 for 40,000 tests with 600,000 RVUs and a variable-labor budget estimated at $49,920 for 2,600 hours at $19.20 per hour for the remaining tests. The relevant range for the monthly variable budget is from 55,001 to 84,000 tests, with the fixed and variable computations being performed in each of the 14 mapped regular cost accounts. But, for illustration purposes, assume the average of $1.28 per test and 10.50 RVUs represent the variable direct labor expense in the relevant range.

The actual for the month is 76,000 tests with 992,000 RVUs and total direct labor of $109,725. The variable-labor cost was $49,725, for 2,550 hours at $19.50 per hour. The direct fixed labor of $60,000 was incurred, but the minimum mix and distribution of tests did not occur; only 39,000 of the baseline tests, representing 585,000 RVUs, were performed. The variable tests were slightly more complex than expected, with an average of 11.00 RVUs and direct labor of $1.32324 per test. Determine the fixed and variable variances for the period.

14.11. The Walnut Grove Memorial Hospital's pathology department has a monthly budget of 80,000 tests, representing 960,000 relative-value units, and a direct labor budget of $105,000. This budget is separated into a fixed-labor budget of $45,000 for 30,000 tests with 435,000 RVUs and a variable-labor budget estimated at $60,000 for 3,200 hours at $18.75 per hour for the remaining tests. The relevant range for the monthly variable budget is from 60,001 to 89,000 tests, with the fixed and variable computations being performed in each of the 14 mapped regular cost accounts. But, for illustration purposes, assume the average of $1.20 per test and 10.50 RVUs represent the variable direct labor expense in the relevant range.

The actual for the month is 82,000 tests with 1,056,500 RVUs and total direct labor of $109,600. The variable-labor cost was $64,600, for 3,400 hours at $19.00 per hour. The direct fixed labor of $45,000 was incurred, but the minimum mix and distribution of tests did not occur; only 29,000 of the baseline tests, representing 420,500 RVUs, were performed. The variable tests were slightly more complex than expected, with an average of 12.00 RVUs. Determine the fixed and variable variances for the period.

Part III

Patient Utilization of Services and Management of Resources

15

Forecasting Health Services by Patients within a Health Care Facility

Introduction

Management of health services requires forecasting and analysis of the episodes of care from many perspectives and purposes. Individuals performing such studies typically have an institutionwide assignment rather than the limited role of a department's management control module or a pricing computation. Traditional studies for monitoring and planning purposes are patient origin and utilization studies, case-mix management studies, and comparisons of physician profiles with those of the medical department or specialty. Other studies are conducted for decision-making purposes, such as the impact of a proposed plant closing, the introduction of new services from medical technology, the departure of a significant medical group from the facility, and a change in the competitive environment.

Medical staffs are also interested in analysis of episodes of care; medical records departments have been responding to these needs for more than two decades in support of medical care evaluation studies. The Joint Commission on Accreditation of Healthcare Organizations (JCAHO) has required the medical records departments to prepare reports on patient episodes of care to meet the needs of the hospital and medical staffs.[1]

Many hospitals participate in a discharge abstracting service so that the medical records departments have summary data from similar facilities that can be used for comparison purposes. Some state hospital associations provide to their members a discharge abstract service;

there are several for-profit corporations that offer discharge abstracting services. The largest nonprofit facility offering abstracting services is the Commission on Professional and Hospital Activities (CPHA); its abstracting service is called Professional Activity Study (PAS). The PAS reports provide a set of comparison data for each category of information in which the health care facility has activities.

Under a fee-for-service arrangement, management of health services is interested in various dimensions of an episode of care. The patient origin and utilization studies focus on social, economic, and demographic characteristics within a region or zip code. The geographical location is the first point of reference that is related to utilization and financial data for that area. An assessment of the outreach for the geographical area is achieved by cross-referencing types of episodes of care and the admitting or referring physicians. Admission and registration information, combined with the utilization and financial logs, provides a large and diverse set of data elements that can be analyzed by various dimensions depending on the decision context directing the study.

Case-mix management studies use the final discharge diagnosis based on *The International Classification of Diseases, 9th Revision, Clinical Modification* (ICD-9-CM).[2] This code structure is explained in the appendix to this chapter. Similar studies are performed for outpatient episodes of care with the ICD-9-CM codes and codes from the *Physicians' Current Procedural Terminology*, fourth edition (CPT-4).[3] Some third party payors prefer the CPT-4 codes because they reflect current medical practice. As of 1987, Medicare has required CPT-4 codes for ambulatory surgery. The case-mix specification is cross-referenced to the physician or medical group providing the care, the financial class of the patient, and the zip code or region of the patient. Any revenue computations by case mix will include information on the financial class of patient so that contractual allowances and adjustments can be determined by the major case-mix codes.

Physician profiles by type of episode of care include selected utilization and financial data for patients treated by a given physician or medical group. Contractual allowances and adjustment by physician can be computed by type of episode of care and by patient origin. The economic impact of different treatment protocols for similar medical problems is determined as part of these analyses.

The framework used in forecasting and analyzing episodes of care is based on coding and classification systems that are understood and applied by the medical staff, nursing personnel, and administrative group. The Uniform Hospital Discharge Data (UHDD) Set provides a minimum set of data elements that must be retained for all inpatients in support of reimbursement; the Uniform Billing System in 1982 (UB82) serves as a standard data set for both inpatients and outpatients.[4] There are some optional fields in UB82, whose contents may vary from state to state, that are required in some states. But there are also defined segments in the UB82 that are uniform across states, including coding and classification entries that are based on the assessments of medical and professional staff.

Patient Origin and Utilization Studies

Patient origin and utilization studies often use UHDD or UB82 defined data elements in the performance of multidimensional comparisons. The unique patient identification number and patient medical record number permit the financial and billing records to be merged with patient admission/registration information, other patient utilization information, and patient abstract and profile data. The admitting physician and the attending physician are identified in these data elements. Some expanded data sets include the medical department designation of the admitting physician; otherwise, this information is available in hospital records. It is important to identify each admitting physician with the appropriate peer group for making comparative assessments.

A separate database is usually established within the computer-based information system that encompasses all identified data elements for each episode of care. Indexes and computational fields are added to a copy of the facility's DBMS in the research or planning database. The extracted episode data in the separate research database provide assurance of accuracy of patient information since the transactions are not inputted a second time. As the extracted data are merged in the research DBMS, standard computer programs create cross-reference indexes based on the extracted data, and these indexes and computational fields become part of the expanded research DBMS. Thus, the research database is an extraction from, and an extension to, the facility's computer-based information systems without having any negative impact on the DBMSs used in day-to-day operations. Certain types of patient origin and utilization studies can be easily performed with the cross-referenced and computational data elements in the research DBMS.

The patient's age, for example, is entered by a code that supports both years and days, as illustrated by Data Element 8 in Exhibit 15.1. But observe that Data Element 9 in Exhibit 15.1 contains twelve age groupings based on the prior data element. When the analysis of episodes of care focuses on pediatrics, the three age groups for under five years are very important; however, for most general types of episodes of care, patients under five can be collectively viewed as a single group. The length of stay is another example of a data element that is defined (Data Element 10 in Exhibit 15.1) and that has an index (Data Element 11).

Many of the data elements in Exhibit 15.1 are aggregations of the total ancillary charges by department for an episode of care. These financial data are based on the discharge statement of account, which must be prepared within five days from the departure or transfer of a patient. The flow of these financial data is from the health care facility's internal records, which show the detailed transactions for each requested service, test, and procedure for a patient. Within the hospital information systems, these transactions are usually captured in the patient order-entry and result-reporting module. After the medical and health care services are provided, then the detailed orders are interfaced with the patient-billing module.

This aggregate set of transaction data is indexed by type of medical and health service so as to permit summary charges for each ancillary department in the patient's final bill. The total ancillary charges by department in Exhibit 15.1 are based on this flow, index arrangement, and aggregation process. The disclosure requirements for the discharge statement of account include the listing of each and every service performed with identification information as to date, label for service, and price or charge. These detailed data for each transaction are similar to the old Medicare logs that were required as supporting documentation under the former reimbursement system, and as before, they are often removed from the active DBMS and retained on separate backup tapes to support requirements for rebilling.

Because of the quantity of data for each patient, the transfer of data to backup storage occurs after the management control reconciliations have been performed for the month. A 35-day hospital stay, for example, might result in a 40- to 50-page report containing the detailed listing of services provided to that patient. The next-to-the-last page of the detailed report contains three summary amounts for the three columns within the detailed listing, as follows:

	Total Amount	Insurance Portion	Patient Portion
Total charges	$xx,xxx.xx	$xx,xxx.xx	$x,xxx.xx
Deductibles and Coinsurance		−x,xxx.xx	x,xxx.xx
Grand total	*$xx,xxx.xx*	*$xx,xxx.xx*	*$x,xxx.xx*

Exhibit 15.1 Patient Origin and Utilization Studies: Data Elements
in Research Database

---

1. Admitting physician identification number
2. Attending physician identification number
3. Department/organizational unit of the attending physician
4. Patient identification number (serves to merge admission, financial, medical records, test ordering/result reporting, utilization, and discharge status data)
5. Discharge date
6. Birth date of patient
7. Admission date
8. Age code (5001 = 1 year, 5002 = 2 years, etc.; 4001 = 1 day, 4002 = 2 days, etc.)
9. Age group (12 age groupings)
   A. less than 6 months
   B. 6 months to 24 months
   C. 2 to 4 years
   D. 5 to 14
   E. 15 to 24
   F. 25 to 34
   G. 35 to 54
   H. 55 to 60
   I. 61 to 64
   J. 65 to 74
   K. 75 to 84
   L. 85 and over

10. Length of stay (LOS)
11. Length-of-stay groupings (11 LOS groups)
    A. 1 day
    B. 2–3 days
    C. 4–6 days
    D. 7–10 days
    E. 11–14 days
    F. 15–20 days
    G. 21–30 days
    H. 31–45 days
    I. 46–70 days
    J. 71–90 days
    K. 91 or more days

12. Admitting diagnosis (ICD-9-CM)
13. Principal diagnosis (ICD-9-CM)
14. Secondary diagnoses (six per ICD-9-CM)
15. Primary procedure codes (six per ICD-9-CM)
16. Major diagnostic category (MDC) per diagnosis related group (DRG) GROUPER

Continued

Exhibit 15.1   Continued

17. DRG per DRG GROUPER
18. List A group (per CPHA)
19. Expected financial class of patient (12 or more payors)

A. Medicare	J. Medicare and Blue Cross
B. Medicaid	K. workers' compensation
C. Blue Cross	L. general assistance
D. commercial insurance	M. medical disability
E. Blue Cross HMO	N. Medicaid assistance no
F. regional HMO	grant (MANG) pending
G. HMO—A	O. self-pay
H. HMO—B	P. other sources
I. Medicare and commercial insurance	

20. Zip code of patient's address
21. Religious preferences (significant for foundation reports)
22. Sex of patient
23. Type of admission

A. referred	E. transfer from nursing home
B. emergency	F. transfer from extended-care
C. elective surgery	facility
D. transfer from other hospital	. . .

24. Disposition status of patient

25. Total charges for episode of care
26. Total charges for room
27. Total charges for ancillary services
28. Total charges for ICU
29. Total charges for intermediate care
30. Total charges for rehabilitation care
31. Total charges for pediatrics care
32. Total charges for room (omits special care units)
33. Total charges for operating/delivery room
34. Total charges for emergency room
35. Total charges for laboratory
36. Total charges for radiology
37. Total charges for medical/surgical supplies
38. Total charges for pharmaceuticals
39. Total charges for inhalation therapy
40. Total charges for physical/occupational/speech therapy
41. Total charges for cardio-graphics
42. Total charges for blood administration
43. Total charges for other medical procedures
44. Total charges for unknown ancillary services

The last page of the financial statement of account prepared for the discharged patient has had a standard format for the past 20 years, illustrated by Exhibit 15.2, which aggregates the detailed data within the statement by category of room and ancillary charges. Data Elements 25 to 44 in Exhibit 15.1 are obtained directly from the last page of the financial statement of account represented by Exhibit 15.2.

Exhibit 15.2   Financial Statement of Account: Last Page of Detailed Report Prepared upon Discharge of Patient

Summary of Charges

Room charges	
ICU room (xx days @ $980.00, etc.)	$ xx,xxx.xx
Intermediate care ICU (xx days @ $430.00, etc.)	xx,xxx.xx
Rehabilitation care (xx days . . .)	xx,xxx.xx
. . .	
Total room charges	$ *xx,xxx.xx*
Ancillary charges	
Operating/delivery room	$ xxx.xx
Emergency room	xxx.xx
Laboratory	x,xxx.xx
Radiology	x,xxx.xx
Medical/surgical supplies	x,xxx.xx
Pharmaceuticals	x,xxx.xx
Inhalation therapy	x,xxx.xx
Physical/occupational/speech therapy	x,xxx.xx
Cardio-graphics	x,xxx.xx
Blood administration	xxx.xx
Other medical procedures	xxx.xx
Unknown (typically something that is not a standard item identified with a department)	xxx.xx
Total ancillary charges	$ *xx,xxx.xx*

*   *   *   [The three columns that follow really appear for each detail line and summary line of the report.]   *   *   *

	Total Amount	Insurance Portion	Patient Portion
Patient payments	$ x,xxx.xx		$ x,xxx.xx
Insurance payments	xx,xxx.xx	$ xx,xxx.xx	
Deductibles and Coinsurance		x,xxx.xx	x,xxx.xx
Grand total	$ *xx,xxx.xx*	$ *xx,xxx.xx*	$ *x,xxx.xx*

The separate research DBMS supporting the analysis of episodes of care contains all elements in Exhibits 15.1 and 15.2.

Some special cost findings by type of episode of care may utilize the detailed data on the backup tapes to obtain mix and distribution of services within an ancillary department. Laboratory charges, for example, can be aggregated by area, such as hematology, chemistry, microbiology, and pathology; there are tremendous differences in the contribution margins among these areas for many health care facilities that must be considered in an informed analysis.

Patient origin and utilization studies are prepared on a regular basis by a health care facility for both inpatients and outpatients. Many of the elements in Exhibit 15.1 focusing on inpatient stay are not included in an outpatient episode, and the references to ICD-9-CM are replaced with CPT-4 for ambulatory surgery and selective outpatient services. Otherwise, the research database is similar for both types of episodes of care. Standard cross-comparisons for inpatients focus on average length of stay (LOS) and average charges by third party payor.

Exhibit 15.3 illustrates the format of patient origin information by region and zip code for three years. Summary information for all regions is initially presented in Exhibit 15.3 (Report 1), followed by the same format of data for each of the regions and by the major zip codes within a given region. There are four standard sets of patient origin reports in the same format as Exhibit 15.3, listed in Exhibit 15.4.

The standard profiles for patient origin studies briefly described in Exhibit 15.4 are structured around the key role of the admitting physician as related to patients from regions and zip codes. Average length of stay (LOS) for all patients from a service area who are admitted by a given physician can be compared with those admitted by other physicians from the same area and for the same reason. A more refined sorting includes the third party payor or financial class of patient.

These standard profiles for patient origin studies permit insights into the behaviors of a given physician's patients from a service area versus the utilization and financial experience of all patients from a geographical location that received services from a given health care entity. Average LOS, total charges, ancillary charges, room and board, and average daily rate or visit rate (per clinic visit) are computed for each segment of patients. The order in which the data are sorted is important. For example, if the focus is on average LOS, then it is average LOS for all patients within a given discharge DRG that were admitted by a given physician, and which are further segmented by the

Exhibit 15.3   Report 1: Patient Origin Information by Region and Zip Code

	Year 1	Year 2	Year 3	Percent Change Year 1–2	Percent Change Year 2–3
Summary Information					
Total hospital discharges	xx,xxx	xx,xxx	xx,xxx	x.xxx	x.xxx
Total days of care	xx,xxx	xx,xxx	xx,xxx	x.xxx	x.xxx
Total hospital charges	xx,xxx	xx,xxx	xx,xxx	x.xxx	x.xxx
Total charges—room and board	xx,xxx	xx,xxx	xx,xxx	x.xxx	x.xxx
Total ancillary charges	xx,xxx	xx,xxx	xx,xxx	x.xxx	x.xxx
Average length of stay	x.xxx	x.xxx	x.xxx	x.xxx	x.xxx
Average daily census	xxx.xxx	xxx.xxx	xxx.xxx	x.xxx	x.xxx
Average charge per patient	$x,xxx	$x,xxx	$x,xxx	x.xxx	x.xxx
Average daily charge	$xxx	$x,xxx	$x,xxx	x.xxx	x.xxx
Region 1 Summary Information Metropolitan					
Total hospital discharges	xx,xxx	xx,xxx	xx,xxx	x.xxx	x.xxx
Total days of care	xx,xxx	xx,xxx	xx,xxx	x.xxx	x.xxx
Total hospital charges	xx,xxx	xx,xxx	xx,xxx	x.xxx	x.xxx
Total charges—room and board	xx,xxx	xx,xxx	xx,xxx	x.xxx	x.xxx
Total ancillary charges	xx,xxx	xx,xxx	xx,xxx	x.xxx	x.xxx
Average length of stay	x.xxx	x.xxx	x.xxx	x.xxx	x.xxx
Average daily census	xxx.xxx	xxx.xxx	xxx.xxx	x.xxx	x.xxx
Average charge per patient	$x,xxx	$x,xxx	$x,xxx	x.xxx	x.xxx
Average daily charge	$xxx	$x,xxx	$x,xxx	x.xxx	x.xxx

. . .

Region 2   West Suburban

. . .

Zip code 60091

. . .

Zip code 60093

. . .

Note: The panel of summary information for Region 1 is repeated for Region 2, Region 3, and so on. The same format of aggregate data is then presented for each major zip code within each region. Thus, there are three levels of aggregate information with the above format—grand total, summary by region, and summary by zip code.

Exhibit 15.4   Standard Profiles for Patient Origin Studies

Report 1:   Patient Origin Information by Region and Zip Code

The demonstration facility has nine regions with a total of 78 major zip codes. Each of the 78 zip codes is supported by a specific report in the format of Exhibit 15.3; thus, there are 88 reports in this format—the grand summary, the nine summaries for regions, and the segment data for 78 zip codes.

Report 2:   Patient Origin Information by Expected Payment Source

The nine regions and the 78 major zip codes are classified by the expected principal payment source based on Data Element 19 in Exhibit 15.1. This three-way sort and reporting of data is first by region, second by zip code, and third by expected payment source. The format for each is identical to the nine reporting categories for three years in Exhibit 15.3.

Report 3:   Patient Origin Information by Medical Department

The nine regions and the 78 major zip codes analyzed in Reports 1 and 2 are classified by the medical department identified with the admitting physician. The seven medical departments have the following distribution of 224 physicians:

Medicine	84
OB/GYN	32
Pediatrics	14
Physician medicine and rehabilitation	2
Psychiatry	8
Surgery and other	78
Neurology	6

This three-way sort and reporting of data is first by region, second by zip code, and third by medical department. The format for each is identical to the nine reporting categories for three years in Exhibit 15.3.

Report 4:   Patient Origin Information by Age and Sex

Data Element 9 within Exhibit 15.1 contained 12 age groupings, but these are combined into 8 age groupings for patient origin reports as follows:

0 to 4 years of age	35 to 54	75 to 84
5 to 14	55 to 64	Over 84
15 to 34	65 to 74	

This four-way sort and reporting of data is first by region, second by zip code, third by age groupings, and fourth by sex of patient. The contents of the report for each segment are the same as the format of Exhibit 15.3.

zip code or geographical unit and separated by financial class of the patient. If the focus is on average charges, then it is the average charges for all patients within a given discharge DRG that were admitted by a given physician, and which are further segmented by the zip code or geographical unit and separated by financial class of the patient.

The formats and contents of these four reports are representative of the standard outputs obtained from computer vendors of shared services for hospitals. There are many other reports prepared for patient origin and utilization studies, but they are typically integrated with case mix and physician profiles. Demographic information on patients is a significant factor in explaining variances in a given physician's practice for a DRG with the same financial class of patient. Patient origin data can also serve as a surrogate for "severity of illness" in certain types of pediatric cases, selective treatments in emergency rooms, and specific episodes handled by clinics. The "presenting condition" of the patient at the point of registration, unfortunately, can be highly related to patient origin data for selective types of episodes of care. These patient origin and utilization data are also used in marketing studies and strategic planning.

Case Mix and Physician Profiles

Physicians within the same medical department at a health care facility may have significantly different profiles of medical practice, including treatments, utilization of services, demographics of patients, financial class of patients, and disposition of patients. The dominant role of the physician in providing medical care influences the approach taken in many case-mix studies. Exhibit 15.5 presents 12 standard profiles of physicians and episodes of care. Each standard screen or profile follows the same format as the nine reporting categories in Exhibit 15.3.

A different approach is taken when the health care facility is assessing the impact of a possible change by a competitor or a third party payor. Otherwise, the primary focus is on a given physician and not upon the related medical department for that physician. Additional reports are prepared on an exception basis depending on the variations in patient data; Report 15, for example, may be partitioned by zip code in those regions with significant variations in aggregate input data.

Medical practice by a group of physicians treating patients with a given disease category and for a defined age and sex status often

Exhibit 15.5   Standard Profiles of Physicians and Episodes of Care

---

Report 5:   Medical Department by Expected Payment Source of Patients

The 224 physicians and seven medical departments cited in Report 3 of Exhibit 15.4 are classified by the expected principal payment source. The summary information in the format of Exhibit 15.3 appears first for medicine, followed by segment data for the financial classes of patients by Data Element 19 in Exhibit 15.1. The next summary information is for OB/GYN, followed by segment data for the financial classes of patients. The same process of a summary and segment data is repeated for the other five medical departments in the demonstration hospital.

Report 6:   Physician Data by Expected Payment Source of Patients

Each of the 224 physicians has a summary followed by segment data for the financial classes of patients. Physicians related to a medical department can be compared to the applicable set of outputs from Report 5.

Report 7:   Physician Data by Region and Zip Code

The information is similar to Report 3 but with a difference in the type of aggregation. This three-way sort and reporting of data is first by physician, second by region, and third by zip code.

*Report 8:   Physician Data by Region, Zip Code, and Expected Payment
            Source*

This four-way sort and reporting of data is first by physician, second by region, third by zip code, and fourth by expected payment source.

Report 9:   Physician Data by Age and Sex

This three-way sorting of data by physician, age, and sex of patient provides baseline information without regard to the episode of care that is useful in long-range planning.

*Report 10:   Case-Mix Information by Expected Payment Source and Medical
             Department*

This three-way sorting of data by DRG or group of CPT-4 codes, expected payment source, and medical department presents summaries that are compared with department data in Report 11.

*Report 11:   Case-Mix Information by Medical Department and Expected Payment
             Source*

This three-way sorting of data by DRG or group of CPT-4 codes, medical department, and expected payment source is compared with information in Report 10.

Continued

Exhibit 15.5   Continued

Report 12:   *Case-Mix Information by Physician, Expected Payment Source and Zip Code Region*

This is four-way sorting of data by DRG or CPT-4 codes, physician, expected payment source, and region based on patients' zip codes. These summaries provide insight into the variations in utilization of services by a given physician for the same type of episode of care.

Report 13:   *Case-Mix Information by Physician, Expected Payment Source, Region, and Zip Code*

This five-way sorting is performed on an exception basis where there are large statistical variations in the individual data elements for a region in Report 12.

Report 14:   *Case-Mix Information by Region and Expected Payment Source*

This three-way sorting of data by DRG or CPT-4 codes, region, and expected payment source provides summaries that can be assessed in terms of changes in medical practice for a region.

Report 15:   *Case-Mix Information by Expected Payment Source and Region*

Medical practice provided by a given facility in a region may be dependent on selected payment sources; Reports 14 and 15 support this type of review and assessment.

Report 16:   *Case-Mix Information by Expected Payment Source and Physician*

The impact of changes in third party payors on case-mix data by physician can be analyzed by the summaries provided in this report.

changes over a year, resulting in a shift in patient profile by DRG. In other cases, one or two physicians may be added to a group, and then the complete physician group may change some parts of the treatment pattern. The DRG classification is very sensitive to both the primary diagnosis by ICD-9-CM code and the procedure codes from ICD-9-CM (volume 3). Changing a surgical procedure code or adding another surgical procedure code can significantly alter the assigned DRG. If there are two dominant surgical procedure codes, then the order in which the DRG coordinator enters these codes into the DRG grouper can alter the resulting assigned DRG.

The DRG coordinator has a major continuing-education role in keeping physicians informed of the resulting DRG from variations in treatment patterns. The DRG coordinator must also work closely with the medical records department so that the final documentation on a discharged patient is compatible with the desired DRG. If there are social and economic changes in the population within the service area during a year, there may be major shifts in the DRGs. Unemployment resulting from closing of a plant or reduction of the work force may be associated with an increase in selected DRGs and with a decrease in others.

Opening of a medical office building or the entry of a competing hospital's clinic within an institution's service area may have dramatic effects on DRGs. If some of the admitting physicians are using the medical office building, there may be a shift in preliminary work occurring at the office building rather than at the hospital's clinic. Presurgical testing may be performed at the office building. Some simple disease entities may be completely handled at the office building. The standard profiles in Exhibit 15.5 support these types of alternative assessments.

Exhibit 15.6 presents information on four DRGs. For the first heart condition (DRG 132), there was an increase in the number of hospital discharges for each of the years while the average length of stay and the days of care decreased. Because of the decrease in the average length of stay, the average charge per patient actually decreased in Year 2 ($8,488 in Year 1 versus $8,372 in Year 2). There was a 51 percent increase in the average charge per patient between Year 2 and Year 3 ($8,372 in Year 2 versus $12,667 in Year 3). There was an 11 percent increase in the average daily charge between Year 1 and Year 2 ($613 in Year 1 versus $681 in Year 2), which moved in the opposite direction than the average charge per patient between Year 1 and Year 2.

The second heart condition (DRG 078) in Exhibit 15.6 constitutes a diagnostic category with a longer length of stay on average than that for the first heart condition. Because of some shifts in average length of stay for DRG 078 over the three years, the average charge per patient increased by 53.6 percent, while that for the previous heart condition (DRG 132) only increased 49.2 percent.

For the third heart condition (DRG 127), there was a significant reduction in the average length of stay (over 15 percent between Year 1 and Year 3) while the average daily charge was increasing by a faster rate. There was a 38.6 percent increase in the average daily charge between the three years ($495 in Year 1 versus $686 in Year 3).

For the fourth heart condition (DRG 122), there was a slower decrease in average length of stay over the three years but with a much higher average charge per patient. There was a 68 percent increase in the average charge per patient over the three years ($8,804 in Year 1 versus $14,795 in Year 3). Because the average length of stay per

Exhibit 15.6 Wilmette Community Hospital: Case-Mix Utilization Information

	Year 1	Year 2	Year 3	Percent Change Year 1–2	Percent Change Year 1–3
Heart Condition #1:					
DRG 132, MDC 05M, Atherosclerosis, Age ≥ 70 and/or CC					
Total hospital discharges	259	267	269	3.089	3.861
Total days of care	3,586	3,283	3,229	(8.450)	(9.955)
Total hospital charges	$2,198,371	$2,235,317	$3,407,492	1.681	55.001
Average length of stay	13.846	12.295	12.004	(11.193)	(13.303)
Average daily census	9.825	8.995	8.847	(8.450)	(9.955)
Average charge per patient	$8,487.92	$8,371.97	$12,667.26	(1.366)	49.239
Average daily charge	$613.04	$680.88	$1,055.28	11.065	72.138
Heart Condition #2:					
DRG 078, MDC 04M, Pulmonary Embolism					
Total hospital discharges	27	34	23	25.926	(14.815)
Total days of care	381	552	292	44.882	(23.360)
Total hospital charges	$197,084	$334,285	$257,914	69.615	30.865
Average length of stay	14.111	16.235	12.696	15.053	(10.031)
Average daily census	1.044	1.512	0.800	44.882	(23.360)
Average charge per patient	$7,299.41	$9,831.91	$11,213.65	34.695	53.624
Average daily charge	$517.28	$605.59	$883.27	17.072	70.752
Heart Condition #3:					
DRG 127, MDC 05M, Heart Failure and Shock					
Total hospital discharges	138	159	226	15.217	63.768
Total days of care	2,021	2,141	2,797	5.938	38.397
Total hospital charges	$1,000,772	$1,232,283	$1,919,398	23.133	91.792
Average length of stay	14.645	13.465	12.376	(8.054)	(15.492)
Average daily census	5.537	5.866	7.663	5.938	38.397
Average charge per patient	$7,251.97	$7,750.21	$8,492.91	6.870	17.112
Average daily charge	$495.19	$575.56	$686.23	16.232	38.581

Continued

Exhibit 15.6 Continued

	Year 1	Year 2	Year 3	Percent Change Year 1–2	Percent Change Year 1–3
Heart Condition #4:					
DRG 122, MDC 05M, Circulatory Disorders with AMI without Cardiovascular Complications Discharged Alive					
Total hospital discharges	96	81	83	(15.625)	(13.542)
Total days of care	1,386	1,170	1,060	(15.584)	(23.521)
Total hospital charges	$845,235	$984,471	$1,227,959	16.473	45.280
Average length of stay	14.438	14.444	12.771	0.048	(11.542)
Average daily census	3.797	3.205	2.904	(15.584)	(23.521)
Average charge per patient	$8,804.53	$12,153.96	$14,794.69	38.042	68.035
Average daily charge	$609.84	$841.43	$1,158.45	37.976	89.961

patient episode was decreased during this period, the average daily charge increased by a higher rate (89.96 percent over the three year period) than the 68 percent increase in average charge per patient.

Exhibits 15.7 and 15.8 examine two of these diagnostic categories from the perspective of principal payment source. Medicare patients typically have the longest length of stay, with the exception of medical disability patients. The average days of care for the fourth heart condition (DRG 122) in Exhibit 15.7 for Year 1 was 17.49 days for Medicare patients versus an average of 14.44 days for all patients. But look at Year 2 and Year 3, where commercial insurance patients under DRG 122 are staying in the hospital longer than Medicare patients. There is also an unusual movement with Blue Cross patients between Year 2 and Year 3 in the average charge per episode ($13,493 in Year 2 versus $10,880 in Year 3) and in the average length of stay (17.3 days in Year 2 versus 10.8 days in Year 3).

The patient episode data reflected for DRG 122 in Exhibit 15.7 are real data for a hospital. The unusual movements in these three years among the financial classes of patients demand further examination by physician practice. Alternatively, there could have been errors in recording of the diagnostic information. An examination by physician group (not shown) did indicate some unusual behavior that demanded the attention of Wilmette Community Hospital's administrative team.

Exhibit 15.7   Wilmette Community Hospital: Case-Mix Information by Expected Payment Source for Heart Condition #4 (DRG 122, MDC 05M, Circulatory Disorders with AMI without Cardiovascular Complications Discharged Alive)

	Year 1	*Year 2*	*Year 3*
Total patients	96	81	83
Total charges	$845,235	$984,471	$1,227,959
Average charges	$ 8,805	$ 12,154	$ 14,795
Total days of care	1,386	1,170	1,060
Average days of care	14.44	14.44	12.77
Medicare patients	43	31	37
Total charges	$449,778	$287,064	$ 591,737
Average charges	$ 10,460	$ 9,260	$ 15,993
Total days of care	752	327	489
Average days of care	17.49	10.55	13.22
Medicaid patients	12	8	10
Total charges	$ 70,010	$116,729	$ 148,388
Average charges	$ 5,834	$ 14,591	$ 14,839
Total days of care	96	160	126
Average days of care	8.00	20.00	12.60
Blue Cross	12	7	8
Total charges	$109,562	$ 94,452	$ 87,040
Average charges	$ 9,130	$ 13,493	$ 10,880
Total days of care	178	121	86
Average days of care	14.83	17.29	10.75
Commercial insurance	22	22	19
Total charges	$163,748	$312,389	$ 296,995
Average charges	$ 7,443	$ 14,200	$ 15,631
Total days of care	278	343	253
Average days of care	12.64	15.59	13.32
Medical disability	1	7	4
Total charges	$ 10,760	$ 83,351	$ 41,499
Average charges	$ 10,760	$ 11,907	$ 10,375
Total days of care	19	105	49
Average days of care	19.00	15.00	12.25
All others	6	6	5
Total charges	$ 41,377	$ 90,486	$ 62,300
Average charges	$ 6,896	$ 15,081	$ 12,460
Total days of care	63	114	57
Average days of care	10.50	19.00	11.40

Exhibit 15.8   Wilmette Community Hospital: Case-Mix Information
by Expected Payment Source for Heart Condition #1
(DRG 132, MDC 05M, Atherosclerosis, Age ≥ 70
and/or CC)

	Year 1	*Year 2*	*Year 3*
Total patients	259	267	269
Total charges	$2,198,371	$2,235,317	$3,407,492
Average charges	$ 8,488	$ 8,372	$ 12,667
Total days of care	3,586	2,283	3,229
Average days of care	13.85	12.30	12.00
Medicare patients	108	97	96
Total charges	$1,041,094	$ 909,086	$1,486,768
Average charges	$ 9,640	$ 9,372	$ 15,487
Total days of care	1,745	1,481	1,428
Average days of care	16.16	15.27	14.88
Medicaid patients	28	38	41
Total charges	$ 223,866	$ 298,267	$ 503,248
Average charges	$ 7,995	$ 7,849	$ 12,274
Total days of care	397	441	531
Average days of care	14.18	11.61	12.95
Blue Cross	31	27	45
Total charges	$ 267,562	$ 288,051	$ 495,562
Average charges	$ 8,631	$ 10,669	$ 11,012
Total days of care	374	360	420
Average days of care	12.06	13.33	9.33
Commercial insurance	55	71	51
Total charges	$ 371,964	$ 470,954	$ 493,126
Average charges	$ 6,763	$ 6,633	$ 9,669
Total days of care	573	612	436
Average days of care	10.42	8.62	8.55
Medical disability	10	18	16
Total charges	$ 53,908	$ 103,261	$ 218,950
Average charges	$ 5,391	$ 5,737	$ 13,684
Total days of care	106	176	209
Average days of care	10.60	9.78	13.06
All others	27	16	20
Total charges	$ 239,977	$ 165,698	$ 209,838
Average charges	$ 8,888	$ 10,356	$ 10,492
Total days of care	391	213	205
Average days of care	14.48	13.31	10.25

DRG 132 presents a typical distribution of average length of stay for Medicare patients over the three years (Exhibit 15.8). The average length of stay for Medicare patients over the three years (16.2, 15.3, and 14.9 days) was longer than for any other category. Some states' Medicaid programs are under such close scrutiny that the spread between Medicare and Medicaid patients may be larger than the 2–3 days reported for this hospital.

Compare the average length of stay in Year 3 for Medicaid patients with that for Blue Cross and commercial insurance. This distribution is the opposite of what is expected: Medicaid patients typically have a shorter length of stay than Blue Cross or commercial insurance patients. Further analysis of this diagnostic group is required by physician practice.

As previously stated, the charge and utilization data presented in Exhibits 15.6 through 15.8 suggested some unusual variations in medical practice depending upon the physician group. Further analysis supported that the medical record charting had been properly performed and that the abstract information was correct. The hospital administrative team implemented a new DRG information tracking system, which provided insights into unusual physician practices during the patient stay and shortly after discharge.

Other Considerations

The financial class of the patient is a very important factor in explaining variation in utilization of services for the same DRG. For example, children covered by Medicaid may stay in the hospital longer than usual for certain types of DRGs under the following circumstances:

1. They were sicker at the point of admission.
2. They have complications.
3. There is no adult in the home on a full-time basis to provide them with care during recovery.

The payment for Medicaid patients is administered by the state, with considerable variation among the states. Some hospitals will permit the child in Medicaid to stay in the hospital during the recovery period even when the state informs the hospital that there is no coverage for the continued stay. Adults in Medicaid tend to have a much shorter length of stay for a given DRG than that experienced by any other financial class of patients.

Medicare patients usually have a longer length of stay and incur more services and charges than any other financial class of patients within a given DRG. Age, complications, and status of patient on admission are factors that contribute to longer stay and higher cost for Medicare patients versus all other groups.

While adult Medicaid patients and Medicare patients represent the two ends of a continuum of the charges and length of stay for a given DRG, Blue Cross patients tend to be near the midpoint of this continuum. HMO patients are between the Medicaid and Blue Cross locations and the commercial insurance patients are between the Blue Cross and Medicare locations. Patients covered by contracts with corporations are similar to commercial insurance patients. Some of the Illinois HMOs are experiencing cost and charges that are similar to those incurred by commercial insurance patients and have not been able to reduce the length of stay of HMO patients by moving some services to outpatient clinics and physician offices.

A significant factor in explaining the variation in cost and length of stay for an episode of care is the age of the patient. Age is a more sensitive factor than suggested by Medicare's payment amounts. Patients that are 85 years of age and older incur more costs and have longer lengths of stay, on the average, than patients 75 to 84 years of age. For some DRGs, patients in the 61–64 age group may have higher average costs and longer lengths of stay than patients 65–70, and from a medical perspective the general physical condition of some 61–64 year olds may not be as good as that of older patients in the same DRG classification.

In the admission or registration of a patient, information is requested on the name and address of the patient's employer and, if applicable, the spouse's employer. The insurance coverage for many patients is through the employer; thus, this information is essential in pursuing reimbursement problems with a third party payor at a future point in time. Identification of employer's name has become of increasing importance in the past five years for accurately projecting health care services. Many employers have changed their insurance carrier, some have become self-insured, and others have created new arrangements for the delivery of health care services. The hospital financial information system contains employer information for the worker, spouse, and dependents (if applicable). The retrieval of employer information is essential for measuring the impact of a plant closing or the cancellation of an agreement with a major employer, or for knowing that the employer has shifted carriers and is now using an HMO that the hospital does not support.

Modular Framework for Decision Making

Planning and management control of health care facilities require patient origin and utilization studies, case mix analyses, and physician profiles. Although these standard reports are helpful in summarizing recent experiences, they are not easily linked as a model in estimating the overall outcomes from different courses of action. The population in each service area must be connected through demand modules to operations of the health care facility that are summarized in forecasted financial statements capturing the outcomes. The links between the demographics of the population in each service area and the forecasted financial statements must be modular to support different health care responses by professionals.

Forecasting health services may be part of a decision context in which management is considering the impact of changes in medical staff, implementation of medical technology, introduction of new competitive forces in the marketplace, shifts in demographic factors, closing of a plant, or restructuring of a facility. The framework of analysis must have a modular approach that accommodates structural changes while retaining the relevant historical experience of the health care facility. The flexibility within the following seven-step approach permits various scenarios for environmental conditions and delivery arrangements that can be compared economically with other proposed structures:

1. Projection of patient admissions and registrations by type of episode of care (DRG or outpatient group)

2. Estimation of the financial class of patients for each type of episode of care

3. Computation of average length of stay by financial class of patient for each type of episode of care

4. Multiplication of average length of stay by financial class of patient times the projected volume of health care episodes

5. Determination of fixed and variable costs by financial class of patient per type of episode of care

6. Projection of revenue by financial class of patient per type of episode of care

7. Matching of projected costs and revenues for the volume of patient episodes of care

Step 1: Projection of patient admissions and registration by type of episode of care (DRG or CPT-4 group)

The first step draws upon the historical experience by type of episode of care within the facility's special database. Known changes in staffing of physicians by medical area, expected developments in competitive conditions, and projected shifts in demographic factors are analyzed in the process of estimating patient admissions and outpatient registrations by type of episode of care.

Inpatient admissions are estimated by DRG, based on adjustments to the hospital's historical experience for known or expected changes and using the latest DRG classification system. Gamma Community Hospital's DRG experience for a portion of its cases is illustrated in Exhibit 15.9. Overall, Gamma is expected to have 13,780 admissions for the coming year. The projected admissions per DRG at Gamma Community Hospital are different in both rate and number from the prior-year experience because a competing outpatient clinic has recently been opened in the service area, and a 500-patient reduction is expected from this clinic.

The most recent discharge experience is given more emphasis than five-year moving averages so that the impact of technological developments and changes in medical practice are appropriately reflected in projected admissions. Gamma Community Hospital had to make adjustments in the data element in the research database specifying the DRG code for some discharges to accommodate major modifications by the federal government in the software for the GROUPER program used in classifying episodes of care. The estimated admissions for two DRGs in Exhibit 15.9 were further modified from the most recent annual experience to show an additional shift in medical practice that is being monitored by a physician group.

Episodes of care for outpatient surgery, ambulatory care services, therapy units, treatment centers, and other health services are estimated in a framework similar to that used for DRGs. The overall volume of outpatient services is estimated for the coming period with as much detail as permitted by the coding systems. The volume of outpatient services as calculated in Step 1 is separated from the classification of services by financial class of patient in Step 2. In forecasting health care services by patient data in a hospital, the term *services* is viewed in the context of the products of the hospital. Each product might be described as an episode of care provided to a patient in a defined diagnostic category.

Exhibit 15.9   Seven-Step Modular Framework for Gamma
Community Hospital: Steps 1 and 2A

		Step 1 Admissions		Step 2A Distribution of Cases			
Episode	*DRG Weight*	*Annual*	*Percent of Total*	*Payor 01*	*Payor 02*	*Payor 03*	*Payor 04*
MDC 01 DRG 014	1.2281	955	6.9303%	0.419	0.279	0.197	0.105
MDC 04 DRG 079	1.8426	403	2.9245	0.371	0.305	0.229	0.095
MDC 04 DRG 089	1.2034	976	7.0827	0.436	0.261	0.216	0.087
MDC 04 DRG 096	0.9739	612	4.4412	0.346	0.306	0.235	0.113
MDC 05 DRG 121	1.6279	658	4.7750	0.358	0.277	0.239	0.126
MDC 05 DRG 122	1.1281	517	3.7518	0.336	0.281	0.274	0.109
MDC 05 DRG 127	1.0195	1,554	11.2772	0.457	0.261	0.168	0.114
MDC 05 DRG 137	0.6315	143	1.0377	0.000	0.416	0.317	0.267
MDC 05 DRG 138	0.8631	710	5.1524	0.298	0.269	0.306	0.127
MDC 05 DRG 140	0.6417	1,089	7.9028	0.468	0.192	0.205	0.135
MDC 06 DRG 148	3.2524	514	3.7300	0.236	0.346	0.302	0.116
MDC 06 DRG 156	0.8382	71	0.5152	0.000	0.394	0.311	0.295
MDC 06 DRG 182	0.7404	803	5.8273	0.348	0.221	0.274	0.157
MDC 08 DRG 209	2.3650	647	4.6952	0.387	0.218	0.277	0.118
MDC 08 DRG 212	1.4611	221	1.6038	0.050	0.396	0.269	0.285
MDC 08 DRG 243	0.6522	383	2.7794	0.314	0.279	0.212	0.195
MDC 10 DRG 296	0.9366	546	3.9623	0.267	0.306	0.281	0.146
MDC 11 DRG 320	1.0250	425	3.0842	0.327	0.282	0.233	0.158
MDC 12 DRG 337	0.6607	317	2.3004	0.367	0.251	0.203	0.179
MDC 14 DRG 372	0.4530	543	3.9405	0.096	0.399	0.318	0.187
MDC 14 DRG 373	0.2988	941	6.8287	0.094	0.396	0.316	0.194
MDC 17 DRG 410	0.4903	394	2.8592	0.367	0.212	0.297	0.124
MDC 18 DRG 416	1.5380	312	2.2642	0.315	0.287	0.229	0.169
MDC 21 DRG 448	0.3470	46	0.3338	0.000	0.402	0.306	0.292
Total		*13,780*	*100.0000%*				

The outputs of Step 1 are total admissions and registrations by
type of episode of care. There are many different decision-making
purposes within health care administration that require aggregate data
by type of inpatient and outpatient episode. The focus in the first step
also facilitates the integration of shifts in demographic factors and
economic conditions into aggregate positions before considering the
financial class of patient.

Step 2: Estimation of the admissions by financial class of patients for each type of episode of care (DRG or CPT-4 group)

The stable distribution of patients by financial class is a thing of the past; in some competitive settings there may be dramatic shifts on an annual basis in the location where medical and health care services are provided for individuals covered by a given insurance carrier or HMO. New contracts between a health care facility and given third party payors may include volume provisions by type of episode of care. Thus, the historical experience of the past distribution of services by financial class of patient merely serves as a point of origin to which adjustments can be made for new contracts, arrangements, and environmental factors.

Gamma Community Hospital is an unusual facility with only four payors; the distribution of cases within a DRG is illustrated in Exhibit 15.9. Payor 01's patients represent 41.9 percent of the total episodes for DRG 014 (specific cerebrovascular disorders); Payor 02's patients, 27.9 percent; Payor 03's patients, 19.7 percent; and Payor 04's patients, 10.5 percent. The distribution for DRG 137 (cardiac congenital and valvular disorders, age 0 to 17) is significantly different: Payor 01, 0 percent; Payor 02, 41.6 percent; Payor 03, 31.7 percent; Payor 04, 26.7 percent. Exhibit 15.9 shows a wide mix and distribution of cases among the four third party payors.

The demographic, economic, and social factors identified with each third party payor will also affect the mix and distribution of cases by the financial class of patients. This variation will typically increase as the number of third party payors increases—to over 30 payor groups in the case of many community hospitals. Most of the decision-making activities within a health care institution require knowledge about the unique utilization experience by payor within a given DRG or outpatient grouping rather than a general weighted-average measure, as given at the bottom of Exhibit 15.10. The matrix in Exhibit 15.9 for the distribution of cases by payor permits adjustments by DRG for expected changes by third party payors in where services are performed.

The outputs of Step 2 are estimated admissions or registrations by payor for each type of episode of care. Gamma Community Hospital's 13,780 admissions in Exhibit 15.9 are distributed by type of episode and payor in Exhibit 15.10. The projected admissions by payor within a DRG in Exhibit 15.10 are used in forecasting revenues, expenses, and contribution margins. In examining the mix and distribution of cases

Exhibit 15.10   Seven-Step Modular Framework for Gamma Community Hospital: Steps 2B and 3

	Step 2B Admissions by Payor				Step 3 ALOS by Payor			
Episode	*Payor 01*	*Payor 02*	*Payor 03*	*Payor 04*	*Payor 01*	*Payor 02*	*Payor 03*	*Payor 04*
MDC 01 DRG 014	400.1	266.4	188.1	100.2	7.4	7.7	7.3	7.1
MDC 04 DRG 079	149.5	122.9	92.3	38.3	9.3	9.6	9.4	9.2
MDC 04 DRG 089	425.5	254.7	210.8	84.9	7.2	7.5	7.3	6.9
MDC 04 DRG 096	211.8	187.3	143.8	69.2	6.0	6.4	5.9	5.7
MDC 05 DRG 121	235.5	182.2	157.5	82.9	8.6	8.9	8.7	8.2
MDC 05 DRG 122	173.7	145.3	141.7	56.4	6.2	6.4	6.1	5.9
MDC 05 DRG 127	710.2	405.6	261.1	177.2	6.2	7.1	6.9	6.5
MDC 05 DRG 137	0.0	59.5	45.3	38.2	3.3	3.2	3.3	3.1
MDC 05 DRG 138	211.6	191.0	217.3	90.2	4.8	5.1	4.9	4.7
MDC 05 DRG 140	509.7	209.1	223.2	147.0	3.9	4.1	3.8	3.7
MDC 06 DRG 148	121.3	177.8	155.2	59.6	14.2	14.3	13.6	13.4
MDC 06 DRG 156	0.0	28.0	22.1	20.9	6.0	5.9	6.1	5.8
MDC 06 DRG 182	279.4	177.5	220.0	126.1	4.9	5.1	5.2	4.8
MDC 08 DRG 209	250.4	141.0	179.2	76.3	11.3	11.1	10.9	10.7
MDC 08 DRG 212	11.1	87.5	59.4	63.0	11.1	11.2	10.8	10.6
MDC 08 DRG 243	120.3	106.9	81.2	74.7	5.0	4.9	4.7	4.5
MDC 10 DRG 296	145.8	167.1	153.4	79.7	6.1	6.3	5.9	5.7
MDC 11 DRG 320	139.0	119.9	99.0	67.2	6.9	6.8	6.7	6.3
MDC 12 DRG 337	116.3	79.6	64.4	56.7	4.2	4.3	4.1	3.9
MDC 14 DRG 372	90.3	375.5	299.2	176.0	3.1	3.2	3.4	2.9
MDC 14 DRG 373	51.0	215.0	171.6	105.3	2.2	2.3	2.1	2.2
MDC 17 DRG 410	144.6	83.5	117.0	48.9	2.6	2.7	2.5	2.4
MDC 18 DRG 416	98.3	89.5	71.4	52.7	7.4	7.3	7.2	6.9
MDC 21 DRG 448	0.0	18.5	14.1	13.4	2.9	2.8	2.7	2.6
Total admissions	*4,595.4*	*3,891.3*	*3,388.3*	*1,905.0*				
Percent	33.4%	28.2%	24.6%	13.8%				

by payor, it should be noted that Medicare is designated at Gamma Community Hospital as Payor 01, which had a range from 0 to 46.8 percent of the cases in Exhibit 15.9. The three DRGs where Payor 01 has a zero volume are for special diseases where the patient is under age 18. But observe in Exhibit 15.10 with DRGs 372 and 373 for normal deliveries that there are 141 estimated Medicare admissions for the coming period. Congress has modified Medicare so that many special groups also are part of this coverage; the 9.5 million Medicare discharges each year contain some episodes in all active DRGs.[5]

Step 3: Computation of average length of stay by financial class of patient for each type of episode of care (DRG)

The average length of stay (ALOS) for each financial class of patient per DRG is subject to change for the projected period because of shifts in medical practice and medical technology. Commercial insurance companies and corporations are also having an impact on ALOS with financial incentives for medical services performed in an outpatient or clinic location. The initial diagnostic testing may be performed in physician offices, and any subsequent therapy may occur at an ambulatory care facility. These changes with third party payors are coordinated with their annual contracts, resulting in two types of behavior in ALOS for the hospital's fiscal year. The ALOS within a DRG is also influenced by demographic, social, and economic factors, and different third party payors provide coverage for patients with various combinations of these factors.

Exhibit 15.10 presents the ALOS by payor for each of Gamma Community Hospital's 24 DRGs. The standard Report 12 in Exhibit 15.5 showing case-mix information by physician, expected payment source, and zip code region will often provide insights into ALOS regarding demographic, social, and economic factors. The ALOS for a DRG across payor groups may be very similar within a certain zip code; thus, the aggregate differences in the rate may be directly related to where the patients live with coverage by a given third party payor.

Selected comparisons of ALOS per DRG by financial class of patient within the last year may suggest a "new arrangement" between physicians and a third party payor. Major differences in ALOS among third party payors may be temporary and directly related to renewal dates of plans. Consequently, the ALOS per DRG in a given health care facility for the coming year may be unrelated to the prior year's experience for the same third party payor.

This third step in the framework permits adjustments in the ALOS matrix in Exhibit 15.10 for known or expected changes by financial class of patient per DRG. The prior year's experience is only an input that must be further analyzed and reviewed in the context of all conditions. Failure to properly study these experiences can lead to unrealistic ALOSs with devastating financial impacts on a hospital.

Step 4: Multiplication of average length of stay by financial class of patient times the projected volume of health care episodes (DRGs)

The ALOS for each financial class of patient per DRG is multiplied by the applicable estimated volume, giving projected patient days of care. Exhibit 15.10 contains the admissions by payor and the ALOS by payor; columns in these two matrices are multiplied, producing total patient days in Exhibit 15.11. The amounts shown for admissions have been rounded in Exhibit 15.10, but the results in Exhibit 15.11 are based on the raw data. For example, the 2,961.1 days for Payor 01 in DRG 014 in Exhibit 15.11 is the result of multiplying the raw data for admissions and ALOS, not the rounded data of 400.1 admissions and 7.4 ALOS in Exhibit 15.10.

The 86,736 total patient days in Exhibit 15.11 are used in budgeting, staffing, planning, and other decision-making activities. The weighted-average ALOSs by payor are helpful in some types of alternative assessments where complete projections are not justified from a cost-benefit perspective.

Step 5: Determination of fixed and variable costs by financial class of patient per type of episode of care

The concept of different costs for various decision-making purposes is certainly applicable to Step 5. The focus is on general measures of effort based on the research database for a given DRG or type of outpatient episode. A more detailed examination is performed in Chapter 16, with the measurement by treatment modality per payor within a DRG.

If medical protocols exist for each major type of episode of care, then the cost data for these services can be extended by financial class of patient within the forecasting model. Where such protocols are not available, average data by financial class of patient can be computed from the backup tapes for the financial statement of account for discharged inpatients and the financial logs for outpatients.

These data sources permit partitioning of fixed costs by area into three categories:

1. Assigned cost based on admission or registration

2. Assigned cost based on length of stay or service time

3. Assigned cost based on total direct charges or services incurred

Exhibit 15.11   Seven-Step Modular Framework for Gamma
Community Hospital: Step 4

| | Step 4 | | | | |
Episode	Total Patient Days Payor 01	Total Patient Days Payor 02	Total Patient Days Payor 03	Total Patient Days Payor 04	Total Days
MDC 01 DRG 014	2,961.1	2,051.6	1,373.4	712.0	7,098.0
MDC 04 DRG 079	1,390.5	1,180.0	867.4	352.2	3,790.2
MDC 04 DRG 089	3,063.9	1,910.5	1,539.0	585.9	7,099.2
MDC 04 DRG 096	1,270.5	1,198.5	848.5	394.2	3,711.8
MDC 05 DRG 121	2,025.9	1,622.2	1,368.2	679.8	5,696.0
MDC 05 DRG 122	1,077.0	929.8	864.1	332.5	3,203.4
MDC 05 DRG 127	4,403.1	2,879.7	1,801.4	1,151.5	10,235.7
MDC 05 DRG 137	0.0	190.4	149.6	118.4	458.3
MDC 05 DRG 138	1,015.6	974.0	1,064.6	423.8	3,478.0
MDC 05 DRG 140	1,987.6	857.3	848.3	544.0	4,237.2
MDC 06 DRG 148	1,722.5	2,543.2	2,111.1	799.0	7,175.7
MDC 06 DRG 156	0.0	165.0	134.7	121.5	421.2
MDC 06 DRG 182	1,369.3	905.1	1,144.1	605.1	4,023.6
MDC 08 DRG 209	2,829.4	1,565.6	1,953.5	816.9	7,165.4
MDC 08 DRG 212	122.7	980.2	642.0	667.6	2,412.5
MDC 08 DRG 243	601.3	523.6	381.6	336.1	1,842.6
MDC 10 DRG 296	889.3	1,052.6	905.2	454.4	3,301.4
MDC 11 DRG 320	958.9	815.0	663.5	423.0	2,860.4
MDC 12 DRG 337	488.6	342.1	263.8	221.3	1,315.9
MDC 14 DRG 372	161.6	693.3	587.1	294.5	1,736.5
MDC 14 DRG 373	194.6	857.1	624.4	401.6	2,077.7
MDC 17 DRG 410	376.0	225.5	292.5	117.3	1,011.3
MDC 18 DRG 416	727.3	653.7	514.4	363.8	2,259.2
MDC 21 DRG 448	0.0	51.8	38.0	34.9	124.7
Total days	*29,636.5*	*25,167.7*	*20,980.7*	*10,951.2*	*86,736.1*
ALOS	*6.45*	*6.47*	*6.19*	*5.74*	*6.29*

Variable costs by area are directly determined from the responsibility-
accounting data and the dedicated cost center assignments. Annual
operating statistics and financial data by the major cost areas permit
calculation of average cost per procedure, test, service, or activity.

There are two phases to Step 5: First, the average variable cost and
the three assignments of fixed costs are determined for each major cost

area. Second, the relevant mix of services by area within a department must be determined for a given episode of care identified by financial class of patient. Here the differences are recognized between third party payors as to services performed at a hospital versus a physician office or clinic.

Direct cost of services provided in each ancillary department must be associated with the patient episodes supported by that department. The patient episodes are expressed in terms of DRGs. A sample of the treatment patterns for *each* DRG can be used in developing an overall budget level of ancillary procedures and activities for the hospital. Average direct cost for these ancillary departments can then be related to the estimated volume of procedures and activities. After this determination, the direct cost of selected procedures can then be mapped to the treatment profile for a given DRG.

As an example, assume the financial class of accounts shows an average laboratory charge of $975 for a given DRG per discharge statements. The two phases within Step 5 focus on the hematology, chemistry, cytology, microbiology, and pathology services within the laboratory. The average variable cost and the three assignments of fixed costs for each of these areas are the point of concentration for these computations. Within a given DRG, the hematology and chemistry services for a given commercial insurance carrier may be less than those for the average Medicare patient because of the location (office or clinic) where such services are performed.

The cost-measurement process in Step 5 is illustrated by the average cost data in Exhibit 15.12 for Gamma Community Hospital's 24 DRGs by payor. The average cost data with these four payors do not contain any shifts in the mix of services according to the second phase of Step 5. The average cost by payor per DRG is based on (1) a constant direct cost per DRG, (2) a variable direct cost component driven by ALOS, and (3) a fixed-cost allocation based on the aggregate direct cost. The sixth column in Exhibit 15.12 shows the constant direct cost per DRG. The variable cost per episode is $200 per day of care, and the ALOS in Exhibit 15.10 is used for computing the average cost by payor per DRG. The support and overhead costs are based on increasing the combined direct cost by 55 percent. Thus, the formula followed in Exhibit 15.12 is

DRG Cost by Payor = {[(ALOS × 200) + Direct cost] × 1.55}

To illustrate the formula, DRG 014 in Exhibit 15.10 shows an ALOS of 7.4, 7.7, 7.3, and 7.1, respectively, for the four payors. The average costs of \$4,154, \$4,247, \$4,123, and \$4,061 are computed as follows for the four payors.

DRG 014 Payor 01 $= \{[(\text{ALOS} \times 200) + \text{Direct cost}] \times 1.55\}$
$\qquad\qquad\qquad = \{[(7.4 \times 200) + \$1,200] \times 1.55\}$
$\qquad\qquad\qquad = [(\$1,480 + \$1,200) \times 1.55]$
$\qquad\qquad\qquad = \$2,680 \times 1.55$
$\qquad\qquad\qquad = \$4,154.00$

DRG 014 Payor 02 $= \{[(7.7 \times 200) + \$1,200] \times 1.55\}$
$\qquad\qquad\qquad = [(\$1,540 + \$1,200) \times 1.55]$
$\qquad\qquad\qquad = \$2,740 \times 1.55$
$\qquad\qquad\qquad = \$4,247.00$

DRG 014 Payor 03 $= \{[(7.3 \times 200) + \$1,200] \times 1.55\}$
$\qquad\qquad\qquad = [(\$1,460 + \$1,200) \times 1.55]$
$\qquad\qquad\qquad = \$2,660 \times 1.55$
$\qquad\qquad\qquad = \$4,123.00$

DRG 014 Payor 04 $= \{[(7.1 \times 200) + \$1,200] \times 1.55\}$
$\qquad\qquad\qquad = [(\$1,420 + \$1,200) \times 1.55]$
$\qquad\qquad\qquad = \$2,620 \times 1.55$
$\qquad\qquad\qquad = \$4,061.00$

Step 6: Projection of revenue by financial class of patient per type of episode of care

The data sources used in Step 5 are also required in Step 6 for estimating patient charges. Revenues by area are determined with an adjustment for contractual allowances by financial class of patient. The deductible portion of a patient bill for most insurance plans creates the possibility of an uncollectible account for a patient with commercial insurance coverage.

Exhibit 15.13 shows the average charges by payor per DRG at Gamma Community Hospital. Payor 01 in Exhibit 15.13 represents Medicare, and the average charges for this payor are based on the DRG weights in Exhibit 15.9 multiplied by the factor of 3,808.56 for Gamma Community Hospital. Thus, the average charge for DRG 014 Payor 01 is the weight of 1.2281 multiplied by the factor 3,808.56 ($1.2281 \times 3,808.56 = \$4,677.29$). The admissions by payor per DRG in Exhibit 15.10 multiplied by the average charges by payor per DRG in Exhibit 15.13 and aggregated for all payors equals the last column in Exhibit 15.13. The summation of these total revenues per DRG is \$58,544,984.79 for the period.

Exhibit 15.12 Seven-Step Modular Framework for Gamma
Community Hospital: Steps 5 and 7

	Step 5 *Average Cost by Payor*				Direct	Step 7
Episode	*Payor 01*	*Payor 02*	*Payor 03*	*Payor 04*	*DRG Cost*	*Total Cost*
MDC 01 DRG 014	$ 4,154	$ 4,247	$ 4,123	$ 4,061	$ 1,200	$ 3,976,691.63
MDC 04 DRG 079	5,828	5,921	5,859	5,797	1,900	2,361,789.16
MDC 04 DRG 089	4,092	4,185	4,123	3,999	1,200	4,016,120.93
MDC 04 DRG 096	3,410	3,534	3,379	3,317	1,000	2,099,251.80
MDC 05 DRG 121	5,456	5,549	5,487	5,332	1,800	3,601,593.27
MDC 05 DRG 122	3,937	3,999	3,906	3,844	1,300	2,034,803.95
MDC 05 DRG 127	3,472	3,751	3,689	3,565	1,000	5,581,776.86
MDC 05 DRG 137	2,108	2,077	2,108	2,046	700	297,232.65
MDC 05 DRG 138	2,883	2,976	2,914	2,852	900	2,068,631.86
MDC 05 DRG 140	2,216	2,278	2,185	2,154	650	2,410,696.43
MDC 06 DRG 148	11,764	11,795	11,578	11,516	4,750	6,008,807.00
MDC 06 DRG 156	2,790	2,759	2,821	2,728	600	196,608.73
MDC 06 DRG 182	2,604	2,666	2,697	2,573	700	2,118,568.55
MDC 08 DRG 209	8,463	8,401	8,339	8,277	3,200	5,430,392.64
MDC 08 DRG 212	5,146	5,177	5,053	4,991	1,100	1,124,687.56
MDC 08 DRG 243	2,247	2,216	2,154	2,092	450	838,352.53
MDC 10 DRG 296	3,286	3,348	3,224	3,162	900	1,785,117.52
MDC 11 DRG 320	3,534	3,503	3,472	3,348	900	1,479,605.20
MDC 12 DRG 337	2,232	2,263	2,201	2,139	600	702,738.60
MDC 14 DRG 372	1,581	1,612	1,674	1,519	400	874,962.51
MDC 14 DRG 373	992	1,023	961	992	200	935,805.68
MDC 17 DRG 410	1,503	1,534	1,472	1,441	450	588,311.74
MDC 18 DRG 416	5,239	5,208	5,177	5,084	1,900	1,619,189.52
MDC 21 DRG 448	1,209	1,178	1,147	1,116	200	52,918.86
Total						$52,204,655.15

Step 7: Matching of projected costs and revenues
for the volume of patient episodes of care

The fifth and sixth steps estimate net revenues and costs per episode of
care by financial class of patient. In Step 7 these per-episode measures
are multiplied by the relevant volume in computing the overall income
and operating expenses for the period. The total admissions by payor
per DRG in Exhibit 15.10 are multiplied by the average costs by payor
per DRG in Exhibit 15.12, resulting in the data in the last column of

Exhibit 15.13 Seven-Step Modular Framework for Gamma Community Hospital: Step 6

Episode	Step 6A				Step 6B
	Average Charges Payor 01	Average Charges Payor 02	Average Charges Payor 03	Average Charges Payor 04	Total Revenue
MDC 01 DRG 014	$ 4,677.29*	$ 4,974.86	$ 4,762.87	$ 4,371.77	$ 4,531,562.56
MDC 04 DRG 079	7,017.65	7,514.15	7,169.06	6,459.26	2,881,735.46
MDC 04 DRG 089	4,583.22	4,872.79	4,678.63	4,273.84	4,540,830.50
MDC 04 DRG 096	3,709.16	3,954.43	3,784.47	3,466.87	2,310,013.40
MDC 05 DRG 121	6,199.95	6,626.95	6,312.44	5,784.97	4,140,679.92
MDC 05 DRG 122	4,296.44	4,561.64	4,385.24	4,025.79	2,257,114.23
MDC 05 DRG 127	3,882.83	4,121.87	3,972.13	3,639.21	6,111,025.99
MDC 05 DRG 137	2,405.11	2,559.54	2,456.42	2,248.01	349,445.16
MDC 05 DRG 138	3,287.17	3,466.58	3,352.77	3,082.45	2,363,948.87
MDC 05 DRG 140	2,443.95	2,561.69	2,498.16	2,304.21	2,677,637.81

MDC 06 DRG 148	12,386.96	13,239.85	12,671.86	11,577.84	6,514,560.30
MDC 06 DRG 156	3,192.33	3,460.68	3,265.76	2,998.38	231,721.38
MDC 06 DRG 182	2,819.86	3,025.54	2,874.71	2,655.44	2,292,187.78
MDC 08 DRG 209	9,007.24	9,772.86	9,184.41	8,418.89	5,922,505.98
MDC 08 DRG 212	5,564.69	6,007.03	5,672.67	5,216.21	1,252,978.61
MDC 08 DRG 243	2,483.94	2,695.08	2,531.07	2,311.67	964,871.59
MDC 10 DRG 296	3,567.10	3,860.07	3,649.14	3,334.09	1,990,597.30
MDC 11 DRG 320	3,903.77	4,185.94	3,973.56	3,648.78	1,682,708.70
MDC 12 DRG 337	2,516.32	2,695.37	2,564.19	2,341.93	805,104.98
MDC 14 DRG 372	1,725.28	1,870.29	1,744.96	1,602.58	959,183.62
MDC 14 DRG 373	1,138.00	1,234.56	1,164.17	1,053.66	1,099,224.93
MDC 17 DRG 410	1,867.34	1,996.06	1,903.28	1,745.36	744,729.86
MDC 18 DRG 416	5,857.57	6,345.56	5,972.29	5,464.95	1,858,752.86
MDC 21 DRG 448	1,321.57	1,433.91	1,341.97	1,225.25	61,862.99
Total					$58,544,984.79

*The DRG weights in Exhibit 15.9 with the factor of 3,808.56 are the basis for computing the Medicare charges per case represented by Payor 01. Thus, DRG 014 with a weight of 1.2281 multiplied by 3,808.56 equals $4,677.29 for Payor 01.

Exhibit 15.12, with a total cost of $52,204,655.15. This same set of admission data in Exhibit 15.10 multiplied by average charge information in Exhibit 15.13 created the total revenue column in Exhibit 15.13, with an aggregate revenue of $58,544,984.79. Thus, Gamma Community Hospital's projected return is $6,340,329.64, which represents 10.8 percent of revenues.

This seventh step is repeated for various scenarios so that the financial impact of alternatives can be quantified and compared with other courses of action. As the projected income and operating expenses are computed for different strategies, the magnitude of the changes in the health care industry by the introduction of PPS can be seen.

A Cost-Finding Example with Differences in Mix of Services

Exhibit 15.14 contains the charge and cost data for DRG XXA with financial class R and financial class S; there is a six-day ALOS for class R and a five-day ALOS for class S. These data show a $1,085 difference in charges ($6,565 versus $5,480) and a $705 difference in cost ($4,945 versus $4,240) for DRG XXA between these two financial classes of patients. The contribution margins are $1,620 for financial class R and $1,240 for financial class S—thus a $380 advantage for the extra day of stay.

Ancillary services are affected by ALOS. A physician's request for a second battery of tests or procedures is not initiated until after the results are known from the previous order. Therapy services may be scheduled so that there is a time interval for the patient's body to respond to the previous service before giving the next application. A reduction in LOS may mean that certain final tests, procedures, therapy services, and activities are performed on an outpatient or clinic basis rather than during the inpatient stay. Thus, a third party payor that is encouraging a shorter LOS will shift ancillary services from the inpatient stay to an ambulatory care, physician office, or clinic location.

Financial class S's profile for a five-day LOS for DRG XXA may not be compatible with the response for financial class R's patients when there is a one-day reduction in LOS. Exhibit 15.15 compares the six-day LOS with a five-day LOS for financial class R and reports a $50 higher contribution margin for this five-day stay than in Exhibit 15.14 for financial class S patients. Two hematology tests, two chemistry tests, one radiology procedure, two respiratory therapy activities, and

Exhibit 15.14   Projecting Revenue and Cost for DRG XXA by
Financial Class

	Financial Class R		*Financial Class S*	
Room	6 days @ $520	$3,120	5 days @ $520	$2,600
Operating room	2 hours @ $450	900	2 hours @ $450	900
Recovery room	1 hour @ $100	100	1 hour @ $100	100
Laboratory:				
Hematology	9 tests @ $25	225	5 tests @ $25	125
Chemistry	8 tests @ $35	280	5 tests @ $35	175
Pathology	6 tests @ $45	270	6 tests @ $45	270
Microbiology	4 tests @ $50	200	4 tests @ $50	200
Radiology	6 units @ $50	300	5 units @ $50	250
Respiratory therapy	9 services @ $80	720	7 services @ $80	560
Physical therapy	6 services @ $75	450	4 services @ $75	300
Total charges		*$6,565*		*$5,480*

Cost finding:

Admission and				
medical records	1 admit @ $120	$ 120	1 admit @ $120	$ 120
Nursing care	6 days @ $140	840	5 days @ $140	700
Room and board	6 days @ $200	1,200	5 days @ $200	1,000
Financial services	1 admit @ $100	100	1 admit @ $100	100
Operating room	2 hours @ $420	840	2 hours @ $420	840
Recovery room	1 hour @ $95	95	1 hour @ $95	95
Laboratory:				
Hematology	9 tests @ $10	90	5 tests @ $10	50
Chemistry	8 tests @ $15	120	5 tests @ $15	75
Pathology	6 tests @ $35	210	6 tests @ $35	210
Microbiology	4 tests @ $40	160	4 tests @ $40	160
Radiology	6 units @ $40	240	5 units @ $40	200
Respiratory therapy	9 services @ $70	630	7 services @ $70	490
Physical therapy	6 services @ $50	300	4 services @ $50	200
Total cost		*$4,945*		*$4,240*

Recap:

Total charges		$6,565	$5,480
Total cost		4,945	4,240
Contribution		*$1,620*	*$1,240*

Budgeting:

ALOS		6 days		5 days
Revenue per				
protocol		$6,565		$5,480
Cost per episode		$2,905		$2,540
Cost per day	6 days @ $340	2,040	5 days @ $340	1,700

Continued

Exhibit 15.14   Continued

	Financial Class R	Financial Class S	Variance
Total charges	$6,565	$5,480	$1,085
Total cost	4,945	4,240	705
Contribution	$1,620	$1,240	$ 380
Ancillary charges:			
Laboratory	$ 975	$ 770	$ 205
Radiology	300	250	50
Respiratory therapy	720	560	160
Physical therapy	450	300	150
Total	$2,445	$1,880	$ 565
Ancillary cost:			
Laboratory	$ 580	$ 495	$ 85
Radiology	240	200	40
Respiratory therapy	630	490	140
Physical therapy	300	200	100
Total	$1,750	$1,385	$ 365
Return from ancillary	$ 695	$ 495	$ 200
Constant charges:			
Operating room	$ 900	$ 900	$ 0
Recovery room	100	100	0
Total	$1,000	$1,000	$ 0
Related cost:			
Operating room	$ 840	$ 840	$ 0
Recovery room	95	95	0
Total	$ 935	$ 935	$ 0
Return from operating	$ 65	$ 65	$ 0
Room charges	$3,120	$2,600	$ 520
Related cost:			
Admission and medical records	$ 120	$ 120	$ 0
Nursing care	840	700	140
Room and board	1,200	1,000	200
Financial services	100	100	0
Total	$2,260	$1,920	$ 340
Return from room	$ 860	$ 680	$ 180

Continued

Exhibit 15.14   Continued

	Financial Class R	Financial Class S	Variance
Contribution margins:			
Ancillary services	$ 695	$ 495	$ 200
Operating and recovery	65	65	0
Room	860	680	180
Total	$1,620	$1,240	$ 380

two physical therapy services are not performed on an inpatient basis for the five-day LOS in Exhibit 15.15 that were accomplished during the six-day LOS in Exhibit 15.14. The set of ancillary services for the five-day LOS in Exhibit 15.15 made a contribution margin of $545 (charges of $1,965 less cost of $1,420).

A comparison of financial class S's five-day LOS in Exhibit 15.14 with financial class R's five-day LOS in Exhibit 15.15 indicates a $50 difference in the contribution margin ($1,240 versus $1,290). Two hematology tests and one chemistry test were deferred for financial class S patients until after discharge; the charges and cost of these tests are given in these exhibits, resulting in the $50 combined increase in contribution margin. If financial and utilization results were available for 25 different patient profiles by financial class for DRG XXA instead of just class R and class S, then additional insights would be available on third party payors and their impact of delivery of health care services. As indicated by Exhibit 15.15, class R's five-day LOS is a different profile than class S's five-day LOS for DRG XXA. The matching of costs and revenue and analysis of utilization must be by financial class of patient; an average of several financial classes can lead to inappropriate conclusions.

Comparison Data

Professional associations identified with the various types of health care facilities typically accumulate utilization, performance, and financial data from participating institutions and then provide a sample of these data to the member facility. This sample information is critical for assessing, evaluating, planning, pricing, and management analysis purposes. Data elements that might disclose the participating

Exhibit 15.15   Impact of LOS on Projecting Revenue and Cost for DRG XXA

	Financial Class R			
	6-Day ALOS	5-Day ALOS	Variance	Comment
Contribution margins:				
Room	860	680	180	N/C*
Operating & Recovery	65	65	0	N/C
Ancillary Services	695	545	150	Lab tests†
Total	$1,620	$1,290	$330	

*N/C: There is no change in the 5-day ALOS for financial class R from the data presented in Exhibit 15.14 for financial class S.

†Lab tests: Two of the hematology tests and one chemistry test that were not performed in the hospital for financial class S in Exhibit 15.14 are included in these ancillary services for financial class R's 5-day LOS. The $20 cost of the two hematology tests versus the $50 charge means a $30 increase in the contribution margin; the $15 cost of the chemistry test versus the $35 charge gives a $20 increase in contribution margin. Thus, there is a $50 combined increase in the contribution margin for 5-day LOS under financial class R ($1,240 in Exhibit 15.14 plus $50 equals $1,290) versus the situation for financial class S. The ancillary services for financial class R's 5-day LOS are computed as follows:

		Cost		Charges
Lab—Hematology	7 tests @ $10	$ 70	7 tests @ $25	$ 175
Lab—Chemistry	6 tests @ $15	90	6 tests @ $35	210
Lab—Pathology	6 tests @ $35	210	6 tests @ $45	270
Lab—Microbiology	4 tests @ $40	160	4 tests @ $50	200
Radiology	5 units @ $40	200	5 units @ $50	250
Respiratory therapy	7 services @ $70	490	7 services @ $80	560
Physical therapy	4 services @ $50	200	4 services @ $75	300
Total ancillary services		$1,420		$1,965

$545

Contribution Margin

institutions including the provider number, name, address, and zip code information, are stripped from any reports or data files transmitted to the member facility. In recognition of patient rights and legal decisions, the extracted patient information does not include data elements that could be used to identify a patient. Unique patient data are provided by the medical records department only in response to court orders.

CPHA's PAS reports for hospitals have always included utilization, performance, and financial data from a sample of other institutions that can be compared with a given health care facility's experience. Some of the state hospital associations accumulate discharge abstract data and annual financial statements from member institutions; a sample of this information is then made available to a participating institution for comparison purposes. Provider numbers, names, and addresses of the facilities in the sample are not disclosed by either CPHA or the state hospital associations. There are other voluntary associations that accumulate and distribute hospital discharge abstract data to participating health care facilities. Some consulting firms have purchased CPHA and other health care data that have been integrated and offer them to their clients on a consulting-fee basis.

Discharge abstract data by payor are available in some areas. A consulting unit in the Blue Cross Association markets this type of data for Blue Cross patients to individual health care facilities. Some states will provide profile data on Medicaid patients that can be used in comparison studies. Medicare information is available on both discharge abstracts and hospital cost reports; the annual revisions in DRGs and rates from PPS are computed from these Medicare provider analysis and review (MEDPAR) data.

The MEDPAR file is based on fully coded diagnostic and surgical data for all Medicare inpatient hospital bills. The MEDPAR public use file contains billing and medical data for Medicare beneficiaries using short-stay hospital inpatient services for a 20 percent sample determined by the terminal digits in the beneficiary's health insurance claim number.[6] Data elements that would identify the hospital have been stripped from the MEDPAR public use file; however, there is an expanded modified MEDPAR file containing 100 percent of Medicare beneficiaries with the hospital data elements.[7] Data elements that would identify the beneficiary are stripped from the MEDPAR files. The purchaser of the 100 percent Medicare file must sign a data use agreement that restricts how the information can be used. HCFA also makes available the cost, statistical, financial, and other information from the Medicare hospital cost report.[8]

The National Hospital Discharge Survey (NHDS) is one of the most widely cited governmental statistical references, and it does not use the expanded modified MEDPAR file or even the 20 percent MEDPAR file. The NHDS is conducted on a sample basis by the National Center for Health Statistics (NCHS). The 1987 NHDS contained 400 participating hospitals with approximately 181,000 abstracts of medical records.[9] Most of the data in the NHDS is obtained on a manual basis directly from the participating hospitals; 17 percent of the 1987 data was purchased from commercial abstracting services. The NHDS reports are aggregated by ICD-9-CM codes, age, sex, and region; there are special reports by bed size and ownership.

Summary

Most community hospitals in the United States have some type of computer-based information system for billing and financial accounting. The UB82 brought uniform structure to commercial insurance billing so that common data elements are identified in each third party payor's files. These common billing data can be merged with admission and medical record information to create a research database for the institution. The research database should be focused on each episode of care (both DRGs and outpatient services) by physician and by patient origin. As indicated in Exhibit 15.1, several of the data elements in the research database are defined groupings designed to facilitate cross-comparisons among patient origins, utilization statistics, financial data, and physician information by episode of care.

Executive management of the health care institution cannot take a passive role concerning the research database. Information in the research database may show poor contracts with third party payors that must be recognized and not renewed. These data may report unusual medical practices of physicians for a given type of episode of care that are identified by utilization of services; an explanation, at least, is needed from physicians for these variations. The research database may reveal shifts in the patient profiles by type of episode of care that may have long-term impact on services provided by the health care institution. The matching of cost and revenue in a DRG or outpatient service by financial class of patient requires information on contractual allowances and adjustments; the absence of such data at this level of detail can only result in misleading assessments.

An analysis of patients by type of treatment or diagnostic category along with the social, economic, and demographic characteristics of patients can be used in computing an average patient profile by disease entity for a given health care facility. An assessment of the population characteristics and economic factors addresses the demand side of the issue. The principal physician group identified with the delivery of medical services can serve as the foundation for profiles of patients identified with a physician group that are summarized by (1) disease entity, (2) utilization of services, (3) demographic and social factors, and (4) financial class and payment behavior. Cross-comparisons of patient profiles for the same disease entity treated by various physician groups provides additional insights for evaluating the delivery of health services.

After the detailed financial statement of account (as illustrated in Exhibit 15.2) has been prepared, the information is removed from the on-line DBMS and retained in a secondary location. The detailed data on each inpatient's episode of care can be retrieved from secondary storage for purposes of aggregating specific types of tests, procedures, activities, operations, and therapy services for selected subsets of patients (such as DRG 112 for physician #367). These discharge logs, utilization records, and financial account information are used in creating profiles by zip code that are cross-referenced to financial class of patients by DRG per admitting physician. Physician profiles for the same type of episode of care are compared within the medical department, and attention is given to differences in social, economic, and demographic characteristics of patients partitioned by the physician providing the services. Typical data elements included in the patient origin and utilization studies are illustrated in Exhibit 15.1.

Common reports for case mix and physician profiles are constantly being revised as more detailed financial and utilization information are available that are cross-referenced to physician and patient origin. The prior year's profiles serve as a frame of reference for measuring change. Variations in medical practice among physicians treating the same general type of patient condition are revealed by these reports. For major medical problems, it is sometimes helpful to partition physicians treating the same type of episode into two or three groups depending on medical practice. Some cardiologists, for example, make extensive use of surgery; other cardiologists defer surgery until the application of medicine has been proven to be ineffective for that patient. Separating cardiologists into these two groups improves the accuracy of annual forecasts of health care services.

A seven-step approach for forecasting health care services permits the use of historical experience with flexibility. Known or expected changes in demand, medical practice, physician groups, third party payor actions, medical technology, and competitive conditions can be accommodated in this modular approach. Changes in the ALOS for the same type of episode of care by financial class of patients can have significant impacts on utilization of services and contribution margins.

Appendix: History of Classifying and Reporting Episodes of Care

Classification of diseases

The coding and classification systems for diseases and procedures did not originate as part of the educational programs of medical schools. *International Classification of Diseases* (ICD), a manual produced by the World Health Organization (WHO) in Geneva, Switzerland, for accumulating morbidity and mortality data, has been adapted for use in hospitals in the United States. Some appreciation of this manual is necessary for selecting appropriate partitions of the code structure in forecasting health services. The origin of this manual partially explains why these coding and classification systems are not just an extension of medical education programs in the United States. As technological advancements occur in medical practice, problems may arise in coding and classification systems that are driven by WHO morbidity and mortality data.

The *International Classification of Diseases* manual is a WHO document providing classification structure for accumulating comparative information on diseases, injuries, and causes of death from a world perspective. The initial hospital adaptation of the ICD manual was dominated by pathologists because of the overall death specification. Some medical records departments in hospitals began in the early 1950s to make adaptations to the ICD manual so that it was more appropriate for hospital use in classifying, storing, and retrieving diagnostic data. The Commission on Professional and Hospital Activities (CPHA) adopted the sixth edition of the ICD manual with similar modifications for use by hospitals participating in CPHA's discharge abstract data program, called Professional Activity Study (PAS).

The AHA and the American Medical Record Association (then the American Association of Medical Record Librarians) jointly established a study group in 1956 to determine the relative efficiencies of coding systems for diagnostic indexing. Although the ICD manual was accepted by this study group as a framework for indexing hospital records, an adaptation was required. A few versions of this adaptation were distributed to hospital personnel. CPHA formalized its adaptation of the ICD manual in 1968 by publishing *Hospital Adaptation of ICDA* (H-ICDA). The many hospitals participating in the PAS program began to use the first edition of the H-ICDA manual. In 1973 CPHA published a revision of the H-ICDA manual (H-ICDA-2), which was implemented in 1974 for all hospitals in the PAS program.[10] Many hospitals not in the PAS program elected to use a different adaptation of the eighth revision of the ICD manual (ICDA-8) prepared by a task force organized by the AHA.[11]

There were many problems with the availability of diagnostic codes for surgical procedures in both the H-ICDA-2 manual and the ICDA-8 manual. Different hospitals used various supplementary schedules of codes in coping with procedures and types of episodes of care not covered in the H-ICDA-2 and ICDA-8 manuals. A utilization review program for Medicare and Medicaid patients was announced by the Department of Health, Education, and Welfare (DHEW), which required a coding system for diagnostic indexing.[12] The American Medical Association (AMA) filed an injunction prohibiting the implementation of the new Medicare and Medicaid utilization review provisions, but AMA reached an informal settlement with DHEW in September 1975. During the 1973–1976 period, AMA assumed a leadership role in working with 22 medical and professional associations in developing *Model Screening Criteria to Assist Professional Standard Review Organizations.*[13]

The coding requirements of the utilization review program brought into focus the limitations of not having procedures and surgical codes in either the H-ICDA or the ICDA manuals. The National Center for Health Statistics and CPHA jointly worked on the creation of a single classification system, based on ICD manuals and adapted for United States hospitals, that would encompass surgical and clinical procedures. The result of this cooperative effort was *The International Classification of Diseases, 9th Revision, Clinical Modification* (ICD-9-CM), published in 1978.[14] The foreword of the ICD-9-CM manual puts in perspective the importance of this new integrated coding system:

> The publication of *ICD-9-CM* constitutes both a national and an international landmark. In the former case it means that one classification of diseases, injuries, impairments, symptoms, and causes of death will supplant the two, or even three or four classification schemes that have confounded and confused clinical and statistical comparisons in the United States for a decade. . . .
>
> With the publication and use of these three volumes, clinicians, medical record administrators, hospital and health services administrators, health planners, PSROs, statisticians, politicians, and the public can be assured that a common classification of diseases and related entities is being used across the country by all agencies, institutions, and geopolitical jurisdictions. . . .
>
> From an international perspective, these volumes represent both a deeper and broader involvement of clinicians, in contrast to pathologists, than has occurred in the preparation of the previous revisions of the

ICD or their adaptations for use in the United States. This involvement implies the worldwide concern with improved health care for the living, in addition to the prior, necessarily limited concern, with improving the reporting of the causes of death.[15]

It is important to realize that medical school graduates prior to 1973 typically did not have extensive training in selecting diagnostic codes to classify an episode of care. Furthermore, medical education programs are concerned with improved health care for the living. The former ICD manuals were not significantly related to the contents of medical education programs, except from the limited perspective of cause of death. This difference in the professional orientation of physicians versus medical records administrators was responsible for misunderstanding and conflicts with both the old ICD manuals and the ICD-9-CM code structure in a complex case.

The new ICD-9-CM manual, published in 1978, has three volumes:

- *Volume 1—Diseases: Tabular List,* 1140 pages.

- *Volume 2—Diseases: Alphabetic Index,* 910 pages.

- *Volume 3—Procedures: Tabular List and Alphabetic Index,* 464 pages

These volumes were required for use in the United States for discharge abstract data on all federal program patients as of 1 October 1979.

To be effective, the coding and classification systems must be understood and applied by the medical staff, nursing personnel, and administrative support units. While there are always statistical and quantitative considerations in forecasting data, most of the complexity in applying these techniques to patients within a hospital relates to the origin of the coding and classification systems and the lack of integration with medical education programs. The macro issue remains as the need for a classification system to express an episode of care within a continuum-of-care context that is integrated with medical education programs. This proposed classification system can then be used in the training of health care professionals, including medical records personnel, discharge planners, health care accountants, and other hospital administrative staff.

History of utilization review reporting

Medical records administrators in community hospitals used the coding and classification systems for indexing patients during the 1970s in support of both retrospective reviews and concurrent reviews. Three different programs mandating utilization review reporting had significant impacts on the role and function of medical records administrators during this period.

Medical care evaluation studies. The oldest type of retrospective review is identified with the formal standards for the medical staff to conduct medical care evaluation studies by the Joint Commission on Accreditation of Healthcare Organizations (JCAHO). JCAHO has mandated medical care evaluation as a fact-finding and educational function for the medical staff. This same JCAHO manual calls for the medical records department to prepare and issue reports required to meet the needs of the hospital and medical staff based on an adaptation of the current revision of the ICD manual.[16]

PSRO reviews. Retrospective and concurrent reviews were part of the program under the Professional Standards Review Organization (PSRO) that was established by the Social Security Amendments of 1972, P. L. 92–603 (dated 30 October 1972). The *P.S.R.O. Program Manual* states that P. L. 92–603 was:

> . . . designed to involve local practicing physicians in the ongoing review and evaluation of health care services covered under the Medicare, Medicaid, and the Maternal and Child Health programs. The legislation is based on the concepts that health professionals are the most appropriate individuals to evaluate the quality of medical services and that effective peer review at the local level is the soundest method for assuring the appropriate use of health care resources and facilities. The PSRO is the means by which the legislation attempts to translate these concepts into practice.[17]

As part of this peer review process, it was envisioned that local physicians, regional and state medical committees, and national specialty groups would participate in the establishment of criteria for evaluating the care given to a patient in a specific diagnostic group. These criteria encompassed six categories:

1. Justification for admission
2. Length of stay
3. Validation of diagnosis and reasons for admission
4. Critical diagnostic and therapeutic services
5. Discharge status
6. Complications[18]

The overall work of the PSRO program was viewed as having three components: admission certification, continued-stay review, and medical care evaluation studies. These activities required the patient's medical record to be updated so that these concurrent reviews could be performed. The medical care evaluation studies under PSRO were similar to the retrospective reviews under JCAHO; frequently, the same analysis might be used for both the PSRO and JCAHO.

Utilization review. While draft copies of the *P.S.R.O. Program Manual* were still being revised by the Bureau of Quality Assurance, DHEW, many observers in the health care field were surprised to see announcements of new programs in other DHEW departments that captured many of the key features in the PSRO program. The Social Security Administration announced a new utilization review program for all Medicare patients, containing admission certification and continued-stay review activities that were very similar to those in the PSRO Program. The Social Rehabilitation Service had a similar announcement covering all Medicaid patients. Both of these concurrent utilization review programs were to be administered by the fiscal intermediary.[19]

The November 1974 DHEW announcements for utilization review were specified as a condition for payment for federal program inpatients administered through the fiscal intermediary. Community hospitals could not afford to take the risk of not implementing a utilization review program even though AMA was legally challenging the authority of DHEW to make the announcements. The legal issue focused on the right of DHEW to specify rules that interfered with the professional relationship between the physician and the patient. As these hospitals implemented concurrent utilization reviews for admission certification and continued-stay review, the role and function of the medical records administrator in hospitals were significantly changed. The medical staff and medical records personnel were the primary participants in the retrospective utilization reviews, with supporting roles performed by nursing personnel. The concurrent utilization reviews administered by the fiscal intermediary brought new participants to the hospital's internal review. Nursing, administrative, and financial personnel joined these concurrent review teams as full members with the medical staff and medical records personnel.

While these programs were emphasizing the importance of medical records, the Institute of Medicine sponsored two studies that indicated a high error rate in the existing practice with the ICDA-8 codes. Hospital discharge data abstracted from patients' medical records where the designation of the principal diagnosis is at the fourth-digit level had a 57.2 weighted percent with no discrepancy for medical records and 65.2 weighted percent for private abstract.[20] These 1974 studies found at the fourth-digit level for Medicare records the weighted percent of abstracts with no discrepancy varied from 36.8 percent for chronic ischemic heart disease to 96.9 percent for inguinal hernia without mention of obstruction.[21]

The findings from the Internal Medicine's 1973–1974 studies were not published for over four years, but copies of the critical results were widely read by members of the health care community. By the time the findings were published in the December 1978 issue of *Medical Care*, the ICD-9-CM manual had been completed, and AMA had published the *Model Screening Criteria to Assist Professional Standard Review Organizations*. Hospital administrators were giving more professional recognition to the position of medical records administrator, and the status of the medical records department had improved. The discharge abstracting services had established editing and screening software within their computer systems that rejected abstract records that were not compatible with criteria. Tremendous progress was made in improving the quality of medical record abstracting data during the late 1970s in all areas.

ICDA code structure

The diagnostic coding structure in the ICD-9-CM manual goes from 000 to 999, with many categories specified at the fourth and fifth level. There are several clusters of codes to designate heart disease; for example, the code 420 is for acute pericarditis. The descriptive material in the manual under the heading "420 Acute Pericarditis" excludes acute rheumatic pericarditis (391.0) and postmyocardial infarction syndrome (Dressler's; 411.0). The first of the four diagnostic codes with the three-digit code 420 requires a cross-referencing as follows:

420.0   Acute pericarditis in diseases classified elsewhere
        Code also underlying disease, as
            actinomycosis (039.8)
            amebiasis (006.8)
            nocardiosis (039.8)
            tuberculosis (017.9)
            uremia (585)

The diagnostic code 420.0 excludes pericarditis (acute) in
    Coxsackie (virus) (074.21)

gonococcal (098.83)
histoplasmosis (115.0–115.9 with fifth-digit 3)
meningococcal infection (036.41)
syphilitic (093.81)

These inclusion and exclusion specifications in the ICD-9-CM manual require health care professionals to be very familiar with the overall classification system for the proper selection of a diagnostic code. In addition to diagnostic code 420.0 (acute pericarditis in diseases classified elsewhere), there are three diagnostic codes under the heading "420.9 Other and Unspecified Acute Pericarditis" with the following labels:

• 420.90: Acute pericarditis, unspecified

• 420.91: Acute idiopathic pericarditis

• 420.99: Other and unspecified acute pericarditis, other

The ICD-9-CM manual contains 14,473 diagnostic codes and 4,086 procedures codes, for a total of 18,559 codes. These counts do not include the code numbers for titles and headings that are in the manual and on the computer tapes supporting the ICD-9-CM volumes. As indicated in the above example of codes beginning with 420, some diagnostic codes are at the fourth level, and others are at the fifth level. In addition, the user has the option of adding to some defined diagnostic codes, resulting in nonuniform codes at the fifth level.

Diagnostic codes at the fourth level and at the fifth level add to the complexity of forecasting health services. When thinking about the 14,473 uniform diagnostic codes, it is important to remember the basic structure of the ICD manual and its original preparation for classification of the causes of death. Ideally, an individual forecasting health services might want a coding system that was based on providing medical and health care services to the living. But, the ICD-9-CM manual is what is currently available and is a tremendous improvement over previous efforts to adapt the ICD manual to patients in U.S. hospitals.

To further illustrate the variations in the level at which diagnostic codes are specified, Exhibit 15.16 presents 23 diagnostic codes and five heading codes under "Ischemic Heart Disease (410–414)" from Volume 1 of the ICD-9-CM manual. The 23 diagnostic codes in Exhibit 15.16 collectively represent 6.5 percent of community hospital discharges, excluding newborn infants.[22] Of these 23 diagnostic codes, 10 have the three digits 410 for acute myocardial infarction, which in aggregate comprise 2.3 percent of community hospital discharges.

Exhibit 15.16 Diagnostic and Heading Codes under "Ischemic Heart Disease (410–414)" in *ICD-9-CM, Volume 1, Diseases*

Diagnostic Codes

410.0 Acute myocardial infarction of anterolateral wall
410.1 Acute myocardial infarction of other anterior wall
410.2 Acute myocardial infarction of inferolateral wall
410.3 Acute myocardial infarction of inferoposterior wall
410.4 Acute myocardial infarction of other inferior wall
410.5 Acute myocardial infarction of other lateral wall
410.6 Acute myocardial infarction, true posterior wall infarction
410.7 Acute myocardial infarction, subendocardial infarction
410.8 Acute myocardial infarction of other specified sites
410.9 Acute myocardial infarction, unspecified site

411.0 Postmyocardial infarction syndrome
411.1 Intermediate coronary syndrome
411.8 Other acute and subacute forms of ischemic heart disease, other

412 Old myocardial infarction

413.0 Angina decubitus
413.1 Prinzmetal angina
413.9 Other and unspecified angina pectoris

414.0 Coronary atherosclerosis
414.10 Aneurysm of heart (wall)
414.11 Aneurysm of coronary vessels
414.19 Aneurysm of heart, other
414.8 Other specified forms of chronic ischemic heart disease
414.9 Chronic ischemic heart disease, unspecified

Heading Codes

410 Acute myocardial infarction
411 Other acute and subacute forms of ischemic heart disease
413 Angina pectoris
414 Other forms of chronic ischemic heart disease
414.1 Aneurysm of heart

Source: CPHA, *The International Classification of Diseases, 9th Revision, Clinical Modification, ICD-9-CM* (Ann Arbor, MI: CPHA, 1978), Volume 1, 366–69.
Note: Descriptive materials under heading and procedure codes are not shown in the above listing.

The procedure coding structure in Volume 3 of the ICD-9-CM manual goes from 01 to 99, with many categories specified at the third and fourth level. For example, the designation code 37 is "Other Operations on Heart and Pericardium." This two digit code is a heading and not a specification of a procedure. There are 38 procedure codes and eight heading codes containing 37 as the first two digits in the ICD-9-CM manual (Exhibit 15.17). Some procedure codes are at the third level (such as 37.0, 37.4, and 37.5), while other procedure codes are at the fourth level (such as 37.10, 37.11, and 37.12). There are 4,086 procedure codes in Volume 3 of the ICD-9-CM manual; there are also descriptive codes specifying headings and titles.

Forecasting health services by the 14,473 diagnostic codes and the 4,086 procedures codes in the ICD-9-CM manual will result in very few cases in a given cell for even the largest community hospitals. *Hospital Statistics: 1990–91 Edition* reports 906 hospitals with 300 beds or more with aggregate admissions of 15.336 million, or an average of 16,927 admissions per hospital in this bed category.[23] Before making any other comparison between the maximum number of diagnostic codes in the ICD-9-CM volumes versus the average annual admissions for a hospital, it should be noted that there are some very unusual diagnostic codes with a low frequency of occurrence on a national basis. On the other hand, codes like acute myocardial infarction of anterolateral wall (410.0) have a relatively high frequency of occurrence.

Prior to ICD-9-CM, the American Medical Association published the *Physicians' Current Procedural Terminology* in 1966, a systematic listing and coding of procedures and services performed by physicians. The fourth edition of the *Physicians' Current Procedural Terminology* is referred to as CPT-4 and is periodically updated to reflect the latest changes in medical practice. Some third party payors require CPT-4 codes for ambulatory surgery, clinic, and outpatient services. A patient classification coding system for other types of outpatient episodes of care is currently being revised as it is being used in a major demonstration project. There are separate research projects for extended-care facilities and nursing homes; thus, there is the potential for three new sets of patient classification systems for outpatient care to be available in the next few years.

Diagnosis related grouping system

Section 101(c) of P. L. 97–248, the Tax Equity and Fiscal Responsibility Act of 1982, mandated the secretary of the Department of Health and

Exhibit 15.17   Procedure and Heading Codes under "37 Other Operations on Heart and Pericardium" in *ICD-9-CM, Volume 3, Procedures*

Procedure Codes

37.0 Pericardiocentesis

37.10 Incision of heart, not otherwise specified
37.11 Cardiotomy
37.12 Pericardiotomy

37.21 Right heart cardiac catheterization
37.22 Left heart cardiac catheterization
37.23 Combined right and left heart cardiac catheterization
37.24 Biopsy of pericardium
37.25 Biopsy of heart
37.29 Other diagnostic procedures on heart and pericardium

37.31 Pericardiectomy
37.32 Excision of aneurysm of heart
37.33 Excision of other lesion of heart

37.4   Repair of heart and pericardium

37.5   Heart transplantation

37.61 Implant of pulsation balloon
37.62 Implant of other heart assist system
37.63 Replacement and repair of heart assist system
37.64 Removal of heart assist system

37.70 Insertion of cardiac pacemaker, not otherwise specified
37.71 Insertion of temporary pacemaker into ventricle
37.72 Insertion of temporary cardiac pacemaker into other and unspecified site
37.73 Insertion of permanent pacemaker into atrium, transvenous route
37.74 Insertion of permanent pacemaker into ventricle, transvenous route
37.75 Insertion of permanent cardiac pacemaker into unspecified site, transvenous route
37.76 Insertion of permanent pacemaker into epicardium
37.77 Insertion of permanent cardiac pacemaker, unspecified approach

37.81 Replacement of transvenous electrode
37.82 Replacement of epicardial electrode
37.83 Removal of transvenous electrode
37.84 Removal of epicardial electrode
37.85 Replacement of cardiac pacemaker pulse generator

Continued

Exhibit 15.17   Continued

37.86 Removal of cardiac pacemaker system
37.89 Other revision of cardiac pacemaker system

37.91 Open check cardiac massage
37.92 Injection of therapeutic substance into heart
37.93 Injection of therapeutic substance into pericardium
37.99 Other operations on heart and pericardium, other

Heading Codes

37   Other operations on heart and pericardium
37.1 Cardiotomy and pericardiotomy
37.2 Diagnostic procedures on heart and pericardium
37.3 Pericardiectomy and excision of lesion of heart
37.6 Implantation of heart assist system
37.7 Insertion of cardiac pacemaker system
37.8 Replacement, revision, and removal of cardiac pacemaker system
37.9 Other operations on heart and pericardium

Source: CPHA, *The International Classification of Diseases, 9th Revision, Clinical Modification, ICD-9-CM* (Ann Arbor, MI: CPHA, 1978), Volume 3, 94–98.
Note: Descriptive materials under heading and procedure codes are not shown in the above listing.

Human Services (DHHS) to develop, in consultation with the Senate Committee on Finance and the Committee on Ways and Means of the House of Representatives, a prospective payment system for hospitals under Medicare. The December 1982 report by Richard S. Schweiker, secretary of DHHS, recommended the 467 diagnosis-related groups (DRGs) developed by researchers at Yale University. The report by the secretary states:

> Discharges will be classified by use of the 1981 version of the Diagnosis Related Group (DRG) classification methodology developed at Yale University. This type of classification system methodology has been extensively tested through actual use over the last 7 years. In addition, New Jersey used the original DRG classification system as the basis for hospital payment for several years, and now uses the 1981 versions of DRGs.[24]

Public hearings were conducted in February 1983; by 20 April 1983, the Social Security Amendments of 1983, P. L. 98–21 had been passed, in which the 467 DRGs were mandated for Medicare.

The 23 major diagnostic categories (MDCs) used as the starting point for the patient classification system are listed in Exhibit 15.18

with cross-references to the applicable DRGs. A review of the titles in Exhibit 15.18 indicates that these MDCs are dominated by organs. Each ICD-9-CM disease code reported as the primary diagnosis for a patient is mapped to one or more of these 23 MDCs. The surgical procedure code along with the sex and age of the patient are used in further partitioning the patient's primary diagnosis into a particular DRG. Other factors may also be used in mapping patient episodes, including complications and discharge alive versus dead.

Health care entities add two more dimensions to the DRGs when performing analysis beyond Medicare payment. These other factors are patient characteristics and location.

There are three facts about the 467 DRGs as of 20 April 1983 that are significant to the quality and utilization issues that emerged in the implementation period. First, there were statistical problems with the original 383 DRGs, and the research team elected to introduce a new structure using the ICD-9-CM codes rather than respond to criticisms of an inability to apply a sample of 690,000 patient records from western Pennsylvania and obtain the same terminal DRGs.[25] The original 383 DRGs were based on ICDA-8 and the 467 DRGs used the ICD-9-CM manuals.

Second, the mandated 467 DRGs were untested as of 20 April 1983 in any major demonstration effort with 12 months of actual experience of working with these DRGs, even though they were developed by December 1981.[26] Contrary to some public statements, the New Jersey demonstration did not use the 467-DRG system but was based on the original 383 DRGs.[27]

Third, there was minimum medical input in the development of the 467-DRG system; this is the primary reason that the December 1981 version had not been approved in 1982 ("on hold") when the Hospital Research and Educational Trust published an analysis of nine patient classification systems.[28] The failure to have sufficient physician input in the initial design of the DRGs caused major problems for some hospitals in partitioning complex inpatient episodes of care.

Changes to DRG classification system

The Prospective Payment Assessment Commission (ProPAC) was established by Congress when PPS was enacted by P. L. 98–21 with responsibilities for maintaining and updating the payment system. There have been many recommendations from ProPAC to the secretary of DHHS that were adopted; some other recommendations are still under review.

Exhibit 15.18   Major Diagnostic Categories Mapped to DRGs

MDC	Name	DRGs
01	Diseases and disorders of the nervous system	DRG 001 to DRG 035
02	Diseases and disorders of the eye	DRG 036 to DRG 048
03	Diseases and disorders of the ear, nose, and throat	DRG 049 to DRG 074
04	Diseases and disorders of the respiratory system	DRG 075 to DRG 102
05	Diseases and disorders of the circulatory system	DRG 103 to DRG 145
06	Diseases and disorders of the digestive system	DRG 146 to DRG 190
07	Diseases and disorders of the hepatobiliary system and pancreas	DRG 191 to DRG 208
08	Diseases and disorders of the musculoskeletal system and connective tissue	DRG 209 to DRG 256
09	Diseases and disorders of the skin, subcutaneous tissue, and breast	DRG 257 to DRG 284
10	Endocrine, nutritional, and metabolic diseases and disorders	DRG 285 to DRG 301
11	Diseases and disorders of the kidney and urinary tract	DRG 302 to DRG 333
12	Diseases and disorders of the male reproductive system	DRG 334 to DRG 352
13	Diseases and disorders of the female reproductive system	DRG 353 to DRG 369
14	Pregnancy, childbirth, and puerperium	DRG 370 to DRG 384
15	Newborns and other neonates with conditions in the prenatal period	DRG 385 to DRG 391
16	Diseases and disorders of the blood-forming organs and immunological disorders	DRG 392 to DRG 399
17	Myeloproliferative diseases and disorders and poorly differentiated neoplasms	DRG 400 to DRG 414
18	Infectious and parasitic diseases (systemic or unspecified sites)	DRG 415 to DRG 423
19	Mental disease and disorders	DRG 424 to DRG 432
20	Substance use and substance induced organic mental disorders	DRG 433 to DRG 438
21	Injuries, poisonings, and toxic effects of drugs	DRG 439 to DRG 455

Continued

Exhibit 15.18   Continued

MDC	Name	DRGs
22	Burns	DRG 456 to DRG 460
23	Factors influencing health status and other contacts with health services	DRG 461 to DRG 467

Source: The New ICD-9-CM Diagnosis Related Groups Classification Scheme, User Manual, prepared by the ICD-9-CM Project Staff, Yale University, School of Organization and Management, Health Systems Management Group (December 1981), Volume 1, 34–35.

ProPac, for example, has extensively analyzed capital payment issues and has made numerous recommendations for including capital in PPS.[29] There are annual recommendations on updating PPS payments, adjustments to the PPS payment formula, quality of care, patient classification and case-mix measurement, DRG classification and weighing factors, technologies, and changing medical practices.

The secretary of DHHS's *Report to Congress* stated there would be testing for DRG "creep," and a 1988 *New England Journal of Medicine* revealed an error rate of 20.8 percent in DRG coding, with 61.7 percent of the errors favoring the hospital.[30] The study was from October 1984 to March 1985, before the 15-page corrections were made in September 1985 to the DRG GROUPER.[31] The article does not clearly distinguish between errors that are associated with design flaws in the DRG GROUPER versus errors by the professional staff in the hospital's medical records department. DHHS's annual revisions in the proposed rules for the DRG system have included changes in more than 100 codes and expanded the number of categories to 477 DRGs in 23 MDCs.[32]

ProPAC analyzed the Medicare discharge data for fiscal year 1984, including diagnostic and procedure information on all 1984 Medicare inpatient hospital bills. As a result of this detailed study, "age over 69" was eliminated from 92 sets of paired DRGs that prior to 1 October 1987 were distinguished by age greater than 69 and/or the presence of a complication or comorbidity (CC).[33]

These 92 sets of paired DRGs represented more than 50 percent of the Medicare cases.[34] Comments by ProPAC staff members conducting the study emphasized the general population included in CPHA's database versus the restricted population for Medicare and DRGs; their conclusion was: "Thus, it appears that it was never appropriate to define DRGs using age in combination with CC for Medicare payment purposes."[35]

The impact of this restricted population is captured by HCFA's comments in the final rule:

> About 70 percent of Medicare beneficiaries hospitalized each year are age 70 or older. About 60 percent of Medicare beneficiaries under age 70 are reported to have CC. As a result, the current split in the paired DRGs based on age over 69 or presence of CC results in about 88 percent of all Medicare cases in the paired DRGs being assigned to the DRGs involving age over 69 and/or CC. The fact that such a substantial majority of Medicare beneficiaries are grouped into these DRGs has the effect of masking significant differences in resource use among patients within the DRG pair because the DRG for older and/or complicated cases includes a mix of extremely sick patients who are very resource-intensive and patients who present no complications and are not very different from younger patients in their average resource use.[36]

HCFA's findings for Medicare beneficiaries indicated that a CC patient without regard to age consumed about 30 percent more resources than a patient without any complications. Concurrently with changing the DRG classification system, there was a recalibration of weights to reflect the utilization of resources.

An ICD-9-CM Coordination and Maintenance Committee was established in September 1985, and new ICD-9-CM codes became effective on 1 October 1986.[37] Because of notification requirements, the new codes could not be used in restructuring of DRGs until 1 October 1987. With this new committee, there are annual additions and exclusions in the ICD-9-CM codes, which are announced by HCFA with the revisions in DRGs and PPS. HCFA also created the CC exclusions list to preclude coding of closely related conditions, duplicate coding, or inconsistent coding that otherwise might be treated as complications or comorbidities.

Among the other major changes that have been made in the DRG system are the modifications in surgical hierarchies. Many patients have multiple surgical procedures, and the resource utilization of these multiple procedures must be considered in the ordering of groups of procedures and in the assignment of cases to DRGs within the MDC.[38] HCFA is making progress in overcoming the flawed structure supporting the initial 467 DRGs. These changes in surgical hierarchies, combined with revised CC under multiple conditions and new ICD-9-CM codes, can move toward more meaningful categories of episodes of care. The improved financial and utilization databases for Medicare patients can then be used in the recalibration efforts for these episodes of care.

Notes

1. JCAH, *Accreditation Manual for Hospitals: Hospital Accreditation Program* (Chicago: JCAH, 1971), Medical Staff section, 6–7.
2. CPHA, *The International Classification of Diseases, 9th Revision, Clinical Modification* (ICD-9-CM) (Ann Arbor, MI: CPHA, 1978).
3. C. M. Fanta, A. J. Finkel, C. G. Kirschner, and J. M. Perlman, *Physicians' Current Procedural Terminology*, Fourth Edition (CPT 1986) (Chicago: AMA, 1986).
4. Uniform Hospital Discharge Data Set has its origins in 1972 and was incorporated in the Social Security Administration's mandated utilization review requirements for 1975. The Uniform Billing System was developed by HCFA in 1982 and implemented by states in 1983 and 1984.
5. *Federal Register* 54 (8 May 1989): 19718–37.
6. DHHS, HCFA, "Medicare Program; Changes to the Inpatient Hospital Prospective Payment System and Fiscal Year 1990 Rates; Proposed Rule," *Federal Register* 54 (8 May 1989): 19657.
7. Ibid.
8. Ibid., 19658.
9. DHHS, Hospital Care Statistics Branch, Division of Health Care Statistics, "1987 Summary: National Hospital Discharge Survey," *NCHS Advance Data from Vital and Health Statistics of the National Center for Health Statistics* 159 (28 September 1988): 12.
10. CPHA Nosology Group, *Hospital Adaptation of ICDA; H-ICDA: Based on International Classification of Diseases (1965 Revision, WHO) and Eighth Revision International Classification of Diseases, Adapted for Use in the United States* (PHS Publication No. 1693), second ed. (Ann Arbor, MI: CPHA, 1973).
11. DHEW, Public Health Service, National Center for Health Statistics, *Eighth Revision: International Classification of Diseases: Adapted for Use in the United States: ICDA*, PHS Publication No. 1693 (Washington, DC: U.S. Government Printing Office, 1968).
12. Medicare: *Federal Register* 39 (29 November 1974): 41603–8, and Medicaid: *Federal Register* 39 (29 November 1974): 41609–18.
13. AMA, *Model Screening Criteria to Assist Professional Standard Review Organizations: Draft* (Chicago: AMA, 1975).
14. CPHA, *ICD-9-CM.*
15. Ibid., iii.
16. JCAH, *Accreditation Manual*, Medical Record Services section, 5–6.
17. DHEW, Office of Professional Standards Review, *P.S.R.O. Program Manual* (Rockville, MD: DHEW, 1974), Chapter I, p. 1.
18. M. J. Goran, J. S. Roberts, M. A. Kellogg, J. Fielding, and W. Jessee, "The PSRO Hospital Review System," *Medical Care* 13 (April 1975): 1–33.

19. T. R. Prince, "Effect of PSRO on Hospital Utilization and Costs," in *Final Report: Private Initiative in Professional Standards Review Organization (PSRO)*, P. D. Sanazaro, Ed. (Ann Arbor, MI: Health Administration Press, 1978), p. 135.
20. L. K. Demlo, P. M. Campbell, and S. Spaght Brown, "Reliability of Information Abstracted from Patients' Medical Records," *Medical Care* 16 (December 1978): 999.
21. Ibid., 1000.
22. DHHS, "Discharge Survey," 6.
23. AHA, *Hospital Statistics: 1990–1991 Edition, Data from the American Hospital Association 1989 Annual Survey of Hospitals* (Chicago: AHA, 1990), 20.
24. R. S. Schweiker, *Report to Congress, Hospital Prospective Payment for Medicare* (Secretary, DHHS, December 1982), 42.
25. W. W. Young, R. B. Swinkola, and D. M. Zorn, "The Measurement of Hospital Case Mix," *Medical Care* 20 (May 1982): 501–12.
26. R. B. Fetter, J. D. Thompson, R. F. Averill, and A. T. Freedman, *The New ICD-9-CM Diagnosis Related Groups Classification Scheme: User Manual*, prepared by the ICD-9-CM Project Staff of Yale University, School of Organization and Management, Health Systems Management Group (December 1981).
27. AHA, "DRGs Creating Cost-Consciousness in New Jersey, Physician Says," *Hospital Week* 16 (10 October 1980): 3.
28. M. P. Plomann, *Case Mix Classification Systems: Development, Description and Testing* (Chicago: Hospital Research and Educational Trust, 1982).
29. *Federal Register* 53 (27 May 1988): 19644.
30. D. C. Hsia, W. M. Krushat, A. B. Fagan, J. A. Tebbutt, and R. P. Kusserow, "Accuracy of Diagnostic Coding for Medicare Payments under the Prospective-Payment System," *New England Journal of Medicine* 318 (11 February 1988): 352–5.
31. A 15-page appendix of corrections to the DRG GROUPER, effective on 1 October 1985, was announced by DHHS as part of "Medicare Program; Changes to the Inpatient Hospital Prospective Payment System and Fiscal Year 1986 Rates; Final Rule," *Federal Register* 50 (3 September 1985): 35736–50.
32. HCFA, "Medicare Program; Changes to the Inpatient Hospital Prospective Payment System and Fiscal Year 1990 Rates; Proposed Rule," *Federal Register* 54 (8 May 1989): 19636–796.
33. *Federal Register* 52 (1 September 1987): 33152.
34. K. F. Price and G. F. Kominski, "Using Patient Age in Defining DRGs for Medicare Payment," *Inquiry* 25 (Winter 1988): 494.
35. Ibid., 502.
36. *Federal Register* 52 (1 September 1987): 33152.
37. *Federal Register* 51 (3 September 1986): 31454.
38. *Federal Register* 54 (8 May 1989): 19639.

Additional Readings

Herr, W. W. "Taking a Deep Breath over Capital Payments," *Healthcare Financial Management* 45 (April 1991): 19–31.

Horn, S. D., P. D. Sharkey, J. M. Buckle, J. E. Backofen, R. F. Averill, and R. A. Horn. "The Relationship between Severity of Illness and Hospital Length of Stay and Mortality," *Medical Care* 29 (April 1991): 305–17.

Katz, S., A. B. Ford, R. W. Moskowitz, B. A. Jackson, and M. W. Jaffe. "Studies of Illness in the Aged—The Index of ADL: A Standardized Measure of Biological and Psychosocial Function," *Journal of the American Medical Association* 185 (21 September 1963): 914–19.

Kuhn, E. M., A. J. Hartz, M. S. Gottlieb, and A. A. Rimm. "The Relationship of Hospital Characteristics and the Results of Peer Review in Six Large States," *Medical Care* 29 (October 1991): 1028–37.

Starfield, B., J. Weiner, L. Mumford, and D. Steinwachs. "Ambulatory Care Groups: A Categorization of Diagnoses for Research and Management," *Health Services Research* 26 (April 1991): 53–74.

Stoskopf, C., and S. D. Horn. "The Computerized Psychiatric Severity Index as a Predictor of Inpatient Length of Stay for Psychoses," *Medical Care* 29 (March 1991): 179–95.

Discussion Questions

15.1. Explain how billing information, patient registration data, and discharge abstract summaries are integrated into a research database to support patient origin and utilization studies.

15.2. Why is a separate research database often established in a health care facility to support patient origin and utilization studies?

15.3. The common data elements in a research database include aggregate ancillary department charges for a patient (Exhibit 15.1). Explain how more detailed data within an ancillary department (such as the laboratory) might be required in patient origin and utilization studies.

15.4. You are engaged to perform an analysis of the variations in medical practice by physicians. Your initial four-way sort of the data in the research DBMS is

a. admitting physician's number by zip codes of patients, DRG, and financial class of patients

b. age of patient by sex of patient, case-mix information, and admitting physician's number

c. case-mix information by physician, expected payment source, and zip code region

d. zip codes of patients, financial class of patients, admitting physician's number, and case-mix information

15.5.   A competitor is opening an outpatient clinic in your service area. Since this competitor is the preferred provider for one of the HMOs, it is expected that this HMO's patients for certain diagnostic categories will begin to use the competitor's hospital with subsequent therapy treatments in the new clinic. In an effort to measure the impact of this activity, your initial sorting of the data in the research DBMS is

   a.   case-mix information by physician, expected payment source, and zip code region

   b.   case-mix information by expected payment source and region

   c.   patient origin information by region, zip code, and medical department

   d.   physician data by region and zip code

15.6.   Explain how the expected payment source affects the average services provided by the same physician to patients within a given DRG.

15.7.   Explain the source of information that is extracted for the research database so that a patient profile by major employers in your service area can be prepared.

15.8.   Your community hospital's management has begun to plan for the coming year, and an informed source states that a local plant may close during the next year. If this event does occur (about an 80 percent probability), most of the employees are expected to accept a transfer to another plant and move with their dependents to the other city. Explain how you would proceed to measure the impact of this potential change on the hospital. (Assume your community hospital has extensive computer-based capabilities, including a hospital financial information system, a patient care information system, a medical record abstracting system, and a separate research database for planning purposes. Review the standard reports in Exhibits 15.4 and 15.5.)

15.9.   Your community hospital's rehabilitation services department has had a shortage of physical and occupational therapists over the past year, and this staffing problem has affected the frequency with which therapy was performed on patients with specific medical conditions. There have also been scheduling problems for outpatients receiving a series of therapy services that were job or occupational related; often the therapy services were extended over a longer period of time with a reduction in the average number of services performed on a patient. Indicate how you measure the impact of this staffing problem on your community hospital. (*Hint*: The therapy services are in a series with the same identification codes, and data on inpatient versus outpatient status of patients are specified in the hospital information system.)

15.10. A tragedy occurred, resulting in the untimely death of a surgeon at your community hospital. While the late surgeon was part of a group, she was the dominant member of the team and the reason for many referrals. Assume a well-known specialist is being recruited and will begin practice in your hospital within five months; information will be sent to various referral sources after the physician begins practice in your facility. Explain how you would proceed to measure the impact of this death and staffing change on your community hospital.

15.11. New admitting and attending physicians began practicing in your community hospital within the past 60 days. It is expected that there will be four additional physicians joining the hospital in the next few weeks with similar medical practice to those who just arrived. Explain how you would proceed to measure the impact of these changes in medical practice for selected DRGs and outpatient services on the revenues and costs of your community hospital.

15.12. A competing community hospital has opened an ambulatory care clinic in your service area during the past four months. Informed sources say a second ambulatory care clinic is scheduled to be opened in another location in your service area within two months. Explain how you would proceed to measure the impact of this new clinic on your hospital.

15.13. Gamma Community Hospital's projected admissions were presented in Exhibit 15.9. Assume that the estimated loss of 500 patients to a competing clinic in the service area does not occur and that the annual admissions are increased by 500 to 14,280. Using 14,280 as a base, determine the number of cases by payor for DRG 148.

15.14. Gamma Community Hospital's ALOS by payor presented in Exhibit 15.10 have been reviewed along with the cost data in Exhibit 15.12. It has been determined that the ALOS for DRG 209 by payor is as follows:

Payor 01	11.3
Payor 02	11.6
Payor 03	11.2
Payor 04	10.8

The analysis of cost data suggested that the direct DRG cost was $3,000 instead of the $3,200 in Exhibit 15.12. Using the revised ALOS and direct DRG cost information, determine the average cost by payor for DRG 209.

15.15. Assume that in your hospital the treatment of selected DRGs and outpatient services will change during the next few weeks as new medical technology is used by physicians. The teaching hospital where this medical technology was developed has published a guideline on these new procedures, and this document is in your community hospital.

Explain how you would proceed to measure the impact of this new medical technology on your community hospital.

15.16. The seven-day LOS and protocol for DRG XXB has been approved with the financial and utilization components shown in Exhibit 15.19. Compute the contributions margin for DRG XXB.

15.17. A third party payor will only approve a five-day LOS for DRG XXB as described above in Question 15.16. Thus, some ancillary services are performed after discharge. The inpatient ancillary services to this third party payor are shown in Exhibit 15.20. Compute the contribution margin for DRG XXB under a five-day LOS.

15.18. Financial class R will support a six-day LOS for DRG XXB as described in Question 15.16, and this results in a contribution margin of $1,200 for inpatient room. The contribution margin for this same effort with a two-day LOS would be

    a. $480

    b. $240

    c. $360

    d. $720

Exhibit 15.19   Financial and Utilization Components for Seven-Day LOS and Protocol for DRG XXB

		Basis of Service	Cost per Service	Charges per Service
Room		per day		$580
Admission and medical records		per admit	$110	
Nursing care		per day	150	
Room and board		per day	190	
Financial services		per admit	130	
Operating room	3 hours	per hour	430	470
Recovery room	1 hour	per hour	125	160
Laboratory:				
Hematology	10 tests	per test	15	30
Chemistry	9 tests	per test	25	40
Pathology	6 tests	per test	30	50
Microbiology	3 tests	per test	45	60
Radiology	5 units	per unit	40	65
Respiratory therapy	8 services	per service	65	90
Physical therapy	12 services	per service	30	45

Exhibit 15.20   Inpatient Ancillary Services to a Third Party Payor for a Five-Day LOS for DRG XXB

		Basis of Service	Cost per Service	Charges per Service
Laboratory:				
Hematology	7 tests	per test	$15	$30
Chemistry	6 tests	per test	25	40
Pathology	5 tests	per test	30	50
Microbiology	3 tests	per test	45	60
Radiology	3 units	per unit	40	65
Respiratory therapy	4 services	per service	65	90
Physical therapy	8 services	per service	30	45

15.19. Financial class R will support a six-day LOS for DRG XXB as described in Question 15.16, and this results in a contribution margin of $1,200 for inpatient room. The contribution margin for this same effort with a three-day LOS would be

   a. $480

   b. $960

   c. $720

   d. $360

15.20. Financial class R will support a six-day LOS for DRG XXB as described in Question 15.16, and this results in a contribution margin of $1,200 for inpatient room. The contribution margin for this same effort with a four-day LOS would be

   a. $360

   b. $960

   c. $720

   d. $480

15.21. Assume that a group of physicians have recently opened a private clinic where outpatient surgery will be performed within their specialty. The physicians will retain their admitting privileges at your community hospital, where complex cases will continue to be treated. Explain how you would measure the impact of this private clinic on your community hospital.

15.22. Assume some of the physical and occupational therapists have recently resigned from your community hospital and will be working with two young physicians who are opening a comprehensive rehabilitation and ambulatory care clinic near your hospital. The two young physicians do not currently have admitting privileges at any hospital. How would you measure the impact of this change on your hospital?

15.23. You have been asked to construct a computer-based model of patient flow in a given ancillary department that provides services to both inpatients and outpatients. Assume that time data are retained in the patient care module for each test or procedure ordered and for each result provided. Further assume there are backup tapes containing the detailed entries and summary information displayed in Exhibit 15.2. In the particular ancillary department under study, there are three distinct medical treatment protocols followed by different physician groups. Prepare a chart showing types of data you might use in your model and the source of each information source.

16

Product Costing and Management

Introduction

Departmental directors are responsible for the services, tests, procedures, treatments, and operations provided by their areas within the approved budgetary guidelines. Variance analysis and management control procedures in a flexible budgeting context are some of the necessary tools used in monitoring these events. The key revenue areas may be organizationally structured as profit centers in which bonuses are given based on performance evaluations; this arrangement encourages monitoring and coordination of departmental activities and resources. The revenue measures used in the analysis by profit center are the average net charges, since the profit center director is typically not a participant in the contractual discussions with third party payors. The performance evaluation in each department is based on expenditures and revenue measures that are controllable by the department director.

Recent changes in the delivery of health care services, financial arrangements between third-party payors and provider groups, and other responses to competitive conditions have created new monitoring requirements that cannot be addressed by profit center directors. Performance data in the profit center with supporting variance analysis will show the changes by volume, price, and relative-value units, but the "real" reason for the shift may be events that are not apparent within the information available to the profit center. An unfavorable variance in the first period might be assumed to be a seasonal fluctuation, based on the standard information available to a profit center, but the reporting of the unfavorable variance in the next period begins to signal that it is something other than a seasonal fluctuation.

The network of support areas within a major health care facility may create an environment in which offsetting movements are not reported by variance analysis. An episode of care may use resources from many departments within the institution, and changes in the protocol of treatment for this diagnostic condition multiplied by the volume of cases may not result in a variance report for any department. Later, when case-mix analysis by physician, expected payment source, and zip code region is performed, the budget analysts are surprised that these variances had not been previously identified. Actions by third party payors may also change the mix and distribution of services in various departments, including emphasizing one protocol of treatment over other protocols.

Products are the health care services provided on an inpatient or outpatient basis within a continuum of care regardless of location. A distinction is made in the designation of a product between a treatment protocol and a diagnostic category; a given diagnostic category may have multiple treatment protocols, with each protocol classified as a product. Within the framework of a continuum of care, the health care facility is concerned with the packaging of its products and with the shift in responsibility to the next provider in those situations where subsequent services are required. Thus, a product is a treatment protocol for a type of episode of care that encompasses all of the "approved" services from the various departments under this method of medical practice, and these approved services for the product should not vary by physician or by third party payor. A given patient may receive additional services beyond those specified in the treatment protocol because of other conditions and complications.

Product management is a new administrative function in health care entities that monitors episodes of care from an organization wide perspective by type of diagnostic condition, physician, third party payor, and patient origin. Treatment protocols for each major type of episode of care are required for the designation of products before the monitoring of these sets of health care services has any meaning. The product analyst performing this new function must have access to the contractual terms and conditions with physicians and third party payors so that all appropriate measures of each treatment protocol are monitored. After this administrative position has been established, the product analyst should be deeply involved in drafting contractual terms and conditions for all physicians and third party payors.

The monitoring of performance against treatment protocols inserts a new dimension in the standard reports showing case-mix information by physician, expected payment source, and zip code region. Actions by third party payors may encourage a change in the medical practice provided by physicians for multiple treatment protocols for the same type of episode of care. Other variations in performance may be directly related to actions by competitors and to new delivery arrangements by other providers in your service area. The responses by the product analyst to the monitoring include revised guidance for staffing, procurement of supplies and services, financial investments, and cash management. These various dimensions and influences impose information requirements on the product analyst that can only be satisfied by extensive use of the research database (Exhibit 15.1), supplemented by detailed transactions supporting the financial statement of account illustrated in Exhibit 15.2.

Third Party Payor Analysis

Profiles of third party payors in the late 1960s emphasized the mix and distribution of patients by primary diagnosis, the presence or absence of a surgical procedure code, the existence of a secondary diagnosis, age, sex, zip code region, status on admission, and financial terms. There were some deductibles and limits on coverage, but the primary consideration in evaluating financial terms was the amount of contractual allowance based on the method of reimbursement: charges, reasonable cost plus 5 percent, or reasonable cost. Commercial insurance companies, in general, paid charges; Blue Cross paid reasonable cost plus 5 percent; and Medicare and Medicaid paid reasonable cost. The profiles of third party payors were important in determining the level of price increases in specific tests, procedures, operations, and health care services. Financial priority was given to price increases for services where the patients were covered by commercial insurance and self-pay. A significant price increase in services primarily for federal program patients only resulted in larger contractual allowances without any substantial change in level of cash receipts to the community hospital.

A few HMOs had been providing financial resources for health care services and monitoring the outcomes for several years, but on a national scale, HMOs were not a major third party payor. This situation changed after the enactment of the Health Maintenance Organization Act of 1973; many new legal entities began to contract with health care providers for patient services. These new entities were not under the same state insurance director that regulated other health care insurance carriers. Special rules and guidelines were applied to HMOs, which typically paid health care providers slightly more than the Blue Cross rate, but significantly less than the regulated plans approved for commercial insurance carriers. This discrepancy in rates between HMOs and commercial insurance carriers was a frustrating problem for insurance executives negotiating with state insurance directors. Since public policy supported the HMOs, some commercial insurance companies responded to the economic dilemma by the merger and acquisition of HMOs.

A confounding problem in the 1970s and early 1980s was the spiraling increase in health care costs; the rate of increase of health care costs was faster than for other consumer goods measured by the consumer price index. Various cost-containment steps were taken, including deductibles and copayments as common features in insurance policies. The cash payments by federal program patients were also increased. State insurance directors did not have the authority to regulate HMOs, but they could limit rate increases for commercial insurance companies. Accepting a regulated cap on a rate increase for premiums, commercial insurance companies were encouraged to alter deductibles, copayments, and excluded areas of coverage. Profiles of third party payors shifted from being grouped in broad categories to payor-specific profiles based on the detailed terms and limits of a given "approved" plan for that entity. Contractual allowances were joined by adjustments in the process of measuring cash receipts for a given third party payor.

Medical technology and changes in medical practice permitted new arrangements and health care delivery systems in the 1980s. Some major employers began to directly contract with health care providers without using a third party payor. HMOs expanded without being subject to rigorous regulatory scrutiny of state insurance directors. The federal government began to approve ambulatory care and rehabilitation clinics that were not affiliated with community hospitals. Some third party payors in competitive environments began to contract with multiple providers for health care services to the same population. The standard reports showing case-mix, physician, patient origin, demographics, utilization, financial, and expected payment source information have assumed new meaning with these recent initiatives by third party payors. There may be financial incentives from third party payors for physicians to offer more services through clinics and their offices rather than through the outpatient facilities at the community hospital. As more services are shifted from the community hospital, there are staffing and fixed support issues that must be considered. The full impact of new initiatives and changes in medical practice may include significant shifts in case mix, physician, patient, and payor profiles. These responses can also be expressed by changes in utilization of services, financial investments, staffing, and cash flows. Projected financial statements for the health care facility must encompass all of these shifts, changes, and movements.

Product Profiles

The approved treatment protocol is a meaningful framework in which to compare changes in medical practice and utilization of services by physician, third party payor, age, sex, and zip code region. The format of standard reports by product profiles contains two parts, as depicted by Exhibit 16.1 for a DRG. Part A encompasses the nine reporting categories for three years, as illustrated in Exhibit 13.3, and Part B presents the detailed data on key ancillary services that may vary by treatment protocol. If the treatment protocol had been for an outpatient episode of care, then the standard report would omit total days of care, total charges—room and board, average length of stay, average daily census, and average charge per patient. Ambulatory surgery and selective outpatient services use the CPT-4 coding structure; some ambulatory care and outpatient services continue to use ICD-9-CM coding for the episode of care.[1]

The research database described in Chapter 15 with its assumed flow, index arrangement, and aggregation process (Exhibit 15.1) does provide the necessary information in Part A of Exhibit 16.1 for both inpatient and outpatient treatment protocols. The specific charge information in Part B by treatment protocol is only available from the detailed transaction data supporting the discharge statement of account and the outpatient billing module.

The product analyst must identify the critical sets of transaction data for an approved treatment protocol based on the backup computer tapes supporting the discharge statement of account and billing modules. After the critical sets of data are designated, the product analyst must specify the aggregation process by treatment protocol. The laboratory charges in Part B of Exhibit 16.1, for example, are illustrated by area in Treatment Protocol A, while most of the other

Exhibit 16.1   Report 17: Case-Mix Information by Product, Physician, Expected Payment Source, and Zip Code Region

---

DRG XX Summary Information
All Treatment Protocols

Part A

				Percent Change	
	Year 1	Year 2	Year 3	Year 1–2	Year 2–3
Total hospital discharges	xx,xxx	xx,xxx	xx,xxx	x.xxx	x.xxx
Total days of care	xx,xxx	xx,xxx	xx,xxx	x.xxx	x.xxx
Total hospital charges	xx,xxx	xx,xxx	xx,xxx	x.xxx	x.xxx
Total charges—room and board	xx,xxx	xx,xxx	xx,xxx	x.xxx	x.xxx
Total ancillary charges	xx,xxx	xx,xxx	xx,xxx	x.xxx	x.xxx
Average length of stay	x.xxx	x.xxx	x.xxx	x.xxx	x.xxx
Average daily census	xxx.xxx	xxx.xxx	xxx.xxx	x.xxx	x.xxx
Average charge per patient	$x,xxx	$x,xxx	$x,xxx	x.xxx	x.xxx
Average daily charge	$xxx	$x,xxx	$x,xxx	x.xxx	x.xxx

Part B [Variable section depending on treatment protocol]

	Current Month		Fiscal Year-to-Date		Last 12 months	
	Amount	Percent*	Amount	Percent	Amount	Percent
Total ancillary charges	xx,xxx	xx.xx	xx,xxx	xx.xx	xx,xxx	xx.xx
Total charges for:						
Hematology	xx,xxx	xx.xx	xx,xxx	xx.xx	xx,xxx	xx.xx
Chemistry	xx,xxx	xx.xx	xx,xxx	xx.xx	xx,xxx	xx.xx
Microbiology	xx,xxx	xx.xx	xx,xxx	xx.xx	xx,xxx	xx.xx
Pathology	xx,xxx	xx.xx	xx,xxx	xx.xx	xx,xxx	xx.xx
Pulmonary function	xx,xxx	xx.xx	xx,xxx	xx.xx	xx,xxx	xx.xx
Radiology	xx,xxx	xx.xx	xx,xxx	xx.xx	xx,xxx	xx.xx
Pharmaceuticals	xx,xxx	xx.xx	xx,xxx	xx.xx	xx,xxx	xx.xx
Inhalation therapy	xx,xxx	xx.xx	xx,xxx	xx.xx	xx,xxx	xx.xx
Physical therapy	xx,xxx	xx.xx	xx,xxx	xx.xx	xx,xxx	xx.xx
Occupational therapy	xx,xxx	xx.xx	xx,xxx	xx.xx	xx,xxx	xx.xx
Speech therapy	xx,xxx	xx.xx	xx,xxx	xx.xx	xx,xxx	xx.xx
Cardio-graphics	xx,xxx	xx.xx	xx,xxx	xx.xx	xx,xxx	xx.xx

Continued

Exhibit 16.1   Continued

DRG XX Summary Information
Treatment Protocol A

Part A

	Year 1	Year 2	Year 3	Percent Change Year 1–2	Percent Change Year 2–3
Total hospital discharges	xx,xxx	xx,xxx	xx,xxx	x.xxx	x.xxx
Total days of care	xx,xxx	xx,xxx	xx,xxx	x.xxx	x.xxx
Total hospital charges	xx,xxx	xx,xxx	xx,xxx	x.xxx	x.xxx
Total charges—room and board	xx,xxx	xx,xxx	xx,xxx	x.xxx	x.xxx
Total ancillary charges	xx,xxx	xx,xxx	xx,xxx	x.xxx	x.xxx
Average length of stay	x.xxx	x.xxx	x.xxx	x.xxx	x.xxx
Average daily census	xxx.xxx	xxx.xxx	xxx.xxx	x.xxx	x.xxx
Average charge per patient	$x,xxx	$x,xxx	$x,xxx	x.xxx	x.xxx
Average daily charge	$xxx	$x,xxx	$x,xxx	x.xxx	x.xxx

Part B [Variable section depending on treatment protocol]

	Current Month Amount	Current Month Percent	Fiscal Year-to-Date Amount	Fiscal Year-to-Date Percent	Last 12 months Amount	Last 12 months Percent
Total ancillary charges	xx,xxx	xx.xx	xx,xxx	xx.xx	xx,xxx	xx.xx
Total charges for:						
Hematology	xx,xxx	xx.xx	xx,xxx	xx.xx	xx,xxx	xx.xx
Chemistry	xx,xxx	xx.xx	xx,xxx	xx.xx	xx,xxx	xx.xx
Microbiology	xx,xxx	xx.xx	xx,xxx	xx.xx	xx,xxx	xx.xx
Pathology	xx,xxx	xx.xx	xx,xxx	xx.xx	xx,xxx	xx.xx
Pulmonary function	xx,xxx	xx.xx	xx,xxx	xx.xx	xx,xxx	xx.xx
Radiology	xx,xxx	xx.xx	xx,xxx	xx.xx	xx,xxx	xx.xx
Pharmaceuticals	xx,xxx	xx.xx	xx,xxx	xx.xx	xx,xxx	xx.xx
Inhalation therapy	xx,xxx	xx.xx	xx,xxx	xx.xx	xx,xxx	xx.xx
Physical therapy	xx,xxx	xx.xx	xx,xxx	xx.xx	xx,xxx	xx.xx
Occupational therapy	xx,xxx	xx.xx	xx,xxx	xx.xx	xx,xxx	xx.xx
Speech therapy	xx,xxx	xx.xx	xx,xxx	xx.xx	xx,xxx	xx.xx
Cardio-graphics	xx,xxx	xx.xx	xx,xxx	xx.xx	xx,xxx	xx.xx

Continued

Exhibit 16.1   Continued

. . .

DRG XX Summary Information
Treatment Protocol A
Third Party Payor YZ

. . .

---

*Percent in each column is based on total hospital charges for the same time period as the columnar heading. While the above example only includes detailed data for ancillary departments, the specified reporting level for other treatment protocols may include room and board charges.

ancillary departments are depicted as totals. The exact aggregation process for Part B will vary by treatment protocol based on the nature and significance of the charges; however, the columnar headings are suggested as a common arrangement for all products. The layout of detailed data in Part B of Exhibit 16.1 emphasizes the distribution in dollars and percent over time for key components with information for the current month, fiscal year-to-date, and totals for the last 12 months.

Exhibit 16.1 illustrates these two parts of the standard product report with headings for DRG XX and Treatment Protocol A. The complete report for Treatment Protocol A under DRG XX will include separate Part A and Part B displays for each physician who uses Treatment Protocol A for DRG XX, separate displays for each payment source by physician, and separate displays for each zip code region for each payment source by physician. The reporting mechanism follows an exception basis of aggregating under the label "other" those situations where there are less than 10 observations within the last 12 months for a physician, for a payment source, or for a zip code region.

The standard screens or profiles emphasizing products are shown as Reports 17–23 in Exhibit 16.2; each of these reports has Part A and Part B data as illustrated in Exhibit 16.1. The information contents of the Part B section are dependent upon the treatment protocol. Reports 17–20 permit a monitoring of the utilization of services based on a given physician's medical practice. Reports 17 and 21–23 provide a foundation for monitoring third party payors and their impact on the utilization of services.

If the physician shifted from one treatment protocol to another during the period, then each of these products for that physician

Exhibit 16.2   Standard Profiles of Products and Physicians

Report 17:   *Case-Mix Information by Product, Physician, Expected Payment Source, and Zip Code Region*

This five-way sorting of data by DRG or CPT-4 group, treatment protocol, physician, expected payment source, and region based on patients' zip codes provide insight into the variations in utilization of services by a given physician for the same type of episode of care under different treatment protocols.

Report 18:   *Case-Mix Information by Products, Physician, Expected Payment Source, Region, and Zip Code*

This six-way sorting is performed on an exception basis when there are large statistical variations in the individual data elements for a region in Report 17.

Report 19:   *Case-Mix Information by Products, ICD-9-CM Diagnostic Codes, and ICD-9-CM Procedure Codes*

Selected medical technologies are designated by unique codes in the ICD-9-CM volumes, and this information can be used in validating the appropriateness of product groupings based on the discharge data for the period. If the episode of care is for outpatient services, then CPT-4 codes and ICD-9-CM codes are used in the same type of assessment.

Report 20:   *Case-Mix Information by Principal ICD-9-CM Diagnostic Code, Secondary ICD-9-CM Codes, and ICD-9-CM Procedure Codes*

This profile of medical practice for the period is compared with the product profiles in Report 19 for indications of changes in practice.

Report 21:   *Case-Mix Information by Product, Zip Code Region, and Expected Payment Source*

This four-way sorting of data by DRG or CPT-4, treatment protocol, region, and expected payment source provides summaries that can be assessed in terms of changes in medical practice for a region.

Report 22:   *Case-Mix Information by Product, Expected Payment Source, and Zip Code Region*

Medical practice provided by a given facility in a region may be dependent on selected payment sources; Reports 21 and 22 support this type of review and assessment.

Report 23:   *Case-Mix Information by Expected Payment Source, Product, and Physician*

The impact of changes in third party payors on case-mix data by product and physician can be analyzed by the summaries provided in this report.

Note: The assigned report numbers are a continuation of the series illustrated in Exhibit 15.5.

is represented by a set of displays under Report 17 in Exhibit 16.2. The differences in length of stay, utilization of services, and financial charges between these treatment protocols are determined by comparing information in the unique displays by physician. The product analyst uses the insights from these comparisons in suggesting revisions in procurement planning, staffing and resource management, cash flow projections, and financial management activities.

Data elements 12–15 of the research database in Exhibit 15.1 were ICD-9-CM diagnosis and procedure codes. The unique ICD-9-CM and CPT-4 codes identified with a given medical technology provide the basis for partitioning and analyzing a given physician's medical practice with respect to a given treatment protocol. Report 19 in Exhibit 16.2 shows the unique experience under this new medical practice by physician with one display that can be compared with a display for the same physician when this medical technology is not used in the treatment protocol. The ICD-9-CM and CPT-4 codes in Reports 19 and 20 provide the basis for assessing if the cumulative experience from the discharge data suggests that there has really been a change in medical practice calling for revisions in products.

Third party payors influence medical practice and the utilization of services; Reports 17 and 21-23 are standard profiles used in assessing actions by third party payors. Financial incentives are such that some third party payors in a competitive environment may use alternative providers for selected services; these movements can only be monitored by detailed charge data depicted in Part B information illustrated by Exhibit 16.1. There are certain health care services that require a significant amount of effort, and yet, the service is not generally priced to cover the total cost. There are other procedures and tests that may have a relatively high contribution margin. A given ancillary department may have a mixture of these types of tests and services that can only be monitored by the detailed data in Part B that vary for treatment protocol.

The laboratory is a good example of a department with a wide variation in contribution margin among areas. There are high volumes of common tests in hematology and chemistry, which supports extensive use of standard instruments and automated equipment. The mix and distribution of tests in microbiology, cytology, and pathology permit only limited use of automated equipment from an economic perspective. There are many types of tests in microbiology and pathology that are unique to a patient's condition, and the technologists can only apply a general framework in the labor-intensive steps. The customary practice in many service areas is for the high volume of hematology and chemistry tests to be priced with a large contribution margin that can be used to subsidize the labor-intensive tests in the other areas of the laboratory department. For example, there can be a $300 pathology test (based on full costing) that is uniquely performed for a surgical patient, who is billed only $125. If the same patient has a few batteries of chemical tests performed, then there is an aggregate contribution margin from that patient to the laboratory.

Product profiles provide monitoring information on responses by third party payors, physicians, and other providers to institutional knowledge about the pricing of health care services in determining where selective activities are performed. If the hematology and chemistry tests, for example, with high contribution margins are performed at an independent clinic or facility, then there are financial problems for a hospital that only performs the microbiology and pathology tests with low contribution margins. The selection of the Part B data for each treatment protocol considers, among other factors, institutional knowledge and pricing arrangements.

Physicians with multiple affiliations may respond to peer pressure in determining the patients that are admitted to a given hospital. This activity can be identified by Report 17 in Exhibit 16.2, which examines case-mix information by products, physician, expected payment source, and zip code region. The partition on the DRG or CPT group by product and payor provides a narrow slice for examining the statistical distribution of episodes of care. The product analyst's study will show if the utilization of services by this physician's patients are outliers versus other physician profiles for the same product and payor.

Physician Attestation

Documentation for billing of a federal program inpatient includes a signed statement by the attending physician on the health services provided to that patient. The contents of this statement have expanded during the past five years to encompass critical ICD-9-CM diagnostic and procedure codes that affect the reimbursement classification by the case-mix system. The required documentation extends beyond the patient's bill; the same information by the attending physician must be present in the medical records. In addition, the hospital must have on file a current signed and dated acknowledgment that the attending physician has received formal notice of the consequences to anyone who misrepresents, falsifies, or conceals essential information required for payment of federal funds under the case-mix system. This formal acknowledgment, signed by the attending physician for a given patient's episode of care, must have been completed within the year prior to the submission of the claim to the fiscal intermediary.

The documentation requirements in Section 412.46 of the federal code, entitled "Medical Review Requirements: DRG Validation," are modified annually as adjustments and corrections are made in the case-mix system. Although these refinements are essential for claims submitted to the fiscal intermediary, a major impact of this section has been on the behavior of physicians, who no longer view a signed discharge statement as a perfunctory task. The wording of the physician attestation requirement in paragraph (a) of 412.46 is as follows:

> The attending physician must, shortly before, at, or shortly after discharge (but before a claim is submitted), attest to the principal diagnosis, secondary diagnoses, and names of major procedures performed. The information must be in writing in the medical record, and, except as provided in paragraph (b) of this section, the physician must sign the statement. Below the diagnostic and procedural information, and on the same page, the following statement must immediately precede the physician's dated signature:
>
> "I certify that the narrative descriptions of the principal and secondary diagnoses and the major procedures performed are accurate and complete to the best of my knowledge."[2]

The physician acknowledgment is addressed by paragraph (c) in the same section, which begins the "Notice to Physicians" with a restatement of the physician attestation and concludes with the following sentence:

> Anyone who misrepresents, falsifies, or conceals essential information required for payment of Federal funds, may be subject to fine, imprisonment, or civil penalty under applicable Federal laws.[3]

This documentation procedure in the medical record by the attending physician for federal program patients is important, but the significance of this process is far beyond claims submitted to fiscal intermediaries. The chart with the physician attestation is subject to medical review and examination by quality assurance. Standard Report 19 in Exhibit 16.2, showing case-mix information by products, ICD-9-CM and CPT-4 diagnostic codes, secondary codes, and procedure codes, may be used in screening for outliers within a treatment protocol.

The patient's final case-mix specification may be different from the expected grouping at an early point in the episode of care.

If the time sequence of events is not captured in the patient's log, then the attending physician may be subject to criticism by peers for unnecessary procedures when, in fact, results from specific tests were not available until a later point in time. The timing of the entries in the log of dictated medical interpretations are extremely critical when these charts are used in malpractice disputes with a jury. If there is no entry, then the typed document of a medical interpretation that is received several hours after a critical event in a treatment episode may be discarded by the jury. But, unnecessary peer pressure may occur shortly after discharge from a medical review or quality assurance examination of a care episode when the log does not contain all the exact times for entries and documents.

Attending physicians are not in a protected position when explaining an episode of care in a legal dispute; they are often criticized by other members of their profession serving as expert witnesses. *The New England Journal of Medicine* and other professional medical journals have emphasized unnecessary procedures in medical practice, and these articles and statements are quoted by expert witnesses against the attending physicians in malpractice cases. The attending physician knows the immediate patient outcome from the services rendered at the time the attestation is being signed. Therefore, it is prudent for the physician to review any modifications and late entries in the chart and records supporting the treatment before signing the document.

Discharge Abstract Data

The document required to support a patient bill is not complete until the medical records contain the physician attestation for federal program inpatients and other third party payors that demand this statement. After the physician attestation is signed and the bill is submitted to the third party payor, there are timing issues concerning when the research database is extracted from the hospital financial information system, the patient order-entry and result-reporting modules, and the medical records module. There are also timing and distribution issues associated with the mix of discharge experiences that are initially available at the end of a period.

Those claims and patient bills that are not processed within 5 days from discharge date are typically not simple cases. They are the exception, the complex case with many secondary diagnoses; often these complex cases have many procedure codes. There may be other contributing factors that are not easily represented by the ICD-9-CM codes. In these cases, the attending physicians are reviewing the charts and documents before signing the attestation block. In other late cases, attending physicians are not available for professional or personal reasons, but the episodes of care are representative of treatment protocols.

Exhibit 16.3 is an example of the distribution of simple and complex cases at a community hospital under the assumption of no adverse behavior by attending physicians and third party payors. The distribution of episodes in this example is generalized from the actual experiences of several community hospitals concerned with the problem; otherwise, all cases would not be closed within 22 days. Note that 660 cases out of 820 standard treatment protocols are available on time (within 5 days after discharge); the remaining 160 cases (20 percent) are not fully available until 22 days after discharge even though these are standard treatment protocols. Hospital administrators use many different types of peer pressure, inducements, incentives, and restrictions (such as admitting privileges) in efforts to reduce the late processing of patient bills because of missing physician attestations.

The 40 exceptional cases that are on time only represent 22 percent of the complex cases; information on 70 of the remaining 140 cases will not be available until 11 to 16 days after discharge (Exhibit 16.3). There are personal and professional reasons that attending physicians may not be available within 5 days after discharge to review charts and sign the physician attestation. Problems in capturing data in medical records and the display of information in charts and documents may be major contributing factors to these delays in signing of physician attestation. There may also be delays because of the late processing of test results and other findings by medical records personnel and other professional staff members. It is prudent for the attending physician to thoroughly review the final charts and records before signing the medical record.

Extracting discharge data for a period without considering the delays represented by Exhibit 16.3 can result in a disproportional mix of simple episodes of care with very little "surprise value" or variances. The cumulative data that are extracted at the end of the current period will reflect major adjustments for the previous period. The monitoring function can keep even with the status, but this informed assessment can only be made after most of the late physician attestation statements have been processed.

Exhibit 16.3   Distribution of Simple and Complex Cases at
Community Hospital

Given:

1. No adverse behavior by attending physicians and third party payors
2. 1,000 discharges for the period
3. 820 discharges after standard episodes of care in accordance with the treatment protocols
4. 180 discharges after complex cases utilizing more resources than budget levels by standard treatment protocols

Signing of Physician Attestation and Billing of Patient	*Standard Treatment Protocols*	*Exceptional Cases*	*Total*	*Cumulative Total*
Early	570	30	600	600
5 days after discharge	90	10	100	700
Subtotal for on time	*660*	*40*	*700*	
6–7 days after discharge	50	17	67	767
8–10 days after discharge	40	20	60	827
11–16 days after discharge	45	70	115	942
17–22 days after discharge	25	33	58	1,000
Total cases	*820*	*180*	*1,000*	

Product Budgeting

A seven-step modular framework for case-mix management was discussed in Chapter 15. The capture of information by this framework may not satisfy the administrative requirements in a highly competitive environment. There are financial incentives for third party payors to capitalize on the shortcomings in the case-mix system and on the institutional knowledge about pricing of services. But these activities by third party payors and other providers can be identified by monitoring treatment protocols partitioned by third party payors and physicians. Changes in application of technology and medical practice can be identified and monitored by examining ICD-9-CM codes within a DRG group or CPT system for outpatient categories. Thus, the episode of care in the seven-step framework may need to be specified at a lower level than the DRG or CPT-4 group in coping with some competitive environments.

The first step in the seven-step modular framework is a projection of patient admissions and registrations by type of episode of care (DRG or outpatient group). In some competitive settings, the first step must be applied by treatment protocol within the DRG or outpatient group in order to accommodate the information requirements of administrative personnel. There are other situations where the first step needs to be at an even more detailed level by treatment protocol partitioned by third party payor within the DRG or outpatient group if the information demands are to be satisfied.

The product analyst has three choices concerning the initial level of accumulating information:

1. By episode of care
2. By treatment protocol within an episode of care
3. By treatment protocol partitioned by third party payor within an episode of care

Regardless of the selection, there is no single specification that is necessarily valid in a highly competitive environment for a metropolitan area. There may be major differences in the critical factors influencing various health care providers. One hospital may have contracts with twelve different HMOs along with the usual array of commercial insurance carriers, Blue Cross, Medicare, Medicaid, and patients supported by other governmental programs. Another hospital may have contracts with three HMOs whose behavior is very similar to traditional third party payors, but the real pressure on this second hospital is coming from corporate contracts with three dominant employers. A different hospital in this same metropolitan area may have many attending physicians with multiple affiliations and problems in the mix and distribution of patients referred to this hospital versus to competing facilities.

The standard reports in Exhibits 15.5 and 16.2 can be used to monitor for these types of movements, but there is no single report that is best for all of these factors. Instead, product analysts can determine from the standard reports the combination of profiles that focuses on the set of unique factors most influencing the given health care facility; those relevant reports can then be used in monitoring activities during the subsequent periods. The approach outlined in the next section discusses alternative partitioning of discharge data to more appropriately meet the needs of a given health care facility.

Projecting Products by Payor for Inpatients

Delta Community Hospital is a 400-bed facility with 14,000 admissions and 40,000 outpatient registrations per year. There are 16 beds in the intensive care unit (ICU), 195 beds in the medical ward, and 189 beds in the surgical ward. The recent occupancy rate for all beds has been 74 percent. The 40,000 registrations are an aggregation of three departments: (1) 25,000 outpatient visits, (2) 12,000 clinic visits, and (3) 3,000 same-day surgeries.

For illustration purposes, there are only three third party payors at Delta Community Hospital, and all inpatient services are grouped into nine case-mix categories, with the ninth category being "other" for all remaining cases. Eight of the nine case-mix groups have a medical treatment protocol and a surgical treatment protocol; the remaining group has a single medical treatment protocol. The demographics and patient origin profiles are different among third party payors, resulting in a variation in utilization of services and length of stay by third party payor within a treatment protocol.

Exhibit 16.4 shows the frequency and distribution of Delta Community Hospital's admissions by treatment protocol per third party payor within a case-mix group. This is a combination of the first two steps in the modular framework of Chapter 15, but the analysis begins at a lower level than the episode of care. The third and fourth steps in the modular framework are accomplished in Exhibit 16.5 with the computation of days of care for each third party payor's patients identified with a given treatment protocol within a case-mix group. Delta Community Hospital has separate wards for the medical versus the surgical admission; thus, the length-of-stay data can be mapped into revenue by bed area. Some medical admissions and some surgical admissions at Delta Community Hospital may have combined stays in the ICU plus the regular ward; Exhibit 16.5 shows this hospital's experience used in projecting ICU days of care.

The frequency distribution of admissions in Exhibit 16.4 was by treatment protocol within a DRG, and the distribution by payor was based on the treatment protocol. This is a more detailed level than the calculation of an average DRG frequency by payor, as illustrated in Exhibit 15.9. The projection of inpatient revenue is also at a more detailed level. Exhibit 16.6 contains detailed projections of revenue for DRG

Exhibit 16.4   Distribution of Inpatient Case-Mix Data by Payor for Delta Community Hospital

Case Mix	Treatment Protocol		Frequency of Admission		Medical Admissions	Surgical Admissions
		Medical	Surgical			
DRG XX1	Med01	Surg01	0.0714	0.0852	999.6	1,192.8
DRG XX2	Med02	Surg02	0.0625	0.0256	875.0	358.4
DRG XX3	Med03	Surg03	0.0213	0.0679	298.2	950.6
DRG XX4	Med04	Surg04	0.0734	0.0908	1,027.6	1,271.2
DRG XX5	Med05	Surg05	0.0604	0.0797	845.6	1,115.8
DRG XX6	Med06	Surg06	0.0471	0.0640	659.4	896.0
DRG XX7	Med07	Surg07	0.0523	0.0225	732.2	315.0
DRG XX8	Med08		0.0419		586.6	
DRG XX9	Med09	Surg08	0.0715	0.0625	1,001.0	875.0
Total					7,025.2	6,974.8

Distribution within Treatment Protocol by Payor

	Medical Treatment Protocols			Surgical Treatment Protocols		
	Payor 01	Payor 02	Payor 03	Payor 01	Payor 02	Payor 03
DRG XX1	584.4	156.6	258.6	567.1	237.0	388.7
DRG XX2	430.8	191.2	253.1	164.1	79.0	115.3
DRG XX3	114.7	79.6	103.9	456.5	170.6	323.5
DRG XX4	223.5	470.0	334.1	285.9	506.7	478.6
DRG XX5	321.7	268.6	255.3	442.2	363.2	310.4
DRG XX6	331.1	132.2	196.1	464.8	180.6	250.5
DRG XX7	365.0	201.3	165.9	160.1	88.0	66.8
DRG XX8	216.4	173.2	197.0			
DRG XX9	513.7	189.3	298.0	439.8	159.5	275.7

XX1 by payor within a medical treatment protocol; Exhibit 16.7 is the revenue for DRG XX1 by payor within a surgical treatment protocol.

The $3,284,149 of charges for Payor 01 in Exhibit 16.6 represents 61.5 percent of total charges for treatment protocol Med01; the patients for Payor 01 consist of 58.5 percent of the total cases. The ALOS for Payor 01's patients is 8.10 days, longer than the 7.60 ALOS for Payor 02's patients and the 6.90 ALOS for Payor 03's patients. With the longer ALOS for Payor 01's patients, the 58.5 percent of the total cases represents 61.4 percent of the total days of care (Exhibit 16.6). While

Exhibit 16.5   Length of Stay by Case-Mix Group and Third Party Payor for Delta Community Hospital

	Days of Care Medical Treatment Protocols			Days of Care Surgical Treatment Protocols		
	Payor 01	*Payor 02*	*Payor 03*	*Payor 01*	*Payor 02*	*Payor 03*
DRG XX1	4,733.4	1,190.4	1,784.3	5,216.9	2,062.0	2,954.4
DRG XX2	4,221.5	1,739.8	1,948.5	1,887.3	782.0	980.0
DRG XX3	665.0	445.9	592.4	2,830.2	1,006.7	1,940.9
DRG XX4	1,765.7	3,525.2	2,539.0	2,344.3	4,002.9	3,733.1
DRG XX5	2,734.2	2,149.2	2,093.4	4,156.6	3,268.7	2,824.8
DRG XX6	2,052.7	846.1	1,235.5	3,114.5	1,174.1	1,653.4
DRG XX7	2,190.0	1,127.2	945.7	976.7	501.8	387.7
DRG XX8	2,034.1	1,472.4	1,634.9			
DRG XX9	4,058.3	1,476.5	2,294.6	3,694.1	1,292.1	2,205.7

Distribution by Bed Area

Admission

Total medical admissions	7,025.2
Total surgical admissions	6,974.8
Total admissions	*14,000*

Length of Stay

Total days of care—medical admission	53,495.7
Total days of care—surgical admission	54,991.1
Total days of care	*108,487*

Revenue by Bed Area

	Days	Rate	Revenue
Total intensive care unit—days of care*	4,369.377	$965	$ 4,216,449
Total medical ward—days of care	52,425.79	360	18,873,286
Total surgical ward—days of care	51,691.59	425	21,968,926
Total room charges	*108,487*		*$45,058,661*

*Delta Community Hospital's experience suggests that 2 percent of the days of care for medical admissions and 6 percent of the days of care for surgical admissions will be spent in the intensive care unit.

Payor 01's patients had the highest average charge per case ($5,620), Payor 02's patients with a shorter ALOS had the highest average charge per day ($703). Payor 03's patients compose 25.9 percent of the total cases but consist of only 23.2 percent of the total days of care since

Exhibit 16.6   Revenues for DRG XX1 Medical Treatment Protocol
Med01 by Payor for Delta Community Hospital

	DRG XX1–Med01	*Payor 01*	*Payor 02*	*Payor 03*
Intensive care unit	$965 per day	$ 91,354	$ 22,976	$ 34,437
Medical ward	$360 per day	1,669,931	419,989	629,507
Surgical ward	$425 per day	0	0	0
Operating and recovery room	$60 per hour	0	0	0
Hematology and chemistry	x tests @ $37	259,459	69,547	86,113
Pathology and microbiology	x tests @ $44	205,697	55,136	68,269
Radiology	x tests @ $30	157,779	42,292	62,063
Outpatient surgical service		0	0	0
Other ancillary services	$590 + $190/day	899,929	226,774	339,610
Total charges	*$5,340,862*	*$3,284,149*	*$836,714*	*$1,219,999*
Percent	100%	61.49%	15.67%	22.84%
Total cases	999.6	584.4	156.6	258.6
Percent	100%	58.46%	15.67%	25.87%
Total days of care	7,708.1	4,733.4	1,190.4	1,784.3
Percent	100%	61.41%	15.44%	23.15%
Average patient days	7.71	8.10	7.60	6.90
Average charge per case	$5,343.00	$5,620.02	$5,341.73	$4,717.77
Average charge per day	$ 692.89	$ 693.83	$ 702.86	$ 683.74

Payor 03's patients have the shortest ALOS for treatment protocol
Med01 and the lowest average charge per case ($684).

Exhibit 16.7 presents similar financial and utilization information
for surgical treatment protocol Surg01 by payor. The data in Exhibits
16.6 and 16.7 are for DRG XX1, and these displays show a shift in
the mix and distribution of patients between the medical treatment
protocol and the surgical treatment protocol. Payor 01 has an almost
equal assignment between the two treatment protocols for DRG XX1
(584 cases in the medical treatment protocol and 567 cases in the

Exhibit 16.7 Revenues for DRG XX1 Surgical Treatment Protocol
Surg01 by Payor for Delta Community Hospital

	DRG XX1–Surg01	Payor 01	Payor 02	Payor 03
Intensive care unit	$965 per day	$ 302,060	$ 119,389	$ 171,058
Medical ward	$360 per day	0	0	0
Surgical ward	$425 per day	2,084,162	823,761	1,180,272
Operating and recovery room	5 hours @ $60	170,117	71,103	116,620
Hematology and chemistry	x tests @ $37	293,736	122,771	143,832
Pathology and microbiology	x tests @ $44	249,505	104,284	136,834
Radiology	x tests @ $30	187,129	78,213	104,958
Outpatient surgical service		0	0	0
Other ancillary services	$590 + $230/day	1,200,483	474,845	680,096
Total charges	$8,815,228	$4,487,192	$1,794,366	$2,533,670
Percent	100%	50.90%	20.36%	28.74%
Total cases	1,192.8	567.1	237.0	388.7
Percent	100%	47.54%	19.87%	32.59%
Total days of care	10,233.3	5,216.9	2,062.0	2,954.4
Percent	100%	50.98%	20.15%	28.87%
Average patient days	8.58	9.20	8.70	7.60
Average charge per case	$7,390.37	$7,913.12	$7,570.87	$6,517.76
Average charge per day	$ 861.43	$ 860.12	$ 870.21	$ 857.60

surgical treatment protocol), but the cases in Exhibit 16.7 represent
only 47.5 percent of the total surgical cases. Payor 02's and Payor 03's
patients are more likely to be treated by a surgical protocol than
by a medical protocol. Payor 02's patients have the highest average
charge per day ($870) for the surgical treatment protocol Surg01; this
outcome is related to the 8.70 ALOS for these patients versus the 9.20
ALOS for Payor 01's patients.

A separate panel of patient's financial and utilization data is
prepared for each treatment protocol by payor. With nine DRGs, Delta

Community Hospital has eight other sets of information that are similar to Exhibits 16.6 and 16.7; this aggregate inpatient experience is then summarized by payor in Exhibit 16.8, with total inpatient charges of $82,856,895. Payor 01's patients represent 44.8 percent of total inpatient charges, 43.4 percent of total cases, and 44.9 percent of total days of care since they have the highest ALOS (8.0 days). Payor 01's patients have the highest average charge per case ($6,103); however, Payor 02's patients, with a slightly shorter ALOS (7.7 days), have the highest average charge per day ($770).

Projecting Products by Payor for Outpatient Services

Exhibits 16.4 to 16.8 illustrate product budgeting by payor for inpatients; the same approach is followed with outpatients, except there is no ALOS for outpatient care. Delta Community Hospital has nine case-mix groups for all outpatient episodes of care; there are three outpatient case-mix groups in each of the three areas, as illustrated in the first column of Exhibit 16.9 with the designations CPT XX1 to CPT XX9. Each outpatient case-mix group based on CPT-4 codes is partitioned by treatment protocol into a type A and a type B product, as specified in the second and third columns of Exhibit 16.9 with designations that indicate where the products are being delivered. The products for the three outpatient case-mix groups in the clinic are labeled Clinic01 to Clinic06; in the outpatient area, Outpt01 to Outpt06; and in the same-day surgery area, SDSurg01 to SDSurg06.

Delta Community Hospital has three third party payors, and each payor's patient profile has a different mix of demographic and patient origin attributes that affect the health services provided. These third party payors also have different financial incentives for providers as to the location of selected support services for outpatient episodes of care. This unique relationship is mapped in Exhibit 16.9 in the projection of registrations by payor within a treatment protocol for an outpatient case-mix group. The nine outpatient case-mix groups, partitioned by a type A and a type B product, and divided by the three third party payors, result in 54 sets of projected registrations, illustrated in the lower section of Exhibit 16.9. The 12,000 projected clinic registrations are separately calculated by payor within a product; the 25,000 outpatient visits and the 3,000 same-day surgery episodes are handled in the same manner as the clinic visits within Exhibit 16.9.

Average charges for an outpatient episode may blend together the differences in mix and distribution of services by payor within

Exhibit 16.8   Total Projected Inpatient Revenues by Payor for Delta
Community Hospital

Combined for All Medical and Surgical Treatment Protocols

Inpatient Charges by Unit	DRG XX1– DRG XX9	Payor 01	Payor 02	Payor 03
Intensive care unit	$965 per day	$1,874,349	$1,085,507	$1,256,592
Medical ward	$360 per day	8,627,685	4,929,550	5,316,051
Surgical ward	$425 per day	9,676,114	5,629,118	6,663,693
Operating and recovery room	x hours @ $60	757,758	494,386	590,145
Hematology and chemistry	x tests @ $37	2,631,513	1,486,030	1,493,276
Pathology and microbiology	x tests @ $44	2,370,621	1,400,718	1,497,531
Radiology	x tests @ $30	1,656,393	977,583	1,016,556
Outpatient surgical service		0	0	0
Other ancillary departments	$590 + x/day	9,523,204	5,594,101	6,308,421
Total charges	$82,856,895	$37,117,637	$21,596,993	$24,142,265
Percent	100%	44.80%	26.06%	29.14%
Total cases	14,000.0	6,081.62	3,646.83	4,271.55
Percent	100%	43.44%	26.05%	30.51%
Total days of care	108,486.7	48,675.45	28,063.06	31,748.25
Percent	100%	44.87%	25.87%	29.26%
Average patient days	7.75	8.00	7.70	7.43
Average charge per case	$5,918.35	$6,103.25	$5,922.12	$5,651.88
Average charge per day	$ 763.75	$ 762.55	$ 769.59	$ 760.43

a treatment protocol. The detailed financial and utilization data are
required for each of Delta Community Hospital's 54 sets of projected
registrations. Exhibit 16.10 presents aggregate data on 18 sets of projected registrations representing the 12,000 clinic visits. Payor 01's
patients constitute 55.1 percent of total clinic charges, compose 48.6
percent of the total visits, and have the highest average charge per
clinic visit. Payor 03's patients have the largest variance in the other
direction, with 25.8 percent of charges, 30.0 percent of the visits, and
the lowest average charge per clinic visit.

Exhibit 16.9   Distribution of Outpatient Episodes of Care Data by Payor for Delta Community Hospital

Case Mix	Treatment Protocol		Frequency of Registration		Type A Registration	Type B Registration
			Type A	Type B		
Clinic Visits						
CPT XX1	Clinic01	Clinic02	0.1854	0.1472	2,224.8	1,766.4
CPT XX2	Clinic03	Clinic04	0.1557	0.1362	1,868.4	1,634.4
CPT XX3	Clinic05	Clinic06	0.2099	0.1656	2,518.8	1,987.2
Total clinic visits					12,000	
Outpatient Visits						
CPT XX4	Outpt01	Outpt02	0.1731	0.1579	4,327.5	3,947.5
CPT XX5	Outpt03	Outpt04	0.1235	0.2508	3,087.5	6,270.0
CPT XX6	Outpt05	Outpt06	0.1366	0.1581	3,415.0	3,952.5
Total outpatient visits					25,000	
Same-Day Surgery						
CPT XX7	SDSurg01	SDSurg02	0.1951	0.1688	585.3	506.4
CPT XX8	SDSurg03	SDSurg04	0.2387	0.2005	716.1	601.5
CPT XX9	SDSurg05	SDSurg06	0.1146	0.0823	343.8	246.9
Total same-day surgery visits					3,000	

Distribution within Treatment Protocol by Payor

	Treatment Protocols Type A			Treatment Protocols Type B		
	Payor 01	Payor 02	Payor 03	Payor 01	Payor 02	Payor 03
Clinic Visits						
CPT XX1	1,211.6	415.4	597.8	892.7	333.3	540.3
CPT XX2	882.4	426.9	559.0	781.1	376.6	476.8
CPT XX3	1,044.0	647.3	827.4	1,013.9	376.6	596.8
Outpatient Visits						
CPT XX4	1,244.2	1,546.6	1,536.7	1,203.6	1,336.6	1,407.3
CPT XX5	1,328.9	888.3	870.4	2,622.1	1,915.5	1,732.4
CPT XX6	1,680.5	787.2	947.3	1,931.2	837.1	1,184.2
Same-Day Surgery						
CPT XX7	285.9	137.5	161.9	242.2	146.6	117.6
CPT XX8	314.3	182.8	219.0	215.7	183.7	202.1
CPT XX9	166.1	68.5	109.2	124.8	51.8	70.4

Exhibit 16.10   Total Projected Clinic Revenues by Payor for Delta
Community Hospital

Outpatient Charges by Unit	*Treatment Protocols*	*Payor 01*	*Payor 02*	*Payor 03*
Hematology and chemistry	x tests @ $37	$ 421,380	$151,311	$273,930
Pathology and microbiology	x tests @ $44	211,725	63,328	83,688
Radiology	x tests @ $30	367,312	120,327	93,672
Outpatient surgical service	x visits @ $420	0	0	0
Other ancillary departments	x visits @ $20	116,516	51,522	71,962
Total charges	*$2,026,673*	*$1,116,933*	*$386,488*	*$523,252*
Percent	100%	55.11%	19.07%	25.82%
Total visits	12,000.0	5,825.80	2,576.09	3,598.11
Percent	100%	48.55%	21.47%	29.98%
Average charge per visit	$168.89	$191.72	$150.03	$145.42

The detailed data by treatment protocol per payor at Delta Community Hospital that are aggregated in Exhibit 16.10 contain larger variances in the mix and distribution of services than suggested by the averages for all clinic visits. For example, some clinic treatment protocols have the highest average charges per visit by Payor 03's patients because of demographic conditions; there are other clinic treatment protocols where Payor 02's patients have the highest average charges per visit. Each of the 18 sets of clinic registration profiles must be analyzed in understanding the expected health care services that may be provided to patients during the coming period.

The aggregate financial and utilization data for outpatient episodes of care at Delta Community Hospital are summarized in Exhibit 16.11 by payor. The information is displayed in four parts with summary charge, visits, and average charge data reported for the three segments (clinic visits, outpatient visits, and same-day surgery episodes). Parts B, C, and D are included for purposes of restricting erroneous assumptions regarding the 40,000 combined registrations for the three segments in Part A beyond the composite distribution of departmental ancillary services by payor. Part B, for example, shows that Payor 01's patients constitute 55.1 percent of total clinic charges, 33.7 percent of total outpatient charges, and 44.9 percent of total same-day surgery charges. Payor 02's and Payor 03's patients make greater use of outpatient visits than they do of clinic visits.

Part D of Exhibit 16.11 shows that Payor 01 has the highest average charge per clinic visit, Payor 02 has the highest average charge per same-day surgery episode, and Payor 03 has the highest average charge per outpatient visit. Payor 01 had the lowest average charge per outpatient visit, which combined with the 40.0 percent portion of total outpatient visits in Part C results in only a 33.7 percent of total outpatient charges in Part B. Payor 03 had the highest average charge per outpatient visit based on 10 percent less volume than Payor 01 but had the combined impact of the highest percent of total outpatient charges in Part B. After examining the summary measures in Exhibit 16.11, the product analyst can go to the detailed reports by treatment protocol for relevant financial and utilization data by payor.

Aggregate Reports

The total projected inpatient revenue by payor in Exhibit 16.8 is combined with the total projected outpatient revenue by payor in Exhibit 16.11 to produce total projected revenues for Delta Community Hospital. Aggregation of financial data by payor is performed simultaneously with the summation of relevant utilization statistics supporting each of the revenue elements by payor. The detailed utilization and statistical measures at Delta Community Hospital have been omitted in the various exhibits in this chapter; however, such data would include the volume of tests, procedures, operations, or activities by major area within each department; relative-value units; and statistical measures of performance. For example, each treatment protocol by payor with revenue from hematology and chemistry tests would contain volume information by groups of tests with aggregate data on relative-value units.

Exhibit 16.12 contains total projected revenues by payor for Delta Community Hospital with supporting utilization and statistical data. Each revenue cell in Part A of Exhibit 16.12 is supported by a series of utilization and statistical measures in Part B. This exhibit shows the aggregation of information by payor on discharges, days of care by area, registrations by area, tests, procedures, and services. In addition, there are volume, relative-value units, and statistical measures of performance for each ancillary department and organizational unit.

Exhibit 16.11 Total Projected Outpatient Revenues by Payor for Delta Community Hospital

Part A
The 40,000 Clinic, Outpatient, and Same-Day Surgery Visits

	Treatment Protocols	Payor 01	Payor 02	Payor 03
Hematology and chemistry	x tests @ $37	$1,208,639	$856,219	$996,092
Pathology and microbiology	x tests @ $44	524,666	288,342	386,310
Radiology	x tests @ $30	627,175	334,647	403,175
Outpatient surgical service	x visits @ $420	566,583	323,740	369,677
Other ancillary departments	x visits @ x	327,378	195,878	226,744
Total charges	$7,635,265	$3,254,441	$1,998,826	$2,381,998
Percent	100%	42.62%	26.18%	31.20%
Total visits	40,000.0	17,185.24	10,658.23	12,156.53
Percent	100%	42.96%	26.65%	30.39%
Average charge per visit	$190.88	$189.37	$187.54	$195.94

Part B
Summary of Outpatient Episodes by Total Charges

	All Payors	Payor 01	Payor 02	Payor 03
Clinic	$2,026,673	$1,116,933	$386,488	$523,252
Percent	100%	55.11%	19.07%	25.82%
Outpatient	$3,386,610	$1,139,536	$1,037,874	$1,209,200
Percent	100%	33.65%	30.65%	35.70%
Same-day surgery	$2,221,982	$997,972	$574,464	$649,546
Percent	100%	44.92%	25.85%	29.23%

Part C
Summary of Outpatient Episodes by Total Visits

	All Payors	Payor 01	Payor 02	Payor 03
Clinic	12,000.0	5,825.80	2,576.09	3,598.11
Percent	100%	48.55%	21.47%	29.98%

Continued

Exhibit 16.11   Continued

	All Payors	Payor 01	Payor 02	Payor 03
Outpatient	25,000.0	10,010.44	7,311.33	7,678.24
Percent	100%	40.04%	29.25%	30.71%
Same-day surgery	3,000.0	1,349.01	770.81	880.18
Percent	100%	44.97%	25.69%	29.34%

Part D
Summary of Outpatient Episodes by Average Charge per Visit

	All Payors	Payor 01	Payor 02	Payor 03
Clinic	$168.89	$191.72	$150.03	$145.42
Outpatient	$135.46	$113.83	$141.95	$157.48
Same-day surgery	$740.66	$739.78	$745.27	$737.97

The information in these aggregate reports are used in forecasting the variable costs and staffing guidelines for the budget period by cost element: direct labor, fringe benefits, supplies, contractual services, utilities, and other expenses. This budgeting process extends beyond the variable costs in the ancillary and operational units directly providing health care services; the variable-cost components of support and administrative units are also forecasted by this process. For example, the days of care, visits, and discharges are used in projecting housekeeping and related support services. At the conclusion of this phase of the budgeting, there would be separate sets of projected variable-costs data for each ancillary, operational, support, and administrative department. The other phase of the budgeting process focuses on fixed costs, addressed in the next section.

Monitoring Product Cost

Hospital and health care facilities are in a unique industry of providing medical and health services to human beings in accordance with given standards of professional practice. There are fixed costs of delivering these services that are not part of the above variable-cost measures, but these expenditures are based on medical review, risk management, quality assurance, and malpractice considerations. The required fixed staffing for a relevant range of activities must be

Exhibit 16.12   Total Projected Revenues by Payor for Delta
Community Hospital

Part A
Total Revenues

	All Payors	Payor 01	Payor 02	Payor 03
Intensive care unit	$ 4,216,450	$ 1,874,350	$ 1,085,507	$ 1,256,593
Medical wards	18,873,286	8,627,685	4,929,550	5,316,051
Surgical wards	21,968,925	9,676,114	5,629,118	6,663,693
Total rooms	$45,058,661	$20,178,149	$11,644,175	$13,236,337
Operating and recovery room	1,842,288	757,758	494,385	590,145
Hematology and chemistry	8,671,770	3,840,152	2,342,249	2,489,369
Pathology and microbiology	6,468,188	2,895,287	1,689,061	1,883,840
Radiology	5,015,527	2,283,567	1,312,230	1,419,730
Other ancillary departments	22,175,726	9,850,582	5,789,979	6,535,165
Outpatient surgical service	1,260,000	566,583	323,740	369,677
Total ancillary and outpatient charges	$45,433,499	$20,193,929	$11,951,644	$13,287,926
Total patient revenue	$90,492,160	$40,372,078	$23,595,819	$26,524,263
Percent	100%	44.61%	26.08%	29.31%

Part B
Utilization and Statistics

	All Payors	Payor 01	Payor 02	Payor 03
Total discharges	14,000.0	6,081.62	3,646.83	4,271.55
Total days of care	108,486.76	48,675.45	28,063.06	31,748.25
Intensive care unit	4,369.38	1,942.33	1,124.88	1,302.17
Medical ward	52,425.79	23,965.79	13,693.20	14,766.80
Surgical ward	51,691.59	22,767.33	13,244.98	15,679.28
Total clinic visits	12,000.00	5,825.80	2,576.09	3,598.11
Total outpatient visits	25,000.00	10,010.44	7,311.33	7,678.24

Continued

Exhibit 16.12 Continued

	All Payors	Payor 01	Payor 02	Payor 03
Total same-day surgery episodes	3,000.00	1,349.01	770.81	880.18
Total hematology tests	234,372.17	103,787.90	63,304.04	67,280.23
Total pathology tests	147,004.26	65,801.97	38,387.74	42,814.55
Total radiology tests	167,184.24	76,118.91	43,740.99	47,324.34
Total outpatient surgical services	3,000.00	1,349.01	770.81	880.18

Note: For illustration purposes, other tests and procedures are omitted.

added to the variable-cost projections. The minimum volumes of tests, procedures, or operations for this fixed staffing are measures of data elements that demand special attention; performance against these minimum volumes should be aggregated in separate data elements in order to facilitate monitoring and management.

These fixed costs are determined by the following process. For each relevant range of registrations and admissions, statistical estimates are made of the mix and distribution of tests, procedures, operations, and activities. The findings are reviewed by physicians and other health care professionals to identify selected "pockets of services" that are not routinely requested by patients but that are essential to support medical practice. These pockets of services are then designated as the minimum volume of tests for fixed-cost computations.

The minimum volume of tests for fixed-cost purposes is a major component in the departmental management control system module discussed in Chapter 12. Special monitoring and variance analyses are performed at the departmental level to provide assurance that the expertise and competence of professional and technical personnel are maintained. These individuals need periodic experience in the labor-intensive performance of these special tests, and the health care facility must document when critical tests are performed for accreditation, medical review, quality assurance, risk management, insurance, and legal purposes. Because of the multiple objectives associated with this minimum volume of tests, these services have traditionally not been priced in the same manner as standard tests; they are frequently priced to earn a much smaller contribution margin. Some very labor-intensive tests may be priced at almost the break-even point.

The monitoring of fixed costs and minimum volumes performed by the product analyst does not duplicate any of the efforts accomplished at the departmental level. Instead, the product analyst is looking at the aggregate financial and utilization experience from an organizationwide perspective, giving primary attention to (1) the third party payors, (2) the physicians or health care professionals providing the care or services, and (3) the changes in medical practice. The second and third dimensions are long-standing concerns in the health care field; the first dimension is a recent emphasis that has become intensified under the fee-for-service arrangement.

Product analysts have a major challenge to monitor third party payors in some of the current competitive environments where change is rampant. Some third party payors display diverse behavior within short periods of time. The existing management of a third party payor may alter various courses of actions because of economic pressures in the competitive environment. In other cases there is a complete change in a third party payor's management without any continuity of objectives and operating procedures. There may be a change in ownership of the third party payor, resulting in new policies, procedures, and management personnel. Bankruptcy of an HMO, insurance company, or other third party payor is becoming a common occurrence; some third party payors have obtained legal protection from the federal court while they restructure their operations and negotiate a settlement for substantial debts to health care facilities. Some health care facilities have all of these types of changes occurring simultaneously in a highly competitive environment.

The monitoring of treatment protocols by payor includes examining those minimum volumes of tests that are typically priced at less than the normal contribution margin. If a given third party payor has a high proportion of these exception tests, then the product analyst has reasonable statistical confidence that this payor's patients are receiving many routine tests and services from another provider. The normal mix and distribution of patients is not occurring from this particular third party payor; hopefully, the contract terms provide for some recovery from this situation.

Summary

Medical review, quality assurance, and risk management are traditional monitoring arrangements in health care institutions that focused on individual episodes of care for both inpatients and outpatients. The profiles of individual physicians by case mix and expected payor were part of the framework in which a peer assessment was made of the treatment in a given episode. This primary emphasis on individual episodes of care has been supplemented by product management's analysis of case-mix data by treatment protocol and payor. The financial and utilization data for a group of episodes of care classified by a treatment protocol within a DRG or outpatient category based on ICD-9-CM and CPT-4 codes are the product management's areas of primary concern.

Changes in the competitive environment have increased the product management's emphasis on the treatment protocol by payor. Some payors have established financial incentives for physicians to use providers other than a hospital for selected types of medical and health care services. When these alternative providers do not offer a full set of services, then these types of episode of care are identified by the detailed financial and utilization data in given ancillary and support departments. The mix and distribution of tests by selected areas within a department present an unusual profile for the treatment protocol in a given case-mix group by physician and provider versus other physicians in Standard Report 17 in Exhibit 16.2 (case-mix information by products, physician, expected payment source, and zip code region).

Information on patients discharged at the end of a month is not available in the research database during the first few days of the next month. Efforts to expedite the review of case-mix data for the prior month can be counterproductive. Simple cases that are compatible with the treatment protocol tend to dominate the set of extracted data (Exhibit 16.3). This erroneous sense of acceptable performance may be dramatically altered at the end of the current month when late patient abstract data for exceptional cases are placed in the research database.

The attending physician must review the overall treatment for a given patient and then sign certain claim forms attesting to the principal and secondary diagnoses and the major procedures performed. If the discharge is for a Medicare patient, the physician acknowledgment must be entered in the medical record for that patient. Any delays in the prompt reporting of test results and their entry in the medical record can pose additional problems to the attending physician because of all the parties performing peer review. The next physician to examine this record may not be on the health care facility's team for medical review, quality assurance, or risk management but may be part of an external "second opinion" group retained by a third party payor. In other cases, the second opinions may be communicated in a legal framework from a malpractice perspective. It is prudent for the physician to fully study all the information within the charts and files before signing the physician attestation.

The seven-step modular framework for case-mix management presented in Chapter 15 included projected costs and revenues for the volume of patient episodes of care. These estimated financial statements did not encompass all support and overhead expenditures that are required for a specified relevant range of activity.

Appendix: Using Case-Mix Index for Payments per DRG

The case-mix index is the measurement of the average DRG weight for a given set of cases based on processing the Medicare provider analysis and review (MEDPAR) data for all fully coded diagnostic and surgical procedure claims of Medicare hospital inpatients. The MEDPAR file contains *charges*, not cost data; thus, the average weight per DRG is currently computed from the provider claim submissions for Medicare discharges. The relative weights for each DRG are measures of the average services consumed by Medicare hospital inpatients in the treatment of these cases based on charges in MEDPAR and excluding outliers. The annual updates to DRGs for PPS include calculations where the Medicare data have been supplemented by information from Maryland and Michigan for low-volume DRGs.

The MEDPAR data for Medicare hospital inpatients indicate that a heart transplant is 100 times more expensive, on the average, than an admission for false labor. Exhibit 16.13 shows that the relative weight for one type of heart transplant classified as DRG 103 is 13.4829, while the false labor classified as DRG 382 is 0.1339; the relative weights for each DRG are used in the payment computation for the hospital under PPS. The importance of age in differentiating within a general category for the amount of services provided to patients in similar cases is illustrated by DRGs 059 and 060 for tonsillectomy and adenoidectomy, where the relative weight increased from 0.2616 to 0.3897 for individuals over age 17. Age is also illustrated in cases with allergic reactions for DRGs 447 and 448, where weights change from 0.3470 to 0.4710 for individuals over age 17. Complications and age are combined in differentiating among services consumed by similar cases with urethral stricture for DRGs 328, 329, and 330, with a range of weights from 0.2788 to 0.6484.

Computations

The computational process applied to DRG weights in determining payment has changed under PPS. Hospitals in rural areas that qualify as a sole community hospital are paid according to a different blend of hospital-specific and regional rates from all other hospitals. There are special adjustments to sole community hospitals covering situations where there is a significant drop in admissions and for new services. PPS has a different payment arrangement for rural referral centers and for cancer hospitals. Some of the PPS administrative rules have been temporarily modified by Congress to benefit selected types of hospitals in the computation of payments. Labor-related and non-labor-related rates are currently computed for the nine federal regions partitioned among (1) large urban, (2) other urban, and (3) rural. There are also national adjusted standardized amounts for labor-related and non-labor-related rates that are separated among (1) large urban, (2) other urban, and (3) rural.

Exhibit 16.14 illustrates the computation process under PPS for fiscal year 1990 at Wilmette Community Hospital. The federal region rate that includes Chicago is higher than the federal national rate; therefore, the 85/15 exceptional processing arrangement is used in computing an adjusted national rate, as presented in Exhibit 16.14. The final factor of 3,808.56 is multiplied by each of the DRGs at Wilmette Community Hospital in determining the regular payment for Medicare hospital inpatients. DRG 382 for false labor is paid $509.97, and the heart transplant case in DRG 103 receives $51,350.43.

As advances in technology are implemented and changes occur in medical practice, DHHS must adjust and recalibrate the relative weights of DRGs so that these measures continue to reflect the relative use of resources without increasing or decreasing the aggregate payments to hospitals under PPS. A normalization factor is applied

Exhibit 16.13   Selected List of DRGs with Relative Weights

DRG Number	Relative Weights	Label
382	0.1339	False labor
391	0.2218	Normal newborn
060	0.2616	Tonsillectomy and/or adenoidectomy only, age 0–17
330	0.2788	Urethral stricture age 0–17
373	0.2988	Vaginal delivery w/o complicating diagnoses
465	0.3301	Aftercare with history of malignancy as secondary diagnosis
448	0.3470	Allergic reactions age 0–17
059	0.3897	Tonsillectomy and/or adenoidectomy only, age > 17
433	0.3999	Alcohol/drug abuse or dependence, left AMA
329	0.4045	Urethral stricture age > 17 w/o CC
372	0.4530	Vaginal delivery with complicating diagnoses
447	0.4710	Allergic reactions age > 17
328	0.6484	Urethral stricture age > 17 with CC
114	1.6133	Upper limb and toe amputation for circ system disorders
269	1.7125	Other skin, subcut tiss and breast procedure with CC
112	1.9203	Vascular procedures except major reconstructive w/o pump
111	2.0376	Major reconstructive vascular proc w/o pump w/o CC
113	2.4586	Amputation for circ system disorders except upper limb and toe
263	2.6338	Skin graft and/or debrid for skin ulcer or cellulitis with CC
285	2.7897	Amputatation of lower limb for endocrine, nutrit and metabol disorders
110	3.5731	Major reconstructive vascular proc w/o pump with CC
472	12.8143	Extensive burns with O.R. procedure
474	13.2512	Respiratory system diagnosis with tracheostomy
103	13.4829	Heart transplant

Source: Federal Register 54 (8 May 1989): 19695–708.

to the new weights so that the average case weight after recalibration equals the average case weight prior to normalization for the same set of cases. After the recalibration and implementation of revised factors into the new GROUPER software program, any increase in the average

Exhibit 16.14   Computation of DRG Rates for FY 1990 for Wilmette
Community Hospital

Step 1. Select the appropriate regional or national adjusted standardized amount considering the type of hospital and designation of the hospital as (1) large urban, (2) other urban, or (3) rural.

Wilmette Community Hospital in Wilmette, Illinois is part of the Chicago area (a large urban area) and is a regular hospital. The federal national rate would normally apply to Wilmette Community Hospital, except that the hospital is in a Census region with a higher regional rate than the national rate. The national adjusted rate is then 85 percent of the federal national rate and 15 percent of the federal regional rate.

	Federal Region IV Rate	*Federal National Rate*	*National Adjusted Rate*
Labor-related rate	2,667.08	2,512.40	*2,643.88*
Non-labor-related rate	960.61	889.89	*950.00*

Computations:

$(2,667.08 \times 0.85) + (2,512.40 \times 0.15) = 2,267.02 + 376.86 = 2,643.88$

$(960.61 \times 0.85) + (889.89 \times 0.15) = 816.52 + 133.48 = 950.00$

Step 2. Multiply the labor-related portion of the standardized amount by the applicable wage index for the geographical area.

The wage index for the large urban area of Chicago is *1.0812*
Labor-related rate from Step 1 = $2,643.88 \times 1.0812 = 2,858.56$

Step 3. Sum the amount from Step 2 and the nonlabor portion of the standardized amount from Step 1.

Labor-related from Step 2	2,858.56
Non-labor-related from Step 1	950.00
Total	*3,808.56*

Step 4. Multiple the final amount from Step 3 by the weighting factors corresponding to the appropriate DRG. Examples are from Exhibit 16.13.

DRG	*Weight*	*Amount*	*Label*
382	0.1339	$ 509.97	False labor
391	0.2218	844.74	Normal newborn
060	0.2616	996.32	T A only, age 0–17
112	1.9203	7,313.58	Vasc proc except major reconstructive
111	2.0376	7,760.32	Major reconstructive vasc proc w/o CC
110	3.5731	13,608.36	Major reconstructive vascular proc CC
474	13.2512	50,467.99	Respiratory system diagnosis w trach.
103	13.4829	51,350.43	Heart transplant

Source: Federal Register 54 (8 May 1989): 19662–708.

case-mix index value for Medicare claims should be attributable to an increase in complexity of cases that are treated or to coding changes.

The accuracy of recalibration of DRG weights is demonstrated by DHHS's reprocessing of the current fiscal year's MEDPAR data that used the current year's GROUPER against the GROUPERs in previous years. Since the same cases are being reprocessed using old versions of the GROUPER, any increases in case-mix index show an inflation factor with a corresponding increase in Medicare expenditures under PPS. Exhibit 16.15 illustrates the result of recalibration for the GROUPER in which 1.35 percent of the overall increase in case-mix index value for fiscal year 1988 versus 1986 is attributable to the recalibration process and changes in the GROUPER software programs. The initial 6.4 percent change in the case-mix index between 1986 and 1988 represents a 5.05 percent increase in complexity of cases and a 1.35 adjustment factor that is eliminated.

Using DRGs for other payors

The unique characteristics of the older Medicare population are beginning to be captured by HCFA's updates to the mandated DRG

Exhibit 16.15   Case-Mix Index Change

Fiscal Year	Discharges	GROUPER Version	Case-Mix Index	Change 1986–1988 Amount	Percent
1986	8,842,953	GROUPER 3	1.2045		
1987	9,501,374	GROUPER 4	1.2367		
1988	9,142,064	GROUPER 5	1.2824	0.0779	0.0779/1.2045 = 6.4%

Reprocessing of 1988 MEDPAR Data

	9,142,064	GROUPER 3	1.2653		
	9,142,064	GROUPER 4	1.2696		
	9,142,064	GROUPER 5	1.2824	0.0171	0.0171/1.2653 = 1.35%

Change:
Case-mix change from 1986 to 1988 of 1.2045 to 1.2824 is 6.4 percent. Reprocessing of 1988 MEDPAR data through GROUPER 3 shows an inflation of 0.0171 in the case-mix index for the same set of discharges, which is a 1.35 percent adjustment factor.

Source: Federal Register 54 (8 May 1989): 19645–46.

system. As the DRG classification system improves for Medicare hospital inpatients, the resulting framework is less appropriate for other third party payors' patients. The elimination of "age over 69" for partitioning Medicare hospital inpatients was implemented after HCFA found there was only a 4 percent variation in utilization of resources based on age when all other factors were held constant.[4] This finding is in marked contrast to the overall population, where CPHA's List A uses age as a key factor for differentiating among patients with similar ICDA codes.

Technological advancements, changes in medical practice, and modifications in the ICD-9-CM codes have made the alternative case-mix methods from the 1970s and early 1980s obsolete. Until there are new classification systems, the mandated DRG system for Medicare hospital inpatients is the only current system that is generally available for use by hospitals. Analysis of the utilization of services for a given payor's patients does not have to stop at the DRG level, but these data are separated by age, sex, and other demographic factors. Standard reports for partitioning case-mix data by various attributes for a given payor and by physician was presented in Chapter 15. Further segmenting of case-mix data by treatment protocol for a given payor is addressed in this chapter with other standard reports.

Notes

1. Fanta et al., *CPT*; CPHA, *ICD-9-CM*.
2. HCFA, "Medicare Program; Changes to the Inpatient Hospital Prospective Payment System and Fiscal Year 1989 Rates; Proposed Rules," *Federal Register* 53 (27 May 1988): 19527.
3. Ibid.
4. *Federal Register* 52(1 September 1987): 33152.

Additional Reading

Chesney, J. D. "Utilization Trends before and after PPS," *Inquiry* 27 (Winter 1990): 376–81.
Finkler, S. A., D. Brooteny, and L. Brown. "Utilization of Inpatient Services under Shortened Lengths of Stay: A Neonatal Care Example," *Inquiry* 25 (Summer 1988): 271–80.
Goldfarb, M. G., and R. M. Coffey. "Case-Mix Differences between Teaching and Nonteaching Hospitals," *Inquiry* 24 (Spring 1987): 68–84.

Olshansky, S. J. "On Forecasting Mortality," *Milbank Quarterly* 66 (1988): 482–530.
Wheeler, J. R. C., and T. M. Wickizer. "Relating Health Care Market Characteristics to the Effectiveness of Utilization Review Programs," *Inquiry* 27 (Winter 1990): 344–51.

Discussion Questions

16.1. A profit center director reviews variance analysis reports and investigates the reasons for significant differences in actual financial results versus budget. How does the review performed by a product analyst differ from the profit center director's study?

16.2. Medical review, quality assurance, and risk management are three traditional monitoring functions of patient care performed in health care facilities; each of these focuses on the episode of care for a given patient. Explain how the product management's activities are different from the traditional monitoring functions.

16.3. The product analyst provides the guidance for extracting the financial and utilization data for a treatment protocol from the various financial and patient care information systems and the medical records modules. Why is a standard retrieval routine not specified for all treatment protocols in place of responding to the guidance of the product analyst?

16.4. Gamma Community Hospital had 3,000 registrations for same-day surgery with the identical frequency distribution for outpatient case-mix groups CPT XX7 to CPT XX9 as in Exhibit 16.9 for treatment protocols by payor. The frequency distribution by payor within a treatment protocol for outpatient episodes of care is shown in Exhibit 16.16. The aggregate financial and utilization data for these 3,000 registrations by payor are shown in Exhibit 16.17. A review of the treatment protocols by payor for outpatient case-mix groups CPT XX7 to CPT XX9 provided the data in Exhibit 16.18. Explain why the average charges per payor are different when the charges per treatment protocol were identical across payor groups.

16.5. Gamma Community Hospital had 12,000 registrations for the clinic with the identical frequency distribution for outpatient case-mix groups CPT XX1 to CPT XX3 as in Exhibit 16.9 for treatment protocols by payor. The frequency distribution by payor within a treatment protocol for outpatient episodes of care is shown in Exhibit 16.16. The aggregate financial and utilization data for these 12,000 clinic visits by payor are shown in Exhibit 16.19. A review of the treatment protocols by payor for outpatient case-mix groups CPT XX1 to CPT XX3 provided the data in Exhibit 16.20. Explain why Payor 01 had 48.55 percent of total clinic

Exhibit 16.16   Delta Community Hospital: Frequency Distribution by Payor within Treatment Protocol—Outpatients

	Treatment Protocols Type A			Treatment Protocols Type B		
	Payor 01	*Payor 02*	*Payor 03*	*Payor 01*	*Payor 02*	*Payor 03*
CPT XX1	0.5446	0.1867	0.2687	0.5054	0.1887	0.3059
CPT XX2	0.4723	0.2285	0.2992	0.4779	0.2304	0.2917
CPT XX3	0.4145	0.2570	0.3285	0.5102	0.1895	0.3003
CPT XX4	0.2875	0.3574	0.3551	0.3049	0.3386	0.3565
CPT XX5	0.4304	0.2877	0.2819	0.4182	0.3055	0.2763
CPT XX6	0.4921	0.2305	0.2774	0.4886	0.2118	0.2996
CPT XX7	0.4885	0.2349	0.2766	0.4783	0.2895	0.2322
CPT XX8	0.4389	0.2553	0.3058	0.3586	0.3054	0.3360
CPT XX9	0.4832	0.1991	0.3177	0.5053	0.2096	0.2851

Exhibit 16.17   Financial and Utilization Data for 3,000 Registrations for Same-Day Surgery

	All Payors	*Payor 01*	*Payor 02*	*Payor 03*
Total charges	$1,905,920	$855,441	$491,599	$558,880
Percent	100.00%	44.88%	25.79%	29.33%
Visits	3,000.00	1,349.01	770.81	880.18
Percent	100.00%	44.97%	25.69%	29.34%
Average charge per visit	$635.31	$634.13	$637.77	$634.96

visits but had 49.18 percent of total clinic charges when the average charge per treatment protocol was identical across payor groups.

16.6.   Exhibit 16.21 shows revenues and utilization data for outpatient case mix CPT XX1 under treatment protocol Clinic01 by payor at Delta Community Hospital. Exhibit 16.21 is based on the 12,000 clinic visits with the distribution illustrated in Exhibit 16.9 and the frequency distribution by payor within the treatment protocol in Exhibit 16.16. Payor 01's patients represent 54.5 percent of the visits but constitute 70.5 percent of the hematology and chemistry tests. The patients of Payor 02 and Payor 03 have smaller utilization rates per visit for hematology and chemistry tests than Payor 01's patients. From studying the financial and utilization data in Exhibit 16.21, explain the reasons for the differences in laboratory and radiology services per visit by payor.

Exhibit 16.18 Average Charge per Visit for Treatment Protocols by Payor for Outpatient Case-Mix Groups CPT XX7 to CPT XX9

	All Payors	Payor 01	Payor 02	Payor 03
CPT XX7 Product SDSurg01	$673.00	$673.00	$673.00	$673.00
CPT XX7 Product SDSurg02	636.00	636.00	636.00	636.00
CPT XX8 Product SDSurg03	643.00	643.00	643.00	643.00
CPT XX8 Product SDSurg04	650.00	650.00	650.00	650.00
CPT XX9 Product SDSurg05	576.00	576.00	576.00	576.00
CPT XX9 Product SDSurg06	569.00	569.00	569.00	569.00

Exhibit 16.19 Financial and Utilization Data for 12,000 Clinic Visits by Payor for Gamma Community Hospital

	All Payors	Payor 01	Payor 02	Payor 03
Total charges	$1,813,741	$891,918	$385,072	$536,751
Percent	100.00%	49.18%	21.23%	29.59%
Visits	12,000.00	5,825.80	2,576.09	3,598.11
Percent	100.00%	48.55%	21.47%	29.98%
Average charge per visit	$151.15	$153.10	$149.48	$149.18

16.7. Two corporations have signed contracts with Delta Community Hospital, and the total clinic visits for the year are expected to increase from 12,000 visits to 18,590. The registration distribution by outpatient case-mix groups, treatment protocols, and payors is the same as presented in Exhibit 16.9; the statistical distribution by payor within a treatment protocol is shown in Exhibit 16.16. Compute the amounts shown in Exhibit 16.21 for outpatient case-mix CPT XX1 with treatment protocol Clinic 01 by payor at Delta Community Hospital under the revised position of 18,590 total clinic registrations.

16.8. A product analyst examining financial and utilization data in Standard Report 17 (case-mix information by product, physician, expected payment source, and zip code region) may require information in certain ancillary areas at organizational levels below a department. Explain this situation and give an example that illustrates the reason for such detailed information.

Exhibit 16.20 Average Charge per Visit by Payor for Gamma Community Hospital

	All Payors	Payor 01	Payor 02	Payor 03
CPT XX1 Product Clinic01	$228.00	$228.00	$228.00	$228.00
CPT XX1 Product Clinic02	154.00	154.00	154.00	154.00
CPT XX2 Product Clinic03	124.00	124.00	124.00	124.00
CPT XX2 Product Clinic04	175.00	175.00	175.00	175.00
CPT XX3 Product Clinic05	131.00	131.00	131.00	131.00
CPT XX3 Product Clinic06	94.00	94.00	94.00	94.00

Exhibit 16.21 Revenues for CPT XX1 Treatment Protocol Clinic01 by Payor for Delta Community Hospital

	All Payors	Payor 01	Payor 02	Payor 03
Hematology and chemistry	$127,148	$ 89,660	$15,369	$22,119
Pathology and microbiology	97,891	53,312	18,276	26,303
Radiology	182,298	109,046	37,383	35,869
Outpatient surgical service	0	0	0	0
Other ancillary services	44,496	24,233	8,308	11,955
Total charges	$451,833	$276,251	$79,336	$96,246
Percent	100%	61.14%	17.56%	21.30%
Total cases	2,224.8	1,211.6	415.4	597.8
Percent	100%	54.46%	18.67%	26.87%
Average charge per visit	$203.09	$228.00	$191.00	$161.00
Tests:				
Hematology and chemistry	3,436.43	2,423.25	415.37	597.80
Percent	100%	70.52%	12.09%	17.40%
Pathology and microbiology	2,224.80	1,211.63	415.37	597.80
Percent	100%	54.46%	18.67%	26.87%
Radiology	6,076.60	3,634.88	1,246.11	1,195.61
Percent	100%	59.82%	20.51%	19.68%

16.9. The contribution margin is not a constant rate among the tests or procedures within some ancillary departments. Explain the reasons for the variation in contribution margins within a given department.

16.10. The physician attestation must now be entered in the medical record for all federal program inpatients. Explain the impact that the physician acknowledgment has on the timing of discharge diagnostic information.

16.11. The Theta Community Hospital employed a product analyst who began to examine discharge abstract data as of 31 July 19X1. The initial study was restricted to discharges during July, and the findings in early August indicated that there were very few exceptional cases. The product analyst in early September extracted discharges for July and August. Similar comparisons were made of the new data and the findings for August suggested that there were very few exceptional cases. But, there were additional discharges for July in the new data that included a disproportional number of exceptional cases. How can the product analyst avoid this problem in October?

16.12. Exhibit 16.22 shows revenues and utilization data for DRG XX2 with surgical treatment protocol Surg02 by payor at Delta Community Hospital. The ALOS is 11.5 for Payor 01's patients, 9.9 for Payor 02's, and 8.5 for Payor 03's; these differences in ALOS are a significant factor in explaining why the average charge per case was between $9,154 and $6,836. From studying the financial and utilization data in Exhibit 16.22, explain the reasons for the difference in average charge per case that are not associated with ALOS.

16.13. Further analysis of Delta Community Hospital's service area suggests that total inpatient admissions will be 15,825 instead of the 14,000 shown in Exhibit 16.4. The distribution of the 15,825 admissions by case-mix groups, treatment protocols, and payors is the same as in Exhibit 16.4; the statistical distribution by payor within a treatment protocol is shown in Exhibit 16.23. Compute the amounts shown in Exhibit 16.22 for DRG XX2 with surgical treatment protocol Surg02 by payor at Delta Community Hospital under the revised position of 15,825 total admissions.

16.14. Changes have occurred in Delta Community Hospital's service area that suggest that total inpatient admissions will be 16,480 instead of the 14,000 shown in Exhibit 16.4. The distribution of the 16,480 admissions by case-mix groups, treatment protocols, and payors is the same as in Exhibit 16.4; the statistical distribution by payor within a treatment protocol is shown in Exhibit 16.23. Compute the amounts shown in Exhibit 16.22 for DRG XX2 with surgical treatment protocol Surg02 by payor at Delta Community Hospital under the revised position of 16,480 total admissions.

16.15. Exhibit 16.24 shows revenues and utilization data for DRG XX2 with medical treatment protocol Med02 by payor at Delta Community Hospital. The ALOS is 9.8 for Payor 01's patients, 9.1 for Payor 02's, and

Exhibit 16.22   Revenues for DRG XX2 Surgical Treatment Protocol Surg02 by Payor for Delta Community Hospital

	All Payors	Payor 01	Payor 02	Payor 03
Intensive care unit	$965 per day	$ 109,273	$ 45,279	$ 56,744
Medical ward	$360 per day	0	0	0
Surgical ward	$425 per day	753,969	312,415	391,521
Operating and recovery room	x hours @ $60	39,387	18,958	27,671
Hematology and chemistry	x tests @ $37	66,793	26,304	34,128
Pathology and microbiology	x tests @ $44	86,651	34,756	40,585
Radiology	x tests @ $30	49,234	21,327	31,130
Outpatient surgical service		0	0	0
Other ancillary services	$590 + $210/day	396,919	164,813	206,395
Total charges	$2,914,252	$1,502,226	$623,852	$788,174
Percent	100%	51.55%	21.41%	27.04%
Total cases	358.4	164.1	79.0	115.3
Percent	100%	45.79%	22.04%	32.17%
Total days of care	3,649.3	1,887.3	782.0	980.0
Percent	100%	51.72%	21.43%	26.85%
Average patient days	10.18	11.50	9.90	8.50
Average charge per case	$8,131.28	$9,153.70	$7,897.73	$6,836.02
Average charge per day	$ 798.57	$ 795.97	$ 797.75	$ 804.24
Tests:				
Hematology and chemistry	3,438.5	1,805.1	711.0	922.4
Percent	100%	52.50%	20.68%	26.82%
Pathology and microbiology	3,681.6	1,969.2	790.0	922.4
Percent	100%	53.49%	21.46%	25.05%
Radiology	3,389.8	1,641.1	711.0	1,037.7
Percent	100%	48.42%	20.97%	30.61%

Exhibit 16.23 Delta Community Hospital: Frequency Distribution by Payor within Treatment Protocol—Inpatients

	Medical Treatment Protocols			Surgical Treatment Protocols		
	Payor 01	Payor 02	Payor 03	Payor 01	Payor 02	Payor 03
DRG XX1	0.5846	0.1567	0.2587	0.4754	0.1987	0.3259
DRG XX2	0.4923	0.2185	0.2892	0.4579	0.2204	0.3217
DRG XX3	0.3845	0.2670	0.3485	0.4802	0.1795	0.3403
DRG XX4	0.2175	0.4574	0.3251	0.2249	0.3986	0.3765
DRG XX5	0.3804	0.3177	0.3019	0.3963	0.3255	0.2782
DRG XX6	0.5021	0.2005	0.2974	0.5188	0.2016	0.2796
DRG XX7	0.4985	0.2749	0.2266	0.5083	0.2795	0.2122
DRG XX8	0.3689	0.2953	0.3358			
DRG XX9	0.5132	0.1891	0.2977	0.5026	0.1823	0.3151

7.7 for Payor 03's; these differences in ALOS are a significant factor in explaining why the average charge per case was between $6,320 and $4,961. From studying the financial and utilization data in Exhibit 16.24, explain the reasons for the difference in average charge per case that are not associated with ALOS.

16.16. With the addition of a new physician group, it is expected that Delta Community Hospital's total inpatient admissions will be 17,775 instead of the 14,000 shown in Exhibit 16.4. The distribution of the 17,775 admissions by case-mix groups, treatment protocols, and payors is the same as in Exhibit 16.4; the statistical distribution by payor within a treatment protocol is shown in Exhibit 16.23. Compute the amounts shown in Exhibit 16.24 for DRG XX2 with medical treatment protocol Med02 by payor at Delta Community Hospital under the revised position of 17,775 total admissions.

16.17. An HMO with a contract at Delta Community Hospital has recently expanded its covered population by the addition of three new employers. It is now expected that Delta Community Hospital's total inpatient admissions will be 21,850 instead of the 14,000 shown in Exhibit 16.4. The distribution of the 21,850 admissions by case-mix groups, treatment protocols, and payors is the same as in Exhibit 16.4; the statistical distribution by payor within a treatment protocol is shown in Exhibit 16.23. Compute the amounts shown in Exhibit 16.24 for DRG XX2 with medical treatment protocol Med02 by payor at Delta Community Hospital under the revised position of 21,850 total admissions.

16.18. A recent article in a professional journal indicated that the standard treatment for a diagnostic condition similar to case mix DRG XX3 has

Exhibit 16.24   Revenues for DRG XX2 Medical Treatment Protocol Med02 by Payor for Delta Community Hospital

	All Payors	Payor 01	Payor 02	Payor 03
Intensive care unit	$965 per day	$ 81,475	$ 33,578	$ 37,606
Medical ward	$360 per day	1,489,335	613,804	687,426
Surgical ward	$425 per day	0	0	0
Operating and recovery room	x hours @ $60	0	0	0
Hematology and chemistry	x tests @ $37	159,382	63,666	74,903
Pathology and microbiology	x tests @ $44	170,582	75,710	77,939
Radiology	x tests @ $30	103,383	40,149	45,549
Outpatient surgical services		0	0	0
Other ancillary departments	$590 + $170/day	718,240	296,357	331,832
Total charges	$5,100,916	$2,722,397	$1,123,264	$1,255,255
Percent	100%	53.37%	22.02%	24.61%
Total cases	875.1	430.8	191.2	253.1
Percent	100%	49.23%	21.85%	28.92%
Total days of care	7,909.8	4,221.5	1,739.8	1,948.5
Percent	100%	53.37%	22.00%	24.63%
Average patient days	9.04	9.80	9.10	7.70
Average charge per case	$5,829.62	$6,319.95	$5,875.20	$4,960.50
Average charge per day	$644.89	$644.89	$645.63	$644.22
Tests:				
Hematology and chemistry	8,053.6	4,308.0	1,720.8	2,024.8
Percent	100%	53.49%	21.37%	25.14%
Pathology and microbiology	7,369.7	3,877.2	1,720.8	1,771.7
Percent	100%	52.61%	23.35%	24.04%
Radiology	6,303.4	3,446.4	1,338.4	1,518.6
Percent	100%	54.68%	21.23%	24.09%

been changed to include a new procedure based on technology. The article cited examples of how the medical treatment protocol with this new procedure had replaced the former surgical treatment protocol for many patients. Explain how the product analyst can monitor if this shift has occurred in the treatment of case mix DRG XX3.

16.19. Explain the following statement: "The fixed staffing and minimum volumes for a given relevant range of activities are the very expenditures that are most vulnerable to actions by third party payors."

16.20. Assume there has been an informal change in medical practice for DRG XX2 under the medical treatment protocol Med02 by payor. Explain how the data in Exhibit 16.24 can be partitioned and analyzed for purposes of measuring the impact of this recent change in medical practice.

16.21. Gamma Community Hospital had 40,000 registrations for the clinic, outpatient area, and same-day surgery with the identical frequency distribution for outpatient case-mix groups CPT XX1 to CPT XX9 as in Exhibit 16.9 for treatment protocols by payor. The outpatient frequency distribution by payor within a treatment protocol at Gamma Community Hospital was identical with the data in Exhibit 16.16. The demographic and patient origin attributes are similar for Gamma Community Hospital's three payor groups, and the actual services provided by payor group per treatment protocol are identical. The aggregate financial and utilization data for these 40,000 outpatient visits by payor for Gamma Community Hospital are shown in Exhibit 16.25.

A. After reviewing the other outpatient information on Gamma Community Hospital in Questions 16.4 and 16.5, explain why Payor 02's patients have 25.60 percent of the hematology tests, 27.19 percent of pathology tests, and 24.22 percent of radiology tests when the treatment protocols for all Gamma Community Hospital payors were identical.

B. Explain why Payor 01's patients had 42.96 percent of total outpatient episodes of care but had 44.26 percent of total charges when the average charge per treatment protocol was identical across payor groups.

16.22. There are six community hospitals in a given service area with identical sets of DRG charges for Medicare hospital inpatients. In each hospital, 50.5 percent of all Medicare patients were assigned to the 95 paired sets of DRGs that in 1986–1987 were partitioned into two groups: (1) no complication or comorbidity (CC) with age under 70 and (2) CC and/or age over 69. The experience in these six community hospitals with respect to the 95 paired DRGs is a mirror of the aggregate national Medicare hospital data as analyzed by ProPAC and reported by K. F.

Exhibit 16.25 Total Projected Clinic Revenue by Payor for Gamma
Community Hospital

	Treatment Protocols	*Payor 01*	*Payor 02*	*Payor 03*
Hematology and chemistry	x tests @ $37	$ 969,207	$ 565,423	$ 673,981
Pathology and microbiology	x tests @ $44	419,101	266,244	293,972
Radiology	x tests @ $30	480,268	252,643	310,189
Outpatient surgical services	x visits @ $420	566,583	323,740	369,677
Other ancillary departments	x visits	327,378	195,878	226,744
Total charges	$6,241,028	$2,762,537	$1,603,928	$1,874,563
Percent	100%	44.26%	25.70%	30.04%
Total visits	40,000.0	17,185.24	10,658.22	12,156.52
Percent	100%	42.96%	26.65%	30.39%
Average charge per visit	$156.03	$160.75	$150.49	$154.20
Total hematology tests	59,692	26,195	15,282	18,215
Percent	100%	43.88%	25.60%	30.52%
Total pathology tests	22,257	9,525	6,051	6,681
Percent	100%	42.79%	27.19%	30.02%
Total radiology tests	34,770	16,009	8,421	10,340
Percent	100%	46.04%	24.22%	29.74%
Total outpatient surgical services	3,000	1,349	771	880
Percent	100%	44.97%	25.69%	29.34%

Price and G. F. Kominski, "Using Patient Age in Defining DRGs for Medicare Payment," *Inquiry* 25 (Winter 1988): 497.

The six community hospitals had 41,580 Medicare discharges, including 21,000 for the 95 paired DRGs that differed only in the presence of a CC and/or age 70 years or older. These 21,000 cases represented $87,225,840 of total charges and 183,220.8 patient days of care. The 3,500 cases in each of the six community hospitals had the characteristics shown in Exhibit 16.26.

Exhibit 16.26 Characteristics of 21,000 Cases for 95 Paired Sets of DRGs

	No CC Age < 70	*CC and/or Age 70+*	*Total*
Cases	560	2,940	3,500
Average charge	$3,289.00	$4,320.00	$4,155.04
Total charges	$1,841,840	$12,700,800	$14,542,640
ALOS	7.070	9.040	8.725
Total patient days	3,959.20	26,577.60	30,536.80

Exhibit 16.27 Distribution of 21,000 Cases for 95 Paired Sets of DRGs

	No CC		*CC*		*Total*
Average charges	$3,439		$4,871		$4,155
Cases	10,500		10,500		21,000
ALOS	7.900		9.550		8.725

	No CC Age < 70	*No CC Age 70+*	*CC Age < 70*	*CC Age 70+*	
Hospital A	560	245	1,100	1,595	3,500
Hospital B	560	2,100	300	540	3,500
Hospital C	560	2,625	100	215	3,500
Hospital D	560	105	600	2,235	3,500
Hospital E	560	315	850	1,775	3,500
Hospital F	560	1,750	200	990	3,500
Total cases	*3,360*	*7,140*	*3,150*	*7,350*	*21,000*

For illustration purposes, assume that DHHS implemented an average charge for the 95 paired sets of DRGs based on the six hospitals' actual experiences for the prior year in which "age over 69" was eliminated as a factor for partitioning. This new charge structure is the same as the weighted averages reported by Price and Kominski for all Medicare hospital inpatients, with charges of $3,439 per case for no CC and $4,871 per case with CC. The overall distribution of the 21,000 cases between the two categories is shown in Exhibit 16.27.

A. Assume the six hospitals had the same experience in the first year under the new charge structure as in the prior year. Compute the total Medicare payments for the 95 DRG pairs in each of the six community hospitals under the revised charge system.

B. Calculate the total patient days of care for the 95 DRG pairs at each of the six community hospitals using the revised data.

C. DHHS recalibrated the weights of the 190 DRGs (the 95 DRG pairs), resulting in revised charges for each DRG. Explain the impact that this recalibration might have on the distribution of total payments among the six community hospitals.

16.23. Using the same data as Question 16.22, assume that the weighted charges for services rendered to the different categories of patients in the 95 DRG pairs and the average length of stay were the same as the national averages calculated by Price and Kominski as follows:

	No CC Age < 70	No CC Age 70+	CC Age <70	CC Age 70+	Total
Average charge	$3,289	$3,510	$4,889	$4,863	$4,155
ALOS	7.07	8.29	9.06	9.76	8.725

A. Compute the total Medicare charges for the 95 DRG pairs in each of the six community hospitals using the above revised charge system.

B. Calculate the total patient days of care for the 95 DRG pairs at each of the six community hospitals using the above data.

C. Compare total charges and patient days for each hospital in Questions 16.22 and 16.23. Remember that these are composite averages for 190 DRGs and as you look at the differences assume the changes are increased by a factor of 20 because of the actual range of charges after the recalibration of DRGs.

16.24. Alpha Community Hospital, located in federal region V, is subject to the national adjusted standardized amounts under the classification of "other urban." The national adjusted standardized amount for labor-related is 2,487.94 and for non-labor-related is 881.22 according to the 8 May 1989 *Federal Register*. The wage index for the urban area in which Alpha Community Hospital is located is 0.9422. Compute Alpha Community Hospital's payments for the 24 DRGs illustrated in Exhibit 16.13. (*Hint*: Apply the relevant steps in Exhibit 16.14.)

Appendix A

Abbreviations and Acronyms

AFDC	Aid to Families with Dependent Children
AHA	American Hospital Association
AHR	*Annual Hospital Report*, 20 February 1980
AICPA	American Institute of Certified Public Accountants
ALOS	average length of stay
AMA	American Medical Association
CAP units	College of American Pathologists work measurement units
CC	complication or comorbidity
CCRC	continuing-care retirement community
CE	credit-enhanced security
CEO	chief executive officer
CON	certificate of need
COTH	Council of Teaching Hospitals
CPAs	certified public accountants
CPHA	Commission on Professional and Hospital Activities
CPI	consumer price index
CPT-4	*Physicians' Current Procedural Terminology*, fourth edition (AMA's expanded and revised coding structure to reflect current medical practice)
CT scanner	computed tomographic scanner
DBMS	database management system
DE	direct expense
DHEW	U.S. Department of Health, Education, and Welfare
DHHS	U.S. Department of Health and Human Services
DLH	direct labor hours
DMCS	departmental management control system
DRGs	diagnosis-related groups

DTI	direct expense transferred in
DTO	direct expense transferred out
ER	emergency room
ESOP	employee stock ownership plan
ESP	economic stabilization program
EUs	equivalent units
FAF	Financial Accounting Foundation
FASB	Financial Accounting Standards Board of the Financial Accounting Foundation
FHA	Federal Housing Administration
FTEs	full-time equivalents
FV	favorable variance
GAAP	generally accepted accounting principles
GASB	Governmental Accounting Standards Board of the Financial Accounting Foundation
GCM	general counsel memorandum by the Internal Revenue Service
GLCA	general ledger chart of accounts
GNMA	Government National Mortgage Association
GNP	gross national product
HCFA	Health Care Financing Administration
H-ICDA	*Hospital Adaptation of ICDA*
HMO	health maintenance organization
ICD	*International Classification of Diseases*
ICDA	*International Classification of Diseases, Adapted for Use in the United States*
ICD-9-CM	*International Classification of Diseases, 9th Revision, Clinical Modification*
ICF	intermediate care facility
ICU	intensive care unit
IRR	internal rate of return
IRS	Internal Revenue Service
JCAH	Joint Commission on Accreditation of Hospitals (name changed to JCAHO in 1987)
JCAHO	Joint Commission on Accreditation of Healthcare Organizations (formerly JCAH)
LOS	length of stay
MC/R center	major cost/revenue center
MDCs	23 major diagnostic categories for DRGs in PPS
MEDPAR	Medicare Provider Analysis and Review data
MSA	metropolitan statistical area

NCHS	National Center for Health Statistics in the U.S. Department of Health and Human Services
NFP	not-for-profit
NHDS	National Hospital Discharge Survey conducted by NCHS
NPRM	notice of proposed rulemaking
NPV	net present value
OB/GYN	obstetrics/gynecology
OCBOA	other comprehensive basis of accounting (not GAAP)
PAS	Professional Activity Study
PHS	Public Health Service
PIP	periodic interim payment
PP&E	property, plant, and equipment
PPS	prospective payment system
ProPAC	Prospective Payment Assessment Commission
PSRO	Professional Standards Review Organization
REIT	real estate investment trusts
RRR	required rate of return
RVU	relative-value units
SHUA	System for Hospital Uniform Accounting
SHUR	System for Hospital Uniform Reporting, 29 September 1978
SNF	skilled nursing facility
SRS	Social and Rehabilitation Service
SSA	Social Security Administration
UB82	Uniform Billing System developed by HCFA in 1982 and implemented by states in 1983 and 1984
UF	unfavorable variance
UHDD	Uniform Hospital Discharge Data Set
WHO	World Health Organization, Geneva, Switzerland
WPPSS	Washington (State) Public Power Supply System

Appendix B

Public Laws

P. L. 849, National Defense Public Works (Lanham Act), 14 October 1940, amended by P. L. 137, 28 June 1941.

> More than 300 hospitals and 500 facilities were constructed with resources from the Lanham Act as amended.

P. L. 725, Hospital Survey and Construction Act (Hill-Burton Act), 13 August 1946.

> Purpose was to construct public and nonprofit hospitals working through the states. P. L. 725 appropriated $75 million for each of the first four years. Congress extended this type of support for more than 20 years. Nursing homes were covered by a 1954 amendment.

P. L. 89–97, Health Insurance for the Aged and Medical Assistance Act, Social Security Amendments of 1965, 30 July 1965.

> The Medicare program (Title XVIII) was created by this act, including the following statement on "reasonable cost of services":

> > The amount paid to any provider of services with respect to services for which payment may be made under this part shall, subject to the provisions of section 1813, be the reasonable cost of such services, as determined under section 1861(v).

> The rules for Medicare were uniform for all states.

P. L. 89–97, Part 2, Grants to States for Medical Assistance Programs, Establishment of Programs, 30 July 1965.

> The Medicaid program (Title XIX) is created by the same act. The states are designated to administer Medicaid, and the act contains general guidelines for all Medicaid programs. The rights of the states on optional features are acknowledged in the act.

P. L. 90–448, Housing and Urban Development Act of 1968, 1 August 1968.

This act added Section 242 to the National Housing Act, entitled "Title XV—Mortgage Insurance for Nonprofit Hospitals." The initial Federal Housing Administration (FHA) Section 242 limited mortgages to $25 million and not to exceed 90 percent of the estimated replacement value of the property.

P. L. 92–78, Housing and Urban Development Appropriation Act of 1971, 10 August 1971.

The Government National Mortgage Association (GNMA), created by the Housing and Urban Development Appropriation Act of 1968, was given $19,543,000 to commence operations.

P. L. 92–213, National Housing Act as Amended, 22 December 1971.

This joint resolution of Congress gave a temporary waiver of certain limitations applicable to the purchase of mortgages by the Government National Mortgage Association. This act combined FHA and GNMA activities in support of mortgages to nonprofit hospitals.

P. L. 92–603, Professional Standards Review, 30 October 1972.

Professional standards review organizations (PSROs) were created by P. L. 92–603. Medical records and coding of patient care became important support areas in hospitals as a result of this act. There are requirements for concurrent review of admissions, continued-stay review, and medical care evaluation studies. SSA and SRS's utilization review requirements in 1974 as a condition for payment reduced the influence of the PSRO program. *Federal Register* 39 (29 November 1974): 41604–19.

P. L. 93–222, Health Maintenance Organization Act of 1973, 29 December 1973.

This act authorized the secretary of DHEW to make grants and enter into contracts with public or nonprofit private entities for planning projects for the establishment of HMOs. Grants and loans may be provided to HMOs serving medically underserved populations.

P. L. 93–579, Privacy Act of 1974, 31 December 1974.

Purpose is to safeguard individual privacy from the misuse of federal records and to provide that individuals be granted access to records concerning them that are maintained by federal agencies. (Medicaid information administered by states is covered by this act.)

P. L. 93–641, National Health Planning and Resources Development Act of 1974, 4 January 1975.

This act established national guidelines for health planning and created the health system agencies.

P. L. 95–142, Medicare-Medicaid Anti-Fraud and Abuse Amendments, 25 October 1977.

The secretary of DHEW shall establish by regulation uniform reporting systems for health services facilities and organizations, including hospitals, skilled nursing facilities, intermediate care facilities, home health agencies, health maintenance organizations, and other types for which payment is made. A draft document entitled "System for Hospital Uniform Reporting or SHUR" was issued on 29 September 1978.

The SHUR document was revised and replaced by the *Annual Hospital Report* (20 February 1980). Required implementation of the *Annual Hospital Report* was announced in the *Federal Register*; however, it was delayed. The prospective payment system in 1983 removed the need for the *Annual Hospital Report*. The SHUR manual and *Annual Hospital Report* document are good references on the status of ancillary departments and work measurement units for the early 1980s.

P. L. 97–35, Omnibus Budget Reconciliation Act of 1981, 13 August 1981.

Section 2101(a), Part C, of Title XVIII of the Social Security Act is amended by adding a new section, "Payments to Promote Closing and Conversion of Underutilized Hospital Facilities." This was seen as a cost-containment initiative; there is a cash payment to a marginal hospital if it will close.

This law also repeals the requirement for the state-administered Medicaid program to reimburse hospitals based on the Medicare reasonable cost. The law also gave the states more flexibility in contracting with health maintenance organizations.

P. L. 97–248, Tax Equity and Fiscal Responsibility Act of 1982, 3 September 1982.

This act represents the most significant revisions in reimbursement regulation since the establishment of the Medicare and Medicaid programs in 1965. The act eliminated (1) inpatient routine nursing salary cost differential, (2) duplicate overhead payments for outpatient services, (3) lesser-of-cost-or-charge provision, and (4) private room subsidy. There were many other reductions under this act. The interim rules for this act were announced in the *Federal Register* on 30 September 1982.

Richard S. Schweiker, secretary of the Department of Health and Human Services, "Report to Congress: Hospital Prospective Payment for Medicare; December 1982."

This 110-page report plus 10 appendices and other supporting documents recommended the establishment of the prospective payment system utilizing the 467 DRGs.

P. L. 98–21, Social Security Amendments of 1983, 20 April 1983.

This act created the prospective payment system for inpatients in the Medicare program following the recommendation of the secretary of DHHS in December 1982.

P. L. 98–369, Deficit Reduction Act of 1984, 18 July 1984.

The Medicare and Medicaid Budget Reconciliation Amendments of 1984 are in this act. A provision restricted the payment of a higher rate in an asset because of an acquisition or merger. This act amended the heading of a section by deleting the words "Professional Standards Review" and inserting "Peer Review." In other places, the words "utilization and quality control peer review organization" were used in place of "professional standards review organization."

P. L. 99–272, Medicare and Medicaid Budget Reconciliation Amendments of 1985, is within the Consolidated Omnibus Budget Reconciliation Act of 1985, 7 April 1986.

This act modified Section 9102 to add one-year for the phased implementation of PPS. The shift from a three-year phased implementation to a four-year period required many changes in the reimbursement arrangements for inpatients in Medicare. There are several changes in the Medicare physician payment provisions and the fees for clinical laboratory services. The secretary of DHHS is mandated to establish within 60 days a Task Force on Long-term Health Care Policies composed of 18 members.

P. L. 99–509, Omnibus Budget Reconciliation Act of 1986, 21 October 1986.

Numerous reimbursement changes in Medicare and Medicaid are contained in this act, including provisions for outpatient surgery and various types of therapy. Payment for hospital capital-related costs were reduced by this act. The secretary of DHHS is mandated by this act to establish a patient outcome assessment research program.

Appendix C

Administrative Rules by Governmental Bodies

DHEW	Department of Health, Education, and Welfare
SSA	Social Security Administration
SRS	Social and Rehabilitation Service
DHHS	Department of Health and Human Services
HCFA	Health Care Financing Administration

DHEW, SSA, Part 405, "Federal Health Insurance for the Aged and Disabled; Limitations on Coverage of Costs under Medicare," *Federal Register* 39 (19 March 1974): 10260–314.

This was a major effort to look at reasonable cost by (1) type of facility, (2) geographical area, (3) size of institution, (4) nature and mix of services rendered, and (5) type and mix of patients treated. While these five dimensions are important, there was no "foundation of what are costs" against which to apply these factors.

DHEW, SSA, Part 405, "Federal Health Insurance for the Aged and Disabled, Revisions in Carriers' Procedural Terminology and Coding," *Federal Register* 40 (21 February 1975): 7637–39.

Current Procedural Terminology (CPT), third edition, published by the American Medical Association, was rejected by this announcement for alternative use in coding. The fourth edition was significantly expanded, and it became the choice coding arrangement for outpatient care.

DHEW, SSA, Part 405, "Federal Health Insurance for the Aged and Disabled; Utilization Review; Conditions of Participation," *Federal Register* 39 (29 November 1974): 41604–8.

Utilization review is required under Medicare for hospitals and nursing homes as a condition for payment.

DHEW, SRS, Part 249, "Services and Payment in Medical Assistance Programs," and Part 250, "Administration of Medical Assistance Programs; Utilization Review," *Federal Register* 39 (29 November 1974): 41609–18.

Utilization review is required under Medicaid for hospitals and nursing homes as a condition for payment.

DHEW, HCFA, "Uniform Reporting Systems for Health Services Facilities and Organizations; Proposed Rule," *Federal Register* 44, (23 January 1979): 4741–44.

The proposed rule pertained to the System for Hospital Uniform Reporting (SHUR) under P. L. 95–142, "Medicare-Medicaid Anti-Fraud and Abuse Amendments," 25 October 1977. (See the public law.)

DHEW, HCFA, "Medicare and Medicaid Programs; Annual Hospital Report; Proposed Rule," *Federal Register* 45 (19 March 1980): 17894–911.

The proposed rule under P. L. 95–142 (1977) was never implemented. (See the public law.)

DHEW, HCFA, "Medicare Program; Proposed Schedule of Limits on Hospital Inpatient General Routine Operating Costs for Cost Reporting Periods Beginning on or after July 1, 1980," *Federal Register* 45 (1 April 1980): 21582–88.

There were several cost-containment initiatives in place combined with the proposed Annual Hospital Reporting Requirements (19 March 1980) for facilities. There were diverse financial responses to these requirements among community hospitals. The *Federal Register* 46 (30 June 1981) contained additional limits on hospital inpatient costs.

DHHS, HCFA, "Medicaid Program; Revocation of Sixty-Day Public Notice of Changes in Method or Level of Reimbursement," *Federal Register* 46 (16 September 1981): 45964–65.

Medicare rates were reduced on 30 June 1981; P. L. 97–35 on 13 August 1981 gave the states the right to make Medicaid payments on a basis other than "reasonable cost" under Medicare. The 16 September 1981 announcement was a "warning" that major changes would be announced in the next two weeks covering the Medicaid program. The revisions in eligibility for the Medicaid program that went into effect on 1 October 1981 were the most drastic in the history of the Medicaid program (1965–1981).

DHHS, SSA, "Aid to Families with Dependent Children; Interim Rule," *Federal Register* 46 (21 September 1981): 46750–79.

These rules implemented the Medicaid provisions of P. L. 97–35, which went into effect on 1 October 1981. Many individuals were no longer eligible for AFDC under the revised rules. States had to seek additional social service coverage for some cases. Others became uninsured.

DHHS, HCFA, "Medicare Hospital Reimbursement Reforms: Limitations on Reimbursable Costs and the Rate of Hospital Cost Increases; Interim Final Rule with Comment Period," *Federal Register* 47 (30 September 1982): 43282–93.

Section 223 of the Social Security Amendments of 1972 (P. L. 92–603) authorized the secretary of DHHS to set limits on the costs that are reimbursed under Medicare. These interim rules pertained to that authority. The real impact of this act was never implemented because of the prospective payment system (PPS). Health care representatives stated they would support PPS if Section 223 requirements were dropped.

DHHS, HCFA, 42 CFR Parts 405, 409, and 489, "Medicare Program; Prospective Payment for Medicare Inpatient Hospital Services; Final Rule," *Federal Register* 49 (3 January 1984): 234–340.

These are the initial rules for the three-year phased implementation of the prospective payment system under Title VI of P. L. 98–21.

DHHS, HCFA, 42 CFR Parts 405 and 412, "Medicare Program; Changes to the Inpatient Hospital Prospective Payment System and Fiscal Year 1986 Rates; Final Rule," *Federal Register* 50 (3 September 1985): 35646–759.

Extensive changes were made in the DRG GROUPER (15 pages of specifications); for example, amputation of a leg ("amputation above knee") was a secondary DRG factor to other procedures under the 1983 DRG GROUPER. Debridement is the cutting away of dead or contaminated tissue from a wound to prevent infection (ICD procedure code 86.22); the 1983 DRG GROUPER reimbursed $8,700 for wound debridement and $3,513 for above-knee amputation. The initial errors in the DRG GROUPER (corrected through the 15 pages of changes) especially penalized diabetic clinics. For example, two amputations in a complex case were reimbursed by the DRG GROUPER at $7,400 while a single amputation was $9,400.

DHHS, HCFA, "Medicare Program; Changes to the DRG Classification System; Proposed Notice," *Federal Register* 52 (19 May 1987): 18885.
The statistically created DRG groups were based on a single, general list of complications and comorbidities in partitioning cases even though in as many as 25 percent of the cases a particular diagnosis may not alter the course of care.

Federal Register 52 (1 September 1987): 33152.
This announcement completed the four-year phased implementation of the prospective payment system. HCFA found that there was only a 4 percent variation in utilization of resources based on "age over 69" when all other factors were held constant. HCFA did not address the more critical age groups (such as over 84) with alternative payment arrangements.

DHHS, HCFA, 42 CFR Parts 412 and 413, "Medicare Program; Changes to the Inpatient Hospital Prospective Payment System and Fiscal Year 1989 Rates; Proposed Rule," *Federal Register* 53 (27 May 1988): 19498–686.
Changes were made in the DRG classification and weighting factors. Physician attestation was added as a requirement. Changes were made in geographic classification, payment for outlier cases, payments to sole community hospitals, referral center criteria, classification of capital-related costs and direct medical education costs, and ceiling on rate of hospital cost increases.
Congress restricted some of the classification changes for designating sole community hospitals and referral center criteria from being implemented for at least 12 months when they were adverse to an existing facility.

DHHS, HCFA, 42 CFR Part 412, "Medicare Program; Changes to the Inpatient Hospital Prospective Payment System and Fiscal Year 1990 Rates; Proposed Rule," *Federal Register* 54 (8 May 1989): 19636–796.
Additional changes were made in complications and comorbidities within the DRG GROUPER. These were addressed in 1987 and partially revised in 1988. This is the next installment in those DRG GROUPER changes. The DRG classification and weighting factors for all DRGs were modified by this 1989 announcement.

DHHS, HCFA, 42 CFR Part 412, "Prospective Payment System for Inpatient Hospital Capital-Related Costs; Proposed Rule," *Federal Register* 56 (29 February 1991): 8476–8535.

This proposed rule specifies a ten-year phased implementation of a new method of reimbursement of capital-related costs.

Appendix D

Accounting and Reporting Guidelines

AICPA   American Institute of Certified Public Accountants
FASB   Financial Accounting Standards Board
GASB   Governmental Accounting Standards Board

Committee on Health Care Institutions, AICPA, *Medicare Audit Guide* (New York: AICPA, 1969).

    This industry audit guide addressed the costs and revenue matching provisions of Medicare. The examinations included three federal government initiatives designed to encourage more hospitals to participate in the Medicare program. First, depreciation can be based on a percentage of operating expenses (especially desirable for donated assets). Second, costs can include the value of services for nonpaid workers (encompasses donated services of religious personnel as cost). Third, an allowance in lieu of recognition of other costs was permitted through 1 July 1969.

Subcommittee on Health Care Matters, AICPA, *Hospital Audit Guide: Industry Audit Guide* (New York: AICPA, 1972).

    The first edition of this audit guide built upon the *Medicare Audit Guide* and encompassed four financial statements for voluntary hospitals: (1) balance sheet, (2) statement of revenues and expenses, (3) statement of changes in fund balances, and (4) statement of changes in financial position. Investor-owned hospitals were told to follow reporting requirements of other investor-owned businesses. Donated services, donated supplies, donated equipment, and donated property continued to receive attention in the *Hospital Audit Guide* since these are important issues in voluntary hospitals.

Proposals to FASB to Amend AICPA Industry Audit Guide on Audits of Hospitals:

Auditing Standards Division, AICPA, "Statement of Position on Clarification of Accounting, Auditing, and Reporting Practices Relating to Hospital Malpractice Loss Contingencies," 1 March 1978.

Auditing Standards Division, AICPA, Statement of Position 78-1, "Accounting by Hospitals for Certain Marketable Equity Securities," 1 May 1978.

Accounting Standards Division, AICPA, Statement of Position 81-2, "Reporting Practices Concerning Hospital-Related Organizations," August 1, 1981.

Auditing Standards Division, AICPA, "Health Care Industry Developments—1989" and "Audit Risk Alert—1989."

Committee on Governmental Accounting and Auditing, AICPA, *Audits of State and Local Governmental Units: Industry Audit Guide.* (New York: AICPA, 1974).

Proposals to FASB to Amend AICPA Industry Audit Guide, Audits of State and Local Governmental Units (1974):

Accounting Standards Division, AICPA, Statement of Position 75-3, "Accrual of Revenues and Expenditures by State and Local Governmental Units," August 1975.

Accounting Standards Division, AICPA, Statement of Position 77-2, "Accounting for Interfund Transfers of State and Local Governmental Units," September 1977.

Accounting Standards Division, AICPA, Statement of Position 78-7, "Financial Accounting and Reporting by Hospitals Operated by a Governmental Unit," 31 July 1978.

This stated that hospitals operated by governmental units should follow the requirements of AICPA's *Hospital Audit Guide.*

Accounting Standards Division, AICPA, Statement of Position 80-2, "Accounting and Financial Reporting by Governmental Units," 30 June 1980.

The 1968 publication of the National Committee on Governmental Accounting (NCGA) is acknowledged as an authoritative source in the area of accounting for state and local governmental units. Encumbrance accounting (commitments) in governmental units was changed.

GASB, "Concepts Statement No. 1; Objectives of Financial Reporting," 1987.

GASB, "Statement No. 7; Advance Refundings Resulting in Defeasance of Debt," 1987.

FASB, "Statement of Financial Accounting Concepts No. 6; Elements of Financial Statements," December 1985.

Committee on Voluntary Health and Welfare Organizations, AICPA, *Audits of Voluntary Health and Welfare Organizations*, 1974.

Accounting Standards Division, AICPA, Statement of Position 89-5, "Financial Accounting and Reporting by Providers of Prepaid Health Care Services," 8 May 1989.

Health Care Committee and the Health Care Audit and Accounting Guide Task Force, AICPA, Audit and Accounting Guide: Audits of Providers of Health Care Services, 1990.
 Amendment to AICPA *Audit and Accounting Guide: Audits of Providers of Health Care Services*.
  Statement of Position 90-8, "Financial Accounting and Reporting by Continuing Care Retirement Communities," 28 November 1990.

Committee on College and University Accounting and Auditing, AICPA, *Audits of Colleges and Universities: Industry Audit Guide* (New York: AICPA, 1973).

Accounting Standards Division, AICPA, Statement of Position 74-8, "Financial Accounting and Reporting by Colleges and Universities," August 1974.

Accounting Standards Division, AICPA, Statement of Position 78-5, "Accounting for Advance Refundings of Tax-Exempt Debt," 30 June 1978.

GASB, Statement 9, "Reporting Cash Flows of Proprietary and Nonexpendable Trust Funds and Governmental Entities That Use Proprietary Fund Accounting," September 1989.
 GASB's cash flow statement is different from FASB Statement 95, "Statement of Cash Flows," in requiring four categories of disclosures: operating, noncapital financing, capital and related

financing, and investing activities. It is similar to FASB's statement with the separate presentation of information about investing, capital, and financing activities not resulting in cash receipts or payments.

GASB, Statement 14, "The Financial Reporting Entity," June 1991.

GASB's Statement 14 presents a framework that differentiates among related organizations, jointly governed organizations, and joint ventures. The treatment of equity interests is not compatible in all respects with FASB's positions. GASB's concept of a financial reporting entity includes organizations in which a primary government is able to impose its will on that unit. It is not necessary that the primary government has a financial investment in the other organization. The government's intent to own stock in a for-profit corporation should determine whether this financial interest is reported as a component or as an investment.

Index

least-squares regression analysis,
417–18; minimum volumes, 415;
pockets of services, 562
Forecasting (health services): case
mix and physician profiles,
479–87; other considerations,
487–88; patient origin studies,
471–78; product budgeting,
547–48; product profiles, 537–
43; projecting products by payor
and type, 549–60; revenue and cost
comparisons, 505–8; third party
payor analysis, 535–37; treatment
protocol within the DRG or CPT
group, 548–49; Uniform Hospital
Discharge Data, 470–71; utilization
studies, 469–78
Freedom of Information Act, 104,
106
Freestanding facilities, 13
Fund accounting, 28
Fundamental accounting equation,
29, 56
Fund balances, 37–38
Funds: general, 19–20, 28, 32–34;
tracing, 91, 97, 134, 371, 372–73;
transfer of, 63, 86–88, 91, 133

General funds, 19–20, 28, 32–34;
unrestricted, 20
Generally accepted accounting
principles (GAAP), 9, 17–18,
27, 91
Governmental Accounting Standards
Board (GASB), 9, 17–18, 38
Government National Mortgage
Association, 125, 588
Grants, 187
Gross charges (by patient category),
62–63
Gross patient revenue, 59–61

Health care entities, characteristics of: control, 10–12; federal
government–owned, 8; framework, three-dimensional, 7, 17;

ownership, 8–10; type of facility,
12–16, 17
Health care facilities by type, 12–16
Health Maintenance Organization
Act, 15, 588
Higgins, John A., 386–87
Hill-Burton Act, 91, 107–8, 112, 587
Hospice, 15–16

Indenture agreements and bond
covenants, 36
Indirect costs, 232
Indirect method for operating
activities, 126
Intermediate care facility, 13–14
International Classification of Diseases (ICD): code structure, 515–
20; conflict with medical education
programs, 512; H-ICDA, 510–11;
H-ICDA-2, 510–11; ICD-9-CM,
470, 473, 481, 511–12, 515–20;
ICDA-8, 511
Investing activities on statement of
cash flows, 122–24; in affiliated
companies, 123; transfers from
donor-restricted funds, 124
Investment in other health care entities, 148–57, 602; affiliates, 135,
138–39; consolidated financial
statement, 152–55; cost method
or cash method of accounting,
148–49; equity or accrual method
of accounting, 149
Investments: cost method of accounting, 148–49; equity method of
accounting, 149; income, 69–70
Investor-owned facilities, 9, 16–18,
29, 39, 135–39

Joint Commission on Accreditation
of Healthcare Organizations
(JCAHO), 15, 469, 513–14
Joint Commission on Accreditation
of Hospitals. See Joint Commission
on Accreditation of Healthcare
Organizations

About the Author

Thomas R. Prince, Ph.D., is a professor of accounting and information systems in the J. L. Kellogg Graduate School of Management at Northwestern University in Evanston, Illinois. He joined the faculty there in 1962, after receiving his Ph.D. from the University of Illinois at Champaign-Urbana, and from 1968 until 1975 he served as chairperson of his department.

In addition to teaching, Professor Prince has served as a consultant to a number of organizations, hospital systems, and government agencies. He was responsible for the installation of laboratory information systems in 12 hospitals and the evaluation, design, implementation, and assessment of hospital information systems in several hospitals and medical centers. He designed over 40 computer programs that were implemented at the Commission on Professional and Hospital Activities for patient origin, physician, and financial assessment. He also had the single-source contract with the federal government for the data structure used in the national PSRO studies. More than one million discharges and medical records have been processed by Professor Prince in various research and consulting engagements.

With awards from the Ford Foundation and Northwestern University, Professor Prince has done postdoctoral studies at Harvard University, the University of Chicago, and the University of Michigan. His current research interests center on the financial management of health care entities, with special emphasis on joint ventures, investments, affiliations, consolidations, and related parties.

Dr. Prince has published numerous books, articles, and reports. His most frequently referenced books are *Extensions of the Boundaries of Accounting Theory* and *Information Systems for Management Planning and Control.* His articles have been published in *Accounting Review, Health*

*Services Research, Journal of Health Administration Education, Hospital &
Health Services Administration,* and *Hospital Progress.* He is also the coau-
thor of many health care reports sponsored by foundations, state and
local governments, and federal agencies.

Also a certified public accountant, Dr. Prince has served on the
Illinois CPA Society's Committee on Health Care Institutions—Hospital
Section. He is a faculty associate of the American College of Health-
care Executives and a member of the Financial Executives Institute
and the American Institute of Certified Public Accountants. Professor
Prince is a past president of the Chicago Chapter of The Institute of
Management Science.